Indigenous Ecotourism

Sustainable Development and Management

———————————————

DEDICATION

To my father – Mervin Vernon Zeppel
(13 July 1922–26 September 2005)

and for S.T.M.
(for your Cree and Ojibway heart)

Ecotourism Book Series

General Editor: David B. Weaver, Professor of Tourism Management, George Mason University, Virginia, USA.

Ecotourism, or nature-based tourism that is managed to be learning-oriented as well as environmentally and socio-culturally sustainable, has emerged in the past 20 years as one of the most important sectors within the global tourism industry. The purpose of this series is to provide diverse stakeholders (e.g. academics, graduate and senior undergraduate students, practitioners, protected area managers, government and non-governmental organizations) with state-of-the-art and scientifically sound strategic knowledge about all facets of ecotourism, including external environments that influence its development. Contributions adopt a holistic, critical and interdisciplinary approach that combines relevant theory and practice while placing case studies from specific destinations into an international context. The series supports the development and diffusion of financially viable ecotourism that fulfils the objective of environmental, socio-cultural and economic sustainability at both the local and global scale.

Titles available:

1. *Nature-based Tourism, Environment and Land Management*
   Edited by R. Buckley, C. Pickering and D. Weaver
2. *Environmental Impacts of Ecotourism*
   Edited by R. Buckley
3. *Indigenous Ecotourism: Sustainable Development and Management*
   H. Zeppel
4. *Ecotourism in Scandinavia: Lessons in Theory and Practice*
   Edited by S. Gossling and J. Hultman

Indigenous Ecotourism

Sustainable Development and Management

_____

Heather D. Zeppel

James Cook University
Cairns, Australia

www.cabi.org

CABI is a trading name of CAB International

CABI Head Office
Nosworthy Way
Wallingford
Oxfordshire OX10 8DE
UK

CABI North American Office
875 Massachusetts Avenue
7th Floor
Cambridge, MA 02139
USA

Tel: +44 (0)1491 832111
Fax: +44 (0)1491 833508
E-mail: cabi@cabi.org
Website: www.cabi.org

Tel: +1 617 395 4056
Fax: +1 617 354 6875
E-mail: cabi-nao@cabi.org

A catalogue record for this book is available from the British Library, London, UK.

A catalogue record for this book is available from the Library of Congress, Washington, DC.

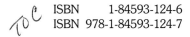

ISBN   1-84593-124-6
ISBN 978-1-84593-124-7

Produced and typeset by Columns Design Ltd, Reading
Printed and bound in the UK by Cromwell Press, Trowbridge

Contents

List of Tables

About the Author

Heather Zeppel is Senior Lecturer in Tourism in the Tourism Program, School of Business at James Cook University Cairns in Queensland, Australia. She has an Associate Diploma (Wildlife and Park Management), BSc, Graduate Certificate of Education, Graduate Diploma (Museum Curatorship) and PhD (Tourism/Material Culture).

Heather lectures on Tourism Issues in Developing Countries, Tourism and the Environment, Tourism Analysis, Australian Ecotourism and Wildlife Tourism Management and Regional Tourism Planning and Foundations of Conference and Event Management.

Her research interests include Indigenous tourism, cultural interpretation, ecotourism, wildlife tourism and sustainable tourism development. Heather's research articles and notes on Indigenous tourism have been published in the *Journal of Travel Research*, *Pacific Tourism Review*, *Tourism*, *Culture & Communication* and *Tourism Management*. She has also written ten book chapters on cultural tourism or Aboriginal tourism and other research reports on *Aboriginal Tourism in Australia* (Zeppel, 1999) and *Indigenous Wildlife Tourism in Australia* (Muloin, Zeppel and Higginbottom, 2001). Her current research examines Aboriginal tourism issues in the Wet Tropics World Heritage Area of Queensland.

Preface

This book had its genesis in the author's previous employment (1981–1984) as a park ranger at Uluru-Katatjuta National Park in the Northern Territory of Australia. This involved working with Anangu Aboriginal people on cultural interpretation and land management issues. Uluru (Ayers Rock) is a major tourism icon and culturally significant area, handed back to Anangu Aboriginal people in 1985.

Starting at Uluru, this interest in conservation and Indigenous cultures continued through to a doctoral study of Iban longhouse tourism in Sarawak, Borneo (1991–1994) and postdoctoral research on Indigenous cultural tourism in Australia, New Zealand and Canada (1996–2000). The initial academic studies of Indigenous tourism in the mid-1990s have now emerged into a major theme or focus at recent tourism or ecotourism conferences in Australia, New Zealand, USA, Canada, Africa and Asia.

This cross-disciplinary research on Indigenous tourism involves tourism, business, geography, anthropology and other areas, along with varied Indigenous groups.

This specific book emerged from an invitation by Professor David Weaver, editor of the CABI Ecotourism Series, to develop a book proposal that focused on Indigenous ecotourism. The subsequent acceptance of this book proposal by CABI indicates a broadening of the academic coverage of ecotourism from certification, policy and management to local communities and Indigenous peoples.

The commissioning editors at CABI, Rebecca Stubbs and Claire Parfitt, helped bring this book to fruition. The author thanks the three reviewers of the original CABI book proposal for their insightful comments and specific suggestions on further topics and issues to cover in a book of this type. In particular, Professor David Weaver provided useful editorial comments throughout the writing of this book. These prompted more in-depth examination of conservation and tourism issues and their impact on Indigenous peoples. Dr Sue Muloin also critically reviewed the first and last chapters of this book. Jenny Thorp and Sue Saunders provided further editorial corrections. The research and writing of this book was assisted by study leave during August 2004 to January 2005. The author thanks the School of Business, James Cook University for this time granted as leave.

The issues pertaining to Indigenous peoples, cultures, land rights, resource use and tourism continue to receive attention from academic researchers, government agencies, NGOs and the private sector.

Recent media coverage of some Indigenous issues that affect tourism include Maori claims to the foreshore, beaches and coastal waters of New Zealand in 2004, and Aboriginal groups in

Northern Australia lobbying for limited trophy hunting of saltwater crocodiles on Aboriginal lands in 2005. Both of these Indigenous claims to lands and use of natural resources are still pending final outcomes, although the Australian government continued to ban the commercial sport hunting of native wildlife.

At the international level, Indigenous groups are pressing for full legal recognition of their claims to traditional territories, biological diversity, cultural resources and traditional knowledge. This book on Indigenous ecotourism links biodiversity conservation and Indigenous rights with global growth in tourism.

The UN Decade of the World's Indigenous Peoples was declared from 1995 to 2004. The research and writing of this book during 2004/05 provided an effective overview of key developments in conservation and ecotourism as they affected Indigenous peoples during this previous decade. Hence, this book provides a summation and appraisal of what has been achieved with Indigenous groups involved in conservation and ecotourism projects on their traditional territories and tribal lands. It also suggests key topics that need further research and critical investigation in this emerging area of Indigenous ecotourism. While the author is non-Indigenous, every effort was made to incorporate Indigenous perspectives on ecotourism as reported in the published literature and case studies. Any errors made in the presentation and interpretation of these case studies about Indigenous ecotourism are inadvertent. The author welcomes feedback or further information about the topics in this book.

Heather Zeppel
Cairns, North Queensland
Australia
22 November 2005

1

The Context of Indigenous Ecotourism

Introduction

This book is concerned with Indigenous-owned and operated ecotourism ventures that benefit Indigenous communities and conserve the natural and cultural environment. Ecotourism enterprises controlled by Indigenous people include cultural ecotours, ecolodges, hunting and fishing tours, cultural villages and other nature-oriented tourist facilities or services. Indigenous involvement in ecotourism is examined through global case studies of Indigenous operators and providers of eco-tourism products. Indigenous ecotourism is defined as 'nature-based attractions or tours owned by Indigenous people, and also Indigenous interpretation of the natural and cultural environment including wildlife' (Zeppel, 2003: 56). The case studies of Indigenous ecotourism ventures in the Pacific Islands, Latin America, Africa and South East Asia illustrate how Indigenous groups are conserving natural areas and educating visitors while developing and controlling ecotourism on Indigenous lands and territories. These case studies, therefore, challenge the common perception of 'minimal involvement in ecotourism by indigenous people in many countries' (Page and Dowling, 2002: 279). Indigenous ecotourism provides an alternative to extractive land uses such as hunting, farming, logging or mining, and it involves Indigenous people in managing tourism,

culture and their own environment. Ecotourism supplements a subsistence lifestyle and aids the transition to a cash economy for many tribal groups. How various Indigenous communities develop and operate tribal ecotourism ventures is a key focus of much recent research in this area.

Worldwide, Indigenous peoples are becoming more involved in the tourism industry, and particularly with ecotourism (Sykes, 1995; Butler and Hinch, 1996; Price, 1996; Mercer, 1998; Ryan, 2000; Mann, 2002; Smith, 2003; Christ, 2004; Hinch, 2004; Ryan and Aicken, 2005; Johnston, 2006; Notzke, 2006). Tourism enterprises controlled by Indigenous people include nature-based tours, cultural attractions and other tourist facilities or services in tribal homelands or protected areas. These Indigenous tourism ventures are largely a response to the spread of tourism into remote and marginal areas, including national parks, nature reserves and tribal territories that are traditional living areas for many Indigenous groups. Indigenous cultures and lands are frequently the main attraction for ecotours visiting wild and scenic natural regions such as the Amazon, Borneo, Yunnan, East Africa and Oceania. Indeed, 'Indigenous homelands rich in biodiversity are the prime target of most ecotourism' (Johnston, 2000: 90). Ecosystems such as tropical rainforests, coral reefs, mountains, savannah and deserts in developing countries are a drawcard for ecotourism, and many of these ecoregions are still inhabited by marginalized Indigenous groups (Weaver, 1998; WWF, 2000). Tourist encounters with these exotic tribal peoples during safaris, mountain trekking and village tours are growing areas of new tourism (Smith, 2003).

The spread of ecotourism into remote areas often coincides with regions that are still the traditional homelands for surviving groups of Indigenous peoples. Tourist experiences with Indigenous peoples now include trekking with Maasai guides in East Africa (Berger, 1996), visiting Indian villages in the rainforest of Ecuador (Wesche, 1996; Drumm, 1998), meeting Inuit people in the Arctic (Smith, 1996a), staying at Iban longhouses in Borneo (Zeppel, 1997) and Aboriginal cultural tours in northern Australia (Burchett, 1992). Small island states or countries with rainforest, reefs and Indigenous groups, especially in the Asia-Pacific region, are also a growing focus for ecotourism ventures (SPREP, 2002; Harrison, 2003). Environmental, cultural and spiritual aspects of Indigenous heritage and traditions are featured in ecotourism, community-based tourism and alternative tourism. New ecotourism enterprises managed by Indigenous groups are featured in travel guides and websites for community tourism and alternative travel (Franke, 1995; Mann, 2000, 2002; Tourism Concern, 2002). Native lands and reserves in developed countries such as Australia, New Zealand, Canada and the USA are also a growing focus for Indigenous tourism (Lew, 1996; Ryan and Aicken, 2005). For example, the USA has 52 million acres of Indian reservation land, often near national parks, with many tribal governments involved in tourism ventures on these lands (Gerberich, 2005). In these colonized countries, Indigenous ecotourism ventures are also found in protected areas that are co-managed with native people having traditional claims over this land. In North America, many Indigenous groups are investing money from land claim settlements, mining or fishing royalties and gaming revenue from tribal casinos in tourism ventures (Ryan, 1997; Lew and van Otten, 1998). In developing countries, some Indigenous groups with communal or legal land titles now derive income from forest or

wildlife resource use rights and from renting or leasing land to tourism operators.

Globally, there is greater public awareness of both environmental impacts and Indigenous peoples. Ecotourism recognizes the special cultural links between Indigenous peoples and natural areas. A growing tourist demand for Indigenous cultural experiences also coincides with the Indigenous need for new economic ventures deriving income from sustainable use of land and natural resources. This global trend is reflected in increasing contact with Indigenous communities living in remote areas and also the opening up of Indigenous homelands for ecotourism (Honey, 1999; Christ, 2004). These Indigenous territories are usually in peripheral areas, away from mainstream development, where Indigenous land practices have maintained biodiversity in 'wilderness' regions and otherwise endangered ecosystems (Hinch, 2004). While Indigenous communities are vulnerable to increased accessibility and contact with outsiders, ecotourism is seen as one way to maintain ecosystems and provide an economic alternative to logging or mining. Indigenous ecotourism involves native people negotiating access to tribal land, resources and knowledge for tourists and tour operators.

With greater legal recognition and control over homeland areas, culture and resources, Indigenous groups in many areas are determining appropriate types of ecotourism development in traditional lands and protected areas. As well as being an exotic tourist attraction, Indigenous peoples are also increasingly the owners, managers, joint venture partners or staff of ecotourism ventures, cultural sites and other tourist facilities. Therefore, the roles of Indigenous people in ecotourism now include landowners, tribal governments or councils, traditional owners, land managers, park rangers, tourism operators and guides. This global expansion of tourism into remote natural areas and Indigenous lands, often in developing countries, has seen increasing concern for sustainable tourism development, particularly with Indigenous groups (Price, 1996; Honey, 1999; McIntosh, 1999; McLaren, 1999; Robinson, 1999; Smith, 2001; Duffy, 2002; Johnston, 2003a, b; Mowforth and Munt,

2003; Sofield, 2003; Gerberich, 2005). For Indigenous peoples, 'land rights are an absolute prerequisite for sustainable tourism' (Johnston, 2000: 92). Legal rights over tribal lands and resources allow Indigenous groups to benefit from ecotourism, through community-owned enterprises, joint ventures and other partnerships.

This book considers the environmental, cultural and economic impacts of Indigenous ecotourism ventures in tribal areas of developing countries. Case studies describe and analyse the approaches adopted by different Indigenous communities in developing and operating ecotourism ventures. These case studies of Indigenous ecotourism ventures are drawn from the Pacific region, South and Central America, South East Asia and Africa. Tropical rainforest areas in the Asia-Pacific region, Latin America and Africa are a main focus for these community-based Indigenous ecotourism projects (Wesche and Drumm, 1999; Mann, 2002; SPREP, 2002; *Tourism in Focus*, 2002a). The savannah and desert regions of Africa along with the Andes Mountains of South America are another key focus. North Asia (i.e. Mongolia) and south Asia (i.e. India, Nepal, Pakistan and Sri Lanka) are not included in this book. In developing countries, ecotourism ventures for Indigenous peoples are mainly implemented with the help of non-government agencies (NGOs) involved in conservation or community development projects. For many Indigenous peoples, controlled ecotourism is seen as a way of achieving cultural, environmental and economic sustainability for the community (Sofield, 1993; Butler and Hinch, 1996; Zeppel, 1998a; Notzke, 2006). Opening up Indigenous homelands to ecotourism, however, involves a balance between use of natural resources, meeting tourist needs and maintaining cultural integrity.

Indigenous Peoples and Tourism

Indigenous peoples

Indigenous peoples are generally regarded as tribal or native groups still living in their homeland areas: 'Indigenous people are the existing descendants of the original people inhabiting a particular region or country' (BSR, 2003). They are considered to be original or First Peoples with unique cultural beliefs and practices closely linked to local ecosystems and use of natural resources (Furze *et al.*, 1996; Price, 1996). According to Russell (2000: 93), Indigenous people are those who 'are generally minority groups in their territories, have developed a unique culture which may include social and legal systems, and whose ancestral connections to a region are pre-colonial'.

The United Nations (UN, 2004) defines Indigenous communities, peoples and nations as those having 'a historical continuity with pre-invasion and pre-colonial societies that developed on their territories', are distinct from other settler groups and want to 'preserve, develop and transmit to future generations their ancestral territories, and their ethnic identity'. This historical continuity is based on occupation of ancestral lands, common ancestry, cultural practices and language. Indigenous peoples are also economically and culturally marginalized and often live in extreme poverty (UNDP, 2004).

The International Labor Organization (ILO) Convention No. 169 on Indigenous and Tribal Peoples defined Indigenous groups as:

> peoples in independent countries who are regarded as indigenous on account of their descent from the populations which inhabited the country, or a geographical region to which the country belongs, at the time of conquest or colonisation or the establishment of present state boundaries and who, irrespective of their legal status, retain some or all of their own social, economic, cultural and political institutions (ILO, 1991, Article 1 cited in Ryan, 2000: 422).

Indigenous peoples are thus the original inhabitants of a region with a special attachment to their lands or territories; have a sense of shared ancestry and self determination; have their own distinct cultures, languages, spirituality and knowledge; their own cultural, political and social institutions based on customary law and collective community living; and have their lands and institutions dominated by other majority groups and modern states (Kipuri, nd). Many Indigenous groups are geographically isolated, economically disadvantaged and socially and politically marginalized. Indigenous peoples make up one third of the world's 900 million extremely poor rural peoples (IFAD, nd). They have often experienced ethnocide, racism and forced removal by other settlers (Maybury-Lewis, 2002). These Indigenous groups are tribal or semi-nomadic pastoralists, hunter-gatherers or shifting cultivators. They mainly have a subsistence economy and rely on natural resources for food and cash.

Different terms used to describe Indigenous groups include ethnic minorities (China, Vietnam, Philippines); tribes (Africa, Americas); hilltribes (Thailand); scheduled tribes or *adivasis* (India); Native American, Indian or Amerindian (North and South America); *Indigenas* (Latin America); Aboriginal (Australia, Canada, Taiwan) and First Nations (Canada). These Indigenous peoples may either be the majority group (e.g. Papua New Guinea, Bolivia) or, more commonly, they are a minority group, particularly in colonized countries such as North America, Australia and New Zealand. Colonized Indigenous groups whose lands are now part of other modern nation states are also called 'fourth world' peoples. Worldwide, there are an estimated 400 million Indigenous peoples (Weaver, 2001). These 5000 tribal or Indigenous groups represent about 5% of the world population. There are 150 million Indigenous people in China and India and some 30 million Indigenous people in the Americas (Healey, 1993). India has 67.76 million *adivasis* recognized as scheduled tribes, living on 20% of the land area, mainly in forests, hills or mountain areas (Bhengra *et al.*, 2002).

Most Indigenous peoples are still found in developing countries, mainly in the southern hemisphere. For example, some 50 million Indigenous people from about 1000 tribes live in tropical rainforests in the equatorial belt of Africa, Asia, Oceania and the Amazon (Martin, 2001). Small, traditional tribes in isolated tropical or desert regions are often seen as endangered cultures, threatened by resource extraction, tourism and cultural change (Raffaele, 2003). New migrants, logging, mining and dams have displaced many tribal groups from their homelands. Organizations such as Cultural Survival (US), Survival International (UK) and Minority Rights Group International campaign for the rights of Indigenous peoples affected by dispossession and development projects on their lands (Janet, 2002). Tribal groups still living a traditional subsistence lifestyle are found in over 60 countries and number 150 million people (Survival International, 1995). However, other Indigenous peoples also now follow a mainstream lifestyle and no longer live in tribal societies based solely on a subsistence economy.

Most Indigenous people are identified by the name of their 'tribe', clan, group, band or nation (Waitt, 1999). Individually, an Indigenous person is one self-identified as Indigenous who is recognized and accepted by an Indigenous group or community as a member. This definition of an Indigenous person as self-identified is followed in Australia, regardless of the mix or proportion of ethnic backgrounds, whereas in Canada there must be proof of native lineage with a minimum of 6% Indigenous ancestry. In New Zealand, people can be entered on the Maori list without knowing their tribe or *iwi*, while in the USA Native Americans need to show direct descent from at least one Indian great-grandparent listed on a tribal or voting list from the early 1900s (Ryan, 1997). In Taiwan, the government requires that Indigenous people still speak their own native language and funds Indigenous language classes. Taiwan has about 400,000 Indigenous people from 12 officially registered tribes (Coolidge, 2004; Yang, 2005). In contrast to these official government designations about Indigenous descent, 'First peoples have a strong sense of their own identity as unique peoples, with their own lands, languages, and cultures. They claim the right to define what is meant by indigenous, and to be recognized as such by others' (Burger, 1990: 16–17). In Africa, recognized Indigenous groups include the nomadic pastoralists of West Africa (e.g. Fulani, Tuareg) and East Africa (e.g. Maasai), the hunter-gather San or Bushmen in southern Africa and the rainforest Pygmies in central Africa. These groups are politically and economically marginalized, and experience discrimination from the dominant Bantu agricultural groups. A coordinating committee for Indigenous peoples of Africa was formed in 1998 to seek official recognition for Indigenous groups and advocate for their rights (IPACC, 2004). Other African politicians claim that all black Africans are Indigenous to Africa and Indigenous peoples are not always recognized as such by African states (Sharpe, 1998; Kipuri, nd). Hence, other traditional and tribal groups in Africa are also covered in this book.

Indigenous peoples and human rights

The terms 'tribal' and 'Indigenous' are both used at the United Nations (UN). However, more people and communities with strong ties to ancestral land now identify themselves as 'Indigenous' where they are marginalized or oppressed. Tribal groups increasingly use the terms 'Indigenous' and 'Indigenous peoples' due to growing national and international recognition of the existence and territorial claims of native groups. Hence, the politics of 'Indigeneity' involves reworking or repositioning the identity of Indigenous people and groups in relation to economic, political or social power (Barcham, 2000; Maaka and Fleras, 2000; Hendry, 2005). The category or status of being Indigenous is then linked to legally asserting cultural, political and economic claims, such as the ownership and use of land, river and sea areas, hunting and fishing rights, cultural or intellectual copyright of Indigenous knowledge and royalties from land use including tourism. Key issues for all Indigenous groups include human rights, use of land and resources (e.g. plants, wildlife, minerals and water), and intellectual and cultural property rights (e.g. traditional ecological knowledge, cultural copyright). The political and legal recognition of Indigenous status (i.e. people and territories) 'entails claim to certain rights over the use, management and flow of benefits from resource-based industries' (Howitt *et al.*, 1996: 3). Increasingly, Indigenous customary claims have been recognized as legal rights in national and international laws and conventions. These include both individual human rights and the collective property claims of Indigenous groups to land and resources (Wilmer, 1993; McLaren, 1998; Pera and McLaren, 1999; Smith, 1999;

Macdonald, 2002; IFAD, 2003; Johnston, 2003). According to Honey (2003), the range of Indigenous rights include fundamental, cultural, Indigenous knowledge and intellectual property, land, protected areas, economic, labour, local communities and a right to sustainable development of ancestral lands.

The International Labor Organization (ILO) Convention No. 169 (1989) is the only international law recognizing the rights of tribal and Indigenous peoples to their cultures, languages and ancestral territories (Osava, 2005; Roy, nd). The ILO has sponsored a website listing of community tourism projects in Latin America, including Indigenous ecotourism ventures (Redturs, nd). World Bank-funded investment projects now require the informed participation of Indigenous peoples for preparation of an Indigenous Peoples Development Plan (Survival International, 2004). The World Bank's policy for Indigenous peoples recognizes their special cultural, social and environmental ties to land. It also supports legal recognition of traditional or customary land tenure through legal land titles or by rights of custodianship and use (World Bank, 1991). This policy of legal land titles was enforced for a forestry loan to Nicaragua. However, an internal operations evaluation found only 29 of 89 World Bank projects affecting Indigenous peoples had any elements of this Plan (Selverston-Scher, 2003). Business for Social Responsibility has also published a document 'Rights of Indigenous Peoples' for companies doing business in the traditional territories of Indigenous groups (BSR, 2003).

Globally, Indigenous issues are represented by key international organizations. For example, the UN set up a Working Group on Indigenous Populations in 1982, yet only established a Permanent Forum on Indigenous Issues in 2000. The Forum is an advisory body to the UN Economic and Social Council addressing Indigenous issues related to culture, the environment, economic and social development, education, health and human rights. Recent activities of this Forum include an international workshop on Indigenous knowledge and a declaration on conserving biological and cultural diversity at sacred natural sites and cultural landscapes (UN, 2005). In 2003, a Global Fund for Indigenous Peoples was established by the World Bank to support this Forum and provide grants to Indigenous organizations (*Cultural Survival Voices*, 2004). A UN *Draft Declaration on the Rights of Indigenous Peoples*, based on human rights and communal property rights, was devised in 1989/90; however, it has still not been formally adopted by the UN or by other organizations. UNESCO's 2001 *Universal Declaration on Cultural Diversity* highlights protecting Indigenous cultural heritage, traditional knowledge and use of natural resources. The UN Commission on Sustainable Development has an Indigenous Peoples' Caucus that prepared an issues paper about Indigenous peoples for the World Summit on Sustainable Development held in Johannesburg, South Africa (UN Commission on Sustainable Development, 2002). A World Social Forum for NGOs, held since 2001, also included Indigenous peoples for the first time in 2005 with 400 people from around 100 Indigenous ethnic groups attending (Osava, 2005).

In addition, the UN Decade of the World's Indigenous People was declared from 1995 to 2004 with the UN International Year for the World's Indigenous People held in 1993 (UNESCO, 2004). There is even a UN International Day of the World's Indigenous People held each year on 9 August! These UN initiatives focus on achieving social, cultural and political recognition for Indigenous peoples. Gaining this recognition was an ongoing process; hence a second UN Decade of the World's Indigenous People was declared from 2005 to 2014. Funding for major Indigenous development projects on bio-diversity conservation or ecotourism is also directed through UN bodies (e.g. UNEP, UNDP) to national governments, aid groups, environment NGOs and Indigenous peoples' organizations. Increasing amounts of funding from international banks and development agencies are being directed towards ecotourism and the sustainable development of Indigenous communities (Halfpenny, 1999; Griffiths, 2004; EBFP, 2005). In 2002, the UN Environment Programme (UNEP) invested over US$7 billion in 320 tourism-related projects with 21 development agencies (Selverston-Scher, 2003). Indigenous groups also represent their territorial claims and cultural interests by establishing their own organizations. For example, the Coordinating Body for Indigenous Organisations of the Amazon Basin (COICA) represents tribal organizations from nine Amazon countries and 2.8 million Amazon Indian people (Osava, 2005). Globally, over 1000 Indigenous organizations advocate for land and resources (Hitchcock, 1994).

Indigenous peoples and biodiversity

Indigenous land practices and cultural knowledge have ensured the conservation of global biodiversity. The UN Commission on Sustainable Development highlighted the key role of Indigenous peoples in the conservation of natural areas and species on their lands:

> Indigenous peoples comprise five per cent of the world's population but embody 80% of the world's cultural diversity. They are estimated to occupy 20% of the world's land surface but nurture 80% of the world's biodiversity on ancestral lands and territories. Rainforests of the Amazon, Central Africa, Asia and Melanesia is home to over half of the total global spectrum of indigenous peoples and at the same time contain some of the highest species biodiversity in the world (UN Commission on Sustainable Development, 2002: 2–3).

The Indigenous Peoples' Biodiversity Network was established in 1997 in Peru and has hosted workshops on Indigenous tourism and biodiversity conservation in Peru, Malaysia, Spain and Panama. Its position is that Indigenous peoples are the 'creators and conservers of biodiversity', with remaining forest areas or global 200 ecoregions with the highest biodiversity linked with surviving Indigenous groups in Asia, Africa, the Americas and Oceania (Nature Conservancy, 1996; Oviedo *et al.*, 2000; Weber *et al.*, 2000; WWF, 2000). The International Alliance of Indigenous and Tribal Peoples of the Tropical Forests, formed in 1992, and the Forest Peoples Programme (FPP) formed in 1990 also represent Indigenous views on conservation, parks and resource development. The UN Convention on Biological Diversity in 1992 recognized the environmental stewardship and traditional dependence of many Indigenous communities on biological resources (Prance,

1998). Article 8(j) requires governments to preserve Indigenous environmental knowledge to help conserve biodiversity and to share equitably any benefits arising from the use of traditional knowledge (Johnston, 2003). Since 1991, the UN's Global Environment Facility (GEF) has funded major projects on biodiversity conservation in developing countries with many including Indigenous lands. GEF funding from 2002 to 2006 was nearly US$3 billion (Griffiths, 2004; GEF Secretariat, 2004). WWF also adopted a policy on Indigenous peoples and conservation in 1996 that recognized the rights of Indigenous peoples to their traditional lands, territories and resources (Weber et al., 2000; Alcorn, 2001; WWF, 2001a, 2005). Over 12 million people, mainly hunter-gatherers and pastoralists, have been removed from their ancestral lands to make way for protected areas, conservation and tourism. They are affected by poverty, limits on resource use and land degradation, with few benefits from tourism (MacKay, 2002; African Initiatives, 2003; Colchester, 2003, 2004; Martinez, 2003; Negi and Nautiyal, 2003; Hill, 2004; Lasimbang, 2004).

Ecotourism is seen as one main way for Indigenous groups to conserve and benefit from biodiversity on their traditional lands (Butcher, 2003). Ecotourism operators in Indigenous territories and protected areas with Indigenous claims also need to negotiate and be aware of the legal rights of Indigenous groups for ongoing use of natural resources. In 2002, new guidelines for tourism in Indigenous territories were drafted under the UN Convention on Biological Diversity. The World Summit on Sustainable Development (UN Commission on Sustainable Development, 2002) and the World Parks Congress in 2003 also included resolutions on the rights of Indigenous peoples in protected areas and conserving biodiversity (FPP, 2003; Larsen and Oviedo, 2005; Scherl, 2005). These are partly a response to the dominance of international agencies funding biodiversity conservation projects. In the mid-1990s, USAID had 105 ecotourism projects in 10 tropical developing countries and also Nepal. These had US$2 billion in funding directed through US conservation NGOs and the private sector (Honey, 1999). Since 2000, three international

conservation NGOs (i.e. WWF, Conservation International and The Nature Conservancy) have together spent US$350 million a year on biodiversity conservation projects in developing countries, which is more than the UN's GEF programme. It is important to note, however, that the political efforts and funding of local NGOs fighting for Indigenous land rights are secondary to these major environmental NGOs funding conservation and ecotourism projects (Chatty and Colchester, 2002; Epler Wood, 2003). The World Conservation Union (IUCN) only recently devised guidelines to involve Indigenous communities in co-managing national parks, protected areas and community conservation areas (Beltran, 2000; Borrini-Feyerabend et al., 2004a,b; Marrie, 2004; Scherl, 2005; Bushell and Eagles, 2006). In many regions, such as Africa, protected areas deny Indigenous rights or involvement in conservation (Negi and Nautiyal, 2003; Nelson and Hossack, 2003; Lasimbang, 2004). Recent IUCN guidelines focus on securing Indigenous rights in legislation together with policies for co-managed protected areas and also support for community conservation and resource management (Borrini-Feyerabend et al., 2004b; Carino, 2004; Grieg-Gran and Mulliken, 2004; Hill, 2004; UNESCO, 2005).

Indigenous territories

Indigenous territories are areas traditionally occupied by Indigenous groups, or are other smaller areas set aside as reserves and reservations for tribal groups in colonized countries. These designated 'territories' include Aboriginal reserves in Australia, Maori reserves in New Zealand, and Indian reservations in North and South America. Examples include the Hopi Indian Reservation in Arizona (USA) which attracts 100,000 tourists annually (Lew, 1999) and Arnhem Land Reserve in the Northern Territory of Australia, which is home to the Aboriginal rock group Yothu Yindi, bark paintings and the yidaki or didgeridoo. In the western USA, cultural tourism on Indian reservations began in the 1960s (Browne and Nolan, 1989). A lucrative form of diversified Indigenous tourism in the USA and Canada are tribally owned casinos on reserve lands with tax-free status for sovereign Indian nations (Lew and van Otten, 1998). In Taiwan, 250,000 ha of land in mountain areas was designated as Aboriginal or native reservations. Farming was limited and ecotourism was encouraged. However, Taiwan's Aboriginal people wanted compensation for limited land use and to independently manage their own reserve lands (Yang, 2005). Indigenous territories with a majority Indigenous population inside modern nation states include self-rule for the Inuit people of Greenland, a part of Denmark, and the newly created Inuit territory of Nunavut in Northern Canada. Other territories are the former tribal homelands (Bantustans) of South Africa and a 'homelands' movement back to traditional Aboriginal lands in Australia. The Torres Strait Islands between Australia and Papua New Guinea are moving towards being a more autonomous region within Australia. Torres Strait Islanders are of Melanesian origin and culturally distinct from the mainland Aborigines of Australia. Countries such as China and Russia also designate provinces or regions as 'ethnic' homelands for minority Indigenous groups (e.g. Tibetan Autonomous Region in China). However, settlers from the majority culture dominate most of these ethnic regions (Weaver, 2001).

Indigenous territories include lands under the legal control of Indigenous groups, with this formal native title defined by nation states, and 'aboriginal', 'customary' or 'communal' title for lands long occupied and used by Indigenous peoples (Hinch, 2001). Most Indigenous groups are pursuing legal title to their traditional lands, reserves and national parks declared on Indigenous lands through treaties, native title claims, land use agreements and other means (MacKay and Caruso, 2004; Weaver, 2006). These Indigenous territories are often in rural and remote areas, are high in biodiversity, wildlife and scenic values and are a focus for traditional life-ways and cultural practices such as art, music, ceremonies and handicrafts. For these reasons 'Indigenous territories are among the most significant of the cultural environments associated with ecotourism' (Weaver, 2001: 262). Indigenous peoples are developing ecotourism and other sustainable ventures based on natural

resources to support the economic development of Indigenous lands. Private operators also seek new locations and products in tribal territories, often in joint ventures or exclusive operating agreements with Indigenous groups.

Indigenous Tourism

Indigenous tourism is referred to as Aboriginal or Indigenous tourism in Australia; as Aboriginal, Native or First Nations tourism in Canada; and Indian or Native American tourism in the USA. It is also referred to as anthropological tourism or tribal tourism (see Table 1.1). According to Hinch and Butler (1996: 9), 'Indigenous tourism refers to tourism activity in which indigenous people are directly involved either through *control* and/or by having their *culture* serve as the essence of the attraction'. In Canada, Parker (1993: 400) defined Aboriginal tourism as 'any tourism product or service, which is owned and operated by Aboriginal people'. In Australia, Aboriginal or Indigenous tourism has been defined as 'a tourism product which is either: Aboriginal owned or part owned, employs Aboriginal people, or provides consenting contact with Aboriginal people, culture or land' (SATC, 1995: 5). Among the Kuna Indians of Panama, Swain (1989: 85) considers Indigenous tourism as 'tourism based on the group's *land and cultural identity* and *controlled from within* by the group'. For Smith (1996b: 299), tribal tourism at Acoma Pueblo, New Mexico (USA) involves '*small scale enterprises* that are labour intensive for an owner, a family, or a small tribe'. Therefore, Indigenous tourism typically involves small businesses based on the inherited tribal knowledge of culture and nature.

Indigenous tourism is sometimes regarded as ethnic tourism (Smith, 1989; Sofield, 1991; de Burlo, 1996; Moscardo and Pearce, 1999). Ethnic tourism always involves some form of direct contact with host cultures and their environment. For Smith (1989), ethnic tourism typically occurs among tribal groups in remote areas with limited numbers of visitors (though 100,000 visitors a year now go trekking among the hilltribes of northern Thailand). Therefore, ethnic and tribal tourism are forms of Indigenous cultural tourism involving tourist contact with Indigenous peoples or their cultural practices (Smith, 2003). However, ethnic tourism also implies contact with immigrant groups who may not be native or Indigenous to a destination. Indigenous people themselves may also be 'ethnic' tourists visiting cultural sites, native reserves or tribal events outside their local area. According to Smith (1996b: 287), the four 'Hs' of habitat, heritage, history and handicrafts define Indigenous tourism as: 'a culture-bounded visitor experience which, quite literally, is a micro-study of man-land relationships'. Hence, Indigenous tourism includes 'that segment of the visitor industry which directly involves native peoples whose ethnicity is a tourist attraction' (Smith 1996b: 283). This includes personal tourism businesses with direct contact between Indigenous hosts and visitors and indirect businesses involving the production and sale of native handicrafts or manufactured 'Aboriginal' products. Indigenous cultural knowledge, ownership and control, then, are key factors defining Indigenous tourism (see Table 1.1). Key aspects of Indigenous tourism products, along with their development and operation, are also related to community-based tourism, cultural tourism, heritage tourism, responsible tourism, pro-poor tourism, nature-based tourism and ecotourism.

Hinch and Butler (1996) distinguish between Indigenous-controlled and Indigenous-themed tourism. Attractions based on Indigenous culture that are owned and operated by Indigenous people represent 'culture controlled' or *Indigenous Cultural Tourism*. Other tourism ventures controlled by Indigenous people, that do not have Indigenous culture as a main theme, represent *Diversified Indigenous Tourism*. These diversified tourist attractions and facilities owned by Indigenous groups include resorts, boat transport or cruises, roadhouses, campgrounds and other visitor services. This infrastructure, including transport and accommodation, is a key part of Indigenous tourism in Canada, the USA and New Zealand. Ryan's (1997) model of Indigenous tourism involved Indigenous ownership and size of the enterprise, amount of Indigenous culture portrayed and the intensity of the visitor experience. Indigenous ownership of tourism and the expansion from culture-based to service-based Indigenous tourism ventures, including ecotourism on traditional lands, has mainly occurred since the 1990s (Zeppel, 1998a, 2001, 2003; Ryan and Aicken, 2005; Notzke, 2006).

Key aspects of Indigenous tourism

Indigenous tourism evolves when Indigenous people operate tours and cultural centres, provide visitor facilities and control tourist access to cultural sites, natural resources and tribal lands.

Indigenous tourist attractions include native museums and cultural villages, nature-based tours, Indigenous festivals or events and Indigenous art galleries. Cultural, environmental and spiritual aspects of Indigenous heritage and traditions are especially featured in Indigenous tourism. Through the 1990s, Indigenous tourism has developed into a new visitor market segment marked by Indigenous ownership and management of cultural attractions, nature tours and other visitor facilities (Getz and Jamieson, 1997; Zeppel, 1998a, d, 2001; Ryan and Aicken, 2005;

Table 1.1. Key features of Indigenous tourism.

INDIGENOUS TOURISM
Also referred to as: Anthropological Tourism; Cultural Tourism; Ethnic Tourism; Tribal Tourism
• Tourism connected with Indigenous culture, values and traditions • Tourism products owned and operated by Indigenous people • Tourism based on Indigenous land and cultural identity, controlled from within by Indigenous groups • Tourism which includes Indigenous 'habitat, heritage, history and handicrafts' • Typically involves small tourism businesses owned by tribes or families • Tourism focused on Indigenous knowledge of culture and nature

Sources: Based on Swain (1989); Parker (1993); Hinch and Butler (1996); Smith (1996a, b).

Notzke, 2006). Many of these Indigenous tourism ventures are community based, developed by native bands, tribal groups, leaders or entrepreneurs living in a native community. Unique aspects of Indigenous history and cultural traditions are included in cultural and heritage tourism, while Indigenous ties to the land and use of natural resources are a part of nature-based tourism and ecotourism (Miller, 1996; Scheyvens, 1999). Ceremonial aspects of Indigenous cultures are also featured in native festivals and special events. Indigenous cultures are frequently the special interest or main motivating factor for tourist travel to exotic destinations, regions and tribal events. However, Indigenous tourism enterprises on tribal lands are often located in rural or remote regions, with limited infrastructure and access by tourist markets (Getz and Jamieson, 1997). For example, there are high transport and tour costs for visiting Nunavut in Arctic Canada or Arnhem Land in Northern Australia. These factors, along with a lack of capital and business skills among Indigenous peoples, also limit the development of Indigenous ecotourism ventures in tribal lands and territories.

Honey and Thullen (2003) reviewed various codes of conduct for Indigenous tourism, ecotourism and sustainable development that were prepared by Indigenous groups, major tourism conferences, the travel industry, ecotourism societies, NGOs, finance or development institutions and government agencies. These codes reaffirmed the rights of Indigenous peoples to control and benefit from tourism, and the responsibilities of tour operators, development agencies and governments for Indigenous groups. This included fair terms for tourism participation, community empowerment and poverty alleviation. For Indigenous peoples, regaining control of Indigenous lands and territories, along with their natural and cultural resources, are integral for self-determination and sustainable development of Indigenous tourism.

Key issues for the development of tourism or ecotourism on Indigenous lands include the legal rights of Indigenous peoples on Indigenous territories, the commodification of Indigenous cultural practices for tourism and the intellectual property rights of Indigenous peoples for the use of their designs and their traditional cultural or biological knowledge in tourism. Indigenous self-determination and control over tourism on Indigenous territories mainly relies on legal title to traditional lands (Hinch, 2004).

Hence, achieving sustainable tourism on Indigenous territories depends on several key factors such as: 'land ownership, community control of tourism, government support for tourism development, restricted access to indigenous homelands and reclaiming natural or cultural resources utilised for tourism' (Zeppel, 1998a: 73). The chapters in this book examine these key issues for Indigenous ecotourism ventures on Indigenous lands or territories in the Pacific Islands, Latin America, Africa and South East Asia.

Indigenous Tourism Rights International

Indigenous Tourism Rights International (ITRI) was established in 1995. Based in the USA, it was formerly known as the Rethinking Tourism Project. It is dedicated to helping Indigenous groups preserve and protect their traditional lands and cultures from the impacts of global tourism (McLaren, 1999, 2003). Their campaigns focus on helping Indigenous groups achieve self-determination and control over tourism. In 2002, ITRI campaigned against the UN International Year of Ecotourism, and organized alternative forums for Indigenous peoples to debate the benefits and impacts of ecotourism activities on their culture and traditional lands (Vivanco, 2002). The International Forum on Indigenous Tourism held in Oaxaca, Mexico in March 2002 generated a declaration on the rights of Indigenous peoples to control tourism on their lands. ITRI has formed a working partnership with the International Indian Treaty Council to promote Indigenous community-based tourism projects and build an Indigenous Tourism Network in the Americas. In 2004, an online ITRI conference titled 'Rethinking Tourism Certification' discussed Indigenous viewpoints on the promotion of global standards for certifying ecotourism or sustainable tourism. These certification programmes, however, give priority to environmental and economic matters rather than to Indigenous issues, as non-Indigenous agencies control these certification schemes with few Indigenous criteria included.

Indigenous Ecotourism

Defining Indigenous ecotourism

The main focus of this book is commercially marketed ecotourism products and ventures operated by Indigenous groups. Key aspects of Indigenous ecotourism include a nature-based product, Indigenous ownership and the presentation of Indigenous environmental and cultural knowledge. Ecotourism includes Aboriginal people and their traditions because of the strong bond between Indigenous cultures and the natural environment. This includes cultural, spiritual and physical links between Indigenous peoples and their traditional lands or natural resources. Indigenous cultural tourism or ecocultural tourism involves 'responsible, dignified and sensitive contact between indigenous people and tourists which educates the tourist about the distinct and evolving relationship between Indigenous peoples and their country, whilst providing returns to the local indigenous community' (TWS (The Wilderness Society), 1999). Indigenous ecotourism then is: 'Tourism which cares for the environment and which involves (Indigenous) people in decision-making and management' (ANTA, 2001). It includes nature-based tourism products or accommodation owned by Indigenous groups and Indigenous cultural tours or attractions in a natural setting. Much of this Indigenous tourism development focuses on community-based ecotourism that benefits local people (Liu, 1994; Drumm, 1998; Sproule and Suhandi, 1998; WWF, 2001b; Tourism Concern, 2002; Fennell, 2003; Chen, 2004; Notzke, 2006). According to Drumm (1998: 198), Indigenous community-based ecotourism involves 'ecotourism programs which take place under the control and active participation of the local people who inhabit a natural attraction'. These ecotourism

enterprises involve Indigenous communities using their natural resources and traditional lands to gain income from tourism. Hence, Indigenous ecotourism ventures involve nature conservation, business enterprise (or partnerships) and tourism income for community development (Sproule, 1996, cited in Fennell, 2003). Hunting and fishing tours are also part of Indigenous ecotourism, (with sustainable use of wildlife resources), although consumptive activities are not usually considered to be 'true' ecotourism (Honey, 1999; Weaver, 2001).

The term Indigenous ecotourism has emerged since the mid-1990s to describe community ecotourism projects developed on Indigenous lands and territories in Latin America, Australia and Canada. Colvin (1994), Schaller (1996) and Wesche (1996) first used the term 'Indigenous ecotourism' to describe community-based ecotourism projects among Indian tribes in Ecuador. Wearing (1996) also presented a paper on training for Indigenous ecotourism development at the Fourth World Leisure Congress. Karwacki (1999) used the term Indigenous ecotourism in reviewing challenges for Indigenous groups seeking to develop ecotourism ventures on their lands, while Beck and Somerville (2002) and Sofield (2002) also referred to Aboriginal (cultural) ecotourism in Australia in this way. Fennell (2003) also refers to Indigenous ecotourism entrepreneurs, while the Mapajo Lodge in Bolivia describe their rainforest programme as Indigenous ecotourism. Furthermore, the Australian National Training Authority (ANTA, 2001) developed an Indigenous Ecotourism Toolbox, which includes case study examples and business plans for communities to set up their own ecotourism ventures. Indigenous Tourism Rights International has reviewed certification programmes and culturally appropriate standards for Indigenous ecotourism. Finally, and most recently, Nepal (2004, 2005) examined capacity building for Indigenous ecotourism on the Tl'axt'en Nation lands in British Columbia, Canada, while Hashimoto and Telfer (2004) reviewed Aboriginal ecotourism in northern Canada. Indigenous ecotourism also occurs in Africa, Asia and Oceania, and is covered in several chapters of this book.

Indigenous views on ecotourism

According to Johnston (2000), there are some key differences between industry definitions of ecotourism and Indigenous views of ecotourism (see Table 1.2). Industry use of ecotourism includes commercializing Indigenous biological and cultural heritage, claims to be environmentally or socially responsible, and uses criteria for sustainability derived without input from Indigenous peoples. Indigenous support for ecotourism, however, involves 'tourism that is based on indigenous knowledge systems and values, promoting customary practices and livelihoods' (Johnston, 2000: 91). Cultural aspects of Indigenous ecotourism include the close bonds between Indigenous peoples and the environment, based on subsistence activities, along with spiritual relationships with the land, plants and animals. However, potential conflicts within Indigenous ecotourism include tourists objecting to traditional hunting activities and tribal people using modern items such as rifles and outboard motors (Hinch, 2001). In East Africa, there are land-use conflicts between hunting companies killing wildlife and the walking or wildlife-viewing safaris run as community ecotourism ventures by the Maasai (*Tourism in Focus*, 2002b).

In addition to generating employment and income, there are often political motivations for Indigenous ecotourism. For many Indigenous groups, ecotourism is used to reinforce land claims, acknowledge cultural identity and land ownership, and regain their rights to access or use tribal land and resources. Ecotourism also shows that tribal land is being used productively to generate income and the ability of Indigenous groups to govern themselves or manage businesses (Hinch, 2001; Weaver, 2001, 2006). For Indigenous peoples, then, sustainable ecotourism development is based on 'conservation of resources and empowerment of local people through direct benefits and control over ecotourism activities' (Scheyvens, 2002: 80). However, government policies on community-based ecotourism and support from environmental NGOs are essential for most Indigenous ecotourism and conservation projects to be implemented.

Most tourism organizations consider Indigenous tourism, ecotourism and wildlife tourism as separate niche or special interest areas of nature-based tourism. Ecotourism Australia (2005), though, defines ecotourism as: 'ecologically sustainable tourism with a primary focus on experiencing natural areas that fosters environmental and *cultural understanding, appreciation and conservation.*'

Table 1.2. Industry and Indigenous perceptions of ecotourism.

Industry Ecotourism
- Ecotourism as any form of industry monopolized tourism
- Marketed as nature, cultural, ethnic or adventure travel
- Commercialize Indigenous bio-cultural heritage, including
- collective property (knowledge) and/or homeland of 'host' peoples
- Claim to be socially and environmentally responsible
- Apply sustainability criteria determined without Indigenous input
- Indigenous cultures commercialized e.g. photographs on brochures
- Few companies obtain prior consent to promote Indigenous peoples
- Few companies negotiate business partnerships or royalty payments

Indigenous Ecotourism
- Ecotourism based on Indigenous knowledge systems and values
- Ecotourism based on promoting Indigenous customary practices and livelihoods
- Ecotourism used to regain rights to access, manage and use traditional land and resources
- Ecotourism used to manage cultural property such as historic and sacred sites
- Takes place under the control and active participation of local Indigenous people
- Includes Indigenous communities in ecotourism planning, development and operation
- Managing Indigenous cultural property in terms of land, heritage and resources
- Negotiating the terms of trade for the use of ecotourism resources, including people

Sources: Based on Drumm (1998); Johnston (2000); Hinch (2001); Hillel (2003).

In this definition, there is a primary focus on the natural environment with a secondary emphasis on cultural heritage, including Indigenous cultures. The International Ecotourism Society (2004), based in the USA, defines ecotourism as 'responsible travel to natural areas that conserves the environment and *improves the well-being of local people*'. The focus, again, is on the natural environment, but with ecotourism providing benefits for local communities. For Honey (1999: 25), ecotourism also 'directly *benefits the economic development and political empowerment of local communities*; and fosters respect for different cultures and for human rights' (see Table 1.3). In Canada, the term Aboriginal tourism is preferred to ecotourism (Hashimoto and Telfer, 2004). Some Indigenous groups also refer to cultural ecotourism or ecocultural tourism, to emphasize that the natural environment and resources are still managed as an Indigenous cultural landscape (Helu-Thaman, 1992; Beck and Somerville, 2002).

Indigenous ecotourism in Australia

In Australia, Indigenous ecotourism ventures include boat cruises, nature-based accommodation, cultural ecotours and wildlife tours operating on Aboriginal lands, National Parks and in traditional tribal areas (Singh *et al.*, 2001; Zeppel, 2003). These Indigenous-owned ecotourism enterprises present unique Indigenous perspectives of the natural and cultural environment, promote nature conservation and provide employment for local Indigenous people (Zeppel, 1998a). Hence, these Indigenous products meet the key criteria of ecotourism as nature based, include environmental education, are ecologically sustainable and support nature conservation (Weaver, 2001). Indigenous nature conservation or 'caring for country' involves traditional landowners or custodians 'looking after the environmental, cultural and spiritual well being of the land' (Aboriginal Tourism Australia, 2005). Looking after Aboriginal sites, landscapes or natural resources and educating visitors about 'country' often motivate Indigenous conserva-

tion ethics in ecotourism or land management. Nganyintja, a *Pitjantjatjara* Elder working with Desert Tracks in Central Australia, stated that: 'carefully controlled ecotourism has been good for my family and my place Angatja' (cited in James, 1994: 12). Many Indigenous tours in natural areas are marketed as cultural tours rather than ecotours, emphasizing the ongoing cultural links between Indigenous tourism operators and their traditional lands.

Indigenous ecotourism ventures, then, focus on Indigenous relationships with the land and the cultural significance of the natural environment, including wildlife. This includes Indigenous use of bush foods and medicinal plants, rock art, landscape features with spiritual significance, creation stories, totemic animals, traditional artefacts and ceremonies and contemporary land use. Such tours educate visitors on Indigenous environmental values, sustainable use of natural resources and 'caring for country'. As Tom Trevorrow, an *Ngarrindjeri* operator of Camp Coorong in South Australia noted, 'We have to look after the environment and we teach visitors the importance of this' (cited in ATSIC, 1996: 29). Indigenous interpretations of nature and wildlife are also important for the maturing ecotourism market (DISR (Department of Industry, Science and Resources), 2000). However, there is limited engagement of the ecotourism industry with Aboriginal peoples in Australia (Dowling, 2001). Gatjil Djerrkura, an Aboriginal keynote speaker at the 2000 ecotourism conference, stated that Aboriginal-owned enterprises should have contemporary business roles to play in Australia's ecotourism industry (*Ecotourism News*, 2000). Indigenous culture is a significant but overlooked part of ecotourism products in Australia. Aboriginal tourism operators also resent 'outsiders setting up tours in their traditional areas, national park permits to visit sites in their own country and ecotourism certification when 'Aboriginal "accreditation" involves approval from elders' (Bissett *et al.*, 1998: 7).

Key Indigenous issues in Australian ecotourism include the following:

- sustainable development of Aboriginal tourism (Burchett, 1992; Altman and Finlayson, 1993);

Table 1.3. Key features of general ecotourism and of Indigenous ecotourism.

Ecotourism	Indigenous ecotourism
1. *Involves travel to natural destinations* Remote regions, protected areas, private reserves	Remote homelands, communal reserves, inhabited protected areas and tribal territories
2. *Minimizes impact* Reduce ecological/cultural impacts of facilities and tourists Sustainable development of non-consumptive industry	Minimize environmental and cultural impacts Sustainable tribal use of natural resources
3. *Builds environmental and cultural awareness* Environmental education of tourists and residents by trained guides	Tribal guides share environmental knowledge Reinforces Indigenous cultural links with land
4. *Provides direct financial benefits for conservation* Tourism funds environmental protection, education and research Park entrance fees, tourist taxes and levies, conservation donations	Tourism funds conservation and community needs Tourist/lease fees, wildlife quotas and NGO funding
5. *Provides financial benefits and empowerment for local people* Park revenue sharing, community tourism concessions and partnerships	Park revenue sharing with local communities Legal land title to negotiate tourism contracts Lease land on reserves and sell wildlife quotas Business owned/co-owned by tribal community
6. *Respects local culture and sensitive to host countries* Culturally respectful of local customs, dress codes and social norms	Promotes ecocultural tourism and learning Tourism complements traditional lifestyle
7. *Supports human rights and democratic movements* Respect human rights; understand social and political situation	Tribal land rights and human rights recognized Indigenous political history acknowledged

Sources: Based on Honey (1999); Blake (2003); Scheyvens (2002); The International Ecotourism Society (2004).

- environmental impacts of tourism (Ross, 1991; Miller, 1996);
- cultural interpretation of heritage sites (Bissett *et al.*, 1998; Howard *et al.*, 2001; Beck and Somerville, 2002); and
- tourism in Aboriginal national parks (Mercer, 1994, 1998; Pitcher *et al.*, 1999; Sutton, 1999; Hall, 2000).

Other industry issues include ecotourism training for Aboriginal people (ANTA, 2001), Aboriginal control of tourism (Trotter, 1997; Pitcher *et al.*, 1999; Zeppel, 2002), ecotourism policies (Zeppel, 2003) and developing Aboriginal ecotourism products (Zeppel,

1998b, c). In Australia, ecotourism is regarded solely as nature viewing activities. Some Aboriginal tours, though, include hunting activities, eating witchetty grubs and plant foods. Tasting wild plant foods may be constrained by environmental laws in protected areas. One Aboriginal tour operator in North Queensland used to let visitors taste rainforest fruits, but a sign in the vehicle now asks guests not to touch or eat anything in the rainforest (Miller, 1996). Telling tourists how Indigenous peoples used to hunt, eat bush foods and utilize the natural environment, as a past practice, contradicts the reality of

Indigenous cultures as alive and still linked to tribal lands. These key issues are similar for all Indigenous peoples involved in ecotourism.

Indigenous involvement in ecotourism

Worldwide, Indigenous involvement and participation in ecotourism occurs with varied levels of ownership and input from Indigenous groups and organizations. Indigenous people may participate in ecotourism as individuals, families, a village or community and through a tribal council or federation (Cater, 1996; Ashley and Roe, 1998; Wesche and Drumm, 1999; Mann, 2002). Indigenous involvement in ecotourism can include full or part ownership, joint ventures, partnerships, services provision (e.g. lodge accommodation, boat transport, guiding and food) and employment by non-Indigenous tourism companies (see Table 1.4). Mann (2002) distinguishes between responsible tours that hire a local Indigenous guide; partnership tours with a tourism business and marketing by an outside operator; and community tours, with enterprises set up, owned and run by an Indigenous community though often with an outside manager. Community-based ecotourism enterprises (e.g. lodges) are owned and managed by communities, with tourism jobs rostered among members and profits allocated to community projects. Family or group initiatives in ecotourism may also employ or involve other community members. Joint ventures involve formal business contracts or exclusive operating agreements between Indigenous communities or tribal councils with non-Indigenous tourism businesses. In joint venture arrangements, the outside operator is responsible for marketing, bringing tourists, a guide and most transport, with the Indigenous group hosting and entertaining visitors. Alternatively, the outside company obtains a long-term lease on Indigenous land, builds tourist facilities and employs local people. The tour operator pays a lease rental fee and/or percentage of profits to the Indigenous group owning or claiming the land. Indigenous people also develop ecotourism ventures in partnership with conservation NGOs, national park agencies, government tourism bureaus, Indigenous organizations, development agencies, university researchers and other local communities (Fennell, 2003). Other related issues with these enterprises include limited community involvement and empowerment in ecotourism, especially by women (Scheyvens, 1999, 2000, 2002; Medina, 2005) business and social challenges for Indigenous groups in developing ecotourism ventures (Karwacki, 1999; Epler Wood, 1999, 2002; Johnston, 2001), and potential conflicts between ecotourism and Indigenous hunting or land use activities (Pleumarom, 1994; Grekin and Milne, 1996; Hinch, 1998; Zeppel, 1998d; Honey, 1999). The chapters in this book assess the nature of Indigenous ownership and involvement in ecotourism ventures on their traditional lands.

UN International Year of Ecotourism

The UN International Year of Ecotourism was held in 2002. It provided a global focus for efforts to link sustainable tourism development with the conservation of natural areas. There were two main international ecotourism conferences sponsored by the UN, one held in

Table 1.4. Indigenous community involvement in ecotourism.

- **Renting land** to an operator to develop while simply monitoring impacts
- Working as occasional, part- or full-time **staff for outside operators**
- Providing **selected services** such as food preparation, guiding, transport or accommodations (or a combination of several or all of these) to operators
- Forming **joint ventures** with outside operators with a division of labour, which allows the community to provide most services, while the operator takes care of marketing
- Operating fully independent **community tourism** programmes
- Enterprise run by **local entrepreneur**, supplying goods and services (guiding, campsites, homestays)

Sources: Drumm (1998: 201); Ashley and Roe (1998: 8).

Quebec (Canada) and the other in Cairns (Australia), which addressed a range of issues including the role of Indigenous groups in ecotourism. The *Quebec Declaration on Ecotourism* stated that ecotourism is sustainable tourism that contributes actively to the conservation and interpretation of natural and cultural heritage. In this Quebec Declaration, ecotourism also 'includes local and indigenous communities in its planning, development and operation, and contributes to their well being' (Hillel, 2002, in Buckley, 2003: xiv). The vision statement for the related *Cairns Charter on Partnerships for Ecotourism* developed in Australia at the end of 2002, states: 'Ecotourism respects the desire of indigenous peoples ... to profitably generate sustainable economic and social development' (Ecotourism Australia, 2002). Article one in this Cairns Charter on Indigenous communities as ecotourism partners reaffirms that Indigenous peoples are recognized for their cultural heritage, provision of access to cultural sites and traditional practices, the requirement of consent for ecotourism projects in homeland areas, support and participation in ecotourism training and encouragement of the tourist appreciation and understanding of Indigenous cultures.

Indigenous groups argued that the UN *International Year of Ecotourism* represented the commercial aspects of using 'ecotourism' to develop global mass tourism, further encroaching on Indigenous territories and the rights of Indigenous peoples. Organizations such as Tourism Concern, the Third World Network and the Rethinking Tourism Project raised key issues relating to the impacts of ecotourism on local communities. Indigenous groups held an alternative meeting in Oaxaca, Mexico in March 2002 to debate the issues from ecotourism development. Some 200 participants from 13 countries in the Americas reviewed case studies of Indigenous tourism projects in local communities. In a Zapotec community in Oaxaca, ecotourism was seen as sharing Indigenous knowledge of sustainable land use, with forest tours an economic alternative to other uses of forest resources (Vivanco, 2002). The *International Forum on Indigenous Tourism* at Oaxaca drafted a declaration reaffirming the rights of Indigenous

groups to manage and control tourism on their lands.

The nature or type of Indigenous ecotourism differs between developed and developing countries (see Table 1.5). This includes the legal status of Indigenous peoples, their lifestyle, type of Indigenous territories, extent of legal rights and land rights and type of support from government agencies or NGOs for ecotourism on tribal lands. Indigenous groups in developing countries are threatened by land incursions, still acquiring legal land titles and rely on support from NGOs to develop ecotourism. This book examines Indigenous participation and control over ecotourism that occurs on tribal lands and protected areas in the developing countries of Oceania, Latin America, Africa and South-east Asia.

Study of Indigenous Ecotourism

There have been a number of books and articles written about Indigenous involvement in ecotourism since the mid 1990s. The first book published on *Tourism and Indigenous Peoples* (Butler and Hinch, 1996) included two chapters about Indigenous ecotourism. One addressed issues with Inuit people in Pond Inlet, Canada, developing and marketing tourism in a remote Arctic area, and also negative tourist responses to traditional Inuit hunting (Grekin and Milne, 1996). The other reviewed community conflicts between customary landowners and local 'big men' in developing a rainforest wilderness walking trail on Guadalcanal in the Solomon Islands (Rudkin and Hall, 1996). Other chapters in the book reviewed cross-cultural issues and the impacts of tourism on local hosts in Bali, Nepal, Thailand, Vanuatu, the Cook Islands, Native American reservations in the USA and Maori tourism in New Zealand. However, this book's inclusion of case studies about Balinese people did not meet the criteria for 'Indigenous' or tribal peoples as defined by the UN (Ryan, 1997).

The book, *People and Tourism in Fragile Environments* (Price, 1996), included five case study chapters of Indigenous peoples and community-based tourism in natural areas.

These included cultural tourism at Zuni Pueblo, New Mexico (USA) (Mallari and Enote, 1996); Inuit hunting and tourism in Nunavut, northern Canada (Smith, 1996a); and the development of Aboriginal tourism on remote Cape York Peninsula in northern Australia (Strang, 1996). Another case study covered the 75,000 Sami people in their Sapmi homeland of northern Scandinavia, where tourism is based on the traditional life of reindeer herding (Pedersen and Viken, 1996). In Kenya, some Maasai people benefit from ecotourism partnerships with safari tour operators on Maasai group ranches and trust land, however, community disputes over income from tourism have increased (Berger, 1996). These five case studies review the key challenges for Indigenous groups in developing ecotourism ventures on tribal lands based on natural and cultural resources.

Chapters on Indigenous ecotourism issues have been included in more recent tourism books. For example, the book *Tourism Development in Critical Environments* included chapters about community-based ecotourism on nature reserves in Belize, with Mayan families involved at Cockscomb Basin Wildlife Sanctuary (Horwich and Lyon, 1999); community tourism in Senegal, Uganda and Namibia in Africa (Echtner, 1999); and tourism on Pueblo Indian reservations in Arizona and New Mexico, south-west USA (Lew, 1999). Books on sustainable tourism and special interest tourism have also included chapters on Indigenous tourism ventures (Zeppel, 1998a, 2001). The *Earthscan Reader in Sustainable Tourism* (France, 1997) included articles about Maasai people and tourism in Kenya and Tanzania, the CAMPFIRE programme in Zimbabwe and ecotourism in the Third World (Cater, 1997). The book *Tourism and Cultural Conflicts* included chapters on

Table 1.5. Indigenous peoples and ecotourism in developed and developing countries.

	Developed countries	Developing countries
Indigenous peoples	Minority cultures Officially recognized as Indigenous Traditional or modern lifestyles Colonized sovereign nations	Majority or minority cultures Varied status as indigenous/tribal/minorities Traditional subsistence economies Colonized or independent nations
Indigenous territories	Mainly government reservations Co-managed Aboriginal national parks Managed by tribal councils and government Tax-free status on reserves (North America)	Ancestral lands and some Indigenous reserves Live inside protected areas, share revenue Managed by Indigenous tribal councils Threatened by resource extraction and settlers
Indigenous rights	Traditional resource use rights No direct wildlife ownership rights Intellectual and cultural property rights Legal title to ancestral lands	Communal resource use rights (forest, reefs) Limited wildlife ownership or use rights No intellectual and cultural property rights Traditional or legal title to ancestral lands
Indigenous ecotourism	Supported by government agencies Funded by government grants Community, family or individual ventures Economic development of tribal areas	Supported by conservation and aid NGOs Funded by development agencies and NGOs Mainly community tourism ventures Economic alternative to extractive land uses

Developed countries/regions = Canada, USA, Australia, New Zealand, Europe, Japan.
Developing countries/regions = Pacific Islands (Oceania), Latin America, Africa, South-east Asia, China, India.

Maori tourism in New Zealand (Ryan, 1998), First Nations peoples managing heritage sites in Canada (Wall, 1998) and cultural property rights for Indigenous tourism in Australia (Whittaker, 1998). *Ecotourism: A Guide for Planners and Managers* (Lindberg et al., 1998), published by The Ecotourism Society, included three chapters reviewing community-based ecotourism ventures in southern Africa (Christ, 1998), Ecuador (Drumm, 1998) and Indonesia (Sproule and Suhandi, 1998). Drumm (1998) reviewed ecotourism ventures in Ecuador managed by Quechua, Huaorani, Napo Runa and Cofan Indians. In contrast, the book *Ecotourism in the Less Developed World* (Weaver, 1998) did not cover Indigenous involvement in ecotourism. Most recently, *Tourism in Destination Communities* included a chapter reviewing Indigenous resource rights in tourism and biodiversity (Johnston, 2003).

There are several published case studies about Indigenous ecotourism projects in the Pacific region. Harrison (2003), in his edited book *Pacific Island Tourism*, included chapters reviewing ecotourism policy in Fiji and community-based ecotourism projects, such as village guesthouses in Vanuatu and trekking on Makira Island in the Solomon Islands. Sofield (2003) in *Empowerment for Sustainable Tourism Development* critically examined the outcomes of village or community-based tourism projects in the Solomon Islands, Fiji and Vanuatu. A manual on *Community-based Ecotourism and Conservation in the Pacific islands* included 14 case studies of ecotourism ventures in community Conservation Areas (SPREP, 2002). The book, *Nature-based Tourism in Peripheral Areas: Development or Disaster?* (Hall and Boyd, 2004) has a chapter on beach *fale* tourism in Samoa (Scheyvens, 2004). In contrast, tourism books on Asia and Africa have included little coverage of Indigenous ecotourism, apart from village tourism and management of national parks. A book on local participation in Latin American tourism included one chapter on Indigenous tourism in Ecuador (de Bont and Janssen, 2002). *A Companion to Tourism* had a chapter on Indigenous peoples and tourism (Hinch, 2004). Scheyvens' (2002) book, *Tourism for Development: Empowering Communities*, included reviews of CAMPFIRE, the

Sunungukai ecotourism venture and Noah's ecocultural tours in Zimbabwe; communal conservancies in Namibia and Zambia; tourism at protected areas and Phinda wildlife reserve in KwaZulu Natal, South Africa; and gorilla tourism in Rwanda and Uganda. However, there was no chapter in this book dedicated to Indigenous tourism or ecotourism.

Since 2000, books on the ecotourism industry, ecotourism policy and ecotourism management have included some chapters or sections on Indigenous ecotourism issues. Zeppel (2003) examined current ecotourism policies for Indigenous peoples in Australia, while Hashimoto and Telfer (2004) reviewed Aboriginal ecotourism in northern Canada. Duffy (2002) included a chapter on threats to community-based ecotourism among Mayan communities in Belize in her book titled *A Trip too Far: Ecotourism, Politics and Exploitation*. Weaver's (2001) book on ecotourism reviewed key issues for ecotourism on Indigenous territories, while Epler Wood (2002) covered the key criteria needed for ecotourism to benefit Indigenous communities. *The Encyclopaedia of Ecotourism* included a chapter on Indigenous territories addressing land claims and Indigenous involvement in ecotourism (Hinch, 2001). Page and Dowling's (2002) book on ecotourism summarized an Indigenous ecotourism project in Capirona, Ecuador, based on research by Drumm (1998). Buckley's (2003) *Case Studies in Ecotourism* provided brief reviews of conservation and ecotourism projects involving Indigenous peoples in Latin America, Australia/NZ, Africa and Asia-Pacific. These studies mainly focused on Indigenous ecotourism in protected areas, on private reserves, at ecolodges and a few ecotours on tribal lands. A manual on *Sustainable Development of Ecotourism* included case studies of several Indigenous ecotourism projects in Africa and Latin America (WTO, 2003). The book *Ecotourism: Management and Assessment* (Diamantis, 2004) has chapters on responsible nature tourism in South African parks, community ecotourism at Lisu Lodge (Thailand) and Il Ngwesi Lodge (Kenya) (Johannson and Diamantis, 2004) and on Canadian Aboriginal ecotourism (Hashimoto and Telfer, 2004).

Indigenous Tourism (Ryan and Aicken,

2005) analysed the commodification and management of Indigenous cultures at various tourist sites, attractions and areas that involve Indigenous peoples. The book reviewed Indigenous tourism in Australia, New Zealand, Canada, USA and Sweden, along with Lijiang (China), Botswana (Africa) and Western Flores (Indonesia). The main focus was on visitor experiences of Indigenous tourism, authenticity in Indigenous cultural tourism products, events and artefacts, and interactions between tourists and Indigenous hosts. One chapter analysed community-based tourism projects among San Bushmen (Basarwa) in the Okavango Delta, Botswana (Mbaiwa, 2005), while others addressed Indigenous ecotourism in western Canada (Nepal, 2005) and at Camp Coorong in South Australia (Higgins-Desbiolles, 2005).

Indigenous ecotourism is included in a new book by Notzke (2006), *The Stranger, the Native and the Land: Perspectives on Indigenous Tourism*. It reviews Indigenous tourism, Indigenous economies, visitor markets for Indigenous tourism, cultural issues in tourism, protected areas, Indigenous ecotourism and community-based tourism. The section on Indigenous ecotourism includes case studies from Canada, Belize and Ecuador, with additional case studies on Indigenous tourism in the Canadian Arctic, Australia and Samoa. There are also other books covering topics relating to Indigenous peoples, conservation, ecotourism and protected areas (Furze *et al.*, 1996; King and Stewart, 1996; Stevens and De Lacy, 1997; Igoe, 2004). In these books, the Indigenous co-management of protected areas and tourism is covered in case studies drawn from East Africa, Nepal, Papua New Guinea, Nicaragua, Honduras, Australia and Canada, along with Alaska and Dakota in the USA.

Articles in tourism journals have mainly reviewed the cultural impacts of tourism on Indigenous groups. From the early to mid-1990s, a few papers addressed key issues for Indigenous tourism development in the USA (Lew, 1996), Arctic Canada (Notzke, 1999), Pacific Islands (Sofield, 1993), Australia (Altman and Finlayson, 1993) and New Zealand (Barnett, 1997; Zeppel, 1998e). Their focus was on Indigenous-owned tourism ventures and managing tourism on tribal

homelands. The few papers published about Indigenous ecotourism projects mainly focus on developing countries, starting with Colvin's (1994) paper on Capirona, Ecuador. Other related papers cover Indigenous property rights in tourism (Johnston, 2000) and empowering women through ecotourism (Scheyvens, 2000). Recent journal articles on natural resource management also refer to Indigenous ecotourism projects.

However, to date, there have been no reports or books addressing Indigenous ecotourism as a specific type of nature-based tourism. Therefore, the chapters in this book provide a global review and analysis of Indigenous ecotourism projects in developing countries (i.e. Pacific Islands, Latin America, Africa and South-east Asia). The chapters review the development and management of Indigenous-controlled ecotourism ventures mainly in tribal homelands and protected areas. The environmental, cultural and economic benefits of different types of Indigenous ecotourism ventures are also evaluated. For Indigenous peoples, achieving sustainable ecotourism depends on asserting legal rights, Indigenous control of land and resources, geographic location, funding or business support and developing effective links with the wider tourism industry.

Key themes in Indigenous ecotourism

Key themes in the published research and case studies about community tourism and Indigenous ecotourism include community development (Russell, 2000; Fennell, 2003; Briedenham and Wickens, 2004), empowerment (Scheyvens, 1999, 2000, 2002; Sofield, 2003; Spenceley, 2004; WTO, 2005) or self-determination (Johnston, 2003a; Hinch, 2004) and sustainable tourism/ecotourism (Epler Wood, 1999, 2002; Robinson, 1999; WWF, 2001b; WTO, 2003; Mat Som and Baum, 2004; Mbaiwa, 2005). Community tourism development became important during the 1990s as many regional and local communities looked for economic alternatives to agriculture, mining and manufacturing. These new avenues included ecotourism, nature tourism and heritage or cultural tourism, initiated either by a top-down government policy approach or by local people starting new ventures (Godde, 1998; Hatton, 2002; WTO, 2002). Small-scale ecotourism promotes local conservation of natural and cultural resources, either individually or through tourism enterprises owned or managed by communities. Local participation, sharing economic benefits and control of tourism were essential for community-based ecotourism (Lash, 1998).

Ecotourism, as a tool for community development, also involves new partnerships with tour operators, government agencies, conservation NGOs, researchers, other Indigenous communities and international groups (Butcher, 2003; Fennell, 2003; Suansri, 2003). According to Mann (2000), community tourism involves local people in decision-making and ownership of tourism, a fair share of profits from tourism ventures and new tourism committees or organizations that represent the community while minimizing environmental and cultural impacts. For Indigenous people, the community is a tribe or village of related members, with shared decision-making and village ownership of forests or reserves held under traditional or legal land titles. For this reason, most Indigenous ecotourism projects are community-based tourism ventures. However, marginalized Indigenous groups require support from NGOs, aid groups and government agencies to control and benefit from community tourism or joint tourism ventures (Lash and Austin, 2003; Smith, 2003).

Successful community-based ecotourism requires the empowerment of community members through local participation and control of tourism decision-making, employment and training opportunities and increased entrepreneurial activities by local people. Empowerment also requires building local capacity to participate in tourism, such as basic tourism awareness courses along with training in languages, business and operational skills. According to Fennell (2003: 159), the process of empowerment involves local people 'holding the will, resources, and opportunity to make decisions within the community'. This process needs to be supported by appropriate policies, education, training and partnerships. Moreover,

'if ecotourism is to be viewed as a tool for rural development, it must also help to shift economic and political control to the local community, village, cooperative, or entrepreneur' (Honey, 2003: 23). Scheyvens (1999, 2002), based on Friedmann (1992), developed an empowerment framework to account for local community involvement and control over ecotourism or other ventures. This community-based model included psychological, social, political and economic empowerment or disempowerment through tourism. Increased status and self-esteem, lasting economic benefits, community development and tourism decision-making are key aspects of empowerment through tourism. Sofield (2003) also proposed that tourism sustainability depends not only on empowering Indigenous communities, but that traditional community mechanisms had to be supported by legal empowerment, along with environmental or institutional change to reallocate power and decision-making on resource use to local communities, supported and sanctioned by states.

In South Africa, despite moves towards local participation in tourism decision-making and training, community tourism projects are limited by a lack of business funding or legal land titles, remote rural locations, tourism seasonality and poor support from other local tourism operators (Briedenham and Wickens, 2004). There is limited commitment from tour operators in supporting Indigenous peoples and their rights to benefit economically from wildlife and traditional lands in South Africa (Woodwood, 1997). However, in 2000/01, bids for new tourism concessions in Kruger National Park included empowerment criteria (20% of bids) such as: 'shareholding by historically disadvantaged individuals or groups (HDI/HDG) (40%), training and affirmative action in employment (20%), business and economic opportunities for local communities (40%)' (Spenceley, 2004: 274). Indigenous ecotourism ventures also required 'resource empowerment' whereby local communities have ownership or use rights of land and resources (Mat Som and Baum, 2004). In the Okavango Delta of Botswana, land trusts for San Bushmen run community tourism ventures or leased land and wildlife quotas to other operators. This promotes wildlife conservation and local economic benefits. However, to be successful, communities require further social and political empowerment through training in managerial skills and use of trust funds, direct resource ownership and more input in land use or wildlife quotas allocated to tourism (Mbaiwa, 2005). Empowering Indigenous communities in tourism depends on enhancing local control through traditional tribal or legal empowerment, and recognition of individual and collective rights to ancestral lands (WTO, 2005). Successful models of community-based ecotourism, such as Capirona in Ecuador (Colvin, 1994), are based on community ownership and management of both natural resources and tourism (Lash, 1998; Sproule and Suhandi, 1998; Sofield, 2003; Mat Som and Baum, 2004).

The sustainable development of ecotourism, then, is based on the integrated elements of ecological, economic and socio-cultural sustainability (WTO, 2003). Ecotourism is based on the conservation of biodiversity, mainly in protected areas, and minimizing the impacts of tourism in natural areas (Garen, 2000; Buckley, 2003). The economic benefits of ecotourism aim to assist nature conservation as well as provide returns to local communities through employment, the purchase of goods and services and fees. Ecotourism and pro-poor tourism projects focus on poverty alleviation and conservation to provide alternatives to traditional subsistence economies and resource use in rural areas (Butcher, 2003; Roe *et al.*, 2004; Epler Wood, 2005). As well as social benefits, ecotourism also aims to foster local cultural practices, crafts and traditions. However, many conservation and community development projects in protected areas, including ecotourism, have had limited community participation through consultation, monetary compensation or employment. Decision-making power about conservation and tourism still lies with NGOs and government agencies, with local communities limited or restricted in resource use (Honey, 1999; Wilshusen, 2000). Intrepid Travel (2002) reviewed the economic, socio-cultural and physical impacts of alternative tourism in 59 rural villages and in first-hand case studies of five villages they visited in South-east Asia. Their findings indicate that while tourism

provides local economic and social benefits, most of the villages had little control over tourism. Doan's (2000) analysis of ecotourism in developing countries suggests that ecotourism in private reserves, including Indigenous areas, was more sustainable and delivered better local benefits than ecotourism in public parks.

However, ongoing Indigenous use of wildlife and natural resources, particularly in protected areas, conflicts with the environmental standards and sustainability criteria of developed nations, western tourists, national park agencies and conservation NGOs (Hinch, 1998; Robinson, 1999). Therefore, negotiating acceptable forms of Indigenous resource use is a key part of many Indigenous ecotourism ventures. These core Indigenous cultural and environmental values influence and shape economic development strategies on tribal lands (Groenfeldt, 2003). A key premise of this book, then, is: 'The nexus between land and culture defines sustainable tourism for Indigenous peoples' (Zeppel, 1998a: 65). In the Cuyabeno Wildlife Reserve of the Ecuadorian Amazon, Indian income from ecotourism depends more on the tourist attractiveness of the natural area, the type of tourism specialization or services offered and the type of local tourism organization or industry structure adopted (e.g. community-run versus joint ventures). Ecotourism had a positive impact on conservation only where tourism changed land use decisions (e.g. no-take areas); and when tourism work reduced the local free time and need for hunting (Wunder, 2000). Wesche (1996) also suggested that as the ecotourism industry in Ecuador reached a consolidation stage, it became more concerned with sustainability and more willing to accommodate Indigenous interests and rights. These key aspects of sustainable ecotourism development are examined in this book in case studies of Indigenous ecotourism.

A framework for Indigenous ecotourism

Indigenous ecotourism occurs within a wider nature-based tourism industry dominated by non-Indigenous tour operators and travel agents. Ecotourism itself is one part of a global tourism industry. Developing countries now attract 30% of all international tourists, with a growth rate of 9.5% per annum since 1990. In addition, 19 of 25 biodiversity hotspots favoured by ecotourism, most with Indigenous populations, are in the southern hemisphere (Christ *et al.*, 2003). As such, Indigenous ecotourism is part of a broader environment that is influenced by non-Indigenous tourism, conservation and development activities (Butcher, 2003; Mowforth and Munt, 2003). Therefore, issues associated with Indigenous control of ecotourism and factors that affect these enterprises need to be considered. Indigenous ecotourism ventures face the same issues of product development, marketing, competition, quality control, training and profitability faced by other small ecotourism businesses (Weaver, 2001; Walpole and Thouless, 2005). However, Indigenous ecotourism businesses also have other objectives, such as asserting territorial rights, maintaining cultural knowledge and practices and providing employment. For many Indigenous people, ecotourism is an alternative to other extractive land uses such as logging, mining (Weaver, 2001), oil drilling, ranching, fishing and sport hunting (*Tourism in Focus*, 2002a, b). However, the development of Indigenous ecotourism is limited by poverty, the lack of infrastructure on reserves, community conflicts over tourism, gaining business knowledge and forming commercial links with the tourism industry.

A framework for Indigenous ecotourism thus needs to consider environmental, cultural, economic and political factors that may limit or control tourism development (Zeppel, 1998a, 2000; Dahles and Keune, 2002; Epler Wood, 2004) (see Table 1.6). Indigenous ecotourism takes place within a global tourism industry, which dominates marketing, transport, accommodation and visitor services (Hinch and Butler, 1996). Socio-political factors that affect Indigenous groups developing ecotourism include land and property rights and overcoming social and economic disadvantage in both developing and industrialized countries. Other external factors that affect the tourism industry, including Indigenous ecotourism ventures, include political unrest in developing countries (e.g. Fiji, PNG, Solomon Islands, Nepal and Peru), terrorism and natural disasters such as cyclones. Therefore, guiding principles for ecotourism in Indigenous territories include community involvement and benefit, small-scale ventures, land ownership and cultural sensitivity (Hinch, 2001). Scheyvens (1999), in her community model, analysed the impacts of ecotourism on local groups in terms of economic, psychological, social and political empowerment. For Honey (1999), 'real' ecotourism also has to empower local people and provide financial benefits. The 'successes' of individual Indigenous ecotourism ventures may also be measured in environmental, social or political outcomes (e.g. land rights) rather than in purely economic terms.

In the suggested framework for Indigenous ecotourism, the environmental and cultural impacts or benefits of ecotourism are treated equally with financial or territorial (i.e. political)

Table 1.6. A framework for Indigenous ecotourism.

Environmental	*Economic*
Indigenous environmental stewardship[a]	Limited capital and equity in tribal areas[b]
Cultural and spiritual values of biodiversity[a]	Lack of reserve infrastructure and services[b]
Preserving environment from harmful use[b]	Tax status and public funding schemes[b]
Subsistence uses of the environment[b]	NGO funding for ecotourism ventures[b]
Cultural/Social	*Political*
Diversity of Indigenous cultures[a]	Indigenous land rights and resource rights[b]
'Traditional' culture and authenticity[a]	Indigenous councils and organizations[a,b]
Intellectual and cultural property rights[b]	Indigenous elders, kinship, local leaders[a]
Poverty and social issues on tribal reserves[b]	Access to Indigenous territories ('title')[b]

[a] Internal cultural, environmental and political factors controlled within Indigenous groups.
[b] Externally determined factors or legal rights of Indigenous groups controlled by nation-states.
Sources: Based on Hinch and Butler (1996); Scheyvens (1999); Johnston (2003).

outcomes for Indigenous groups. Economic and political criteria are key motivators for Indigenous ecotourism, while environmental and cultural criteria are outcomes for Indigenous groups involved in ecotourism. For example, Gerberich (2005) applied cultural, environmental, socio-economic and political factors to assess the sustainability of tourism on American Indian reservations. All four factors had to be considered, as economic development through tourism is contingent on protecting cultural and environmental resources. Retaining cultural integrity in tourism is paramount, while a native land ethic or holistic approach to ecosystem management assured sustainability of natural resources. Socio-economic benefits derive from employment and tourism income funding healthcare, childcare and housing. The political factors revolve around Indian sovereignty and tribal ownership of land and resources. In the USA, tourism development on Indian reservations maintained tribal cultures and reinforced autonomous powers.

Rationale and Need for this Book

Despite the growing global popularity of ecotourism, there has been no book to date examining Indigenous involvement in ecotourism ventures. This book, then, builds on other recent books published about ecotourism policy, certification and management. Current books on Indigenous peoples and protected areas also have limited consideration of ecotourism. Previous research and reports on Indigenous ecotourism are published widely across academic, government and conservation sectors. Compiling and analysing this diverse information on Indigenous ecotourism ventures provides the main rationale for this book. The lessons learned from these case studies of tribal ecotourism ventures will benefit Indigenous groups, tourism operators, government agencies, conservation groups, consultants, researchers and tertiary students, including Indigenous students.

This Indigenous involvement in ecotourism is examined in developing countries, mainly the approaches adopted by different Indigenous communities in operating ecotourism ventures. Case studies of Indigenous ecotourism ventures

in developing countries are reviewed in chapters for the Pacific Islands, Latin America, east, southern and West Africa and South East Asia. These examples highlight the key role of government policies on Indigenous lands or wildlife and conservation NGOs in supporting Indigenous resource management and ecotourism projects. Information about these Indigenous ecotourism case studies is summarized for each continent or region, with an overview of key issues at the end of each chapter. The final chapter in this book discusses key factors for the sustainable development of Indigenous ecotourism ventures in tribal lands and protected areas.

Methods and Case Study Approach

This book summarizes information about Indigenous ecotourism ventures published in English in tourism books and journals; in reports and manuals from conservation NGOs; government organizations or ecotourism operators; and on Websites for Indigenous communities or organizations. These selected case studies either describe Indigenous ecotourism products and/or critically evaluate the operation of selected Indigenous ecotourism ventures in more detail. These examples meet the key criteria for Indigenous ecotourism, as nature-based attractions, lodges or tours owned or part-owned by Indigenous people. There is a focus on the conservation and community benefits of these different Indigenous ecotourism projects.

The criteria for an Indigenous business to qualify as ecotourism in this book (Weaver, 2001) are:

- nature-based product or setting;
- manage environmental or cultural impacts;
- environmental education based on Indigenous culture;
- conservation of natural environment; and
- benefits for Indigenous communities.

Additional measures for defining community-based ecotourism involving Indigenous groups are:

- ecotourism activity based in community or tribal territory;

- community or its members have substantial control and involvement;
- major benefits from ecotourism remain in the community; and
- ecotourism venture approved by community or tribal council (Wesche and Drumm, 1999).

The published research reviewed in this book largely provides a non-Indigenous perspective of Indigenous ecotourism, since it is mostly non-Indigenous people (including the author of this book) who write the majority of case studies about tribal tourism ventures (Hinch, 2004; Ryan and Aicken, 2005; Johnston, 2006; Notzke, 2006). However, Indigenous views of tourism, culture, conservation and natural resources are reported in these case studies. The researchers, advisers and consultants working on developing ecotourism ventures with tribal groups generally did so with the permission and support of relevant Indigenous groups and organizations. Hence, the role of government agencies and conservation NGOs in developing Indigenous ecotourism is also reviewed along with alternative Indigenous perspectives and approaches to ecotourism.

The benefits, therefore, of compiling diverse case studies of Indigenous ecotourism projects are to:

- provide a broad global overview of Indigenous ecotourism ventures;
- establish key 'best practice' models for communities and NGOs to follow;
- compare Indigenous ownership and involvement in ecotourism projects;
- identify development and management issues for Indigenous ecotourism;
- analyse the incorporation of Indigenous cultural perspectives in ecotourism; and
- assess sustainability based on economic, cultural, political and environmental criteria.

This book establishes Indigenous ecotourism as a new field of study within the disciplines of tourism, community development, natural resource management and conservation and Indigenous studies.

Conclusion

This chapter has reviewed relevant literature and established a context for the study of Indigenous ecotourism as a global trend in new tourism. Indigenous ecotourism is defined as nature-based attractions or tours owned by tribal groups, which feature Indigenous cultural knowledge and practices linked to the land. Tourists are increasingly visiting Indigenous peoples and their tribal lands around the world. Areas of high biodiversity, such as tropical rainforests, are linked with surviving groups of Indigenous peoples. Key factors driving Indigenous involvement in ecotourism include gaining legal rights to land, preventing other extractive land uses and cultural revival. Many Indigenous groups are now owners and operators of ecotourism ventures located on traditional homelands and protected areas. Indigenous control over ecotourism on tribal lands includes approval, ownership, partnerships and joint ventures. Ideally, Indigenous ecotourism will sustain and conserve natural areas, maintain Indigenous lifestyles and provide benefits for Indigenous communities. The review of Indigenous ecotourism ventures in this book illustrates how and why different Indigenous groups are involved in ecotourism. Indigenous land and cultural identity are central to this trend. Indigenous ecotourism also operates within a broader framework of economic, political, cultural and environmental factors, which are examined in the chapters that follow.

References

African Initiatives (2003) *Whose Land is it Anyway? The Cost of Conservation.* Briefing Paper. African Initiatives and Ujamaa-Community Resource Trust. http://africaninitiatives.gn.apc.org/articles/conserve. htm (accessed 17 November 2005)

Alcorn, J.B. (2001) *Good Governance, Indigenous Peoples and Biodiversity Conservation: Recommendations for Enhancing Results Across Sectors.* Biodiversity Support Program, WWF. http://www.worldwildlife.org/bsp/publications/ (accessed 17 November 2005)

Altman, J. and Finlayson, J. (1993) Aborigines, tourism and sustainable development. *Journal of Tourism Studies* 4(1) , 38–50.

ANTA (Australian National Training Authority) (2001) *Indigenous Ecotourism Toolbox.* ANTA Website. http://www.dlsweb.rmit.edu.au/toolbox/Indigenous/ecotourismtoolbox/ (accessed 17 November 2005)

Ashley, C. and Roe, D. (1998) *Enhancing Community Involvement in Wildlife Tourism: Issues and Challenges.* IIED Wildlife and Development Series No. 11. International Institute for Environment and Development, London.

ATA (Aboriginal Tourism Australia) (2005) *Welcome to Country. Cultural Protocols.* Aboriginal Tourism Australia Website. http://www.ataust.org.au/pdf/WTC%20Brochure.pdf (accessed 17 November 2005)

ATSIC (Aboriginal and Torres Strait Islander Commission) (1996) *On Our Own Terms: Promoting Aboriginal and Torres Strait Islander Involvement in the Australian Tourism Industry.* ATSIC, Canberra, Australia.

Barcham, M. (2000) (De)constructing the politics of Indigeneity. In: Ivison, D., Patton, P. and Sanders, W. (eds) *Political Theory and the Rights of Indigenous Peoples.* Cambridge University Press, Cambridge, UK, pp. 137–151.

Barnett, S. (1997) Maori tourism. *Tourism Management* 18(7), 471–473.

Beck, W. and Somerville, M. (2002) Embodied places in indigenous ecotourism: The Yarrawarra research project. *Australian Aboriginal Studies* 2002(2), 4–13.

Beltran, J. (ed.) (2000) *Indigenous and Traditional Peoples and Protected Areas: Principles, Guidelines and Case Studies.* Best Practice Protected Area Guidelines Series No. 4. IUCN.

Berger, D.J. (1996) The challenge of integrating Maasai tradition with tourism. In: Price, M.F. (ed.) *People and Tourism in Fragile Environments.* John Wiley, Chichester, UK, pp. 175–197.

Bhengra, R., Bijoy, C.R. and Luith, S. (2002) *The Adivasis of India.* Minority Rights Group International. http://www.minorityrights.org/Profiles/profile.asp?ID=2 (accessed 17 November 2005)

Bissett, C., Perry, L. and Zeppel, H. (1998) Land and spirit: Aboriginal tourism in New South Wales. In: McArthur, S. and Weir, B. (eds) *Australia's Ecotourism Industry: A Snapshot in 1998.* Ecotourism Association of Australia, Brisbane, Australia, pp. 6–8.

Blake, B. (2003) The tourism industry's codes for indigenous peoples. In: Honey, M. and Thulen, S. (eds) *Rights and Responsibilities: A Compilation of Codes of Conduct for Tourism and Indigenous and Local Communities.* Center on Ecotourism and Sustainable Development and The International Ecotourism Society. http://205.252.29.37/webarticles/anmviewer.asp?a=14 (accessed 17 November 2005)

Borrini-Feyerabend, G., Kothari, A. and Oviedo, G. (2004) *Indigenous and Local Communities and Protected Areas: Towards Equity and Enhanced Conservation.* http://www.iucn.org/themes/ceesp/ Publications/TILCEPA/guidelinesindigenouspeople.pdf (accessed 30 May 2006). Best Practice Protected Area Guidelines Series No. 11. IUCN.

Borrini-Feyerabend, G., Pimbert, M., Farvar, M.T., Kothari, A. and Renard, Y. (2004b) *Sharing Power: Learning by Doing in Co-Management of Natural Resources Throughout the World.* IIED and IUCN/CEESP/CWMG, Cenesta, Tehran. http://www.iucn.org/themes/ceesp/Publications/sharingpower. htm (accessed 30 May 2006)

Briedenham, J. and Wickens, E. (2004) Community involvement in tourism development: White elephant or empowerment? In: Weber, S. and Tomljenovic, R. (eds) *Reinventing a Tourism Destination: Facing the Challenge.* Institute for Tourism Zagreb, Zagreb, Croatia, pp. 167–177.

Browne, R. and Nolan, M. (1989) Western Indian reservation tourism development. *Annals of Tourism Research* 16(3), 360–376.

BSR (Business for Social Responsibility) (2003) *Rights of Indigenous Peoples.* Issue Briefs. BSR Website. http://www.bsr.org/CSRResources/IssueBriefDetail.cfm?DocumentID=49771 (accessed 17 November 2005)

Buckley, R. (2003) *Case Studies in Ecotourism.* CABI, Wallingford, UK.

Burchett, C. (1992) Ecologically sustainable development and its relationship to Aboriginal tourism in the Northern Territory. In: Weiler, B. (ed.) *Ecotourism Incorporating the Global Classroom.* Bureau of Tourism Research, Canberra, Australia, pp. 70–74.

Burger, J. (1990) *The Gaia Atlas of First Peoples: A Future for the Indigenous World.* Penguin, Ringwood, Australia.

Bushell, R. and Eagles, P.F.J. (eds) (2006) *Tourism and Protected Areas: Benefits Beyond Boundaries.* CABI Publishing, Wallingford, UK.

Butcher, J. (2003) New moral tourism, the third world and development. In: *The Moralisation of Tourism: Sun, Sand ... and Saving the World?* Routledge, London, pp. 113–136.

Butler, R. and Hinch, T. (eds) (1996) *Tourism and Indigenous Peoples.* International Thomson Business Press, London.

Carino, J. (2004) Indigenous voices at the table: Restoring local decision-making on protected areas. *Cultural Survival Quarterly* 28. http://209.200.101.189/publications/csq/csq-article.cfm?id=1739 (accessed 29 November 2005)

Cater, E. (1996) *Community Involvement in Third World Ecotourism.* University of Reading, Reading, UK.

Cater, E. (1997) Ecotourism in the Third World – problems and prospects for sustainability. In: France, L. (ed.) *The Earthscan Reader in Sustainable Tourism.* Earthscan, London, pp. 68–81.

Chatty, D. and Colchester, M. (eds) (2002) *Conservation and Mobile Indigenous Peoples: Displacement, Forced Settlement and Sustainable Development.* Berghahn Books, Oxford, UK.

Chen, C.C. (2004) Indigenous community development through ecotourism: A case study. *Journal of Rural Development* 23, 491–512.

Christ, C. (1998) Taking ecotourism to the next level: A look at private sector involvement with local communities. In: Lindberg, K., Epler Wood, M. and Engeldrum, D. (eds) *Ecotourism: A Guide for Planners and Managers,* Vol. 2. The Ecotourism Society, Vermont, USA, pp. 183–195.

Christ, C. (2004) A road less travelled. *Conservation Frontlines online.* Conservation International. http://www.conservation.org/xp/frontlines/people/focus32-1.xml (accessed 17 November 2005)

Christ, C., Hillel, O., Matus, S. and Sweeting, J. (2003) *Tourism and Biodiversity: Mapping Tourism's Global Footprint.* Conservation International and UNEP.

Colchester, M. (2003) *Salvaging Nature: Indigenous Peoples, Protected Areas and Biodiversity Conservation.* World Rainforest Movement and Forest Peoples Programme. http://www.forestpeoples.org/publications/salvaging_nature_eng.shtml (accessed 29 November 2005)

Colchester, M. (2004) Conservation policy and indigenous peoples. *Cultural Survival Quarterly* 28. http://209.200.101.189/publications/csq/csq-article.cfm?id=1738 (accessed 29 November 2005)

Colvin, J.G. (1994) Capirona: A model of indigenous ecotourism. *Journal of Sustainable Tourism* 2, 174–177.

Coolidge, T. (2004) In 10 years Taiwan's indigenous peoples redefined their image. *Cultural Survival Voices* 3. http://209.200.101.189/publications/csv/csv-article.cfm?id=75 (accessed 17 November 2005)

Cultural Survival Voices (2004) Indigenous peoples at the United Nations. *Cultural Survival Voices* 3. http://209.200.101.189/publications/csv/csv-article.cfm?id=71 (accessed 17 November 2005)

Dahles, H. and Keune, L. (eds) (2002) *Tourism Development and Local Participation in Latin America.* Cognizant Communication Corporation, New York.

de Bont, C. and Janssen, W. (2002) Indigenous people and local participation in tourism: Two case studies from Ecuador. In: Dahles, H. and Keune, L. (eds) *Tourism Development and Local Participation in Latin America.* Cognizant Communication Corporation, New York, pp. 115–129.

de Burlo, C. (1996) Cultural resistance and ethnic tourism on South Pentecost, Vanuatu. In: Butler, R. and Hinch, T. (eds) *Tourism and Indigenous Peoples.* International Thomson Business Press, London, pp. 255–277.

Diamantis, D. (ed.) (2004) *Ecotourism: Management and Assessment.* Thomson, London.

DISR (Department of Industry, Science and Resources) (2000) *National Indigenous Tourism Forum Proceedings Report: Tourism – The Indigenous Opportunity.* DISR, Canberra, Australia.

Doan, T.M. (2000) The effects of ecotourism in developing countries: An analysis of case studies. *Journal of Sustainable Tourism* 8, 288–304.

Dowling, R. (2001) Oceania (Australia, New Zealand and South Pacific). In: Weaver, D.B. (ed.) *The Encyclopaedia of Ecotourism.* CABI, Wallingford, UK, pp. 139–154.

Drumm, A. (1998) New approaches to community-based ecotourism management: Learning from Ecuador. In: Lindberg, K., Epler Wood, M. and Engeldrum, D. (eds) *Ecotourism: A Guide for Planners and Managers,* Vol. 2. The Ecotourism Society, Vermont, USA, pp. 197–213.

Duffy, R. (2002) *A Trip Too Far: Ecotourism, Politics and Exploitation.* Earthscan Publications, London.

EBFP (Environmental Business Finance Program) (2005) Ecolodges : *Exploring Opportunities for Sustainable Business.* International Finance Corporation. http://ifcln1.ifc/ifctext/enviro.nsf/Content/EBFP_Ecolodge (accessed 17 November 2005)

Echtner, C.M. (1999) Tourism in sensitive environments: Three African success stories. In: Singh, T.V. and Singh, G. (eds) *Tourism Development in Critical Environments.* Cognizant Communication Corporation, New York, pp. 149–162.

Ecotourism Australia (2002) Cairns Charter on Partnerships for Ecotourism. Ecotourism Australia. http://www.ecotourism.org.au/cairnscharter.asp

Ecotourism Australia (2005) What is ecotourism? Ecotourism Australia. http://www.ecotourism.org.au
Ecotourism News (2000) Aborigines offer ecotourism more than just the didgeridoo. *Ecotourism News (Ecotourism Association of Australia)* Spring 2000, 6.
Epler Wood, M. (1999) Ecotourism, sustainable development, and cultural survival: Protecting Indigenous culture and land through ecotourism. *Cultural Survival Quarterly* 23. http://209.200.101.189/publications/csq/csq-article.cfm?id=1431&highlight=ecotourism (accessed 17 November 2005)
Epler Wood, M. (2002) Ecotourism and indigenous communities. In: *Ecotourism: Principles, Practices & Policies for Sustainability.* UNEP, Paris and The International Ecotourism Society, Vermont, USA, pp. 44–45.
Epler Wood, M. (2003) *Community conservation and commerce.* EplerWood Reports, October 2003. EplerWood International. http://www.eplerwood.com/images/EplerWood_Report_Oct2003.pdf (accessed 17 November 2005)
Epler Wood, M. (2004) *Evaluating ecotourism as a community and economic development strategy.* EplerWood Reports, October 2004. EplerWood International. http://www.eplerwood.com/images/EplerWood_Report_Oct2004.pdf (accessed 17 November 2005)
Epler Wood, M. (2005) *Stepping up: Creating a sustainable tourism enterprise strategy that delivers in the developing world.* EplerWood Reports, October 2005. EplerWood International. http://www.eplerwood.com/images/EplerWood_Report_Oct2005.pdf (accessed 17 November 2005)
Fennell, D.A. (2003) Ecotourism development: International, community, and site perspectives. In: *Ecotourism: An Introduction,* 2nd edn. Routledge, London, pp. 150–170.
FPP (Forest Peoples Programme) (2003) *WPC Recommendation 24: Indigenous peoples and protected areas.* World Parks Congress 2003. http://www.forestpeoples.org/documents/conservation/bases/wpc_base.shtml (accessed 29 November 2005)
France, L. (ed.) (1997) *The Earthscan Reader in Sustainable Tourism.* Earthscan, London.
Franke, J. (1995) *Walking the Village Path: A Worldwide Guide to Community-Generated Tourism Projects.* First Nations Health Project, Portland, Oregon, USA.
Friedmann, J. (1992) *Empowerment: The Politics of Alternative Development.* Blackwell, Cambridge.
Furze, B., De Lacy, T. and Birckhead, J. (1996) Indigenous people. In: *Culture, Conservation and Biodiversity.* John Wiley, Chichester, UK, pp. 126–145.
Garen, E.J. (2000) Appraising ecotourism in conserving biodiversity. In: Clark, T.W., Willard, A.R. and Cromley, C.M. (eds) *Foundations of Natural Resources Policy and Management.* Yale University Press, New Haven, USA, pp. 221–251.
GEF Secretariat (2004) Protected areas and the Global Environment Facility. In: *Biodiversity Issues for Consideration in the Planning, Establishment and Management of Protected Areas Sites and Networks.* CBD Technical Series No. 15. Secretariat of the Convention on Biological Diversity, Montreal, 111–115.
Gerberich, V.L. (2005) An evaluation of sustainable Indian tourism. In: Ryan, C. and Aicken, M. (eds) *Indigenous Tourism: The Commodification and Management of Culture.* Elsevier, Oxford, UK, pp. 75–86.
Getz, D. and Jamieson, W. (1997) Rural tourism in Canada: Opportunities and entrepreneurship in Aboriginal tourism in Alberta. In: Page, S.J. and Getz, D. (eds) *The Business of Rural Tourism: International Perspectives.* International Thomson Business Press, London, pp. 93–107.
Godde, P. (1998) *Community-based Mountain Tourism: Practices for Linking Conservation with Enterprise.* Mountain Forum and The Mountain Institute, West Virginia, USA. http://www.mountainforum.org/rs/pub/ec.cfm (accessed 17 November 2005)
Grekin, J. and Milne, S. (1996) Toward sustainable tourism development: The case of Pond Inlet, NWT. In: Butler, R.W. and Hinch, T.D. (eds) *Tourism and Indigenous Peoples.* Thomson Business Press, UK, pp. 76–106.
Grieg-Gran, M. and Mulliken, T. (2004) *The Commercial Record of Community-based Sustainable Use Initiatives.* IIED, London.
Griffiths, T. (2004) Help or hindrance? The Global Environment Facility, biodiversity conservation, and indigenous peoples. *Cultural Survival Quarterly* 28. http://209.200.101.189/publications/csq/csq-article.cfm?id=1740 (accessed 29 November 2005)
Groenfeldt, D. (2003) The future of indigenous values: Cultural relativism in the face of economic development. *Futures* 35, 917–929.
Halfpenny, E. (1999) The state and critical issues relating to international ecotourism development policy. In: *Australia – The World's Natural Theme Park: Proceedings of the Ecotourism Association of Australia 1999 Conference.* Ecotourism Association of Australia, Brisbane, pp. 45–52.
Hall, C.M. (2000) Tourism, national parks and Aboriginal people. In: Butler, R.W. and Boyd, S.W. (eds) *Tourism and National Parks.* John Wiley, Chichester, UK, pp. 51–71.
Hall, C.M. and Boyd, S. (eds) (2004) *Nature-based Tourism in Peripheral Areas: Development or Disaster?* Channel View Publications, Clevedon, UK.

Harrison, D. (ed.) (2003) *Pacific Island Tourism*. Cognizant Communication Corporation, New York.

Hashimoto, A. and Telfer, D.J. (2004) Canadian Aboriginal ecotourism in the north. In: Diamantis, D. (ed.) *Ecotourism: Management and Assessment*. Thomson, London, pp. 204–225.

Hatton, M.J. (2002) The character of community-based tourism. In: *Community-based Tourism in the Asia-Pacific*. CTC, APEC & CIDA. http://www.cullin.org/cbt/index.cfm?section=chapter&number=1 (accessed 17 November 2005)

Healey, K. (1993) *Indigenous Peoples*. Issues for the Nineties, Vol. 10. Spinney Press, Australia.

Helu-Thaman, K. (1992) Ecocultural tourism: A personal view for maintaining cultural integrity in ecotourism development. In: Hay, J.E. (ed.) *Ecotourism Business in the Pacific: Promoting a Sustainable Experience*. Conference Proceedings. Environmental Science, University of Auckland, Auckland, New Zealand, pp. 24–29.

Hendry, J. (2005) *Reclaiming Culture: Indigenous Peoples and Self Representation*. Palgrave Macmillan, London.

Higgins-Desbiolles, F. (2005) Reconciliation tourism: Challenging the constraints of economic rationalism. In: Ryan, C. and Aicken, M. (eds) *Indigenous Tourism: The Commodification and Management of Culture*. Elsevier, Oxford, UK, pp. 223–245.

Hill, R. (2004) *Global Trends in Protected Areas: A Report on the Fifth World Parks Congress*. Rainforest CRC, Cairns, Australia. http://www.acfonline.org.au/uploads/res_protected_areas.pdf (accessed 29 November 2005)

Hillel, O. (2003) Foreword. In: Buckley, R. (ed.) *Case Studies in Ecotourism*. CABI, Wallingford, UK, pp. xiii–xiv.

Hinch, T. (1998) Ecotourists and indigenous hosts: Diverging views on their relationship with nature. *Current Issues in Tourism* 1, 120–124.

Hinch, T. (2001) Indigenous territories. In: Weaver, D.B. (ed.) *The Encyclopaedia of Ecotourism*. CABI, Wallingford, UK, pp. 345–357.

Hinch, T.D. (2004) Indigenous peoples and tourism. In: Lew, A.L., Hall, C.M. and Williams, A.M. (eds) *A Companion to Tourism*. Blackwell, Malden, MA, USA, pp. 246–257.

Hinch, T. and Butler, R. (1996) Indigenous tourism: A common ground for discussion. In: Butler, R. and Hinch, T. (eds) *Tourism and Indigenous Peoples*. International Thomson Business Press, London, pp. 3–19.

Hitchcock, R.K. (1994) Endangered peoples: Indigenous rights and the environment. *Colorado Journal of International Environmental Law and Policy* 5, 11.

Honey, M. (1999) *Ecotourism and Sustainable Development: Who Owns Paradise?* Island Press, Washington DC, USA.

Honey, M. (2003) Summary of major principles regarding tourism and indigenous peoples and local communities. In: Honey, M. and Thullen, S. (eds) *Rights and Responsibilities: A Compilation of Codes of Conduct for Tourism and Indigenous and Local Communities*. Center on Ecotourism and Sustainable Development and The International Ecotourism Society. http://205.252.29.37/webarticles/articlefiles/rightsandresponsibilities.pdf (accessed 17 November 2005)

Honey, M. and Thullen, S. (eds) (2003) *Rights and Responsibilities: A Compilation of Codes of Conduct for Tourism and Indigenous and Local Communities*. Center on Ecotourism and Sustainable Development and The International Ecotourism Society. Reports. http://205.252.29.37/webarticles/anmviewer.asp?a=14 (accessed 17 November 2005)

Horwich, R.H. and Lyon, J. (1999) Rural ecotourism as a conservation tool. In: Singh, T.V. and Singh, S. (eds) *Tourism Development in Critical Environments*. Cognizant Communication Corporation, New York, pp. 102–119.

Howard, J., Thwaites, R. and Smith, B. (2001) Investigating the roles of the indigenous tour guide. *Journal of Tourism Studies* 12, 32–39.

Howitt, R., Connell, J. and Hirsch, P. (eds) (1996) *Resources, Nations and Indigenous Peoples: Case Studies from Australasia, Melanesia and Southeast Asia*. Oxford University Press, Melbourne, Australia.

IFAD (nd) Indigenous peoples. Fact sheet. IFAD, Rome. http://www.ifad.org/media/events/2005/ip.htm (accessed 18 May 2006)

Igoe, J.J. (2004) *Conservation and Globalization: A Study of National Parks and Indigenous Communities from East Africa to South Dakota*. Thomson/Wadsworth, Belmont, CA, USA.

International Fund for Agricultural Development (IFAD) (2003) *Indigenous Peoples and Sustainable Development: Discussion Paper*. Roundtable Discussion Paper for the 25th Anniversary Session of IFAD's Governing Council. IFAD, Rome. http://www.ifad.org/media/events/2005/ip.htm (accessed 18 May 2006)

Intrepid Travel (2002) *Literature Review: Impacts of Alternative Types of Tourism in Rural Village Communities in Less Developed Countries*. Responsible Travel Research. http://www.intrepidtravel.com/rtresearch.php (accessed 17 November 2005)

IPACC (2004) *About IPACC.* Indigenous Peoples of Africa Coordinating Committee. http://www.ipacc.org.za/whatisipacc.asp (accessed 17 November 2005)

James, D. (1994) Desert tracks. In: *A Talent for Tourism: Stories about Indigenous People in Tourism.* Commonwealth Department of Tourism, Canberra, Australia, pp. 10–12.

Janet, S.C. (2002) *Development, Minorities and Indigenous Peoples: A Case Study and Evaluation of Good Practice.* Issues Paper. Minority Rights Group International. http://www.minorityrights.org/Dev/mrg_dev_title9_ip2/mrg_dev_title9_ip2.htm (accessed 17 November 2005)

Johansson, Y. and Diamantis, D. (2004) Ecotourism in Thailand and Kenya: A private sector perspective. In: Diamantis, D. (ed.) *Ecotourism: Management and Assessment.* Thomson, London, pp. 288–312.

Johnston, A. (2000) Indigenous peoples and ecotourism: Bringing indigenous knowledge and rights into the sustainability equation. *Tourism Recreation Research* 25, 89–96.

Johnston, A. (2001) Ecotourism and the challenges confronting indigenous peoples. *Native Americas* 18, 42–47.

Johnston, A.M. (2003a) Self-determination: Exercising indigenous rights in tourism. In: Singh, S., Timothy, D.J. and Dowling, R.K. (eds) *Tourism in Destination Communities.* CABI, Wallingford, UK, pp. 115–134.

Johnston, A.M. (2003b) *Protected areas, tourism and biodiversity conservation: Benefits to Indigenous peoples.* http://www.tilcepa.org/CDDocs/Tourism/html/TourismJohnstone.htm (accessed 17 November 2005)

Johnston, A.M. (2006) *Is the Sacred for Sale? Tourism and Indigenous Peoples.* Earthscan, London.

Karwacki, J. (1999) Indigenous ecotourism: Overcoming the challenge. *The Ecotourism Society Newsletter,* First Quarter 1999.

King, D.A. and Stewart, W.P. (1996) Ecotourism and commodification: Protecting people and places. *Biodiversity and Conservation* 5, 293–307.

Kipuri, N. (nd) Indigenous peoples in Kenya – An overview. http://www.whoseland.com/paper6.html (accessed 17 November 2005)

Larsen, P.B. and Oviedo, G. (2005) Protected areas and indigenous peoples. The Durban contributions to reconciliation and equity. In: McNeely, J.A. (ed.) *Friends for Life: New Partners in Support of Protected Areas.* IUCN, Gland, Switzerland, pp. 113–128.

Lash, G. (1998) What is community-based ecotourism? In: Bornemeier, J., Victor, M. and Durst, P.B. (eds) *Ecotourism for Forest Conservation and Community Development Seminar.* RECOFTC Report No. 15. RECOFTC, Bangkok, Thailand, pp. 1–12. http://www.recoftc.org/site/index.php?id=22 (accessed 17 November 2005)

Lash, G.Y.B. and Austin, A. (2003) *The Rural Ecotourism Assessment Program (REAP): A Guide to Community Assessment of Ecotourism as a Tool for Sustainable Development.* The International Ecotourism Society. http://www.ecotourism.org/index2.php?onlineLib/searchResult.php (accessed 17 November 2005)

Lasimbang, J. (2004) National Parks: Indigenous resource management principles in protected areas and indigenous peoples of Asia. *Cultural Survival Quarterly* 28 (1). http://209.200.101.189/publications/csq/csq-article.cfm?id=1746 (accessed 17 November 2005)

Lew, A.A. (1996) Tourism management on American Indian lands in the USA. *Tourism Management* 17, 355–365.

Lew, A.A. (1999) Managing tourism-induced acculturation through environmental design on Pueblo Indian villages in the US. In: Singh, T.V. and Singh, S. (eds) *Tourism Development in Critical Environments.* Cognizant Communication Corporation, New York, pp. 120–136.

Lew, A.A. and van Otten, G.A. (eds) (1998) *Tourism and Gaming on American Indian Lands.* Cognizant Communication Corporation, New York.

Lindberg, K., Epler Wood, M. and Engeldrum, D. (eds) (1998) *Ecotourism: A Guide for Planners and Managers,* Vol. 2. The Ecotourism Society, North Bennington, Vermont, USA.

Liu, J. (1994) *Pacific Islands Ecotourism: A Public Policy and Planning Guide.* Pacific Business Center Program, University of Hawaii, USA.

Maaka, R. and Fleras, A. (2000) Engaging with Indigeneity: Tino rangatiratanga in Aotearoa. In: Ivison, D., Patton, P. and Sanders, W. (eds) *Political Theory and the Rights of Indigenous Peoples.* Cambridge University Press, Cambridge, UK, pp. 89–112.

Macdonald, T. (2002) Nicaraguan Indians at the Inter-American Court of Human Rights: Internationlizing indigenous community landrights. *Harvard Review of Latin America,* winter. http://www.fas.harvard.edu/~drclas/publications/revista/tourism/macdonald.html (accessed 30 March 2006)

MacKay, F. (2002) *Addressing Past Wrongs – Indigenous Peoples and Protected Areas: The Right to Restitution of Lands and Resources*. FPP Occasional Paper. Forest Peoples Programme. http://www.forestpeoples.org/publications/addressing_past_wrongs_eng.shtml (accessed 29 November 2005)

MacKay, F. and Caruso, E. (2004) Indigenous lands or national parks? *Cultural Survival Quarterly* 28. http://209.200.101.189/publications/csq/csq-article.cfm?id=1737 (accessed 29 November 2005)

Mallari, A.A. and Enote, J.E. (1996) Maintaining control: Culture and tourism in the Pueblo of Zuni, New Mexico. In: Price, M.F. (ed.) *People and Tourism in Fragile Environments*. John Wiley, Chichester, UK, pp. 19–31.

Mann, M. (2000) *The Community Tourism Guide*. Earthscan and Tourism Concern, London.

Mann, M. (2002) *The Good Alternative Travel Guide*, 2nd edn. Earthscan and Tourism Concern, London.

Marrie, H. (2004) Protected areas and indigenous and local communities. In: *Biodiversity Issues for Consideration in the Planning, Establishment and Management of Protected Areas Sites and Networks*. CBD Technical Series No. 15. Secretariat of the Convention on Biological Diversity. Montreal, 106–110.

Martin, G. (2001) People of the forest. In: Holing, D. and Forbes, S. (eds) *Rain Forests*. Insight Guides. Discovery Travel Adventures. Discovery Communications, London, pp. 36–43.

Martinez, D. (2003) Protected areas, indigenous peoples, and the western idea of nature. *Ecological Restoration*, 21, 247–250.

Mat Som, A.P. and Baum, T. (2004) Community involvement in ecotourism. In: Weber, S. and Tomljenovic, R. (eds) *Reinventing a Tourism Destination: Facing the Challenge*. Institute for Tourism Zagreb, Zagreb, Croatia, pp. 251–260.

Maybury-Lewis, D. (2002) Indigenous peoples. In: *Indigenous Peoples, Ethnic Groups, and the State*, 2nd edn. Allyn and Bacon, Boston, MA, USA, pp. 1–46.

Mbaiwa, J.E. (2005) Community-based tourism and the marginalized communities in Botswana: The case of the Basarwa in the Okavango Delta. In: Ryan, C. and Aicken, M. (eds) *Indigenous Tourism: The Commodification and Management of Culture*. Elsevier, Oxford, UK, pp. 87–109.

McIntosh, I. (1999) Ecotourism: A boon for Indigenous people? *Cultural Survival Quarterly* 23. http://209.200.101.189/publications/csq/csq-article.cfm?id=1418&highlight=ecotourism (accessed 17 November 2005)

McLaren, D. (1998) *Rethinking Tourism and Ecotravel: The Paving of Paradise and How You Can Stop It*. Kumarian Press, West Hartford, CT, USA.

McLaren, D.R. (1999) The history of Indigenous peoples and tourism. *Cultural Survival Quarterly* 23.

McLaren, D.R. (2003) Indigenous peoples and ecotourism. In: Honey, M. and Thullen, S. (eds) *Rights and Responsibilities: A Compilation of Codes of Conduct for Tourism and Indigenous and Local Communities*. Center on Ecotourism and Sustainable Development and The International Ecotourism Society, pp. 1–8. Reports. http://205.252.29.37/webarticles/anmviewer.asp?a=14 (accessed 17 November 2005)

Medina, L.K. (2005) Ecotourism and certification: Confronting the principles and pragmatics of socially responsible tourism. *Journal of Sustainable Tourism* 13, 281–295.

Mercer, D. (1994) Native peoples and tourism: Conflict and compromise. In: Theobald, W.F. (ed.) *Global Tourism: The Next Decade*. Butterworth Heinemann, Boston, USA, pp. 124–145.

Mercer, D. (1998) The uneasy relationship between tourism and native peoples: The Australian experience. In: Theobald, W.F. (ed.) *Global Tourism*, 2nd edn. Butterworth Heinemann, Oxford, UK, pp. 98–128.

Miller, G. (1996) Indigenous tourism – A Queensland perspective. In: Richins, H., Richardson, J. and Crabtree, A. (eds) *Ecotourism and Nature-based Tourism: Taking the Next Steps*. Ecotourism Association of Australia, Brisbane, Australia, pp. 45–57.

Moscardo, G. and Pearce, P.L. (1999) Understanding ethnic tourists. *Annals of Tourism Research* 26, 416–434.

Mowforth, M. and Munt, I. (2003) *Tourism and Sustainability: Development and New Tourism in the Third World*. Routledge, London.

Nature Conservancy (1996) *Traditional Peoples and Biodiversity Conservation in Large Tropical Landscapes*. The Nature Conservancy.

Negi, C.S. and Nautiyal, S. (2003) Indigenous peoples, biological diversity and protected area management – policy framework towards resolving conflicts. *International Journal of Sustainable Development and World Ecology* 10, 169–179.

Nelson, J. and Hossack, L. (eds) (2003) *Indigenous Peoples and Protected Areas in Africa: From Principles to Practice*. Forest Peoples Programme. http://www.forestpeoples.org/publications/p_to_p_africa_eng.shtml (accessed 29 November 2005)

Nepal, S.K. (2004) Indigenous ecotourism in central British Columbia: The potential for building capacity in the Tl'azt'en Nations territories. *Journal of Ecotourism* 3, 173–194.

Nepal, S.K. (2005) Limits to indigenous ecotourism: An exploratory analysis from the Tl'azt'en Territories, Northern British Columbia. In: Ryan, C. and Aicken, M. (eds) *Indigenous Tourism: The Commodification and Management of Culture.* Elsevier, Oxford, pp. 111–126.

Notzke, C. (1999) Indigenous tourism development in the Arctic. *Annals of Tourism Research* 26, 55–76.

Notzke, C. (2006) *The Stranger, the Native and the Land: Perspectives on Indigenous Tourism.* Captus University Press, North York, Ontario.

Osava, M. (2005) World Social Forum: Indigenous peoples claim their own space. Quechua Network. 5 February 2005. http://www.quechuanetwork.org/news_template.cfm?news_id=2454&lang=e (accessed 17 November 2005)

Oviedo, G., Maffi, L. and Larsen, P.B. (2000) *Indigenous and Traditional Peoples of the World and Ecoregion Conservation: An Integrated Approach to Conserving the World's Biological and Cultural Diversity.* WWF and Terralingua. http://www.iucn.org/bookstore/ (accessed 17 November 2005)

Page, S. and Dowling, R.K. (2002) Community-based ecotourism: Management and development issues. In: *Ecotourism.* Pearson Education, Harlow, UK, pp. 244–247.

Parker, B. (1993) Developing Aboriginal tourism – opportunities and threats. *Tourism Management* 14, 400–404.

Pedersen, K. and Viken, A. (1996) From Sami nomadism to global tourism. In: Price, M.F. (ed.) *People and Tourism in Fragile Environments.* John Wiley, Chichester, UK, pp. 69–88.

Pera, L. and McLaren, D. (1999) Globalization, tourism and indigenous peoples: What you should know about the world's largest 'industry'. http://www.planeta.com/ecotravel/resources/rtp/globalization.html (accessed 17 November 2005)

Pitcher, M., van Oosterzee, P. and Palmer, L. (1999) *'Choice and Control': The Development of Indigenous Tourism in Australia.* Centre for Indigenous Natural and Cultural Resource Management, Northern Territory University, Darwin, Australia.

Pleumarom, A. (1994) The political economy of tourism. *The Ecologist* 24, 142–148.

Prance, G.T. (1998) Indigenous non-timber benefits from tropical rain forest. In: Goldsmith, F.B. (ed.) *Tropical Rain Forest: A Wider Perspective.* Chapman and Hall, London, pp. 21–42.

Price, M.F. (ed.) (1996) *People and Tourism in Fragile Environments.* John Wiley, Chichester, UK.

Raffaele, P. (2003) *The Last Tribes on Earth: Journeys Among the World's Most Threatened Cultures.* Pan Macmillan, Sydney, Australia.

Redturs (nd) Network of Communitarian Tourism of Latin America. Redturs. Sponsored by ILO. http://www.redturs.org/inicioen/inicio/index.php (accessed 17 November 2005)

Robinson, M. (1999) Collaboration and cultural consent: Refocusing sustainable tourism. *Journal of Sustainable Tourism* 7, 379–397.

Roe, D., Goodwin, H. and Ashley, C. (2004) Pro-poor tourism: Benefiting the poor. In: Singh, T.V. (ed.) *New Horizons in Tourism: Strange Experiences and Stranger Practices.* CABI, Wallingford, UK, pp. 147–161.

Ross, H. (1991) Controlling access to environment and self: Aboriginal perspectives on tourism. *Australian Psychologist* 26, 176–182.

Roy, C.K. (nd) The ILO and its work on indigenous and tribal peoples. ILO. UN Development Programme. http://www.undp.org.vn/projects/vie96010/cemma/RAS93103/014.htm (accessed 17 November 2005)

Rudkin, B. and Hall, C.M. (1996) Unable to see the forest for the trees: Ecotourism development in Solomon Islands. In: Butler, R. and Hinch, T. (eds) *Tourism and Indigenous Peoples.* International Thomson Business Press, London, pp. 203–226.

Russell, P. (2000) Community-based tourism. *Travel & Tourism Analyst* 5, 87–14.

Ryan, C. (1997) Book review: Tourism and Indigenous Peoples. *Tourism Management* 18, 479–480.

Ryan, C. (1998) Some dimensions of Maori involvement in tourism. In: Robinson, M. and Boniface, P. (eds) *Tourism and Cultural Conflicts.* CABI, Wallingford, UK.

Ryan, C. (2000) Indigenous peoples and tourism. In: Ryan, C. and Page, S. (eds) *Tourism Management: Towards the New Millennium.* Pergamon, Oxford, UK.

Ryan, C. and Aicken, M. (eds) (2005) *Indigenous Tourism: The Commodification and Management of Culture.* Elsevier, Oxford, UK.

SATC (South Australian Tourism Commission) (1995) *Aboriginal Tourism Strategy.* SATC, Adelaide, Australia.

Schaller, D.T. (1996) Indigenous Ecotourism and Sustainable Development: The case of Rio Blanco, Ecuador. MA Thesis, University of Minnesota. Educational Web Adventures. http://www.eduweb.com/schaller (accessed 17 November 2005)

Scherl, L.M. (2005) Protected areas and local and indigenous communities. In: McNeely, J.A. (ed.) *Friends for Life: New Partners in Support of Protected Areas.* IUCN, Gland, Switzerland, pp. 101–111.

Scheyvens, R. (1999) Ecotourism and the empowerment of local communities. *Tourism Management* 20, 245–249.

Scheyvens, R. (2000) Promoting women's empowerment through involvement in ecotourism: Experiences from the Third World. *Journal of Sustainable Tourism* 8, 232–249.

Scheyvens, R. (2002) *Tourism for Development: Empowering Communities.* Prentice Hall, Harlow, Essex, UK.

Scheyvens, R. (2004) Growth of beach *fale* tourism in Samoa: The high value of low-cost tourism. In: Hall, C.M. and Boyd, S. (eds) *Nature-based Tourism in Peripheral Areas: Development or Disaster?* Channel View Publications, Clevedon, UK.

Selverston-Scher, M. (2003) Indigenous peoples and international finance and development institutions. In: Honey, M. and Thullen, S. (eds) *Rights and Responsibilities: A Compilation of Codes of Conduct for Tourism and Indigenous and Local Communities.* Center on Ecotourism and Sustainable Development and The International Ecotourism Society, pp. 148–151. Reports. http://205.252.29.37/webarticles/anmviewer.asp?a=14 (accessed 17 November 2005)

Sharpe, B. (1998) Forest people and conservation initiatives: The cultural context of rainforest conservation in West Africa. In: Goldsmith, F.B. (ed.) *Tropical Rain Forest: A Wider Perspective.* Chapman and Hall, London, pp. 75–97.

Singh, S. *et al.* (2001) *Aboriginal Australia* and *the Torres Strait Islands: Guide to Indigenous Australia.* Lonely Planet, Melbourne, Australia.

Smith, L.T. (1999) *Decolonizing Methodologies: Research and Indigenous Peoples.* Zed Books, London, and University of Otago Press, Dunedin, NZ.

Smith, M.K. (2003) Indigenous cultural tourism. In: *Issues in Cultural Tourism Studies.* Routledge, London, pp. 117–132.

Smith, V.L. (1989) Introduction. In: Smith, V.L. (ed.) *Hosts and Guests: The Anthropology of Tourism,* 2nd edn. University of Pennsylvania Press, Philadelphia, pp. 1–17.

Smith, V.L. (1996a) The Inuit as hosts: Heritage and wilderness tourism in Nunavut. In: Price, M.F. (ed.) *People and Tourism in Fragile Environments.* John Wiley, Chichester, UK, pp. 33–50.

Smith, V.L. (1996b) Indigenous tourism: The four Hs. In: Butler, R. and Hinch, T. (eds) *Tourism and Indigenous Peoples.* International Thomson Business Press, London, pp. 283–307.

Smith, V.L. (2001) Sustainability-Heritage tourism and indigenous peoples. In: Smith, V.L. and Brent, M. (eds) *Hosts and Guests Revisited: Tourism Issues of the 21st Century.* Cognizant Communication Corporation, New York, pp. 187–200 [198–199].

Sofield, T. (1991) Sustainable ethnic tourism in the South Pacific: Some principles. *Journal of Tourism Studies* 2, 56–72.

Sofield, T.H.B. (1993) Indigenous tourism development. *Annals of Tourism Research* 20, 729–750.

Sofield, T.H.B. (2002) Australian Aboriginal ecotourism in the Wet Tropics rainforest of Queensland, Australia. *Mountain Research and Development* 22, 118–122.

Sofield, T.H.B. (2003) *Empowerment for Sustainable Tourism Development.* Pergamon, New York.

Spenceley, A. (2004) Responsible nature-based tourism planning in South Africa and the commercialisation of Kruger National Park. In: Diamantis, D. (ed.) *Ecotourism: Management and Assessment.* Thomson, London, pp. 267–280.

SPREP (South Pacific Regional Environment Programme) (2002) *Community-based Ecotourism and Conservation in the Pacific Islands: A Tool Kit for Communities.* SPREP, Apia, Samoa.

Sproule, K.W. and Suhandi, A.S. (1998) Guidelines for community-based ecotourism programs: Lessons from Indonesia. In: Lindberg, K., Epler Wood, M. and Engeldrum, D. (eds) *Ecotourism: A Guide for Planners and Managers,* Vol. 2. The Ecotourism Society, Vermont, USA, pp. 215–236.

Stevens, S. and De Lacy, T. (1997) *Conservation through Cultural Survival: Indigenous Peoples and Protected Areas.* Island Press, Washington DC, USA.

Strang, V. (1996) Sustaining tourism in far north Queensland. In: Price, M.F. (ed.) *People and Tourism in Fragile Environments.* John Wiley, Chichester, UK, pp. 51–67.

Suansri, P. (2003) *Community Based Tourism Handbook.* REST, Bangkok, Thailand. http://www.rest.or.th/training/handbook.asp (accessed 17 November 2005)

Survival International (1995) *Tourism and Tribal Peoples.* Survival International, London.

Survival International (2004) *Importance of Rights to Development.* Survival International Website. http://www.survival-international.org/ (accessed 17 November 2005)

Sutton, M. (1999) Aboriginal ownership of National Parks and tourism. *Cultural Survival Quarterly* 23, 55–56.

Swain, M.B. (1989) Gender roles in indigenous tourism: Kuna mola, kuna yala, and cultural survival. In: Smith, V.L. (ed.) *Hosts and Guests: The Anthropology of Tourism*, 2nd edn. University of Philadelphia Press, Philadelphia, USA, pp. 83–104.

Sykes, L. (1995) Welcome to our land. *The Geographical Magazine* 67, 22–25.

The International Ecotourism Society (2004) *Definition and ecotourism principles*. TIES. http://www.ecotourism.org/index2.php?what-is-ecotourism (accessed 17 November 2005)

Tourism Concern (2002) Press statement and briefing: *Why Tourism Concern is cautious about the International Year of Ecotourism*. http://www.tourismconcern.org.uk/media/2002/ecotourism%20press%20statement.htm (accessed 17 November 2005)

Tourism Concern (2004) *What is community tourism? Tourism Concern*. http://www.tourismconcern.org.uk/resources/community_what_is.htm

Tourism in Focus (2002a) Communities choosing ecotourism. *Tourism in Focus (Tourism Concern)* 42, 10–11.

Tourism in Focus (2002b) The hunting ecotourism conflict in Tanzania. *Tourism in Focus (Tourism Concern)* 42, 12–13.

Trotter, R. (1997) Land rights, tourist rights: Whose rights? *Media and Culture Review* 1, 1 and 10.

TWS (The Wilderness Society) (1999) *Tourism in Natural Areas Policy*. 16 May 1999. TWS Website. http://www.wilderness.org.au/member/tws/projects/General/tourism.html (accessed 17 November 2005)

UN (United Nations) (2004) *The Concept of Indigenous Peoples*. Permanent Forum on Indigenous Issues, United Nations, New York. http://www.un.org/esa/socdev/unpfii/news/news_workshop_doc.htm (accessed 17 November 2005)

UN (United Nations) (2005) News and events. UN Permanent Forum on Indigenous Issues. UN. http://www.un.org/esa/socdev/unpfii/news/news_2.htm (accessed 17 November 2005)

UN Commission on Sustainable Development (2002) *Dialogue Paper by Indigenous People*. Addendum No. 3. UN Economic and Social Council. Redturs Website. Documents. ttp://www.redturs.org/ (accessed 17 November 2005)

UNDP (United Nations Development Programme) (2004) *UNDP and Indigenous Peoples: A Practice Note on Engagement*. Indigenous Peoples. UNDP. http://www.undp.org/cso/ip.html (accessed 17 November 2005)

UNESCO (2004) The UN Decade for world's indigenous peoples. UNESCO. Social and Human Activities. http://www.unesco.org.id/activities/social/197.php (accessed 17 November 2005)

UNESCO (2005) *Local and Indigenous Knowledge of the Natural World: An Overview of Programmes and Projects*. International Workshop on Traditional Knowledge, Panama City, 21–23 September 2005. http://www.un.org/sea/socdev/unpfii/news_workshop_tk.htm (accessed 17 November 2005)

Vivanco, L.A. (2002) Ancestral homes. *Alternatives Journal* 28, 27–28.

Waitt, G. (1999) Naturalizing the 'primitive': A critique of marketing Australia's indigenous peoples as 'hunter-gatherers'. *Tourism Geographies* 1, 142–163.

Wall, G. (1998) Partnerships involving indigenous people in the management of heritage sites. In: Robinson, M. and Boniface, P. (eds) *Tourism and Cultural Conflicts*. CABI, Wallingford, UK.

Walpole, M.J. and Thouless, C.R. (2005) Increasing the value of wildlife through non-consumptive use? Deconstructing the myths of ecotourism and community-based tourism in the tropics. In: Woodroffe, R., Thirgood, S. and Rabinowitz, A. (eds) *People and Wildlife: Conflict or Coexistence?* Cambridge University Press, Cambridge, UK, pp. 122–139.

Wearing, S. (1996) Training for indigenous ecotourism development. In: *Proceedings of the 4th World Leisure Congress, Cardiff, Wales*. http://www.worldleisure.org/events/congresses/previous_congresses/congress1996.html (accessed 17 November 2005)

Weaver, D.B. (1998) *Ecotourism in the Less Developed World*. CAB International, Wallingford, UK.

Weaver, D.B. (2001) Indigenous territories. In: *Ecotourism*. John Wiley Australia, Milton, Australia, pp. 256–262.

Weaver, D.B. (2006) Indigenous territories. In: *Sustainable Tourism: Theory and Practice*. Elsevier, Oxford, pp. 143–146.

Weber, R., Butler, J. and Larson, P. (eds) (2000) *Indigenous Peoples and Conservation Organizations: Experiences in Collaboration*. WWF. http://www.worldwildlife.org/bsp/publications/ (accessed 17 November 2005)

Wesche, R. (1996) Developed country environmentalism and indigenous community controlled ecotourism in the Ecuadorian Amazon. *Geographische Zeitschrift* 3/4, 157–198.

Wesche, R. and Drumm, A. (1999) *Defending our Rainforest: A Guide to Community-based Ecotourism in the Ecuadorian Amazon*. Accion Amazonia, Quito, Ecuador.

Whittaker, E. (1998) Indigenous tourism: Reclaiming knowledge, culture and intellectual property in Australia. In: Robinson, M. and Boniface, P. (eds) *Tourism and Cultural Conflicts.* CABI, Wallingford, UK.

Wilmer, F. (1993) What indigenous peoples want and how they are getting it. In: *The Indigenous Voice in World Politics.* Sage, Newbury Park, CA, USA, pp. 127–161.

Wilshusen, P.R. (2000) Local participation in conservation and development projects: Ends, means, and power dynamics. In: Clark, T.W., Willard, A.R. and Cromley, C.M. (eds) *Foundations of Natural Resources Policy and Management.* Yale University Press, New Haven, USA, pp. 288–326.

Woodwood, S. (1997) Report – 'Cashing in on the Kruger': The potential of ecotourism to stimulate real economic growth in South Africa. *Journal of Sustainable Tourism* 5, 166–168.

World Bank, The (1991) *Operational Directive. Indigenous peoples.* OD 4.20. September 1991. Safeguard Policies. The World Bank. International Finance Corporation. http://www.ifc.org/ifcext/enviro.nsf/AttachmentsByTitle/pol_IndigPeoples/$FILE/OD420_IndigenousPeoples.pdf (accessed 17 November 2005)

WTO (World Tourism Organization) (2002) *Enhancing the Economic Benefits of Tourism for Local Communities and Poverty Alleviation.* WTO, Madrid.

WTO (World Tourism Organization) (2003) *Sustainable Development of Ecotourism: A Compilation of Good Practices in SMEs.* WTO, Madrid.

WTO (World Tourism Organization) (2005) Local control. In: *Making Tourism More Sustainable: A Guide for Policy Makers.* UNEP and WTO, Madrid, pp. 34–36.

Wunder, S. (2000) Ecotourism and economic incentives – an empirical approach. *Ecological Economics* 32, 465–479.

WWF (World Wildlife Fund) (2000) *Map of Indigenous and Traditional Peoples in Ecoregions.* World Wildlife Fund, Gland, Switzerland.

WWF (2001a) *The Hundested recommendations for donor best practice. Indigenous peoples and biodiversity governance.* WWF http://www.worldwildlife.org/bsp/publications/asia/hundested/hundested.html (accessed 17 November 2005)

WWF (2001b) *Guidelines for Community-based Ecotourism Development.* July 2001. WWF International. http://www.wwf.no/pdf/tourism_guidelines.pdf (accessed 17 November 2005)

WWF (2005) *WWF statement of principles on indigenous peoples and conservation.* WWF. Policy. http://www.panda.org/about_wwf/what_we_do/policy/people_environment/indigenous_people/index.cfm (accessed 17 November 2005)

Yang, W.T. (2005) The development of ecotourism business in Taiwan's native reservation areas. In: *Exploring the Ecotourism in Taiwan, 11–12 October 2005.* Department of Environmental Resources Management, Transworld Institute of Technology, Taiwan, pp. C-89–C-94.

Zeppel, H. (1997) Meeting 'Wild People': Iban culture and longhouse tourism in Sarawak. In: Yamashita, S., Din, K.H. and Eades, J.S. (eds) *Tourism and Cultural Development in Asia and Oceania.* Universiti Kebangsaan Malaysia, Bangi, Malaysia, pp. 119–140.

Zeppel, H. (1998a) Land and culture: Sustainable tourism and indigenous peoples. In: Hall, C.M. and Lew, A. (eds) *Sustainable Tourism: A Geographical Perspective.* Addison Wesley Longman, London, pp. 60–74.

Zeppel, H. (1998b) Tourism and Aboriginal Australia. *Tourism Management* 19, 485–488.

Zeppel, H. (1998c) Indigenous cultural tourism: 1997 Fulbright Symposium. *Tourism Management* 19, 103–106.

Zeppel, H. (1998d) Selling the dreamtime: Aboriginal culture in Australian tourism. In: Rowe, D. and Lawrence, G. (eds) *Tourism, Leisure, Sport: Critical Perspectives.* Hodder Headline, Sydney, Australia, pp. 23–38.

Zeppel, H. (1998e) Issues in Maori tourism. *Pacific Tourism Review* 1, 363–370.

Zeppel, H. (2000) Ecotourism and indigenous peoples. *Issues: All Australian Educational Magazine*, 51, July.

Zeppel, H. (2001) Aboriginal cultures and indigenous tourism. In: Douglas, N., Douglas, N. and Derrett, R. (eds) *Special Interest Tourism: Context and Cases.* John Wiley Australia, Brisbane, Australia, pp. 232–259.

Zeppel, H. (2002) Indigenous tourism in the Wet Tropics World Heritage Area, North Queensland. *Australian Aboriginal Studies* 2002/2, 65–68.

Zeppel, H. (2003) Sharing the country: Ecotourism policy and indigenous peoples in Australia. In: Fennell, D.A. and Dowling, R.K. (eds) *Ecotourism Policy and Planning.* CABI, Wallingford, UK, pp. 55–76.

2

The Pacific Islands: Village-based Ecotourism in Community Rainforests

This chapter reviews Indigenous ecotourism and village-based tourism ventures in the Pacific Islands. It first reviews tourism in the Pacific Islands and programmes promoting community-based ecotourism ventures. Case studies of community ecotourism in conservation areas are described for the South Pacific Biodiversity Conservation Programme (SPBCP) and other ecotourism projects supported by environmental NGOs. Village ecotourism ventures in community-owned forests are reviewed for the Solomon Islands, Fiji, Vanuatu, Papua New Guinea, Samoa and Micronesia. Key issues for the development of village ecotourism in the Pacific Islands are discussed in the conclusion.

Introduction: Ecotourism in the Pacific Islands

There are 22 Pacific Island countries and territories, covering the three main regions of Micronesia in the north Pacific, Melanesia in the west Pacific and Polynesia in the south Pacific (see Table 2.1). Small Pacific island nations typically rely on foreign aid, agriculture, fishing, logging and tourism for an income. Tourism is an important part of the economy in the Cook Islands (nearly 50% of GDP), Fiji, French Polynesia, New Caledonia, Niue, Palau, Samoa and Vanuatu (SPTO, 2001; Treloar and Hall, 2005). There were

about 2.5 million visitors to the Pacific Islands in 2000, compared to 23 million in the Caribbean. Guam, Northern Marianas, Fiji and French Polynesia attract two-thirds of all tourist arrivals in the Pacific (Harrison, 2003). There are some 1500 tourism businesses in Oceania, with the majority being small companies. Apart from air access to the main islands of each country (except Tokelau and Pitcairn Islands), some 90% of smaller islands in the south Pacific can only be reached by boat (Martel, 2001). Across the Pacific region, the main tourism focus is on cultural, adventure and nature tourism, along with marine tourism and diving. A 1992 conference discussed key issues for developing ecotourism in the Pacific (Hay, 1992), while conservation and tourism agencies have promoted the economic benefits of ecotourism ventures for local landowners (Liu, 1994; Scheyvens and Purdie, 1999; Sofield, 2003a, b). Ecotourism is a new industry sector developed by conservation agencies and tourism organizations in Samoa, Fiji, Vanuatu and Solomon Islands (Weaver, 1998a, b; Zeppel, 1998). Home-stay visits and village-based tourism are promoted in several island nations but, overall, the Pacific region lacks 'a consistent approach to ecotourism and village-based tourism' (Harrison, 2003: 22).

Pacific island peoples still largely rely on subsistence agriculture and fishing, and most land areas and marine resources in these Pacific island countries are in recognized community

Table 2.1. Pacific island countries and ecotourism programmes.

Micronesia ('small islands')	Polynesia[a] ('many islands')	Melanesia ('dark islands')
Federated States of Micronesia[b]	American Samoa (US)	Papua New Guinea[c] (Ecotourism Melanesia)
(Yap, Truk, Pohnpei, Kosrae)	Samoa (National Ecotourism Program)	New Caledonia (Fr)
Guam (US)	Cook Islands (NZ)	Solomon Islands[c] (Solomons Village Stay)
Marshall Islands[b]	Niue (NZ)	Fiji[c] (Ecotourism and Village-based Tourism)
Northern Marianas (US)	Tonga	Vanuatu (Wantok Environment Centre)
Palau[b]	French Polynesia (Fr)	
Kiribati[c]	Wallis and Futuna (Fr)	
Nauru	Tuvalu[c]	
	Tokelau (NZ)	
	Pitcairn Islands (UK)	

[a] Hawaii is Polynesian but is part of the USA. [b] Former US territories. [c] Former UK territories. Fr: France; NZ: New Zealand; US: United States; UK = United Kingdom.

ownership (Martel, 2001). Hence, ecotourism ventures in the Pacific Islands are largely village- or community-based enterprises. Several small-scale community ecotourism projects, such as rainforest walking trails, village guest houses, ecolodges and tours, have been developed with donor assistance in the Solomon Islands, Fiji, Vanuatu, Samoa and other countries (Weaver, 1998; Dowling, 2001; Harrison, 2003). These ecotourism projects provide some income for local villagers and are an incentive for communities to conserve tropical rainforests and coral reefs. Ecotourism ventures proposed by a community, rather than individuals, are more acceptable for development donors as they focus on income generation and social benefits as well as conservation (Sofield, 1992). Indigenous ecotourism ventures are largely based on community-owned Conservation Areas rather than National Parks as customary tenure of land and sea areas include most of the remaining biodiversity in the Pacific (Weaver, 1998a; Martel, 2001). The Pacific Islands has one of the lowest percentages of public protected areas (< 1%), (a major ecotourism venue in other areas) mainly due to traditional ownership of land. For example, Fiji's first National Park was only declared in 1989 (Weaver, 1998a). Hence, Indigenous ecotourism takes place in community conservation areas or other protected areas that recognize village ownership and management of these sites. Through the 1990s, western

consultants, foreign donors and conservation agencies (NGOs) were heavily involved in developing community-based ecotourism ventures in the Pacific Islands.

South Pacific Biodiversity Conservation Programme: Community Ecotourism

Community-based ecotourism ventures were developed as part of the South Pacific Biodiversity Conservation Programme (SPBCP) that ran from 1993 to 2001. SPBCP was managed by the South Pacific Regional Environment Programme (SPREP) and funded by the Global Environmental Facility, through UNDP, with US$10 million over 8 years in the 1990s (Turnbull, 2004). The SPBCP had 26 members including Australia, NZ, USA, France and the 22 Pacific island nations. The main aim of SPBCP was supporting the preservation of forest and marine areas in 17 community-owned Conservation Areas (CA) covering 1.4 million hectares of land and sea across 12 Pacific island countries. From 1997, SPBCP funded 12 CA ecotourism initiatives assisted by Conservation Area Support Officers and village-based training workshops on developing and managing ecotourism activities. These CA ecotourism projects were established by local communities to provide alternative income, support conservation activities and promote sustainable development of Pacific island communities

(Martel, 2001; Buckley, 2003a). The CA ecotourism ventures included village lodges, forest trails, guided tours and marine or wetland activities. Some ecotourism ventures were initiated entirely by local communities. An ecotourism development manual published by SPREP (2002) included 14 case studies of community ecotourism ventures in 11 Pacific countries (see Table 2.2).

The Conservation Area Support Officers in each country wrote up the SPBCP ecotourism projects. These case studies described the natural attractions, location and village ownership of each CA, the ecotourism achievements, steps taken, lessons learned and other technical advice from supporting staff in conservation or tourism (SPREP, 2002). Seven of these CA community ecotourism projects were co-funded by other aid organizations (e.g. Australia, NZ, Japan) or conservation NGOs (e.g. WWF, TNC). CA ecotourism products developed by communities included village-owned lodges, beach *fales* or huts (7), guided tours, walking trails, interpretive signs and brochures (see Table 2.3). Koroyanitu Heritage Park won a Fiji ecotourism award in 1996. However, remoteness, limited transport access, low visitor numbers, lack of funding or training, issues in marketing new products and industry

control of hotels and dive tourism (e.g. Palau in Micronesia) limited the development of CA ecotourism projects in several countries (e.g. Solomon Islands, Kiribati, Pohnpei, Niue). The Pohnpei Watershed CA did not receive enough visitors or income for upkeep of walking trails that are now overgrown. The Komarindi CA community ecotourism project also stopped operating due to ethnic unrest in the Solomon Islands since 1999.

Community ownership of land and ecotourism activities includes clan, village or family groups. At Sa'anapu-Sataoa CA, Samoa, family groups own beach *fale* accommodation while the infrastructure and tours within the reserve are community owned. At Uafato CA, however, chiefs prefer that all tourism is community-based rather than hosted by individual families. Overall, community income from ecotourism includes fees from guided tours, CA entry fees, lodge or *fale* accommodation, provision of food, handicraft sales, interpretive trails, yacht anchorage fees (Arnarvon Marine CA) and shop sales of environmental products or visitor donations (Takitumu CA). Financial benefits from ecotourism in Koroyanitu Heritage Park (Fiji) are directed to community development, such as an education fund (60%) and project

Table 2.2. Community ecotourism initiatives in SPBCP Conservation Areas.

Conservation Area (CA)	Area (ha)	Ecotourism features
Arnavon Marine CA, Solomon Islands	8,720	Coral reefs, Arnavon Islands
Komarindi CA, Solomon Islands	19,300	Catchment area, forest, birds, archaeological cave
Vanua Rapita, Solomon Islands[a]		Coral islands, reefs, bush walks, villages, custom sites
Vatthe CA, Vanuatu	2,276	Lowland rainforest, rare birds, black-sand beach
Koroyanitu Heritage Park, Fiji	2,984	Forest, birds, archaeological sites, trekking tours
Ha'apai CA, Tonga	10,000 km^2	Coral atolls, marine life, 62 islands, Tongan lifestyle
Huvalu Forest CA, Niue	6,029	Rainforest, birds, bats, coconut crab, flying fox
Sa'anapu-Sataoa CA, Samoa	75	Mangrove forest, birds, beach areas
Uafato CA, Samoa	1,306	Rainforest, waterfalls, birds, *Ifilele* trees, wood carving
Takitumu CA, Cook Islands	155	Catchment area, endangered birds, *kakerori* bird
Na'a Tarawa CA, Kiribati		Tarawa Atoll, coral reef, marine life, diving
Ngaremeduu CA, Pohnpei		Coral reefs, mangroves, archaeological sites
Pohnpei Watershed CA, Pohnpei		Artificial islands, Nan Madol archaeological site
Rock Islands CA, Palau	800 km^2	Limestone islands, marine lakes, jellyfish, turtles
Utwa Walung Marine CA, Kosrae		Wetlands, jungle, mangroves, lagoons, reef area

[a] Non-SPBCP Case Study – Ecotourism lodge in Marovo Lagoon, supported by WWF South Pacific.
Sources: Martel (2001: 91); SPREP (2002); Buckley (2003a: 63).

Table 2.3. Community ecotourism products and funding support in SPBCP Conservation Areas.

Conservation Area (CA)	Ecotourism products	Year began	Funding support
Arnavon Marine CA, Solomon Islands[a]	Rest house, marine tour	1995	TNC
Komarindi CA, Solomon Islands[a]	Ecotour	1998	
Vanua Rapita, Solomon Islands[b]	Rapita Lodge, ecotours	1995	WWF South Pacific
Vatthe CA, Vanuatu	Vatthe Lodge, ecotours	1996	NZODA
Koroyanitu Heritage Park, Fiji[a]	Lodge tours, trekking	1990/94	NZODA, JANPECC
Ha'apai CA, Tonga[a]	Beach *fales*, ecotours, festival	1997	AusAID (guides, beach)
Huvalu Forest CA, Niue	Ecotour, signs, brochure	1998	
Sa'anapu-Sataoa CA, Samoa[a]	Beach *fales*, boardwalk, signs	1998	Keidanren Foundation
Uafato CA, Samoa[a]	CA sign, group tours	1999	
Takitumu CA, Cook Islands	Bird tours, shop, brochure	1997	
Na'a Tarawa CA, Kiribati[a]	Signs, day tour	1998	
Ngaremeduu CA, Pohnpei[a]	Kayaking tour, heritage tour	1998	
Pohnpei Watershed CA, Pohnpei	Walking trails, booklet		TNC (booklet)
Rock Islands CA, Palau[a]	Kayak/canoe, resorts, trail	1998	
Utwa Walung Marine CA, Kosrae	Mangrove canoe tour, huts, visitor centre, boardwalk	1997	National Congress Seacology (solar power)

[a] Ecotourism project supported by local government/tourism agency or local NGO.
[b] Non-SPBCP case study.
TNC: The Nature Conservancy; WWF: World Wildlife Fund; NZODA: New Zealand Overseas Development Assistance; AusAID: Australian Agency for International Development; JANPECC: Japan Pacific Economic Cooperation Committee.
Source: SPREP (2002).

management and maintenance (40%). At Takitumu CA (Cook Islands), ecotourism funds the *karekori* bird recovery programme and provides some benefits for landowners. Takitumu CA had 624 visitors in 2001. At Vatthe CA (Vanuatu), 90% of tourism income from Vatthe Lodge goes to two communities. The Lodge receives 200 visitors a year and is a member of the Vanuatu Islands Bungalow Association marketed by Island Safaris. At Rapita Lodge (Solomon Islands), income is directed to the community (63% for salaries, dividends and development fund), local businesses (25% for food, fuel, supplies) and others (12% to government and churches) (SPREP, 2002).

Community ecotourism products in these SPBCP Conservation Areas focused on natural scenery and wildlife rather than Indigenous cultural traditions or identity. Product interpretation at these sites (i.e. signs, tours) featured Indigenous ecological knowledge rather than cultural performances or displays. Indigenous issues in nature conservation and traditional practices were discussed on CA guided tours. The SPREP programme focused on biodiversity conservation and environmental management, rather than the social structures, land tenure and political issues that affected island communities (Turnbull, 2004). There were no data or research on tourist satisfaction with Indigenous tours in Conservation Areas, or whether Indigenous culture and identity was a key motivation for joining these ecotours.

Conservation NGOs and Village-based Ecotourism

Biodiversity Conservation Network

The SPBCP ecotourism projects built on the experiences of other conservation agencies developing community enterprises in the Pacific. From 1993 to 1999, the Biodiversity Conservation Network (BCN), managed by WWF, worked on 20 projects across the Pacific and Asia region that supported community-based enterprises for nature conservation. The BCN was a part of the Biodiversity Support Program funded by USAID as a consortium of

WWF, The Nature Conservancy and the World Resources Institute. BCN community ecotourism projects in the Pacific were in East Bauro, Makira Island (Solomon Islands) with Conservation International (CI), in addition to Crater Mountain Wildlife Management Area and the forests of Lakekamu Basin (PNG). The BCN enterprise approach to community-based conservation involved a direct link to biodiversity, generating economic, social and environmental benefits for stakeholders and involving communities. These integrated conservation and development projects, including ecotourism, were developed to conserve nature and give local communities a sustainable alternative to logging and hunting activities. In 1997, BCN added online 'Marketspace' to promote their ecotourism projects and other community-based forest enterprises. The local staff and partner NGOs involved in these BCN ecotourism projects also assessed the environmental and socio-economic impacts along with the financial viability of ecotourism businesses. BCN reports evaluated rainforest ecotourism in Crater Mountain and Lakekamu Basin (PNG) and trekking in the highlands of Makira Island (Solomon Islands). The Makira Island Trek won an ecotourism award but ecotourism in Lakekamu Basin was not a success due to landowner disputes, lack of tourist arrivals and focus on ecological research (see next sections).

Seacology: island conservation

The Seacology Foundation, based in the US, aims to conserve island ecosystems by providing funding to support the preservation of environments and Indigenous cultures on islands around the world. Seacology funds community centres, schools, water tanks, wharfs, roads and other community facilities in exchange for island villages preserving rainforest and marine areas. They also provide funding and materials for infrastructure and conservation in protected areas and other community ecotourism projects. Village leaders control these Seacology projects deciding how funds will be used for conservation and community schemes. The focus is mainly on

island conservation projects in developing countries. Seacology has an advisory board of island environmentalists as well as a scientific advisory board. Pacific members of Seacology's Island Advisory Board include representatives from Yap, Palau, Pohnpei, PNG, Samoa, Cook Islands, Tonga, Kosrae, Saipan, Vanuatu and Fiji. On Savaii Island in Samoa, the Director of Seacology provided US$85,000 in 1989 to establish the Falealupo Rainforest Preserve. In 1997, Seacology funded construction of the Falealupo Canopy Walkway to help the local community generate income from ecotourism. At the Tafua Samoa Rainforest Preserve on Savaii, Seacology funded the Tafua Conservation Centre, walking trails and signs for the preserve. In Micronesia, Seacology funded the installation of solar power at the Visitor Centre for Utwa-Walung Conservation Area in Kosrae and constructed an ecotourism hostel on And Atoll in Pohnpei. In 2003, Seacology funded restoration of the historic Tamilyog Stone Path on Yap, along with a forest reserve.

Conservation International, The Nature Conservancy and WWF South Pacific

Other American NGOs involved with community ecotourism projects in the Pacific Islands include Conservation International and The Nature Conservancy. Conservation International helped develop and promote the Makira Island Ecotrek in the Solomon Islands and is involved with other conservation and tourism projects in Milne Bay, PNG. The Nature Conservancy funded visitor facilities, such as a booklet in Pohnpei Watershed Conservation Area (Micronesia) and a rest house in Arnavon Marine Conservation Area, Solomon Islands. Together with WWF, The Nature Conservancy was a member of the Biodiversity Conservation Network in the Pacific. WWF South Pacific funded the Rapita Lodge near Michi Village on Marovo Lagoon, Solomon Islands as their flagship project for rainforest conservation in the western Pacific. International conservation NGOs have provided significant regional funding for community ecotourism projects in the Pacific Islands. However, as Fagence (1997) noted, there is a lack of coordination among these ecotourism projects funded by conservation NGOs and no overall strategies for promoting ecotourism once the projects end. Village ecotourism projects funded by NGOs are described for Solomon Islands, Samoa and in Micronesia.

Solomon Islands

The Solomon Islands are a chain of islands north east of Papua New Guinea with a population of around 400,000 people spread across a land area of 28,000 km². About 90% of people in the Solomon Islands are dependent on subsistence agriculture and fishing and only 2% of the land is cultivated (Buckley, 2003). Many islands have been affected by commercial logging clear felling the rainforests.

The Solomon Islands receive around 12,000 visitors a year, with a focus on dive tourism (Macalister et al., 2000; Buckley, 2003b). Village disputes over land ownership based on traditional land tenure systems and ethnic unrest since 1999 have limited tourism development in the Solomon Islands. In the 1980s and 1990s, local villages and chiefs were under intense pressure from logging companies to sell timber for cash. Conservation NGOs and government agencies supported village-based ecotourism ventures to preserve tropical rainforest and provide alternative income (WWF, 2000). In the Solomon Islands, ecotourism enterprises need the support of local communities who own the land (Sofield, 1993, 2003a; Michaud et al., 1994). Ecotourism ventures reviewed in this section are Komarindi Ecotours near Honiara, forest walking trails on Guadalcanal and Makira Island, Rapita Lodge on Marovo Lagoon and the Solomons village homestay network.

Komarindi Ecotours

Komarindi Ecotours took place in Komarindi Conservation Area with 19,300 ha of forest highlands and the main water supply for the capital city of Honiara. The traditional owners

of the CA began planning and training for ecotourism development in 1997. Two ecotours began in October 1998, a half-day Nature and Custom Tour focusing on Poha Cave, Melanesia's oldest rock art, and a 1 day Village and Rainforest Trek visiting the Lakuili village of Veramboli (Macalister et al., 2000). Fifty tourists provided net income of SI$1500 for the community. However, fighting between tribal groups in Honiara meant Komarindi Ecotours closed in early 1999. Tour guides trained in the project gained casual work with other tour operators. Ecotourism training raised the level of environmental and cultural awareness and developed a community-owned business (SPREP, 2002). However, in a small visitor market, Komarindi Ecotours were unable to secure visits from cruise ship visitors and more marketing and site infrastructure was required while the day tour relied on the village visit (Macalister et al., 2000). The local community needed to diversify its activities rather than rely solely on tourism.

In 1991/92, government agencies, SPREP and TNC, devised plans for the Komarindi Catchment Conservation Area. A hydroelectric scheme was proposed that did not eventuate. Along with a resource rent for traditional landowners, other income-generating activities proposed for the area were guided rainforest walks, overnight adventure tours at traditional camps, sale of handicrafts and establishing board walks and canopy observation decks on the Lungga Plateau. Other commercial ventures suggested for Komarindi were a butterfly observatory, sale and breeding site and selling forest products such as ngali nuts (Thomas et al., 1993). However, these relied on external funding and links with hotels and tour operators. Other tours proposed by Komarindi Ecotours, but not developed, were a weekend walk and cross-island trek (Macalister et al., 2000).

Guadalcanal Track

The island of Guadalcanal, with a land area of 5300 km², is the largest island in the Solomon Islands. The southern 'weather coast' of Guadalcanal has a rugged mountain range covered with tropical rainforest along the full length of the island. The region has poor quality agricultural land, malaria and natural disasters such as cyclones. The subsistence use of natural resources from forests, the marine and freshwater environments is also based on customary (*kastom*) ownership of land (Rudkin and Hall, 1996). In 1988, the Australian High Commissioner, and part owner of Vulelua Resort, proposed an indigenous ecotourism development for the Lauvi area of southern Guadalcanal. As an alternative to rainforest logging, he suggested a rainforest wilderness trail crossing the island of Guadalcanal controlled by 'an indigenous company of customary landowners' (Sofield, 1992: 96). The proposed walk started at Aola on the northern coast of Guadalcanal, near Vulelua Resort, and ended at Lauvi Lagoon on the southern 'weather coast' by a light airstrip. Soon after, a local area council applied for funding to build a tourist resort at Lauvi supported by a parliamentary member from the Lauvi area. A nature tourism plan was prepared for the Lauvi Lagoon area. While the Solomon Islands Ministry of Tourism and Aviation and the Guadalcanal Provincial Government supported the proposed tourist resort at Lauvi Lagoon, local landowners who used forest resources and the lagoon area for fishing were not consulted (Rudkin and Hall, 1996). Tourism reports evaluated the natural resources in Lauvi Lagoon as tourist features rather than customary use of land and sea resources for subsistence needs. In this ecotourism proposal, the environment was seen as an individual rather than collective resource.

The Guadalcanal Rainforest Trail included the conservation of a ten-mile wide corridor across the width of the island as a forest 'protected area.' The walk visited four villages, with overnight stays in thatched huts, dancing and traditional *umus* (feasts) for tourists. It provided some employment and supported traditional lifestyles. However, villages along the proposed walking trail also used scarce resources to host visitors. Sofield (1992: 96) stated the walk would be ecologically sustainable as it used 'annually renewable resources'. However, *umus* were only prepared for special occasions since they required large amounts of wood to heat stones and

vegetation to wrap a large variety and quantity of foods that would have been *tambu* (taboo) until at a sustainable level (Rudkin and Hall, 1996). Villagers would need to obtain these extra resources from reserved areas. Members of local villages also provided the free labour for constructing and maintaining the walking trail. The first Guadalcanal Walk in July 1992 visited four villages with total income for the locals of SI$3000 (Sofield, 1992). The distribution of this income to chiefs, villagers providing tourist services or to support conservation was not explained. According to Rudkin and Hall (1996), this proposal focused on the conservation and economic benefits of ecotourism, mainly for 'big men', NGOs and the resort owners, while the social benefits of ecotourism for villagers were limited by extra resource demands.

The complex negotiations with four villages and Melanesian tribal rivalry also disrupted the walk. For these reasons, village-based ecotourism treks along the Guadalcanal Track did not go ahead.

Makira Island EcoTrek

On Makira Island, to the east of the main island of Guadalcanal in the Solomon Islands, a responsible tourism project based on trekking was developed with local villages. This ecotourism project aimed to assist in rainforest conservation and provide some cash income for Melanesian villagers still leading subsistence lifestyles (Gould, 1995). The Solomon Islands Development Trust (SIDT), together with two international conservation agencies, Maruia Society (NZ) and Conservation International (CI, USA), developed this project. The Makira Conservation Area of 63,000 ha was first established with local Bauro people. In 1995, this Conservation in Development consortium received a grant of US$347,574 from the Biodiversity Conservation Network (BCN) to develop village enterprises, such as the trekking tour, providing technical assistance to the Bauro community in ecotourism product development, training and monitoring (Russell and Stabile, 2003). The Makira Island Ecotrek involved 6 days of strenuous walking through highland rainforest, staying in villages, eating local food and watching panpipe dancing. Only three tours a year were planned, with a maximum of 15 people, to minimize impacts. *Conde Nast Travel* magazine featured the Makira trek as a key ecotourism experience in the South Pacific (Russell, 1998). An initial visit to Makira Island to experience the trek was also made in 1994 by a New Zealand adventure travel company and, in 1995, by One World Travel from Australia (Volkel-Hutchison, 1996). One World Travel, a Community Aid Abroad company, and Conservation International started advertising the Makira Island ecotrek in 1996. While One World Travel featured the tour in their brochure, pamphlets and talks, no bookings were made. CI featured this Makira ecotrek in their online 'Ecotravel Center', with the tour booked through an agent in Honiara (CI, 2001). By the end of 1997, there had been eight tours with three more treks planned in 1998 (Russell and Stabile, 2003). A BCN Program Officer joined a Makira Trek in 1998 from the key funding body for this project.

A 1995 survey found the Bauro communities were cash poor, with intensive subsistence use of natural resources and several taking cash from logging companies. This sustainable, community-based ecotourism venture involved several villages in a 5-day walk across the Bauro highlands. Guides and porters accompanied the group of six people. The first night was spent in a leaf hut owned by the local manager of the ecotour. At other villages, the group heard pan pipers, saw custom activities, bought crafts and joined in dancing. Trekkers received gift bowls, headdresses and beads. The wage rates paid for tourist services were decided by the trek leader, who was a local teacher, together with the community leaders. Payments were made to guides, porters, carvers, weavers, caterers, hosts, entertainers, builders and decorators. The payments to individuals involved over 400 transactions on each trekking tour (Russell, 1998). The first Makira ecotreks began in September 1996 and July 1997, with cash benefits for villages. The July 1997 ecotour brought in US$2500 to Makira communities or 40% of the yearly cash earned in Highland villages. The village of Togori put all their earnings from hosting the ecotour into a fund

for community works (US$510) while the highland Bauro communities made payments to individuals (US$1780) with a smaller amount in a community fund (US$600). Some people used tourism income to buy bullets used to shoot pigeons, sold in coastal markets. However, one Bauro elder also wanted to set aside all his land for conservation (Russell and Stabile, 2003).

This Makira ecotrek conserved rainforest, brought some cash benefits and supported cultural practices, such as carving, dancing and playing panpipes. Key issues were the difficulties of negotiating community-based conservation, reliance on the local tour leader and setting up an ecotourism enterprise in a rugged and remote location like Makira. Staff from SIDT, Conservation International and One World Travel assisted the Bauro communities in developing this Makira ecotrek. This included local ownership, community-wide participation, renewing cultural pride, guide training and marketing the tour. The local benefits from community participation in ecotourism, however, were tempered by the need for economic sustainability of the venture. One World Travel marketed responsible tourism and ethical travel to small groups while CI supported other mainstream travel agencies marketing the Makira trip to generate a regular flow of tourist groups (Volkel-Hutchison, 1996). This included using a local inbound tour operator and packaging the Makira trek with visits to other community lodges in Marovo Lagoon (Russell, 1998; Russell and Stabile, 2003). With limited tours (three a year) and visitor numbers (max. 15), generating income from other ventures, such as nut oil processing, were also necessary to support conservation and ecotourism in Makira.

Rapita Lodge, Marovo Lagoon

The Marovo Lagoon is a large coral reef lagoon along one side of the islands of New Georgia, Vangunu and Ngatokae in the western Solomon Islands. The 100 km-long coral reef and island ecosystem has a population of 11,000 people living in 50 villages. Ninety per cent of the Marovo Lagoon is owned by 15 Indigenous subgroups (*butubutu*) with rights to use land and marine resources. Income from local use of natural resources and ecotourism (128 beds over 10 years) was estimated to be worth SI\$15.2 million in Marovo Lagoon (LaFranchi, 1999). Diving on coral reefs and wrecks in the Marovo Lagoon and upmarket dive resorts are the main tourist attractions in this area (Hviding, 2003).

Rapita Lodge on Marovo Lagoon consists of three local guesthouses that accommodate 12 to 15 people. Operating since 1995, the lodge is owned and managed by the Michi Village who built the guesthouses using local materials such as mangrove wood, with walls of sago and nipah palm thatching. The lodge is on a small island in the Marovo Lagoon with bungalows built out over the water. The Tobakokorapa Association runs Rapita Lodge as a cooperative venture whereby village members buy shares to receive dividends. The Tobakokorapa Association, with three clans and 350 members, owns the Rapita Lodge. Income from the Lodge is directed to the community (63% for salaries, dividends and development fund), local businesses (25% for food, fuel and supplies) and others (12% to government, churches) (SPREP, 2002). WWF assisted in training villagers to operate the lodge while the Japanese Environment Corporation provided start-up funding. The lodge has a manager and village members take shifts for the cleaning, cooking, bar and restaurant. Guided tours run from the lodge include bush medicine tours, village visits and river safaris. Income from Rapita Lodge has allowed the community to stop logging on customary land and ban fishing in some reef areas (Buckley, 2003b).

Rapita Lodge was the first village-owned ecotourism resort developed in the Solomon Islands. WWF South Pacific supported Michi Village during their development of Rapita Lodge in 1994. The village first proposed a tourist lodge during a WWF Community Resource Conservation Planning exercise. Village members formed their own working groups on construction, operations, visitor activities, housekeeping, for food preparation and grounds management while WWF field staff facilitated planning and training sessions where community members put forward their own ideas. This generated a feeling of community ownership, control and responsibility for Rapita Lodge (Martin, 1994; WWF, 2000). Michi villagers sell their food products to the resort, work in shifts and receive annual dividends. The lodge provides local employment at Michi Village and helps to conserve natural resources such as forest and reefs (*South Pacific Currents*, 2001). Rapita Lodge is promoted on the website for WWF South Pacific (Rapita Lodge, 2004; WWF, 2004).

Hviding and Bayliss-Smith (2000) provide a critical review of WWF's ecotourism project at Michi. As a flagship project for rainforest conservation in Marovo Lagoon, WWF provided initial funding of A\$140,000 for Michi and the Rapita Lodge. A chiefly son of Michi Village worked for WWF in Gizo through the 1990s and steered WWF towards an ecotourism project in Michi. The lodge was built 100 metres offshore from the village on a tiny island, using unpaid village labour and local building materials. WWF proposed a composting toilet but villagers wanted a septic system installed. A stay at the lodge is an all inclusive charge including meals (SI\$85). Extra fees are charged for boat transfers, guided activities, 'custom dancing' and hire of snorkelling gear. Rapita Lodge, though, was just one part of an overall Resource Management Plan for the landowners of Michi Village, with community nature reserves declared over inshore areas where tourists snorkelled and rainforest areas.

Community members also hired a bulldozer in mid-1996 to level a ridge for a new village site about 1 km away. The chief's son working for WWF threatened to burn Rapita Lodge to stop the village relocation and potentially losing staff. Hence, this ecotourism project also created social divisions among Michi villagers, reinforcing the role of 'bigmen' in controlling local villages (Hviding, 2003).

Hviding and Bayliss-Smith (2000) also questioned the financial viability of Rapita Lodge. A profit of SI\$16,000 was paid in full by the Rapita Lodge to Michi Village after the first 6 months of operation in 1995. Village members working at the lodge were originally paid weekly wages. However, the manager, assistant manager, caterers, boatmen and activity groups were all then paid according to monthly profits. Money was also set aside to replace capital items such as outboard motors. For the resort to break even it needed an average of 25% occupancy (four guests) or to be profitable, six guests. Rapita Lodge achieved 7% occupancy in its first year and 13% in the second, with 26% occupancy in August–September 1997. Tourists at the lodge came from Europe, North America and Australia. The average stay at Rapita Lodge was 3 days, while villagers preferred tourists to stay for a week.

The Maruia Society conservation NGO from New Zealand was involved in a World Heritage Programme (WHP) for Marovo Lagoon. The impetus was seeking World Heritage listing of Marovo as the largest island-enclosed lagoon in the world. This generated village requests to fund ecotourism projects. Some 54 landowning groups in Marovo applied to the Area Council for permits to build tourist lodges. All were approved but only two were built. In 1987 though, nine families in one village raised NZ$5000 to build a six-bed tourist lodge by selling shells, fish and vegetables and also money earned by relatives in Honiara with jobs. Profits were used to extend and upgrade the lodge. The Makikuri Lodge opened in 1986 and was run by an extended family. Other Marovo landowners wanted business grants from WHP to build their lodges. One locally owned tourist lodge was upgraded for a visit by tourism wholesalers to boost local support and interest (Lees and Evans, 1993). A Marovo Lagoon Ecotourism Association was formed in 1996, with a focus on community and family-run ecotourism lodges, handicrafts, water taxis and allied ventures (Halfpenny, 1999). By 1997, there were 11 ecolodges in Marovo (Hviding and Bayliss-Smith, 2000). Seven lodges received financial support from WHP funded by a NZ bilateral aid project. The WHP dealt with individuals rather than communities and they mainly funded upgrades to existing lodges (e.g. toilets) or new projects approved by villages but run by the sons of chiefs (Hviding and Bayliss-Smith, 2000). In Marovo Lagoon, ecotourism was about rainforest conservation and not overall community benefits.

Village homestays in the Solomon Islands

Solomons Village Stay was established in 1996 as a network of village stays in lagoon or coastal areas of various island provinces around the Solomon Islands. Visitors stayed in small guest bungalows built of local materials next to their host family, ate traditional food and joined in with daily village activities. The village stays were limited to one group or booking at a time and limited to 10 visits a month. This village stay network was 'the first village ecotourism venture of its type in the South Pacific' (Solomons Village Stay, nd). The village stays offered an alternative to rainforest logging by providing some cash income for host families (Hayes, 1997). Most village stay hosts were local community and church leaders who acted as interpreters and guides, provided meals and organized cultural activities for visitors. Tourists paid US$33 per person per night for accommodation, guides and meals. Other traditional village-based activities were free, except motorized canoe trips. Some 'custom' fees were also payable to local landowners for visiting cultural sites or private areas.

An Australian teacher set up the Solomons Village Stay network with sponsorship and support from the Solomon Islands Tourist Authority and Solomon Airlines (Hayes, 1997). The village stays were, at first, booked through agents in Brisbane, Queensland and Honiara in the Solomon Islands. A website for Ecotourism Melanesia later allowed direct email bookings and payment for village stays. In 2001, this website described eight village stay localities and activities, mainly in the Western Province (Solomon Islands Ministry of Commerce, 2001a, b, c).

The Guadalcanal village stays were not promoted on this site after the ethnic unrest of 1999–2000. The Solomons Village Stay network also booked other village-operated nature lodges and resorts located near the main village, but with separate facilities (e.g. dining area) and activities for tourists. Another 15 to 20 lodges run by families or communities were added to this site in mid-2001. In 2005, there were 11 village stays and 10 ecolodges listed, with all but three found in the Western Province.

Lipscomb (1998) reviewed impediments to village-based tourism as the main form of Indigenous tourism enterprise in the Solomon Islands. While the guesthouses were built with local labour and materials, capital input was required to purchase water tanks, plumbing, bedding, canoes, outboard motors and other equipment. With low operating costs, 'break even' occupancy rates are as low as 10 to 15%. Other issues such as accessibility and location of village stays also affect viability. Lagoon areas are a key attraction, especially Marovo, Roviana and Vona Vona around New Georgia Island, but the village stays are much dispersed with transport access limited to air or boat connections. Training for villagers in food preparation, health and hygiene and provision of water supply and toilet facilities are further issues. Cultural impediments for village-based tourism are the customary land tenure system, jealousy, family and tribal allegiances, big men and local power hierarchies. There was also limited marketing of village-based tourism to international visitors, while conservation NGOs (eg. WWF, CI, NZ) had spent large amounts of money developing village-based tourism enterprises.

Conservation NGOs and some village leaders promoted the development of village stays and nature lodges as an alternative to rainforest logging. In the Marovo Lagoon, driven by external funding and support from conservation NGOs, numerous village guesthouses were established in the 1990s. However, low visitor numbers in the Solomon Islands, low occupancy rates and limited marketing meant that these could not all be sustained (Ell, 2003). The economic and social benefits of village tourism mainly flow to host families in positions of leadership. The conservation outcomes of village stays and ecolodges are limited to local level protection of some rainforest and reef areas. Links between village stays and the thriving dive industry (e.g. boats and dive resorts) are also poorly developed in the Solomon Islands.

Government legislation for building standards and tourism development plans that exclude peripheral areas also inhibit the building and operation of village-owned guesthouses in the Solomon Islands. In North Malaita, villagers built a guesthouse on a man-made island constructed in the Lau lagoon. The two huts were opened in 1988, with four Canadian tourists spending 3 weeks in the village. A Canadian anthropologist, who had previously worked in the Lau lagoon area, sent these visitors. The charge was $50 a week per person with visitors joining in with village activities, such as fishing and gardening. Other backpackers also stayed at the guesthouse, which generated tourism income of $4000 by 1990. Despite being opened by a government minister in 1989, the guesthouse was not licensed, with the villagers also refusing to pay a bed tax or other fees. By 1996, the community no longer provided the labour needed to rebuild the guesthouse and rethatch the roof (Sofield, 2003a).

On Rennell Island, a local landowner obtained a grant of $12,000 from the Provincial Development Fund in 1989 to build a tourist guesthouse. The Tainui guesthouse was built out over Lake Te Nggano, near the village of Niupani. Based on a traditional Polynesian longhouse, the 18-bed guesthouse was built of milled and local timber with glass windows. The Ministry of Tourism advised that European toilets, showers and a kitchen were also required but the $10,000 in extra funding for this could not be obtained. Joint venture partners could not invest since the lodge did not meet official building codes. The Tainui guesthouse still opened in 1990 with 90 visitors in the first 6 months (Sofield, 2003a). Government regulations limited the operation of Indigenous-owned guesthouses. The Kiakoe Lakeside Lodge on Lake Tenggano was promoted on the Solomons Village Stay website.

Fiji

Fiji has more than 330 islands, with the two largest islands being the main island of Viti Levu and Vanua Levu. Fiji has a population of 780,000 people, with 60% living in rural areas (Bricker, 2003).

Indigenous Fijians own 85% of the land area of Fiji, held by local *mataqali* landowning groups. In Fiji, native-held land is leased and administered by the Native Lands Trust Board (NLTB). This land ownership system affects foreign investment in tourism, employment of Fijians from local villages and frequent disputes over access to leased land or villages providing tourist services to resorts (Harrison, 1998). Fiji has a mass tourism industry focused on beach resorts along the Coral Coast of the main island, Viti Levu and the Yasawa Islands to the west. In 1999, Fiji received 409,955 visitors and the tourism industry generated US$600 million. Tourism employs around 45,000 people in Fiji (Bricker, 2002). Beach tourism, nature tourism and Fijian culture are the main tourist attractions. Ecotourism in Fiji has grown since the mid-1990s and mainly takes place on Indigenous land (Turnbull, 2004). Indigenous Fijian participation in ecotourism is mainly in village-based ecotourism.

Ecotourism and Village-based Tourism in Fiji

Since the mid-1990s, Fiji promoted the economic and social benefits of ecotourism for rural villages. New Zealand (US$300,000) and the ILO (US$161,000) funded this village-based ecotourism (Bricker, 2002). The Fiji Ecotourism Association was formed in 1995 to encourage sustainable practices in tourism. Members included the Native Land Trust Board, airlines, beach resorts, Sheraton Hotel and Fiji Pine. The NLTB has been involved in major ecotourism projects and conservation in rural areas, including Taveuni (Bouma Falls) and Viti Levu (Abaca and Koroyanitu Park) (Harrison and Brandt, 2003). One objective of the ecotourism association was to assist local Fijians to become more involved in ecotourism activities. The Association created a Fiji Ecotourism and Village-Based Tourism Policy, adopted in 1999 by the Ministry of Tourism as a national policy and strategy for developing ecotourism and village tourism (Harrison, 1997; Harrison and Brandt, 2003; Harrison *et al.*, 2003). In this policy, ecotourism was defined as nature-based experiences and responsible travel that respected local cultures and conserved the social environment by 'respecting the aspirations and traditions of those who are visited and improving the welfare of the local people' (cited in Bricker,

2002: 272). Ecotourism was based on conservation and delivering benefits for rural Fijian people (Narayan, 2000; Tokalau, 2005). The strategy outlined five key principles for developing ecotourism in Fiji. These were environmental conservation, social cooperation, complement mass tourism, information and infrastructure development. The policy recognized that ecotourism is strongly linked to village-based community tourism in Fiji (Dowling, 2001). This village-based ecotourism in the outer islands and near resorts complements the mass tourism industry in Fiji (Van't Stot, 1996; Weaver, 1998). The traditional land tenure system ensures a high level of local Fijian control and participation in ecotourism ventures at Koroyanitu and Rivers Fiji on Viti Levu, Bouma Falls on Taveuni Island and other localities. Village ecotourism ventures in Fijian National Heritage Parks, such as Koroyanitu and Bouma, recognize Indigenous ownership and management of lands in these protected areas.

Koroyanitu National Heritage Park

Koroyanitu National Heritage Park (KNHP) in western Viti Levu has 250 km^2 of never logged tropical montane forest. With pressure on the area from logging and mining interests, local chiefs and landowners set aside their land to be protected as Koroyanitu NHP in 1993. Eighteen landowners in six local villages owned the land area covered by the KNHP. Abaca and Navilawa villages operated their own tourism ventures in KNHP, with income directed to an education fund (60%) and project management and maintenance (40%). Navilawa began overnight trekking tours in 1990, while Abaca began tourism operations in 1994. Koroyanitu NHP won a Fiji ecotourism award in 1996 (SPREP, 2002). The Abaca Cultural and Recreation Park and Abaca Ecotourism Cooperative Society were formed in 1993 (Gilbert, 1997). Abaca Park includes an ecolodge, walking trails to scenic and historic sites and guided tours. SPBCP, New Zealand aid (NZODA) and the Japan Pacific Economic Cooperation Council's (JANPECC) Pacific Ecotourism Prospects project funded ecotourism development in KHNP. Fiji Pine, a government forestry agency, provided ecotourism workshops for Abaca villagers in 1996 and 1997 (Godde, 1998). Local villagers from Abaca and Navilawa provide trekking and guided tours of 1 to 3 days within the Park to mountain and forest areas. Trekkers stay in a 12-bed lodge near Abaca or experience home-stay accommodation with a Fijian family (Buckley, 2003d). Navilawa completed 12 overnight hikes in KNHP in 2001, with assistance from a trek trainer (SPREP, 2002). In 1999/2000, NZODA funding assistance for Koroyanitu Park included an upgrade of visitor facilities, training for guides and bookkeeping, field guides and handbooks for trek leaders, launching the Mt Batilamu trek, and holding a tourism industry Open Day to promote the new features (Bricker, 2002). Abaca villagers established a tree nursery, replanted logged areas and opposed logging of the forest. Women sold crafts, developed a medicinal plant garden and participated more in community matters. A four-wheel-drive truck purchased for the ecotourism venture also transported local children to school (Gilbert, 1997).

Bouma National Heritage Park

Bouma NHP on Taveuni Island is a community-owned and -operated tourism venture. Bouma Falls is a popular tourist destination that brings in several thousand dollars a year for the landowners. It has 7 km of walking tracks through 2000 ha of community-owned rainforest. In 1991, the entrance fee was US$3.50. The local *mataqali* land-owning group initially set aside the Tavoro Forest Park and Reserve to protect the rainforest from logging. A young Fijian man from a nearby village convinced a Fijian priest and the elders from Bouma to withdraw from logging and develop an ecotourism venture (Young, 1992; Buckley, 2003e). The land-owning group first achieved consensus on developing the project at Bouma Falls then approached the NLTB for help. In 1989, the Native Lands Trust Board (NLTB) and Fiji Pine, a government forestry agency, provided planning assistance to help develop visitor facilities at Bouma Falls. The New Zealand

government provided NZ$60,000 to fund the walking tracks, picnic areas, toilets, visitor centre and signs. The walking trail and the visitor centre were built on communal land outside the village, while women made handicrafts sold at the visitor centre. Visitors arrived by bus or taxi, payed the Park entrance fee and walked up to the falls.

The Park opened in March 1991 and by November tourist entry fees had totalled US$8000. The money paid for staff wages and maintenance, with the remaining 50% used to pay school fees and build new houses. Staff included a receptionist, two groundsmen and guides for tour groups. At Bouma Falls, the local village initiated and managed ecotourism on their land for communal benefit. In 1992, a member of the land-owning group living in the capital city of Suva organized his own tours to the Park and planned to collect the entrance fees for his benefit (Young, 1992). NZ$140,000 was also spent on extending the forest pathway into 200 ha of secondary forest above the main waterfall and on other small buildings, with NZ$20,000 for a forest management plan (Lees and Evans, 1993). In 1999/2000, NZODA funding assistance for Bouma NHP included field handbooks for guides, interpretive signs, ongoing training, tourism awareness workshops in five villages, the launch of a tourist transport service and a marine park tour (Bricker, 2002). In 2002, Bouma NHP won the British Airways Tourism for Tomorrow Award. Over 10 years, Bouma received NZ$450,000 in funding assistance from NZAID. Other village ecotourism ventures in Fiji are unlikely to receive the same amount of donor funding and support as Bouma NHP.

Rivers Fiji, Viti Levu

Rivers Fiji provides white-water rafting trips organized with local villages on the main island of Viti Levu. The 1- and 2-day river trips take place on the Wainikoroiluva River starting at Nakavika village, and on the Upper Navua River, starting at Nabukelevu village. The total tour capacity on each river trip is 36 passengers. Local landowners at these villages receive land-use fees, lease payments and employment as guides. Rivers Fiji began in

1998 and is a partnership between two Americans and one Fijian. They invested US$500,000 in this Fijian rafting business. To operate these rafting trips, Rivers Fiji gained approval from land-owning groups who controlled access to the rivers. They negotiated an exclusive use agreement with the villages and invested in lease access to the river, with an improved road and bridge. Their lease with the Native Land Trust Board restricts other extractive land uses. Local villagers made decisions on tour scheduling, guide selection and employment and community protocol for the tourism operation with Rivers Fiji. Eight people from each village were trained as rafting guides, along with a local manager and assistant manager (see Table 2.4). Rivers Fiji has educated the local communities, guides and guests on 'leave no trace' principles and protected the river corridor on Upper Navua Gorge with a conservation lease (WTO, 2000; Buckley, 2003f). The conservation and community benefits make this an ecotourism venture.

Rivers Fiji (2004) brought ecotourism development into the rural hinterland of Fiji, with rafting trips on rivers that flowed through tropical rainforest. The inland villages that controlled river access, Nakavika and Nabukelevu, mainly relied on subsistence farming and the sale of timber. Rivers Fiji consulted with all the villages along each river. After 2 years of negotiation, Rivers Fiji developed a formal agreement with the NLTB, representing local landowners, for a legal agreement maintaining long-term river access. Rivers Fiji signed a formal lease with Nabukelevu village to protect their investment in roads and bridges used to access the river.

The 50-year lease of the road involved a one-off payment to NLTB and an annual fee for exclusive use of the road. To prevent logging and gravel extraction near a waterfall, Rivers Fiji negotiated a linear biosphere reserve along the Navua River in their lease, approved by villagers and NLTB. At Nakakiva, Rivers Fiji presented the landowners with a whale's tooth, the traditional Fijian way to conclude agreements and contracts.

Fees are paid to landowners for disembarking tourists, lunch sites, trekking to a waterfall and take-out areas. The fees went to the village community fund (18%), caretaker of the waterfall (18%) and the rest to land-owning groups along the river. Community funds were used to improve village facilities and build schools. Rivers Fiji built thatched huts, developed trails and an overnight camp, employing local men or village groups earning cash for team projects. Families took turns in working as porters, with income used to buy fuel for the village generator. Visitors paid fees to stay overnight at Nakakiva village and locals also wanted to provide tent accommodation (Bricker, 2001, 2003).

Devokula Village, Oavalu Island

Devokula is a cultural village presenting traditional Fijian activities, along with *bures* and a dormitory for visitor accommodation. It opened in November 1996 and is located 13 km from the historic capital of Levuka on the island of Oavalu. Devokula is built on land owned by the adjacent Fijian village of Aravudi. It includes a performance area for traditional dances (*mekes*) with a traditional

Table 2.4. Rivers Fiji: supporting conservation through village-based ecotourism in Fiji.

Area	Local community	Ecotourism income
RIVERS FIJI: Whitewater Rafting US (OARS) and Fijian partners, US$500,000 invested *Viti Levu, Fiji*		
Upper Navua River, Wainikoroiluva River	Nabukelevu village Nakavika village	Land use fees, lease payments Employment of eight local guides (four from each village) Exclusive use agreement with landowners Villagers agree on employment and project benefits NLTB lease excludes logging and extractive land uses

OARS: Outdoor Adventure River Specialists (California, USA); NTLB: Native Lands Trust Board.
Sources: WTO (2000); Bricker (2001, 2003); Buckley (2003)f; Rivers Fiji (2004).

priest's *bure*. The thatched village is built of local material using split logs to reduce the number of logs required. A conch shell is blown to announce visitor arrivals and a gift of kava root is presented. Cultural activities at the village include bark cloth production, basket and mat weaving and food production. Local people dressed in traditional costume perform a daily dance show for tourists. The younger son of the village chief in Aravudi developed Devokula Village mainly to preserve Fijian culture and employ young people. Local villagers also sold garden produce and fish to Devokula for tourist meals. Day tours to Devokula were marketed and booked through a travel agency in Levuka owned by Americans. Some day tourists also flew in from the main island of Viti Levu to visit Devokula. By July 1997, only 40 tourists had stayed overnight at the cultural village. Hotel and resort owners saw Devokula as a threat rather than an added attraction. The chief of Aravudi also paid outsiders to clear tracks to a waterfall and an inland village, since local people would not do this work (Fisher, 2003).

Other village-based ecotourism projects in Fiji

In the early 1990s, the NLTB funded a tourism development project for a landowning group at Waikatakata on the Coral Coast. The village owned rainforest, waterfalls and hot springs. A tourist track through the forest and a visitor centre were built with aid funds. Both were largely unused, with regrowth around the visitor centre, while the storm-damaged walking track fell into disrepair. There was landowner conflict over ownership and benefits from use of communal resources (Lees, 1992).

Waikatakata village was located next to a luxury tourist resort and most villagers worked in the resort. The NLTB project involved landowners giving their time freely to develop and run the project. Some landowners already guided tourists into the forest and kept the profits for their own benefit. Villagers employed at the resort for wages gained little by working on this local tourism project (Young, 1992).

A village-based ecotourism venture, Fiji's Hidden Paradise Resort on a remote area of Vanua Levu, was owned and run by Raviravi community. An Australian investor helped establish the resort, which accommodated 15 guests in three *bures* (thatched huts). Swimming, snorkelling, fishing and village activities were promoted to visitors. Natural attractions were a remnant patch of rainforest, mangrove forest, coral reef and gardens. The resort was closed due to low visitation (Sinha and Bushell, 2002).

A Fijian entrepreneur on the historic island of Ovalau operates the Lovoni ecotourism venture. He is a member of the chiefly group owning land between Levuka and the mountain village of Lovoni. Niumaia gives guided tours along ancestral trails crossing communally owned land. At Lovoni village, tourists present the chief with a *sevu sevu* or gift, enjoy a meal with traditional stories and stay the night. While Niumaia is an independent operator, his tourism venture needed approval from the chief.

This approval and his status as an elder of the chiefly group gave him the right to access and bring tourists to his native village. In exchange for this approval and hosting tourists, Nimuaia shared a percentage of his profits with the chief, who distributed this money to the village (Godde, 1998). Ecotourism projects are used by Fijian chiefs to maintain their control over natural resources, through kinships links in the communal system, and by gaining access to NGO funds or industry fees (Turnbull, 2004).

In 1997, the International Labour Organization (ILO) proposed an Ecotourism sub-programme in Fiji to develop jobs for local Fijians, with funding of US$161,000 from 2000 to 2002 (Bricker, 2002). The programme initially included any village-based economic activities, such as coral and pearl farming and bamboo furniture-making, but these were later removed from the ecotourism list of 23 projects. Two ILO pilot projects in village-based ecotourism were opened in November 2000. The Nasesnibua ecotourism venture, with 40 employees, included horseback riding, trekking, a *billi billi* (bamboo raft) ride, a base camp, trekking and a visit to a waterfall. Another 20 villagers were employed at the Wailotua Caves project that hoped to expand into trekking. Another two ecotourism projects were due to open in 2001, creating 60 more jobs for native Fijians. The ILO programme relied on government support from the National Centre for Small Business Development, which provided financial and technical assistance for local ecotourism operators beginning new projects (Bricker, 2002).

Fijian Village Homestay

A Queensland marketing and media entrepreneur established the Fijian Village Homestay network and online booking service (FijiBure.com) in 2003. It was set up as a humanitarian venture to assist Fijian villages to gain some direct income from tourism. The entrepreneur was on honeymoon in Fiji and was asked by locals how they could get involved in tourism. A Fijian homestay costs F$70 (US$242). Tourists participated in traditional Fijian village life and daily activities, such as kava ceremonies, singing, horse riding, mat making and spear fishing on coral reefs. By March 2004, five Fijian villages participated in this homestay programme, including Namatakula, Namuamua and Navutulevu on the main island of Viti Levu. Over 100 guests had visited these Fijian villages by August 2004. The maximum was up to ten visitors at one village. Visitors were encouraged to bring a small gift, such as powdered kava or school items. Income from tourism was used to upgrade public toilets, build a guesthouse and community hall and purchase bedding and mattresses. New villages added in March 2004 were Beqa Island (Naiseuseu), Korovisilou at Waidroka Bay and Navoro near Tavuni Hill. Other adventure walking treks and rafting or kayaking trips with Fijian guides were also added later in 2004. Fijians were to be given direct ownership of the booking website, FijiBure.com, while the Fiji Ministry of Tourism endorsed the Fijian Village Homestay network. In February 2005, Namatakula Homestay featured on the Australian media travel programme, *Getaway*. There were now eight villages in the homestay network, on Viti Levu and the Yasawa Islands (FijiBure, 2005).

Vanuatu

Vanuatu is an archipelago of 83 islands between the Solomon Islands and New Caledonia. Some 53,000 visitors came to Vanuatu in 1998, most on package holidays staying at resorts in Port Vila. Thirty per cent of tourists (11,500) also visit the outer islands of Vanuatu for nature-based adventure and scuba diving, up from 15% in 1991. Most tourists go to Tanna (4600), Espiritu Santo (4000), Malekula (1000), Ambryn (650) and 1200 to other islands. Ten tour operators in Port Vila now offer ecotourism trips to the outer islands, where visitors stay in local guesthouses (Black and King, 2002).

Island Safaris of Vanuatu is the main inbound operator selling package tours to the outer islands. It won the 2002 Skal Ecotourism Award in the category of Beaches, Coasts and Islands. Unique ecotourism activities on the outer islands of Vanuatu include snorkelling or diving on coral reefs, rainforest, swimming with dugongs (Epi and Tanna), viewing active volcanoes (Tanna and Ambryn), Pentecost land diving and visiting custom villages (Vanuatu Tourism, 2005).

Vanuatu Islands Bungalow Association

Tourist accommodation on the outer islands of Vanuatu mainly comprises guesthouses, locally built thatched hut bungalows and small-scale resorts with basic facilities. The bungalows and guesthouses built of local materials are owned and operated by a village community or managed by one family. These basic tourist guesthouses are a popular rural business option (de Burlo, 2003). There are some 20 small resorts and bungalows in the outer islands built by village communities. Most of these local bungalows are members of the Vanuatu Islands Bungalow Association (VIBA), an association set up to represent and promote these Indigenous operators. A rural tourism adviser based in Port Vila supported and promoted the village bungalows. In 1998, a marketing brochure for these bungalows and tours was circulated to travel agents and airlines in the main tourist markets of Australia (55%), New Zealand and New Caledonia. The

European Union, NZ, South Pacific Forum Secretariat, Vanair and the Vanuatu Chamber of Commerce funded this Association (Decloitre, 1998).

VIBA and Vanair, the domestic airline for Vanuatu, jointly owned Island Safaris, the local travel agency organizing package tours to outer islands including Ambryn, Aneityum Island in the far south and the remote Banks and Torres group of islands at the northern end of Vanuatu (Vanuatu Tourism, 2005). The Wantok Environment Centre (WTEC), a local conservation NGO, also promoted 72 locally owned bungalows and 13 conservation areas on 19 outer islands of Vanuatu (Wantok Environment Centre, 2005a).

The bungalows provide guided tours of the surrounding area with local people working as tour guides. The tours include walks to forests, village gardens, custom village tours and dances and boat and walking tours. According to the manager of Island Safaris, the main tourist drawcards on the outer islands were the activity and tour parts of the package tours, rather than the food or bungalow accommodation (Black and King, 2002). In 1999, guide training to improve tours run through local bungalows was provided to 51 people at six VIBA bungalows on Tanna, Ambryn and Epi. The participants were bungalow owners, bungalow staff and community members involved in tours. Three-day training programmes covered tour planning, interpretation, visitor safety, briefings, tourism impacts and benefits and guiding skills. Training issues included transport to the outer islands, bad roads, poor weather, language skills, limited tours and few female guides (Black and King, 2002). Donors funded further tour guide training on the outer islands of Vanuatu to improve visitor services. Local ownership of natural sites, visitor entrance fees and social ties are other issues in island tourism.

In the early 1980s, a local man on South Pentecost was encouraged by Vila tour operators to build a tourist guesthouse for visitors arriving to see the land diving. He used his own money to build the guesthouse and pay insurance, and obtained a loan from the Development Bank of Vanuatu for a generator and stove. Regarded as a business leader, he formed a committee to guide others in tourism business. He also ran the village store, sold copra and established an agricultural cooperative. Money from these businesses, including the guesthouse, was used to assist supporters and put into traditional activities, such as grade-taking rituals for higher social status. While the guesthouse was closed in 1988 due to limited occupancy, it supported the social achievements of the owner as a local leader. From this local perspective, the tourist guesthouse was a success in social and cultural terms, rather than meeting development goals of ensuring income or conserving natural resources (de Burlo, 2003).

Aelan Walkabaot Long Vanuatu

Aelan Walkabaot Long Vanuatu is a website promoting independent travel around the outer islands of Vanuatu. It features 72 local bungalows and 13 community-owned conservation areas on 19 islands. This ecotourism website and a 'birds online' website were developed by a volunteer working for the Wantok Environment Centre (WTEC), a local conservation NGO established in March 2004 and based on the island of Espiritu Santo, Vanuatu. The aim of this WTEC travel website is to promote low impact tourism, rural development and local nature conservation (*Bubu Shell*, 2005; Wantok Environment Centre, 2005a, b, c). The village bungalows are linked with key natural attractions, wildlife and cultural activities in the islands. Some lodges are located near Vatthe, Lake Fanteng and Duviara Conservation Areas (Santo, Ambryn and Ambae), at Loru Rainforest or Nabi Protected Areas (Santo and Malekula) and other marine conservation or marine protected areas (Efate, Epi and Malekula) managed by local communities. Twenty-three guesthouses were also members of the Vanuatu Islands Bungalows Association (VIBA), with the ecotourism website a joint project between WTEC and VIBA to assist rural nature conservation. The Director of WTEC, who formerly managed the Vanuatu Protected Areas Initiative from 1993 to 2004, also supported these community ecotourism ventures.

Vatthe Conservation Area, Espiritu Santo

The communities of Sara and Mantantas, in northern Espiritu Santo, established the Vatthe Conservation Area in 1996 to protect the forest from logging. The villages of Sara and Mantantas are 40 km apart on opposite sides of the forest. They refused to take money from logging companies and their chiefs talked to SPBCP about saving the forest. In return for declaring the forest as Vatthe CA, the chiefs wanted electricity, running water, a health clinic and a school in their villages. Other agencies provided these facilities. A local soccer star helped resolve the long-running feud between the two villages in order to protect the forest (*Focus*, 2001). Vatthe has 2300 ha of lowland rainforest and 80% of Vanuatu's bird species are represented. A local chief initiated the idea for a community ecotourism venture and the project began in 1995 with a moneybox. The villagers built a guesthouse in 1996 and six bungalows were added in 1997. A local woman was trained to be lodge manager. The ecotourism venture is centred on Vatthe Lodge, with a restaurant/office at Mantantas village and guided tours including forest tours, village garden tours and coconut crab hunts. Sara village provide a custom-village and garden tour, but some tensions remain (Martel, 1999). The lodge receives around 200 tourists a year, including group tours such as the Royal Forest and Bird Protection Society from NZ, and generates annual income of VT$1.5 million, with 90% going to the community. Vatthe Lodge is a member of the Vanuatu Island Bungalow Association and marketed by Island Safaris, a key inbound operator (SPREP, 2002). At the end of 2004, Conservation International provided US$20,000 to Vatthe Conservation Area to compensate a landowner. A Trust Fund also supported environmental activities in Vatthe and other community conservation areas (*Bubu Shell*, 2005).

Pentecost land diving

Land diving (*naghol*) takes place each year on Pentecost Island, a remote area 200 km north of Port Vila. Eight traditional or custom villages perform this ritual, building a 30 m platform from which men and boys leap off with a vine tied around their ankle. The ritual is performed to ensure a good yam harvest, with four to eight land dive ceremonies taking place in April/May when the vines are supple and springy. In the 1980s, local chiefs established the South Pentecost Tourism Council to manage the *naghol* event and gain economic benefits from tourism (Sofield, 2003b). The Council controlled the preparation rituals, chose the participants and sites and the number of jumps. They also set visitor entrance and filming fees and the total number of tourists allowed. There was a US$410 entrance fee for tourists using their video camera to film the *naghol* (de Burlo, 1996, 2003).

In 1988, there were eight jumps with 40 visitors each, while in 1989 there were four jumps with 50 visitors at each jump. Tourists paid US$340 each to see the event on a day tour from Port Vila (Sofield, 1991). Marketing of the Pentecost land dive was done by the government agency, Tour Vanuatu, at a 3% commission rate, with half of the *naghol* tickets sold to overseas travel wholesalers.

The 1988 entrance fee was US$85 and the *naghol* villages earned over U$27,000, while the 1989 entrance fee was US$106 and the villages earned US$21,200 for community projects (Sofield, 1991). The community purchased group items, such as an outboard motor boat, while individuals were paid according to their role, status and gender, with US$10–20 for men and US$2–5 for women (de Burlo, 1996). Maximum benefits were gained by local Indigenous ownership and control of the *naghol* event on Pentecost, supported by marketing from Tour Vanuatu and the Vanuatu National Tourism Office.

Papua New Guinea

In Papua New Guinea (PNG), ecotourism involves 'rural-based small-scale natural *and* cultural attractions' (Weaver, 1998a: 196). In 1998, PNG had 67,000 visitor arrivals with tourism generating K$251 million. Key ecotourism areas are the Highlands and Sepik River, with their tribal diversity and crafts; the coastal areas of Madang, Lae and outer islands for diving; and the rainforest and unique wildlife, such as Birds of Paradise. High transport and tour costs and tribal fighting limit the growth of tourism in PNG (Douglas, 1998). Up-market tourists join cruise ships on the Sepik River and stay at expensive lodges like Ambua Lodge in the Highlands. Community participation is essential for ecotourism in Papua New Guinea, where local clans own over 90% of the land under customary tenure and 80% live in rural areas. The aim of the 1996 national tourism policy was to preserve PNG's natural and cultural heritage for tourism and generate local employment, with a focus on ecotourism. Ambua Lodge and the Kumul development were examples of ecolodges supported by local communal landowners (Bosselman et al., 1999). In 2005, ecotourism training workshops for local villagers were held in the Western Highlands. There are some locally built guesthouses, such as in the Tufi area, but they do not support nature conservation (Ranck, 1987). Conservation NGOs in PNG mainly promote community ecotourism as an alternative to logging, mining and hunting. WWF is working with Bahinemo people in the Hunstein Range of the Upper Sepik River (Carter and Davie, 1996; Wearing and McDonald, 2002). Conservation International (CI) supports ecotourism projects linked with reef and forest preservation in the Milne Bay region. From 1995 to 1998, the Biodiversity Conservation Network (BCN) funded rainforest research and community-based ecotourism in Crater Mountain and the Lakekamu Basin. These conservation-based ecotourism projects are described along with others in the Oro Province and the Highlands.

Crater Mountain Wildlife Management Area

The Crater Mountain Wildlife Management Area (WMA) is 75 km west of Goroka in the Highlands of PNG. It covers 2700 km^2 of lowland rainforest, montane forests and grassland, with 220 bird species and 84 mammal species. Local landowners from 22 family clans in five villages established the Crater Mountain Wildlife Management Area in

1993. It was supported by enterprises such as ecotourism, a research station and artefact stores. Ecotourism enterprises were three village-owned guesthouses with tours to a bat cave, bird of paradise display site, suspension bridge and Crater Mountain lookout. Tourists could also stay in a local village. Research-based ecotourism for visiting scientists included two research stations, assisted by PNG staff and trained local observers from villages paid by scientists to help in data collection. Four artefact stores in the WMA also generated K$10,000 a year in craft sales (CASO Link, 1998). The Research and Conservation Foundation of PNG and the Wildlife Conservation Society (USA) developed this ecotourism project at Crater Mountain, with funding of US$575,057 from BCN. They provided technical assistance and training for local communities in village tourism and research-based ecotourism. A 1997 survey found income from research ecotourism had reduced the export of wildlife among five clans but not local use of natural resources (BCN, 1997a; Johnson, 1999).

Ragianna Birds of Paradise and other endemic tropical birds are found in rainforest around Herowana village on the northern perimeter of the Crater Mountain WMA. Researchers and bird watching tourists stay in a traditionally-built guesthouse at this village. Tourists were taken on treks to see Ragianna and Magnificent Birds of Paradise in their display trees or dance grounds, and the maypole bowers constructed and decorated by a Macgregor's Bowerbird. Local Gimi people acted as bird guides and carriers on these bird treks. Other activities were talking to local people, sleeping in bush huts and stopping at village markets to buy produce and artefacts such as string bags or billums. This Gimi income from tourism met basic needs and also provided an incentive to maintain the rainforest (Freeman, 2005).

Lakekamu Basin

Research-based ecotourism was also developed in the lowland rainforests of Lakekamu Basin, a 2500 km^2 area threatened by logging and mining activities. The project partners at

Lakekamu were Conservation International (USA), Foundation for the Peoples of the South Pacific (PNG) and the local Wau Ecology Institute, with BCN funding of US$508,062. Community members received land-use fees from scientists, payments for research and field assistance services, money for providing food and lodging, as well as working as guides and porters (Salafsky, 1999). Research scientists visited a tropical field station at Lakekamu that generated income of US$1028, with US$302 paid to landowners in 1997. Local communities built guesthouses, with Kakoro Lodge generating income of US$390 in 1997. French participants completed a review of adventure tourism products in Lakekamu, with the information sent to Lonely Planet for their PNG guidebook. However, hunting and fishing activities increased among local Kovio people and other groups in the Lakekamu Basin as the community ecotourism project generated minimal extra income. The people who set up Kakoro Lodge panned for gold to earn money to furnish the lodge and buy food for the opening. Local men who helped build the research station also panned for gold when their work ended, destroying one of the creeks (BCN, 1997b). Other problems were landowner disputes which saw the research station moved to a new site in 1996, no long-term lease signed with communities, locals building guest houses with few visitor arrivals, and no marketing or implementation of the adventure tourism activities (Salafsky, 1999). Conservation International continued this Lakekamu project, with the support of local landowners.

Oro conservation project

This conservation project in Oro Province is based around protecting rainforest habitat for the Queen Alexandra Birdwing butterfly, the world's largest butterfly. AusAID funded the project from 1995 to 1999, working with local villages, the PNG Department of Conservation and Environment and Oro Provincial Government. Big rainforest trees with a rare species of vine used as a food plant by the butterfly all occur on customary-owned land, especially on the Managalase Plateau. Ten

local people recorded sightings of the butterfly on nectar and food plants in their villages and nearby rainforest. Ecotourism facilities included an eight-bed lodge built at Ondahari village, with income from tourists paying to watch butterflies around vines and nectar plants and to walk in the rainforest. Other income was from insect trading with local families harvesting butterflies for sale through an agency in Lae. These activities depended on villages retaining primary rainforest as butterfly habitat (Hibberd, 1997). In 2001, Ecovitality, an American NGO, conducted the first ecotour of the Managalase Plateau, with profits supporting conservation and assistance in marketing forest products for ten local clans. The clans formed community-based organizations to prevent logging of their forest (Ecovitality, nd).

Greenpeace Pacific has campaigned to prevent commercial logging of forests for the 3000 Maisin people living in nine villages along Collingwood Bay in Oro Province. The Maisin declaration of 1994 opposed commercial logging and clearing forest for agriculture in 38,000 ha of their forest. For cash income, alternative enterprises, such as village-based tourism and making tapa cloth decorated with traditional designs were developed. Greenpeace assisted the Maisin people to establish Maisin Tapa Enterprises, marketing their crafts overseas with profits shared among the communities. A solar powered telephone was installed with funds raised from tapa sales. Forest conservation was supported among the Maisin, but village tourism enterprises were not described (Greenpeace, 2004).

Milne Bay

Conservation International is promoting reef and rainforest preservation, along with ecotourism, in the Milne Bay region and offshore islands on the south-eastern tip of mainland Papua New Guinea. Milne Bay province has mountain forests and the largest reef, coastal and island ecosystems in PNG. Biological surveys of the rich marine ecosystems and coral reefs in Milne Bay began in 1997. The Global Environment Facility provided funding to

CI and the provincial government for the Milne Bay project in 2000. This included marine conservation and sustainable use options, including ecotourism. Local villages were involved in managing Marine Conservation Areas and dive tourism in Milne Bay. The divers paid a fee to local landowners for use of their reefs. New village guesthouses also operate in Milne Bay (Milne Bay Tourism Bureau, 2004). The Napatana Lodge in Alotau opened in 2001, as the first ecolodge in Milne Bay Province. The lodge is built of bush materials and employs local staff. Food was bought locally and cooked the traditional way in clay pots. Napatana Lodge promoted local culture and encouraged visitors to stay at village guesthouses along the coast and islands. This outreach programme provided training and promoted village adventure tours (Napatana Lodge, nd). This tourism income encouraged local villagers to support conservation and sustainable development.

Ambua Lodge, Southern Highlands

The Ambua Lodge Tourist Resort, owned by Trans Nuigini Tours, is a partnership with the Huli clan in the Southern Highlands of PNG. Built on a high ridge overlooking the Tari Basin, the lodge comprises 40 cabins with a central dining/lounge room, nature trails through a forest area and an environmental research base. The lodge was built in a traditional hut style using Huli labour in 1989/90. The Huli people of the Tari region are renowned for their unique wigs made of bird feathers and ceremonial attire. Ambua Lodge provided cultural interaction with the Huli people while the surrounding rainforest had ten species of Birds of Paradise (Bosselman et al., 1999). Some 50 Huli people work at the lodge, which has an expatriate manager. This remote lodge had ten managers in 2 years as Huli staff left due to tribal battles (Douglas, 1998). Huli people from local villages also sold fruit and vegetables to the lodge, gave cultural performances and sold crafts to visitors. The lodge funded a community health centre, paid 'gate fees' to bring tourists to Huli villages famous for the Huli wigmen and used small guest houses in local villages for trekking tours. A senior Huli employee worked among Huli people to help conserve wildlife in the Tari Gap area affected by local hunting for food and Birds of Paradise for feathers (Bates, 1992). Ambua Lodge won a PATA Gold Heritage Award in 1992 for culturally sensitive and ecologically responsible tourism. The up-market lodge is linked with other tourist facilities in Madang and in the Sepik River area.

Kokop village ecotourism centre, Western Highlands

The Kokop village is an eight-bedroom hut or ecolodge built of local materials in the Western Highlands region. Opened in 1998, the lodge was developed by a local man from the Kentiga tribe of 3000 people, part of the Melpa cultural group. Kokop village is a 45-minute drive west of Mt Hagen. The ecolodge in the middle of Kokop Village was surrounded by the 30 ha Wopkola Rainforest and located near the Turulg River and Inbilg Waterfalls. The lodge also provided day tours of rural villages in the Western and Southern Highlands, with local guides and porters (Yuimb, 2004). In 2000, the Kokop Village Eco-Forestry Development Organisation (KVEDO) was established to support reforestation and conservation of the Wopkola rainforest. From 2000 to 2004, KVEDO raised US$7413 to fund the planting of 10,000 seedlings in the Wopkola Rainforest, run as a private nature conservation site. Other rural villages were also assisted with reforestation, conservation and ecotourism projects, covering 23,000 people from seven tribes in the Highlands. Ecotourism in PNG was also promoted through an online tourism website and an inbound tour company based in Mt Hagen. One local man from Kokop Village, educated in the USA, set up all these initiatives, which linked ecotourism with conservation, reforestation and community development (KVEDO, 2004).

Ecotourism Melanesia

Ecotourism Melanesia is a travel company and website which provides a booking service for small village guest houses, lodges and homestay accommodation operated by local people in Papua New Guinea and the Solomon Islands. A local individual, family or community group operated these village homestays, guesthouses or rural tourist lodges, mainly built of bush materials. These were either basic with tourists eating local food and bathing in waterfalls, or improved with separate guest rooms and some western facilities or meals. Most tour wholesalers do not market these village guesthouses. Ecotourism Melanesia supported ecotourism and sustainable community-based tourism in the south-west Pacific region. It promoted travel in rural areas, with tourism income giving rural villages an alternative to mining and logging. Ecotourism Melanesia is based in Port Moresby and operated by an Australian who worked as a teacher and developed links with rural villages in PNG.

The village homestays were mainly located in Milne Bay Province, including the Trobriand Islands, around Madang, in the Tufi coastal area of Oro Province, with a few in the Sepik,

Western and Gulf Provinces (see Table 2.5). The company also provided packaged eco-tours of PNG based around trekking, culture, wildlife and diving (Ecotourism Melanesia, nd). Support for nature conservation projects was not mentioned, but village ecotours and local conservation areas were promoted in PNG.

These included the Ohu Butterfly Conservation Area for birdwing butterflies and guided nature walks with the Wasab ecotourism development project and Mt Masur Sanctuary near Madang. The 47,000 ha Kamiali Wildlife Management Area, with Kamiali guesthouse and Lababia village, were also featured.

The Village Development Trust based in Lae helped Lababia people to oppose logging and to set aside this area for conservation with the Kamiali guesthouse used for ecotourism accommodation and training courses. The World Bank provided K150,000 in 1996 to build the guesthouse, which had annual income of K150,000, with 50% going to the Kamiali Development Trust (*Post-Courier*, 2002).

Table 2.5. Village guesthouses, homestays and lodges in Papua New Guinea.

Milne Bay Province (10)
Faiava villagestay and Bolu Bolu guesthouse, Goodenough Island
Kinanale guesthouse and Galahi villagestay, Samarai
Vakuta Island homestay and Kiriwina lodge, Trobriand Islands
Esaala women's guesthouse, Normanby Island
Mumunu guesthouse, Salamo; Misima guesthouse; Napatana lodge, Alotau
Oro Province (5)
Orokaiva villagestay, Tufi villagestays (Jebo villagestay and beach bungalow, Siu, Orotoaba)
Kokoda mountain view lodge
Morobe Province (2)
Kamiali guesthouse, Salamaua (Kamiali Wildlife Management Area)
Mukulapmang guesthouse, Erap valley
Madang Province (8)
Wasab ecotourism village guesthouse (Wasab Ecotourism Development Project)
Barem village guesthouse (Mt Masur Sanctuary), Keki ecolodge, Udisis villagestay
Siar Island lodge, Samun Island lodge
Ohu village homestay (Ohu Butterfly Conservation Area)
Kanganaman village guesthouse, Middle Sepik
Gulf Province (7)
Kakoro lodge, Hinowattie guesthouse and Uyana guesthouse, Lakekamu Basin
Kikori guesthouse, Baimuru guesthouse
Moveave villagestay and Makara village homestay, Malalaua
Western Province (3)
Kubu village longhouse, Balimo
Lake Murray guesthouse, Morehead guesthouse

Source: Ecotourism Melanesia (nd).

Samoa

Western Samoa is an independent Polynesian nation of 163,000 people, where the traditional way of life (*fa'a Samoa*) has been retained. This includes social customs, *matai* or chiefs, land tenure and use of natural resources. The majority of Samoans live in rural areas and most of Samoa is communal land (81%). Villages charge access or custom fees for tourists to visit local beaches, waterfalls, rest huts, parking and for activities like swimming or surfing (Perrottet, 1996; Twining-Ward, 1998; Buckley, 2003g). In 1997, Samoa received 68,000 visitors, but only 30% were tourists on holiday. Less than 25% of all tourists go to the island of Savaii (Twining-Ward, 1998). In Samoa, all tourism operations need to be negotiated with local villages and chiefs. A 1989/90 study identified 18 coastal sites on Savaii and Upolu with ecotourism potential, where local villages could generate income through user fees and serve as environmental caretakers for the sites (Pearsall, 1993).

National Ecotourism Program

The Western Samoa Visitors Bureau established a National Ecotourism Program in the mid-1990s to promote village-based ecotourism and support conservation (Van't Stot, 1996; Lindgren *et al.*, 1997; Weaver, 1998a). The alternative tourism products included ecovillages and ecolodges on Savaii, Upolu and Manono Islands. The Bureau also provided finance for coastal villages to build simple beach *fales* or huts to rent out to visitors, with 30 in Upolu, four in Savaii and one on Manono (Twining-Ward, 1998; Scheyvens, 2002, 2005). Samoan ecovillages established their own conservation area, have new village laws to protect wildlife, retain their village customs and traditions and participate in community tourism projects (Sooaemalelagi *et al.*, 1996; Sooaemalelagi *et al.*, 1999; Imai and Kikuchi, 2000). Tourists paid US$20 per night to stay at Samoan villages like Uafato and share in the daily activities of rural life (Perrottet, 1996). Visitors were also encouraged to help with rural development

tasks and environmental restoration projects (water supply, reafforestation, etc.). A website for the Program focused on promoting ecotourism and sustainable tourism in Samoa, while the allied Samoan Ecotourism Network functioned as an inbound tour operator that promoted tours and ecovillages to travel wholesalers in Europe, Australia and the USA.

In 1996, Samoan ecovillages received two small groups per month, with at most 12 to 15 visitors (Sooaemalelagi *et al.*, 1996). At Uafato village, chiefs prefer that all tourism is community-based rather than hosted by individual families. However, at Sataoa village, family groups own beach *fale* accommodation, while the infrastructure and tours within the Sa'anapu-Sataoa Conservation Area are community owned. A tourism centre, walking trail from Sataoa village to the mangrove lagoon and a canoe tour of the mangroves was provided. Revenue from canoe trips was divided among the boat owner (50%), paddler (25%) and community fund (25%) (UNESCO, 2000; SPREP, 2002). Other issues were the village pastor or chief banning tourism on a Sunday or fining families with beach *fales* for not joining communal activities (Twining-Ward, 1998). By the end of 1999, there were 44 registered beach *fales* operating in Samoa.

Beach *fales*

The *fales* charged US$20–33 a night for accommodation, bedding and two local meals (Green Turtle Holidays, nd). Backpackers, surfers, Samoans returning from overseas and domestic visitors stayed at the beach *fales*. Toilets and shower facilities for the beach *fales* were built with grants from the AusAID Tourism Development Fund. NZAID funded two *fale* business seminars in 1998 and 1999 and a manual for beach *fale* owners, with a Tourism Support Fund providing matching dollar grants for *fale* owners to upgrade facilities (Scheyvens, 2002, 2005). These locally owned village tourism projects are meant to benefit rural areas. In 1996, less than 1% of the NZ$30 million from tourism in Samoa went to local villages hosting tourists (Knight, 1997; Sooaemalelagi *et al.*, 1999). According to Sofield (2003a), the European

Community provided US$1.5 million to build six bungalows in the Samoa village tourism programme. This 'model' of village tourism could not be applied in other Pacific Island countries that lacked access to this amount of aid funding. By 2003, Ecotour Samoa claimed that community tourism in Samoa generated substantial local income. However, there is little research or data on the economic benefits of village-based tourism in Samoa. The beach *fales* also caused environmental impacts from sewage and wastewater in the coastal living zone (Scheyvens, 2005).

Ecotour Samoa

Ecotour Samoa is a small business based in Apia, run by a Samoan woman and her Australian husband, a wildlife veterinarian who came to Samoa in 1990 on a forestry aid programme. The owners started this ecotourism business mainly to provide an alternative to Samoan villages logging their rainforest areas. They have actively promoted the benefits of ecotourism in Samoa, in particular village-based ecotourism (Sooaemalelagi *et al.*, 1996; Knight, 1997; Miller and Malek-Zadeh, 1997; Ecotour Samoa, 2004). The main product involves tourists staying in rural Samoan villages, where guests sleep in beach huts (*fales*), eat local food and join activities such as guided walks and kayaking. Some 20 villages are involved in this ecotourism programme, with tourists transported to the villages in a company bus decorated with a large bat design. Ecotour Samoa also provides a low-cost volunteer programme where tourists assist host villages with conservation and cultural projects, including training local guides. The owners follow Samoan cultural protocol, the tours generate income for local communities and the company provides environmental education for villages, government agencies and tourists (Buckley, 2003g). They invited western researchers to help develop village-based ecotourism in Samoa and also established an ecocamp for youths from rural villages.

As a privately owned company, Ecotour Samoa has successfully negotiated and marketed village-based ecotourism without assistance from foreign donors or government agencies. In American Samoa, a National Park on land leased from seven villages has a homestay programme operated by 17 families. The National Park included land and sea areas on Tutuila, Ta'u and Ofa Islands. This ecotourism programme provided local benefits and park services for visitors (Travel Maxia, 2005). A similar scheme linking village homestays with parks has not been developed in (Western) Samoa.

Falealupo and Tafua Canopy Walkways, Savaii

Villages on Savaii at Falealupo and Tafua established community rainforest reserves with funding support from conservation NGOs (Pearsall, 1993; Cox and Elmqvist, 1997). The Falealupo rainforest on Savaii Island in Samoa was saved when Dr Paul Cox, an ethnobotanist, raised US$85,000 in 1989 to help villagers pay off loggers and keep the forest (Cox, 1999). His organization, Seacology, an NGO for island conservation, built the Falealupo Rain Forest School in 1993 in exchange for Falealupo village protecting 30,000 acres of rainforest. In 1997, Seacology funded construction of the Falealupo Rainforest Canopy Walkway to help the local community generate income from ecotourism that supports a retirement fund for village elders. The canopy walkway was removed in 2002 over safety concerns with some anchoring trees. Seacology, with Nu Skin International, funded the building of a new tower and aerial walkway at Falealupo linked to existing observation platforms. The Falealupo Walkway reopened in 2003.

Tafua Rainforest Reserve on Savaii Island was established in 1990 with funds from Seacology, WWF Sweden and Christie Brinkley (Seacology, 2002). The reserve is protected by a 50-year agreement between three villages on Tafua Peninsula and the Swedish Society for the Conservation of Nature. The lowland rainforests at Tafua were severely damaged by Cyclone Ofa in 1990, but have since recovered (Pearsall, 1993). In 2002, Seacology funded the construction of a canopy walk with ladders, lookout platforms and suspended walkways in Tafua reserve (Seacology, 2002). Seacology also established the Tafua Conservation Centre, walking trails and signs for the reserve. The tourist entry fee of US$3 is paid at a village house by the entrance track to the reserve (Buckley, 2003h). Tafua villages use the money for ongoing management of the canopy walkway and reserve.

Cook Islands, Niue and Tonga

SPREP community ecotourism projects were also developed in the Cook Islands, Niue and Tonga (SPREP, 2002). The Takitumu Conservation Area on Rarotonga, Cook Islands, conserves key habitat for the *kakerori* bird. A recovery programme in Takitumu saw bird numbers increase from 29 in 1989 to over 220 by 2002. Three tours a week were conducted in Takitumu with a limit of ten people in a group. The area received 624 tourists in 2001, representing 2% of visitors to the Cook Islands. The tour cost NZ$45 and generated NZ$28,000 in income, with visitor donations of a further NZ$493. The CA also has a shop in Rarotonga selling environmental products. This income funds wages for one person, the bird recovery effort, administration costs and a website as well as development and maintenance of the area. The tour is marketed to visitors on Rarotonga, with advertising in travel and birding magazines.

In Niue, the Huvalu Conservation Area covers 6003 ha of rainforest with birds, bats and coconut crabs. The two villages of Hakupu and Liku share the area and alternate in providing guided ecotours of the forest with talks on conservation practices along with a visit to the village and Information Centre for craft sales. Signs and information *fales* (huts) provide local environmental information about the forest (Talagi-Hekesi, nd). The conservation ecotour is marketed by Niue Tourism Office, but operates infrequently. Niue is a small raised coral island, between Tonga and the Cook Islands. With limited flights and high airfares, there are few tourists with 1729 visitors in 1998 (De Haas, 2003). Swimming with humpback

whales is promoted as a new activity on Niue, together with a forest tour in Huvalu.

In Tonga, the Ha'apai Conservation Area covers 62 coral atolls spanning 150 km. There are budget beach *fales* (huts) on 'Uiha and Uoleva islands run by families with island tours including marine activities, interpretive walks and coconut weaving. Island tours are marketed through a local café. With AusAID funding, training was provided for local guides, and visitor facilities provided at three beaches. Brochures were produced on Lifuka in addition to snorkelling and beach-combing areas. The Ha'apai region has limited access and competes with the more popular Vava'u islands in northern Tonga.

Micronesia

The Micronesian islands of Saipan (Northern Marianas), Guam, Palau and Pohnpei (FSM) in the northern Pacific are mass tourism destinations attracting dive tourists from Japan, Taiwan and America. There has been a review of forest tourism (Wylie, 1994) and community ecotourism in marine parks (SPREP, 2002). On Pohnpei, a local village established the Enipein Marine Park around mangrove areas, located 2 hours by boat or road from the main town of Kolonia. They received training funds for young people to build 14 traditional lagoon canoes. The people of Enipein ran a day tour with a canoe trip in the mangroves, picnic lunch and a *sakau* or kava ceremony for US$35. Tourists heard stories about local plants and animals and traditional practices. Enipein village formed a corporation to manage the ecotourism project and further plans included visitor accommodation and other tours. Conservation issues included litter and using mangrove resources (timber, crabs) in the Park (Valentine, 1993).

The SPBCP evaluated community ecotourism in five marine conservation areas of Micronesia. The community-owned marine areas were remote with few visitor facilities (Kiribati), few visitors (Pohnpei Watershed), and competed with a dive tourism industry in the Rock Islands (Palau). Ecotourism is a large part of Utwe-Walung Conservation Area on Kosrae Island, established in 1996. Activities include mangrove canoe tours, other ecotours, a visitor centre and picnic huts (SPREP, 2002). The visitor centre was funded by the National Congress of Kosrae, with Seacology funding the installation of solar power (18 solar panels and 32 batteries) at the centre. In 2000, the Seacology Prize for the *Island Indigenous Conservationist of the Year* went to Madison Nena, the Conservation Area Support Officer in Kosrae, for his role in establishing Utwe-Walung CA (Wortle, 2001).

The Conservation Society of Pohnpei created fact sheets and brochures for the community-managed Lenger Marine Protected Area and a visitor brochure promoting ecotourism in Pohnpei. The island conservation NGO, Seacology, constructed an ecotourism hostel with solar power on And Atoll (Pohnpei), owned by an Indigenous family, with the area becoming a marine reserve with no fishing.

On Yap, Seacology funded restoration of the historic Tamilyog Stone Path, in exchange for 75 acres of forest alongside the path being set aside as a protected reserve by the Dalipebinaw Council. There was a guided tour of the village of Bechyal on Yap with the traditional community house, chief's house, traditional shell money, a sailing canoe and fish traps. However, the chief of Bechyal was not sharing the entrance fees with other people who owned land in the village (Mansperger, 1992).

Conclusion

In the Pacific Islands, Indigenous ecotourism ventures mainly depend on donor assistance (e.g. SPREP, NZ, Australia, Japan and the ILO) and support from conservation NGOs (e.g. Conservation International, WWF, The Nature Conservancy and Seacology). These ecotourism projects focus on rainforest areas with high conservation value, provide an alternative to logging rainforest and are community-based enterprises. Indigenous ecotourism ventures in the Pacific are largely based on community-owned Conservation Areas rather than National Parks due to customary tenure and ownership of land and sea areas. Environmental NGOs fund ecotourism ventures as an incentive for communities to conserve tropical rainforests and

coral reefs. While donor funds protect selected rainforest areas with single-focus ecotourism projects these have limited benefits for other villages or the region as a whole. Donor agencies also view Indigenous ecotourism as conservation or community development projects rather than a business enterprise, since community-owned and -operated ecotourism ventures often supplement a subsistence economy. Ecotourism ventures proposed by a community are more acceptable for development donors as they focus on income generation and social benefits along with conservation. While there are community efforts to manage and distribute income, village leaders and chiefs mainly benefit from ecotourism projects. Overall, there is a lack of coordination among village ecotourism projects funded by conservation NGOs or donor agencies in the Pacific Islands and no overall strategies for promoting ecotourism once the projects end.

Most community ecotourism products in conservation areas and heritage parks (Fiji) focus on natural scenery and wildlife, rather than Indigenous cultural traditions or identity. Product interpretation mainly features Indigenous ecological knowledge rather than cultural performances or displays. Some traditional cultural practices (e.g. crafts, music and dance) are supported or revived through village ecotourism at other sites. However, there are no data or research on tourist satisfaction with Indigenous tours in natural areas or whether Indigenous culture is a key motivation for joining these ecotours. Village interest in supporting ecotourism ventures also depends on other opportunities for cash income from hotel work, donor projects, to selling timber, fish, forest products or agricultural crops.

Local interest in protecting rainforest areas from logging has motivated several ecotourism projects. However, local participation in a cash economy also influences the success of these ecotourism sites.

Fiji, Samoa, Solomon Islands and Vanuatu provide government support for community ecotourism to bring benefits of tourism to villages in rural areas, generate local income and to support conservation. However, the sustainability of these ecotourism ventures is affected by communal land tenure issues, conflicts over individual versus community gain from tourism, donor funding for set up costs but not operational support or marketing, small visitor markets, remoteness and limited integration with the private tourism industry. Many village ecotourism ventures in the Pacific have failed or had limited success because of these factors. Some industry operators, such as rafting trips by Rivers Fiji and Tour Vanuatu with the Pentecost land dive, have negotiated ecotourism agreements with local villages. This is supported by government legislation on Indigenous land ownership and business ventures. Apart from icon sites or 'hybrid' ecotourism products combined with adventure, culture or recreational activities, there is limited integration of village ecotourism with the tourism industry.

References

Bates, B. (1992) Impacts of tourism on the tribal cultures and natural environment in Papua New Guinea. In: Weiler, B. (ed.) *Ecotourism Incorporating the Global Classroom.* Bureau of Tourism Research, Canberra, pp. 75–78.

BCN (Biodiversity Conservation Network) (1997a) *Ecotourism in the Rainforests of Crater Mountain, Papua New Guinea.* BCN. http://www.worldwildlife.org/bsp/bcn/projects/crater97.htm (accessed 17 November 2005)

BCN (Biodiversity Conservation Network) (1997b) *Eco-tourism in the Forests of Lakekamu Basin, Papua New Guinea.* BCN. http://www.worldwildlife.org/bsp/bcn/projects/lakekamu97.htm (accessed 17 November 2005)

Black, R. and King, B. (2002) Human resource development in remote island communities: An evaluation of tour-guide training in Vanuatu. *International Journal of Tourism Research* 4, 103–117.

Bosselman, F.P., Peterson, C. and McCarthy, C. (1999) Case study: Papua New Guinea. In: *Managing Tourism Growth: Issues and Applications.* Island Press, Washington DC, pp. 265–269.

Bricker, K.S. (2001) Ecotourism development in the rural highlands of Fiji. In: Weaver, D. (ed.) *Tourism and the Less Developed World: Issues and Case Studies.* CABI, Wallingford, UK, pp. 235–249.

Bricker, K.S. (2002) Planning for ecotourism amidst political unrest: Fiji navigates a way forward. In: Honey, M. (ed.) *Ecotourism and Certification: Setting Standards in Practice.* Island Press, Washington DC, pp. 265–297.

Bricker, K.S. (2003) Ecotourism and Rivers Fiji. In: Honey, M. and Thullen, S. (eds) *Rights and Responsibilities: A Compilation of Codes of Conduct for Tourism and Indigenous and Local Communities.* Center on Ecotourism and Sustainable Development and The International Ecotourism Society. Reports. http://205.252.29.37/webarticles/articlefiles/rightsandresponsibilities.pdf (accessed 17 November 2005)

Bubu Shell, The (2005) WTEC launches two ecotourism websites. *The Bubu Shell: WTEC Quarterly Newsletter* 1, 2. http://www.positiveearth.org/newsletters.htm (accessed 17 November 2005)

Buckley, R. (2003a) Community ecotourism in the South Pacific Biodiversity Conservation Program. In: *Case Studies in Ecotourism.* CABI, Wallingford, UK, pp. 62–63.

Buckley, R. (2003b) Rapita Lodge, Solomon Islands. In: *Case Studies in Ecotourism.* CABI, Wallingford, UK, p. 46.

Buckley, R. (2003c) Rennell Island, Solomon Islands. In: *Case Studies in Ecotourism.* CABI, Wallingford, UK, pp. 89–90.

Buckley, R. (2003d) Abaca Village and Recreation Park, Fiji. In: *Case Studies in Ecotourism.* CABI, Wallingford, UK, p. 48.

Buckley, R. (2003e) Rivers Fiji. In: *Case Studies in Ecotourism.* CABI, Wallingford, UK, pp. 60–61.

Buckley, R. (2003f) Tavoro Forest Park, Fiji. In: *Case Studies in Ecotourism.* CABI, Wallingford, UK, pp. 61–62.

Buckley, R. (2003g) Ecotour Samoa. In: *Case Studies in Ecotourism.* CABI, Wallingford, UK, pp. 55–57.

Buckley, R. (2003h) Tafua Canopy Walkway, Samoa. In: *Case Studies in Ecotourism.* CABI, Wallingford, UK, p. 61.

Carter, R.W. and Davie, J.D. (1996) (Eco)tourism in the Asia Pacific region. In: Richins, H., Richardson, J. and Crabtree, A. (eds) *Ecotourism and Nature-based Tourism: Taking the Next Steps.* Ecotourism Association of Australia, Brisbane, pp. 67–72.

CASO Link (1998) Crater Mountain Wildlife Management Area Papua New Guinea. *CASO Link* (SPREP) 7.

Cox, P.A. (1999) *Nafanua: Saving the Samoan Rain Forest.* W.H. Freeman, New York.

Cox, P.A. and Elmqvist, T. (1997) Ecocolonialism and indigenous-controlled rainforest preserves in Samoa. *Ambio* 22. http://www.ambio.kva.se/ (accessed 17 November 2005)

de Burlo, C. (1996) Cultural resistance and ethnic tourism on South Pentecost, Vanuatu. In: Butler, R. and Hinch, T. (eds) *Tourism and Indigenous Peoples.* International Thomson Business Press, London, pp. 255–277.

de Burlo, C.R. (2003) Tourism, conservation and the cultural environment in rural Vanuatu. In: Harrison, D. (ed.) *Pacific Island Tourism.* Cognizant Communication Corporation, New York, pp. 69–81.

De Haas, H. (2003) Sustainability of small-scale ecotourism: The case of Niue, South Pacific. In: Luck, M. and Kirstges, T. (eds) *Global Ecotourism Policies and Case Studies: Perspectives and Constraints.* Channel View Publications, Clevedon, UK, pp. 147–165.

Decloitre, P. (1998) Away from the beaten tracks. *Pacific Islands Monthly* April, 34.

Douglas, N. (1998) Tourism in Papua New Guinea: Past, present and future. *Pacific Tourism Review* 2, 97–104.

Dowling, R. (2001) Oceania (Australia, New Zealand and South Pacific). In: Weaver, D.B. (ed.) *The Encyclopaedia of Ecotourism.* CABI, Wallingford, UK, pp. 139–154.

Ecotourism Melanesia (nd) *Ecotourism Melanesia About us.* http://www.em.com.pg/emaboutus.htm (accessed 17 November 2005)
Community-based ecotourism. http://www.em.com.pg/PNG/special%20interests/PNGecotourism.htm
Village guest houses and homestays. http://www.em.com.pg/PNG/accommodation/PNGaccvillage.htm

Ecotour Samoa (2004) *Samoa Travel Ecotourism Holidays.* http://www.ecotoursamoa.com (accessed 17 November 2005)

Ecovitality (nd) *Ecovitality, Papua New Guinea, Tour Operator/Non-Governmental Organization.* SIDS Ecotourism Success Stories. http://www.sidsnet.org/eco-tourism/ecovital.html (accessed 17 November 2005)

Ell, L. (2003) Striving towards ecotourism in the Solomon Islands. ECOCLUB.com. E-Paper Series Number 8. May 2003. http://www.ecoclub.com/library/epapers/8.pdf (accessed 25 May 2006)

Fagence, M. (1997) Ecotourism and Pacific island countries: The first generation of strategies. *Journal of Tourism Studies* 8, 26–38.

FijiBure (2005) *Fiji holidays at traditional Fijian village homestay.* http://www.fijibure.com/ (accessed 17 November 2005)

Fisher, D. (2003) Tourism and change in local economic behavior. In: Harrison, D. (ed.) *Pacific Island Tourism.* Cognizant Communication Corporation, New York, pp. 58–68.

Focus (2001) Soccer hero wins a battle for conservation. *Focus* (AusAID), June 2001, 9.

Freeman, A. (2005) An Eastern Highland's fling. *Wingspan* 15, 30–33.

Gilbert, J. (1997) The Koroyanitu development programme, Fiji. In: *Ecotourism Means Business.* GP Publications, Wellington, New Zealand, pp. 25–32.

Godde, P. (1998) Community-based mountain tourism in Fiji. Article from Community-Based Mountain Tourism Conference, 22 April 1998. The Mountain Forum. http://www.mtnforum.org/rs/pub/econf reports/Community-BasedMountainTourism.pdf (accessed 17 November 2005)

Gould, J. (1995) Protecting Pacific forests. *Habitat Australia* 23, 14–15.

Greenpeace (2004) *Working Together. Reclaiming Paradise. The Paradise Forest.* Greenpeace Forests. http://www.paradiseforest.org/reclaiming_paradise/ (accessed 17 November 2005)

Green Turtle Holidays (nd) *Western Samoa Beach Fales.* Green Turtle Holidays Samoa. http://www.green turtlesamoa.com/accommodation/beach-fales.html (accessed 17 November 2005)

Halfpenny, E. (1999) The state and critical issues relating to international ecotourism development policy. In: *Australia – The World's Natural Theme Park: Proceedings of the Ecotourism Association of Australia 1999 Conference.* Ecotourism Association of Australia, Brisbane, pp. 45–52.

Harrison, D. (ed.) (1997) *Ecotourism and Village-based Tourism: A Policy and Strategy for Fiji.* Ministry of Tourism, Transport and Civil Aviation, Suva, Fiji.

Harrison, D. (1998) The world comes to Fiji: Who communicates what, and to whom? *Tourism, Culture and Communication* 1, 129–138.

Harrison, D. (ed.) (2003) Themes in Pacific Island tourism. In: Harrison, D. (ed.) *Pacific Island Tourism.* Cognizant Communication Corporation, New York, pp. 1–23.

Harrison, D. and Brandt, J. (2003) Ecotourism in Fiji. In: Harrison, D. (ed.) *Pacific Island Tourism.* Cognizant Communication Corporation, New York, pp. 139–156.

Harrison, D., Sawailau, S. and Malani, M. (2003) Ecotourism and village-based tourism: A policy and strategy for Fiji. In: Harrison, D. (ed.) *Pacific Island Tourism.* Cognizant Communication Corporation, New York, pp. 157–170.

Hay, J.E. (ed.) (1992) *Ecotourism Business in the Pacific: Promoting a Sustainable Experience.* Conference Proceedings. Environmental Science, University of Auckland, Auckland.

Hayes, A. (1997) Village tourism in Solomon Islands. *Ecotourism Association of Australia Newsletter* 6, 4.

Hibberd, J. (1997) The world's largest butterfly still flies in PNG. *Focus* (AusAID) March, 19–22.

Hviding, E. (2003) Contested rainforests, NGOs, and projects of desire in Solomon Islands. UNESCO. Blackwell, Oxford, pp. 539–553.

Hviding, E. and Bayliss-Smith, T.P. (2000) Rumours of utopia: Conservation and eco-tourism. In: *Islands of Rainforest: Agroforestry, Logging and Ecotourism in Solomon Islands.* Ashgate, Aldershot, pp. 291–320.

Imai, M. and Kikuchi, M. (2000) Commons and environmental conservation: Some attempts of ecotourism in Samoa. *Technical Bulletin of Faculty of Horticulture Chiba University* 54, 105–114.

Johnson, A. (1999) *Lessons from the Field 3: Measuring Our Success: One Team's Experience in Monitoring the Crater Mountain Wildlife Management Area Project in Papua New Guinea.* BCN. http://www.world wildlife.org/bsp/bcn/learning/Lessons/lesson2/lessons-BCN_2.htm (accessed 17 November 2005)

Knight, S. (1997) Culture without the shock. *The New Zealand Herald,* Travel & Leisure, 15 April, D1, D3.

Kokop Village Eco-Forestry Development Organization (KVEDO) (2004) Kokop Village Eco-Forestry Development Organization (KVEDO), Incorporated. http://www.geocities.com/skyfdn/kvedo.html (accessed 17 November 2005)

LaFranchi, C. (1999) *Islands Adrift? Comparing Industrial and Small-scale Economic Options for Marovo Lagoon Region of the Solomon Islands.* Greenpeace Pacific. http://www.paradiseforest.org/downloads/marovo_report.pdf (accessed 17 November 2005)

Lees, A. (1992) Ecotourism – restraining the big promise. In: Hay, J.E. (ed.) *Ecotourism Business in the Pacific: Promoting a Sustainable Experience.* Conference Proceedings. Environmental Science, University of Auckland, Auckland, pp. 61–64.

Lees, A. and Evans, B. (1993) Helping conservation pay: Village microenterprise development in the Solomon Islands. In: *Fifth South Pacific Conference on Nature Conservation and Protected Areas,* Vol. 2. Conference Papers. SPREP, Apia, Western Samoa, pp. 181–193.

Lipscomb, A.J.H. (1998) Village-based tourism in the Solomon Islands: Impediments and impacts. In: Laws, E., Faulkner, B. and Moscardo, G. (eds) *Embracing and Managing Change in Tourism: International Case Studies.* Routledge, London, pp. 185–202.

Liu, J.C. (1994) *Pacific Island Tourism: A Public Policy and Planning Guide.* Office of Territorial and International Affairs, Honolulu.

Macalister, R., daWheya, N. and Trewwenack, G. (2000) A promising start: Komarindi Ecotours – Development of community ecotourism on Guadalcanal, Solomon Islands. SPREP Paper. terra firma associates, Cairns.

Mansperger, M.C. (1992) Yap: A Case of benevolent tourism. *Practicing Anthropology* 14, 10–13.

Martel, F. (1999) Skills development programme in virtual reality! *CASO Link* (SPREP) 10, 1–3.

Martel, F. (2001) The role of the South Pacific Regional Environment Program in community ecotourism development. In: Varma, H. (ed.) *Island Tourism in Asia and the Pacific.* World Tourism Organization, Madrid, pp. 87–102.

Martin, D. (1994) Old Michi village tourism project. *Wildlife News (WWF)* 69, Sept–Nov.

Michaud, J., Maranda, P. *et al.* (1994) Ethnological tourism in the Solomon Islands: An experience in applied anthropology. *Anthropologica* 36, 35–56.

Miller, J. and Malek-Zadeh, E. (1997) The ecotourism equation: Measuring the impacts. *Bulletin Series, Yale School of Forestry and Environmental Studies* 99.

Milne Bay Tourism Bureau (2004) *Ecotourism.* http://www.milnebaytourism.gov.pg/eco.html (accessed 17 November 2005)

Napatana Lodge (nd) Napatana Lodge. Ecotourism in Papua New Guinea. http://www.napatanalodge.com/ (accessed 17 November 2005)

Narayan, P.K. (2000) Ecotourism in Fiji: Potential and constraints. *Contours* 10, 10–15.

Pearsall, S. (1993) Terrestrial coastal environments and tourism in Western Samoa. In: Wong, P.P. (ed.) *Tourism vs Environment: The Case for Coastal Areas.* Kluwer Academic, Dordrecht, pp. 33–53.

Perrottet, T. (1996) Grace & fervour. *The Weekend Australian,* Review Travel, 14–15 December, 16.

Post-Courier (2002) Villagers benefit from conservation. *Post-Courier* PNG, 28 February. http://www.em.com.pg/PNG/provinces/Morobe/kamialiarticle.htm (accessed 17 November 2005)

Ranck, S.R. (1987) An attempt at autonomous development: The case of the Tufi guesthouses, Papua New Guinea. In: Britton, S. and Clarke, W.C. (eds) *Ambiguous Alternative: Tourism in Small Developing Countries.* University of the South Pacific, Suva, pp. 154–166.

Rapita Lodge (2004) *Rapita Lodge.* WWF South Pacific Website. http://wwwpacific.org.fj/ (accessed 17 November 2005)

Rivers Fiji (2004) *Ecotourism and Rivers Fiji.* http://www.riversfiji.com/ecotourism.htm (accessed 17 November 2005)

Rudkin, B. and Hall, C.M. (1996) Unable to see the forest for the trees: Ecotourism development in Solomon Islands. In: Butler, R. and Hinch, T. (eds) *Tourism and Indigenous Peoples.* International Thomson Business Press, London, pp. 203–226.

Russell, D. (1998) *The beauty and danger of ecotourism: Trekking the highlands of Makira Island, Solomon Islands.* Biodiversity Conservation Network. http://www.worldwildlife.org/bsp/bcn/results/ecotour.htm (accessed 17 November 2005)

Russell, D. and Stabile, J. (2003) Ecotourism in practice: Trekking the highlands of Makira Island, Solomon Islands. In: Harrison, D. (ed.) *Pacific Island Tourism.* Cognizant Communication Corporation, New York, pp. 38–57.

Salafsky, N. (1999) *Lessons from the Field: Linking Theory and Practice in Biodiversity Conservation.* BCN. http://www.worldwildlife.org/bsp/bcn/learning/Lessons/lesson2/lessons-BCN_2.htm (accessed 17 November 2005)

Scheyvens, R. (2002) *Growth and benefits of budget beach fale tourism in Samoa.* DevNet Conference 2002. http://devnet.massey.ac.nz/papers/Scheyvens,%20Regina.pdf (accessed 17 November 2005)

Scheyvens, R. (2005) Growth of beach *fale* tourism in Samoa: The high value of low-cost tourism. In: Hall, C.M. and Boyd, S. (eds) *Nature-based tourism in peripheral areas: Development or disaster?* Channel View Publications, Clevedon, pp. 188–202.

Scheyvens, R. and Purdie, N. (1999) Ecotourism. In: Overton, J. and Scheyvens, R. (eds) *Strategies for Sustainable Development: Experiences from the Pacific.* UNSW Press, Sydney, pp. 212–225.

Seacology (2002) Samoa – Tower/walkway construction for the Falealupo Rainforest Preserve. *Seacology,* September/October (Fall) 2002, 6. http://www.eacology.org/news/index.cfm (accessed 17 November 2005)

Sinha, C.C. and Bushell, R. (2002) Understanding the linkage between biodiversity and tourism: A study of ecotourism in a coastal village in Fiji. *Pacific Tourism Review* 6, 35–50.

Sofield, T. (1991) Sustainable ethnic tourism in the South Pacific: Some principles. *Journal of Tourism Studies* 2, 56–72.

Sofield, T. (1992) The Guadalcanal Track ecotourism project in the Solomon Islands. In: Hay, J.E. (ed.) *Ecotourism Business in the Pacific: Promoting a Sustainable Experience.* Conference Proceedings. Environmental Science, University of Auckland, Auckland, pp. 89–100.

Sofield, T.H.B. (1993) Indigenous tourism development. *Annals of Tourism Research* 20, 729–750.

Sofield, T.H.B. (2003a) Empowerment at the national level: Solomon Islands. In: *Empowerment for Sustainable Tourism Development.* Pergamon, New York, pp. 191–223.

Sofield, T.H.B. (2003b) Empowerment and sustainability through village ownership: The *Ghol,* Vanuatu. In: *Empowerment for Sustainable Tourism Development.* Pergamon, New York, pp. 259–284.

Solomon Islands Ministry of Commerce (2001a) *Solomon Islands ecotourism.* http://www.angelfire.com/biz/solomonsvillagestay/ (accessed 17 November 2005)

Solomon Islands Ministry of Commerce (2001b) *Village homestays in the Solomon Islands* [Ecotourism Melanesia]. http://www.angelfire.com/biz/solomonsvillagestay/svsinfo.html (accessed 17 November 2005)

Solomon Islands Ministry of Commerce (2001c) Nature lodges and other ecotourism accommodation in Solomon Islands. http://www.angelfire.com/biz/solomonsvillagestay/lodges.html (accessed 17 November 2005)

Solomons Village Stay (nd) Solomon Islands village homestays, Solomon Islands rustic resorts and eco-lodges. http://www.solomonsvillagestay.8k.com/lodges.html (accessed 17 November 2005)

Sooaemalelagi, L., Hunter, S. and Brown, S. (1996) Alternate tourism development in Western Samoa. Paper presented at *3rd Pacific Indigenous Business Conference,* 11–13 December, 1996, Sydney, Australia.

Sooaemalelagi, L., Brown, S., Martel, F. and Dolgoy, R. (1999) The ecotourism operation was a success, but the patient died: A case study from Western Samoa. *Yale Bulletin* 99 (*The Ecotourism Equation: Measuring the Impacts*). http://www.yale.edu/environment/publications/bulletin/099pdfs/99sooaemalagi.pdf (accessed 17 November 2005)

South Pacific Currents (2001) Rapita Lodge: A world away from it all. *South Pacific Currents* (WWF South Pacific) *14*, April. http://www.wwfpacific.org.fj/ (accessed 17 November 2005)

SPREP (South Pacific Regional Environment Programme) (2002) *Community-based Ecotourism and Conservation in the Pacific Islands: A Tool Kit for Communities.* SPREP, Apia, Samoa.

SPTO (South Pacific Tourism Organisation) (2001) Eco-tourism development. In: *Regional Tourism Strategy for the South and Central Pacific.* Deloitte & Touche Emerging Markets. SPTO, Suva, Fiji, p. 56.

Talagi-Hekesi, I. (nd) Huvalu Forest Conservation Tours. SIDS Ecotourism Success Stories. http://www.sids net.org/eco-tourism/niue.html (accessed 17 November 2005)

Thomas, P., Worboys, G. and Farago, A. (1993) The Komarindi catchment conservation area model: Providing for sustainable management of conservation areas through a resource rent and other income generation. In: *Fifth South Pacific Conference on Nature Conservation and Protected Areas*, Vol. 2. *Conference Papers.* SPREP, Apia, Western Samoa, pp. 171–179.

Tokalau, F. (2005) The economic benefits of an ecotourism project in a regional economy: A case study of Namuamua Inland Tour, Namosi, Fiji Islands. In: Hall, C.M. and Boyd, C.M. (eds) *Nature-Based Tourism in Peripheral Areas: Development or Disaster?* Channel View Publications, Clevedon, pp. 173–187.

Travel Maxia (2005) National Park promotes American Samoa village homestay program – American Samoa. Pacific Islands Report, SPTO, August 2001. South Pacific Ecotourism Travel News. http://www.travel maxia.com/eco/index.cfm (accessed 17 November 2005)

Treloar, P. and Hall, C.M. (2005) Introduction to the Pacific Islands. In: Cooper, C. and Hall, C.M. (eds) *Oceania: A Tourism Handbook.* Channel View Publications, Clevedon, pp. 165–321.

Turnbull, J. (2004) Explaining complexities of environmental management in developing countries: Lessons from the Fiji Islands. *The Geographical Journal* 170, 64–77.

Twining-Ward, L. and Twining-Ward, T. (1998) Tourism development in Samoa: Context and constraints. *Pacific Tourism Review* 2, 261–271.

UNESCO (2000) *Field trip to Saanapu-Sataoa.* CSI Papers. http://www.unesco.org/csi/pub/papers/samoa8b. htm (accessed 17 November 2005)

Valentine, P.S. (1993) Ecotourism and nature conservation: A definition with some recent developments in Micronesia. *Tourism Management* 14, 107–115.

Van't Stot, J. (1996) Pacific Islands seek ecotourism solutions: Tough choices are ahead. *Ecotourism Society Newsletter* 2nd quarter, 1–3.

Vanuatu Tourism (2005) *Island Safaris Vanuatu.* http://www.vanuatutourism.com/vanuatu/export/sites/VTO/ en/operators/island_safaris.html (accessed 17 November 2005)

Volkel-Hutchison, C. (1996) Creating awareness: Responsible tourism – an issue for anthropologists? Paper presented at the Australian Anthropological Society Conference, 2–4 October 1996. Charles Sturt University, Albury, Australia.

Wantok Environment Centre (2005a) *Aelan Walkabaot Long Vanuatu.* Wantok Environment Centre. http://www.positiveearth.org/bungalows/ (accessed 17 November 2005)

Wantok Environment Centre (2005b) *About island bungalows and travelling in Vanuatu.* Wantok Environment Centre. http://www.positiveearth.org/bungalows/introduction.html (accessed 17 November 2005)

Wantok Environment Centre (2005c) Vanuatu conservation areas directory. Wantok Environment Centre. http://www.positiveearth.org/bungalows/conservation.htm (accessed 17 November 2005)

Wearing, S. and McDonald, M. (2002) The development of community-based tourism: Re-thinking the relationship between tour operators and development agents as intermediaries in rural and isolated area communities. *Journal of Sustainable Tourism* 10, 191–206.

Weaver, D.B. (1998a) Magnitude of ecotourism in the South Pacific. In: *Ecotourism in the Less Developed World.* CABI, Wallingford, UK, pp. 195–196.

Weaver, D.B. (1998b) Strategies for the development of deliberate ecotourism in the South Pacific. *Pacific Tourism Review* 2, 53–66.

Wortle, O. (2001) Kosrae goes solar. *Environment Newsletter* (SPREP), 63 (January–March), 1, 7.

WTO (2000) Rivers Fiji: Tourism development and conservation through white-water adventure trips. In: *Sustainable Development of Tourism: A Compilation of Good Practices.* WTO, Madrid, pp. 47–51.

WWF (2000) *Solomon Islands – ecotourism.* WWF South Pacific. http://www.wwfpacific.org.fj/ (accessed 17 November 2005)

WWF (World Wide Fund for Nature) (2004) *WWF Solomon Islands.* http://www.wwfpacific.org.fj/where_ we_work/solomons/index.cfm (accessed 17 November 2005)

Wylie, J. (ed.) (1994) *Journey Through a Sea of Islands: A Review of Forest Tourism in Micronesia*. USDA Forest Service, Honolulu.

Young, M. (1992) Ecotourism – profitable conservation. In: Hay, J.E. (ed.) *Ecotourism Business in the Pacific: Promoting a Sustainable Experience*. Conference Proceedings. Environmental Science, University of Auckland, Auckland, pp. 55–60.

Yuimb, S.K. (2004) *Kokop village ecotourism centre Papua New Guinea*. http://www.geocities.com/kokopvillage/ (accessed 17 November 2005)

Zeppel, H. (1998) Land and culture: Sustainable tourism and indigenous peoples. In: Hall, C.M. and Lew, A. (eds) *Sustainable Tourism: A Geographical Perspective*. Addison Wesley Longman, London, pp. 60–74.

3

Latin America: Rainforest Ecotourism, Andes Mountains and Indian Territories

This chapter reviews Indigenous ecotourism enterprises in South America and Central America. Collectively, the countries in this region are known as Latin America as they were mainly colonized by Spain or Portugal (i.e. Brazil). Many Latin American countries have policies for community-based tourism integrating nature and culture, but most village ecotourism projects rely on funding and support from conservation NGOs and other foreign aid (Dahles and Keune, 2002). A brief overview is first provided on Indigenous peoples and the ecotourism industry in Latin America. Case studies are presented of Indigenous ecotourism ventures in Ecuador, Peru, Chile, Bolivia, Venezuela, Colombia, Guyana, Suriname, French Guiana and Brazil. Other sections review several Indigenous ecotourism ventures, such as ecolodges, in the rainforest areas of the Amazon region. This is followed by case studies of Indigenous ecotourism enterprises in Belize, Mexico, Guatemala, Honduras, Panama, Costa Rica and on the Carib Territory, Dominican Republic in the Caribbean. The case studies reflect what has been published in English and include most Indigenous ecotourism projects. The last section discusses key issues and challenges for developing Indigenous ecotourism ventures in Latin America.

Introduction: Ecotourism in Latin America

There are 13 million Indigenous people in Central America and over 15 million in South America, with most living in highland regions, rainforest and rural areas. Indigenous groups are a significant part of the population of Bolivia (66%), Guatemala (60%), Peru (40%), Ecuador and El Salvador (21%). Mayan, Aztec, Quechua and Aymara peoples are the main groups (Healey, 1993). In Latin America, Indigenous peoples are referred to as *Indigenas*, Indians and Amerindians. Some 1 million Indigenous peoples live in the tropical rainforests of the Amazon region extending over Brazil, Peru, Ecuador, Bolivia and five other countries. Latin American countries are biodiversity 'hotspots' for rainforest ecosystems and tropical wildlife but are affected by land use conflicts, civil wars, political instability, mining, oil extraction and deforestation with inadequate laws or funding to manage protected areas or defend Indigenous territories (Tourism Concern, 1994; Brandon, 1996; Gray *et al.*, 1998; Newing and Wahl, 2004). There is little guardianship for the rights of Indigenous peoples who are marginalized groups in rural regions of Latin America. Some Indigenous groups have gained legal title to their lands, used for subsistence activities and farming (Ingles, 2002).

Ecotourism ventures provide a means to preserve natural resources and make a living in some tribal areas. The southern countries of Chile, Argentina, Paraguay and Uruguay have few Indigenous ecotourism ventures, possibly due to more intensive colonization of land and the Indigenous groups.

The Otavalo Declaration (2001) and San Jose Declaration (2003) reaffirmed the rights of Indigenous peoples to benefit from rural community-based tourism projects in their traditional territories. While ecotourism in Latin America has grown since the 1990s, local participation from rural and Indigenous people in ecotourism projects ('*proyectos ecoturisticos*') is still limited (Mader, 2003; Ecotribal, 2005).

In Central America, Costa Rica and Belize have well-developed ecotourism industries, linked to resort tourism on the Caribbean coast and dominated by US investors. Here, Indigenous communities often provide 'cultural add-ons' to nature-based tourism (Weaver, 2001: 291; Mowforth and Munt, 2003). In South America, private ecotourism operations are established around gateway areas, such as Quito (Ecuador), Manaus (Brazil), La Paz (Bolivia), Iquitos (Peru) and Leticia (Colombia). Since the 1990s, Indian groups have developed small-scale ecotourism ventures, such as jungle ecolodges and rainforest tours, in the Amazon basin and the Andes, attracting tourists from the US and Europe. These joint ventures or community-based ecotourism programmes provide an economic alternative to logging and agriculture, support Indigenous land claims and commitment to conservation and strengthen Indigenous culture (Wesche and Drumm, 1999; de Bont and Janssen, 2003; Mader, 2004). As with the Pacific Islands, environmental NGOs assist Indigenous groups in the Amazon to develop ecotourism and preserve tropical rainforest areas. Tribal organizations, local NGOs, development groups, government agencies, multilateral institutions, American researchers and private operators also support Indigenous ecotourism ventures in Latin America (Edwards *et al.*, 1998).

A website on community tourism in Latin America features about 50 Indigenous ecotourism ventures, in Ecuador (30), Bolivia (6), Peru (4), Costa Rica (3), Guatemala (3) and Colombia (2) (Redturs, nd). These include ecolodges, homestays, guiding and transportation services in parks and rural areas.

Indigenous Ecotourism in South America

Ecuador

Tourist attractions in Ecuador include the Andes highlands, Amazon rainforest and diverse Indian cultures, such as Quechua, Shuar, Huaorani, Otavalenos and others (de Bont and Janssen, 2002). Ecuador has a wide range of community ecotourism enterprises, owned and operated by Indian groups mainly in the rainforest Amazon region. These have developed in response to outside tour operators and to prevent incursions by oil and logging companies on Indian territories (Irvine, 2000; Krenke and Murillo, 2005). Some 104,000 Indian people had claims to 75% of the 138,000 km^2 Ecuadorian Amazon, compared to Brazil where 139,000 Indians had claimed only 21% of the 6.2 million km^2 of the Brazilian Amazon (Irvine, 2000). With strong Indigenous political organizations, Ecuadorian Indian groups have legal control over large areas of the Amazon, and more political autonomy at the local level to control tourism activities (Drumm, 1998; Zografos and Oglethorpe, 2004; Boniface and Cooper, 2005). A federation or association of Indian villages (e.g. RICANCIE) often represents or organizes several community ecotourism ventures. Guidelines for managing ecotourism activities in Ecuador were published by CONAIE, a confederation of Amazon Indigenous groups (Blangy, 1999). The Plurinational Federation of Community Tourism of Ecuador (FEPTEC) also supports and promotes ecotourism ventures developed by Indigenous groups in the Amazon, Andes and coastal regions. These Indigenous ecotourism projects complement farming and subsistence activities. However, there is limited support from the Ecuador government for village tourism (de Bont and Janssen, 2002). A National Forum on

Community Participation in Ecotourism held in Quito in 1997, recommended tourist guidelines, local Indian guides, zoning areas for ecotourism and those community agreements with external agencies (e.g. NGOs, operators) include financial and operational details. Limitations for Indigenous ecotourism ventures include remoteness, communication, and access to visitor markets, competition with private operators and also between communities and obtaining finance and training (Drumm, 1998; de Bont and Janssen, 2003). One project evaluated international visitor markets (ecotour operators, US study abroad and non-profit travel programmes) for Indigenous ecotourism at two sites in Amazonian Ecuador (Epler Wood, 2004). The next sections review Indigenous community-based ecotourism ventures in Ecuador.

Community-based Ecotourism in Ecuador

A travel guide for the Amazon region of Ecuador lists 33 community-based ecotourism ventures operated by Quechua, Cofan, Secoya, Siona, Zaparo and Achuar Indian groups. These ventures provide accommodation in village huts or cabins, rainforest tours, wildlife viewing and cultural activities (see Table 3.1). They are strategically located along rivers or lakes and either nearby or in nature reserves (Wesche, 1996; Epler Wood, 1998; Wesche and Drumm, 1999). A website for community tourism ventures in Latin America also lists 42 ecotourism ventures with Indian involvement in Ecuador. Twenty-eight of these Indian ecotourism projects were in the Ecuadorian Amazon, with others in the high Andes and coastal or mountain areas in or around nature reserves and national parks. The Quechua (16), Huaorani (3), Shuar (3), Siona (1), Shiwiar (1) and other Indian groups operated these ecotourism ventures either as self-managed community enterprises or in partnership with other tour operators (Redturs, nd). While Quechua tourism ventures in the RICANCIE network of Napo province began in the early 1990s, most other Indian tourism ventures in Ecuador have only been established since 2000. The Amazon rainforest region is a day's journey from the capital Quito, although many Indian tourism ventures are in remote areas with limited access by light

Table 3.1. Community ecotourism ventures in the Amazon region, eastern Ecuador.

Indian group	Location	Type of venture (CB, Pr, Partnership, JV)
Achuar	Kapawi	Partnership (Canodros S.A.)
Cofan	Zabalo, Dureno	CB, Pr, JV (Transturi)
Huaorani	Quehueire'ono	CB, Partnership (Tropic Ecological Adventures)
Huaorani	Tiguino	Partnership (Kempery Tours)
Quechua	Capirona, Rio Blanco, Playas de Cuyabeno and 22 other villages	CB, Pr, RICANCIE Network, Amazanga Tours, Atacapi Tours
Secoya	Piranha Tour	Pr (community-supported)
Siona	Biana, Orahueaya, Puerto Bolivar	CB, CB, Pr
Zaparo	Llanchamacocha-Jandiayacu	CB

Ecotourism attractions and activities
* Rainforest, flooded forest, waterfalls, caves, rivers, lagoons, lakes, hot springs, look outs, salt licks, animal rehabilitation centre, canopy tower (Playas de Cuyabeno), treetop rope and pulley system (Zabalo).
* Jungle walks, swimming, fishing, spearfishing, snorkelling, inner tubing, canoeing, swing from lianas, community work (*minga*), wildlife viewing, gold panning (Chuva Urcu and Sapollo).
* Petroglyphs, museum, dance, music, handicrafts, pottery, *shaman* (healer), medicinal plant garden, *chicha* drink, blowgun demonstration, basket weaving, hammock weaving, healing ritual, farewell ceremony, face painting, myths and legends, food preparation, fish-trap construction, fire making, dart making, hut construction.
* Wildlife viewing – freshwater dolphins, monkeys, peccaries, caiman, anaconda, jaguar, ocelot, boar, reptiles, insects, butterflies, tapir, turtles, fish, birds (500 species): parrots, scarlet macaw, toucan.

CB, community based; Pr, private; JV, joint venture. *Source:* Wesche and Drumm (1999).

planes or lengthy canoe trips. These community ecotourism enterprises were developed with the support of Indigenous organizations, local foundations, conservation NGOs and private tourism operators. Indian ecotourism supports nature conservation by retaining primary forest areas, controlled subsistence hunting and setting aside reserves on Indigenous territories where hunting and cultivation is prohibited (e.g. Zaparo and Cofan). Community-based ecotourism ventures are reviewed for the Quechua, Cofan, Huaorani, Achuar and Shiwiar Indians in the Amazon rainforest area of north-eastern Ecuador.

Quechua Indians at Capirona, Rio Blanco and Cuyabeno

In Ecuador's Napo Province, in the Amazon Basin, 24 Quechua Indian families at Capirona independently initiated a small ecotourism project in 1989 (Lemky, 1992; Silver, 1992; Colvin, 1994; WRI, 1996; Zeppel, 1998; Page and Dowling, 2002). With community sales of maize and a loan from a regional Indigenous federation, the Quechua villagers at Capirona constructed a tourist lodge and visitor centre. The Capirona territory of 2000 ha is 75% forest with the ecotourism venture preventing oil development and unauthorized visits by tourist groups. The Federation of Indigenous Organisations of Napo (FOIN) and the Jatun Sacha Foundation provided initial funding (Wesche and Drumm, 1999). The American co-owners of Jatun Sacha, a nearby biological research station, supplied US tourists completing rainforest courses to Capirona (Wesche, 1996). A Capirona visit included guided walks led by the shaman's son, jungle trails, canoeing, cultural programmes and swimming. Assisted by a German NGO, Capirona printed flyers and distributed these in the regional city of Tena. They attracted 50 visitors in the first year, mainly students, and then targeted study groups from US universities. The Capirona guesthouse was promoted through travel agents in the capital city of Quito and by Indigenous organizations that also provided training in tourism and hospitality. In 1992, a research team from the University of California prepared practical strategies for managing community ecotourism at Capirona (Colvin, 1994). Visitor numbers grew from 12 in 1989 up to 700 by 1995 (Buckley, 2003a). Income from ecotourism at Capirona paid workers and also funded schools and health care centres.

The Capirona community encouraged other Quechua villages at Rio Blanco to establish tourism businesses, to spread the impacts of tourism. In 1995, the village of Rio Blanco attracted some 158 visitors to their ecotourism project (Schaller, 1996, 1998). This generated income of US$6000 with US$2400 distributed to local families. Loans used for construction, and development of the community ecotourism project, were repaid in 1 year. Tourists spent their time in forest areas, less than 50% of community land at Rio Blanco, while locals worked in farming and cash crops. Income from forest ecotourism, however, reduced the need to clear further areas. Tourists arrived at Rio Blanco on biological tours and as small groups of independent visitors. A limit was set of 300 visitors a year at Rio Blanco. Traditional Quechua music and dances, with performers in grass skirts and red body paint, were revived for tourists (Schaller, 1996). For Capirona and Rio Blanco, the benefits of controlled ecotourism could be affected by a downturn in tourist numbers, competition between villages or with local tour operators (Buckley, 2003a). A growing network of Quechua villages involved in ecotourism requires varied programmes (Colvin, 1994, 1996; Wesche and Drumm, 1999).

Quechua involvement in ecotourism at Capirona was motivated by the limited economic returns from tourism run by outside operators (Hutchins, 2002). This same reason also generated other community ecotourism projects among Quechua villages. The communities of Anangu and Panacocha cut down trees across streams to stop tour operators entering lakes in their territory. The Anangu control a lagoon that has 400 bird species and other rainforest wildlife with basic accommodation on a sleeping platform. Community members pooled their labour and resources to build new tourist cabins at Anangu Lake. The Napo Wildlife Centre, with 10 cabins, opened in 2003 as a partnership between the Anangu community, EcoEcuador, a local conservation NGO, and Tropical Nature, a company promoting conservation through ecotourism. Community members staff the lodge and work as guides. The Napo wildlife lodge is located on a 70-acre private reserve within Yasuni National Park (Rogers, 2004; TNT, 2004c). Another Quechua group set up their own company, Amazanga, working with the Quechua Federation to operate tours along the Middle and Lower Napo (Drumm, 1998). At Playas de Cuyabeno, the Quechua work at a floating hotel, but in 1996 they built four tourist cabins. A canopy observation tower was later built around a tall tree in the Cuyabeno Reserve. They host groups brought in by five tour operators and received 1000 tourists in 1997/98 (Wesche and Drumm, 1999).

The San Isla Quechua community on the Napo built the small Sani Lodge on Challuacocha Lake. For 15 years, members of the Sani Isla community worked for other lodges in the area as canoe drivers, tour guides, chefs and housekeepers. In the early 1990s, the community received title to 17,000 ha of rainforest and a local man suggested building a small lodge for 16 guests as a community-owned ecotourism venture. Sani Lodge employs a naturalist and co-administrator while another lodge nearby manages customer service and hospitality. Profits from tourism are put in a community fund to build a school and hire teachers. The community will declare the forest around the lodge a private reserve to prevent poaching of animals and illegal harvesting of plants (Sani Lodge, 2004). The lodge is part of a new group, Ecuador Verde, promoting volunteer work at five community tourism ventures. Projects at Sani include managing the lodge, teaching English and wildlife species counts (Ward, 2004).

Napo communities and RICANCIE network

In 1993, nine communities established the RICANCIE network in the regional city of Tena, assisted by the Federation of Indigenous Organisations of Napo (FOIN). RICANCIE is the Network of Indigenous Communities of the Upper Napo for Intercultural Exchange and Ecotourism. The network promotes community ecotourism ventures, provides guiding courses, organises tour bookings and the transport or other logistical arrangements for visiting communities. RICANCIE defends Quechua territory within the Grand Sumaco Biosphere Reserve from mining and oil companies while providing tourism income for 200 families (RICANCIE, 2004). The nine Quechua communities in the RICANCIE network were Capirona, Chuva Urcu, Cuya Loma (or Suru Panka), Galeras, Huasila Talag (or Takik Sacha), Machacuyacu, Rio Blanco, Runa Huasi and Salazar Aitaca (RICANCIE, 2004). With funding from a community development NGO, Ayuda en Accion, RICANCIE developed tourist cabins made of traditional materials and walking trails in the jungle. Capirona guidelines were developed to minimize cultural impacts of tourists in the villages. Prices are fixed for tourism programmes in the member communities, with a package price of US$60 for a stay of more than 2 days. In 1997, the 12 communities in the RICANCIE network had a capacity of 200 beds and received 800 visitors, with 1200 visitors in 1996. The network attracted visitors from foreign universities, research NGOs and nature tourists, mainly from the US and Europe. Ecotourism has generated income, motivated other sustainable community ventures and revitalized the cultural knowledge of elders and women. Tourism income was used to purchase motorized canoes and a radio communication system and invested in handicrafts and farming. RICANCIE became a legally recognized corporation in 1997 to gain finance and promote its community ecotourism products (Drumm, 1998; Wesche and Drumm, 1999; Edeli, 2002; Buckley, 2003b). At Expo 2000 in Germany, RICANCIE participated in the Indigenous Communities display. In March 2004, RICANCIE protested against oil exploitation in Indian territories of the Amazon rainforest of Ecuador with other Indian organizations.

Yachana Lodge

In 1995 a local NGO, the Foundation for Integrated Education and Development

(FUNEDESIN), constructed Yachana Lodge on the banks of the Upper Napo River. The initial lodge investment was US$120,000 (WTO, 2003a). The goal of this NGO is protecting Ecuador's rainforest by educating and empowering local people through conservation and community development. The name 'Yachana' is a Quechua word meaning a place of learning. The 40-person lodge is in the small community of Mondana, surrounded by 3600 acres of tropical rainforest. Since 1995, Yachana Lodge has hosted 4500 visitors and generated $1 million dollars with 100% of profits invested in conservation, healthcare and community development projects. Local Indigenous guides accompany all visitor excursions, manage cultural interactions with Quechua people and explain their environmental knowledge of the rainforest. Visitors can spend time with local families, make traditional pottery, learn how *chicha* drink is made from yucca, be spiritually cleansed by a Quechua healer and join a canoe ride to pick up school children. Yachana Lodge won the 2004 *Conde Nast Traveler* ecotourism award (Yachana Lodge, 2004). Profits from Yachana Lodge and the Yachana Gourmet chocolate facility, using locally grown organic cacao, support the Mondana medical clinic and agricultural projects including a farm and tree nursery. Yachana Lodge and the other related projects employ 54 local community members, with 52% Indigenous Quechua people. Since 1994, FUNEDESIN bought over 3600 acres of rainforest, with donations from Rainforest Concern and individuals that adopted an acre of forest. In 2002, it was declared a protected forest in the buffer zone around Gran Sumaco National Park. Another 150 acres was purchased in 2002 to establish the Amazon Centre for Conservation, Education and Sustainability and provide environmental education courses for teachers and schoolchildren (FUNEDESIN, 2004). Yachana Lodge also set technical standards for ecotourism.

Cofan Indians and Cuyabeno Wildlife Reserve

Tourists have visited the Cofan people since 1978 guided by Randy Borman, the son of American missionaries, who lives as a Cofan chief. Tourists initially joined Cofan hunting trips, but were outraged at the killing of toucans. In 1984, the Cofan moved away from areas used by oil companies to found a new community at Zabalo in the Cuyabeno Wildlife Reserve. The Zabalo community owns and manages over 100,000 ha of forest. In 1993 the Cofan at Zabalo took direct action to stop an illegal oilrig on their territory (Tidwell, 1996). An ecotourism venture was developed at Zabalo to help preserve the rainforest. This attracted mainly US visitors brought in by Wilderness Travel (Wunder, 2000). Randy Borman established a community-run tourism company with ten Cofan families that together built four tourist cabins and walking trails. Community members gained income from handicraft sales, as canoe drivers and guides, maintenance and construction workers. Other Cofan groups sold their crafts to Zabalo for resale in their tourist craft market (Borman, 1999).

Ecotourism income at Zabalo provided $500 annually for each Cofan person (Blangy, 1999). Since 1991, up to four groups with 12 tourists from a large Ecuador tour operator were brought to Zabalo twice a week. Zabalo hosted 3000 visitors annually, most on day visits to the interpretation centre and craft market. Some 200 visitors a year went on 10-day forest trekking programmes with Cofan guides (Borman, 1999). The Cofan tourism operations include community-owned and managed cabins, a community enterprise by Randy Borman, a joint venture and private tourist cabins built by Cofan in other areas of the reserve (Wesche and Drumm, 1999). Zabalo has formed a joint venture with Transturi for Aguarico Trekking, with 9/10 days of trekking with Cofan guides for US$2300. Transturi market the trek and provide transport. Profits from the trek are shared 50/50. Twice a week, tourists from the Transturi floating hotel visit the Zabalo Museum, join a guided jungle walk (US$2) and buy handicrafts (Wunder, 2000). On a forest trek, tourists are lifted up on a treetop rope and pulley system for views over the forest canopy. To support conservation, the Cofan zoned their territory into subsistence hunting areas with a monthly quota set for each family and an ecotourism area where no hunting was allowed (Wesche, 1996). Fines were levied for overhunting or killing key wildlife species such as toucans and parrots. A community turtle nursery project has also reintroduced over 4000 young turtles to the river. Key tourism issues were legalizing Zabalo as a travel agency; marketing trips and communication with tour operators (Borman, 2001). Tourist arrivals at Zabalo have declined as communities nearby developed similar ventures with cheaper access for tour operators (Drumm, 1998; Buckley, 2003c). At Misahualli, a town in the Ecuadorian Amazon and departure point for 50% of jungle tours, about 10% of Quechua Indians work in tourism, with 60 guides and a few canoe operators, while none owned tourist hostels (de Bont and Janssen, 2002).

Indigenous ecotourism income in Cuyabeno Reserve

The Cuyabeno Wildlife Reserve was created in 1979 to preserve biodiversity and allow sustainable resource to benefit Indigenous groups living in the area (Hinojosa, 1992; Dunn, 1995). Lobbying from tourism operators and Indian groups saw the Cuyabeno Reserve extended in 1991. Wunder (2000) evaluated the economic benefits and conservation incentives of ecotourism at three Indigenous communities in Cuyabeno Reserve – Zabalo (Cofan), Puerto Bolivar/San Pablo (Siona-Secoya) and Zancudo/Playas de Cuyabeno (Quechua). Some 14–20 Ecuadorian travel agencies operate in the Reserve visited by 5000 tourists a year since 1991 when the Reserve doubled in size to 400,000 ha. The Cofan at Zabalo independently provides local tourist services and has a trekking joint venture with the agency Transturi. At Puerto Bolivar and San Pablo, community members provide canoe and accommodation services. The Siona people at Puerto Bolivar guide rainforest walks where tourists sleep on raised platforms with sleeping pads and mosquito nets purchased by the Rainforest Action Network using tourism income (MLF, 2004a). The Secoyas at San Pablo have signed a Letter of Agreement with the agency Etnotur covering

transport provision and cultural presentations, medical services, donations for local festivals and US$5 for each tourist visiting the community.

Some 39 Quechua people work at Transturi's floating hotel 'Flotel Orellana' on the Aguarico River. In 1994, Zancudo community signed a Letter of Agreement with Transturi where the company provides tourism employment, goods (one head of cattle a month, food items and school uniforms) and services (river and air transport, pay teacher salary and education courses). In return, Zancudo ensured exclusive access for Transturi, protected natural resources and ceased hunting in the tourism area. However, Transturi does not employ native guides, while local employment and cash transfers were reduced due to financial problems. Tourism income mainly derived from wage labour for Transturi (Zancudo 58%, Playas 78%), handicraft sales (Zabalo 34%, but 31% went to Associates profits), canoe transport and tips (San Pablo 27%/24%) and canoe transport and salaries (Puerto Bolivar 46%/20%). Most tourism income derived from salary work, transport provision and cultural services provided for private tour agencies rather than solely community-owned ecotourism. Tourism income as a proportion of total village income was 100% (Zabalo), 95% (Zancudo) and 80–90% (Puerto Bolivar) for natural areas, with hunter gather lifestyles and small-scale subsistence agriculture. Tourism income in degraded natural areas was lower at Playas (25–35%) and San Pablo (15–25%) where cattle ranching, agricultural crops (coffee, cocoa) and timber sales provided other income (Wunder, 2000).

Conservation benefits of ecotourism included greater environmental awareness and bans on subsistence hunting in tourism zones at Zabalo, in the Cuyabeno lake area by Sionas of Puerto Bolivar. It also reduced time for hunting at Zancudo, with men working at the Transturi floating hotel.

Siona-Secoya hunters reported illegal poaching and protected rare species in the Reserve (Hinojosa, 1992). The monthly cattle transfer by Transturi was a protein substitution scheme at Zancudo, but other sheep were eaten rather than bred. Handicrafts and food sales provide income but increase local use of wood or feathers and cleared farmland. At Playas and San Pablo, ecotourism income occurs in natural areas away from the villages and has not reduced local land use for commercial agriculture. Recently, Indigenous groups, tour operators and environmentalists formed the Association for the Defence of Cuyabeno, gaining a Presidential Decree to stop oil exploration in the eastern Imuya zone.

Huaorani Indians and Tropic Ecological Adventures

The Huaorani people live in and around Yasuni National Park, a UNESCO Biosphere Reserve. Conflicts with tour groups have seen outboard motors and cameras confiscated by the Huaorani. Tour operators and guides also resisted attempts by the Huaorani to organize payment of tourist fees. Fees of US$50–$100 to enter Huaorani territory were often not paid by guides, delayed or competitively negotiated with individuals (Smith, 1993; Braman, 2002). In 1995, a tour company based in Quito, Tropic Ecological Adventures, established a partnership with one Huaorani village at Quehueri'ono. The community sought an economic alternative to working as labourers for oil companies. After nine months of negotiation, a tourist cabin was built in the forest 45 minutes away from the community. Tropic brought eight tourists once a month for a stay of up to 6 days. The tour operator used Huaorani canoes, drivers and guides and trained local cooks to prepare food. Only manioc, papaya and bananas were purchased locally to minimize impacts on local food. Visitor fees and salaries for tourist services were paid at a community meeting when each tour group arrived. Money was shared equally among families, with an extra US$5 per person paid to a Huaorani organization. Visitors donated money for training workshops, solar panels and radios and helped establish the Accion Amazonia Foundation (Drumm, 1998; Buckley, 2003d). Tropic's 'Amazon Headwaters with the Huaorani' tour won the 1997/1998 ToDo award for socially responsible ecotourism operator and best ecotourism programme. Some 10% of profits at Tropic Ecological Adventures are donated to environmental

programmes including the Huaorani People's Organization (ONHAE) and the Huaorani at Quehueri'ono. However, the Huaorani visit was combined with a trip to the Galapagos Islands, as the community-based ecotourism programme was less marketable or profitable on its own. The Huaorani airstrip was also closed while competition increased between Amazon operators in 1999/2000 due to political instability (PPT, 2001). Tropic Ecological Adventures also promoted Indigenous ecotours with the Cofan (Zabalo), Achuar (Kapawi Lodge) and the Quichua (Huacamayos) (Tropic Ecological Adventures, 2004).

Huaorani Indians and Bataburo lodge

Bataburo lodge, opened in 1997, was a partnership between Huaorani Indians and Kempery Tours, a Swiss-Ecuadorian travel agency. The lodge and a canopy tower were located on the Tiguino River in Huaorani Reserve, 90 km from the town of Coca (Puerto Francisco de Orellana). In 1996, Kempery Tours signed a contract with the Federation of the Huaorani (ONAHE) to build a tourist lodge that would be handed over to the Huaorani people in 15 years. Half of the tourist entrance fee went to the Huaorani village of Tiguino and half to the Federation. Under pressure from oil exploration companies, tourism provided alternative income for the 2200 Huaorani people. The 4–10 day tours featured Huaorani or Quechua guides interpreting the rainforest, wildlife and Huaorani culture including blowpipes and the use of forest plants for weapons, houses and medicinal remedies. The traditional Huaorani village of Bameno with chief Kem Pere was also visited (Kempery Tours, nd). The small village of 50 people still used blowpipes to hunt monkeys, macaws and tapir for food. Roads, logging and oil had more impacts than local Huaorani hunting of these animals (Foster Parrots, 2003).

Achuar Indians and Kapawi Lodge

The Kapawi Lodge is a partnership between a private tour operator, Canodros S.A. and the Federation of Ecuadorian Achuar Nationalities

(FINAE), representing five communities. It is located in the 5000 km² Kapawi Ecological Reserve in a remote rainforest area near the border with Peru. The lodge has 20 waterfront cabins built over a lagoon. The facility uses solar power, biodegradable soap, a septic system, electric canoe motors and raised boardwalks, with recyclable waste flown out by plane. Some 150 Achuar people were hired to build the lodge with jungle materials and no metal nails were used in construction. The lodge opened in 1996 and employs 22 Achuar (70% of staff) including three Spanish-speaking Achuar guides. Canodros is training Achuar staff in lodge management and language skills. Tourists visit nearby Achuar villages for local meals, *chicha* drink, shamanic rituals, buy handicrafts and try using a blowgun. In 1998, 520 tourists visited Kapawi on a package deal with 11 operators. The lodge operator, Canodros, pays US$2000 per month to FINAE for land rental and usage rights, with a yearly increase of 7%, plus US$10 per tourist. Tourism income is divided between the five Achuar communities in FINAE. In return, the Achuar provide access to airstrips, provide building materials and labour, limit hunting to areas outside the ecotourism zone and share their environmental knowledge. With a total development cost of US$2 million, Kapawi was the most expensive ecotourism project in the Amazon Basin of Ecuador (Rodriguez, 1999, 2000). The Kapawi Lodge made a profit for the first time in 2001, five years after it opened in 1996. Full management of Kapawi Lodge will be given to the Achuar by 2011 (Wesche and Drumm, 1999). Achuar have teamed up with an NGO, Pachamama Alliance, to create a GIS profile of the area and promote ecotourism at Kapawi Lodge. The lodge operation has prompted other NGOs to develop education, communication and transportation services for the Achuar (Kapawi Ecolodge, 2004). The Achuar and Shuar peoples oppose oil drilling in their tribal territories (Forero, 2004; Krenke and Murillo, 2005).

Ikiam Shiwiar

The Ikiam Shiwiar community ecotourism project in the province of Pastaza began in 2001. The 67,000 ha Shiwiar territory between the Rio Conambo and Rio Corrientes rivers has six communities. The 659 Shiwiar people, related to the Achuar, have their own tribal organization, ONSHIPAE. The lowland rainforest and lagoons in the Shiwiar region include macaws, parrots, caimans, capybaras, monkeys and collared peccaries. The Shiwiar provided a 6-day tour at US$200, with accommodation in cabins, boat transport, a guide, meals and canoe trips. This community-managed project aimed to use tourism income to help preserve the forest and wildlife in Shiwiar territory. From 2000–2004, research teams from the UK and Ecuador conducted a Shiwiar ethno-biological study. This assisted tourism, as they employed Shiwiar guides and helped fund ONSHIPAE. A workshop on tourism held in three communities found some Shiwiar were not sure what a tourist was or thought they would lose control of their tribal territory (Redturs, nd; SRI, 2004). Ecotourism depends on community support.

Quijos river valley

The Quijos river valley in eastern Ecuador is a gateway to the Amazon region. The scenic mountain landscapes of this river valley are 94% covered by ecological and biosphere reserves.

The Quijos township municipality is promoting ecotourism development in this valley area. In the area above 3200 m are common lands belonging to three Quechua communities located in two reserves on the Antisana and Cayambe volcanoes. The communities of El Tambo, Jamanco and Oyacachi make communal land-use decisions and maintain an open grassland landscape with grazing. They have also ventured into tourism, with El Tambo running horseback tours around Artisana volcano, while Jamanco and Oyacachi built basic thermal resorts to attract visitors. These communities lacked finance, access to visitor markets or business and English language training. Hence, this limited their community tourism as most visitors went to private reserves and ecolodges. Water extraction projects and other damaging land use practices also threatened communal lands. The protected areas of Quijos river valley needed to recognize unique Quechua cultural links with this landscape and promote these as part of rural ecotourism in the tropical Andes of Ecuador (Marglin, 1995; Brown and Mitchell, 2000; Sarmiento *et al.*, 2000; Chaurette *et al.*, 2003).

Runa Tupari

Runa Tupari is a Quechua-owned travel company based in the city of Cotacachi. Key natural features in this area of the Andes were the Cotacachi Volcano, Cuicocha Lake and the 24,000 ha Cotacachi-Cayapas Ecological Reserve. This reserve extended from a tropical zone at 300 m up to 4939 m in the high Andes. There were over 500 bird species, including the Andean condor, and 20,000 plant species, including the biggest orchid flower in the world. Guided tours of this area by Runa Tupari included guesthouse accommodation (US$20 a night) at four rural Quechua communities. The Cotacachi Farmers Organisation Union (UNORCAC) started this community tourism project in 2001. In the Quechua language, Runa Tupari means 'meeting the indigenous population'. The Runa Tupari travel agency was co-owned by UNORCAC, Quechua communities, the Native Guides Association and a Lodges Association. The tours visited volcanic crater lakes and waterfalls, with Quechua music, rituals, mats woven from totara plants and weaving shawls also demonstrated. Runa Tupari Native Travel trained the guides who lived at the local Quechua communities (Redturs, nd; Runa Tupari, nd).

Other Quechua tours of the Andes were available at the Pulingui Santa Ana Tourist Centre, near the city of Riobamba and the Chimborazo Fauna Reserve, and at Caranqui village in La Esperanza.

Peru

Posada Amazonas

This rainforest lodge in the Amazon region of Peru is a joint venture between a Peruvian tour company, Rainforest Expeditions and a community landholding group, the Native Community of Infierno (CNI), representing 80 families of the indigenous Ese'eja people and mestizo migrant groups that lived along the Tambopata River. A tourism joint venture agreement was signed in May 1996 with 60% of profits to CNI and 40% to the company with management divided 50/50. Several Ese'eja had worked for Rainforest Expeditions and in 1995 they lobbied for a tourism lodge in their area, in the buffer zone of Tambopata National Reserve. The Infierno community owned the land and infrastructure and provided labour for their 60% share of revenue from the Posada lodge until 2018 (IFC, 2004). Rainforest Expeditions has exclusive ecotourism rights at Posada Amazonas with CNI members unable to establish a competing community or individual tourism venture. After 20 years, the entire lodge operation will belong to CNI (Stronza, 1999; Nycander, 2000; Nycander and Holle, nd). The contract also specified the land-use terms, the rights and obligations of either party, the role of the community ecotourism committee, shared responsibility for decision-making and conflict resolution procedures (Holle, 1998). A 2000 ha communal nature reserve was declared around the lodge, with locals limiting their use in exchange for jobs and a share of profits (Ramirez, 2001a). A grant from the McArthur Foundation and a loan from the Peru-Canada fund were used for lodge construction and community training (Stronza, 1999).

Posada Amazonas lodge opened in 1998. The 30-room lodge is built of palm, bamboo and other forest materials. The venture also includes a 40 m tower to observe the rainforest canopy, forest trails and a catamaran. The lodge staff and guides are mainly community members, while cultural activities include ethnobotanical walks and visiting local farms (RE (Rainforest Expeditions), 2004). The Posada Amazonas lodge is a 3-hour boat ride from the city of Puerto Maldonado and a stopover for 40–50 tourists a day that travel up the Tambopata River, a tributary of the Amazon system. Rainforest Expeditions already operated a lodge, Tambopata Research Centre 5 hours upriver located near a large macaw clay-lick featured in *National Geographic*. The Tambopata Reserve covers

15,000 km^2, with intact cloud forest and the watershed of three rivers in the Amazon (Buckley, 2003e). Some 10,000 tourists annually visited the Tambopata area (Holle, 1998).

Posada Amazonas lodge provides an overnight stop for ecotourists on their way to Bahuaja-Sonene National Park. Rainforest Expeditions chose the CNI area as the only native titled community in an area with colonists and a prime area for viewing rare species like the giant otter and harpy eagle. The CNI area was in a buffer zone for the national park with limits on forest extraction and agricultural expansion. The 80 CNI families are spread over 10,000 ha of forest along the Tambopata River and received title to this land in 1976 (RE, 2004). Legal title to land areas was essential for ecolodges and nature conservation (Yu et al., 1997). The lodge is located half-a-day's paddle by dugout canoe from the community centre. Some local NGOs were opposed to the Ese'eja agreement with a private company and community members needed more time to discuss the project. Women were not informed about the tourism agreement signed by men. NGOs and legal staff from a local Indigenous federation explained the legal details of the contract to community members. Key project staff visited families, using graphs to explain the tourism business and their role as partners, while an anthropologist gave several families disposable cameras to record what local attractions they wanted tourists to see and activities or areas not open to tourists (Holle, 1998; Stronza, 2000, 2005).

The CNI community formed a ten-person ecotourism coordination committee to organize community labour and oversee construction of the lodge. Groups worked in weekly rotation, to clear forest, weave palm thatch (20 families), cut wood (15 families) and collect wild cane (10 families) while 65 families installed posts, laid floorboards and cut forest trails (Holle, 1998; Nycander and Holle, nd). Community members worked in the lodge for wages, or sold food, materials and crafts. Other benefits were a competitive income ($65/month more than other lodges), improved nutrition and new skills. In 2000 lodge profits of $14,000 were distributed among the 80 families of CNI

(Ramirez, 2001a). The lodge employed over 50 local people who earned 38% more from tourism than farming or hunting. People who gained tourism income were clearing less forest areas for agriculture and hunting fewer animals or less often. Other people sold Brazil nuts, fish, food crops, timber, fuel wood, charcoal, game meat or pelts and raised cattle for income. Goods were transported 20 km by truck on a dirt road to Puerto Maldonado. On average, CNI household income from extracting natural resources equalled ecotourism income. Some people talked about using tourist income to buy chainsaws and motorized boats that would facilitate clearing or hunting. The extraction of timber and palm increased to build the lodge, but these areas naturally regenerated (Pani, nd; Stronza, nd).

CNI members have slowly taken on the new role of owners and active partners in managing Posada Amazonas as a community venture. The World Bank provided $50,000 for an Artisans Rediscovery Project to improve local crafts made for sale. However, tourism focused on traditional Ese'eja culture caused ethnic tensions at the end of 1999. The mestizo and non-Ese'eja CNI members had become the main lodge workers, while the Ese'eja wanted to form a separate urban community to control their own future. Rainforest Expeditions made a decision to give equal representation of 50/50 to ethnic groups at Posada lodge (Yoshihara, 2000; Gardner, 2001). In March 2005, Posada Amazonas and US partners hosted a 1-week ecolodge planning and management course, with the lodge regarded as a leading model of business and community-based ecotourism (Epler Wood, 2004; Pyke and Stronza, 2004; Stronza, 2005).

Wildlife species and key habitats have been protected as key ecotourism resources in the CNI area. The 1996 lodge contract prohibited the Ese'eja hunting wildlife species of interest to tourists, such as jaguar, macaws, harpy eagles and otters (Nycander and Holle, nd). Community members located four harpy eagle nests and nests for other raptors such as crested eagles, hawk eagles and king vultures. The endangered harpy eagle is highly sought after by birdwatchers. Tourists returning from Tambopata Research Centre stopped at

Posada to view a harpy eagle nest. Local people who found a harpy eagle nest became a guardian, protecting the site and recording eagle activity with a fee paid every time tourists visited a nest. The community also conserved forest areas within an 800-m radius of the nest and 500 m on either side of access trails, protecting 600 ha. When seven more harpy eagle nests were discovered, the community ecotourism committee decided that guardians had to clear and maintain the shortest trail to the nest and only received a tourist fee for nests actually visited. Forest around lakes with giant river otters and forest in front of a parrot and macaw clay-lick was protected with hunting banned around three mammal clay-licks (Holle, 1998). Community attitudes to wildlife and conservation changed due to ecotourism at Posada Amazonas. The harpy eagle became a community symbol while locals ceased hunting macaws for food (Yoshihara, 2000).

Machiguenga Center for Tropical Research

The Machiguenga Center for Tropical Research is a rainforest lodge on the Urubamba River in the lowland Amazon region of Peru. It is 100% owned and operated by the Machiguenga Indians of Timpia, who decided to build the lodge in 1997 with funding from Peru Verde, a local conservation NGO and CEDIA, an Indigenous rights group. Two American natural guides spent 3 months training the Machiguenga in tour guiding, English phrases and lodge operations. Tourists ate local food, went on forest walks, visited a macaw and parrot clay-lick, bought handicrafts and listened to storytelling. The lodge, which opened in 2000, aims to generate tourism income while helping to protecting the rainforest from timber harvesting and mining (Royce and Palmer, nd). The lodge is the only accommodation near a spectacular 3-km-long canyon on the Urubamba River, within 400,000 acres of rainforest and cloud forest protected as the Machiguenga Megantoni National Sanctuary. The Machiguenga Timpia Indians, with 829 people in 126 families, are the largest and most politically active of some 22 Indian communities with title to their lands

in the lower Urubamba area (Maud, 2003). The Timpia community owns 89,000 acres of intact rainforest, with three major macaw clay-licks visited by all three large macaw species in the Amazon lowlands. The US McArthur Foundation funded the lodge, with ten rooms, through Peru Verde and the Centre for the Development of the Amazonian Indian (CEDIA), with ongoing advice and training. The US Wildlife Conservation Society funded workshops on tourism training for the Machiguenga people and also wildlife research (MLF, 2004b).

Casa Matsiguenka Lodge

The Casa Matsiguenka Lodge is located in the buffer zone of Manu National Park. The 17,163 km^2 Manu protected area covers 12% of Peru with tropical rainforest in 85% of the park. Manu had 1200 types of butterflies, 1000 bird species, 13 monkey species, giant otters, the harpy eagle, jaguar and black caimans. Macaw clay-licks, lagoons and lakes were other natural attractions. Matsiguenka Indian communities lived in the buffer zone of the park, along the Madre de Dios River.

The Yomibato Indian community built the Casa Matsiguenka Lodge with 24 beds as a joint venture. Cultural activities and guided tours to Salvador Lake and Otorongo Lagoon were offered. The lodge cost US$35 per night. The 300 Yomibato people received 50% of tourism income from the lodge, spent on local education and health facilities (Redturs, nd).

Heath River Wildlife Center

The Heath River Wildlife Center opened in 2002 near the rainforest border with Bolivia. The lodge with six bungalows is owned and operated by the Ese'eja Sonene people who work as guides on wildlife and ethno-botanical tours of the forest. The Peruvian NGO, Peru Verde, donated the lodge to the Ese'eja with support from Tropical Nature, an NGO promoting conservation through ecotourism in Latin America. The lodge, marketed by Tropical Nature Travel (2004a, b), is located near a macaw clay-lick and promotes tourist interaction with the Indigenous Ese'eja rainforest people.

Ampiyacu and Yanamono rivers

Tourist boats from Iquitos (Peru) and Leticia (Colombia) regularly visit Indian communities along tributary rivers of the Amazon. These Indian villages depend on subsistence crops, forest products, hunting and fishing with little cash income. Performing dances and selling handicrafts to visitors on river cruises is a valued income source at Bora, Witotos and Yagua villages on the Ampiyacu River and a Yagua village next to a tourist lodge on the Yanamono River, east of Iquitos (Ingles, 2001). Amazon Tours and Cruises first visited the Boras and Witotos communities in 1973 and in 1992 first visited the Yagua village. These Indian communities host tourists about twice a month for about 2 hours, with 10–40 people in a group mainly from the USA (58%) and Europe (40%). Tourists donated pens, paper, money and books to local schools; traded T-shirts and hats; and bought Indian handicrafts, such as natural fibre hammocks, bags, baskets and paintings on tree bark. Communities are paid $20–50, depending on group size, with money divided among all the dancers. Since 1997, larger cruise ships with 80–100 passengers visited these villages during April and May. On arrival, tourists are taken to a ceremonial roundhouse where villagers explain their lifestyle and perform dances. The communities visited by tourists also used these roundhouses for their own traditional ceremonies. The villagers negotiated with boats the amount of tourists they hosted and the amount of money earned. Without tourist income, the villagers would clear more forested land to grow agricultural crops to sell. Cash was needed for school fees, clothes, food, radios, tools, household items and fuel for generators.

The Yagua community on the Yanamono River, Palmares II, was located opposite a tourist lodge built in 1964 by Explorama Lodges. In 1999, the lodge received 4558 tourists, with 62% from America. Tourists visited the Yagua community to buy handicrafts daily during peak season and once

a week at slow times. In the early 1990s, the village stopped performing dances for tourists to spend more time fishing and growing market crops. Village interest in their ritual ceremonies decreased as elders died. With the help of a researcher and local guide, villagers negotiated with the lodge owner to once again perform dances. The lodge contributed money for materials to construct a new ceremonial roundhouse at Palmares II. The tourist dance performances resumed at the end of 1999 for payment from the lodge, with young people learning dance rituals and maintaining their cultural identity (Ingles, 2001).

Tourism income at these Indian villages helped preserve forested areas by reducing the need to sell timber or clearing more land to grow market crops (Ingles, 2001, 2002). Forest resources also provided natural materials for crafts, while dance performances helped maintain cultural heritage.

Vicos farmstays, Huaraz

The Vicos community was a group of 800 Quechua families living in ten neighbourhoods in the Central Andes of Peru, near the city of Huaraz and the Huascaran Biosphere Reserve. The Quechua lived along the highest mountain range in Peru and used natural resources in the reserve area (Torres, 1996). The Mountain Institute (MI) supported an ecotourism project, funding the building of seven guesthouses next to farmer's houses. The sites were selected for their panoramic views and the diversity of crops at Quechua agricultural sites. The farmers provided their labour and some construction materials. Visitors were to be rotated among the guesthouses, with a maximum stay of 3 days at one site. TMI provided training for farmers on visitor services, but there were no English language guides. Agro-ecotourism, mountain climbing with Quechua guides and hot springs were other attractions.

A local NGO, Urpichallay, collected cultural information on local crops and assisted in the project. A communal visitor centre in the Vicos community charged visitor fees (Ramirez, 2001a). This Cuyaquihuayi tourism project in Vicos commenced in 2001 and the first tourists visited in 2002. It cost tourists US$25 per day to visit the Vicos community. Tourism profits went to communal projects (Mountain Institute, 2005a). The conservation benefits of this ecotourism project were not described.

At Olleros, 30 km from Huaraz, lama treks went 37 km along an old Inca trail to Chavin de Huantar. Twelve local people formed a tourism group, purchased lamas and hosted tourists at their houses (Redturs, nd)

Humacchuco homestay tourism, Huaraz

The Mountain Institute also developed Humacchuco homestay tourism on the border of the Huascaran Biosphere Reserve, as part of their Andes community tourism programme. It was the first tourism project in the Cordillera Blanca of Peru with lodging and guides provided by Quechua Indians. For US$30 per person per night, tourists stayed in five guesthouses built near a Quechua family in the community of Unidos Venceremos. The guesthouses were built in 2000, while the first tourists arrived in 2001. Visitor activities included hiking on mountain trails to forests, lakes and ruins, music, cultural activities, crafts such as basketwork, wool blankets and textiles dyed with local plants and joining agricultural work. Local food and drink was provided, including roast guinea pig (cuy), sold to visitors in a tourist centre at Lake Chinancocha (Mountain Institute, 2005b). Since 1999, The Mountain Institute developed community conservation and ecotourism projects with Quechua villages in Huarascan Reserve. The new Andean School for Mountain Studies hosted study tours to Humacchuco, Vicos, and other sites.

Inca nani (Inca road) project

The Inca road was a stone highway, 27 feet wide, built throughout the vast Inca Empire across present-day Ecuador and Peru (Muller, 2000). The Andes in Peru has one of the best remaining sections of this Inca road. This mountain area of Peru area is poor, underdeveloped and home to descendants of the Inca, the Quechua people. The Mountain Institute is developing a community tourism project based around the Inca road, known as Inca nani in the local Quechua dialect. The Great Inca Trail project was started by IUCN to protect the archaeological sites. In 2003, The Mountain Institute held consultation workshops with local Quechua villages along the Inca road between Yauya and Huanunco Viejo. In 2004/05, American tourists hiked the Inca road, providing feedback on the experience and visitor services in the local villages. This community tourism project aimed to preserve the Inca road and provide income for the Quechua (Mountain Institute, 2005c).

Taquile Island, Lake Titicaca

Taquile is a small island of 754 ha inhabited by 1850 mainly Quechua people. The island is 3–4 hours by boat from the regional capital of Puno. The community lives by agriculture, fishing and selling woven textiles with traditional and environmental designs made from alpaca or sheep wool. Up until 1990, the Taquile community controlled most tourism services (i.e. entrance fee, boat transport, restaurants and guesthouses) and all stages of textile weaving sold through two community-run artisan stores. The woven textiles had a fixed price and community law prohibited private sales to tourists. Island committees managed daily tourist services such as accommodation, transportation, weaving, food and a reception group to meet arrivals and collect the entrance fee of 1 sol (40 cents). In 1996, while 86% of Taquile residents gained tourism income, 74% of tourism revenue went to restaurants (nine private, one community-owned) and 19 boat owners (four 'cooperatives' and 15 private), with 16% earned from tourist lodging and craft sales. By 1997, the Taquile operated only 19 of 62 boats used for tourist transport, charging just $8 for a round trip, while Puno agencies charged $45. In the 1980s, islanders had an official monopoly of boat transport with families sharing boat ownership and management (Healy and Zorn, 1983a, b). A Peruvian anti-monopolization law in the early 1990s affected Taquile community self-management as outsiders took over transport and guide services. There was 91% leakage of gross tourism revenue while islanders purchased boat motors, fuel, food and wool supplies from Puno or outsiders (Mitchell, 1998, 2001, 2004; Mitchell and Eagles, 2001; Mitchell and Reid, 2001). The conservation benefits of ecotourism on Taquile Island were not mentioned in the reports.

Tourists also visit floating reed islands in the Bay of Puno, on the western side of Lake Titicaca, home of the Uru people. Some 2500 Urus are claimed to live on 45 islands in the bay. Attractions include Uru houses and canoes woven of totara reeds, and the brightly coloured clothing of women who also wear bowler hats. The Uru sell handicrafts and receive tips for posing in photographs. However, Uru people stopped living on the islands full-time some 50 years ago. According to a Bolivian tour operator, the Uru dress in traditional clothing for tourist day-jobs on the floating islands, then return to their homes in the city of Puno. The Uru use tourist income to buy modern appliances and clothing. Instead of native spirituality based on nature, the Uru were converted to Christianity (Tidwell, 2001). While the Uru people gained income from tourism, the conservation benefits were not described. The islands of Anapia and Yuspiqui, with 1200 Indian people, provided boat transportation, guesthouse accommodation, food and guided tours. This tourism project began in 1997 as a business alliance between the Anapia community and a tour operator in Puno, All Ways Travel. At Llachon community above Lake Titicaca, a local Quechua man provided visitor accommodation and tours (Redturs, nd).

Chile

Mapuche ethnic tourism

There are over 1 million Mapuche Indigenous people in southern Chile. The Mapuche live in the high Andes Mountains, depending on native forest resources and agriculture for their livelihood. The *Araucaria* monkey-puzzle tree or *pewen* is an important source of food seeds and wood for Mapuche in the mountain forests. The term Mapuche means 'people of

the land' and covers several sub-groups such as the Mapuche Pehuenche. Some 500,000 Mapuche people (Pehuenche and Huilliche) in southern central Chile still live in close association with forests. Commercial logging of native forests and conversion of their traditional lands to private or industrial landownership threatens the Mapuche. Two thousand reservations in the 1970s were reduced to just 665 by the 1980s. A new Indigenous Law passed in 1993 prohibited land sales; but people used gaps in the law to still buy Mapuche land. Forest conservation and cultivating seedlings in nurseries for reforestation of cleared areas were a priority for the Mapuche (Herrman, 2005). Indigenous land claims and timber plantations provided impetus for ecotourism and other forest resources as alternative ways for the Mapuche to derive income (Armesto *et al.*, 2001). WWF also supported the Mapuche in forest-based ecotourism businesses, helping to conserve coastal temperate rainforests threatened by logging (WWF, 2004).

A rural tourism project was also developed for ten Mapuche families in the Antonio Hueche community, based around agriculture and cultural performances held in a *ruca* or traditional house, with local homestay accommodation provided. The Institute for Agricultural Development and Indigenous Corporation (CONIDA) supported this Mapuche ethnic tourism project that began in 1998. Swedish tourists visited Weche-Ruca or traditional house to experience Mapuche culture in Chile. This project employed local people as guides, entertainers and in crafts, funding bathrooms and education for families. It was also part of the Chilean Association for Rural Tourism (WTO, 2003c).

Bolivia

Chalalan Ecolodge

The 1.8 million hectare Madidi National Park in the Bolivian Amazon is the location of the Chalalan Ecolodge, reached with a 4–6-hour boat ride along the Tuichi River and 1-hour walk through forest. The local Quechua-Tacana community of San Jose de Uchupiamonas started the lodge in 1995 with a US$1.45 million grant from the Inter-American Development Bank. Conservation International (CI) provided training for local staff in lodge management, marketing, food preparation, guiding and wildlife monitoring. In 2001, CI transferred all shares, giving full control and ownership of the lodge to the San Jose community (Cahill, 2004). Some 74 local families receive income from employment at the ecolodge (CI, 2004a). The lodge accommodates 24 visitors in three local-style cabins, with solar-powered running water, and views of Chalalan Lake. Three hundred and forty bird species were found in this area (Redturs, nd). Activities include canoe trips and guided forest walks, with 25 km of hiking trails in Madidi National Park. Wildlife includes monkeys, peccaries, macaws and jaguar. Tourists also visit local wood carvers such as Pascual Valdez who sells caiman, hawk and jaguar carvings. The ecolodge provides employment and income for local families, as an economic alternative to logging and hunting. About 40 villagers manage and own the ecotourism business (Pyke and Stronza, 2004). Families who helped build Chalalan receive $80 per year, while 50% of tourism revenue funds community health and education services. Tourism income bought a satellite dish and antenna for radio and telephone communication plus a new middle school with a computer and solar panel. The new school and tourism work at Chalalan Ecolodge saw locals returning to San Jose village (ENS, 1999; Buckley, 2003f; Rome 2003a, b; CI, 2004a). Chalalan Lodge was promoted on Conservation International's Ecotravel Centre.

Mapajo Ecolodge

The Mapajo Ecolodge is located at the community of Asuncion de Quiquibey within the Pilon Lajas Indigenous Territory and Biosphere Reserve of 400,000 ha. The community of 280 people was from Moseten and Chiman (Shimanes) Indigenous groups. The Mapajo Indigenous ecotourism project and ecolodge was developed during 1999–2001 by PRAIA, an Ecuador NGO

supporting Amazon Indigenous groups. The Asuncion de Quiquibey community provided materials and labour for the ecolodge while Canada, Britain and France provided aid funding and technical assistance for the US$185,496 project in the UNESCO Man and the Biosphere programme (Schulze, nd). A website for Mapajo Ecolodge in Spanish and English features 4-, 5- and 6-night package tours (Mapajo, nd). Both Mapajo Ecolodge and Chalalan Ecolodge are promoted as part of Madidi.com, set up in 1998 by a US biologist to promote Indigenous ecotourism in the Madidi region of Bolivia (Madidi.com, 2004). Other Aymara and Quechua people provided 1-day tours of rainforest areas and community enterprise projects at Rurrenabaque, in the external zone of Pilon Lajas Reserve. The communities received 21% of tourism income, with other costs for transportation, lunch, taxes and travel agents. The National Academy of Science of Bolivia supported these tours at Rurrenabaque (Redturs, nd).

Che Guevara Trail

The new Che Guevara Trail in south-east Bolivia follows the path taken by the revolutionary leader on his last journey. It runs from the regional city of Santa Cruz to Vallegrande and then ends at La Higuera where Che Guevara died in 1967. The trail crosses seven remote municipalities in Santa Cruz and Chuquisaca, poor rural areas of Brazil. The project aimed to help 500 Guarani Indigenous families living along the route. Local people were employed as official guides on the trail, provided visitor services such as food and accommodation, sold crafts and produce and worked on cultural projects. A part of each person's salary went towards local community projects. The Bolivia office of CARE International managed this project, which it intended to hand over to the local community. The British Department for International Development (DFID) and Bolivian Ministry for Tourism provided US$610,000 to fund this Trail. Since 2001, tourism facilities were improved along the route with the Che Guevara Trail launched in October 2004. The trail aimed to draw international tourists to a rural area of Bolivia, and also to help revive the tourism industry affected by riots in La Paz when the Bolivian President was deposed in 2003 (*Developments*, 2004). The Foundation for Cultural, Historical and Ethno-ecotourism Development was established to manage this ecotourism project in the Santa Cruz region. Bolivia has promoted ethno-ecotourism since 1994, by linking natural areas with local culture for sustainable tourism development (Schluter, 2001).

Agua Blanca Lodge and Lagunillas Lodge, Apolobamba

The Agua Blanca Lodge and the Lagunillas Lodge were located in Andean villages at 3600 m in the Apolobamba protected area, 360 km from the capital city of La Paz. Quechua and Kallawaya ethnic groups lived in this mountain region. The lodges provided a base for trekking tours in the high Andes. Archaeological sites, local handicrafts, textile crafts and diverse bird species were other attractions. At Agua Blanca, local people built the lodge and formed an association for tour guides and porters. Other local associations managed ecotourism at Agua Blanca Lodge and the Yurax Uno museum. Technical assistance, support and training for local people at Agua Blanca and Lagunillas were provided by COBIMI, a Bolivian NGO focused on biodiversity conservation (Redturs, nd).

Venezuela

Pemon people and Angel Falls

In Venezuela, the Indigenous Pemon people host 100 visitors a day at Angel Falls, the highest waterfall in the world. The tourists fly in from a beach resort on Margarita Island. The Pemon guide visitors to the falls and serve them a meal, receiving $25 per visitor from a package costing $70. The Pemon also built ten traditional cabins situated one hour from their village to accommodate overnight groups, with tourism income funding a local school and health clinic. A state-run hydroelectric

company, Edelca, is promoting 'mucoposadas' or guesthouses among the Pemon indigenous communities to develop ecotourism. This is supported by the Venezuela NGO Tropical Andes, founded in 1997, funded by the EU, a Spanish NGO and the Andean Development Corporation ($1.4 million), with 11 guesthouses operating in the Andean highlands. Campesinos (peasants) from the Andean highlands recently shared their hosting experiences with the Pemon (Marquez, 2004). Angel-Eco Tours also set aside 5% of their annual income for Indigenous groups living in Canaima National Park to maintain Pemon cultural practices and build community facilities (WTO, 2003b).

Amazonas region

In 1994, Canadian agencies funded a workshop on Indigenous People in Ecotourism, attended by 70 Amazonian Indians. From this, the Amazonas native organization ORPIA published a Canadian First Nations training manual for Indigenous communities to retain control of ecotourism (Walker, 1996; Gines, 1999). In the Amazonas region, there are conflicts between tour operators visiting Indigenous groups, while tourist camps and lodges are illegally built on Indian land (Colchester and Watson, 1995). During 1996 to 1998, the Canadian International Development Research Centre provided funding of CAD$261,720 to develop Indigenous ecotourism in the southern Amazonas region of Venezuela. This region included some 60,000 Indigenous people from 19 Indigenous nations who comprised 70% of the population and were affected by uncontrolled tourism impacts and resource development. An anthropologist held workshops in eight pilot communities to develop a code of ethics for ecotourism and environmental best practice criteria. An Ethnocultural Council was recommended to ensure that ecotourism was in agreement with local culture; and another Council of Representatives with a member of each family to ensure that ecotourism activities were carried out. The IRDC project focused on impact assessment rather than technical training or business skills. Four Indigenous communities participated in a pilot ecotour from 22 October to 5 November 1998. The group of seven tourists travelled in a motorized canoe, ate local food (e.g. alligator, piranha, cassava and manioc), traded for handicrafts and watched traditional dances and a blowgun competition. Consultants on the trip recommended training in business management, accounting, food preparation for special diets and local guides learning English (Shore, 1999). Other conservation benefits were not mentioned.

On the Carua River, the Ye'Kuanas people had their rights recognized by the government to manage a forest reserve. They built guest cabins and hosted tourists from a Caracas tour agency (Blangy, 1999). There are 17 Indigenous groups in the northern Amazonas region of Venezuela. Seventy-five per cent of land in the Caura River Basin is the territory of the Yek'wana people, with ecotourism and crafts promoted as new sources of income (Flores, 2005). Amazonas was developing as a new ecotourism destination. Key attractions included Angel Falls, 40% of bird species, 43 National parks and 31 Indigenous tribes. An ecotourism expo and trade show of ecotourism products was held in Venezuela in 2002/03 and 2005. It also promoted best practices to protect natural areas and help local communities benefit from ecotourism (Expoecoturismo, 2005).

Colombia

Tourist boats from Leticia in southern Colombia regularly visit Indian communities along tributary rivers of the Amazon. The Amacayacu park and visitor centre is located 65 km from Leticia. This park has the largest area of tropical rainforest in the Colombian portion of the Amazon. Indian guides and interpreters from the local Tikuna culture provide rainforest tours, boat transportation, food, cultural shows and hammock beds in the four local communities of El Vergel, Mocagua, Macedonia and Palmeras. The main activities were hiking, boating, fishing, wildlife and visits to Tikuna Indian villages. The local NGO, Siempre Colombia, supported Indian groups around Amacayacu in developing and managing tourist services to generate alternative income (Redturs, nd).

The Alta Guajira Desert in the far north of Colombia has cactus, lagoons, dunes, the Macuira Hills and 200 km of coastline. This arid Guajira region included the Wayuu ethnic territory and other Indigenous tribes. Twenty five Indigenous families operated ecotours through Kai Ecotravel, providing accommodation on Wayuu farms or hammocks in beach shelters, transportation, food and the sale of Wayuu handicrafts. A German NGO, 'Only one world' supported the development of Kai Ecotravel. Trekking, textile workshops, dance shows and Wayuu festivals were also featured (Redturs, nd).

Guyana

The country of Guyana, a former British colony, has retained 80% of its tropical rainforest. The 850,000 residents only occupy 3% of the land area. There are nine Amerindian tribes that mainly (70%) live in the interior of Guyana, including the Arawak (15,000), Makushi (7000), Wapishanas (6000), Warrau and Patamuna (4700 each), Akawaio (3800), Carib (2700) and others. There are some 50,000 Amerindians, over 6% of Guyana's population (Iwokrama, 2004). Sixteen per cent of Guyana and 77 land areas were designated as Amerindian territory, with Amerindians being the poorest group (Vereecke, 1994). Only 50% of Amerindians had legal title to parts of their customary lands (Forest Peoples Project, nd). In 1999, there were over 75,000 visitors in Guyana. Nature tourism has been promoted since the early 1990s, while a National Plan for Ecotourism Development was prepared for Guyana in 1997 (Ecovision, nd). The rainforest, wildlife and diverse Amerindian groups were key parts of this plan for ecotourism. Developing Indigenous community tourism was a priority area in Guyana (CPEC, 2002), involving negotiations on Indigenous rights in Guyana's protected areas (LaRose, 2004).

Makushi Indians and Iwokrama reserve

Some 6000 Makushi Indians live in the rainforest interior of Guyana. The Guyanese government supports ecotourism as an economic opportunity for Indian groups. The Makushi village of Surama became involved in ecotourism by hosting researchers and students visiting Iwokrama, a 371,000 ha international rainforest reserve established in 1996. The director at Iwokrama research camp coordinated accommodation for visitors at nearby Makushi villages. From 1995, American university students visited Surama village, learning about Makushi culture and rainforest ecology. Payments were made to the community council for accommodation and use of facilities (US$20 per person per day), while individuals were paid for services as cooks, guides and teachers (US$7–10 per day). Makushi men led hunting and fishing tours or demonstrated weaving, while women were paid to demonstrate cassava production and lectured on health and childcare. By 1998, tourism fees were used to build visitor quarters at Surama with a kitchen, toilet and showers. Tourism money also met the needs of older women or mothers of small children with absent male relatives. Hosting visitors at Iwokrama involved 11 Makushi villages, with a maximum of 20 guests at each village. Other projects were a UN-cassava production centre and Oxford University ethno-botany project (Dilly, 2003). Volunteers from the UK also helped build and run ecolodges at Iwokrama to benefit Indian groups.

By 2004, the forest reserve acted as a booking agent and promoted various ecotourism businesses in the Iwokrama forest and Rupununi wetlands. These included a field station with visitor cabins, a new canopy walkway opened in 2003, satellite camps and walking trails. Community ecotourism ventures promoted at Indian villages were a mountain nature trail and cabin 305 metres above Aranaputa village, Surama village and Makushi culture with ancient petroglyphs or rock engravings at Fairview village. With 21 households and 110 mainly Makushi residents, Fairview or Kurupukari was the only Indian village in the forest reserve. Another 13 villages in the North Rupununi District had 3500 residents who were 91% Amerindian (Iwokrama, 2004). Iwokrama forest had 900 tourists in 2004, up from 347 in 2003. A joint venture agreement to manage the Iwokrama

canopy walkway was signed with Community and Tourism Services, a new company set up by Surama village and two private operators, Rock View Lodge and Wilderness Explorers (Iwokrama, 2005a). The company policy was to provide benefits to Indigenous communities, with schools from eight villages visiting the walkway. Rock View Lodge in North Rupununi had few tourism benefits for Annai village (Cattarinich, 2003). The Makushi village of Surama operated the Carahaa Lodge Camp, Surama guesthouse, canoe trips on the Burro Burro River and guided walks in the rainforest, savannah and up Surama Mountain. Tapirs, giant river otters and spider monkeys were key attractions at Surama. A private company, Wilderness Explorers (nd), supported Surama with marketing sales and administration, while tours were operated and managed by Makushi. Part of every tour fee went to a village fund used for community development projects or to pay medical expenses. In 2002, Surama had 445 tourists.

Local community involvement in ecotourism and links with the private sector were key parts of the new ecotourism development strategy for Iwokrama (Maud, 2003). Twenty-five local Indian people were trained as Iwokrama Rangers, while another 13 people from North Rupununi were trained as licensed tour guides in 2003.

The Canadian International Development Agency (CIDA) funded the community tourism programme at Iwokrama including tour guide training, the new canopy walkway, Surama lodge and the nature trail at Aranaputa. The Iwokrama canopy walkway was the first private sector–community partnership in Guyana (Olsder, 2004). The Iwokrama Centre, since 2002, also worked with the North Rupununi District Development Board (NRDDB) to develop the mountain trail at Aranaputa and the village lodge at Surama. These community tourism products were promoted to tour operators, as part of the new strategy for sustainable business development involving Indians in Iwokrama (*Iwokrama Newsletter*, 2003, 2004).

A 1999 survey found over 80% of Amerindians in the Rupununi region lived below the poverty line. An Indian member of NRDDB was only appointed to the Iwokrama

Board in 2002. An ecotourism revolving fund scheme, supported by CIDA, was set up for NRDDB Indian communities to borrow CDN$3000–5000 to set up small-scale ecotourism products linked to conservation (Allicock, 2003). Iwokrama forest derived income from selective timber harvesting, tourism (US$200,000 in 2004) and training services, with a UNDP loan of US$300,000 needed to cover costs (Iwokrama, 2005b).

Project Guyana

Project Guyana is an ecotourism initiative of Foster Parrots, an American NGO committed to the protection and conservation of parrots in their natural habitat. In 2002 and again in 2004, the Director and Chairman of Foster Parrots met with Amerindian people to discuss a new initiative to protect wild parrots and benefit local people in the Rupununi district of southern Guyana. A local MP, who was an Arawak Amerindian and now the Director of Project Guyana, supported this parrot ecotourism. The Indian village of Nappi, at the Kanuku Mountains, set aside 250 square miles of their territory for parrot conservation and this was the site for the first ecolodge, Benab, built in 2005. A local bird group led by a Makushi Indian tour guide also built a small lodge and camping area on Eagle Mountain. This area had five species of macaws, the harpy eagle, the world's largest eagle and giant anteaters. Birder's Exchange donated bird watching equipment to this local Indian bird group. Guyana was one of only two countries in South America that still legally exported parrots and other wildlife. Selling birds and animals provided some income for Amerindians but local wildlife populations were declining. Hence, Foster Parrots supported this local ecotourism project to provide alternative income for Amerindians based on conservation. Ecolodges, camping areas, a bird hide and local crafts were supported. Planting Ete palms and fruit trees used as food by wild macaws, installing nest boxes and rearing chicks for reintroduction were other aspects of this ecotourism project (Foster Parrots, 2004).

Karanambu ranch

Karanambu ranch in the savannah region of Guyana was a well-known ecotourism destination due to the owner's conservation of endangered giant river otters. In 1995, a feasibility study examined the development of a protected area on the ranch linked with development programmes for local Macusi Indian groups. However, the issue of Indian land rights and continued reliance on using natural resources meant a protected area was not feasible. Instead, a scientific research station was established on Karanambu ranch, linked with a smaller nature reserve. This ecotourism development and farming wildlife provided income and employment for local Macusi Indian communities (Shackley, 1998). The type of land use or reserve designation influenced these ecotourism options for Indian groups.

Shell beach

Shell Beach on the north-west Atlantic coast of Guyana is an important nesting area for four species of endangered marine turtles (olive ridley, leatherback, hawksbill and green turtles). Two communities of Arawak and Carib Indians lived at Almond Beach and Gwennie Beach, as subsistence farmers and fishermen, killing turtles for their meat and collecting turtle eggs to sell in local markets. Since 1989, conservation efforts by turtle researchers involved local people in protecting turtle nests at Almond Beach. The Guyana Marine Turtle Conservation Society and WWF Guianas also coordinated sea turtle protection, educational camps and a women's group at Almond Beach making basket liners from coconut fibre or coir. Since 2001, WWF has negotiated with local stakeholders to establish a Shell Beach protected area, with ecotourism regarded as a conservation management tool (Olsder, 2004; Shell Beach Adventures, nd). A social survey and tourism feasibility study were conducted for this (Roberts, 2003; WWF, 2005a).

Suriname

The Republic of Suriname, on the north-east coast of South America, has retained 80% of its tropical Amazon rainforest, more forest than all of Central America. The rainforest in Suriname has 674 bird species, 200 mammal species and 130 species of reptiles. It is part of the Guyana Shield, a biodiversity hotspot. Ninety-five per cent of the population of 450,000 people live in the capital city of Paramaribo, with just 5% living in other small rural villages. A former Dutch colony, Suriname has five Indigenous Amerindian tribes, including the coastal Caribs, Arawaks and the Trios, Wajanas and Akurios living in the interior (Mets, 2005a). Some Amerindians were involved in marine turtle ecotourism at Galibi and rainforest ecotourism át Palumeu in Suriname.

Galibi Nature Reserve

The Galibi Nature Reserve in north-east Suriname has major nesting beaches for marine turtles such as olive ridley, leatherback, hawksbill and green turtles (WWF, 2005b). The 400 ha reserve was declared in 1969 on the ancestral lands of the Indigenous Kalinya people that still lived in this area (Pane, 2004). The local Foundation for Nature Conservation in Suriname (STINASU), WWF Guianas and Dutch NGOs supported the conservation of marine turtles at Galibi reserve. STINASU built a lodge and facilities to support turtle research and ecotourism at Galibi. The reserve can only be visited by boat, with access to the reserve through two Amerindian villages of Carib Indians living at the mouth of the Marowijne River. The 750 Caribs (or Kalinya) mainly lived by fishing and cultivating cassava and other food plants. There was controlled harvesting of marine turtle eggs by the Caribs at Galibi, except the olive ridley which had a total ban, for sale to Javanese communities in Suriname. STINASU managed the Galibi reserve and worked with the two Carib villages that formed their own foundation for sustainable nature management in 1997 (Olsder, 2004). In 2005, this Carib nature foundation received a grant of US$6500 from WWF Guianas to purchase a boat to transport tourists to the reserve. In 2001, WWF (2005c) funded a visitor and activity centre located near both Carib villages. Ecotourism provided jobs for local Caribs who

worked as reserve staff and tour operators, protecting the beaches from poachers of turtle eggs (Lindsay, 2003). The Kalinya people also seek recognition of their land rights, full management of the protected area and local conservation of marine turtles (Pane, 2004).

Palumeu jungle lodge

The jungle lodge at Palumeu, with six cabins built of local materials, was located in the southern interior of Suriname, 270 km from the capital city of Paramaribo. The lodge was built at the junction of the Tapanahony and Palumeu rivers, near Palumeu, an Amerindian village, with 200 residents from the Trios and Wajanas tribes. The Amerindian villagers lived a subsistence lifestyle based on fishing, garden plots and hunting game. Local people worked at the lodge, led boat trips by dugout canoes and guided rainforest treks to Poti Hill. Tourists learnt about the Amerindian lifestyle, tried bow and arrow shooting, bought local crafts and enjoyed traditional Indian music. Other activities were fishing, paddling a canoe, bird watching or visiting gardens. The Trios and Wajanas depended on tourism income to purchase clothes, tools, pots, outboard motors and other necessities (Mets, 2005b). Palumeu was managed by METS, Movement for Ecotourism in Suriname, a travel company established since 1962. The jungle lodge was developed with the approval of the Amerindian villagers. This company promoted community ecotourism at Palumeu village, working towards local management of the lodge. The village received part of the income from each tour as a cash donation. They worked with Dutch donor agencies, supporting a school, medical clinic, freezer, hydroelectricity and sustainable agriculture projects, handicrafts and an Indian artist at Palumeu village. Palumeu jungle lodge was marketed in the Netherlands, Switzerland, UK and Curaçao (Netherlands Antilles) (Mets, 2005c).

French Guiana

Ecotourism has been promoted in French Guiana since 1995, with a charter for nature conservation signed by environmental, tourism, national park, scientific agencies and communities. Protected areas, wildlife, local communities and environmentally friendly accommodation with a WWF logo were the focus of ecotourism development in French Guiana. In this small French territory by Suriname, Amerindians (4%) included the Galibi, Arawak, Wayana, Emerillon, Wayampi and Palikur peoples (Tourisme Guyane, nd). 60,000 to 75,000 tourists a year visit French Guiana.

Amana nature reserve

The 14,800 ha Amana nature reserve along the north-west coast of French Guiana is also a major nesting area for marine turtles. The Awala and Yalimapo beach in the reserve is the world's most important nesting site for leatherback turtles, the largest marine turtle species. During May–June, over 200 leatherback turtles may nest in one night at this beach. The Amana reserve was established in 1998 and was managed in partnership with two local Carib Indian villages, Mana and Awala. The local Amerindians provided visitor accommodation in small huts and advised visitors on seeing marine turtles (Godfrey and Drif, 2001; Olsder, 2004). An Amerindian organization, Kulalasi, helps protect the western turtle nesting beaches and provides guided tours for visitors in the area. Six local rangers were hired by the reserve. WWF-France has funded turtle conservation in this area since 1997, working with the reserve staff and Kulalasi in managing tourists and turtle research at Amana reserve (WWF, 2005d).

Brazil

The Amazon rainforest in western Brazil is the main focus for conservation and ecotourism development. This mainly occurs with private ecolodges and tour operators based around the city of Manaus. The government and industry are trying to develop ecotourism in Brazil. However, logging, mining and clearing for agriculture are depleting the Amazon rainforest (Schluter, 2001). Despite having an

ecotourism policy since 1994, Brazilian efforts to develop ecotourism have been ad hoc and driven by market demand. In 1996, the Indian Affairs agency FUNAI first supported tourism in Indian reserves, as ten Indigenous groups had proposed ecotourism projects (Healy, 1996). There are around 350,000 Indian people remaining in Brazil, from over 200 tribes, with about 50 groups living in remote areas still not contacted. Brazil does not officially recognize tribal land ownership or rights. Hence, farmers, loggers, mining companies and others often invade these Indian land areas. Indian reserves are controlled by the state and Indian people are still considered minors (Hill, 2004; Survival International, 2005). In the Amazon, community ecotourism projects involve Indian groups living in protected areas, such as the Mamiraua Sustainable Development Reserve. Other conservation and ecotourism projects have been established on Indigenous lands in the Amazon, such as the Kayapo Indigenous Territories and the Xingu River in Para state, where a local Indian NGO and The Body Shop developed the Tataquara Lodge. Other environmental NGOs in Brazil support rainforest projects linking scientific research with ecotourism. Some of these projects include Indigenous peoples.

Indigenous Ecotourism in Brazil's Amazon

Despite the sheer size of the Brazilian Amazon, 60% of the entire Amazon region, there are few Indigenous ecotourism ventures. There are some 220 Indigenous tribes in the Amazon region of Brazil, with Amazon Indian reserves encroached on by illegal settlers, agriculture, logging, mining, roads and hydroelectric dams. Six million people live in the Amazon rainforest, the poorest region of Brazil (da Silva, 2005). Of Brazil's 441 Indigenous reserves, 80% are in the Amazon (CI, 2005a). Indigenous lands cover 20% of the Amazon region, compared to 146 protected areas covering 12.4% of the Amazon, of which 8.3% are sustainable use reserves (Prance, 1998; da Silva, 2005). Prior to the 1990s, the Brazilian government was reducing the size of Indian reserves in the Amazon (Redford and Stearman, 1993). However, the current focus is now sustainable development of Indigenous territories in the Amazon, with environmental NGOs helping to conserve biodiversity in key areas (Amazon Coop, 2004). Rainforest research and Indigenous ecotourism projects are key aspects of this approach.

Private ecotourism companies benefit from rainforest conservation (Carr et al., 1993). The Amazon ecotourism industry in Brazil is also unregulated, led by market demand from international tourists, with little involvement of local communities or Indian tribes (Diegues, nd; Ruschmann, 1992; Garcia et al., 2004). A 1992 study of eight jungle lodges and one tourism boat on the Amazon River at the city of Manaus found they contributed little to conservation, visitor education or resource protection, while only 27% of employees were local people. While WWF (2001) promoted community ecotourism, the National Parks, nature reserves and Indigenous areas in the Brazilian Amazon were poorly funded, lacked infrastructure and were too far from Manaus for tourist access (Wallace and Pierce, 1996). The 11.5 million hectare Kayapo Indigenous Territories had a scientific research station with entrance fees and work as guides for the A'Ukre community. Fourteen other Kayapo communities also sought help with conservation projects and the defence of their land. This Kayapo land was the largest area of tropical rainforest controlled by a single Indigenous group. Income from scientific activities provided the Kayapo with an alternative to logging mahogany trees (CI, 2005b).

Tataquara Lodge, Xingu River

The Tataquara Lodge is located on a small island in the Xingu River, 140 km from the city of Altamira in the Brazilian State of Para. The lodge with 15 rooms is owned and operated by the Amazon Co-op, representing six Indian tribes with a total population under 3000 people who own 6 million ha of rainforest. The Co-op was set up in 1998 to promote sustainable development projects for member tribes. The Body Shop Foundation (UK) provided funding in 1999 to build Tataquara

Lodge from local materials. The lodge uses solar power, treats wastes, recycles and uses biodegradable organic soaps made from medicinal plants on a farm and laboratory owned by Amazon Co-op in Altamira. Visitor activities at the lodge include fishing, canoeing, wildlife viewing and forest walks. Local Indian people work at the lodge. There are no visits to nearby villages, instead Indians visit the lodge to sell crafts, perform songs and dances, tell stories and meet guests (Amazon Coop, 2004).

Mamiraua Sustainable Development Reserve

The Mamiraua Reserve was established in 1990. It covers over 1 million ha of flooded forest in the Amazon region and includes 12,000 Indian people who continue hunting, fishing and farming. These Indigenous inhabitants were regarded as part of the reserve, protecting the area from exploitation, and contributing to management decisions, such as fishing of lakes and catch quotas (Freitas et al., 2004). The Mamiraua Reserve is a core project of the Wildlife Conservation Society that has maintained an ecological research station in the area since 1989. Some 90 scientists and support staff conduct wildlife research in Mamiraua and the Amana Reserve, which was created in 1997. Mamiraua is the largest area of protected rainforest in the Amazon, with 3000 lakes managed by local groups. A network of floating stations equipped with radios and 100 volunteer wardens are used to monitor the Reserve, reducing poaching and illegal logging (Guynup, 2002). The Society supports community development projects like a fishing cooperative, forest management, arts and crafts and ecotourism. A floating lodge accommodated visitors, with ecotourism income employing local people (WCS, 2004). Indigenous groups required further support to develop ecotourism (Freitas et al., 2004).

Indigenous Ecotourism in the Amazon Rainforest, South America

The Amazon region of 7.5 million km^2 covers nine countries and 44% of South America

(Garcia *et al.*, 2004). The Amazon River, with its 1100 tributaries, is the heart of this rainforest area. There are 20 million people living in the Amazon, with 1 million of these being Indian people from 420 tribal groups (Schluter, 2001). In the nine countries covering the entire Amazon rainforest region, there are about 2.8 million Indigenous peoples (Osava, 2005). In the Amazon rainforest, most Indigenous ecotourism ventures are found in the eastern sectors of Ecuador, Peru and Bolivia (see Table 3.2). Community ecolodges operated by Amazon Indian groups have been developed with substantial support from international conservation and development agencies (e.g. Yachan and Chalalan) or as joint ventures with private companies (e.g. Kapawi and Posada Amazonas). Community-owned guesthouses in Ecuador's Amazon were developed as community initiatives, with support from local NGOs and Indian tribal organizations, and some international help at the first site of

Table 3.2. Key Indigenous ecotourism ventures in the Amazon rainforest, South America.

Product/year began	Location, country	Indian group	Donor/support agencies
Community ecolodge			
Yachana Lodge 1995	Upper Napo River, ECU	Quechua	FUNEDESIN, Rainforest Concern
Chalalan Ecolodge 1995	Madidi NP, Bolivia	Quechua	IADB, Conservation International
Kapawi Lodge 1996	Kapawi Reserve, ECU	Achuar	Canodros, Pachamama Alliance
Tataquara Lodge 1996	Xingu River, Brazil	Assurini	Amazon Coop, Body Shop Foundation
Bataburo Lodge 1997	Huaorani Reserve, ECU	Huaorani	Kempery Tours, Huaorani Federation
Posada Amazonas 1998	Tambopata River, Peru	Ese'eja	Rainforest Expeditions, Canadian Aid McArthur Foundation, World Bank
Machiguenga Centre for Tropical Research 2000	Urubamba River, Peru	Machiguenga	McArthur Foundation, Peru Verde NGO Wildlife Conservation Society, CEDIA
Casa Matsiguenka Lodge	Madre de Dios River, Peru	Matsiguenka	
Mapajo Ecolodge 2001?	Madidi NP, Bolivia	Moseten/ Chiman	Canada, Britain, France, PRAIA
Heath River Wildlife Centre 2002	Tambopata River, Peru	Ese'eja	Tropical Nature, Peru Verde NGO
Napo Wildlife Centre 2003	Yasuni NP, Ecuador	Quechua	Tropical Nature, EcoEcuador NGO
Community guesthouse			
Capirona Lodge 1989	Napo, Ecuador	Quechua	FOIN, Jatun Sacha Foundation, German NGO, University of California
Rio Blanco 1995?	Napo, Ecuador	Quechua	Loan
Playas de Cuyabeno 1996	Napo, Ecuador	Quechua	Transturi wages-Flotel Orellana
Sani Lodge 1995?	Napo, Ecuador	Quechua	Ecuador Verde (volunteers)
RICANCIE Network 1993	Napo, Ecuador	Quechua	FOIN, Ayuda en Accion NGO
Mucoposadas 2004	Venezuela	Pemon	Tropical Andes NGO, Edelca
Community ecotours			
Zabalo 1984	Cuyabeno Reserve, ECU	Cofan	Transturi visitors, Aguarico Trekking
Huaorani 1995	Yasuni NP, Ecuador	Huaorani	Tropic Ecological Adventures
Pilot ecotour 1998	Amazonas, Venezuela	4 villages	IDRC (Canada)
Other tourism agreements			
San Pablo 1990s	Cuyabeno Reserve, ECU	Secoyas	Etnotur (canoes, dances, $5 visitor fee)
Zancudo 1990s	Cuyabeno Reserve, ECU	Quechua	Transturi Flotel (jobs, goods, services, limit on hunting, protect resources)
Boras and Witotos 1973	Ampiyacu River, Peru	Boras, Witotos	Amazon Tours and Cruises (dances)
Yagua 1992	Ampiyacu River, Peru	Yagua	Amazon Tours and Cruises (dances)

ECU: Ecuador; FUNEDESIN: Foundation for Integrated Education and Development (Ecuador); IADB: Inter-American Development Bank; PRAIA: El Program Regional de Apoyo a los Pueblos Indigenas de la Cuenca del Amazonas (Ecuador); FOIN: Federation of Indigenous Organisations of Napo (Ecuador); IDRC: International Development Research Centre; CEDIA: Centre for the Development of the Amazonian Indian (Peru)

Capirona. Indian guided ecotours are provided through ecolodges and community guest-houses. Some ecotours are promoted as joint ventures with private operators, like the Cofan at Zabalo (Transturi) and the Huaorani (Tropic Ecological Adventures). Other Indian communities in Ecuador, Peru and Bolivia have agreements with travel agencies to protect resources and provide services, such as dance performances and canoe transport. The uneven development of Indigenous ecotourism ventures in the Amazon region depends on location, accessibility and resource features (e.g. intact rainforest, lakes, wildlife and macaw licks) along with legal land title, donor funding, agency support and private tourism agreements.

Community networks (e.g. RICANCIE for the Napo River, Ecuador) and allied resource projects in forest use or rainforest research also support Indian ecotourism ventures. Pilot ecotours began in 1998 at four Indian villages in the Amazonas region of Venezuela. However, there are no Indigenous ecotourism ventures in the Amazon area of Colombia. A new project, funded by the EU, developed six eco-routes in the Tierra Adentro region that promoted Indigenous cultures (Eco-Index, 2004a).

Amazonian Ecotourism Exchange

In 2003, the Critical Ecosystem Partnership Fund of Conservation International (CI) provided a grant of US$143,895 for three ecotourism workshops in South America. The Amazon Ecotourism Exchange involved Indigenous leaders, tour operators (Rainforest Expeditions, Canodros), CI and researchers from three community ecotourism lodges in Peru (Posada Amazonas), Ecuador (Kapawi Lodge) and Bolivia (Chalalan Ecolodge). The 35 participants discussed common experiences of ecotourism management in remote areas (Pyke and Stronza, 2004). Local leaders set the workshop topics of ecotourism products, partnership terms, distributing income, transferral of ownership to communities, tourism impacts and managing resources. The exchange focused on lessons learned, compared partnership models, defined best ecotourism practices for environmental management and

cultural impacts. Local standards were set for involving Indigenous groups in ecotourism projects (Eco-Index, 2004b).

The hosted ecotourism exchange was held over 3 months for a total of 20 days, on-site at each lodge. The best ecotourism model was a community–tourism company–NGO alliance that complemented other projects, defined partner roles and a structure for sharing earnings (Rainforest Alliance, 2004a). Communities wanted access to NGO funding for other projects rather than full ownership of lodges. NGOs provided training for communities, research and monitored impacts, and linked with operators. Tour companies provided marketing and business management expertise for communities (CI, 2004b). At Kapawi, the Achuar received a monthly lease payment, but did not feel like owners or managers. Tourists are strictly controlled at Kapawi, with all meetings mediated by an Achuar guide. At Chalalan and Posada Amazonas, tourists stay in the lodge and do not visit the local community. Lodges need to be located away from community living areas, farming, fishing and hunting sites. The ecotourism exchange fostered new alliances and radio communication between the three lodges, with plans for joint marketing of their ecotourism businesses (Rome, 2003c; Rainforest Alliance, 2004a, b).

Indigenous Ecotourism in Central America:

Belize

Toledo Ecotourism Association

In 1990, local Mayan, Garifuna and Creole residents established the Toledo Ecotourism Association (TEA) in southern Belize, working with a guesthouse owner in Punta Gorda to develop a village guesthouse programme, with tourists rotated between participating local villages in the Mayan foothills. Key objectives of TEA are to fund alternatives to slash and burn agriculture, improve health and education, protect the environment and culture, share tourism benefits and limit the number of visitors. Starting in 1991, the TEA used local resources to construct tourist guesthouses in five Indigenous villages (Mopan and Kek'chi Maya) at a total cost of US$1646. Small numbers of tourists started arriving at TEA guesthouses in 1993. WWF and The Nature Conservancy provided grants to upgrade the five guesthouses and build other tourist facilities (e.g. museum, craft area). The Belize government provided hospitality training (Mahler, 1997). Initial problems were local hotels and lodges in the city of Punta Gorda opposing the village scheme, delays in obtaining money and materials and rivalries and political disputes between villages in TEA (Beavers, 1995a, b). Eight other village guesthouses were built in this area in 1995 funded by USAID (US$26,193), through the Belize Enterprise for Sustained Technology (BEST) and the UK. For a time, these UK- and USAID-funded guesthouses were in competition with locally built TEA guesthouses (Mowforth and Munt, 2003), but these have now been included in the overall programme. By 1995, about 600 tourists had stayed at the TEA guesthouses. However, village income and visitor numbers remained low due to minimal promotion and lack of administrative staff for TEA (Beavers, 1995a, b).

The 30 Mayan villages in Toledo District practise subsistence agriculture and lack basic amenities, while commercial logging, road construction and shifting cultivation impact on the rainforest. Some 10,000 Kekchi and Mopan Maya people in Toledo (64%) live in basic huts with no electricity or plumbing. Foreigners and wealthy people in Belize also controlled 95% of all tourism in Toledo. An American in Punta Gorda who operated a travel agency and guesthouse coordinated the TEA Mayan Guest House Program. The Program integrated small-scale tourism, conservation and better farming practices. Visitors were rotated between villages to control tourist access and numbers. Other visitor activities were nature trails, medicinal plants, crafts and Mayan ruins. Rates in 1995 were US$20 a night for accommodation, US$3 for meals and US$10 for guided tours. Mayan villages used tourism income for sustainable agriculture, clinics and other community needs (Mahler and Wotkyns, 1995). A TEA conservation fund also supports local ecotrails

and village protected areas (Beavers, 1995a, b). In 2001, TEA members participated in monitoring bird species around their areas (Wartinger, 2001).

The Toledo Ecotourism Association now includes ten villages, with seven to nine families in each village involved in hosting tourists. The participating Kekchi or Mopan Maya villages were Laguna, Blue Creek, Pueblo Viejo, San Jose, San Miguel, San Antonio, San Pedro Columbia, Santa Elena/Santa Cruz and the Garifuna village of Barranco. Each guesthouse is built like a village house and accommodates four to eight people. There was no running water, flush toilets or electricity at the guesthouses. Visitors eat with local families, with each meal in a different house. Households in each village share the provision of tourist services, such as running the guesthouse, cooking meals and guiding forest walks. Other activities were guided tours to Mayan ruins, caves and waterfalls, along with horseback riding or canoeing. The average daily amount earned by the Association from tourists was US$35 per day for meals, accommodation, dances and handicraft sales (Edington and Edington, 1997). Local families providing tourist services receive 80% of tourism income, with 20% kept in a village fund or used to fund administration of TEA. In 1996, there were 219 members of TEA (Toledo Ecotourism Association, nd). Money from tourism increased village incomes by 25%, mainly from word-of-mouth referrals (Buckley, 2003g). In Belize, local Mayan guides were also designated as village site guides and paid a lower licence fee of US$5 rather than US$70 (Duffy, 2002). This assisted rural groups, such as TEA, to operate tours at Mayan villages in southern Belize.

One of the key objectives of TEA is to share tourism benefits within and between Indigenous villages. Favouritism in the allocation of tourists to family households for meals (for payment) was a problem in the past, with one family suspended from the scheme. The competing guesthouse scheme funded by USAID and BEST also created social divisions within Mayan villages. A second guesthouse was built in Laguna Village, in direct competition with a TEA guesthouse. The UK Overseas Development Administration also funded construction of a second guesthouse in a TEA village. This foreign aid funding ignored cooperative community action and the TEA principle of rotating tourists to different villages for a fair distribution of tourist benefits (Mowforth and Munt, 2003). Village income from tourism is affected by their location, transport links, local organization and lobbying within TEA. Plenty International, an American NGO supporting tribal peoples, produced a promotional video, fliers and brochures for TEA. In 2000, they also launched a website for TEA promoting the village guesthouses, Mayan ecotours and crafts (Wartinger, 2001). The Mesoamerican Ecotourism Alliance and Tide Tours (Toledo Institute for Development and Environment) do not market TEA. These two groups mainly promoted natural attractions and ecotourism in Belize protected areas (Horwich and Lyon, 1999). A website for southern Belize (2005a, b) promoted the villages in TEA and also the Maya village homestay network.

The TEA won a 'ToDo' world prize for socially responsible tourism from a German NGO in 1996, by helping ten local villages (nine Mayan and one Garifuna) in Belize to organize, operate, control and directly benefit from community ecotourism operations. However, the Belize Tourist Board did not publicize or promote this tourism award or the TEA programme. Belize funding for conservation and ecotourism has not been given to TEA. The Belize government has resisted a proposed Mayan eco-park in Toledo, while illegal logging and wildlife poaching on Mayan forest reserves affects their ecotourism potential (Duffy, 2002). When logging licences were granted around Mayan villages in 1995/96, TEA demonstrated against the Malaysian logging company involved and developed an alternative Mayan Teken-Sy eco-forestry enterprise based on salvaging timber for furniture and carvings. The TEA also linked the village guesthouses with mountain eco-trails, medicinal plants and furniture. The eco-trails went through forest areas protected by villagers to attract wildlife and be a source of medicinal plants. Plenty Belize supported TEA with computers, training, grant proposals, crafts and other rural projects (TEA, nd).

The Maya Village Indigenous Experience, a homestay programme, was formed in 1990 by an American couple that managed the Toledo Visitor Information Centre in Punta Gorda. For a US$5 fee, tourists were connected with a Mayan host family, with visitors paying US$7 for board (Mahler and Wotkyns, 1995). Tourists stayed with rural Mayan families in their home, slept in a hammock, bathed in the river and ate local food. They joined in with daily activities, such as land tilling and food preparation. Village women sold crafts while men guided tourists to see caves, Mayan ruins, and forest areas. Mayan families in the host programme paid US$2 a month to fund hotel taxes and license fees. After a workshop on tourism regulations, the Mayan villagers took over administration of the homestay programme. Village chiefs assigned tourists to families, but some individuals started similar tourism projects, causing disputes. By 1996, this programme included 26 families in six villages and had hosted 300 tourists (Steinberg, 1997). This homestay scheme complemented the TEA guesthouse programme. In 2005, three Mayan villages were listed in this homestay network (SouthernBelize.com, 2005b).

Mexico

There are more than 50 Indigenous groups in Mexico, with a total of 10 million people or 10% of the population being Indians (Momsen, 2002). These include the Mayan, Nahua, Totonacos, Otomis and other Indigenous people. Referred to as *Indigenas*, these Indigenous groups are mainly found in the Yucatan Peninsula, the Chiapas Highlands, Central Valley, Isthmus of Tehuantepec and the Sierra Norte of Puebla (Greathouse-Amador, 2005). There are 62 officially recognized Indigenous groups in Mexico (Nauman, 2002). Some Mayan groups in Yucatan, Chiapas, Oaxaca (Carballo-Sandoval, 1999; Ramirez, 2001b) and Veracruz have developed ecotourism ventures (AMTAVE, 2005). In 1999, the first trade conference on adventure tourism and ecotourism was held in Mexico City. The states of Veracruz, Oaxaca, Michoacan and Morelos promoted their community-run ecotourism projects. These included the San

Juan Nuevo Parangaricutiro forest tourism venture near Paracutin Volcano and community museums in Oaxaca. Since 2001, the Oaxaca Ecotourism Fair has promoted community-run lodges and museums (Mader, 2002, 2003). However, Mexico has a mass tourism industry based around beach resorts on the Pacific and Caribbean coast. There has been minimal collaboration between Mexican tourism and environmental government departments in developing ecotourism projects. Under Mexican law, ecotourism operators must consult with Indigenous communities to enter their territory, but do not pay fees as natural features were owned by the state government (Tiedje, 2005). Local consultation or impact assessment was not often done in Mexican ecotourism (Greathouse-Amador, 1997; Cruz et al., 2005). Environmental and community NGOs have supported a few Indigenous ecotourism projects in Mexico. These include a Mayan forest and ecotours in Yucatan, the Lacandona forest in Chiapas, reforestation in Oaxaca, an eco-hotel in Puebla and ecotours by Huichol Indians.

Punta Laguna, Yucatan Peninsula

At Punta Laguna, a local Mayan community initiated an ecotourism project, attracting tourists travelling between Mayan ruins on the Yucatan Peninsula (Zeppel, 1998). This local ecotourism project evolved from the determination of one man, Serapio Canul, to protect forest areas and wildlife from exploitation, particularly a troupe of resident spider monkeys. The area also contained Mayan archaeological sites at Coba visited by 70,000 tourists annually (Brown, 1999; Pi-Sunyer et al., 2001). Mayan people hunted and sold wild game, such as parrots and badgers, to tourists along the Coba road (Juarez, 2002). From the mid-1980s, outside tour operators brought groups to see the spider monkeys and forest. Tourists taking a forest tour with Sr Canul either left a tip or donation. Serapio trained his sons to guide visitors and made more forest trails. Local tour guides also brought visitors to Punta Laguna. In 1989, a Mexican conservation agency, Pronatura, provided funds for a visitor reception area and tourist brochure. In June 2002, after a decade of conservation support

from local Mayan people and a local NGO, Pronatura-Peninsula de Yucatan (PPY), an area of 5237 ha was set aside as a Flora and Fauna Protected Area, Otoch Ma'ax Yetel Kooh (House of the monkey and panther). Since 1990, PPY paid Serapio Canul a monthly wage to act as watchman for the forest.

The Punta Laguna ecotourism project has provided valuable income for 20% of a poor community lacking modern facilities. Tourism income is derived from working as forest guards, research assistants, tour guides and by women selling handicrafts. In 1996, a tourism operator from the resort town on Cancún sought to run an ecotourism business with a contract providing all tourist services at the forest site with local people paid a daily salary. However, Serapio decided not to sign the contract and most of the tourism income still went to his family – with sons and nephews working as tourist guides and only women from his family selling crafts. In 2001, some 1600 tourists visited the area, mostly on 552 tourist buses, generating US$21,000 ($1 entry fee, $15 guide fee and $15,600 salary from PPY to Serapio). This caused local resentment of Serapio's family and, by the end of 2002, community members gained control of tourism in the protected area that now had to abide by a new management plan and advisory committee to share tourism income (Frapolli, 2003). Other issues for sustainability were the impacts of growing tourist numbers on forest trails and wildlife. Over 50% of Mexico's forests are now owned and managed by local communities, including Indigenous groups, with collective land grants and control of forest resources. A new forestry law in 1997 also supported local use of forests by self-governing rural communities. There were 290–479 community forest enterprises, providing income and employment from timber, other forest products and ecotourism (Bray et al., 2003). At San Juan village, tarantulas were now sold since a Mayan theatre performance attracted few tourists (Momsen, 2002).

Sian Ka'an Reserve and Mots Maya, Yucatan Peninsula

The Sian Ka'an Biosphere Reserve in Yucatan has local Mayan people providing nature-based activities such as bird watching, kayaking, snorkelling, fishing and visiting Mayan archaeological sites. Sian Ka'an is 2 hours south of the resort area of Cancún on the Yucatan Peninsula which receives 5 million visitors annually (Pi-Sunyer et al., 2001). Community Tours Sian Ka'an was an alliance of four Mayan cooperatives with 69 members that lived in Punta Allen and Muyil within the reserve. Sian Ka'an, a world heritage site, was Mayan for 'where the sky is born'. Assisted by Rare Conservation, the ecotourism alliance was formed to diversify activities, minimize visitor impacts and distribute tourism benefits more equitably among members. Five per cent of tourism revenue went towards conservation. Rare Conservation worked with farmers and fishermen in Sian Ka'an for 5 years to develop this local ecotourism business. The UNEP, UNESCO, UN Foundation, Mexican government and Aveda Corporation supported this project. In July and August 2004, Community Tours Sin Ka'an had 200 visitors, with guides earning 30% more than others visiting the reserve (Rare, 2004). By 2005, the business employed 33% of workers in the reserve, with tourism income benefiting 75% of local families. Community Tours Sin Ka'an had 30–40% of tourism business, in an area that received 30,000 visitors a year (Rare, 2005a; Sian Kaan Tours, 2005). A new Sian Ka'an visitor centre had rooms, a lookout tower, ecotours and training courses (Bravo, 2004).

Five young Mayan people also formed Mots Maya (Maya Roots) as an ecotourism business on the Yucatan providing kayaking and bird watching tours. Grants from Rare Conservation, along with training as guides and ecotourism entrepreneurs and the Mexican National Indigenous Institute, supported their ecotours and a kayak-making business (Rare, 2003a). The business aimed to support Mayan culture and communities. However, the Sian Ka'an Reserve established in 1986 restricted Mayan harvesting of lobster, shells and turtles, limiting Mayan use of subsistence food resources or selling seafood to tourists. Local Mayans were also excluded from beach areas where hotels charged tourist access fees (Juarez, 2002). Ecotourism aimed to provide alternative income for local people.

Lacandona forest, Chiapas

The Lacandona forest in Chiapas, south-east Mexico, was the focus of an ecotourism project in the Frontera Corozal community of Chol Indians. The Chol Indians, a Mayan group, had colonized this rainforest area in 1976 and used small plots for crops and grazing. Date palms and timber were also harvested, along with fishing and hunting local wildlife such as deer, peccaries, armadillo and birds. The Lacandona rainforest, along the border with Guatemala, was a biologically diverse area that included five protected areas and an Indigenous community reserve. The Mayan archaeological sites of Yaxchilan and Bonampak were also found in this area, with Chol people providing boat transport on the Usumacinta River to Yaxchilan. The Chol Indian community of Frontera Corozal, located on the border with Guatemala, had 4762 residents in 954 households. This Lacandona community tourism project focused on local Chol households in the ecotourism centre of Escudo Jaguar (Jaguar Shield). It included river transport, cabins/restaurant and a women's food business section. This tourism organization was set up in 1990 by 55 local landowners but by 1994 was reduced to 17 members that owned boats or had economic resources. In 1995, the Escudo Jaguar group received funding from Conservation International to build three cabins and to buy lifejackets for riverboats. A Mexican entrepreneur worked with CI to build the Ixcan Station, an ecotourism and research centre, developed with the Ixcan community who also managed this venture (Ramirez, 2001b).

Since 1996, the group received funding and technical support from Mexican government agencies (e.g. Economic and Social Development, Tourism and the National Indigenous Institute) for equipment and other infrastructure. This support was linked to the Montes Azules ecotourism circuit developed in the mid-1990s to provide tourism income for communities living around the Montes Azules Biosphere Reserve. By 2002, Escudo Jaguar had 37 members who were co-owners/managers and 24 local employees in tourism. In 2000, the wives of the 37 members were included in Escudo Jaguar and set up a tortilla factory. The cabin/restaurant section derived 66% of income from tourism while the river transport group derived 41% from tourism. Households with employees at Escudo Jaguar gained 61% of their income from tourism, but with low seasons and limited income from other sources some were migrating to the USA. The 37 members of Escudo Jaguar derived more income from tourism and other activities. However, another local group, Tikal Chilam, now competed with Escudo Jaguar for river transport. Government and technical support, and NGO funding, assisted local involvement in ecotourism. Community support, income from other activities and wider tourism networks were needed to grow Chol ecotourism in the Lacandona forest (Cruz et al., 2005).

Oaxaca

In the early 1980s, five large hotels and other beach resort facilities were built along the Pacific coast of Oaxaca, when a 30 km coastal strip was taken over by the Mexican Tourist Development Fund. The region had 50,000 people from four Indigenous groups living in 150 subsistence communities. To build the resorts, local Indigenous communities were removed from coastal fishing villages, highland forests logged and migrant workers brought in. Indigenous people were offered menial jobs, while the rate of deforestation and erosion increased. In the early 1990s, a Mexican NGO, the Centre for Ecological Support (CSE) started reforestation programmes with affected Indigenous groups, funded by Mexican and international sources. Bungalows were constructed to offer ecotourism services based on sharing reforestation techniques. The Sheraton Hotel financially supported this forest conservation project, with local tourism agencies directing clients to this community project. There were plans to charge hotels for the water used from reforested catchment areas (Barkin and Bouchez, 2002). Environmental restoration of the forest area by Indigenous groups provided conservation and community benefits and, thus, was a form of ecotourism (Foucat, 2002). In Oaxaca, other community forest enterprises use income from logging to support ecotourism, and to develop other ventures such as water bottling

and tapping resin (Bray et al., 2003). In the northern Sierra region of Oaxaca, the eight communities of Pueblos Mancomunados developed rural trails and country roads for ecotourism hiking and biking on their own 29,000 ha forest area (Ramirez, 2001b).

Cuetzalan, Puebla

Cuetzalan, in Puebla State, is a weekend getaway for tourists from Mexico City and the city of Puebla. The town of Cuetzalan is located in a hilly area with colonial Spanish architecture and Indigenous Nahua Indians that comprise 82% of the population. The natural scenery and ethnic groups at Cuetzalan also attracted international tourists. Since the late 1980s, Nahua women formed a cooperative to make arts and crafts. In the mid-1990s, one-third of the Nahua women in this cooperative decided to build a tourist hotel in Cuetzalan. Mestizos owned most hotels, shops and restaurants in Mexico. Using their own income, together with funding received from Mexican and international organizations, they bought land and constructed the hotel. The women also received training in how to operate and manage a hotel and restaurant. The Taselotzin hotel opened in September 1997. It was the first ecotourism hotel owned and managed by Indigenous women in Mexico. Nahua cultural heritage and natural attractions were integrated with accommodation at this hotel, as the women delivered courses on Nahua culture, language and traditions to visitors and students. The natural environment and use of plants for medicine were also featured. With growing tourism, the Nahua became more aware of the need for conservation and environmental protection. This hotel revived interested in the Nahua language and culture, and provided local tourism income. The mestizos also had a new respect for the Indigenous Nahua people (Greathouse-Amador, 2005).

Huichol Indians

The Huichol Indians or Wixarikari live in the Sierra Madre mountain areas of western

Mexico. The Huichol have reclaimed 30,000 ha (115 square miles) of their tribal territory after 172 legal cases over 15 years. Other lawsuits based on agrarian law reform were expected to reclaim another 30,000 ha of Huichol land. The aim was to establish a Huichol protected area in 10 to 12 years on this territory. The Huichol homeland area covered 1740 square miles where the Huichol lived in family villages and small towns spread across four states – Jalisco, Nayarit, Durango and Zacatecas. Subsistence agriculture based on native corn, hunting, gathering and spiritual rites to maintain natural areas are the basis of communal Huichol culture. This has maintained trees, plants and wildlife in Huichol territory in contrast to adjacent areas cleared for cattle. The Huichol are also renowned for their yarn art and bead art based on traditional designs. Twelve years ago some 80,000 ha of Huichol land was taken over by loggers, cattle grazing and marijuana crops, causing major environmental degradation. A project for the reconstruction of Wixarika tribal territory focuses on conservation and sustainable development of this area, including ecotourism and organic agriculture. The 50,000 Huichol people are supported by a local NGO, the Jalisco Indigenous Groups Support Association, set up in 1990 to protect Huichol land, culture and biodiversity. An ecotourism or visitors programme was proposed at Huichol community assemblies and planning workshops. In 2001, tourists from Finland paid US$1000 each to camp and learn about Huichol culture from their hosts. Twenty per cent of the money went to an environmental fund to help establish a protected area. The Huichol built cabins with a ceremonial circle in the middle to host tourists in this Blue Deer visitors project (Nauman, 2002). Other agriculture projects and training in resource management also supported Huichol land use.

Singayta, Nayarit

Singayta is a rural village near San Blas in Nayarit state, with traditional style wood and mud huts with thatched roofs and a forest area with 260 bird species. Most of the villagers were Huichol or Cora Indians. Changes in

Mexican land law saw communal titles in *ejidos* or agricultural collectives converted to individual titles. The 40 families in the San Blas Ejido of Singayta favoured selling their forest area to ranching and logging interests for cash. The main source of village income was selling palm fronds used to thatch roofs, cutting wood, gathering oil nuts and hunting. These local natural resources were severely impacted by Hurricane Kenna in October 2002. A local NGO, the Mangrove Environmental Protection Group or El Manglar, then worked with local people in Singayta to preserve the forest area and generate alternative income from ecotourism, handicrafts and a plant nursery specializing in wild orchids. In 2003, an environmental eco-centre was built by townspeople on land obtained by El Manglar in Singayta. Ecotours focused on traditional houses and fruit trees in the town, along with plants, birds and other wildlife in the forest area. Ornithologists provided ecotourism training and advice about the songbirds, shore birds and migratory birds in the area. Canoe tours through mangrove estuaries; a horse drawn cart tour; the renting of horses, donkey carts and bicycles; and an outdoors kitchen were other visitor services provided. A gift shop sold local Huichol artwork. The villagers also planted 3000 trees in a reforestation effort. The Global Green Grants Fund assisted Singayta to develop ecotourism and establish the Ecological Community of Singayta, as well as fund a uniform T-shirt, signs and publicity for the project (El Manglar, 2003; Singayta, 2004).

Guatemala

Ecomaya

Ecomaya is a company that markets two Spanish language schools in San Andres and San Jose and three community ecotourism ventures in the Peten area of northern Guatemala. Ecomaya was established in 1998 by ten community businesses, assisted by Conservation International (CI), to jointly market their ecotours and language schools (CI, 2004c). The Maya Kek'chi and Maya Itza ethnic groups lived in this area. More than 200 local families provide services for Ecomaya businesses (Redturs, nd). The Peten region includes the Mayan Biosphere Reserve of 17,000 km^2, established in 1990, with rainforests and scarlet macaws, and Mayan ruins at Tikal, Yaxha and El Mirador. The Peten region has had widespread deforestation due to colonization by migrants (311,314 in 1990), with land clearing for shifting cultivation and also subsistence hunting of wildlife. To address these environmental impacts, several conservation NGOs developed forestry management and tourism projects in the Mayan Biosphere Reserve (Sundberg, 1997; Norris et al., 1998; Hearn and Santos, 2005; Wallace and Diamente, 2005). Funded by USAID, three Mayan conservation trails were developed in the Biosphere Reserve to protect wildlife and deter looting at Mayan sites. In 1993, Conservation International (CI) helped three local communities set up ecotourism businesses, providing guided tours of Mayan ruins at Mirador, bat caves and breeding areas of scarlet macaws. The tours are jointly promoted as Mayan EcoTrails. CI helped set up these Mayan ecotourism ventures as economic alternatives to logging, agricultural land clearing and hunting in the Maya Biosphere Reserve (Ecomaya, 2004). The forest ecotours in the Reserve were managed and operated by community ecotourism committees that supplied equipment, pack mules, guides, cooks and interpreters on 2- to 4-day ecotours (Conway, 1998). The Paso Caballos community in Peten won a conservation award in 2002 for protecting the scarlet macaw.

San Andres and San Jose Spanish schools

In 1993, CI and ProPeten, a Guatemalan NGO, created a Spanish language school in the village of San Andres. This community-owned school provided Spanish language courses combined with homestay accommodation and ecotours. Some 56 teachers, homestay hosts and administrators collectively owned the school, which employs more people than a local sawmill. By 1997, the school was already a sustainable business, paying an annual bonus of US$200 to cooperative members (Rohr and Gines, 1998). The language school attracts

1800 tourists a year from America and Europe and employs 100 local people, of whom 60% were previously hunting, illegally felling timber or clearing farm land. A study in 2000 found local families working at the school reduced their hunting and their slash-and-burn agriculture plots. Social pressure against hunting increased while community-managed private reserves were set up (CI, 2004c; UNEP, 2002). In 1998, a second Spanish language school was established in the town of San Jose, to help support a 36 km^2 nature reserve that was set aside by the Mayan Itza people and managed by the local Bio-Itza Association. Students at the school also learn about traditional Mayan cultural activities and participate in conservation projects such as reforestation, environmental education and nature trails (CI, 2004c). Ecomaya soon reached an annual turnover of US$250,000 fuelled by the 60% growth in tourism to Guatemala from 1996 to 1999. In 2001, the local ecocertification scheme, Alianza Verde, recognized the community businesses in Ecomaya while other Peten tourism operators joined the Ecomaya group in 2002 (Buckley, 2003h).

Conservation Tours Tikal

Conservation Tours Tikal is a community-based ecotourism business set up by five Mayan people that provides guided tours of rainforest and Mayan ruins in Tikal National Park. The American NGO, Rare Conservation, provided nature guide training and ecotourism entrepreneurship courses for the Mayan people living in communities next to the park. They had previously hunted wildlife. Five per cent of income from Conservation Tours Tikal went towards projects such as cleaning up local watersheds and environmental talks in schools. Most of the tour income stayed in the local Mayan community. US$16,000 was earned from these Mayan nature tours at Tikal in the first few months of 2003. The business was promoted by RARE conservation and by the Mesoamerican Ecotourism Alliance (Rare, nd). In 2005, Conservation Tours Tikal hosted 363 tourists and employed people from 19 local families. The tours generated over US$30,000 in income (US$6000 in profit), with over 56% of this income from ecotourism retained in three local Mayan communities (Rare, 2006a).

San Pedro Volcano

Mayan communities in the San Pedro region have established a monopoly over tourism to the 3000 m volcano topped with cloud forest. They operate guesthouses, provide guided tours and transport and own souvenir shops. Tourist access to the San Pedro volcano is by boat across Lake Atitlan or by road. Local Mayan people prevented the entry of foreign-owned companies and resisted government authorities to control access to the volcano (Parent, 1995). While the Maya benefited economically from tourism, government is poor at providing infrastructure and services in rural areas (Buckley, 2003i). American anthropology students also stay with local families and study the impacts of tourism on Mayan communities around Lake Atitlan, during an annual summer school (May–July).

Alta Verapaz

In the Coban region of Guatemala, the local NGO, Proyecto Ecological Quetzal (PEQ) promoted ecotourism in two key forest areas with Mayan Q'eqchi' communities. The project began in 1988 with German students monitoring rare quetzal birds in the forests of Alta Verapaz, with 145 birds per km^2. PEQ, mainly funded by Germany and the USA, promoted ecotourism, handicrafts and sustainable agriculture to protect the forests and provide alternative income for poor villagers in the Alta Verapaz area. PEQ has two ecotourism programmes where tourists stay with Mayan host families in Chicacnab (cloud forest) and at Rokja Pomtila (sub-tropical rainforest). Visitors walk into these remote areas and stay in basic rural huts, attracted by the birds, wildlife, plants and scenery (PEQ, 2002). PEQ also helped Mayan women at Chicacnab make and sell aromatic candles to visitors. In the Chisec region of Alta Verapaz, Mayan Q'eqchi' people managed guiding and visitors at four attractions based around caves,

lakes, tropical rainforest, underground rivers and ruins (Redturs, nd).

Quehueche ecotourism centre

The Quehueche ecotourism project involves a rural guesthouse along with other Mayan cultural activities or natural attractions. Forest walks explained the benefits of forest resources while Mayan ceremonies, music, dance, food and crafts were also shared. The village of Quehueche was chosen from among 18 villages to develop community tourism based on conserving natural resources. The guesthouse was built with support from the Ak'Tenamit Association, a Mayan NGO, and the RECOSMO project funded by Holland and UNDP. Some 30 Q'eqchi' Mayan villages were located in the rainforest area of Rio Dulce National Park in eastern Guatemala. Since 2001, the Ak'Tenamit Association supported two ecotourism projects at Quehueche village that had relied on corn crops, selling timber and illegal hunting. With tourism income, local hunting and corn farms in the forest decreased. Nineteen families and artists provided guiding and cultural services or sold items to visitors. The village tourism committee and participating families received part of the tourism income. The 19 families already earned more from 50 tourists than from corn. The rivers were also kept cleaner, while hunting of icon species, such as ocelot and jaguar, decreased. The village of Quehueche belonged to the Guatemala Sustainable Tourism Network and RECOSMO (WTO, 2003d).

Honduras

Rio Platano Biosphere Reserve

The 830,000 ha Rio Platano Biosphere Reserve and World Heritage site was declared in 1980. It includes rainforest, tropical wildlife, rivers and lagoons. The area includes Miskito Indians, who live by shifting agriculture, subsistence hunting and fishing and cash income from selling agricultural or forest products (e.g. timber, dugout canoes, wild game and wildlife). Three Indigenous groups, the Miskito (43%), Tawahka (1%) and Pesch (1%) live in the Reserve area, along with the Garifuna (3%), an African-Arawak group, and Mestizos (52%) (Eco-Index, 2004c). Forty thousand people lived in the Reserve, which had basic services, limited employment and poverty. Located in eastern Honduras, the large Reserve has no government enforcement, resources or staff to stop illegal logging and forest clearing for agriculture. Ecotourism development in the Reserve has been assisted by environmental NGOs (e.g. WWF), development agencies (USAID, US Peace Corps and Japan), and an Indigenous organization, MOPAWI (Mosquitia Pawisa), partly funded by WWF. MOPAWI was the sole agency managing the northern zone of the Biosphere Reserve for sustainable management of natural resources and conservation integrated with development of local communities. A local Indigenous organization and local ecotourism committee were formed to manage activities in the Biosphere Reserve.

The community of Las Marias on the Platano River, with 350 Indigenous residents, is located at the centre of the Reserve. Tourism activities at Las Marias boomed in 1992/93 causing environmental and social impacts. There was increased hunting and fishing to feed tourists, with guides providing wild game for visitors. A 1993 report to WWF stated the local tribal council was divided, with family and ethnic conflicts to gain control over tourism and collect the US$2 entrance fee to the Reserve. Some 23% of families received income from tourism and spent less time on subsistence agriculture. To address these tourism impacts, MOPAWI conducted a participatory planning process to develop a 5-year conservation and ecotourism development plan, assisted by a US Peace Corps volunteer, and implemented with funding from WWF. The planning process took 10 weeks, supported by MOPAWI.

The tourism focus groups included tribal elders, women, tribal council, teachers and religious leaders. Community goals included equitably sharing the profits and opportunities of ecotourism, minimizing tourism impacts and controlling services provided to ecotourists. An ecotourism committee devised a short-term action plan to meet these village goals. This included regulations prohibiting tourists from eating endangered wildlife and buying live animals or artefacts made from animal products. Guides also banned hunting and fishing during jungle trips. The guide association started a guide rotation system and, by mid-1995, all families gained tourism income. From March 1994–April 1995, the community of Las Marias earned US$11,731 from tourism, with most income going to the guides. Women also formed a cooperative and sold traditional crafts to tourists (Nielsen and Munguia, 1998; Horochowski and Moisey, 1999, 2001). Ten Garifuna and Miskito people also obtained a grant of US$189,000 from the UN to construct ecolodges and guesthouses and manage environmental projects such as nesting beaches used by sea turtles in the Rio Platano Biosphere Reserve (Rare, 2003b). Garifuna people in north-west Honduras were positive about tourism growth (Horochowski and Moisey, 1999, 2001).

Pech Indians in the Olancho region of the Rio Platano Biosphere Reserve also developed ecotourism projects in 1997/98, assisted by volunteers from the US Peace Corps. Based in the village of El Carbon, these projects included hammocks and bags made for tourists and sold through a local centre. USAID provided a grant to build two guesthouses, to accommodate tourists and provide a base for hikes to nearby waterfalls and ruins, guided by locals from a Pech community group (Parent, 1999). These ecotourism ventures aimed to provide Pech communities with economic alternatives to clearing rainforest for cattle pasture, banana plantations, slash-and-burn forest swidden agriculture and hunting.

In 2003, the Miskito Indian people won the UNDP Equator Prize for establishing ecotourism in Rio Platano Reserve. An ecotourism committee coordinated local tour guides, handicrafts, restaurants and small business management. One hundred Miskito families received tourism income from working as river guides, six families provided room and board for visitors and six more carried supplies along rivers. For participating Miskito families, their annual income increased from US$500 to US$12,000. However, broader Miskito Indian involvement in Reserve management was still needed (Hill, 2004).

In 2005, 'La Ruta Moskitia', a community ecotourism enterprise, was launched in the Rio Platano area. This ecotourism venture, with a Miskito Indian coordinator, benefited five Indigenous communities. Tours of the Rio Platano Reserve included rainforest, wildlife (e.g. parrots, monkeys, jaguars and manatees), horseback riding, tubing and boat rides as well as the food, dance and music of the Pech, Miskito and Garifuna peoples. The first tour hosted by 'La Ruta Moskitia' took place in July 2005. Rare Conservation, the UN Foundation, UNESCO, the Honduras government and local communities took 4 years to develop this new ecotourism enterprise. Rare Conservation built ecolodges and supported local tour operators with marketing, customer service and business development. In the village of Belen, a former lobster diver managed a restaurant and cabins used by travellers. This Belen ecotourism enterprise and other tour operations were supported to deliver local benefits from conservation. Other tour operators were also visiting Rio Platano, the largest area of lowland rainforest north of the Amazon. The Moskitia or Mosquito Coast region and Rio Platano Biosphere Reserve are featured on the Honduras tourism website (Rare, 2005b, 2006b).

Panama

San Blas Kuna

In Panama, the San Blas Kuna Indians, numbering some 50,000 people, largely control tourism in their homeland area of the San Blas Archipelago. Living on 50 offshore islands, the San Blas Kuna are mainly known for the colourful outfits worn by women, especially the *mola* blouse (Swain, 1989). The Kuna reservation or *comarca*, established in 1938, covers 5000 km^2 and includes 370 coral islands and a portion of the mainland. In the mid-1970s, Kuna opposition to a large hotel proposal on one island led to violent and forced expulsion of other non-Kuna resort and tour boat operators from the area. In 1990, three small hotels were owned and managed by Kuna families, with tourists flown in from Panama City in light planes (Chapin, 1990). The Kuna region now hosts 5000 hotel guests

and 30,000 cruise ship visitors. In 1996, the Kuna General Congress passed a statute to control tourism in Kuna Yala or Kuna lands, preventing foreign ownership or investment in tourism plus a tourist tax of US$1 per visitor at Kuna hotels. In 1999, only three of 15 Kuna hotels paid this tax, at US$10–15 per month, while cruise ships paid US$300 per visit ($150 to the Congress and US$150 to the local community), but were largely unregulated. Environmental degradation caused by effluent from cruise ships and hotels was a problem. Since only four hotels had a septic system (Snow and Wheeler, 2000). Cruise ship tourists, however, can spend US$1500 in a single visit on Kuna crafts (Snow, 2001). The benefits of tourism in San Blas are unevenly spread while Kuna people are still affected by poverty, child malnutrition, basic facilities, community division and limited work (Bennett, 1997, 1999). In 2000, the Foundation for the Promotion of Indigenous Knowledge developed a strategic plan for ecotourism with pilot projects in three communities, training five Kuna as ecotourism guides, and devised solid waste management plans (*Eco-Exchange*, 2001; People and Planet, 2002; Eco-Index, 2004d).

While the Kuna gain income from island tourism, handicrafts and hotels, a plan to establish nature tourism in a Kuna wildlife reserve of 60,000 ha on the mainland was less successful (Chapin, 1990, 2000; Zeppel, 1998). In 1983, the Kuna launched the PEMASKY project for management of this Kuna Park with a US$425,000 grant from the Inter-American Foundation and research support from American environmental agencies (e.g. WWF and the Smithsonian Tropical Research Institute). The Kuna biosphere reserve was established to prevent the Panama government developing this 'unused' forest area and to protect Kuna territory (Archibald and Davey, 1993; Dunn, 1995; Igoe, 2004). The project centre at Nusagandi included a dormitory and office with nature trails and jungle field stations. Scientists completed biological surveys of the reserve and hired Kuna assistants. Project staff sought to link ecotourism at Nusagandi with ethnic tourism on the offshore Kuna islands. However, only small groups of tourists arrived, no Kuna links were made with travel agents in

Panama City or the USA and conservation NGOs did not promote this Kuna reserve. Despite the attraction of a primary rainforest, the region had very poor roads, limited access, lacked visitor transportation to Nusagandi and had basic tourist facilities. It was difficult for North Americans to get tourist visas, with no support from the Panama government for developing ecotourism in natural areas (Chapin, 1990, 2000). Hence, Kuna ecotourism was not viable in this area. The Kuna PEMASKY project ended in the late 1980s.

Embera Indians and Chagres National Park

A USAID-funded study reviewed community ecotourism in the Panama Canal watershed, where local communities lived in the buffer zones of five protected areas and within Chagres Park. Some 1500 Embera and Wounan Indians lived in the Park. Tourism to these communities began in 1993. Embera cultural ecotourism received support from the Panamanian Institute for Tourism, a local tourism NGO, USAID, US Forest Service and Peace Corps (Kohl, 2003). Some 100–200 tourists a month visit the villages in high season and 20–50 a month in the rainy season. In 1995, one Embera village with 68 people earned US$7000 from an entrance fee of $5–10 per tourist and selling handicrafts. Village leaders negotiated their own deals with tour operators without sharing income with other communities. Tour operators also made verbal agreements for prices not kept or asked Indians to wear traditional clothing, thatch their huts, not use tin roofs and minimize use of plastic. While tourism was an economic alternative to selling timber, there was a shortage of the plants needed to weave baskets and make other tourist handicrafts (Snow and Wheeler, 2000). Only the Embera communities had ecotourism ventures, however marketing and visitors were controlled mainly by outside tour operators. Embera ownership of ecotourism was thus limited. Local groups were interested in community tourism, but government support was limited (Lumpkin, 1998).

Wekso Ecolodge

The Wekso Ecolodge on the Teribe River in Panama is a community ecotourism enterprise of the Naso people. It is located on the border of the La Amistad Biosphere Reserve with the largest area of rainforest in Central America. The harpy eagle and quetzal are found in the rainforest around Wekso Ecolodge, with the Reserve visited by 75% of migratory birds in the western continental area. The small lodge has three rooms and visitors eat traditional Naso meals. Conservation International supported the Naso people in developing Wekso lodge at a former jungle training camp. A non-profit organization, Grupo Odesen (Organisation for the Sustainable Development of Naso Ecotourism) was set up in 1995 by 11 Naso communities on the Teribe River to manage the lodge and distribute income. The lodge provides employment and income for some 20 families in the Naso community (CI, 2004d). Visitors can walk along forest trails, ride on a traditional raft and visit local Naso villages. The lodge has helped the Naso to retain their traditions, language and plant knowledge through interpretive jungle walks, an Indigenous museum and cultural centre, a Shaman's apprentice programme for young Naso people to learn about traditional medicine, and selling handicrafts (Buckley, 2003j; CI, 2004d). The Naso also received financial support from the US Critical Ecosystem Partnership Fund for new lodge infrastructure, a business plan, Naso medicinal plant gardens as a new attraction and promoting Wekso to tour operators in Panama City (Eco-Index, 2004e; Rome, 2004).

Nicaragua

Community ecotourism at Pearl Lagoon

In 2004, a Nicaraguan Indigenous organization (MIRAAS) and the Foundation for Sustainable Development (FUNDESO) supported rural ecotourism in four Indigenous communities on the Pearl Lagoon. Ninety Indigenous families lived in two nature reserves along the coast of eastern Nicaragua. This South Atlantic Autonomous Region of Nicaragua was a poor area where Mayagna, Miskito and Rama Indian groups lived in the coastal forest areas. Since 2001, the Government of Nicaragua has been legally demarcating and titling Indigenous lands. The ecotourism project funded the building of tourist cabins in two Indigenous communities at Pearl Lagoon, hiking trails and model farms. Denmark, Finland and Nicaragua funded this rural ecotourism project (US$75,000). Education on sustainable use of natural resources and tour guide training were also provided (Eco-Index, 2004e). Sustainable development of this region was linked to local environmental awareness and ecotourism.

Costa Rica

Talamanca ecotourism network

The Talamanca Mountains and rainforest in south-eastern Costa Rica are part of the La Amistad Biosphere Reserve World Heritage site. The Talamanca, with a large area of Atlantic moist forest, has 65% of Costa Rica's Indigenous population, including the Bribri and Cabecar groups (The Nature Conservancy, 2005). The Talamanca Corridor area was an area of high biological diversity with 90% of plants in Costa Rica, 350 bird species, 58 mammals, 51 reptiles and 43 amphibians. 25,000 people lived in this Talamanca Corridor region, a poor region of Costa Rica. Small-scale rural ecotourism ventures were established to support nature conservation and organic farming of cocoa, coffee and banana crops (Scialabba and Williamson, 2004). The Talamanca Ecotourism Network represented 16 local organizations or businesses mainly set up by local farmers and Indigenous groups involved in tourism. The Talamanca-Caribbean Biological Corridor Association (TCBCA), a conservation project, and a local NGO the ANAI Association launched this ecotourism network in 1998 to provide alternative income in the Talamanca area. The network with 203 members was financed by UNDP, Spain, Britain and a Costa Rica-Canada debt swap fund. The network helped to conserve 10,000 ha of forest, supported 21 local conservation or tourism initiatives such as bird watching and trained 60 local guides (Eco-Index, 2004f).

The TCBCA also helped to conserve 4000 ha of forest on private land, with 17.4% on Indigenous lands (The Nature Conservancy, 2005). The Talamanca Ecotourism Network linked with organic farming had also generated $450 million and 250 jobs. This Talamanca conservation and community development initiative won the 2002 UN Equator Prize (Jukofsky and Murillo, 2002).

There were two Indigenous organizations in the Talamanca Ecotourism Network for the Kekoldi and the Bribri groups. Ecotourism and organic farming provided local income, as the sale of wood was not allowed in Indigenous territories. Since 1995, the Indigenous Kekoldi group on Costa Rica's Caribbean coast provided bird tours to a site well known for watching migrating birds of prey and managed a nursery for green iguanas that tourists paid $2 to enter. The Kekoldi hunted the iguana, with the nursery used to reintroduce captive-bred iguanas into local forests (Redturs, nd). Tourism income supported the iguana nursery and other Kekoldi community projects. This ecotourism ethic of 'care for the earth' (or Kekoldi's keepers) was the meaning of the Kekoldi Wak Ka Koneke Association (Murillo, 2003). The Kekoldi Association was set up in 1994 to protect the forest and land through conservation and sustainable development. The association had 25 affiliated members from Bribri and Cabecar groups. The Stibraupa organization of female artisans represented the Bribri Indigenous group with their small ecolodge on the Yorquin River, forming the border between Costa Rica and Panama. This cabin for eight guests, Casa de Mujeres, was thatched with palm fronds. There was also a camping area for 20 people. Tourists travelled to the lodge by dugout canoe. The Yorquin area had 500 ha of protected forest, with sections owned by several Bribri families. Organic farming, rainforest walks, medicine plants, local Bribri food and traditions were shared with visitors. Hikes were taken in the community-owned forest of 1500 ha that had rivers, streams and thermal springs. Families sold fresh produce and crafts to visitors. The main benefit of this village-based ecotourism was that Bribri men stayed in the community instead of seeking other work. A 2-day tour cost US$50. This village ecotourism project began in 1997, with annual tourism income of US$2500–3000 (Murillo, 2003; Eco-Index, 2004g). Individual Bribri people donated their time for river transportation, food, cooking and serving and cultural presentations. Tour fees went to a community fund used for the needs of members (Blake, 2003). Fifteen Bribri families benefited from the Stibraupa association, with income from tourism, crafts and organic crops. The tours to Kekoldi and the Bribri reserve were promoted by ACTUAR, an association promoting community-based rural tourism in Costa Rica. Set up in 2001, the association supported over 20 rural tourism ventures around Costa Rica (ACTUAR, 2005a, b).

Ecotourism activities among other Indigenous groups in southern Costa Rica were supported by ARADIKES, a local NGO that supported reforestation, cultural projects and ecotourism, and opposed a hydroelectric dam. The directors of ARADIKES were people from six Indigenous groups. This forest conservation project, funded by Canada and Horizons of Friendship, began in 1993. The tourism projects included selling Indigenous art, a hostel in Terraba, ecological and cultural tours, and horse and walking trips in La Amistad International Park (Eco-Index, 2004h). Indigenous groups living in and around La Amistad Park were the key focus of conservation and ecotourism projects. The Boruca Indigenous community also led tours of the Cerro Sagardo de Cuasran area (Redturs, nd).

Dominican Republic, Caribbean

Carib Territory, Dominica

The Carib Indians on Dominica are the last Indigenous group living in the Caribbean. The Carib community of 2700 people received title to their mountainside reserve of 1500 ha in 1987. The Caribs live by selling garden produce and commercial crops. They also produce handicrafts made for sale to tourists such as baskets, handbags, place settings, hats, mats, fans and miniature canoes. These items are sold at roadside craft shops made from tree branches and palm thatching. Caribs also work as tour guides, taxi drivers and manage small guesthouses. In 1993, the Caribs developed a plan to promote community-based ecotourism, based on reviving crafts, music, dances and medicinal knowledge and conservation of the reserve (Haysmith and Harvey, 1995). Tourist dance performances were held in a traditional Carib longhouse with handicrafts sold at a stall outside (Joseph, 1997). With funding from the Caribbean Development, the community planned to build a model Carib village and guesthouses for tourists to stay with villagers. Conservation projects aimed to replant watersheds and grow plants used for making woven crafts, with ecotourism increasing forest values (Slinger, 2000). In 2000, US students helped Carib tour guides develop an ecotrail while Plenty International, a US village-based NGO, funded Carib education on land use and environmental issues (Wartinger, 2001).

Conclusion

Since the 1990s, Indian groups in Latin America have developed small-scale ecotourism ventures, such as jungle ecolodges and rainforest tours, in the Amazon basin and in Central America. Aided by legal land title and growing Indigenous political organization, several Indian groups have negotiated ecotourism agreements or contracts allowing access by private operators in exchange for lease fees, visitor entry fees, employment, support for community projects, transport and other tourism services. This has mainly occurred in the rainforest regions of Ecuador, Peru and Bolivia, where Indigenous groups have a stronger presence. The Amazon region of north-eastern Ecuador has a wide range of 35 community-owned Indian ecotourism ventures. These community-based ecotourism programmes provide an economic alternative to logging, mining and agriculture, fund school and healthcare facilities in communities and strengthen Indigenous cultures. In exchange, Indian groups limit land clearing and hunting in tourism areas. Indian ecotourism ventures are strategically located along rivers and lakes, nearby or in nature reserves (e.g. National Park, Biosphere/Wildlife Reserve) and at Indian communities with legal title to their lands. Conservation NGOs and other donor agencies (e.g. USAID and Inter-American Development Bank) have assisted Indian groups to develop ecotourism projects and preserve tropical rainforest areas. Some private companies in Ecuador and Peru have developed exclusive joint ventures and partnerships with Indian groups to develop ecolodges or operate ecotours in community areas (e.g. Kapawi Ecolodge, Posada Amazonas and Tropic Adventures).

The accessible Amazon rainforest region in the eastern sectors of Ecuador, Peru and Bolivia is a key focus for ecolodges and other Indigenous ecotourism ventures on Indian reserves or protected areas. Problems such as growing competition, low visitation rates and security issues limit these enterprises. Other limiting factors include basic tourism infrastructure, little name area recognition for remote areas and continued dependency on funding, staff training and marketing support from environmental NGOs and industry partners (Dahles and Keune, 2002). Some Amazon rainforest areas, such as the Cuyabeno Reserve in Ecuador, are still threatened by oil drilling.

In contrast to Ecuador, the vast Amazon region of Brazil has few Indigenous ecotourism ventures, apart from Tataquara Lodge and Mamiraua Reserve. Indian reserves in the Brazilian Amazon are poorly protected and threatened by extractive activities while there is no industry regulation of tourism. The same factors may also apply to Colombia, which has a tourism centre at Quito in the Amazon, but has very few Indigenous-owned ecotourism ventures. Suriname and French Guiana have Indigenous ecotourism at turtle nesting areas.

Tribal organizations, conservation NGOs, local NGOs, development agencies, researchers and private tourism companies all support Indigenous ecotourism ventures in Latin America. Conservation NGOs fund ecotourism projects to conserve biodiversity while local NGOs and tribal agencies develop a range of ventures to support Indian groups (e.g. Tataquara Lodge, Brazil; and Yachana Lodge, Ecuador).

In Guyana, the Iwokrama Forest assisted local Indian villages with community ecotourism ventures, supported by the North Rupununi District Development Board and using Canadian aid funding. With ecotourism, Indian groups retain primary forest areas, conserve key wildlife species, control or limit subsistence hunting, set aside nature reserves and reduce land clearing for cultivation. Most Indian reserves are still affected by illegal logging, poaching, settlers and land clearing for agriculture. A community ecotourism venture may limit these incursions or the extractive use of natural resources.

Rural Indian ecotourism is ancillary to mass tourism at beach resorts, archaeological sites and cities, especially in Central American countries. The Mayan forest at Punta Laguna and Sian Ka'an on the Yucatan Peninsula attracts tourists from Cancún on the Caribbean coast of Mexico. Other Indigenous ecotourism ventures in Central America such as Spanish schools, forest tours or lodges also rely on links with the mainstream tourism industry or marketing networks with conservation NGOs (e.g. Ecomaya, Guatemala; and Talamanca Ecotourism Network, Costa Rica). The uneven development of Indigenous ecotourism ventures in Latin American countries depends on their location, accessibility and resource features along with land title for Indian reserves, funding, agency support, government assistance for ecotourism and tourism agreements with private operators. Community networks (e.g. RICANCIE in Ecuador; and Toledo Ecotourism Association in Belize) and allied resource projects such as agriculture, forest products and language schools can also support Indian ecotourism ventures.

The expansion of Indigenous ecotourism ventures in Latin America suggests that conservation NGOs, many Indian groups and the tourism industry see these projects as a solution to environmental and community concerns. However, growth may not be matched by market demand for these products.

References

ACTUAR (2005a) Bribri Indigenous Reserve rural adventure in Yorkin. Community-based Rural Tourism in Costa Rica (ACTUAR). Rural Adventures. http://www.actuarcostarica.com/ingles/bribri_yorkin.htm (accessed 17 November 2005)

ACTUAR (2005b) Kekoldi. Community-based Rural Tourism in Costa Rica (ACTUAR). Rural Adventures. http://www.actuarcostarica.com/ingles/kekoldi.htm (accessed 17 November 2005)

Allicock, S. (2003) Developing partnerships between the North Rupununi District Development Board (NRDDB) and the Iwokrama International Centre Programme for Rainforest Conservation and Development. Indigenous Rights in the Commonwealth Caribbean and Americas Regional Expert Meeting, Georgetown, Guyana, 23–25 June, 2003. http://www.iwokrama.org/library/pdfdowload/ NRDDB%20%20Iwokrama%20by%20S.%.Allicock.pdf (accessed 17 November 2005)

Amazon Coop (2004) The ecotourism business of the Amazon Coop. http://www.amazoncoop.org/ (accessed 17 November 2005)

AMTAVE (2005) Communities. Mexican Association of Adventure Tourism and Ecotourism. http://www.amtave.org/publish.php?cons=15 (accessed 17 November 2005)

Archibald, G. and Davey, S. (1993) Kuna Yala: Protecting the San Blas of Panama. In: Kemf, E. (ed.) *The Law of the Mother: Protecting Indigenous People in Protected Areas.* WWF/CEC/IUCN.

Armesto, J.J., Smith-Ramirez, C. and Rozzi, R. (2001) Conservation strategies for biodiversity and indigenous peoples in Chilean forest ecosystems. *Journal of the Royal Society of New Zealand* 31, 865–877.

Atkinson, D. (2004) Che. http://guidebookwriters.com/samples/david-atkinson.html (accessed 17 November 2005)

Barkin, D. and Bouchez, C.P. (2002) NGO-community collaboration for ecotourism: A strategy for sustainable regional development. *Current Issues in Tourism* 5, 245–253.

Beavers, J. (1995a) *Community-based Ecotourism in the Maya Forest: Six Case Studies From Communities in Mexico, Guatemala, and Belize.* The Nature Conservancy, USAID/Mayafor Project.

Beavers, J. (1995b) The Toledo Ecotourism Association (TEA) and its philosophy. TIES Online Library. Indigenous/Community Ecotourism. http://www.ecotour.org/ (accessed 17 November 2005)

Bennett, J. (1997) San Blas: The role of control and community participation in sustainable tourism development. Masters Thesis, University of North London, UK.

Bennett, J. (1999) The dream and the reality: Tourism in Kuna Yala. *Cultural Survival Quarterly* 23.

Blake, B. (2003) The tourism industry's codes for indigenous peoples. In: Honey, M. and Thullen, S. (eds) *Rights and Responsibilities: A Compilation of Codes of Conduct for Tourism and Indigenous and Local Communities.* Center on Ecotourism and Sustainable Development and The International Ecotourism Society. http://205.252.29.37/webarticles/anmviewer.asp?a=14 (accessed 17 November 2005)

Blangy, S. (1999) Ecotourism without tears. *UNESCO Courier* July–August, 32–34.

Boniface, B. and Cooper, C. (2005) Ecotourism in the Ecuadorian Amazon. In: *Worldwide destinations casebook: The geography of travel and tourism.* Elsevier, Oxford, pp. 238–244.

Borman, R. (1999) Cofan: Story of the forest people and the outsiders. *Cultural Survival Quarterly* 23, 48–50.

Borman, R. (2001) Forest tourism: Can computers save a rainforest? People and ecotourism. http://www.peopleandplanet.net/doc.php?id=131 (accessed 17 November 2005)

Braman, S. (2002) Creating Huaorani discourse on tourism. *Cultural Survival Quarterly* 25. http://209.200.101.189/publications/csq/csq-article.cfm?id=1402&highlight=ecotourism (accessed 17 November 2005)

Brandon, K. (1996) *Ecotourism and Conservation: Key Issues.* World Bank Environment, Paper 033. World Bank, Washington DC.

Bravo, L. (2004) Sian Ka'an visitor centre sustainable training centre. http://www.ecotravelmexico.com/ Press_Release_Sian_Kaan_Visitor_Center.htm (accessed 17 November 2005)

Bray, D.B., Merino-Perez, L., Negeros-Castillo, P., Segura-Warnholtz, G., Torres-Rojo, J.M. and Vester, H.F.M. (2003) Mexico's community-managed forests as a global model for sustainable landscapes. *Conservation Biology* 17, 672–677.

Brown, D.F. (1999) Mayas and tourists in the Maya world. *Human Organization* 58, 295–304.

Brown, J. and Mitchell, N. (2000) Culture and nature in the protection of Andean landscapes. *Mountain Research and Development* 20, 212–217.

Buckley, R. (2003a) Quichua communities, Ecuador. In: *Case Studies in Ecotourism.* CABI, Wallingford, UK, pp. 145–147.

Buckley, R. (2003b) RICANCIE and the Napo Runa, Ecuador. In: *Case Studies in Ecotourism*. CABI, Wallingford, UK, pp. 147–148.

Buckley, R. (2003c) The Cofan and Cuyabeno Wildlife Reserve, Ecuador. In: *Case Studies in Ecotourism*. CABI, Wallingford, UK, p. 150.

Buckley, R. (2003d) TROPIC and the Huaorani, Ecuador. In: *Case Studies in Ecotourism*. CABI, Wallingford, UK, pp. 148–150.

Buckley, R. (2003e) Posada Amazonas and Tambopata Reserve and Research Centre, Peru. In: *Case Studies in Ecotourism*. CABI, Wallingford, UK, pp. 134–135.

Buckley, R. (2003f) Chalalan Ecolodge, Bolivia. In: *Case Studies in Ecotourism*. CABI, Wallingford, UK, pp. 133–134.

Buckley, R. (2003g) Toledo Ecotourism Association, Belize. In: *Case Studies in Ecotourism*. CABI, Wallingford, UK, pp. 143–144.

Buckley, R. (2003h) Ecomaya, Guatemala. In: *Case Studies in Ecotourism*. CABI, Wallingford, UK, pp. 151–152.

Buckley, R. (2003i) San Pedro volcano, Guatemala. In: *Case Studies in Ecotourism*. CABI, Wallingford, UK, pp. 152–153.

Buckley, R. (2003j) Wekso Ecolodge, Panama. In: *Case Studies in Ecotourism*. CABI, Wallingford, UK, pp. 132–133.

Cahill, T. (2004) Madidi National Park, Bolivia: Call of the wild. *National Geographic Traveler* 21, 52–58.

Carballo-Sandoval, A. (1999) *Community Involvement in Sustainable Ecotourism: The Case of the Mexican Caribbean Area*. University of Reading, Reading, UK.

Carr, T.A., Pedersen, H.L. and Ramaswamy, S. (1993) Rainforest entrepreneurs: Cashing in on conservation. *Environment* 35, 12–15.

Cattarinich, X. (2003) *Report on the Development of the North Rupununi Tourism Impact Monitoring Tool*. Ecotourism Unit, Iwokrama International Centre. http://www.iwokrama.org/library/pdfdownload/XavierCattarinich2003.pdf (accessed 17 November 2005)

Chapin, M. (1990) The silent jungle: Ecotourism among the Kuna Indians of Panama. *Cultural Survival Quarterly* 14, 42–45.

Chapin, M. (2000) *Defending Kuna Yala: PEMASKY, the Study Project for the Wildlands of Kuna Yala, Panama*. USAID Biodiversity Support Program, Washington DC.

Chaurette, E., Sarmiento, F.O. and Rodriguez, J. (2003) A protected landscape candidate in the tropical Andes of Ecuador. *Parks* 13, 42–51.

CI (Conservation International) (2004a) Chalalan Ecolodge, Bolivian Amazon. The Ecotravel Centre. Ecotourism Destinations. http://www.ecotour.org/destinations/chalalan.htm (accessed 17 November 2005)

CI (Conservation International) (2004b) Host to host: Lessons learned. Critical Ecosystem Partnership Fund. http://www.cepf.net/xp/cepof/in_focus/2003/July2003lessons.xml (accessed 17 November 2005)

CI (Conservation International) (2004c) Guatemala (Bio-Itza, Eco-Escuela de Espanol, Ecomaya, Mayan Trails). The Ecotravel Center. Ecotourism Destinations. http://www.ecotour.org/destinations/ (accessed 17 November 2005)

CI (Conservation International) (2004d) Wekso Ecolodge, Panamanian Lowland Rainforest. The Ecotravel Centre. Ecotourism Destinations. http://www.ecotour.org/destinations/wekso.htm (accessed 17 November 2005)

CI (Conservation International) (2005a) Indigenous reserves a force for conservation. Conservation Frontlines online. http://www.conservation.org/xp/frontlines/protectedareas/focus31-2.xml (accessed 17 November 2005)

CI (Conservation International) (2005b) Kayapo Indigenous Territories: Preserving ancestral lands. Conservation Frontlines online. http://www.conservation.org/xp/frontlines/people/parkprofile24-5.xml (accessed 17 November 2005)

Colchester, M. and Watson, F. (1995) Impacts of ecotourism in Venezuela. Planeta.com. http://www.planeta.com/planeta/95/195ven.html (accessed 17 November 2005)

Colvin, J.G. (1994) Capirona: A model of indigenous ecotourism. *Journal of Sustainable Tourism* 2, 174–177.

Colvin, J.G. (1996) Indigenous ecotourism: The Capirona programme in Napo province, Ecuador. *Unasylva* (FAO) 187(47).

Conway, K. (1998) Creating ecologically based businesses in the Maya Biosphere Reserve. IDRC Canada. http://web.idrc.ca/en/ev-5133-201-1-DO_TOPIC.html (accessed 17 November 2005)

CPEC (2002) Guyana tourism. Caribbean Program for Economic Competitiveness. http://www.cpechrd.org/guytourism.htm (accessed 17 November 2005)

Cruz, R.E.H., Baltazar, E.B., Gomez, G.M. and Lugo, E.I.J.E. (2005) Social adaptation: Ecotourism in the Lacandon forest. *Annals of Tourism Research* 32, 610–627.

Dahles, H. and Keune, L. (eds) (2002) *Tourism development and local participation in Latin America.* Cognizant Communication Corporation, New York.

da Silva, J.M.C. (2005) Aggressive development in Brazilian Amazon galvanises forces for sustainable development. Conservation Frontlinesonline. Conservation International. http://www.conservation.org/xp/frontlines/protectedareas/focus31-1.xml (accessed 17 November 2005)

de Bont, C. and Janssen, W. (2003) Indigenous people and local participation in tourism: Two case studies from Ecuador. In: Dahles, H. and Keune, L. (eds) *Tourism Development and Local Participation in Latin America.* Cognizant Communication Corporation, New York, pp. 115–129.

Developments (2004) The Che revolution. *Developments: The International Development Magazine,* 27. http://www.developments.org.uk/data/issue27/bolivia-che.htm (accessed 17 November 2005)

Diegues, A.C. (nd) The myth of wilderness in the Brazilian rainforest. Theme on Culture and Conservation. IUCN/CEESP. http:/www.iucn.org/themes/ceesp/culture.html (accessed 9 May 2006)

Dilly, B.J. (2003) Gender, culture, and ecotourism: Development policies and practices in the Guyanese rain forest. *Women's Studies Quarterly* 31, 58–75.

Drumm, A. (1998) New approaches to community-based ecotourism management: Learning from Ecuador. In: Lindberg, K. Epler Wood, M. and Engeldrum, D. (eds) *Ecotourism: A Guide for Planners and Managers,* Vol. 2. The Ecotourism Society, Vermont, pp. 197–213.

Duffy, R. (2002) Ecotourism and Indigenous communities. In: *A Trip Too Far: Ecotourism, Politics and Exploitation.* Earthscan, London, pp. 98–126.

Dunn, A. (1995) *Summaries of Some Recent Project Approaches to Conservation and Development.* Rural Development Forestry Network, ODI. http://www.odifpeg.org.uk/publications/rdfn/18/d-i.html (accessed 17 November 2005)

Eco-Exchange (2001) The Kuna of Panama aim to develop a new kind of tourism: On their own terms. *Eco-Exchange* June–July 2001. http://www.rainforest-alliance.org/programs/neocomm/newsletter/ (accessed 17 November 2005)

Eco-Index (2004a) Ecotourism in special management areas: Tierra Adentro zone, Cauca, Colombia. Eco-Index. Rainforest Alliance. http://www.eco-index.org/search/results.cfm?projectID=782 (accessed 17 November 2005)

Eco-Index (2004b) Amazonian host to host: Ecotourism exchanges in the tropical Andes. Eco-Index. Rainforest Alliance. http://www.eco-index.org/search/results.cfm?projectID=390 (accessed 17 November 2005)

Eco-Index (2004c) Rio Platano Reserve Integrated Management Program. Eco-Index. Rainforest Alliance. http://www.eco-index.org/search/results.cfm?projectID=135 (accessed 17 November 2005)

Eco-Index (2004d) Program to promote indigenous alternative tourism in Panama. Eco-Index. Rainforest Alliance. http://www.eco-index.org/search/results.cfm?ProjectID=176 (accessed 17 November 2005)

Eco-Index (2004e) Weckso ecotourism project. Eco-Index. Rainforest Alliance. http://www.eco-index.org/search/results.cfm?ProjectID=714 (accessed 17 November 2005)

Eco-Index (2004f) Talamanca community tourism network. Eco-Index. Rainforest Alliance. http://www.eco-index.org/search/results.cfm?ProjectID=407 (accessed 17 November 2005)

Eco-Index (2004g) La Casa de las Mujeres. Eco-Index. Rainforest Alliance. http://www.eco-index.org/search/results.cfm?ProjectID=405 (accessed 17 November 2005)

Eco-Index (2004h) Regional Aboriginal Association of Dikes (ARADIKES), Costa Rica. Eco-Index. Rainforest Alliance. http://www.eco-index.org/search/results.cfm?ProjectID=846 (accessed 17 November 2005)

Ecomaya (2004) EcoTrails and Spanish schools. http://www.ecomaya.com/ (accessed 17 November 2005) Tikal Connection. Maya Biosphere, Spanish Schools, Eco Trails. http://tikalcnz.com/ (accessed 17 November 2005)

Ecotribal (2005) Welcome to ecotribal. http://www.ecotribal.com/content/index.php (accessed 8 February 2006)

Ecovision (nd) Ecovision – promoting tourism in Guyana. http://www.ecovision.org.gy/mission.html (accessed 17 November 2005)

Edeli, D. (2002) Selling culture without selling out: Community eco-tourism in the global economy. *Harvard Review of Latin America,* Winter. http://www.fas.harvard.edu/~drdas/publications/revista/tourism/Edeli.html (accessed 30 March 2006)

Edington, J.M. and Edington, M.A. (1997) Tropical forest ecotourism: Two promising projects in Belize. In: Stabler, M.J. (ed.) *Tourism and Sustainability: Principles to Practice.* CABI, Wallingford, UK, pp. 163–168.

Edwards, S.N., McLaughlin, W.J. and Ham, S.H. (1998) *Comparative Study of Ecotourism Policy in the Americas – 1998. Volume II Latin America and the Caribbean.* University of Idaho and Organization of American States. http://www.oas.org/tourism/VIIEPS.pdf (accessed 17 November 2005)

El Manglar (2003) Mangrove environmental protection group. http://www.elmanglar.com.singataya.html (accessed 17 November 2005)

ENS (Environmental News Service) (1999) Chalalan Ecolodge, Bolivia. The Ecotravel Center. ENS.

Epler Wood, M. (1998) *Meeting the Global Challenge of Community Participation in Ecotourism: Case Studies and Lessons from Ecuador.* The Nature Conservancy, Virginia.

Epler Wood, M. (2004) Annual Report: Epler Wood International 2003. http://www.eplerwood.com/news.php (accessed 17 November 2005)

Expoecoturismo (2005) News. Expoecoturismo. http://www.expoecoturismo.com/siteenglish/newsintro.htm (accessed 17 November 2005)

Flores, A.L. (2005) Venezuela journal: CI and the Yek'wana peoples in Venezuela's Caura Basin. Conservation Frontlines online. Conservation International. http://www.conservation.org/xp/frontlines/people/fieldnotes31.xml (accessed 17 November 2005)

FNV (First Nations Vacations) (2000) First Nations Vacations. http://www.guidedculturaltours.com/fnv/ (accessed 17 November 2005)

Forero, J. (2004) Kapawi journal: Ecuador Indians fend off oil companies with tourism. *The New York Times* 19 January 2004, A4.

Forest Peoples Project (nd) South America – community mapping in Guyana. http://www.forestpeoples.org/templates/projects/south_america.shtml (accessed 17 November 2005)

Foster Parrots (2003) Eco-tourism? Quito, Ecuador. http://www.fosterparrots.com/etecuador.html (accessed 17 November 2005)

Foster Parrots (2004) Eco-tourism? Project Guyana. http://www.fosterparrots.com/etguyana.html (accessed 17 November 2005)

Foucat, V.S.A. (2002) Community-based ecotourism management moving towards sustainability in Ventanilla, Oaxaca, Mexico. *Ocean & Coastal Management* 45, 511–529.

Frapolli, E.G. (2003) Local participation and biodiversity conservation: The natural protected area *Otoch Ma'ax Yetel Kooh*, in the Yucatan Peninsula (Mexico). PhD thesis. Autonomous University of Barcelona, Spain. http://www.h-economica.uab.es/tercicle/econecol/publications/eduardo_garcia.pdf (accessed 17 November 2005)

Freitas, C.E.C., Kahn, J.R. and Rivas, A.A.F. (2004) Indigenous people and sustainable development in Amazonas. *International Journal of Sustainable Development and World Ecology* 11, 312–325.

FUNEDESIN (2004) Amazon Ecotours (Yachana Lodge), Rainforest Conservation. Foundation for Integrated Education and Development. http://www.funedesin.org/ (accessed 17 November 2005)

Garcia, B., Gasques, J.G. and Bastos, E.T. (2004) Ecotourism in the Amazon. IEMSS 2004 Conference. http://www.iemss.org/iemss2004/pdf/ecotourism/garcecot.pdf (accessed 17 November 2005)

Gardner, S. (2001) Peru's rainforest natives pin future on ecotourism. Reuter News Service. 10 October 2001. Environmental News. Planet Ark. http://www.planetark.com/dailynewsstory.cfm (accessed 17 November 2005)

Gines, M.J. (1999) Indigenous management of eco-tourism in the Amazon (Venezuela). IDRC Canada. http://web.idrc.ca/es/ev-40438-201-1-DO_TOPIC.html (accessed 17 November 2005)

Godfrey, M.H. and Drif, O. (2001) Developing sea turtle ecotourism in French Guiana: Perils and practicalities. *Marine Turtle Newsletter* 91, 1–4.

Gray, A., Newing, H. and Parellada, A. (1998) *From Principles to Practice: Indigenous Peoples and Biodiversity Conservation in Latin America.* Forest Peoples Programme with IWGIA & AIDESEP.

Greathouse-Amador, L.M. (1997) Ethnic, cultural, and ecotourism. *American Behavioral Scientist* 7, 936–943.

Greathouse-Amador, L.M. (2005) Tourism and policy in preserving minority languages and culture: The Cuetzalan experience. *Review of Policy Research* 22, 49–58.

Guynup, S. (2002) Rain forest expert saves his Amazon 'neighbourhood'. National Geographic News, National Geographic Today, 17 December 2002. http://www.nationalgeographic.com/news/2002/12/ (accessed 17 November 2005)

Haysmith, L. and Harvey, J. (1995) *Nature Conservation and Ecotourism in Central America.* Wildlife Conservation Society, New York.

Healy, G.H. (1996) Tourism policy in Brazil: Development alternatives and environmental consequences.

Nicholas School of the Environment. http://www.nicholas.duke.edu/people/faculty/healy/BRAZIL_h.html (accessed 17 November 2005)

Healy, K. and Zorn, E. (1983a) Lake Titicaca's campesino controlled tourism. *Grassroots Development* 6/7, 5–10.

Healy, K. and Zorn, E. (1983b) Lake Titicaca's campesino controlled tourism. In: Annis, S. and Hakim, P. (eds) *Direct to the Poor: Grassroots Development in Latin America.* Lynne Reinner, Boulder, Colorado, pp. 45–56.

Healey, K. (1993) *Indigenous Peoples.* Issues for the Nineties, Vol. 10. Spinney Press, Australia.

Hearne, R. and Santos, C. (2005) Tourists' and locals' preferences toward ecotourism development in the Maya Biosphere Reserve, Guatemala. *Environment, Development and Sustainability* 7, 303–318.

Herrman, T.M. (2005) Knowledge, values, uses and management of the *Araucaria araucana* forest by the indigenous Mapuche Pwenche people: A basis for collaborative natural resource management in southern Chile. *Natural Resources Forum* 29, 120–134.

Hill, R. (2004) *Global Trends in Protected Areas: A Report on the Fifth World Parks Congress.* Rainforest CRC, Cairns. http://www.acfonline.org.au/uploads/res_protected_areas.pdf (accessed 29 November 2005)

Hinojosa, F.C. (1992) The Cuyabeno Wildlife Reserve. In: Redford, K.H. and Padoch, C. (eds) *Conservation of Neotropical Forests: Working from Traditional Resource Use.* Columbia University Press.

Holle, K. (1998) Tambopata: Community owned venture redefines ecotourism. Planeta.com Website. http://www.planeta.com/planeta/98/0598tambo.html (accessed 17 November 2005)

Horochowski, K. and Moisey, R.N. (1999) The role of environmental NGOs in sustainable tourism development: A case study in northern Honduras. *Tourism Recreation Research* 24, 19–29.

Horochowski, K. and Moisey, R.N. (2001) Sustainable tourism: The effect of local participation in Honduran ecotourism development. In: McCool, S.F. and Moisey, R.N. (eds) *Tourism, Recreation and Sustainability: Linking Culture and the Environment.* CABI, Wallingford, UK, pp. 163–175.

Horwich, R.H. and Lyon, J. (1999) Rural ecotourism as a conservation tool. In: Singh, T.V. and Singh, S. (eds) *Tourism Development in Critical Environments.* Cognizant Communication Corporation, New York, pp. 102–119.

Hutchins, F.T. (2002) Ecotourism and global connections among the Quichua in Ecuador's Amazon. PhD thesis, University of Wisconsin, Madison.

Igoe, J.J. (2004) Indigenous protected areas – the Kuna park. In: *Conservation and Globalization: A Study of National Parks and Indigenous Communities from East Africa to South Dakota.* Thomson/Wadsworth, Belmont, California, pp. 159–161.

Ingles, P. (2001) Performing traditional dances for modern tourists in the Amazon. In: Santana, G. (ed.) *Tourism in South America.* The Haworth Hospitality Press, New York, 143–159. Co-published in the *International Journal of Hospitality & Tourism Administration* 1, 143–159.

Ingles, P. (2002) Welcome to my village: Hosting tourists in the Peruvian Amazon. *Tourism Recreation Research* 27, 53–60.

IFC (International Finance Corporation) (2004) Rainforest Expeditions, Peru. In: *Ecolodges: Exploring opportunities for sustainable business.* International Finance Corporation, pp. 37–41. http://ifcln1.ifc.org/ifctext/enviro.nsf/Content/EBFP_Ecolodge (accessed 17 November 2005)

Irvine, D. (2000) Indigenous federations and the market: The Runa of Napo, Ecuador. In: Weber, R., Butler, J. and Larson, P. (eds) *Indigenous Peoples and Conservation Organizations: Experiences in Collaboration.* WWF, pp. 21–46. http://www.worldwildlife.org/bsp/publications/ (accessed 17 November 2005)

Iwokrama (2004) Indigenous people. Iwokrama Centre. http://www.iwokrama.org/people/indigenouspeople.htm (accessed 17 November 2005)

Iwokrama (2005a) Iwokrama International Centre makes major strides in 2004; announces key initiatives for 2005. Press Release, 4 January 2005. Iwokrama Centre. http://www.iwokrama.org/news/pressreleases/ (accessed 17 November 2005)

Iwokrama (2005b) Government of Guyana secures support for Iwokrama from the United Nations Development Programme. Press Release, 11 January 2005. http://www.iwokrama.org/news/press releases/ (accessed 17 November 2005)

Iwokrama Newsletter (2003) Local community and private sector consortium wins Iwokrama canopy walkway concession, Communities move ahead with ecotourism products. *Iwokrama E-mail Newsletter* October 2003, 2. http://www.iwokrama.org/newsletter/octissue.html (accessed 17 November 2005)

Iwokrama Newsletter (2004) First community guide training course completed in Guyana. Canopy walkway opening. *Iwokrama E-mail Newsletter* February 2004, 1. http://www.iwokrama.org/newsletter/febissue.html (accessed 17 November 2005)

Joseph, G. (1997) The Indigenous people of the Caribbean. In: Wilson, S.M. (ed.) *Five Hundred Years of Indigenous Resistance*. University Press of Florida, Gainesville.

Juarez, A.M. (2002) Ecological degradation, global tourism, and inequality: Maya interpretations of the changing environment in Quintana Roo, Mexico. *Human Organization* 61, 113–124.

Jukofsky, D. and Murillo, K. (2002) Global prize awarded to sustainable development initiative in Talamanca mountains of Costa Rica. *Eco-Exchange*, November–December 2002. Rainforest Alliance. Neotropics Communications. http://www.rainforest-alliance.org/programs/neocomm/newsletter/2002/nov02-1.html (accessed 17 November 2005)

Kapawi Ecolodge (2004) Kapawi Ecolodge & Reserve. http://www.kapawi.com/html/en/home/aboutus.htm (accessed 17 November 2005)

Kempery Tours (nd) Bataburo lodge. Kempery Tours. http://www.kempery.com/ecuador_amazon_bataburo lodge.htm (accessed 17 November 2005)

Kohl, J. (2003) Embera ecotourism: Keeping civilization at arm's length. *Native Peoples* September/October. http://jonkohl.com/publications/nativepeoples.htm (accessed 17 November 2005)

Krenke, M. and Murillo, K. (2005) Indigenous groups and NGOs use creative approaches to save lands in Ecuadorian Amazon from oil companies. Rainforest Alliance. http://www.rainforest-alliance.org/programs/newcomm/newsletter/2005/sept05-1.html (accessed 17 November 2005)

La Rose, J. (2004) In Guyana, indigenous peoples fight to join conservation efforts. *Cultural Survival Quarterly* 28. http://209.200.101.189/publications/csq/csq-article.cfm?id=1741 (accessed 17 November 2005)

Lemky, K.M.K. (1992) The Amazon rainforest ecotourism industry of Napo, Ecuador. MA thesis, University of Ottawa.

Lindsay, H.E. (2003) Ecotourism: The promise and perils of environmentally-oriented travel. Ecotourism. Cambridge Scientific Abstracts. http://moe.csa.com/hottopics/ecotour1/oview.html (accessed 17 November 2005)

Lumpkin, T. (1998) Community based ecotourism in the Panama Canal watershed: Executive summary. May 1998. Planeta.com. http://www.planeta.com/planeta/99/0799panama.html (accessed 17 November 2005)

Mader, R. (2002) Latin American ecotourism: What is it? *Current Issues in Tourism* 5, 272–279.

Mader, R. (2003) Latin American ecotourism: What is it? In: Luck, M. and Kirstges, T. (eds) *Global ecotourism policies and case studies*. Channel View Publications, Clevedon, pp. 100–107.

Mader, R. (2004) Spotlight on Indigenous groups and tourism in Ecuador. World Travel Directory. http://www.planeta.com/ecotravel/south/ecuador/ecind.html (accessed 17 November 2005)

Madidi.com (2004) About Us, Links-Ecolodges. http://www.palouse.net/alanperry/aboutus.html (accessed 17 November 2005)

Mahler, R. (1997) Community's control their tourism destiny in rural Belize. http://www.planeta.com/planeta/97/1197belize.html (accessed 17 November 2005)

Mahler, R. and Wotkyns, S. (1995) Toledo district. In: *Belize: A Natural Destination*. John Muir Publications, Santa Fe, New Mexico, pp. 154–166.

Mapajo (nd) Indigenous ecotourism. Mapajo Ecolodge. http://h7887.serverkompetenz.net/mapajo (accessed 17 November 2005)

Marglin, F.A. (1995) Development or decolonisation in the Andes? *Futures* 27, 869–882.

Marquez, H. (2004) Venezuela pushes ecotourism in the tropical Andes. Global Information Network, New York, 23 (September), 1.

Maud, H. (2003) The Iwokrama story – a Commonwealth cliff-hanger. *The Round Table* 371, 477–485.

Mets (2005a) Info about Suriname, Surinamese cultures. Mets Travel & Tours. http://www.metsresorts.com/en/suriname/index.html (accessed 17 November 2005)

Mets (2005b) Palumeu. Mets Travel & Tours. http://www.metsresorts.com/en/junglelodges/palumeu.html (accessed 17 November 2005)

Mets (2005c) Profile. Mets Travel & Tours. http://www.metsresorts.com/en/general/profile.html (accessed 17 November 2005)

Mitchell, R.E. (1998) Community integration in ecotourism: A comparative case study of two communities in Peru. MSc thesis in Rural Planning and Development, University of Guelph, Ontario.

Mitchell, R.E. (2001) Community perspectives in sustainable tourism: Lessons from Peru. In: McCool, S.F. and Moisey, R.N. (eds) *Tourism, Recreation and Sustainability: Linking Culture and the Environment*. CABI, Wallingford, UK, pp. 137–162.

Mitchell, R. (2004) Community tourism in Peru: The island of Taquile, Lake Titicaca. http://www.planeta.com/planeta/00/0010/peru.html (accessed 17 November 2005)

Mitchell, R.E. and Eagles, P.F.J. (2001) An integrative approach to tourism: Lessons from the Andes of Peru. *Journal of Sustainable Tourism* 9, 4–28.

Mitchell, R.E. and Reid, D.G. (2001) Community integration: Island tourism in Peru. *Annals of Tourism Research* 28, 113–139.

MLF (Macaw Landing Foundation) (2004a) Cuyabeno. Ecotourism. http://www.cnnw.net/~cuyabeno.html (accessed 17 November 2005)

MLF (Macaw Landing Foundation) (2004b) Timpia and the Machiguenga Center. Ecotourism. http://www.cnnw.net/~mlf/timpia.html (accessed 17 November 2005)

Momsen, J.H. (2002) NGOs, gender and indigenous grassroots development. *Journal of International Development* 14, 859–867.

Mountain Institute, The (2005a) Welcome to Vicos, Peru! Andean Tourism. The Mountain Institute. http://www.mountain.org/work/andes/ttourism/vicos.cfm (accessed 17 November 2005)

Mountain Institute, The (2005b) Humacchuco homestay tourism. Andean Tourism. The Mountain Institute. http://www.mountain.org/work/andes/ttourism/humacchuco.cfm (accessed 17 November 2005)

Mountain Institute, The (2005c) Inca Nani – The Great Inca Road. Andean Tourism. The Mountain Institute. http://www.mountain.org/work/andes/ttourism/incanani.cfm (accessed 17 November 2005)

Mowforth, M. and Munt, I. (2003) Government control/community control. In: *Tourism and Sustainability: Development and New Tourism in the Third World.* Routledge, London, pp. 224–234.

Muller, K. (2000) *Along the Inca road: A woman's journey into an ancient empire.* Adventure Press, National Geographic Society, Washington DC.

Murillo, K. (2003) In Costa Rica's Talamanca Mountains: Tourism network connects farmers, communities with nature. *Eco-Exchange Newsletter*, February–March 2003. Rainforest Alliance. http://www.rainforest-alliance.org/programs/neocomm/newsletter/2003/mar03-1.html (accessed 17 November 2005)

Nauman, T. (2002) Reclaiming a territory and the culture that goes with it. *Changemakers Journal*, February. http://www.changemakers.net/journal/02february/nauman.cfm (accessed 17 November 2005)

Newing, H. and Wahl, L. (2004) Benefiting local populations? Communal reserves in Peru. *Cultural Survival Quarterly* 28. http://209.200.101.189/publications/csq/csq-article.cfm?id=1742 (accessed 17 November 2005)

Nielsen, E. and Munguia, O. (1998) Community participation in wildlands management: A case of indigenous efforts to plan and manage sustainable ecotourism in the Rio Platano Biosphere Reserve, Honduras. The World Bank/WBI CBNRM Initiative. http://srdis.ciesin.org/cases/honduras-004.html (accessed 17 November 2005)

Norris, R.J., Wilber, S. and Marin, L.O.M. (1998) Community-based ecotourism in the Maya forest: Problems and potentials. http://www.planeta.com/planeta/98/0598mayaforest.html (accessed 17 November 2005)

Nycander, E. (2000) Posada Amazonas. In: *Sustainable Development of Tourism: A Compilation of Good Practices.* WTO, Madrid, pp. 143–145.

Nycander, E. and Holle, K. (1996) Rainforest expeditions: Combining tourism, education and research in southwest Amazonian Peru. *Yale School of Forestry and Environmental Studies Bulletin* 99, 169–181.

Nycander, E. and Holle, K. (nd) The Ese'eja native community of Tambopata, Peru: Protecting harpy eagles and macaws to show their guests. TIES Online Library. Community/Indigenous Tourism. http://www.ecotourism.org/ (accessed 17 November 2005)

Olsder, K. (2004) *Sustainable Ecotourism in the Guiana Shield Region.* A Working Document for the Guiana Shield Initiative. Netherlands Committee for IUCN, Amsterdam.

Osava, M. (2005) World social forum: Indigenous peoples claim their own space. Quechua Network, 5/2/05. http://www.quechuanetwork.org/news_template.cfm?news_id=2454&lang=e (accessed 17 November 2005)

Page, S. and Dowling, R.K. (2002) Community-based ecotourism: Management and development issues. In: *Ecotourism.* Pearson Education, Harlow, UK, pp. 244–247.

Pane, R. (2004) Protected areas in Suriname: A voice from Suriname's Galibi Nature Reserve. *Cultural Survival Quarterly* 28. http://209.200.101.189/publications/csq/csq-article.cfm?id=1744 (accessed 29 November 2005)

Pani, R. (nd) Traditional forest use and ecotourism at the Infierno native community: Two different income generating activities and their impact on local peoples economies. Masters Thesis. Research Papers on the Ese'ejas. Posada Amazons, Rainforest Expeditions. http://www.perunature.com/info07.asp (accessed 17 November 2005)

Parent, D. (1995) Cloudforest: A journey to the summit of volcano San Pedro. http://www2.planeta.com/ (accessed 17 November 2005)

Parent, D.A. (1999) Indigenous-based and commercial ecotourism in La Mosquitia, The Olancho Pech. http://www.garrobo.org/mosquitia/pecdap.html (accessed 17 November 2005)

People and Planet (2002) A new kind of tourism in Panama. http://www.peopleandplanet.net/doc.php?id=1437 (accessed 17 November 2005)

PEQ (Proyecto Ecologico Quetzal) (2002) Low impact tourism. PEQ Website. http://www.ecoquetzal.org/ (accessed 17 November 2005)

Pi-Sunyer, O., Thomas, R.B. and Daltabuit, M. (2001) Tourism on the Maya periphery. In: Smith, V.L. and Brent, M. (eds) *Hosts and Guests Revisited: Tourism Issues of the 21st Century*. Cognizant Communication Corporation, New York, pp. 122–140.

PPT (Pro Poor Tourism) (2001) Case Study 6: Tropic Ecological Adventures, Ecuador. Pro-Poor Tourism. http://www.propoortourism.org.uk/ecuador_sum.html (accessed 17 November 2005)

Prance, G.T. (1998) Indigenous non-timber benefits from tropical rain forest. In: Goldsmith, F.B. (ed.) *Tropical Rain Forest: A Wider Perspective*. Chapman and Hall, London, pp. 21–42.

Pyke, E. and Stronza, A. (2004) *Amazon Exchange: Effects of Ecotourism on Indigenous Culture* (DVD). The International Ecotourism Society.

Rainforest Alliance (2004a) Amazonian host to host: Ecotourism exchanges in the tropical Andes. Eco-Index. http://www.eco-index.org/search/results.cfm?projectID=390 (accessed 17 November 2005)

Rainforest Alliance (2004b) Stories from the field. Interview with Amanda Stronza, Director of the Amazonian Exchange. February 2004. Eco-Index. http://www.eco-index.org/nws/stories/2004/february.cfm (accessed 17 November 2005)

Ramirez, M. (2001a) Appendix 4 Some Peruvian examples of ecotourism initiatives. In: *Adventures in Agrobiodiversity: Ecotourism for Agrobiodiversity Conservation – A Feasibility Study*. IPGRI Innovation Fund 2001. International Plant Genetic Resources Institute, Colombia, pp. 69–71. http://www.ecoturismolatino.com/eng/ecotravellers/alternative/alternative.htm (accessed 17 November 2005)

Ramirez, M. (2001b) Appendix 3 Mexico's environment for ecotourism. In: *Adventures in Agrobiodiversity: Ecotourism for Agrobiodiversity Conservation – A Feasibility Study*. IPGRI Innovation Fund 2001. International Plant Genetic Resources Institute, Colombia, pp. 59–68. http://www.ecoturismolatino.com/eng/ecotravellers/alternative/alternative.htm (accessed 17 November 2005)

Rare (nd) Conservation Tours Tikal offers Guatemalan adventure, economic opportunity. RARE Conservation. http://www.rareconservation.org/contentmgr/feature_story_1.jsp?fid=85 (accessed 17 November 2005)

Rare (2003a) Kayaking for conservation: Mayan entrepreneurs launch eco-tour business in the Yucatan. Rare Enterprises. http://www.rareconservation.org/programs_enter_casestudy.htm (accessed 17 November 2005)

Rare (2003b) Community entrepreneurs raise $189,000 in UN grants for Rio Platano. RARE Conservation. http://www.rareconservation.org/contentmgr/feature_story_3.jsp?fid=86 (accessed 17 November 2005)

Rare (2004) Communities forge unprecedented partnership for sustainable tourism in the Yucatan. Feature story. November 2004. http://www.rareconservation.org/feature.ctsk.htm (accessed 17 November 2005)

Rare (2005a) Rare enterprise in Mexico wins Conde Nast traveller award. Feature Story. September 2005. http://www.rareconservation.org/feature_story2condenast.htm (accessed 17 November 2005)

Rare (2005b) La Ruta Moskitia: An adventure for local Honduran entrepreneurs and tourists alike. Feature Story. September 2005. http://www.rareconservation.org/feature_story3larumo.htm (accessed 17 November 2005)

Rare (2006) Commitment to Tikal pays off: Local entrepreneurs in Guatemala sustain successful ecotourism enterprise. Feature Story January 2006. http://www.rareconservation.org/feature_story3_ctt.htm (accessed 1 March 2006)

Rare (2006b) Honduran entrepreneurs discover the business of conservation. Feature Story, February 2006. Rare Conservation. http://www.rareconservation.org/feature_story1.htm (accessed 22 May 2006)

RE (Rainforest Expeditions) (2004) Posada Amazonas. http://www.perunature.com/lodges.asp (accessed 17 November 2005)

Redford, K.H. and Stearman, A.M. (1993) Forest-dwelling native Amazonians and the conservation of biodiversity: Interests in common or in collision? *Conservation Biology* 7, 248–255.

Redturs (nd) Welcome to the portal of living cultures of Latin America. Network of Communitarian Tourism of Latin America. Sponsored by the ILO. http://www.redturs.org/inicioen/inicio/index.php (accessed 17 November 2005)

RICANCIE (2004) Community-based eco-tourism in the upper Napo River of Ecuador. http://ricancie.nativeweb.org/en/body.html (accessed 17 November 2005)

Roberts, J.S. (2003) *An investigation into community-NGO partnerships: Options and challenges for developing ecotourism as a conservation management tool at Shell Beach*. University of Kent, Canterbury. Guyana Marine Turtle Conservation Society. http://www.gmtcs.org.gy/research/papers.html (accessed 17 November 2005)

Rodriguez, A. (1999) Kapawi: A model of sustainable development in Ecuadorian Amazonia. *Cultural Survival Quarterly* 23, 43–44.

Rodriguez, A. (2000) Kapawi: The story of an Ecuadorian ecolodge. Planeta.com. http://www.planeta.com/planeta/00/0006eckapawi.html (accessed 17 November 2005)

Rogers, C. (2004) Feathers, fur and jungle waters in Ecuador. *The New York Times*, Travel, 1 August 2004. http://travel2.nytimes.com/2004/08/01/travel/01ecuador.html (accessed 17 November 2005)

Rohr, B. and Gines, C. (1998) Combining education and conservation in the Mayan Biosphere Reserve. IDRC Canada. http://web.idrc.ca/en/ev-5043-201-1-DO_TOPIC.html (accessed 17 November 2005)

Rome, A. (2003a) Partnerships for community-based ecotourism. E/The Environmental Magazine. Environmental News Network. 31 December 2003. http://www.enn.com/news/2003-12-31/s_9204.asp (accessed 17 November 2005)

Rome, A. (2003b) The meeting of two worlds in the Bolivian Amazon. Critical Ecosystem Partnership Fund. Conservation International. http://www.cepf.net/xp/cepf/in_focus/2003/July03chalalan.xml (accessed 17 November 2005)

Rome, A. (2003c) Ecotourism exchange in the Amazon advances community-based ecotourism. Critical Ecosystem Partnership Fund. http://www.cepf.net/xp/cepf/in_focus/2003/july.xml (accessed 17 November 2005)

Rome, A. (2004) Expanding ecotourism opportunities for the Naso people of northern Panama. CEPF News. http://www.cepf.net/xp/cepf/news/in_focus/2004/april_feature.xml (accessed 17 November 2005)

Royce, K. and Palmer, A. (nd) Community based tourism: Machiguenga Center for Tropical Research. TIES Online Library. Community/Indigenous Ecotourism. http://www.ecotourism.org/ (accessed 17 November 2005)

Runa Tupari (nd) Runa Tupari Native Travel. http://www.runatupari.com/ingles/quienes.htm (accessed 17 November 2005)

Ruschmann, D.M. (1992) Ecological tourism in Brazil. *Tourism Management* 13, 125–128.

Sani Lodge (2004) Sani Lodge Rio Napo Ecuador Amazon. http://www.sanilodge.com/ (accessed 17 November 2005)

Sarmiento, F.O., Rodriguez, G., Torres, M., Argumedo, A., Munoz, M. and Rodriguez, J. (2000) Andean stewardship: Tradition linking nature and culture in protected areas of the Andes. *The George Wright Forum* 17, 55–69.

Schaller, D.T. (1996) Indigenous ecotourism and sustainable development: The case of Rio Blanco, Ecuador. MA thesis, University of Minnesota. Educational Web Adventures. http://www.eduweb.com/schaller (accessed 17 November 2005)

Schaller, D. (1998) Growing pains in indigenous ecotourism: The case of Rio Blanco. *Contours* 8, 27–29.

Schluter, R. (2001) South America. In: Lockwood, A. and Medlik, S. (eds) *Tourism and Hospitality in the 21st Century.* Butterworth Heinemann, Oxford, pp. 181–191.

Schulze, J.C. (nd) Proyecto Indigena de Ecoturismo 'Mapajo', Cuenca del Amazonas, Brazil. Madidi.com. Links-Ecolodges. http://www.palouse.net/alanperry/links.html (accessed 17 November 2005)

Scialabba, N.E.H. and Willamson, D. (2004) Organic cacao agro-forestry in the Talamanca-Caribbean Biological Corridor, Costa Rica. In: *The Scope of Organic Agriculture, Sustainable Forest Management and Ecoforestry in Protected Area Management.* Environment and Natural Resources Working Paper No. 18. Annex: Example 3. FAO, Rome. http://www.fao.org//docrep/y5558e/y5558e00.htm (accessed 17 November 2005)

Shackley, M. (1998) Designating a protected area at Karanambu ranch, Rupununi savannah, Guyana: Resource Management and indigenous communities. *Ambio* 27, 207–210.

Shell Beach Adventures (nd) Welcome to Shell Beach. http://www.sbadventures.com/home_page.htm (accessed 17 November 2005)

Shore, K.J. (1999) Testing the waters: Indigenous ecotours in Venezuela. IDRC Explore Reports. IDRC Website http://web.idrc.ca/en/ev-5133-201-1-DO_TOPIC.html (accessed 17 November 2005)

Sian Kaan Tours (2005) Community Tours Sian Ka'an. http://www.siankaantours.org/english/eng_ctsk.html (accessed 17 November 2005)

Silver, I. (1992) Capirona: An experiment in local control. *Cultural Survival Quarterly* 16, 54–58.

Singayta (2004) Final report for Global Greengrants Fund. Donation 50-078. San Blas, Nayarit, January 15, 2004. Ecotourism in Singayta, Mexico. Global Greengrants. http://www.singayta.com/ (accessed 17 November 2005)

Slinger, V. (2000) Ecotourism in the last Indigenous Caribbean community. *Annals of Tourism Research* 27, 520–523.

Smith, R. (1993) *Crisis under the Canopy: Tourism and other Problems Facing the Present Day Huaorani*. Abya Yala, Quito.

Snow, S.G. (2001) The Kuna general congress and the statute on tourism. *Cultural Survival Quarterly* 24.

Snow, S.G. and Wheeler, C.L. (2000) Pathways in the periphery: Tourism to Indigenous communities in Panama. *Social Science Quarterly* 81, 732–749.

SouthernBelize.com (2005a) Toledo Ecotourism Association (TEA) http://www.southernbelize.com/tea.html (accessed 17 November 2005)

SouthernBelize.com (2005b) Maya village homestay network. http://www.southernbelize.com/homestays.html (accessed 17 November 2005)

SRI (Shiwiar Rainforest Initiative) (2004) The project. http://cuyacocha.hypermart.net/project.htm (accessed 17 November 2005)

Steinberg, M.K. (1997) Tourism development and indigenous people: The Maya experience in southern Belize. *Focus (The American Geographical Society)* 44, 17–20.

Stronza, A. (nd) Brief analysis of the economic impacts of Posada Amazonas. Research Papers on the Ese'ejas. Posada Amazons, Rainforest Expeditions. http://www.perunature.com/info07.asp (accessed 17 November 2005)

Stronza, A. (1999) Learning both ways: Lessons from a corporate and community ecotourism collaboration. *Cultural Survival Quarterly* 23, 36–39. http://209.200.101.189/publications/csq/csq-article.cfm?id= 1438&highlight=ecotourism (accessed 17 November 2005)

Stronza, A.L. (2000) Because it is ours: Community-based ecotourism in the Peruvian Amazon PhD thesis, University of Florida, Florida.

Stronza, A. (2005) Hosts and hosts: The anthropology of community-based ecotourism in the Peruvian Amazon. *National Association for the Practice of Anthropology Bulletin* 23, 170–190.

Sundberg, J. (1997) NGO landscapes: Conservation in the Maya Biosphere Reserve, Peten Guatemala. NGOs in Tourism and Conservation Conference. http://www.planeta.com/planeta/97/1197maya.html (accessed 17 November 2005)

Survival International (2005) Indians in Brazil. Survival International. http://www.survival-international.org/ (accessed 17 November 2005)

Swain, M.B. (1989) Gender roles in indigenous tourism: Kuna mola, kuna yala, and cultural survival. In: Smith, V.L. (ed.) *Hosts and Guests: The Anthropology of Tourism*. 2nd edn. University of Philadelphia Press, Philadelphia, pp. 83–104.

The Nature Conservancy (2005) Talamanca-Caribbean Biological Corridor. Parks in Peril. The Nature Conservancy. http://parksinperil.org/wherewework/centralamerica/costarica/protectedarea/talamanca/ (accessed 17 November 2005)

Tidwell, M. (1996) *Amazon Stranger: A Rainforest Chief Battles Big Oil*. Lyons and Burford, New York.

Tidwell, T. (2001) Uru life more than a tourist attraction. *Cultural Survival Quarterly* 25 .

Tiedje, K. (2005) People, place and politics in the Huasteca, Mexico. *Anthropology Today* 21, 13–17.

TNT (Tropical Nature Travel) (2004a) Heath River Wildlife Centre. http://www.tropicalnaturetravel.com/ travel/lodges/heath-river-wildlife-centre (accessed 17 November 2005)

TNT (Tropical Nature Travel) (2004b) Tambopata – Madidi Wilderness. http://www.tropicalnaturetravel. com/travel/peru/tambopata.shtml (accessed 17 November 2005)

TNT (Tropical Nature Travel) (2004c) Napo Wildlife Center. http://www.tropicalnaturetravel.com/travel/ lodges/napo.html (accessed 17 November 2005)

Toledo Ecotourism Association (TEA) (nd) The Toledo Ecotourism Association. Plenty International. http://www.plenty.org/mayan-ecotours/index.htm (accessed 17 November 2005)

Torres, M. (1996) Participatory planning for ecotourism development in the Peruvian highlands. In: Miller, J.A. and Malek-Zadeh, E. (eds) *The Ecotourism Equation: Measuring the Impacts*. Yale F&ES Bulletin 99. Yale University, New Haven.

Tourism Concern (1994) Rainforest s.o.s. *In Focus* 13, 8.

Tourisme Guyane (nd) Ecotourism, Culture and history, Regional nature park. Tourist Board of French Guiana. http://www.tourisme-guyane.com/en/nature/ecotourisme.htm (accessed 17 November 2005)

Tropic Ecological Adventures (2004) The Amazon rainforest. http://www.tropiceco.com/html/ amazonintro.html (accessed 17 November 2005)

UNEP (United Nations Environment Programme) (2002) Environmental impacts of tourism. Sustainable Tourism. http://www.uneptie.org/pc//tourism/sust-tourism/env-conservation.htm (accessed 17 November 2005)

Vereecke, J. (1994) *National Report on Indigenous Peoples and Development*. UNDP Guyana. http://www.sndp.org.gy/undp-docs/nripd/ (accessed 17 November 2005)

Walker, L. (1996) Aboriginal tourism in Venezuela: Walking lightly on the land. IDRC. http://archive. idrc.ca/books/reports/1996/21-02e.html (accessed 17 November 2005)

Wallace, G.N. and Pierce, S.M. (1996) An evaluation of ecotourism in Amazonas, Brazil. *Annals of Tourism Research* 23, 843–873.

Wallace, T. and Diamente, D.N. (2005) Keeping the people in the parks: A case study from Guatemala. *National Association for the Practice of Anthropology Bulletin* 23, 191–218.

Ward, N. (2004) Volunteering in South America: Top Ecuadorian eco-lodges seek talented help. *Transitions Abroad*, May/June. http://www.transitionsabroad.com/publications/magazine/0405/volunteer_in_south_america/ (accessed 17 November 2005)

Wartinger, L. (2001) Plenty 2000 Projects Review-Carib Territory, Dominica, Toledo Ecotourism Association. *Plenty Bulletin*, Spring, 17. http://www.plenty.org/PB17_1/review2000.html (accessed 17 November 2005)

WCS (Wildlife Conservation Society) (2004) Flooded forest – Ecotourism, community development. http://www.floodedforest.com/ff-research/ff-eco_tourism (accessed 17 November 2005)

Weaver, D.B. (2001) Central America, South America. In: *Ecotourism*. John Wiley Australia, Milton, Queensland, pp. 290–295.

Wesche, R. (1996) Developed country environmentalism and indigenous community controlled ecotourism in the Ecuadorian Amazon. *Geographische Zeitschrift* 3/4, 157–198.

Wesche, R. and Drumm, A. (1999) *Defending our Rainforest: A Guide to Community-based Ecotourism in the Ecuadorian Amazon*. Accion Amazonia, Quito.

Wilderness Explorers (nd) Surama Village. http://www.wilderness-explorers.com/surama_village.htm (accessed 17 November 2005)

WRI (World Resources Institute) (1996) Lessons in tourism development from Belize and Costa Rica and community-led tourism in Ecuador. In: Sizer, A., *Profit Without Plunder: Reaping Revenue from Guyana's Tropical Forests Without Destroying Them*. WRI. http://biodiv.wri.org/pubs_description.cfm?PubID=2730 (accessed 17 November 2005)

WTO (2003a) Yachana Lodge: Ecotourism project by an NGO (FUNEDESIN). In: *Sustainable Development of Ecotourism: A Compilation of Good Practices in SMEs*. WTO, Madrid, pp. 101–103.

WTO (2003b) Proyecto Ecoalianza (Ecoalliance Project). In: *Sustainable Development of Ecotourism: A Compilation of Good Practices in SMEs*. WTO, Madrid, pp. 287–291.

WTO (2003c) Turismo Rural Weche-Ruca: Mapuche ethnic tourism. In: *Sustainable Development of Ecotourism: A Compilation of Good Practices in SMEs*. WTO, Madrid, pp. 75–77.

WTO (2003d) Plan Grande Quehueche Ecotourism Centre. In: *Sustainable Development of Ecotourism: A Compilation of Good Practices in SMEs*. WTO, Madrid, pp. 119–122.

Wunder, S. (2000) Ecotourism and economic incentives – an empirical approach. *Ecological Economics* 32, 465–479.

WWF (2001) Developing tools for community-based ecotourism in Brazil. In: *Guidelines for Community-based Ecotourism Development*. WWF International, 9.

WWF (2004) WWF in Chile – our work. http://www.panda.org/about_wwf/where_we_work/latin_america_and_caribbean/where/chile/our_work/index.cfm (accessed 17 November 2005)

WWF (2005a) Shell Beach. Sea Turtle Conservation in the Guianas. WWF-Guianas. http://www.panda.org/about_wwf/where_we_work/latin_america_and_caribbean/where/guianas/our_work/index.cfm (accessed 1 November 2005)

WWF (2005b) Galibi Nature Reserve, Suriname. Sea Turtle Conservation in the Guianas. WWF-Guianas. http://www.wwfguianas.org/expedition_Galibi.htm (accessed 1 November 2005)

WWF (2005c) Stidunal receives ecotourism grant. Sea Turtle Conservation in the Guianas. WWF-Guianas. http://www.wwfguianas.org/Galibi_grant.htm (accessed 1 November 2005)

WWF (2005d) Amana Nature Reserve. Sea Turtle Conservation in the Guianas. WWF-Guianas. http://www.wwfguianas.org/expedition_Amana.htm (accessed 1 November 2005)

Yachana Lodge (2004) Yachana Lodge. http://www.yachana.com/ (accessed 17 November 2005)

Yoshihara, F.M. (2000) Sustainable development: A business model for the millennium. Kellogg National Leadership Program. Research Papers on the Ese'ejas. Posada Amazons, Rainforest Expeditions. http://www.perunature.com/info07.asp (accessed 17 November 2005)

Yu, D.W., Henrickson, T. and Castillo, A. (1997) Ecotourism and conservation in Amazonian Peru: Short-term and long-term challenges. *Environmental Conservation* 24, 130–138.

Zeppel, H. (1998) Land and culture: Sustainable tourism and indigenous peoples. In: Hall, C.M. and Lew, A. (eds) *Sustainable Tourism: A Geographical Perspective*. Addison Wesley Longman, London, pp. 60–74.

Zografos, C. and Oglethorpe, D. (2004) Multi-criteria analysis in ecotourism: Using goal programming to explore sustainable solutions. *Current Issues in Tourism* 7, 23–43.

4

East Africa: Wildlife and Forest Ecotourism, the Maasai and Community Lands

This chapter reviews community ecotourism ventures in East Africa located on Maasai group ranches in Kenya and Tanzania, at other local villages in Tanzania and on forest reserves in Uganda. It first provides an overview of ecotourism in East Africa and key issues for community ecotourism development. This includes the role of Indigenous communities and landowners, donor agencies, conservation NGOs and private investors in developing and managing ecotourism on community-owned lands. Indigenous peoples in East Africa include pastoralists such as the Maasai (Kenya, Tanzania) and Samburu (Kenya), hunter-gatherers such as the Hadzabe and Dorobo (Tanzania), the coastal Swahili and other tribal groups. These Indigenous peoples have varied land titles, where governments legally recognized traditional or communal land tenures and also some user rights over wildlife. As with Latin America, community-based ecotourism in Africa is regarded as a key tool for biodiversity or wildlife conservation and also community development. Case studies review wildlife tourism and forest-based ecotourism ventures owned or leased by Indigenous groups in Kenya, Tanzania and Uganda. There is a particular focus on Indigenous ecotourism in 'Maasailand', covering both protected areas and Maasai group ranches. The conservation outcomes and community benefits of these varied

Indigenous ecotourism ventures in East Africa are discussed at the end of this chapter.

Introduction: Ecotourism in East Africa

Ecotourism in East Africa mainly involves viewing wildlife in national parks and private game reserves. It is dominated by safari-based mass tourism in the East African countries of Kenya, Tanzania and Uganda. Ecotourism lodges and other visitor facilities are located within or adjacent to protected areas and wildlife reserves in these countries. Local elites and companies own private game reserves or lease concession areas with up-market lodges that cater to wealthy tourists. Government agencies manage wildlife and national parks, established on tribal lands during colonial times, with varied revenue sharing of park income from tourism with adjacent local communities. This has mainly benefited communities living near park areas with high visitation (Barbier, 1992; Weaver, 1998; Hackel, 1999; Watkin, 1999; Weinberg, 2000; WTO, 2001; Borrini-Feyerabend and Sandwith, 2003). Since 1997, the African Travel Association has held an annual cultural and ecotourism symposium, promoting African ecotourism products to the travel industry. These products mainly feature Indigenous culture as an exotic add-on to a wildlife safari. Since the mid-1990s there has been a strong government and NGO focus on ecotourism in Kenya, Tanzania and Uganda, linking wildlife conservation with community benefits from tourism on traditional lands. There is an Ecotourism Society of Kenya, set up in 1996, that supports community ecotourism such as joint venture ecolodges on group ranches and a business mentorship programme to help communities (ESOK, 2004a, b). Uganda has a Community Tourism Association (UCOTA) representing local villages. Government policies and programmes in East African countries also support the economic development of rural communities, including tourism ventures, and national parks directing income, jobs and services to nearby villages. New tourism partnerships and joint ventures also promote the benefits of ecotourism for local groups.

In March 2002, an East African regional conference on ecotourism was held in Nairobi, Kenya. Organized by the African Conservation Centre, the conference included some 200 participants from community ecotourism ventures, conservation NGOs, wildlife agencies, national parks and the tourist industry in Kenya, Tanzania and Uganda. The conference focused on developing community-based ecotourism to benefit local people in rural areas. Case studies were presented on community-managed ecotourism at Il Ngwesi Lodge and Shompole Lodge on Maasai group ranches in Kenya (Hatfield, 2003a, b) and Buhoma Rest Camp at Bwindi Forest in Uganda (Namara, 2003). The conference focused on ecotourism as a business involving different sectors (i.e. communities and landowners, donors/NGOs, private investors and government), and the impacts of ecotourism, along with the management, marketing and financing of ecotourism by international donor agencies to benefit local communities (Watkin et al., 2002; Watkin, 2003a, b). Factors limiting community involvement in ecotourism were a lack of government policy or technical assistance, uneven benefit sharing, resource rights and tenure issues (Goodwin, 2001; Yunis, 2001; Kamuaro, 2002). Most Indigenous ecotourism ventures in East Africa are located on community-owned lands such as Maasai group ranches in Kenya/Tanzania, local villages in Tanzania and on forest reserves in Uganda.

Kenya: Wildlife-based Ecotourism on Maasai Lands

The Indigenous peoples of Kenya are nomadic and pastoral communities such as the Maasai, Samburu, Rendille, Borana, Turkana, Somali and others. In total, these pastoralist groups numbered 6 million people, comprising 25% of Kenya's population and occupying 88% of the arid regions. These nomadic pastoralists in northern and southern Kenya rely on their herds of cattle, goats, sheep and camels. Sixty per cent of people live below the poverty line in Kenya with the majority being marginalized pastoralists. About 90% of protected areas in Kenya such as national parks (Amboseli, Tsavo) and game reserves (Masai Mara, Samburu, Marsabit and Turkana) were established on the better pastoral grazing lands used by groups such as the Maasai and Samburu (Kipuri, nd). Significant wildlife populations are also found on these open rangelands and famous game reserves of Kenya.

Ecotourism in Kenya based on viewing wildlife was aided by the 1977 government ban on hunting. Wildlife safaris focus on popular National Parks such as Amboseli, Masai Mara, Tsavo, Nairobi and Lake Nakuru. Nairobi and Mombasa are the main tourist gateways for safaris and coastal tourism. In 1993, 64% of tourists stayed on the Kenyan coast, 19% in Nairobi and 9% in game park lodges. More Americans participate in safari tourism while Europeans prefer visiting coastal areas (Weaver, 1998). Lodges and tented camps on privately owned game reserves and Maasai group ranches in Kenya target up-market ecotourists (Harman, 2001). Since 1994, the Kenya Wildlife Service (KWS) has targeted ecotourism and community participation in national parks, aided by revenue sharing of park income with adjacent local communities. In Kenya, 70% of wildlife lives outside protected areas and Maasai group ranches were encouraged to set aside land areas for wildlife conservation and tourism (Smith, 2001). Ongoing land use conflicts in buffer zones around parks, wildlife impacts and problems with KWS payments to local authorities rather than landowning groups limit this scheme (Sindiga, 1995; Coupe et al., 2002; Coffman, 2004). The Maasai people on group ranches in Kenya directly collect fees from tourists and safari operators using their tribal lands for lodges, camps and tours based on viewing wildlife.

The Ecotourism Society of Kenya (ESOK) and Kenya Wildlife Service (KWS) promote wildlife conservation and community benefits of ecotourism (Okech, nd). Eight joint venture ecolodges on Maasai (seven) and Samburu (one) group ranches (e.g. Olonana Basecamp, Cottars, Saruni, Borana, Il Ngwesi, Koija Starbeds and Kampi Ya Kanzi) were awarded a bronze eco-rating from ESOK in 2003/04 (ESOK, 2004c). Kenyan government policies and programmes encourage these community-based ecotourism ventures, with the KWS providing funding for local tourist and wildlife enterprises through its Wildlife for Development Fund set up in 1993 (Berger, 1996; Barrow et al., 1998; Reid, 2003). The KWS 1996 Parks beyond Parks programme also supported local people setting up tented camps and tourist activities in land areas near parks for wildlife conservation (Reid et al., 1999; Okungu, 2001; Rutten, 2002a, b). Wildlife conservation was linked with ecotourism and community development (Honey, 1998; Norton-Griffiths, 1998; Johnstone, 2000; Scheyvens, 2003; APTDC, 2004a; Johansson and Diamantis, 2004). A Wildlife Extension Project funded by NGOs helped negotiate tourism contracts with Maasai people from 1984 to 1989, leading to the formation of a Community Wildlife Service within KWS (Berger and Ntiati, 2000). The East African Wildlife Society, African Conservation Centre (ACC) and African Wildlife Foundation (AWF) also support community-based ecotourism and conservation on tribal lands in Kenya. They provide funding and training, negotiate with tourism investors and support management, marketing and organizational development of local communities implementing ecotourism projects. USAID, the European Union and other American or European donor agencies provide key funding for Indigenous ecotourism and conservation in Kenya. Most community-owned ecotourism ventures are located on Maasai group ranches in Laikipia, northern Kenya and around protected areas in southern Kenya.

Maasai People and Tourism

There are some 400,000 Maasai people in Kenya. The Maasai are an eastern Nilotic group of pastoralists that has occupied the Great Rift Valley of Kenya since the 15th century (Survival International, 2003). Maasailand extends from north central Kenya down to the central rangelands of northern Tanzania. National boundaries often cut across the traditional lands of Indigenous groups like the Maasai. In the early 1900s, treaties with the British split Maasailand in Kenya into a northern reserve at Laikipia and three southern reserves at Transmara, Narok and Kajiado bordering Tanzania. About 40% of Kenya's tourism income is generated from wildlife safari tours visiting national parks in Maasailand – Masai Mara, Nairobi, Amboseli and Tsavo West (Western, 1992). In 1973, Maasai people were evicted from Amboseli National Park with 25,000 Maasai landowners now living on group ranches in the Amboseli ecosystem (Smith, 2001). In the early 1990s, Maasai people were also excluded from grazing their livestock in the Masai Mara and Samburu reserves. Maasai cattle grazing maintained natural ecosystems and wildlife populations in rangeland areas. However, Maasai people are moving from nomadic pastoralism to settled agriculture and a cash economy, with many communities involved in conflicts over ownership of land, wildlife and natural resources (Ole Ndaskoi, 2001; Martyn, 2004). Excluded from these national parks, the Maasai people in Kenya and in Tanzania have had few benefits from participation in tourism (Monbiot, 1994, 1995; van der Cammen, 1997; Akama, 1999, 2002; Coast, 2002; Forest Peoples Project, 2003; Varat and Anand, 2003). Some Maasai leaders leased land to acquire shares in early hunting and safari tourism operations. These elite Maasai landowners control most resources in Maasailand, including tourism. Other Maasai groups seek to regain control over their homelands. Over 1.5 million acres of Maasai land in Kenya was lost to tourism, farming and other developments from 1978–1998 (Dapash and Kutay, 2005).

Many Maasai people have settled along tourism routes and near park entrance gates to sell their handicrafts, pose for paid photographs, dance and demonstrate Maasai cultural practices at cultural *bomas* or tourist villages around Amboseli and Masai Mara for minimal income (Boynton, 1997; Douglis, 2001; Wishitemi and Okello, 2003; Okello *et al.*, 2003a, b; Igoe, 2004). Some Maasai individuals or groups have developed tourism ventures such as cultural villages; are partners in safari businesses; owners of lodges and game viewing vehicles; own shops and bars in tourist trading centres; and lease land to private companies to build tourist camps and hotels. A few Maasai individuals signed away land and resource rights to conservation organizations and hunting operators who then owned the land (Goodman, 2003). Tourism facilities on private or communal land has increased use of resources and denuded the land around some Maasai settlements. Predators attacking livestock and local people also affect Maasai villages near parks. Hence, the Maasai people often kill lions (Sindiga, 1995; Berger, 1996; Wishitemi and Okello, 2003; Gutkin, 2004). In Maasailand, the sustainable management of wildlife tourism will increasingly involve more equitable arrangements with Maasai communities over compatible land uses, sharing wildlife revenues, ownership of lodges and joint ventures with safari operators. Maasai ecotourism joint ventures such as Campi ya Kanzi (Kuku group ranch), Il Ngwesi Lodge, Loisaba and Saruni Camp were members of The International Ecotourism Society (Sikoyo and Ashley, 2000; Eco-Resorts, 2002; UNDP, 2002, 2004; *EcoCurrents*, 2005). These new ecotourism ventures are mainly on Maasai group ranches.

Maasai Group Ranches

In colonial times, Maasai communal areas were legally registered as trustlands administered by local authorities. After Kenyan independence in 1963, government policy promoted private land ownership with Maasai trustlands converted into individual properties or communal group ranches. Most Maasai trustland is now privately owned, with many group ranches subdivided into smaller

individual land areas that are sold to others, fenced for cultivation or leased to agriculturalists. This trend to land privatization and increased cultivation on group ranches around Amboseli and Masai Mara will affect wildlife movements and also revenue from wildlife tourism (Smith, 2001; Lamprey and Reid, 2004). Some 75% of Maasai territory on group ranches and trustlands surrounding parks and reserves is arid or semi-arid rangelands with abundant wildlife. A growing population has increased grazing pressure and conflicts with wildlife on Maasai lands. Other Maasai are combining pastoralism with ecotourism on their lands, setting up their own tour ventures or leasing tourism concession areas for ecolodges or wildlife conservation reserves on group ranches (Wishitemi and Okello, 2003). Ecotourism is growing in Maasailand. Several Maasai group ranches in Laikipia and near Amboseli, Tsavo West and Masai Mara are combining cattle rearing with up-market ecotourism ventures for smaller groups and forming partnerships with safari tour operators and hotels. Community ecotourism joint ventures on Maasai land include Il Ngwesi Lodge, Porini Camp and Shompole Lodge (Okello *et al.*, 2003a, b; Responsible Travel, 2004). Game scouts are also employed to protect rhinoceros, elephant and lions in conservation areas on Maasai group ranches.

Imbirikani group ranch set aside land in the Chyulu Hills for ecotourism, with land leased to a safari operator for a small up-market ecotourism lodge, Ol Donyo Wuas. The lodge employed local Maasai people, linked women bead workers with a handicraft designer, developed a wildlife management plan and wildlife cropping licence and started rearing ostriches. Tourism revenues were placed in a Community Trust fund and used for projects such as reforestation and building a dam. In the mid-1980s wildlife extension workers funded by the African Fund for Endangered Wildlife assisted negotiations between the safari operator and Maasai members of Imbirikani group ranch (Berger 1993, 1996). In the early 1990s, Maasai group ranches around Amboseli submitted plans for wildlife conservation and tourism development on their land to KWS, conservation NGOs and foreign donors to gain funding (Reid, 2003).

Other Maasai group ranches at Kuku and Kimana also set aside wildlife conservation areas and negotiated contracts for tented camps and safari lodges (Berger, 1996; Buysrogge, 2001).

The next section reviews community and conservation benefits of ecotourism lodges located on Maasai group ranches in Kenya (see Table 4.1). These include Il Ngwesi Lodge, Sarara Camp, Tassia Lodge and Koija Starbeds in Laikipia, northern Maasailand; Loita Hills and the Masai Mara area; and Shompole Lodge and ecotourism joint ventures on Maasai community conservation areas at Kuku, Kimana, Eselenkei and Imbirikani group ranches near Amboseli National Park in southern Kenya.

Il Ngwesi Lodge

The 8700 ha Il Ngwesi group ranch on the Laikipia Plateau in northern Kenya combines Maasai livestock rearing and wildlife-based ecotourism. Up until the early 1990s, the area

survived on subsistence Maasai pastoralism. A tented camp was set up in 1982 on the Il Ngwesi ranch, but poaching made wildlife viewing difficult (Waithaka, 2002). The Il Ngwesi Lodge was built in 1995 with funds donated through the Kenya Wildlife Service and with the technical assistance and support of Lewa Wildlife Conservancy, a Kenyan NGO based on a neighbouring ranch. The lodge has six thatched cottages with open air showers. Solar systems are used for water heating and electricity with water coming from a spring and gravity-fed to the lodge. Visitor activities include walking, game drives, a hand-reared black rhino and a cultural *boma* demonstrating Maasai traditional skills and practices such as hunting, hut building, bee keeping, dancing, medicinal plants and cattle husbandry. Tourists from Lewa Downs, Borana Ranch and Tassia Lodge also visit the Il Ngwesi Maasai cultural village. There were three cultural centres (*bomas*) and five mobile campsites on the Il Ngwesi ranch.

About 50 Maasai people worked at the lodge while the cultural *boma* employed 31

Table 4.1. Community ecotourism ventures on Maasai group ranches, Kenya.

Ecotourism venture, year	Group ranch/location	Ecotourism partners/agencies
Ol Donyo Wuas, 1995	Imbirikani GR, Kajiado	Lodge operator, African Fund for Endangered Wildlife
Il Ngwesi Lodge,[a] 1996	Il Ngwesi GR, Laikipia	Lewa Wildlife Conservancy, LWF, KWS, Tusk Trust (UK), USAID
Sarara Camp, 1997	Sarara and Sabache GR, Laikipia (*Samburu community*)	Namunyak Wildlife Conservation Trust Tusk Trust, KWS, LWC, Acacia Trails
Tassia Lodge, 2001	Lekurruki-Tassia GR, Laikipia	Borana Ranch, LWF
Porini Ecotourism, 2000	Eselenkei GR, Kajiado *Eselenkei Conservation Area*	Tropical Places, KWS, IFAW, ACC Tusk Trust and Care for the Wild (UK)
Koija Starbeds,[a] 2002	Koija GR, Laikipia	African Wildlife Foundation, LWF, Loisaba Wilderness, USAID
Campi ya Kanzi,[a] 2002	Kuku GR, Kajiado *Kuku Conservation Area*	Luca Safari
Shompole Lodge, 2002	Shompole GR, Kajiado	African Wildlife Foundation, ACC, Art of Ventures
Olgulului Tented Camp, 2003	Olgulului GR, Kajiado	AWF, Serena Hotels
Saruni Lodge,[a] 2003?	Koiyake-Lemek GR, Masai Mara	Lodge operator (Italy)
Shompole Mara Camp, 2004	Ol Kinyei GR, Masai Mara	Art of Ventures

[a] Bronze Eco-rating awarded from Ecotourism Society of Kenya in 2003/04.
Sources: Berger (1996); Johnson (2004); Grieves-Cook (2002); Rutten (2002a, b); Stewart (2003); AWF (2002, 2004); ACC (2004a, b, c).
LWF, Laikipia Wildlife Forum; ACC, African Conservation Centre; KWS, Kenya Wildlife Service; IFAW, International Fund for Animal Welfare.

people (i.e. 17 men and 14 women) (Waithaka, 2002). Tourism profits at Il Ngwesi support 499 Maasai households and some 6000 people, funding school bursaries, a primary school and three nursery schools, water supplies, health schemes, cattle dips and ranch operations. Occupancy of the lodge is stated to be 60–70% based on word-of-mouth marketing. In 2000, the lodge hosted 1000 visitors and generated US$85,000 in tourism revenue (USAID, 2002a). Tourism income derived from annual concession fees (93%), bed night levy (85%), tourist camps (44%) and curio shops selling artefacts (42%). Il Ngwesi Lodge is marketed on the websites for Lewa Wildlife Conservancy and Laikipia Wildlife Forum in northern Kenya. Il Ngwesi was the first community-owned and managed lodge in Kenya and has won several awards, including the 2002 UNDP Equator Prize and 1997 British Airways 'Tourism for Tomorrow' best ecotourism destination award (UNDP, 2002; LWC, 2004). It is regarded as a role model for other community ecolodges in East Africa (Thomas and Brooks, 2003). While Il Ngwesi Maasai people strongly supported any tourism venture, the ranch needed to diversify into other income-generating projects.

In 1996, the Il Ngwesi Conservation Area was established as a wildlife sanctuary to conserve biodiversity and develop ecotourism. The conservancy covered 20% of group ranch land. To develop wildlife-based ecotourism, the Maasai at Il Ngwesi established strict regulations and also prevented livestock grazing in some areas around the wildlife sanctuary (Waithaka et al., 2003). A community-owned trust is responsible for land and wildlife management at Il Ngwesi. Eight local game scouts are employed to protect wildlife and limit poaching which, in the 1970s and 1980s, wiped out all the rhinoceros and threatened elephants (Waithaka et al., 2003). As a result of wildlife patrols at Il Ngwesi and surrounding ranches, the area has some 400 elephants and wildlife has increased threefold (EA-Ecoconsult, 2002a; LWC, 2004). Key wildlife species have been reintroduced from Lewa Downs to Il Ngwesi group ranch including giraffe, waterbuck and black and white rhino. A biodiversity survey found the wildlife sanctuary at Il Ngwesi had higher

species richness, grass cover, tree density and ecological diversity than surrounding areas. Il Ngwesi also had higher numbers of endangered species such as elephants, gerenuk, cheetahs, greater kudu and other species (Waithaka, 2002). The success of ecotourism at Il Ngwesi increased sustainability of wildlife conservation across the region.

Lewa Wildlife Conservancy conducts training and wildlife conservation workshops and supports vehicle maintenance, communications and accounting at Il Ngwesi ranch. LWC has led wildlife conservation efforts with private and group ranches in Kenya (Johnson, 2004). A 2002 marathon on LWC raised US$12,299 each for Il Ngwesi and Namunyak Wildlife Conservation Trust and funded other community projects (Uncharted Outposts, 2004a). The success of Il Ngwesi saw nine other Maasai group ranches establish the Naibunga Conservancy covering 172 km^2 in 2002. Ecotourism facilities constructed in this new conservancy include the Koija Starbeds and a lodge at Kijape. The Il Polei cultural *manyatta* (village) and *bandas* (round huts) were planned at Il Motiok (Waithaka, 2002).

At the end of 2004, the Laikipia Wildlife Forum took 30 local community members from the Naibunga Conservancy on a study tour of Maasai ecotourism ventures in northern Tanzania. In the Laikipia District of Kenya, Maasai communities were co-owners of tourism lodges and campsites and received a share of net profits rather than a set rental or access fee (Sand County Foundation, 2004a).

Sarara Camp

With the success of tourism at Il Ngwesi, the 30,350 ha Sarara and Sabache group ranches based around the Matthews Mountains in northern Kenya established the Namunyak Wildlife Conservation Trust in 1995 to develop ecotourism. Sarara group ranch is a Samburu community, a pastoralist group related to the Maasai. In 1997, with funding from the Tusk Trust (UK), Namunyak constructed a small luxury tented camp called Sarara. Namunyak Trust was a 50% shareholder of Sarara Camp in partnership with Acacia Trails who marketed the site to international visitors while

Namunyak manages the camp. Sarara Camp employs 15 local staff, generating US$15,000 a year in tourism income from accommodation, satellite camps and guided walking trails with Samburu game scouts. Tourism revenue is used to build wells and hospitals, support small business ventures and fund education bursaries. The Namunyak Trust employs 12 game scouts, with two additional rangers funded by Save the Elephants to protect a seasonal population of 1500 elephants and key species such as Grevy's zebra, a free-ranging black rhino group and African wild dogs. The Namunyak conservation area was a key dispersal region for elephants and other wildlife. Save the Elephants (nd), a local NGO, supported Samburu conservation of elephants by funding community game scouts, monitoring of elephants with radio collars covered in Samburu beadwork and school education programmes (Kuriyan, 2002). Since 2002, Elephant Watch Safaris funded scholarships for Samburu high school students and other training. Game scouts also protect and monitor key conservation zones on Namunyak such as Ol Donyo Sabache, a basalt mountain hosting nine owl species and 62 diurnal birds of prey. Namunyak game patrols, with KWS and LWC, have eliminated poaching in the area and increased local security (Johnson, 2004). LWC also assisted with the 30,000 ha Sera Wildlife Conservancy in north Kenya.

Tassia Lodge

North of Il Ngwesi, the 6000 ha Lekurruki-Tassia group ranch with 500 Maasai families also established a community wildlife conservation and ecotourism programme. They received legal title deeds to their land in March 1999 (Tassia Lodge, 2001). Maasai elders approached the manager of Borana Ranch for tourism advice and help (Stewart, 2003). With initial funding provided by privately owned Borana Ranch, the community built a small tourist lodge and bunkhouse at Tassia in 2000.

Tassia Lodge with six cottages opened for tourists in November 2001 and is booked by

groups as a unit. The trading company for Tassia was registered as Lekurruki Community Conservation Lodge. Local Mokogodo Maasai people run Tassia Lodge, with visitor activities including forest walks and game drives. No trees were cut down to build Tassia Lodge, an eco-friendly lodge with electricity from solar panels, water gravity-fed from a spring and hot water from paraffin heaters. Tourism income is divided among the community and used for schools, wells and health centres (LWC, 2004). Tassia Lodge is marketed on the Laikipia Wildlife Forum website for tourism in northern Kenya. A proposal for a similar ecotourism venture on 6230 ha Kuri Kuri group ranch, where the Maasai community of 700 families sought 100% ownership of a tented camp, did not eventuate (ACC, 2004).

Koija Starbeds

The Koija Starbeds is a lodge with large rolling beds set on a half-covered platform overlooking the Ewaso Ngiro River and Mt Kenya in northern Kenya. Tourists can view the night sky from the unique 'starbeds' that were developed by the African Wildlife Foundation with two pastoral Maasai communities on Koija group ranch. Koija Ranch was established in 1976 for 1000 Maasai households. A severe drought in 2000 saw Maasai people surviving on relief food. The group ranch had no bank account nor had title deeds to the land. AWF facilitated a contract between Koija ranch and Oryx Ltd, a conservation-based tourism company, to build the Koija starbeds. USAID funded construction of the starbeds and trained six Maasai people to operate the facility. Oryx employed a community liaison officer and assisted Koija with marketing, management and logistics. Two women's groups were trained in weaving, jewellery design and beadwork while Maasai youth established cultural performance groups. Group ranch leaders were trained in leadership, record keeping and management (USAID, 2002b). The successful venture has created new jobs for local Maasai people, supported health schemes and provided local scholarships for secondary education. A private ranch, Loisaba Wilderness, provided skills and construction equipment while the Koija community provided land for the Starbeds and set aside a 500 ha wildlife reserve with restricted livestock grazing. The starbeds facility is linked with a community wildlife conservation programme in support of ecotourism (AWF, 2004d). The Koija Starbeds is a joint venture between Loisaba Wilderness (Oryx Ltd) and the Laikipiak Maasai from Koija community. Tourists at Koija Starbeds are hosted and guided by local Maasai and Samburu people (Carey, 2002; LWF, 2004). AWF, Loisaba Wilderness and the Laikipia Wildlife Forum all market the Koija Starbeds, now located at two sites on the Ewsao River.

Loisaba is a private ranch employing staff and guides from local Maasai and Samburu tribes who are full partners in this integrated tourism project supporting wildlife conservation and education (Loisaba Wilderness, 2004). This tourism partnership between Loisaba ranch, leased by American and British families, and the neighbouring Koija Maasai group ranch began in 1999. Tourists at Loisaba were initially brought to Koija to watch Maasai dancing. Loisaba built the first starbeds then provided a loan to the Koija Maasai to build their own starbeds. Tourists paid US$50 per person to visit the Koija Maasai and a further bed fee of US$30 per night for the Koija starbeds. The Loisaba Community Trust assisted the Koija Maasai with schools, a health clinic and cow dip. Loisaba supported other Koija ventures such as bee keeping, beadwork, leather tanning and furniture, and marketed the Koija Starbeds. A Maasai community development coordinator was a key part of the ecotourism partnership between Loisaba and the Koija group ranch. The Koija wildlife reserve was opened for herding during a severe drought where families lost half of their cattle and goats while men hunted zebras for meat. Other Maasai and Samburu people from nearby areas also moved their livestock onto Koija (Botha and Kasana, 2003). In late 2004, the pressure of drought in Laikipia saw Maasai herders tear down fences and invade many private ranches to graze their livestock. This also resulted from long-standing disputes over ownership of land leased as private ranches in Maasai areas (Dapash and Kutay, 2005).

Shompole Lodge

The 62,869 ha Shompole group ranch has 1404 members mainly of Maasai origin. It is located 35 km from the town of Magadi in Kajiado District, about 130 km south of Nairobi. Since 1997, the African Conservation Centre (ACC) and AWF worked with the Shompole community in developing an ecotourism venture with a private operator, Art of Ventures. An eco-lodge was proposed for Shompole at a 1999 Ecoforum. The Shompole group ranch also set aside 10,000 ha as a conservation area. However, it was difficult to access the region with only limited ACC funds for wildlife rangers. Working with the Shompole community and investor, ACC submitted a proposal for ecotourism infrastructure funding. The Shompole ecotourism project received a grant of KSh12 million from the EU-funded Biodiversity Conservation Program to construct roads, an airstrip, and community buildings; and buy equipment for rangers to improve tourism and conservation efforts (ACC, 2002).

Shompole Lodge opened in 2002. Set on the Nguruman escarpment, it overlooks the Great Rift Valley. The lodge is jointly owned by the travel company, Art of Ventures, and the Shompole group ranch that contributed 4050 ha of land and local building materials (wood, thatch, river rock) for 30% ownership of the venture. Three-quarters of the group ranch members were paid to construct Shompole Lodge, earning US$75,000 in wages for an area where average monthly cash income was less than US$2. These workers now build roads and infrastructure in the group ranch area. Forty local Maasai people work as service staff at the lodge, which has an expatriate manager. Art of Ventures contributed capital funding and their tourism expertise to set up and run the lodge. A jointly owned company, Maa O'Leng, was set up between Art of Ventures and Shompole group ranch to manage the tourism business and lodge. The company falls under the Shompole Trust that distributes profits from community shareholding in the lodge to ranch projects that benefit local people. Tourists at Shompole pay a US$20 conservation fee, with 50% directed to community development and 50% to wildlife conservation. The long-term aim is that Shompole Maasai will eventually own 80% of the lodge and company, purchasing more shares in the business over a 15-year period. Beadwork made by Maasai women is sold at the lodge gift shop while lodge furniture made by community members from dead fig wood is marketed abroad (Russell, 2002). Maasai involvement in ecotourism has increased the economic value of local wildlife, previously seen as predators or grazing competitors. Fees from ecotourism are used for school bursaries, health centres, improving livestock and bee keeping, along with Maasai wildlife conservation efforts, supported by EU funding (Stewart, 2003).

A survey of 238 residents (75% male) from Shompole (50%) and Olkiramantian group ranches in Magadi found that 88% wanted more tourists to visit the area. Local people derived tourism income from direct employment (n=12), entry fee payments (n=45), campsite charges (n=48), tour guiding (n=>41), walking safaris (n=33), donkey safaris, a cultural *manyatta* (one), photography fees and bird shooting (n=13) (see Table 4.2). Only 28 respondents were employed in wildlife-based tourism activities in the area, with 30 employed outside the area. More wildlife-based income and higher entry fees for a conservation area would improve tourism revenue on the group ranches. Factors limiting tourism development and promotion were poor communication between group ranch committees and locals; no coordination of tourism studies, plans or work allocations; little progress after tourism workshops and seminars; lack of business and tourism

knowledge; nepotism; and no conservation trust master plan (Warinda, 2001).

Ol Donyo Wuas, Imbirikani Group Ranch

The 129,895 ha Imbirikani Group Ranch in Kajiado District has 10,000 Maasai households. Income from livestock rearing and crop farming is supplemented with wildlife income from bird shooting licences, wildlife cropping, campsite charges and revenue sharing from KWS used to fund and set up Ol Donyo Wuas lodge in the Chyulu Hills. Ten local game scouts were employed to guard wildlife in the area, which competes with cattle for water and grass in the dry season. In 1987, Imbirikani leased some land for tourism at an annual charge of KSh50,000 while from 1984 to 1986 the ranch received KSh23,100 from bird hunting. A survey of 202 household heads found 74% had encountered tourists within the group ranch in the past year. Tourist activities included walking safaris, camping, hiking, horse riding and bird shooting. The average annual revenue estimated from tourism per hectare on Imbirikani was KSh5816. In 1995, Imbirikani ranch leased some land in the Chyulu Hills to a safari operator for a small up-market ecotourism lodge, Ol Donyo Wuas, with 18 beds. Income from the private tourism operator was KSh1.5 million, including gate fees, lease fee and a bed night levy. Tourism revenues were placed in a Community Trust fund. Obstacles to community tourism development were leadership and age group conflicts, political divisions, poor understanding of law, member rights and insecurity about

Table 4.2. Tourism activities and revenue at Shompole and Olkiramantian group ranches.

Tourism activity	Engaged in activity (%)	Total revenue (KSh$)
Walking safaris	16.0	135,000
Donkey safaris	18.1	109,700
Entry fee	18.9	107,750
Campsite charges	20.2	100,300
Tour guiding	17.2	76,400
Bird shooting	16.0	56,900
Cultural manyatta	2.1	23,000
Direct employment	5.0	18,900
Photography	13.9	16,000

Source: Warinda (2001: 48).

land tenure on the group ranch (Warinda, nd). Guests at Ol Donyo Wuas are informed about problems facing the Maasai land owners and environment and can donate funds to the Maasailand Preservation Trust for community projects. These projects include reforestation, dams, local schools, scholarships, medical treatment, 11 game scouts, a women's beading workshop and game counts. In 2000, these Trust projects employed 18 Maasai people and generated US$30,000 in wages and infrastructure on the ranch. Ol Donyo Wuas and the Trust employed 53 people and generated US$81,000 in income (Uncharted Outposts, 2004b). Ol Donyo Wuas was an enduring partnership (Berger and Ntiati, 2000).

Porini Ecotourism, Eselenkei Conservation Area

Porini Ecotourism is a luxury safari camp in the Eselenkei Conservation Area, a game reserve on the 75,000 ha Eselenkei group ranch, just to the north of Amboseli National Park. The camp has four luxury tents and hosts a maximum of eight guests per day. The project began in 1996 with meetings between the manager of Porini Ecotourism and elected leaders of the Eselenkei Maasai community. In 1997, Porini Ecotourism and the local Maasai community agreed to set aside 57,000 ha of land as a wildlife conservation reserve. Ten local game scouts were employed to patrol the Eselenkei reserve and protect wildlife. The company pays an annual lease fee (US$6500) and an entry fee for each tourist paid directly into the community bank account. The community received US$500–1200 per year as income from gate fees and tourist bed charges (Ogutu, 2002). The 15-year lease, signed in 1997, is for exclusive rights to the conservation area. The Kenyan Wildlife Service provided a legal officer to prepare the tourism agreement while ACC ran tourism seminars to explain the project to the community. Porini Ecotourism developed the tourism infrastructure in the Eselenkei reserve (60 km of roads, two waterholes, dams, safari camp and vehicles) at a total cost of US$275,000. This included the tour operator providing US$150,000, a loan of

US$100,000 from the International Fund for Animal Welfare and additional grants of US$25,000 from Care for the Wild and Tusk Trust (UK).

Porini is an acronym for 'protection of resources (Indigenous and natural) for income' and also a Swahili word meaning 'in the wild'. Seventy kilometres of roads in the Eselenkei reserve and waterholes for game viewing were constructed with local Maasai labour. Locals from 25 families were employed on the road maintenance teams, as borehole attendants, game scouts, drivers and as camp staff. This included monthly salaries for 26 local staff and another 20 casual workers. Maasai families also sold firewood, charcoal, goats and other food items to the tourism camp (Ogutu, 2002). Porini Ecotourism also provided US$8000 for Maasai community projects such as uniforms for community game scouts, deepening a livestock waterhole, repairing a windmill pump and donating funds to schools. Tourism income has funded local schools and improved water supplies, but some community leaders have lacked accountability in using tourism funds. Hence, Porini Ecotourism paid for repairs to community water supplies at their request and deducted these amounts from usual lease payments. This ensured tourism income was allocated and spent on community projects. Paying school fees was the main use with other women's business groups not supported by the male group ranch committee (Ogutu, 2002). Conservation benefits included wildlife returning to the Eselenkei Conservation Area, with more elephants seen in May 2001 than in the preceding 15 years. Locals no longer speared or snared wildlife on the ranch while community game scouts hired by Porini Ecotourism assisted the KWS to protect wildlife in the Amboseli area (EA-Ecoconsult, 2002b; Grieves-Cook, 2002; Buckley, 2003a). The Maasai *morans* (warriors) from other areas were each fined US$19 for killing wildlife. Lion numbers increased from 0 to 14, with giraffe, birds and other bush wildlife numbers doubling (Ogutu, 2002).

Rutten (2002b) provides an alternative view of Porini ecotourism at Eselenkei group ranch. The area officially became part of a group ranch in 1988 and some 2500 to 3500 Maasai live on the ranch. A 20-acre campsite was developed on Selengei River in 1988 for bird watchers. Camping fees and bird-shooting fees provided the community with an annual income of KSh50,000–100,000. In 1995, a former game warden at Amboseli started discussions with the Maasai about a wildlife reserve on Eselenkei ranch. He introduced a British tour operator, Tropical Places, to the group ranch committee. The initial proposal was for a 60-bed lodge, lease fee, entrance and bed night fees linked to a 7000 ha reserve. The company sought an exclusive 20-year lease, with a revised proposal including waterholes, tracks and observation platforms. KWS provided trips for ranch members to other community wildlife sanctuaries to gain support. In April 1996, ranch members allocated 16 ha to Tropical Places to build a lodge and offered a 15-year lease. Other issues were local employment, providing tourist facilities and allowing cattle inside the conservation area in the dry season. In November 1996, Tropical Places accepted these terms and established a company called Porini Ecotourism for this project. The company required exclusive use rights and formal registration of Eselenkei Conservation Area.

An agreement was signed in April 1997 for a 15-year lease of Eselenkei Conservation Area, setting an annual lease fee and visitor entrance/bed night fees that would increase by 10% each year. Livestock was not permitted near tourist facilities while Maasai dwellings and cattle enclosures were forbidden in the conservation area. There was a 5-km exclusion zone around the area for other wildlife tourism activities. Conflicts arose when the Maasai Porini liaison officer employed family members on tourism jobs. Ecotourism training and study tours were mainly for Maasai people on the group ranch committee and their relatives (Ogutu, 2002). The ranch committee also allowed subdivision of the tourist area into four sites of 10 acres each. In 1999, the project manager for Porini burnt Maasai huts built in the conservation area. Maasai from the neighbouring Mbuko group ranch also poisoned three leopards that had killed cattle moved into the conservation area during a drought in 1999/2000. Some Maasai youths also poached wildlife on Eselenkei to sell as game meat in Nairobi (Ogutu, 2002).

The tourism agreement was reconfirmed in September 1999 with the conservation area at 5000 ha. A conservation area committee was set up to manage the distribution of fees from Porini, but internal conflicts saw this divided with half of the payments going to the group ranch committee. In February 2000, Tropical Places advertised tours to Eselenkei and brought UK journalists to the site. The 60-bed lodge was not built and with a maximum of eight guests per day, the venture provided an average return of US$5–8 per year for each person ($30 per family) on Eselenkei group ranch. The entrance fee was changed to a one-time rather than daily fee while the Kenyan shilling devalued by 1.5% annually, above the 10% annual increase in fees. The Maasai gave up previous income from bird hunting and lost access to a grazing area, with wildlife conflicts and community conflicts over tourism income. In early 2002, ranch committee members were accused of stealing money from the conservation account. The tour operator made an estimated profit of US$156,540 annually, after Eselenkei fee payments (US$23,780), labour (US$25,000) and running costs (US$75,000) were deducted. A new contract should reflect the real market price of leasing Maasai land for wildlife tourism (Rutten, 2002b). The Kenyan Wildlife Service also paid Eselenkei US$12,500 annually for wildlife grazing (Ogutu, 2002).

Campi ya Kanzi, Kuku group ranch

The 'Campi ya Kanzi' is located in a concession on the Kuku group ranch. A Kuku Community Conservation Area was declared on the ranch, forming a wildlife corridor between the Amboseli, Tsavo West and Chyulu National Parks. The ranch is home to 3000 Maasai people. The up-market camp has seven guesthouses for a maximum of 12 visitors and is managed by an Italian couple. They also run Luca Safaris, a travel company. Tourists at Campi ya Kanzi pay a conservation fee of US$30 per person per day, used to fund Maasai community projects such as schools, medical care and conservation activities. Visitor activities include game walks, game drives, bird watching and visiting a game tracker's house in the Maasai village (Luca Safari, 2002). No trees were cut to build the camp that also uses solar power, reuses grey water and composts food scraps. Thirty-five local Maasai people worked at the camp in cooking, camp maintenance and housekeeping. The camp reflects the policy of KWS for local people to be involved in conserving wildlife (Uncharted Outposts, 2004b). In 2000, Campi ya Kanzi established the Maasai Wilderness Conservation Trust, with conservation fees and visitor donations funding schools, a medical clinic and 16 game scouts who protect wildlife on Kuku ranch. In total, the Trust employed 70 Maasai people on tourism projects (Environmental Business Finance Program, 2004). The 'Simba Project' also compensated Maasai not killing lions for livestock lost to predation (Uncharted Outposts, 2004a).

The Kuku Maasai community and KWS jointly developed the Kuku community conservation area. Ranch members sought community ownership of the conservation area due to the economic benefits from tourism and to avert individual conflicts over compensation for wildlife damage and attacks. Kuku group ranch was about to be subdivided, with members engaging in agricultural expansion while still supporting conservation and tolerating wildlife grazing freely on the land. The estimated net tourist revenue of US$116,240 for Kuku conservation area was extrapolated from tourist visitation to the nearby Tsavo and Amboseli national parks. A survey of potential tourists found 82% were willing to visit a community wildlife sanctuary where tourism revenue supported local people and conservation. Tour operators were willing to visit or develop marketing partnerships for Kuku sanctuary. Suggested tourist activities for Kuku were walking safaris, horse and camel safaris, bird hunting and cultural attractions, supported by a marketing partnership with national parks. KWS, local conservation NGOs, the ranch committee and community elders supported the Kuku sanctuary. Kuku members wanted a new local committee to ensure revenue sharing from tourism; but members did not want their land leased to foreign tourism investors who might restrict access to natural resources or lack understand-

ing of Maasai culture. Maasai elders sought community ownership or co-management with a tourism investor and training provided for local people. To stop a land grab by investors or local elites, a formal legal status for Kuku sanctuary was needed (Okello et al., 2003a, b). The Kuku conservation area had a greater diversity of large mammal species than Amboseli Park, but also had to maintain local Maasai access to water, grazing pasture and plant resources (Okello, 2005a–c).

Wildlife Tourism on Amboseli Group Ranches

In 1996, Kimana Community Wildlife Sanctuary was declared as the first conservation area on a group ranch in Kenya. Kimana ranch is one of several Maasai group ranches around Amboseli Park. Funding for a tourism resort at Kimana wildlife sanctuary was provided by KWS and USAID. The KWS also trained local game scouts and provided a road network in the sanctuary, (APTDC, 2004b). A local management committee was established for the sanctuary, but the community had limited skills and education for managing a tourism business. The KWS focused on biodiversity preservation rather than community participation in goal setting, capacity building and shared decision-making (Reid and Sindiga, 1999). Equitable revenue sharing from community tourism was not achieved at Kimana Wildlife Sanctuary and the area was leased to a private tourism investor (Buysrogge, 2001; Okello et al., 2003a, b). The group ranch earned KSh0.25 million when they operated the sanctuary while the African Safari Club paid KSh7 million annually for the Kimana tourism concession area (Wishitemi and Okello, 2003). A British tour operator constructed a luxury lodge and paid Kimana a tourist fee of US$12 per night. Despite this revenue, a local school and clinic had not been built by 2002 (Mowforth and Munt, 2003a).

The Kuku, Kimana and Imbirikani group ranches near Amboseli are the focus of a 5-year research project (2003–2007) by the School for Field Studies (2005). These Maasai group ranches form a wildlife corridor and dispersal area between Amboseli and Tsavo National Parks. The research examines the impact of land use changes, wildlife conservation and ecotourism enterprises on Maasai people living in this area. Maasai views on wildlife conservation and use of natural resources and Maasai cultural *bomas* were covered. The subdivision of group ranches into areas of individual tenure, the decline of Maasai pastoralism based on cattle grazing and the fencing of land used for cultivation on Kimana in 1997 all impact on wildlife movements and tourism in the Amboseli region (Western, 1994; Okello and Kiringe, 2004; Okello, 2005b).

In 2001, Olgulului ranch near Amboseli redeveloped a 19-year-old public campsite along a key elephant migration corridor, with funding support and assistance from USAID, KWS and the AWF. Olgulului ranch had 3600 Maasai households registered as members. Another ecotourism joint venture with Serena Hotels was for a 20-bed tented camp at Lemomo Hill, beside the elephant migration route. Olgulului ranch set aside a 4000 ha conservation area for this venture while Serena Hotels marketed cultural products made by local Maasai people (*CORE-net*, 2001). Olgulului ranch also leased an exclusive concession area at Esiteti Hill to a safari company and operated the Enkong-Ookankere *boma* or Maasai cultural village that brought tourist benefits to women and poorer people.

Five Maasai cultural villages at Amboseli each earn KSh400,000 a year (Berger and Ntiati, 2000). Some *bomas* supported 200 households but obstructed elephant migration routes (Douglis, 2001). Guides took 'gate fees' from tourists and demanded a commission from *bomas* (Mbaria, 2003). Other Maasai 'villages' at tourist lodges also competed with community *bomas* (Ongaro and Ritsma, 2002; Dapash and Kutay, 2005; van der Duim *et al.*, 2005).

Wildlife Tourism on Masai Mara Group Ranches

In the 1970s, Maasai group ranches were established north and east of the Masai Mara National Reserve. Maasai people were evicted from Masai Mara Reserve in 1974 and restricted from using the area for water, firewood or grazing livestock (Francis, 2002). During the 1980s and 1990s the Maasai people in this area diversified into tourism, agriculture and leasing land to commercial farmers (Cultural Survival, 1999). Maasai group ranches and rangelands in this region are part of the wildlife dispersal area around the Mara reserve. However, the increasing Maasai population and land cultivation have seen wildlife populations in the Masai Mara decline by 70% over 20 years while tourism has increased tenfold in the reserve (Walpole *et al.*, 2003). Wildlife-based tourism in the Masai Reserve attracts 150,000–200,000 visitors annually, earning US$20 million or 8% of all Kenyan tourism revenue. According to Olerokonga (1992), 98% of 260 employees at tourist camps in the Mara Reserve were Maasai. The reserve is also a major source of income for the Narok County Council that manages the area. In 1996, Mara Reserve generated income of US$3.85 million for Narok Council, with 19% remitted to Maasai group ranches and the rest spent on schools, roads and health services in the district (Kareithi, 2003). Since the mid-1990s, however, little or no money was actually remitted to group ranches around the Mara reserve, with less than 1% of this revenue going back to local communities (Walpole and Leader-Williams, 2001; Martyn, 2004). The Narok Council also made the Maasai group ranches collect the tourist entry fee of KSh2400 for the Mara Reserve. To oppose this measure, Siana Trust blocked tourist entry to the reserve while four group ranches wanted the accounts of Narok Council to be audited (UNPO, 2005). The KWS also shared 25% of tourism earnings from the Masai Mara with adjacent group ranches (Berger and Ntiati, 2000). Some Maasai people benefited from ecotourism and cultural *bomas* or villages set up for tourists (Irandu, 2004). The Olonana Masai Cultural Centre near Kwicha Tembo employed 70 Maasai people (Honey, 1999a). However, in 2001, out of 46,331 people living in this Mara area, 36,138 lived below the poverty line (Martyn, 2004).

Maasai group ranches in the Mara region generate US$10 million from wildlife tourism with $3.8 million from agriculture and $2.4 million from livestock. However, 98% of tourism earnings in the Mara are accrued by private operators with tourism generating just 14% of profits on group ranches, mainly from employment, bed night and visitor fees (Norton-Griffiths, 1995). Luxury safari operators are negotiating exclusive use of tourism operations on group ranches, to avoid tourist overcrowding in the Masai Mara Reverse, but this mainly benefits a local Maasai elite of ranch leaders. The Koiyaki ranch earns US$40,000 a year from a sole use contract with a safari operator, while the Lemek ranch kept all wildlife tourism revenue from entry fees and bed night fees, earning $500,000 a year, and was being sued by Narok Council (Norton-Griffiths, 1995). The Koiyaki-Lemek group ranch covered 1490 km². Some 25 companies lease land on Koiyaki and neighbouring group ranches, working with the Maasai to conserve wildlife. Maasai landowners set aside all of Koiyaki and half of Lemek group ranches for wildlife tourism. The Koiyaki-Lemek Conservation Trust charged game viewing fees and had contracts with 25 tour operators that leased their campsites on Maasai land (Berger and Ntiati, 2000; Walpole and Leader-Williams, 2001). The Saruni Camp (2005) with six luxury lodges worked with the Olokirisia local Maasai community on the Koiyaki-Lemek group ranch. A Maasai Wellbeing Space used massage and wellness treatments based on local Maasai use of medicinal plants. Saruni Lodge, owned by Italians, employed Maasai guides and trackers and visited Maasai communities. The Tembo Camp with three large tents was located 10 km from Saruni on the Ole Yaile Conservancy.

The Olchoro O'rowu Association included eight local Maasai families that had legal title to their land. This land area of 8903 ha supported about 500 Maasai people in extended families. The Olchoro O'rowu Association was set up in 1992. A Kenyan man, who had leased land in this area for farming, established this association and went to court for the right to collect tourism revenue. The Narok County Council also had to pay back the association US$467,000 in prior tourism revenue. Four luxury lodges paid a land rent of US$333,333 to the association,

which also charged an entrance fee of US$20 per visitor. Thirty per cent of tourism income was divided among the eight Maasai families, 30% went to management and 4% to community projects such as schools, a medical clinic and wells. A rhino protection project was set up by the association, with support from NGOs and 6% of tourism income. However, two neighbouring Maasai group ranches demanded compensation for tourist game viewing on their lands when the tourists stayed at lodges on the association's land. Like KWS, the association started sharing their tourism revenue with these neighbouring Maasai group ranches (Honey, 1999a).

Private campsites on Maasai land along the Talek River with views over the Masai Mara have been fenced. Maasai people from the Koiyaki group ranch owned 11 campsites at Talek trading centre. They set up a Koiyaki Camp Owners' Association to collect booking fees and bed night levies directly from operators. The Mpuai Women's Group also built the Enkiyo Enkorien Cultural Village near Talek (Berger and Ntiati, 2000). Base Camp Masai Mara on the Talek River is a joint venture between one Maasai group and a Swedish/Norwegian tourism business. The camp with 15 tents has a 42-year lease with Ole Taek group ranch to use their land, plus a bed night levy of US$5 per guest. Additional fees are paid for village tours and walking safaris while 27 Maasai people are employed at Base Camp as guides, gardeners and service staff. Base Camp promoted cultural exchange, livelihood benefits and conservation efforts. Tourists are taken to a Maasai *boma* or village to meet women and children and purchase crafts and beaded bracelets. The Friends of Conservation NGO worked with Base Camp in an Arts and Crafts project for 200 Maasai women. Base Camp also used solar power and bio toilets and recycled grey water on to trees planted along the Talek River. A wood lot was planted with fast growing trees for the Maasai people to use as firewood (Francis, 2002; Lindkvist, 2002a, b).

In July 2004, the Shompole Mara luxury tented camp opened on Ol Kinyei Wildlife Conservancy, 1 hour north of the Masai Mara National Reserve. The camp with six tents and a wildlife conservation reserve are located on Ol Kinyei group ranch. Visitor activities include game drives and walking safaris with Maasai guides and visiting the Ol Kinyei Maasai people to experience their culture. Ol Kinyei is the first wildlife game conservancy on a ranch in the Masai Mara area (Shompole, 2004). This luxury Mara camp is linked with Shompole Lodge in Kajiado, another Maasai joint venture. The Siana Springs Tented Camp is located on the Siana group ranch, 8 km from the eastern boundary of the Masai Mara Reserve. The luxury camp with 38 tents is set in a forest around Siana Springs, the largest natural spring in the Mara area. Local Maasai people made up 60% of the camp staff. The camp owners, Intrepid Safari Company, built a local primary school and continue to fund its development (Porini, 2004). A wildlife conservation area was also developed with the Maasai Siana Wildlife Trust.

The Siana group ranch, to the north-east of Mara Reserve, had 13,700 residents who were mainly rural Maasai people. The Siana Wildlife Trust received US$27 per day from tourists staying on the group ranch with this income paying for school fees, teachers and medical bills for residents (MAO, nd). Oropile Camp paid concession fees and camp fees to the local village and reserve fees to the Trust.

The Mara Intrepids camp had 30 luxury tents above a bend in the Talek River, near the Mara reserve. Instead of buying firewood, the Mara Intrepids tented camp gave a briquette-making machine to Kolong village and buys cow-dung fuel briquettes made by local Maasai women (Harman, 2001). At the Mara Explorer camp, briquettes made from coffee husks were used for heating water. Both of these Mara camps supported a Community Development Fund to equip schools and clinics for Maasai people. Guests could visit local Maasai communities (*manyattas*) and see these facilities (Porini, nd). Conservation Corporation Africa (CCA, 2003) operated two luxury safari camps at Kwicha Tembo on the western border of Mara reserve on a tourism concession leased from the Maasai. Guests went on bush walks with a Maasai guide in traditional attire and also visited Maasai cultural villages.

Wildlife conservation and ecotourism compete with agricultural land uses on Maasai group ranches. In 2003, Koiyaki group ranch was subdivided into individual plots of 60 ha

for 1020 ranch members. Increased cultivation and fencing will further exclude wildlife and affect tourism income that currently generates about US$10 per hectare for wildlife-based enterprises in natural landscapes. This wildlife tourism income depends on unfenced and undeveloped rangelands. Group ranches around Amboseli are also being sub-divided, and growing more crops (Miaron, 2003). Maasai landowners will need to amalgamate many small plots of 60 ha for viable wildlife conservancies on private land. Tour operators also plan to directly compensate Maasai landowners to keep land open for wildlife in prime game viewing areas east of the Mara River. In the wider Mara area the full cost of this wildlife compensation for landowners would amount to $18.5 million each year (Norton-Griffiths, 1995).

Agricultural use of land will increase on group ranches as income from cultivating maize and millet at US$50–100/ha exceeds wildlife tourism income by 300%. Interviews with 200 Maasai household heads from four group ranches found future land use of subdivided individual plots included livestock (82%), cultivation (53%) or tourism (27%). Wildlife would continue grazing on Maasai land, but in more confined areas. Wildlife use options included ecotourism and hunting services collectively managed by Maasai wildlife associations and conservation easements with government or tour operators restricting land use to livestock grazing and wildlife (Sindiga, 1995; Seno and Shaw, 2002). Maasai support for wildlife conservation depends on equitable distribution of tourism income between leaders and members of group ranches (Thompson and Homewood, 2002; Lamprey and Reid, 2004). Maasai income from tourism was used to build houses and campsites, buy cars, pay for education and acquire more livestock that could increase local land degradation (Berger and Ntiati, 2000). Game scouts were also employed by Maasai group ranches to protect wildlife for tourism (Walpole, 2004).

Loita Hills

The Loita Maasai, numbering around 25,000 people, opposed plans to turn a forest area on

Loita Hills known as 'The Forest of the Lost Child' into a game reserve. In particular, the Loita Maasai wish to avoid the environmental degradation and impacts of mass tourism caused by the proliferation of lodges and safari vehicles in the nearby Masai Mara Reserve. For the self-sufficient Loita Maasai, however, the Forest of the Lost Child provides a watershed, a cattle grazing area in the dry season, a source of medicinal herbs and is of ceremonial significance (Carrere, 1994). The Loita forest is used for age grade ceremonies every 7 years, and the blessing for female fertility performed by a *laibon* or spiritual healer (Maasai Trails, 2004). Instead of gazetting the forest area as a game reserve or allowing safari lodges and minibuses access, the Loita Maasai wanted to develop low-key tourist facilities such as tented camps. Tourist activities include forest walks with Loita elders and visiting villages bordering the forest area to participate in Maasai daily life (Stewart, 2003). Many private tour companies bring small groups on trekking or horseback safaris, with Loita Maasai working as guides.

The 33,000 ha Loita Forest is 320 km south-west of Nairobi. Surrounding the forest are Loita Maasai *bomas* or settlements. The dense forest is a source of water, trees, leaves, grass and medicinal plants, and can only be approached on foot. In the early 1990s, the Narok District Council sought to develop the Loita Forest for mass tourism, as an extension to the Maasai Mara Reserve. Narok Council members planned to lease the forest to a consortium to construct a large tourist hotel and roads. In response, the Loita Maasai produced pamphlets and articles, joined local networks and set up the Loita Naimina Enkiyio Conservation Trust. The Trust, controlled by ten Maasai Loita elders, aimed to preserve the Loita forest for local use. In 1994, the Loita Trust filed a lawsuit against Narok Council, who held the forest as trust land, to gain legal entitlement to Loita forest. Their legal case referred to article 8(j) of the Convention on Biological Diversity, signed by Kenya, to respect and maintain Indigenous knowledge, practices and sustainable use of biodiversity (Stephenson, 1999). Narok Council granted the Loita and Purko Maasai ownership rights to Loita Forest in October 2002.

In 2004, the Loita Maasai protested against a KSh200 million project for this forest funded by the World Conservation Union (IUCN). One local Maasai was killed and others injured during these protests. The Maasai objected to an outside organization controlling use of the Loita forest. The project was put on hold until consensus was reached among all stakeholders in the forest project.

In 1995, a Loita ethnobotany project was initiated to record Loita Maasai knowledge and use of forest plants (Maundu *et al.*, 2001). The Loita plant use project was funded by UNESCO and implemented under the Loita Naimina Enkiyio Conservation Trust. The project was a step towards community management of Loita forest by the Loita Maasai people. To protect forest resources, Loita Maasai established the Loita Development Foundation forming a partnership with a Dutch NGO, Stichting Loita Maasai. Five programme areas support Maasai conservation and economic enterprises in the Loita area, including ecotourism. A Dutch veterinarian, European Kenyan and a Loita Maasai man set up a small-scale ecotourism business, *Maasai Trails*. The venture provides trekking walks of 6–9 days through the Loita forest with Maasai guides and donkeys (Maasai Trails, 2004). Forest wildlife includes birds and colobus monkeys. This ecotourism business run by the Maasai highlights the need for forest conservation and is an alternative source of community income (Loita Maasai, 2004).

West of the Loita Hills, the Olarro Lodge is located on the 150,000 acre Maji Moto group ranch. The lodge is just 35 km from the Masai Mara Game Reserve with panoramic views over the Mara plains. Olarro is Maasai for buffalo, and the ecolodge works with the Maasai people who continue to graze their cattle along the hills (Let's Go Travel, 2004). There were no other details on this ecolodge. The Otarakuai Kitilikini group ranch in the Loita Hills also has a safari camp, with a conservation fee for each traveller paid to the tribal council, which is used to fund a school and clinic (Deeper Africa, 2005).

Maasai tours

Other tours with Maasai involvement include the *Maasai Culture and Wildlife Safari* run by an

Australian woman and her Maasai husband. This 3-week tour to Maasai villages in the Loita Hills commenced in the early 1990s. Tourists camped near a Maasai village, had language lessons, went on guided forest walks with Maasai guides, visited Maasai homes and joined traditional ceremonies. Part of the tour fee went to a trust fund for the local Maasai community (Carlisle, 1993; Oddie, 1994). Trekking Warrior Expeditions operates around the Masai Mara Reserve. An American business graduate and a Maasai man, Paul Ole Kuyar, run the small company. The business partners support community campsites and employ two local guides in the Mara region (Trekking Warrior, 2004). Into Africa operate fair trade safaris in Kenya visiting a Maasai marketplace and homesteads at Narok. Set up in 1998, it employs Maasai guides and supports schools and community projects (Rahman, 2002).

Wildland Adventures operates tours in partnership with the Maasai Environmental Resource Coalition (MERC, 2003a), a community organization protecting Maasai land rights and promoting conservation. Local Maasai community leaders led the Maasai Land Safari, with trip proceeds going to MERC. The trip included game viewing in the Masai Mara and Amboseli and wildlife walks with Maasai guides. On the first Maasailand safari in August 2003, 14 participants donated US$6000 to rebuild a well in Meshannani village, near Amboseli Park (Dapash and Kutay, 2005). Other Maasai beading safaris focused on craftwork made by Maasai women in Amboseli (Kenya), with a new beading cooperative funded from donations to MERC in 2003 plus other Maasai beading groups in Sinya and Tarangire (Tanzania). The tours included a Maasai guide and MERC membership (Wildland Adventures, 2005).

These ecotours with MERC began in 2003 to promote Maasai culture and land issues (Kutay, 2003; Mbaria, 2003). MERC represented Maasai groups in Kenya and Tanzania, including tourism ventures.

Community ecotourism ventures in northern Kenya

The Kijabe group ranch in northern Kenya is developing an exclusive ecolodge for 12 guests on a 5000 acre wildlife conservation area. The 15,000 acre Kijabe group ranch was established in 1976 for 100 Maasai families. In 1999, Maasai elders in the regional town of Ol Malo asked some US advisers for help in developing their ranch. They proposed a wildlife area and an ecotourism lodge run and hosted by the Kijabe community. Funding for the Kijabe ecotourism project was obtained from the Ford Foundation (US$100,000), USAID, Wildlife Trust and Impala Trust (USA). The private investor, Anjuan Ltd, already managed a lodge on Ol Malo ranch. The project will also develop art and craft projects with Maasai women and children (Uncharted Outposts, 2004a). The US Earthwatch Institute has also established a Samburu Heartlands Conservation Research Centre on Kijabe ranch.

The Kalacha Camp is located at a permanent oasis in the Chalbi Desert of far northern Kenya. The camp is built from palm trunks and palm leaves woven into mats for the walls and roof. The camp was established with funding from the European Union to provide income for local Gabbra people. Visitor activities include walking around the palm-lined oasis, photographing desert scenery, visiting the Gabbra village and shooting sandgrouse that flock at the springs (Uncharted Outposts, 2004c). Conflicts between bird watchers and bird shooters and the community benefits were not described.

CORE Community Ecotourism Ventures

From 1999 to 2003, the Conservation of Resources through Enterprise (CORE) programme funded by USAID has supported conservation-linked ecotourism businesses in Kenya. These community enterprises include ecolodges on Maasai group ranches in Laikipia District, Siana Springs Tented Camp in the Masai Mara, Lion Rock Tsavo tented camp in LUMO Community Wildlife Sanctuary, Mwaluganje Elephant Sanctuary and ecolodges on Maasai group ranches near Amboseli (see Table 4.3). The CORE programme also supported cultural centres, craft projects and a mangrove boardwalk. These community ecotourism projects were

Table 4.3. CORE community ecotourism enterprises in Kenya.

Name of enterprise, year began	Enterprise type	Location
Siana Springs Tented Camp, 2002?	Ecolodge	Masai Mara
Koija Starbeds, 2002	Ecolodge	Laikipia
Kijabe Ecolodge, 2003?	Ecolodge	Laikipia
Ngutuk Ongiron Lodge, 2003?	Ecolodge	Laikipia
Lion Rock Tsavo Tented Camp, 2003	Ecolodge	Taita Taveta
Kasiagu bandas (huts) for 5 villages, 2001	Ecolodge	Taita Taveta
Elerai/Entonet Lodge	Ecolodge	Amboseli
Imbirikani Lodge	Ecolodge	Amboseli
Olgulului/Lolarrashi Tented Camp	Ecolodge	Amboseli
Shompole Ecolodge, 2002	Ecolodge	Amboseli
Mwaluganje Elephant Sanctuary, 1995	Sanctuary and Stationery	Kwale, South Coast
Wasini Women's Group, 2001	Boardwalk and Crafts	Wasini, South Coast

Other CORE enterprises include: Il Polei Cultural Manyatta, Laikipia; Ewaso and Otiti Women's Groups Crafts and Jewellery, Laikipia; Amboseli Cultural Centres Manyattas, Amboseli; Dupoto and Shompole Women's Groups, Crafts and Jewellery, Amboseli.
Source: CORE-net (2002a, b, c).

funded by grants from the Enterprise Development Fund of USAID, private tourism investors (i.e. hotels and safari operators), local communities, other donor agencies and the Biodiversity Conservation Program of the European Union (*CORE-net*, 2001). The African Wildlife Foundation and Kenya Wildlife Service also supported these ecotourism projects.

The Lion Rock Tsavo Camp in south-western Kenya is a joint venture between Tsavo Park Hotels and LUMO Community Wildlife Sanctuary, managed by a Trust from three community ranches. The tented camp is located on the 144,470 acre LUMO conservation area set up in 2001. Developed at a cost of KSh30 million, the Lion Rock Tsavo camp is the first community partnership with an Indigenous Kenyan for an ecolodge in a wildlife sanctuary. The Lion Rock Camp opened in 2003, employing local people and purchasing local farm produce. Key challenges were sharing tourism benefits between three ranches, co-management of the camp, setting up a management board for the LUMO sanctuary and working with nearby parks and sanctuaries (*CORE-net*, 2002a).

The Kasiagu community *bandas* (round huts) were built in five villages around the base of Mt Kasiagu in the Taita-Taveta District of south-east Kenya. Funding for the *bandas* was provided by USAID to provide an alternative income for subsistence farmers living in the area. The huts were owned and operated by five villages that set up their own tourism companies with community members purchasing a company share for KSh534. Overseas student volunteers rent the Kasiagu *bandas* and participate in conservation projects or local community service. Savannah Camps and Lodges negotiated exclusive use of the Kasiagu *bandas* with a 10-year lease. The annual lease fee was US$20,000 with a 10% annual increase. In the first operating year of 2001/02, the company generated revenue of US$38,000 for the Kasiagu community *bandas* (USAID, 2002c).

Kiswahili women on Wasini Island own and manage a 1 km boardwalk through mangrove forest and coral gardens that opened in 2001. KWS, USAID, IUCN and the Netherlands Wetlands and Conservation Training Program funded the boardwalk and trained local Muslim women in business management and leadership. The project employs three local women trained in bookkeeping and as tour guides while tourism income funded school fees for girls and also maintenance of the boardwalk. In 2002, the boardwalk entrance fees generated income of US$6500 with US$2000 being used to set up a craft shop and US$2800 paid as dividends to members. The project supported mangrove conservation and raised local awareness of marine ecology. It also increased female benefits from tourism in the nearby Kisite Mpunguti Marine Park and in managing resources (*CORE-net*, 2002c; USAID, 2003).

Mwaluganje Elephant Sanctuary

The Mwaluganje Elephant Sanctuary opened in 1995. It is located 35 km from the coastal city of Mombasa and southern beach resorts that attract 600,000 tourists a year. The sanctuary has around 150 elephants and other wildlife such as impala, bushbuck, sable, warthog, leopard, birds and butterflies. The forest area formed an elephant corridor in the Shimba Hills that was farmed by local Duruma and Digo people. Prompted by elephant raids on crops and property damage, in 1993 over 200 families ceded their farmlands to establish the 36 km^2 Mwaluganje Elephant Sanctuary, with support from KWS, the Eden Wildlife Trust and environmental NGOs (Knicker-brocker and Waithaka, 2005). A community conservation association was formed in 1994 to manage the sanctuary. Local families are now shareholders that receive annual dividends based on one share for each acre of land ceded. In 1997, the sanctuary generated US$29,000 in gate entry fees. There were revenue sharing conflicts until the sanctuary land owned by farmers was surveyed and adjudicated. Sanctuary payments ranged from KSh60,000 to KSh200,000 per family (Cocheba and Ndriangu, 1998). In 2001, the sanctuary paid US$23,763 in wages to 13 staff and dividends of US$25,641 to 160 share-holders. Tourism revenue has built classrooms, paid school fees and improved roads and water supply. With USAID funding, a manager and other staff from the local community were trained to run the sanctuary. The Mwaluganje Elephant Sanctuary is community-owned but run by the KWS.

The East African Wildlife Society also developed a marketing plan and promotion material for the sanctuary, along with a website and familiarization visit by 21 south coast tour operators and travel agents. A private investor built a lodge in the sanctuary paying US$800 per month for this concession. The Travellers Mwaluganje Elephant Camp has 20 luxury tents facing a traditional elephant trail in the sanctuary. A related project is producing stationery products made from elephant dung, sold at the sanctuary. Production of these paper products employs two people and generates extra income of KSh25,000 per month. In 2002, Mwaluganje Elephant Sanctuary had 17 employees and paid over KSh2 million in dividends to 232 shareholders (*CORE-net*, 2002b; USAID, 2002d). In June 2004, UK students with Camps International helped develop a tourist information centre and shop, provide signage and trail marking, conducted elephant research and wildlife education.

Ngomongo Villages

The Ngomongo Villages are located 10 km north of Mombasa. The villages represent 10 tribal groups in Kenya with their huts, utensils, gardens, crops, domestic animals, and staff demonstrating traditional practices. The ten tribes are the Maasai, Kalenjin, Taita, Akamba, Mijikenda, Pokot, Turkana, Luo, El Molo and Rendille peoples. Visitors participate in hands-on cultural activities such as archery, grinding grain, tasting tribal foods, fishing, visiting a witch doctor and tribal dances. The villages occupy a 6.5 ha area on the site of a former barren limestone quarry. Re-vegetation of the quarry began in 1991 led by the efforts of one local man, Dr Fredrick Gikandi. Tree seedlings were obtained from the government and from seed banks and a tree nursery set up by the local community who helped with the tree planting. The 80 tree species grown had food and medicinal uses. Two natural ponds were excavated to form wetlands and a bird sanctuary with over 50 bird species was established, attracting wild birds like Egyptian geese. Cultural tourism was added to ensure sustainability and income for the tree planting work (Ngomongo Villages, nd). The cultural village opened in 1998 and receives around 8000 visitors a month, mostly school groups and foreign students (Ochieng, 2004). Fifteen thousand trees were planted at the Ngomongo site and visitors are invited to plant a tree in their home country. Ngomongo is a sustainable eco-cultural tourist village and a model of land reclamation. Local people formed an NGO to extend tree planting to nearby farming communities. Dr Gandiki invested US$200,000 in this revegetation project at Ngomongo. In 2001 he was awarded the UN Global 500 Roll of Honor award for his environmental work. From 2002 to 2004, Ngomongo was nominated as one of three finalists in the Sustainable Tourism Awards of *Smithsonian Magazine*.

Kaya Kinondo forest

The 30 ha Kaya Kinondo forest is located on Diani beach, a tourist resort area on the south coast. The forest is sacred to the Digo community who used it to commune with ancestral spirits and perform offerings, collect medicinal plants and build ritual structures. The kaya forests were threatened by growing demand for farmland, timber extraction, sand mining and tourist hotels. WWF and the Kenyan Coastal Forest Conservation Unit, set up in 1992, worked to conserve biodiversity in these sacred kaya forests of the Mijikenda tribes in southern Kenya (Githitho, 1998, 2002; Sacred Land, 2004). Some 38 kaya forests were gazetted as national monuments legally managed by local communities (Salehe, 2004). The Kaya Kinondo forest had 187 plant species, 45 butterfly species, over 48 bird species, the colobus monkey and the rare golden-rumped elephant shrew. The Ford Foundation (US) provided funding to set up the Kaya Kinondo Ecotourism Project in 2001 that was managed by Digo people from two villages. The project aimed to generate income from ecotourism and conserve the sacred forest. A Kinondo guide, often a traditional healer, led tours of the forest, explaining medicinal plant uses and community practices. Handicrafts made by Digo women were sold at the forest entrance. Tourists in shorts or miniskirts had to cover their legs with a sarong and certain forest areas were either off limits or photography was banned. Tourists also visited a village and local school (Gaceru, 2003). Other activities included conservation awareness, promoting the site to local hotels, a cultural centre for visitors, a brochure and website information for WWF and Alliance

Hotels and site management (Enchanted Landscapes, 2004). During 2003/04, over US$5000 was generated from tourism in the Kaya forest (Salehe, 2004). Tourism revenue funded schools and local community projects. In 2004, the Kaya Kinondo Ecotourism Project was granted US$19,915 from the Critical Ecosystem Partnership Fund, to develop further ecotourism activities and protect the forest area.

Tanzania: Village-based Ecotourism on Community Lands

Tourism in Tanzania is based around the northern safari circuit of Serengeti, the Ngorongoro Crater, Lake Manyara and Mt Kilimanjaro, based out of Arusha and Nairobi, Kenya. In 2001, Tanzania earned US$275 million from tourism, 12% of GDP, second only to agriculture as an export earner (Nelson, 2004, 2005a). Mt Kilimanjaro, the highest mountain in Africa, receives around 20,000 visitors a year. The popular island of Zanzibar received 100,000 tourists in 1998 and is dominated by foreign-owned beach resorts on the eastern coast of this island. Cultural and nature-based tours of Menai Bay, dolphin tours, fishing villages, spice tours and the Jozani forest were also promoted on Zanzibar (Eco and Culture Tours, nd). The 1998 Tanzania tourism policy promoted sustainable tourism that improved the economy and livelihood of local people. The 1994 national policy for Tanzania National Parks (TANAPA) and 1998 wildlife policy also encouraged tourism development either outside park boundaries or near the periphery to benefit neighbouring communities. TANAPA promoted community-based tourism ventures and other income-generating activities to alleviate poverty for people living adjacent to Tanzania's protected areas. A Community Conservation Service was set up in 1989 by TANAPA to assist socio-economic development of park communities (Bergin, 1998; Honey, 1999b). Community wildlife management areas around protected areas also allowed local villages to benefit from wildlife. TANAPA guidelines for ecotourism included investors employing local people, financial gain for locals, improved social facilities and environmental protection through partnerships with communities (Melamari, 2001; Kileo, 2004; Sand County Foundation, 2004b). The Ministry of Natural Resources and Tourism in Tanzania supported conservation partnerships with local communities, NGOs and the private sector.

During the 1990s, forest-based ecotourism was promoted in the Eastern Arc Mountains of Tanzania. The 1998 Tanzania Forest Policy emphasized joint management of Forest Reserves based on active community participation in using and protecting forests. Conservation agencies worked with local communities to develop alternative activities based on forest resources, including ecotourism. These forest management and biodiversity conservation programmes in the East Usambara, Uluguru, and Udzungwa mountains were implemented by the Forestry Division of the Ministry of Natural Resources and Tourism with funding from USAID, European Union, Finland, Denmark and the UK. The next section reviews community ecotourism projects in the Amani Nature Reserve (East Usambara), Nogutu village (Uluguru), Udzungwa National Park and the Jozani Forest, Zanzibar.

Village-based Ecotourism in Community Forests

Amani Nature Reserve, East Usambara Mountains

Amani Nature Reserve is part of the 83,600 ha East Usambara Biosphere Reserve, in the Eastern Arc Mountains of Tanzania – one of 25 global biodiversity hotspots with over 2000 plant species. The high numbers of endemic and range-restricted birds, such as the Uluguru bushshrike and Udzungwa partridge, were also a major attraction for birdwatchers (Butchart, 2003). Amani Reserve was established in May 1997. Formerly a botanic garden, the key ecotourism attractions were the forest, mountain viewpoints, waterfalls and forest birds. The reserve was financed by the Amani Nature Reserve Conservation Fund, with the government of Finland providing financial assistance from 1991 to 2002. Facilities in the reserve included walking trails, hiking and

driving routes with trail leaflets and signs, a map and guidebook for the area. Nine trails were set up, extending from the reserve to local villages. There were two visitor guesthouses in the reserve, one near the entrance and the other in the upland plateau. Some 20% of tourism revenues from the Amani Reserve were directed to community development projects. The reserve has 18 trained tour guides from local villages who retain 60% of guiding fees. A shop at the reserve also sold local handicrafts, while cultural tourism activities were promoted in the buffer zone villages. The Amani Reserve received around 2000 visitors a year, mainly people interested in local biodiversity of species such as butterflies, birds, frogs and plants. However, the road to the reserve was in poor condition with a four-wheel-drive vehicle needed in the rainy season, local people were averse to visitors and high management costs were not covered by visitor arrivals. While the 1998 Tanzania Forest Policy supported ecotourism and community participation in forest use and management, there were no tools or regulations for implementing ecotourism projects (Sawe, 2002; Buckley, 2003b).

The reserve collaborated with local people to preserve the forest. Villagers around the Amani Nature Reserve were allowed to enter the forest twice a week to collect dead wood that had fallen from trees. Hunting in the reserve was forbidden and villagers could not pursue baboons that destroyed their crops. Ecotourism was developed as a sustainable forest use and source of income for the reserve and local communities. Forest trails led through tea plantations to nearby villages. The Tanzanian government had limited funds to maintain the reserve after western donors ended their financial assistance for forest management. The East Usambara Mountains were to be developed as a stopover for tourists travelling between Zanzibar and the safari circuit in northern Tanzania (Houtzager, 2000). A WWF project supports community-based forest management in the East Usambara Mountains, for ten village forest reserves, 15 government forest reserves and 28 villages with 135,000 people. It promotes sustainable use of forest resources and ecotourism activities to benefit local people (WWF, 2005).

Nogutu Village, Uluguru Mountains

The Uluguru Mountains are an outlying ridge of the Eastern Arc Mountains in Tanzania. The forest with endemic mammals, reptiles and birds, covers two mountain blocks rising to 2600 m. There are 14 forest reserves on the Uluguru Mountains, covering 404 km^2 on the mountain and foothills. The area has intensive agriculture with 1.5 million Luguru people living around the Uluguru Mountains. Around 100,000 Luguru people live on the mountain itself, growing fruit and vegetable crops for sale. In the mid-1990s the European Union began conservation work on the Uluguru Mountains followed in 1999 by Danish agencies with the Wildlife Conservation Society of Tanzania and BirdLife International (Eastern Arc, 2002). The key focus was on protecting forest reserves with the local people.

The Mountains Conservation Society of Tanzania established community-based ecotourism projects in three Uluguru villages, to support forest conservation and provide alternative income. In July 2000, the villages of Nogutu, Ruvuma and Morningside, located a 1–3 hour walk from the regional city of Morogoro on the main road to Dar es Salaam, were advised to develop ecotourism projects. A Dutch development consultant and Dutch students assisted with this ecotourism project in 2001. Ecotours to Nogutu Village focused on local culture and daily activities such as mat making, brick factory, coconut chair factory, traditional dances and local food including 'ugali' made from cassava, local beer 'pombe' and a local soft drink 'togwa.' A team of 14 women prepared lunch while nine women and six men performed traditional dances and drumming. From Nogutu village, tourists hiked through the forest to Madola village, with mountain views, wooden handicrafts and a witch doctor. A 3-hour hike also went to Morningside village, with camping equipment hired to visitors.

The Mountains Conservation Society of Tanzania (MCST) played a major role in marketing and promoting the Uluguru Mountains ecotourism project. Tour brochures were printed and distributed at tourist sites in Dar es Saalam and at the society's regional office in Morogoro. Visitor reservations were made through the MCST offices and local guides took visitors from Morogoro to the villages for the tour. The village chairman was informed by mobile phone of the date and arrival time of visitors. Tourists paid for the tour at Nogutu village, with the money divided among local groups and guides by a set fee chart. A coordination fee was paid to MCST for brochures, phone bills and office rent. Ten per cent of tourism income went to a village conservation fund with trees planted to restore watersheds (Salum Madoweka, Mountain Forum email list, 24 April, 2002).

Udzungwa Mountains

The Udzungwa Mountains are also part of the Eastern Arc Mountains in Tanzania. A US$2.9 million forest management and biodiversity conservation project began in the Udzungwa Mountains in 1999. Uncontrolled harvesting of forest products by local communities was degrading the area. The Udzungwa forests were a critical watershed area, had high biodiversity and endemism, and were culturally important. Joint forest management agreements were prepared for two reserves and 16 community development enterprises were initiated for sustainable use of forests (Eastern Arc, 2002).

Since 1992, WWF was involved in conserving and establishing Udzungwa Mountains National Park, the only part of the Eastern Arc mountain range with intact forest cover from low to high altitudes. The park included Udzungwa Mountain, at 2576 metres, with dense rainforest and rare fauna including endemic primates, the iringa red colobus and sanje-crested mangabey. The Udzungwa Mountains National Park is one of the top ten forests in Africa for bird conservation, with endemic birds such as the udzungwa partridge and rufous-winged sunbird. WWF led conservation awareness campaigns and supported village enterprises such as tree nurseries and bricks made from rice husks. WWF also worked with the Community Conservation Service of Tanzania National Parks (TANAPA) to develop community-based conservation and involve local communities in park planning and management. Park infrastructure was developed with funding from the UK and visitor numbers were increasing. Local villages identified business opportunities from ecotourism, supported by women and youth groups, with WWW assisting TANAPA in developing park ecotourism facilities (Kasulwa, 2000).

Jozani Forest, Zanzibar

The Jozani Forest and larger Jozani-Chwaka Bay Conservation Area are a key area for ecotourism in Zanzibar or Unguja Island. The Conservation Area was established in 1993, with funding from Austria. It includes mangrove forests, the southern part of Chwaka Bay and Jozani Forest, the first forest area established on Zanzibar. Jozani Forest was a secondary growth forest replanted with red mahogany from 1948 to the 1980s. The 33,000 ha forest had small populations of endangered fauna species such as endemic Zanzibar red colobus monkeys, civets, dikdik, Ader's duiker and Sykes monkeys. Jozani Forest had 700 red colobus monkeys and another 300 in the Conservation Area, out of a total island population of 2350 (Khatib, 2000; Myers, 2002). The red colobus was a key ecotourism attraction with no fear or aversion to humans, as local people considered it poisonous and it was not hunted. The village of Jozani-Pete next to Jozani Forest set up an environmental committee to develop ecotourism. They constructed a 1-km boardwalk through mangroves at the southern road entrance to Jozani Forest, funded by the Netherlands and CARE Tanzania. Villagers worked as authorized guides for tours in the southern part of Jozani Forest. Tourists paid an entry fee of US$10 for the boardwalk and forest tour. In 1997, Jozani Forest had 17,360 visitors generating US$63,612 in entry fees. US$5075 was allocated to seven villages around the Jozani Forest, while a grant of US$5970 went to the village advisory committee and US$747 on administration. Visitor donations went to a Community Development Fund (Khatib, 2000). The village committee installed two gates and regular forest patrols to reduce illegal cutting of poles while Charawe village was fined for cutting red mahogany. In

contrast, Chwaka and other villages in the Conservation Area had not benefited from ecotourism (Archabald, 2000). Conservation measures for fishing, mangroves and wildlife were not followed in Chwaka village, the site of eight donor-funded environmental research projects in the 1990s. Ideas of conservation and development set by external agencies reduced social cohesion and village-led conservation efforts (Myers, 2002). Economic and political inequalities affected local interest in conservation and ecotourism at Jozani-Chwaka Bay Conservation Area.

Marine Ecotourism in Zanzibar and Pemba

Menai Bay Conservation Area, Zanzibar

The Menai Bay Conservation Area of 470 km^2 is the largest marine protected area in Zanzibar. In 1994, WWF established a conservation programme to address over-fishing, with the marine reserve declared in 1997. USAID, the British government and Switzerland also funded this WWF programme. By 2003, 19 local villages in the Menai Bay area were involved in this WWF conservation programme. Village conservation committees were set up to control illegal fishing with dynamite and nets in Menai Bay. Mangrove replanting, bee keeping, tree nurseries and tourism were also supported in some villages to provide alternative local income and support conservation. The village of Kizimkazi Dimbani in the eastern part of Menai Bay had paved road access, and received more resources and support from the WWF programme, including tourism. The village also received many day visitors, with this area of Menai Bay receiving 10,000 tourists in 1998. Two hundred bottlenose and humpback dolphins were found in the waters around Kizimkazi and fishermen from this village used their boats to take tourists out on dolphin watching or dolphin swimming tours in the bay. Guidelines about boats not pursuing dolphins and swimmers staying close to the boats were often ignored. However, 5 years earlier local people in Menai Bay had been killing dolphins for meat (Eliah, 2000). Half of the fishermen used boats with outboard motors to conduct these dolphin tours or to fish. To generate revenue for the conservation programme, tour operators were levied at US$2 for each visitor. Both local fishermen and tour operators opposed this tourist tax, as they saw few benefits from this revenue. Residents of Fumba village in western Menai Bay gained few benefits from tourism, or the programme. Village committees in Fumba were not supported, while a new village committee set up at Kizimkazi Dimbani, which received more tourism and programme resources, strengthened local structures. The lack of patrols to prevent illegal fishing in the Bay also affected conservation and tourism (Levine, 2004).

Mnemba Island Lodge

A community-based marine tourism programme also operates at Mnemba Island Lodge, an exclusive beach resort operated by Conservation Corporation Africa (CCA). The 1.5 km-round Mnemba Island is located off the north-east cost of Zanzibar, and is part of the 20 km Mnemba Atoll. The Mnemba Conservation Area was declared in 1997. The marine wildlife on this coral island include green turtles, whale sharks, humpback whales, dolphins, rich coral reefs and numerous tropical fish. CCA purchased the island lease in 1996 for US$4 million and worked with the nearby communities of Matemwe and Muyumi to improve nature conservation and minimize impacts of the lodge. The Africa Foundation provided more than US$40,000 to build clinics, schools, other community projects, alternative fishing practices based on fish aggregation devices placed in 300 m of water, and rescued fishing boats. Forty staff from nearby villages worked at the lodge, with other local income from a vegetable garden and collecting waste from local hotels. CCA spent US$5000 per month purchasing local produce and fish. Daily charges for water activities such as diving and snorkelling were put into a community fund. Environmental activities adopted by CCA with the local communities were turtle monitoring and protection of the Mnemba Atoll. A 200 m no-go zone with no

fishing or shell collecting was established around Mnemba Island. CCA managed this island conservation area with the Mnemba Island Marine Conservation Area established in 2002. To encourage local support for marine conservation and prevent over-fishing, four local communities received 1 million Tanzanian shillings from the Mnemba Marine Area in 2003. Local support for the Mnemba Island Lodge and Marine Area mainly came from community development projects (Wildwatch, 2003; WTO, 2003c).

Misali Island Conservation Association

Misali Island is a small forest-covered island, 0.9 km long and 500 metres wide, surrounded by coral reefs. The island beaches have nesting green and hawksbill turtles while divers are attracted to the reefs. Misali is located west of Pemba Island, and north of Zanzibar. Some 1640 fishermen from 29 coastal communities on Pemba Island fished on the reefs around Misali and left offerings in the caves. Developers sought a lease to turn Misali Island into a luxury Indian Ocean resort that would exclude other users. Lobbying by fishers and environmental agencies led the Zanzibar Government to declare Misali Island and its surrounding reefs a protected marine conservation area in 1998. Ten per cent of the marine conservation area was a non-extractive zone with no fishing (Garcia, 2005). The Misali Island Conservation Area covered 22 km^2 while Misali Island became a community-managed ecotourism site with controlled fishing. A management committee of fishers, government and NGOs set use limits with no fishing on Misali's coral reef and also no fishing with dynamite, poison or tightly woven nets. The Misali Island Conservation Association of mainly local fishermen was set up in 1998 to manage and monitor use of the area. This included 12 local communities around Pemba Island and 34 groups in fishermen's associations. Visitor charges to Misali Island offset fishing restrictions with tourism revenue divided among member villages (Abdullah *et al.*, 2000). Forty per cent of tourism revenue went to the local community and 60% to conservation management (Mwangi, 2002).

The Misali Island Conservation Project was based on Islamic principles of conservation for the Muslim fishermen, supported by CARE International-Tanzania, US Foundations, the Islamic Foundation for Ecology and Environmental Sciences and WWF (Khalid, 2003). A small-scale tourism project started in 1997 with four Misali fishers trained as guides. A tour operator in Stonetown, Zanzibar, transported tourists to Pemba Island on a high-speed ferry, where visitors made day trips to Misali. Tourists and divers at Misali gave a voluntary US$10 donation shared among the local fishers (Ziegler, 1998). During 2001–2004, British NGOs assessed marine resources around Misali for a new management plan.

Maasai Community Ecotourism in Tanzania

There was 10% annual visitor growth in Tanzania during the 1990s, leading to overcrowding at key national parks in the northern safari circuit of Serengeti, Ngorongoro Crater and Lake Manyara. Private tour operators started walking safaris and bush camping trips on communal or village lands that were wildlife dispersal areas near parks and reserves. Walking trips were prohibited or restricted inside parks while the villages added a cultural element to safari tours, not found in protected areas. Tanzanian wildlife and tourism policies also supported tourism ventures on community-owned lands. Changes to land laws allowed village councils to negotiate contracts with private tour operators. These contracts for walking or vehicle safaris, camping trips and tented camps included set fees for access, visitor services and a per person bed night payment. These community tourism fees ranged from US$5 to US$45 depending on the type of safari operation. For these reasons, community-based ecotourism grew in northern Tanzania in the 1990s, particularly among Maasai pastoral groups near Tarangire and Serengeti National Parks. These Maasai village ecotourism ventures have expanded since 2000, providing a significant source of income in rural areas of northern Tanzania (Nelson, 2004). Ololosokwan, a

Maasai village on the eastern edge of Serengeti earns US$50,000 annually from various tourism ventures. Maasai villages around Tarangire Park earn US$10,000 annually from safari tourism (Nelson, 2005a). The next sections review Maasai community ecotourism ventures around both Tarangire and Serengeti.

Ecotourism in Tarangire and Serengeti

Tarangire Conservation Area

Tarangire Conservation Area covers a major wildlife migration route adjacent to Tarangire National Park. It is a tourism joint venture with the Maasai people, and is the only area in Tanzania with night game drives. Other tourist activities are foot safaris, fly camping and visiting a local Maasai village. The Tarangire Conservation Area is a 40,000-acre wildlife management area leased to the East African Safari Company by local Maasai villages (Sikar, 1996; Igoe, 2002). In return for conserving wildlife, the Maasai receive revenue from each tourist entering the area, funding schools, clinics, water-pumps, boreholes and women's projects. Tourism income and employment has reduced deforestation, wildlife poaching and charcoal making. There are two eco-lodges in the Conservation area, Boundary Hill Lodge overlooking Gosuwa and Silale swamps and Naitolia Lodge on the Lemiyon Plains. Maasai craftsmen built the lodges from local materials and village councils are on the board of directors (East Africa Safari, nd). The International Finance Corporation funded the construction of these eco-lodges in Tarangire Conservation Area. The Maasai village of Lokisale, with 4000 residents, jointly owned the Boundary Hill Lodge, which opened in 2002 (Friends of the Earth, nd). It was the first lodge in Tanzania with local Maasai community shareholding (50%) (East Africa Safari, nd). The Maasai community of Minjingu also had a 25,000 ha wildlife concession area on the north-west side of Tarangire National Park set aside for conservation and ecotourism. The Tarangire River Camp with 18 luxury safari tents operated in this concession area (Africa Wilderness, nd). Hunting groups opposed these community joint ventures with ecotourism operators at Tarangire. One ecotourism company in partnership with Maasai was threatened with revocation of its licenses (MERC, 2003b).

Oliver's Camp

Oliver's Camp is a small ecotourism operation on community-owned land leased from two Maasai villages located in the eastern wildlife dispersal area for Tarangire National Park in northern Tanzania. The owners of Oliver's Camp spent a year negotiating with Maasai villagers about tourism. Younger Maasai people wanted to farm or sell the land while women and village elders supported ecotourism and conservation. Boundaries also had to be demarcated for the Maasai villages. The camp owners proposed a wildlife conservation area of 20 km^2 at Emboreet village for the campsite and a larger wilderness activity area of 320 km^2 at Loboir Soit village used for walking safaris and wilderness camping. The operators sought a 99-year lease agreement where Maasai villagers agreed not to graze livestock, farm or burn land, or cut trees for charcoal in the core wildlife conservation area. Villagers retained grazing and water rights in the larger activity area, but harassment or killing of wildlife was discouraged. In return, the camp paid a US$12 wildlife conservation fee (per-tourist per-day), divided between the two villages. The Tanzanian government wildlife department supported this tourism proposal by Oliver's Camp. An initial 6-month agreement was reached while Oliver's Camp funded meetings and trips for a year to discuss the long-term lease with the Maasai village councils. Oliver's Camp was established in 1992. The $12 tourist levy was paid during this stage. A village bank account was opened to receive tourism payments and a 33-year lease agreement was signed with each village. Tourism payments into this village account were made every 2 months. From October 1992 to early 1997, income of US$40,000 from tourist fees was paid directly to the two Maasai villages. This tourism revenue was used to maintain a village water pump, build a borehole and cattle dip, expand a school and buy food during a drought. The

camp owner found that identifying village boundaries and checking village title deeds or land documents was required for this venture. One village signed a lease agreement for the camp and received tourism income knowing the site belonged to another village. Four Maasai people (out of 16 staff) were employed at Oliver's Camp. The camp owners also paid US$20 per person per day to access and use Tarangire National Park (Christ, 1994, 1998; Honey, 1999b; Buckley, 2003b).

Dorobo Tours and Safaris

Dorobo Tours operates walking safaris and mobile camps in the Maasailand region of northern Tanzania. Owned by three brothers, Dorobo Tours supports community management of natural resources, Indigenous cultures and conservation of wilderness to benefit local people (Christ, 1998). The brothers were children of American missionaries and grew up with the Maasai people. They were concerned about increased impacts on Maasai from agriculture, cutting trees and low prices for cattle. The company promoted the value of wildlife tourism for Maasai communities in the Simanjiro plains to the east of Tarangire National Park, as an alternative to economic pressures to expand agriculture. Five-year exclusive lease agreements were signed with three Maasai villages to bring tourists into their wilderness areas. Longer-term leases were seen to alienate villagers from their own land areas. The Maasai villages first obtained legal titles to their land and got the Wildlife Division to excise their areas from hunting concessions. Dorobo Tours paid annual concession fees of US$500 per year to each village and tourist levies of US$10–20 per night, with a total of US$50,000 paid to the three Maasai villages over the 5-year period. Village income from tourism was used to buy a truck, construct an office building and restore a borehole. Small ecotourism operations such as Dorobo Safaris and Oliver's Camp, however, could still have their areas reclaimed as hunting blocks. The owners noted in 1997 there was no official policy, framework or government support for ecotourism in Tanzania, documenting their community involvement to assist other ecotourism partnerships with private operators. Dorobo Tours also established the Dorobo Fund for Tanzania with guest donations used for training villagers on resource management and handling tourism revenue (Christ, 1994, 1998; Honey, 1999b; Buckley, 2003b). According to Nelson (2000) one Maasai village near the Tanzania–Kenya border earned several thousand US$ per year in tourist entrance fees but did not use this to cover annual school fees for 94 children whose parents were too poor to pay the fees. The Maasai leaders of the village expected aid agencies or western donors to pay for their education and social needs.

Manyara Ranch

In April 2001 the African Wildlife Foundation purchased the 17,800 ha Manyara Ranch from the Tanzanian Government, the first acquisition by the new Tanzanian Land Conservation Trust that aimed to acquire key wildlife areas. This working ranch in AWF's 'Maasai Steppe Heartland' formed a key wildlife corridor between Tarangire and Lake Manyara National Parks. The Manyara Ranch was held jointly with local pastoral communities under the Trust. It also provided education and social services for Maasai communities. Funding from the Brown Foundation and other agencies funded the relocation of Manyara Ranch Primary School. Other AWF priorities were establishing a new ranch management structure, improving wildlife conservation and seeking private investment in tourism on the ranch. Potential biodiversity enterprises for the Trust included up-market tourism, cultural tourism and a research centre or field school. These enterprises aimed to provide economic opportunities in village conservation areas and share wildlife income with local communities (AWF, 2003, 2004e). For the Maasai, tourism income was seen as a 'gift or donation' not directly linked to saving wildlife (Nelson, 2000).

Lake Natron

Lake Natron is a 60-km-long pink soda lake in northern Tanzania, extending from Lengai to Mount Shompole on the border with Kenya.

The lake is renowned as a breeding area for 80% of East Africa's lesser flamingos that congregate there in the millions. Other water birds such as the Chestnut-banded Plover were also found in the marshlands and carbonate water of Lake Natron, listed as a Ramsar site for wetlands of international importance. Wildebeest, oryx and lions occur around the lake. The Maasai 'mountain of god', Oldoinyo Lengai, a 2300 m volcano, is 25 km from Lake Natron. Since 2000, tourism has included Lake Natron and climbing Lengai. However, local people at remote rural villages have only recently realized they had legal rights to control access by tourists and tour operators to their lands. At Engare Sero, a Maasai village at the southern end of Lake Natron, tour operators built camps without entering contracts or paying for tourism activities. New partnerships arrangements with the Ujamaa Community Resource Trust and up-market safari operators at Engare Sero will ensure local people derive benefits from ecotourism (Nelson, 2005b).

Serengeti Ecotourism and Cultural Centre

The Serengeti Ecotourism and Cultural Centre, located at the western edge of Serengeti National Park, featured the culture of the Sukuma people, a tribe of 5 million people in north-west Tanzania. The Serengeti Ecotourism Centre provides a campsite, traditional *bandas* (round huts), meals and a craft shop. The Centre employs local people and part of the tourism revenue supports community development projects such as clean water and craft making. It claims to be the only facility in the western corridor of Serengeti where the needs of local people are integrated with conservation efforts. The Serengeti Cultural Centre features a resident traditional healer, royal drums, artefacts, Sukuma dances, and village tours of farm animals, tasting traditional food, and fishing at Lake Victoria. The Centre also provides tours of Kamani Forestry Reserve and the Sukuma Museum (SECUCE, 2004). Special study tours focus on savannah vegetation, small mammals and Sukuma village culture.

In 1959, the Maasai people were moved from the Serengeti into Ngorongoro

Conservation Area. The Serengeti National Park became a wildlife reserve with no livestock grazing or human settlement. Tourism in the Serengeti involves safari tour operators and luxury tented camps owned by outsiders. Over 90,000 tourists a year visit the Serengeti Park. Rapid population growth along with drought and land degradation has seen local communities encroach on the Serengeti protected area for grazing, cultivation, collecting fuel-wood and illegal hunting of wildlife for meat with some 200,000 ungulates taken each year. Pastoral groups in Tanzania have been further dispossessed by government policies on nationalization of pastoralists' land into state farms, while villagization and village titling restricted movement and land use planning for productive uses is converting property rights from communal to private tenure (Mwamfupe, 1998). These have limited local involvement in tourism while land use conflicts have increased pressure on protected areas. At Serengeti, local people received 19% of park fees, which was then spent on schools, health clinics and other facilities. Twenty-three villages around Serengeti Park also had locally administered Wildlife Management Areas (Serengeti Park, 2000). Others see community-based tourism as an alternative livelihood for the Maasai in northern Tanzania (Goodman, 2002, 2003). At Ololosokwan, a Maasai village on the eastern boundary of Serengeti, village control of access and rights to land has delivered tourism income of US$50,000 (Nelson and Makko, 2005).

Klein's Camp, northern Serengeti

Klein's Camp comprises ten safari cottages along the edge of the Kuka Hills, overlooking the main migration route for wildlife in the Serengeti. This wildlife-rich area borders Serengeti to the west and the Masai Mara in Kenya to the north. The camp, operated by Conservation Corporation Africa (CCA), was located in a 10,000 ha concession area leased from Maasai people. This included exclusive use of 3000 acres where the cottages were located and shared use of 22,000 acres of land used by the Maasai to graze their cattle and also for safari game drives and bush walks. A

joint committee of CCA managers and local Maasai managed the tourism concession area, which had fees of US$30 per person per day. The Maasai community received annual income from the CCA lease while the Africa Foundation funded community development projects such as a clinic, crafts market and wild honey (Charnley, 2005). Maasai crafts were sold at the lodge craft shop and tourists visited local Ololosokwan Maasai homesteads or manyattas. The camp also offered 1–3 hour interpretive wilderness walks with Maasai trackers that explained Maasai use of plants for medicine (CCA, 2002).

Ngorongoro Conservation Area

The 8290 km^2 Ngorongoro Conservation Area (NCA) includes the Ngorongoro Crater, an acclaimed wildlife viewing area and World Heritage site. Tourism income at Ngorongoro is US$3.7 million annually (Boyd et al., 1999). According to 1975 game parks legislation, NCA is required to conserve natural resources and also safeguard the interests of Maasai people. The NCA is home to 42,000 Maasai pastoralists living in 16 villages. Some NCA revenue is used to build community facilities for pastoralists such as schools, a health clinic, grain stores, a cattle dip and water systems. In 1995/96, the NCA budget allocated for community development was unused and local Maasai had little input into park management. A 1996 general management plan for NCA was widely opposed by the Maasai (Taylor and Johansson, 1996; Nelson and Hossack, 2003). The Maasai in NCA also lacked title deeds to their houses and did not have secure access to land and resources while tourist hotels on the crater rim had acquired land titles (Lane, 1996). Profits from safari tourism at Ngorongoro Crater mainly go to foreign-owned travel enterprises while local Maasai communities are poverty-stricken and lack representation on the Ngorongoro Conservation Area Authority (NCAA) (Olerokonga, 1992; Carrere, 1995; Kaisoe and Seki, 2001).

In 1974/75, Maasai and other tribal people were removed from Ngorongoro and Olmoti Craters and banned from cultivating crops. In the 1980s, the Maasai were also prevented from collecting tree resin or burning grasses in highland areas. A 1987 raid on Maasai maize plots in NCA led to fines and prison terms but the ban on cultivation was lifted in 1992 due to child malnutrition. With the removal of the Maasai, increased wildlife poaching saw numbers of rhinoceros decline by 80%. Excluded from grazing and wildlife tourism, Maasai people line the roads to sell handicrafts and pose in traditional dress to solicit tourist tips for taking photographs in a 'Maasai theme park with models' (Mowforth and Munt, 2003a; Igoe, 2004). A few educated Maasai people work as tour guides and conservation area staff at Ngorongoro Crater. Twelve per cent of households earned tourism income at NCA, compared to 86% of households at Talek in the Masai Mara, Kenya (Ashley and Elliott, 2003).

There are three Maasai cultural *bomas* for tourists in the NCA and new walking safaris led by Maasai guides with pack donkeys are growing in popularity among visitors. Twenty-five young Maasai men were employed as guides on walking safaris, promoted by NCAA to diversify tourism. The six wards in NCA formed tourism committees to manage walking safari campsites and wanted tourism revenue paid directly to these Maasai wards rather than the park. Norwegian aid money and the National Outdoor Leadership School supported these Maasai walking safaris, which began in 2001. These Maasai tours visited Olmoti and Empakaai Craters, Munge River Waterfall and trekked to the base of Oldoinyo Lengai, a volcanic cone. The Maasai guides prepared Maasai tea, told cultural stories and provided information on hyenas and other wildlife. The guides earned US$25–30 a day plus tips. This income supplemented a rural lifestyle based on cattle and small gardens. However, the NCA was expected to soon ban Maasai farming in Ngorongoro Crater, increasing their reliance on tourism (DeLuca, 2005). Ten per cent of NCA income, US$550,000, is currently given as revenue to the Maasai Pastoral Council which wants half of the NCA income. Lack of secure land titles and limited political control over their village land and activities limited Maasai involvement in ecotourism at Ngorongoro or forming NCA joint ventures with operators like Dorobo Safaris (Honey, 1999b; Charnley, 2005).

In the late 1980s, tribal groups including the Maasai and agriculturalist groups were also evicted from Mkomazi Game Reserve in Tanzania, bordering Tsavo West National Park in Kenya. International NGOs rehabilitated the reserve, patrolling to exclude livestock, and reintroduced African wild dogs and black rhinoceros to the reserve. In contrast, Maasai groups living on group ranches around Tsavo, Amboseli and Masai Mara in Kenya received a share of tourism revenue and income as game scouts that protected wildlife (Fratkin and Wu, 1997). They also developed other ecotourism joint ventures.

In Tanzania, the 75,000 acre Sinya concession area bordered Kenya's Amboseli National Park. It included 10 luxury tents in Kambi ya Tembo or Elephant Camp, with views of Mount Kilimanjaro. Large bull elephants with big tusks and other abundant wildlife were key attractions at Sinya. The camp provided walking safaris led by Maasai guides, and cultural interaction at Maasai *bomas*, local markets, schools or traditional ceremonies. Kibo Safaris (nd) operated the Sinya private concession and supported community projects for the Sinya Maasai such as water pumps, the school and clinic. Sinya village earned over US$20,000 from safari tourism ventures in the area (Nelson, 2005a).

Community Ecotourism *versus* Safari Hunting

Wildlife conservation on parks and reserves in northern Tanzania often excludes the needs of local Indigenous groups and any community benefits from tourism. Other tribal land in Tanzania has been allocated as hunting blocks to private companies, with Indigenous people fined for trespassing, grazing or hunting in these game reserves. Safari hunting generates revenues of US$10 million annually for the Tanzanian government (Lewis and Jackson, 2005). The Loliondo game controlled area in northern Tanzania, next to the Serengeti and Ngorongoro, was sold in 1992 as a 20-year hunting lease with local Maasai people opposing abuses of commercial hunting in this region (Honey, 1999b; Odhiambo, 2000; Botha, 2003). Hunting concessions increased from 47 in 1989 up to 140 in 1997 and cover 20% of Tanzania. Most of the hunting areas are on communal lands next to protected areas, with 85% of communal lands and game-controlled areas allocated for hunting and just 15% used for ecotourism ventures. A 1998 Wildlife Policy, however, allowed local villages to designate Wildlife Management Areas for conservation. The villages owned the land and user rights to wildlife while the government owned wildlife resources (Redford et al., 1995; Goldman, 2001). New contracts between villages and ecotourism operators were challenged by hunting groups, as the policy was not yet in legislation (MERC, 2003b). Hence, there are ongoing conflicts between hunting companies and the walking safaris or wildlife viewing safaris run as community ecotourism ventures by the Maasai, particularly in the Tarangire area (Tourism in Focus, 2002; MERC, 2003b). These conflicts have escalated since 2000, with new regulations by the Tanzanian government prohibiting ecotourism in hunting blocks that largely cover village lands near key wildlife areas. This will prohibit or limit community ecotourism ventures in most areas of rural Tanzania. The central government directly receives income from safari hunting, and also wants to regulate and control safari tourism, including ventures on communal lands (Nelson, 2005a). Apart from some new Maasai ventures, wildlife tourism and safari hunting has been of little benefit to most tribal people in Tanzania (Nelson, 2000; Ole Ndaskoi, 2001). Wildlife conflicts and damage to crops or people, and poaching, reduce the benefits of sharing hunting or tourism income in parks with local people (Johannesen and Skonhoft, 2005). A recent exception is villages in buffer zones around the Selous Game Reserve that gain economic benefits from hunting, tourism lodges and campsites.

Selous Game Reserve

The Selous Game Reserve covers an area of 48,000 km^2 and has 60% of Tanzania's elephant population. The reserve is a World Heritage Area and the largest uninhabited protected area in Africa. In the late 1980s elephant and rhino poaching was widespread in the reserve, with elephant numbers reduced from 110,000 in 1976 to 55,000 in 1986 (Baldus et al., 2003; GTZ, 2004). In 1987, the Tanzania Wildlife Division implemented a Selous Conservation Programme funded by the German government, GTZ – a German NGO, and other donors (German Bank for Reconstruction and Development, African Development Bank, European Union, WWF and the Frankfurt Zoological Society). Bank loans funded access and trunk roads in the northern tourist part of Selous along with construction, training and conservation work. The programme supported community-based conservation and sustainable utilization of wildlife in local villages around the reserve. Fifty-one villages in the Selous buffer zone now manage their own wildlife areas and share in conservation benefits (Ndunguru and Hahn, 1998). The Jukumu Society is a community organization employing local game scouts to patrol the Wildlife Management Area of 21 villages in the northern buffer zone of the Selous Reserve. They also run a tourist campsite. Other villages joined together to lease their land for a tourist lodge. Three hundred village game scouts patrol buffer zones that cover a total of 8600 km^2 around the Selous Game Reserve (Baldus et al., 2003).

With a reduction in wildlife poaching and community involvement in conservation, reserve income from safari hunting (90% of total) and photographic wildlife tourism (10%) significantly increased. In 2001, Selous Game Reserve had 4802 tourists and 482 legal hunters. From 1991 to 2001, revenue from wildlife tours increased 15-fold to US$299,000 while hunting revenue trebled to US$3.6 million. Six tourist camps operate in the northern sector of the reserve and 20 hunting companies utilized 44 hunting blocks in the Reserve sold at a cost of US$7500 each per year. Some hunting blocks are sub-let for higher amounts. Hunting companies need to meet minimum quotas set by the Tanzania Wildlife Division; species hunted were buffalo, antelope, leopard, lion and up to 50 elephants per year. Private companies also provided funds and maintained roads and airstrips. Villages around the Selous Reserve had wildlife hunting quotas set for local consumption or sale, but harvested only 30–80% of their quota. Some villages sold part of their quotas to resident hunters, received voluntary payments from hunting companies, and charged fees for fishing. Under the 1998 Wildlife Policy and community conservation laws, villages receive a major share of revenue from wildlife on their land.

In 1994, a 'retention fund scheme' was established whereby 50% of the income generated at Selous, about US$1.8 million/year, was kept by the reserve for wildlife management and investment. From 1999 to 2002, 11% of the reserve retention fund, US$890,000, was voluntarily used to construct roads and schools in four adjoining districts. The law requires only that 10% of hunting revenues in Selous reserve were paid to local districts. In the northern Selous, a 19-village wildlife society, the District Council and village governments received twice the amount of wildlife revenues to that paid as wages or allowances to individuals. There was limited creation of wildlife enterprise opportunities or linking tourism to local villages (Ashley *et al.*, 2002). Apart from the Jukumu Society, there were limited economic benefits from sustainable use of wildlife on village Wildlife Management Areas. Local village elites also gained most project benefits from the Selous Conservation Program, with mismanagement of village wildlife revenues (Gillingham, 1998; Gillingham and Lee, 1999).

In Tanzania, 16 pilot projects have been started on village Wildlife Management Areas (WMAs). However, private investors are buying land in villages or areas around game reserves and national parks to build tourist lodges and camps before WMAs are declared. Hence, investors need not pay communities or share tourism income, as required in WMAs under the 1998 Wildlife Policy. Regulations for WMAs allow for community investment, leases, joint ventures and other wildlife enterprises. Village Councils can also make by-laws imposing taxes and levies on tour operators or set key conditions for selling village land to private investors but most villagers lack awareness of these rights. The Land Commissioner could prohibit construction of hotels and lodges in villages around protected areas or the Tourism

Minister could put a caveat on development in potential WMAs (Gastorn, 2003). Village land purchases and lodge constructions are often not completed according to Tanzanian legislation.

Tanzania Cultural Tourism Coordination Office

The Tanzania cultural tourism programme was begun in 1995 by a Dutch development agency, SNV. They developed a programme of cultural tours in local villages guided by local residents (SNV, 1999; Earthfoot, 2003). The selected villages were located close to natural attractions, with 70–80% of their economy based on forest products or agriculture. SNV provided local people with training and advice on running tours for foreign visitors. Each trained guide received an identity card from the cultural tourism programme. SNV funded tour guide training, marketing materials and programme management costs. The cultural tours were initiated with tour operators and promoted by the Tanzania Tourist Board. Pilot cultural tours began at the villages of Longido, Ng'iresi and Mto wa Mbu. With their success, a joint five-year programme developing cultural tourism in north-eastern Tanzania began in 1997. The Tanzanian Cultural Tourism Coordination Office handled bookings and itineraries for the village tours (see Table 4.4).

Daily costs of the cultural tours varied from US$10–15 to $20–25 per person per day. In 1996, the cultural tours attracted 600 visitors increasing to 3700 tourists in 1999, with direct income to villagers of US$53,658 from guiding fees, meals and accommodation while the Village Development Fund accrued US$14,215 (WTO, 2002a). In 2001, 7600 visitors provided direct income of US$59,756 and village fund revenue of US$25,609 (Sikar, 2002). Tourism income was used for school facilities, education trust funds, energy-saving stoves, health clinics, a cattle dip, and agricultural projects.

The guided tours involved local agricultural and fishing activities, forest walks, historic areas, visiting homes, local craft enterprises, a traditional healer, camel treks, and other development projects (see Table 4.4). Bird watching, butterflies, monkeys, forest reserves and mountain scenery were also featured. The

Table 4.4. Village tours in Tanzania cultural tourism programme.

Village	Location	Tribal group	Nature-based attractions
Kisangara Chini	Kilimanjaro	Pare	Kindoroko Mountains
	Southern Pare Mtns	Pare	Chome Forest Reserve, Tona Mountains, Shengena peak, Mbaga Hills, waterfalls
	Northern Pare Mtns	Pare	Kindoroko Forest Reserve, Lake Nyumba ya Mungu
Pangani	Pangani Coast	Swahili	Coral, beaches, Pangani River, hippo pools, crocodiles, green turtle, dolphins
Ilkiding'a	Mount Meru	Wa-arusha	Njeche canyon, Leleto hill, Ilkisongo viewpoint
Ng'iresi	Mount Meru	Wa-arusha	Kivesi Hill (old volcano with natural forest)
Babati and Hanang	Arusha	Barbaig	Mount Hanang, Lake Babati, birds
Lushoto and Soni	Usambara Mtns	Shambaa	Kwa mongo Mountain, butterflies, viewpoints, waterfalls, Masumbae forest reserve, birds
Mto wa Mbu	Arusha		Miwaleni Lake, old baobab trees, Bala Hill
Longido	Longido Mountain	Maasai	Birdwatching walks, Mt Longido, walking safaris
	Ruins of Engaruka	Maasai	Birdwatching, Oldoinyo Lengai Mountain
Mkuru	Arusha	Maasai	Camel safaris, birdwatching, Ol Doinyo Landaree
Mulala	Arusha		Marisha River, birds, monkeys, Lemeka Hill
Mamba and Marangu	Kilimanjaro	Chagga	Views of Mt Kilimanjaro, waterfalls, caves
	Mbeya		Ngosi Crater Lake, mountain peaks, natural bridge

Source: Tanzania Cultural Tourism Coordination Office (2003).

programme was designed to be environmentally friendly with villagers establishing tree nurseries and tree plots to reduce their use of forests for fuel wood and timber, using biogas systems for energy and improved cooking stoves to reduce wood use. Tourism income increased local awareness of nature conservation in village areas. Nineteen village communities now participate in this ecotourism project with jobs for more than 100 villagers as tour guides, or selling food and crafts. In 2001, SNV set up the Tanzania Association of Cultural Tourism Organisation (TACTO) to continue with training and programme management (WTO, 2002a). However, with the withdrawal of SNV, this new organization did not develop as planned and there was declining cooperation between the participating villages and their cultural tourism packages offered in rural areas of Tanzania (Kobb and Olomi, 2002; Verburg, 2003; van der Duim *et al.*, 2005).

Uganda: Forest-based Ecotourism with Local Communities

Conservation efforts in Uganda have developed ecotourism based on viewing forest primates and bird watching. Six new national parks were declared by 1993, with mountain gorilla tracking permits issued in Bwindi and Mgahinga in 1993 followed by chimpanzee tracking in Kibale Forest and the Budongo Forest Reserve (US$10–40). Tourism infrastructure such as the airport and tourist hotels in national parks was rebuilt, following the end of the civil war in 1986. By the late 1990s, Uganda received 160,000 tourists, generating US$6.6 million in revenue. This declined after eight tourists were murdered at Bwindi in 1999 but with improved park security is growing again (Ringer, 2002). Other community ecotourism ventures such as campsites and guided walks were developed in Uganda's national parks and forest reserves. Government policies support community tourism, local benefits from conservation and revenue sharing from parks. The Uganda Tourist Board and Uganda Community Tourism Association (UCOTA) promoted these community ecotourism ventures.

In 1993, the Uganda Forest Department devised a new policy that forests were to be managed for tourism, recreation, environmental education and amenity uses, along with timber production. Half of the Uganda forest estate was set aside for conservation and the other half for timber extraction. Non-consumptive forest uses such as ecotourism aimed to provide income for local communities and government. Key objectives for ecotourism development were providing forest recreational activities, increasing public awareness of Uganda's forests and linking nature conservation with tourism benefits for local communities. The policy also supported local people managing forest areas for employment and conservation benefits. Uganda's tropical forests are biologically diverse ecosystems supporting 20,000 plant species, over 1000 bird and butterfly species and rare species such as mountain gorillas. In 2001, there were five ecotourism sites in Uganda's forest reserves: Busingiro and Kaniyo Pabidi in Budongo forest, and one each in Mabira, Mpanga and Ntanda forests. Other community ecotourism centres were located by wetlands or lakes and in Bwindi and Mgahinga National Parks (Aulo, 2001).

Uganda Community Tourism Association (UCOTA)

Formed in 1998, the Uganda Community Tourism Association (UCOTA) represents community-based ecotourism and handicraft enterprises. Members of UCOTA operate tourism enterprises such as campsites, community guides and trackers, rest camps, craft centres, dance groups, food facilities and cultural heritage sites. Communities living near forest reserves, national parks and scenic areas developed these small-scale tourism enterprises in order to capitalize on growth in tourism to Uganda during the 1990s. Government policies also promoted community ecotourism to benefit rural groups and conservation (Ringer, 2002). Half of Uganda's 20 million people live in rural areas, subsisting on farming, gathering forest products and hunting, with annual income at half the national average of US$300 (Williams, 2001). UCOTA arose out of an USAID-funded training workshop in 1995 for 27 community-based tourism entrepreneurs around national parks that focused on visitor services, management skills and using local resources and rural products (Victurine, 2000). UCOTA helps rural

communities to plan, manage and develop tourism activities, with technical support, training workshops, handicraft sales, marketing, and a reservations service. The rural tourism enterprises are linked with community development projects and marketed by UCOTA (Williams *et al.*, 2001; Sebunya, 2002; UCOTA, 2003). Two American zoos (North Carolina, Cleveland) and the European Union provided initial funding to UCOTA for an adviser's salary, office rent, trade shows, vehicle expenses, training workshops and marketing. UCOTA also completed a chimpanzee ecotourism evaluation project and workshops for Heritage Trails Uganda, while sales of handicrafts now cover office operation costs. UCOTA works in partnership with the Uganda Wildlife Authority and communities near protected areas. Ecotourism projects supported by UCOTA include Buhoma community restcamp (Bwindi NP), Mgahinga campground (Mgahinga NP), Bigodi Wetland Sanctuary and Lake Bunyonyi (see Table 4.5).

During the 1990s, community ecotourism ventures such as campsites and guided walks were developed in Uganda's national parks and forest reserves. The Uganda Wildlife Authority and Uganda Forest Department supported these community ecotourism enterprises. At Mabira and Mpanga forest reserves, local communities provide guided bird walks and visitor accommodation.

Wetlands comprise 25% of Uganda's habitats and are a key attraction for bird watchers. At Bigodi Wetland Sanctuary and at Lake Nkuruba Nature Sanctuary, next to Kibale Forest, community-guided walks view birds and five primate species in forest areas. Local boatmen now punt tourists across the Mabamba Swamp to see the prized shoebill with a clog-shaped bill, the largest living bird, and other bird species. Fishermen that killed the shoebill as a bad luck omen now see it is a source of tourism revenue. Bird watching tours with knowledgeable local guides are growing in Uganda (Briggs, 2003). The Kibale Association for Rural and Environmental Development provides guided walks around Bigodi Wetland Sanctuary. From 1999 to 2001, the wetland had an average of 1000 visitors annually generating income of US$3000. Forty per cent

Table 4.5. Community ecotourism projects in Uganda.

Buhoma Community Restcamp, Bwindi Impenetrable Forest National Park
Attractions: mountain gorillas, birds (350 species), butterflies;
Facilities: 4 huts for 20 guests, campground, picnic shelter, restaurant and bar, village guided tours, handicrafts;
Community Development: schools, health clinic equipment, maize-grinding mill, women's club building.

Mgahinga Community Campground, Mgahinga Gorilla National Park
Attractions: mountain gorillas, mountain climbing;
Facilities: huts for 12 guests, campground facilities, shelter, medicinal garden, overland campground;
Community Development: primary schools, stretcher service.

Bigodi Wetland Sanctuary, next to Kibale Forest National Park
Attractions: wetland walk, birds, primates (chimpanzees, colobus, mangabey);
Facilities: boardwalk, pathway, trained guides, tree house, reception building, kiosk;
Community Development: Bigodi secondary school library.

Lake Bunyoni
Attractions: bird watching, yellow-spotted otter, lake scenery, swimming, canoeing;
Facilities: tents for 20 guests, campground facilities, restaurant, canteen, island trail, community tours;
Community Development: maize mill, orphan's care, agroforestry.

Busingiro and Kaniyo Pabidi ecotourism sites, Budongo Forest Reserve
Attractions: chimpanzee tracking, monkeys, birds, mahogany forest, forest trails;
Facilities: huts for 9 guests, campground facilities, picnic hut, visitor centres, guided forest walks, handicrafts;
Community Development: schools, health clinics, water supply, environmental education programme.

Mabira and Mpanga Forest Reserves
Attractions: birds, forest;
Facilities: campground, guided bird walks.

Ruboni Community Campground, near Ruwenzori National Park
Attractions: Ruwenzori Mountains, forest walks, guided cultural walks;
Facilities: camping, food, dance performances;
Community Development: adult education, medical care.

Lake Nkuruba Nature Reserve
Attractions: crater lake, forest, colobus monkeys, birds;
Facilities: campground, huts, meals, mountain bike hire, guided walks;
Community Development: education programmes, school library and classrooms.

Sources: Ajarova (2001); Aulo (2001); Williams (2001); Langoya and Aulo (2002); Briggs (2003); UCOTA (2003).

of this income was spent on community projects (WTO, 2003a).

Uganda Wildlife Authority

In 1994, the Uganda National Parks Service (now Uganda Wildlife Authority) reintroduced a policy of revenue sharing with local communities. A pilot project at Bwindi and Mgahinga national parks saw 20% of income from mountain gorilla tracking fees go to local communities. All Uganda parks then set aside 12% of total income for revenue sharing with adjacent communities; this amount increased in 1996 to 20% but with park income from gate fees only (US$10–20/day). At Bwindi and Mgahinga this reduced the pool of park funds derived mainly from gorilla tracking permits rather than entry fees (Adams and Infield, 2003; Buckley, 2003c). During 1993 to 1998, Mgahinga, Bwindi and Kibale national parks distributed US$83,000 of tourism revenue to local communities, used to build 21 schools, four health clinics, a bridge and road. The Uganda parks revenue sharing policy with nearby communities was resumed in 2001 (Archabald and Naughton-Treves, 2001). Gorilla trekking fees provide 90% of the annual budget for Uganda Wildlife Authority (Ringer, 2002). In contrast, at Lake Mburo National Park, the park service in 2001 signed contracts with the Rurambira Wildlife Utilisation Association, set up by local landowners and a private Ugandan operator, to allow trophy hunting of animals such as impala with a fixed quota and fees paid to landowners. Illegal hunters poached wild animals in Lake Mburo which received 10,000 visitors. Trophy fees could generate US$90,000 with an additional US$80,000 from sport hunting packages (Averbeck, 2003).

Community Involvement in Mountain Gorilla Tourism

Mountain gorillas are the main tourist attraction at Mgahinga Gorilla National Park and Bwindi Impenetrable Forest National Park in south-west Uganda (Weber, 1993; Litchfield, 2001). The Ugandan population of 300 mountain gorillas includes 50 troupes or family groups in 325 km^2 of Bwindi and three gorilla troupes in 34 km^2 of Mgahinga (Buckley, 2003c). The 330 km^2 Bwindi Forest, with half of the remaining mountain gorillas, was declared a World Heritage site in 1994 (Lepp, 2002). In 1999, Bwindi had 2100 tourists while Mgahinga received 1718. Both parks were declared in 1991, with 1300 illegal peasant farmers removed from Mgahinga in 1992, compensated by USAID and resettled elsewhere. These parks were the ancestral lands of Indigenous Batwa hunter gatherer peoples (Zaninka, 2001). Locals could still collect water, gather plants and place beehives in the forest (Ham, 1995; Wild and Mutebi, 1996; Archabald and Naughton-Treves, 2001). After community negotiations, 20% of Bwindi was allocated for multiple use, and 40% to research and tourism, with the remainder a gorilla core zone (Dunn, 1995). Gorilla tracking tours began in both parks in 1993, with park service guides and trackers leading tourists through the forest to spend a maximum time of 1 hour with the gorillas. Bwindi has three habituated troupes while Mgahinga has one gorilla troupe habituated to human contact. Mgahinga has ten gorilla permits a day, with seven permits sold in advance to commercial operators. The daily gorilla tracking permit fee was US$280 at Bwindi and US$175 at Mgahinga. This covered the cost of trackers, park guides, visitor facilities, permit administration, and park patrols. Since 1992, over 20,000 tourists trekked to see Bwindi mountain gorillas (Lepp, 2002).

Since 1994, 12.5% of Bwindi gorilla permit revenues and 20% of Mgahinga entrance fees were shared with local communities, compensating for crop damage caused by gorillas (Echtner, 1999; Litchfield, 2001). This included three communities up to 3 km from the Mgahinga park boundary and 19 of 21 communities up to 7 km from the Bwindi boundary (Adams and Infield, 2001, 2003; Archabald and Naughton-Treves, 2001). From 1995 to 1997, communities around Bwindi received 8% of the US$280 gorilla-tracking fee but, from 1998, this changed to 20% of the US$25 park entrance fee (Vieta, 2002). By 2000, Bwindi Impenetrable National Park (BINP) tourism revenue of US$52,000 was spent on 20 community projects such as schools, roads and clinics (Borzello, 2001; Lepp, 2002). However, local residents at Mgahinga claim they mainly derived income from selling food to the campsite restaurant (Buckley, 2003c). Twenty per cent of gorilla-tracking permits were given to adjacent local farmers who gained income from leading tours (Fennell, 2003). In 1990, the International Gorilla Conservation Program provided funding of US$4 million for gorilla conservation (Mowforth and Munt, 2003b). The World Bank GEF provided another US$4.3 million in 2001 for the Mgahinga Bwindi Impenetrable Forest Conservation Fund Trust (Kabananukye, 1998; Hamilton et al., 2000; Borzello, 2001; Nelson and Hossack, 2003). The Trust supported community projects, the training of park staff and park management in multiple-use zones and research. However, local Batwa people felt the Trust excluded them from using local resources and gaining benefits from the park (Zaninka, 2001).

Communities around Bwindi and Mgahinga also operate tourist campgrounds with locals employed as camp staff, and income from tourist meals, food and craft sales, guiding services and cultural entertainment. Campground staff received training in food preparation to improve tourist meals and in managing cash flow by reinvesting in improved visitor facilities (Victurine, 2000). At Mgahinga, the Amagyembere Iwacu community camp was rehabilitated in 2004. Around Bwindi, habituated mountain gorillas often slept and fed on farms at Ntungamo village. In 2001, the villagers constructed a tourist campground and hostel at Ntungamo to gain income from tourism, modelled on the successful Buhoma rest camp (Lepp, 2002). Since 2001, the FAO supported local communities around Bwindi with small-scale enterprises such as handicrafts, honey, oyster mushrooms and tour guiding. The Buhoma Village Walk visited cultural sites and a traditional medicinal healer. This village tour had 148 tourists in 2003/04 (FAO, 2004).

Buhoma community restcamp, Bwindi Impenetrable Forest

The Buhoma restcamp is located at Bwindi Impenetrable National Park (BINP). In 1992, community leaders from ten villages in the adjoining Mukona Parish formed the Buhoma Community Campground Development Association (BCCDA) to promote community development, provide tourism employment, to establish tourist accommodation and train local people in campground and financial management plus visitor and food services (Ajarova, 2001). The new association worked with American volunteers at BINP and was awarded US$9000 from the US Peace Corps' Small Project Assistance Grant to build two accommodation bandas (round huts), toilets and showers. The community-run Buhoma campground opened in December 1993 for visitors to BINP. The BCCDA association has over 5000 local members represented by the Community Campground Council of 16 village members, plus a BINP ranger and BINP community conservation warden and two US Peace Corps volunteers. The Council assisted campground staff and reviewed community project proposals.

The BCCDA and Buhoma restcamp has

been supported by key partner organizations such as park staff of BINP and the Institute for Tropical Forest Conservation (ITFC) that rented land to the association for USh50,000 per year. The International Gorilla Conservation Program (IGCP) provided funding and training workshops for campground staff (e.g. visitor handling, record keeping, catering) and rebuilt a picnic hut destroyed by a terrorist attack on visitors at Bwindi in 1999. The Uganda Community Tourism Association (UCOTA) provided training and ongoing technical assistance to BCCDA while also marketing the Buhoma restcamp. North Carolina Zoological Park donated a 10,000 litre water tank to BCCDA, along with school blackboards. From 1993 to 1995, site infrastructure included four bandas for 20 guests, staff quarters, tea sheds and a picnic shelter. In 1996, a kitchen and a reception area with a bar, shop and dining area were added for visitors. Tourists waiting for gorilla permits also joined guided community walks to experience local cultural activities such as beer brewing and basket making. Other areas for income from community tourism were traditional music and dance, crafts, storytelling, bird watching and village waterfalls (Ajarova, 2001). Women in the Buhoma Rural Tourist Enterprise sold food, mats and pottery items, generating US$4444 in 1994 and US$33,333 in 2000 with income used to build local schools (Sebunya, 2002).

From 1993 to 2000, the Buhoma restcamp generated tourism income of US$96,488. BCCDA used US$6572 of this revenue to fund seven community projects in Mukono Parish including the construction of classrooms, staff rooms, a store and kitchen at four local schools, equipment and furniture for two health clinics and a new maize-grinding mill. Direct community benefits of tourism include eight full-time staff employed at the Buhoma campground, a centre for cultural entertainment groups, selling local handicrafts, a local market for farm produce and funding community projects. These improvements to tourism facilities and services were a larger kitchen area, repairs to shelters, a reliable water supply for showers, heating water and improved rubbish disposal. New two-person bandas and a water supply system for the park and campground were needed (Ajarova, 2001). Key issues were training BCCDA staff in financial planning and disbursing revenue for projects. Other investors bought land at Buhoma and compete with the community rest camp (Lepp, 2002).

The Ruwenzori Mountains ecotourism project

The Ruwenzori Mountains National Park is located in a high altitude region of west Uganda. The Bakonzo people are the Indigenous group living around the mountains. Local communities started an ecotourism project in this area, funded from arts and crafts and cultural performances. The ecotourism business, Ruwenzori Mountaineering Services, guided visitors on the mountains. This employed local porters and guides while local food and crafts were sold to visitors. The area received 200–400 visitors a year. Free tree seedlings were provided to local people for reforestation of this area (WTO, 2003b). However, the Ruwenzori Mountains Service had a 30-year tourist concession for guiding, was dominated by one local family, with poor service and sporadic payments to guides. While 8% of park receipts from tourism were also given to community projects, the local collection of specified forest resources was more important than sharing income from tourism (Hamilton, 2000). In 2005, the German government provided a grant of USh48 million to rehabilitate tourist facilities, construct toilets and train more local guides for the Ruwenzori Mountaineering Services. Two hundred and fifty foreign tourists climbed the Ruwenzori Mountains from January to April 2005 (Nzinjah, 2005).

Busingiro ecotourism site, Budongo Forest Reserve

The Busingiro ecotourism site is a zone dedicated to conservation and tourism in Budongo Forest Reserve in north-west Uganda. The 825 km^2 Budongo forest is the largest mahogany forest in East Africa. It has high biodiversity with 600 to 800 chimpanzees, the largest wild population in Uganda, along with black and white colobus, blue and red-tailed monkeys, and rare bird species. Tourists pay a forest entry fee, take guided nature walks or participate in chimpanzee-tracking tours with a maximum of six people per group. Since 1992, six groups of chimpanzees were habituated to human contact (EA-Ecoconsult, 2002c). The Uganda Forest Department developed the Busingiro ecotourism project in collaboration with five local communities in the Masindi District. The European Union provided project funding of US$2 million for vehicles, supporting staff, forest infrastructure (trails, picnic facilities, camp sites, visitor centres and huts) and local environmental education programmes. Some 200 km of forest trails were built in the forest while local craftsmen built campsite facilities and visitor *bandas* (round huts) from grass. The campsites opened in 1995. A second ecotourism site was also developed at Kaniyo Pabidi in the north-east part of the forest reserve also with a resident chimpanzee population. Profits from chimpanzee tours and camping fees supported 17 local communities (Litchfield, 2001).

Threatened by logging proposals and illegal pit sawing in 1991, half of the Budongo forest reserve was dedicated to conservation and half to timber production. Ecotourism development at Budongo forest began in 1993 preceded by community consultations, interviews with tour operators and a survey of tourist needs. Local communities provided input to an ecotourism advisory committee with elected tourism advisers informing forest staff on visitor facilities and illegal activities. Local people worked as guides, caretakers, trail cutters and cooks, and helped protect the forest area, while private investors include lodge-owners. Twenty-eight local people (20 men and eight women) ran the Busingiro project. Local women also sold handicrafts and food at the ecotourism site. Forty per cent of entry and camping fees went to the Community Development Fund and 60% covered wages and maintenance. Initially 40% of all tourism revenue went to the community. However, this was revised with fees from forest entry, camping and chalet use put in the Community Fund, of which 60% was used for project maintenance and 40% for other community projects. All the tour guiding revenue went towards guide wages, equipment and trail maintenance (Godde, 1998). The Busingiro project made a profit in the peak visitor months of July–September and December–February. By 2000, the project was to be managed as a tourism concession by local people (Langoya and Long, 1997). The Uganda Tourist Board and tour operators marketed the Busingiro site and chimpanzee tracking tours. Visitor numbers slowly increased from 354 in 1994, generating revenue of US$1000, to 967 in 2000 earning US$6300. Tourism revenue is used for primary schools, health centres, water supplies and other activities such as bee keeping and vegetable growing (Aulo, 2001; Langoya and Aulo, 2002; Buckley, 2003c). Since 1990, the Budongo Forest Project (2003) also supported research on chimpanzees and forest use by local people.

Ethiopia

Bishangari Nature Reserve and Lodge

The Bishangari Nature Reserve is located on the east shore of Lake Langano, 235 km from the capital city of Addis Abada. The forest and wetlands with 300 birds and many mammal species is a 'biodiversity site of national significance'. The local name of 'bishangari' means sweet water. An ecolodge with nine bungalows, a restaurant, tree bar and souvenir shop was developed at the nature reserve by an Ethiopian family-owned business. The lodge, which opened in November 2001, used solar power and conserved the adjacent forest area by planting trees and using alternative sources of fuel such as biogas. Bishangari was Ethiopia's first ecolodge. It was first proposed by FARM Africa, a British NGO, but Ethiopian laws supported development by local business ventures. The lodge development cost US$270,588 with 70% funded from commercial bank loans. Clean water and a health clinic were provided for local people with a Bishangari community fund supporting other projects such as tree planting. Workshops on forest and wildlife management were also held. Twelve local people were hired during

construction (seven labourers, five guards) with 35 local staff employed to run Bishangari Lodge. Local handicrafts were also sold at the lodge (WTO, 2002b; Bishangari Lodge, 2004).

In 2002, there were only two community-based tourism projects in Ethiopia initiated by NGOs such as SNV (Holland), SOS Sahel and GTZ (Germany). These NGOs were setting up an Ethiopian Forum for Community Tourism to improve rural livelihoods and preserve natural areas. Other small community enterprises around sites of tourism interest also required assistance (Mark Chapman, Greentour Email list, July 2002). A local NGO, Tourism in Ethiopia for Sustainable Future Alternatives (TESFA), was established in 2003 and funded by Save the Children UK. From 2004–2007, TESFA community tourism projects aim to assist rural villages of Amhara people by developing trekking routes around Lalibela. A tourism camp and cottages (*tukuls*) for trekkers were built at the mountain communities of Mequat Mariam and Wajela. The daily tourism fee of US$35 paid for accommodation, meals, a guide and porters, assisting a village development fund used for a grinding mill (TESFA, nd). While the Ethiopian government promoted sustainable development and poverty alleviation through tourism there was little offered support for ecotourism ventures (Sukkar, 2002).

Conservation and Community Benefits of Ecotourism, East Africa

Community-based ecotourism projects in East Africa are mainly based on conserving wildlife and forest areas (see Table 4.6). Wildlife-based ecotourism ventures have been developed on Maasai group ranches in Kenya and Tanzania since key wildlife dispersal areas are located on Maasai land around the heavily visited parks and reserves of southern Kenya and northern Tanzania. Land titles granted since the 1970s enabled Maasai and other groups to negotiate joint ventures with private tourism operators, with tribal lands leased for tented camps, ecolodges and game viewing activities. Lease conditions for wildlife conservation areas and ecotourism facilities on group ranches limit Maasai settlement, grazing, hunting wildlife

Table 4.6. Conservation and community benefits of Indigenous ecotourism in East Africa.

Wildlife-based Ecotourism

Maasai group ranches, Kenya and Tanzania

Wildlife Conservation Areas on group ranches – Lease agreements for ecolodges, *bandas* and tented
  camps;

No hunting, no Maasai homesteads or cattle enclosures, limited grazing, no extractive uses;

Annual lease fees, entrance fees, bed night levies, game viewing fees, employment as service staff and
  guides;

Revenue Sharing (KWS, TANAPA), Local Game Scouts for Wildlife Patrols, Wildlife Monitoring.

Mwaluganje Elephant Sanctuary, Kenya

Local land ceded for sanctuary, elephant corridor, traveller's lodge, game scouts and guides, annual
  dividends.

Mountain gorilla tourism, Uganda

Revenue sharing (UWA), compensation for crop damage, employment as trackers and guides;

Community campsites (Bwindi and Mgahinga), meals, handicrafts, village tours, dance performances.

Selous Game Reserve, Tanzania

Revenue sharing (10% hunting fees), building roads and schools, assist village *Wildlife Management
  Areas:* 300 game scouts, Jukumu Society campsite, hunting concessions, lease for tourist lodge.

Forest-based Ecotourism

Busongoro Forest Reserve, Uganda: 2 ecotourism sites, camping facilities, guided tours, and
  chimpanzees;

Amani Nature Reserve, Tanzania: Collection of dead wood only, guided tours, walking trails,
  guesthouses;

Jozani Forest, Zanzibar: Replanted mahogany forest, red colobus monkey, boardwalk, walking trails,
  tours;

Kaya Kinobo Forest, Kenya: Sacred kaya forest, medicinal plant use, guided tours, handicraft sales;

Loita Hills, Kenya: Loita Naimina Enkiyio Conservation Trust, Maasai-owned sacred forest, trekking
  tours.

Other Ecotourism Ventures

Misali Island, Tanzania: reef conservation zone, fishing restrictions, Islamic ethics in nature conservation;

Ngomongo Villages, Kenya: Reforestation of quarry site, tree planting, wetlands, birds, cultural activities;

Wasini Boardwalk, Kenya: Conservation of coral gardens and mangrove forest, entry fee and handicraft
  shop;

Serengeti Ecotourism Centre, Tanzania: campsite, *bandas*, meals, craft shop, clean water and craft
  making;

Cultural Tourism Program, Tanzania: guided tours, accommodation, meals, forest walks, handicrafts,
  treks.

KWS, Kenya Wildlife Service; TANAPA, Tanzania National Parks; UWA, Uganda Wildlife Authority.

and other extractive activities. However, Maasai gain wildlife-related income from tourism lease fees, bed night levies, entry fees, employment as service staff and guides, handicraft sales and other activities. This provides an economic value for wildlife on Maasai lands. Some tourism operators also financially compensated Maasai for not killing lions but some neighbouring group ranches still retaliated by killing predators that ate livestock (Walpole and Thouless, 2005). Only one group ranch near the Masai Mara reserve in Kenya, Koiyaki, has been set aside entirely for wildlife conservation and ecotourism. On other group ranches, Maasai continue cattle grazing and increasingly also the cultivation of agricultural crops. This increases local human conflicts with wildlife and restricts the movements of migrating animals. In southern Kenya, local farmers ceded their land to set up the Mwaluganje Elephant Sanctuary in an elephant migration corridor. In Uganda, community campsites at Bwindi and Mgahinga parks provide local benefits from mountain gorilla tourism. Revenue sharing by park agencies with local communities and income from wildlife-based ecotourism on group land was spent on schools, health clinics and water supplies. Apart from the employment of game scouts at group ranches or village areas there was little Indigenous investment of tourism income in wildlife conservation work.

Indigenous people developed ecotourism projects to gain economic benefits from wildlife and forests on tribal lands. These ecotourism projects were community-owned or developed as joint ventures with private operators. Ecotourism ventures also provided an alternative income to grazing, agriculture and using forest resources. A cash income from ecotourism was needed to fund schools, education, health clinics and water supplies for growing populations. However, there were often conflicts over the division and use of ecotourism income for community facilities and individual needs. Ecotourism agreements reinforced land use based on nature conservation and wildlife conservation in designated areas of tribal lands and group ranches. According to Nelson (2000), some Maasai village leaders still expected aid agencies or western donors to pay for education and social services, rather than taking responsibility for their own community development and using tourism revenue for this purpose. Tourism income used for community projects was seen as another 'gift or donation' and not linked to conserving wildlife. Kenyan community outreach programmes also found village expectations and perspectives of ecotourism were affected by accountability, business responsibility and donor support as a 'right' (ESOK, 2004b). All of these Indigenous ecotourism ventures were developed with funding and support from conservation NGOs, development agencies, international donors from the US and Europe, forest departments and government wildlife departments in Kenya, Tanzania and Uganda.

Revenue sharing by government parks and wildlife agencies since the early 1990s delivered some economic and social benefits for local communities living around protected areas in East Africa. Tourist entrance fees to parks and hunting concessions (Tanzania) funded infrastructure in local communities. These fees equated to a rent for land use that partly compensated local people for not using natural resources in protected areas. Park agencies also supported community conserva-

tion and ecotourism projects on their lands. While park revenue-sharing schemes delivered financial and social benefits, local people had little input into how parks or tourism projects operated. Exceptions were the joint venture tourism enterprises or land leasing arrangements negotiated on Maasai group ranches. Despite the increase in tourism benefits for Indigenous groups in East Africa, these 'development and ecotourism projects rarely lead to real empowerment of local people' (Honey, 1999: 257).

Forest-based ecotourism has been developed in the Eastern Arc Mountains of Tanzania, Jozani forest on Zanzibar; in forest reserves and national parks in Uganda; and in the Loita Hills and Kaya Kinobo forest of southern Kenya. These ecotourism ventures aim to prevent further human encroachment into forest areas and to provide an alternative source of income for local communities. Local people could still collect forest products but no hunting or cultivation is allowed in these forest reserves. In these small-scale ecotourism ventures, community members worked as forest guides and operated visitor facilities such as boardwalks, walking trails and campsites. In Uganda, the Forest Department and Wildlife Authority supported community-based ecotourism ventures in forest areas and wetlands. In Kenya and Tanzania, community ecotourism in forests was mainly supported by conservation NGOs.

The Loita Maasai asserted their ownership of the Loita Hills in Keyna and guided trekking tours in this forest. Income from forest ecotourism ventures supported local employment and some community facilities. In forest areas managed by Indigenous groups, there are no lease agreements with private operators.

Conclusion

In East Africa, Indigenous ecotourism ventures are mainly located on tribal lands around national parks and game reserves. Up-market ecolodges and tented camps are located on Maasai-owned group ranches around the Masai Mara, Amboseli, Tsavo West and Laikipia in Kenya, and near Tarangire or

Serengeti in Tanzania. These ecotourism facilities are owned and managed by Maasai people or they involve joint ventures with safari operators and hotels. The latter involve exclusive lease agreements that limit Maasai grazing activities in wildlife conservation areas set aside on group ranches. Secure land titles and new wildlife laws in Kenya and Tanzania allow Indigenous people to charge tourism operators and financially benefit from wildlife on their lands. However, there was some conflict between ecotourism and trophy hunting of wildlife in Tanzania. Indigenous groups provide other ecotourism services such as campsite facilities, boardwalks and guided tours in forest reserves of Uganda, the Eastern Arc Mountains of Tanzania, in Zanzibar and south-east Kenya. The Cultural Tourism Program in Tanzania also involves Indigenous

guided tours of forest areas. Limited collection of forest resources is still allowed by Indigenous peoples in many areas of East Africa. Other community ecotourism ventures include the Mwaluganje Elephant Sanctuary and Wasini mangrove boardwalk in southern Kenya where local members received annual dividends. The development of Indigenous ecotourism ventures in East Africa since the mid-1990s has relied on support from government forest and wildlife departments and funding from international conservation agencies, along with capacity building, training and marketing support by local conservation NGOs and other development agencies. Programme support over a minimum 5-year period was needed to negotiate tourism leases and establish new Indigenous ecotourism ventures on tribal lands in East Africa.

References

Abdullah, A., Hamad, A.S., Ali, A.M. and Wild, R.G. (2000) Misali Island, Tanzania: An open access resource redefined. Digital Library of the Commons. http://dlc.indiana.edu/documents/dir0/00/00/01/93/ (accessed 17 November 2005)

ACC (African Conservation Corporation) (2002) Shompole group ranch. The Shompole ecotourism project. http://www.conservationafrica.org/Reports.htm (accessed 17 November 2005)

ACC (African Conservation Corporation) (2004) An ecological evaluation of Il Ngwesi community conservation project. http://www.conservationafrica.org/ecotourism_biodiversity.htm (accessed 17 November 2005)

Adams, W. and Infield, M. (2001) Park outreach and gorilla conservation: A study of Mgahinga Gorilla National Park, Uganda. In: Hulme, D. and Murphree, M. (eds) African Wildlife and Livelihoods: The Promise and Performance of Community Conservation. Heinemann, London.

Adams, W. and Infield, M. (2003) Who is on the gorilla's payroll? Claims on tourist revenue from a Ugandan National Park. World Development 31, 177–190.

Africa Wilderness (nd) Tarangire River Camp. http://www.africawilderness.com/river/central_river.html (accessed 17 November 2005)

Ajarova, L. (2001) Involvement of local communities in ecotourism: Buttoma community-Bwindi Impenetrable National Park. Seminar on Planning, Development and Management of Ecotourism in Africa, Mozambique, 5–6 March 2001. http://www.world-tourism/sustainable/IYE/Regional_Activities/ Mozambique/ (accessed 17 November 2005)

Akama, J.S. (1999) Marginalization of the Maasai in Kenya. Annals of Tourism Research 26, 716–718.

Akama, J. (2002) The creation of the Maasai image and tourism development in Kenya. In: Akama, J. and Sterry, P. (eds) Cultural Tourism in Africa: Strategies for the New Millennium. Proceedings of the ATLAS Africa International Conference, December 2000, Mombassa. ATLAS, Arnhem, pp. 43–54.

APTDC (African Propoor Tourism Development Centre) (2004a) About us. http://www.propoortourism-kenya.org/about_us.htm (accessed 17 November 2005)

APTDC (African Propoor Tourism Development Centre) (2004b) Propoor Tourism Success Stories. http://www.propoortourism-kenya.org/successstories.htm (accessed 17 November 2005)

Archabald, K. (2000) Can revenue-sharing save wildlife? A case study of Jozani Chakwa Bay Conservation Area, Zanzibar, Tanzania. MSc thesis, University of Wisconsin.

Archabald, K. and Naughton-Treves, L. (2001) Tourism revenue-sharing around national parks in Western Uganda: Early efforts to identify and reward local communities. Environmental Conservation 28, 135–149.

Ashley, C. and Elliott, J. (2003) 'Just wildlife?' or a source of local development? Natural Resource Perspectives, 85. http://www.odi.org.uk/nrp/ (accessed 17 November 2005)

Ashley, C., Mdoe, N. and Reynolds, L. (2002) *Rethinking Wildlife for Livelihoods and Diversification in Rural Tanzania: A Case Study from Northern Selous.* LADDER Working Paper No. 15. University of Norwich, East Anglia. http://www.odg.uea.ac.uk/ladder/doc/wp15.pdf (accessed 17 November 2005)

Aulo, M.G.M. (2001) Development of ecotourism and other natural areas of Uganda: The case of the Budongo Forest Reserve. Seminar on Planning, Development and Management of Ecotourism in Africa, Mozambique. http://www.world-tourism/sustainable/IYE/Regional_Activities/Mozambique/ (accessed 17 November 2005)

Averbeck, C. (2003) A park is not an island: Linking different wildlife management strategies in the area of Lake Mburo National Park, Uganda. In: Bissonette, J.A. and Storch, I. (eds) *Landscape Ecology and Resource Management: Linking Theory with Practice.* Island Press, Washington DC, pp. 283–298.

AWF (African Wildlife Foundation) (2003) Manyara Ranch: A corridor and more. http://www.awf.org/news/12656 (accessed 17 November 2005)

AWF (African Wildlife Foundation) (2004a) Heartland community lodges. Kilimanjaro Heartland. http://www.awf.org/safari/ecokili.php (accessed 17 November 2005)

AWF (African Wildlife Foundation) (2004b) Heartland community lodges. Samburu Heartland. http://www.awf.org/safari/ecosamburu.php (accessed 17 November 2005)

AWF (African Wildlife Foundation) (2004c) Suggested eco-travel facilities – Heartland community lodges. http://awf.org/safari/ecotravel.php (accessed 17 November 2005)

AWF (African Wildlife Foundation) (2004d) Koija Starbeds. http://www.awf.org/success/starbeds.php (accessed 17 November 2005)

AWF (African Wildlife Foundation) (2004e) Manyara Ranch. http://www.awf.org/success/manyara.php (accessed 17 November 2005)

Baldus, R., Kibonde, B. and Siege, L. (2003) Seeking conservation partnerships in the Selous Game Reserve, Tanzania. *Parks: Conservation Partnerships in Africa* 13, 50–61.

Barbier, E.B. (1992) Community-based development in Africa. In: Swanson, T.M. and Barbier, E.B. (eds) *Economics for the Wilds: Wildlife, Wildlands, Diversity and Development.* Earthscan, London, pp. 103–135.

Barrow, E., Gichoi, H. and Infield, M. (1998) *Summary and Key Lessons from a Comparative Review and Analysis of Community Conservation in East Africa.* IUCN, East Africa Regional Office. http://www.iucn.org/places/earo/pubs/forest/KEYLESSO.PDF (accessed 17 November 2005)

Berger, D. (1993) *Wildlife Extension Participatory Community Based Tourism Development: Why, What and How?* Ministry of Environment and Tourism, Windhoek.

Berger, D.J. (1996) The challenge of integrating Maasai tradition with tourism. In: Price, M.F. (ed.) *People and Tourism in Fragile Environments.* John Wiley, Chichester, pp. 175–198.

Berger, D. and Ntiati, P. (2000) Milking the wild herd: Maasailand. In: Weinberg, P. (ed.) *Once We Were Hunters: A Journey with Africa's Indigenous People.* Mets & Schilt, Amsterdam & David Philip, Cape Town, pp. 75–102.

Bergin, P. (1998) The Community Conservation Service Centre: An institutional innovation in promoting and supporting community based wildlife management in East Africa. The World Bank/WBI's CBNRM Initiative. http://srdis.ciesin.columbia.edu/cases/tanzania-012.html (accessed 25 May 2006)

Bishangari Lodge (2004) Bishangari Lodge [Ethiopia]. http://www.bishangari.com/acco.htm (accessed 17 November 2005)

Borrini-Feyerabend, G. and Sandwith, T. (2003) From 'guns and fences' to paternalism to partnerships: The slow disentangling of Africa's protected areas. *Parks: Conservation Partnerships in Africa* 13, 1–5.

Borzello, A. (2001) Ecotourism successes: Gorillas in the mist. http://www.peopleandplanet.net/doc.php?id=1108 (accessed 17 November 2005)

Botha, K. and Kasana, E.O. (2003) Building bridges in the bush. *Cultural Survival Quarterly* 27. http://209.200.101.189/publications/csq/csq-article.cfm?id=1726 (accessed 17 November 2005)

Botha, T. (2003) Killing the killing fields of Loliondo. MERC. http://www.maasaierc.org/killingthekilling.html (accessed 17 November 2005)

Boyd, C., Blench, R., Bourn, D., Drake, L. and Stevenson, P. (1999) Reconciling interests among wildlife, livestock and people in Eastern Africa: A sustainable livelihoods approach. *Natural Resources Perspectives* 45, June. Overseas Development Institute (UK). http://www.odi.org.uk/nrp/45.html (accessed 17 November 2005)

Boynton, G. (1997) The search for authenticity: On destroying the village in order to save it. *The Nation,* 6 October, 18–20.

Briggs, P. (2003) Secret safaris [Uganda]. *Africa Geographic* 11, 58–68.

Buckley, R. (2003a) Eselenkei Conservation Area, Kenya. In: *Case Studies in Ecotourism.* CABI, Wallingford, UK, p. 33.

Buckley, R. (2003b) Oliver's Camp, Tanzania; Dorobo Tours and Safaris, Tanzania; Amani Nature Reserve, Tanzania. In: *Case Studies in Ecotourism*. CABI, Wallingford, UK, pp. 22–23, 27, 42–43.

Buckley, R. (2003c) Bwindi and Mahinga, Uganda; Busingiro, Uganda. In: *Case Studies in Ecotourism*. CABI, Wallingford, UK, pp. 38–42.

Budongo Forest Project (2003) Introduction to the Budongo Forest Project. http://www.budongo.org/index_introduction.html (accessed 17 November 2005)

Butchart, D. (2003) Islands in a savanna sea – the Eastern Arc Mountains. Wildwatch. http://www.wildwatch.com/resources/other/easternarc.asp (accessed 17 November 2005)

Buysrogge, W. (2001) Sustainable Safaris? Participation of the Maasai in Tourism Development on Kimana Group Ranch, Adjacent Amboseli National Park. MSc thesis, Wageningen University, Wageningen.

Carey, S. (2002) Proud warriors or useless blankets? Star gazing with El-Murrani in northern Kenya. http://www.responsibletravel.com/Copy/Copy101086.htm (accessed 17 November 2005)

Carlisle, H. (1993) Warriors, wildlife and wilderness: Walking adventures in Kenya. *Simply Living* 7, 92–93.

Carrere, R. (1994) Kenyan indigenous people battle to save sacred forest. *Third World Resurgence* 51, 2–3.

Charnley, S. (2005) From nature tourism to ecotourism: The case of the Ngorongoro Conservation Area, Tanzania. *Human Organization* 64, 75–88.

Christ, C. (1994) Taking ecotourism to the next level. In: Lindberg, K., Epler Wood, M. and Engeldrum, D. (eds) *Ecotourism: A Guide for Planners and Managers*. Ecotourism Society, North Bennington, Vermont, pp. 183–195.

Christ, C. (1998) Taking ecotourism to the next level: A look at private sector involvement with local people. In: Lindberg, K., Epler Wood, M. and Engeldrum, D. (eds) *Ecotourism: A Guide for Planners and Managers*. Vol. 2. Ecotourism Society, North Bennington, Vermont, pp. 183–195.

Coast, E. (2002) Maasai socioeconomic conditions: A cross-border comparison. *Human Ecology* 30, 79–106.

Cocheba, D.J. and Ndriangu, J. (1998) The Golini-Mwaluganje Community Elephant Sanctuary: A community conservation poised for success but plagued by an elephant management dilemma. Digital Library of the Commons. http://dlc.indiana.edu/archive/00000037/ (accessed 17 November 2005)

Coffman, J.E. (2004) Buying (into) and selling conservation among Maasai in southern Kenya. In: Moseley, W.G. and Logan, B.I. (eds) *African Environment and Development: Rhetoric, Programs, Realities*. Ashgate, Aldershot, UK, pp. 161–188.

Conservation Corporation Africa (CCA) (2002) Klein's Camp Northern Serengeti Tanzania. http://www.ccafrica.com/ (accessed 17 November 2005)

Conservation Corporation Africa (CCA) (2003) Kwicha Tembo Masai Mara Kenya. http://www.ccafrica.com/ (accessed 17 November 2005)

CORE-net (2001) Conservation profile of the greater Amboseli ecosystem. *CORE-net* 3, 1–3. http://www.eawildlife.org/swara/index.htm (accessed 17 November 2005)

CORE-net (2002a) The USAID director visits Lion Rock Tsavo Camp in LUMO. *CORE-net* 5, 6. http://www.eawildlife.org/swara/index.htm (accessed 17 November 2005)

CORE-net (2002b) Mwaluganje Elephant Sanctuary: From cornfields to wildlife sanctuary. *CORE-net* 5, 1. http://www.eawildlife.org/swara/index.htm (accessed 17 November 2005)

CORE-net (2002c) Wasini Island women's group. *CORE-net* 5, 3. http://www.eawildlife.org/swara/index.htm (accessed 17 November 2005)

Coupe, S., Lewis, V., Ogutu, Z. and Watson, C. (2002) *Living With Wildlife: Sustainable Livelihoods for Park-Adjacent Communities in Kenya*. ITDG Working Papers. Intermediate Technology Development Group.

Cultural Survival (1999) Ecotourism in the Masai Mara: An interview with Meitamei Ole Dapash. *Cultural Survival Quarterly* 23. http://209.200.101.189/publications/csq/csq-article.cfm?id=1111&highlight=ecotourism (accessed 17 November 2005)

Dapash, M.O. and Kutay, K. (2005) The Maasai people, Indigenous stewards living among parks, ranches, and tourism. *EcoCurrents* (TIES) First quarter 2005, 3–4, 6.

Deeper Africa (2005) Ethical tourism. http://www.deeperafrica.com/ethical-tourism.html (accessed 17 November 2005)

DeLuca, L. (2005) Maasai walking safaris in Tanzania take travelers off the beaten path. *EcoCurrents* (TIES) First quarter 2005, 7.

Douglis, C. (2001) Cultural bomas: Business and show biz. *African Wildlife News* 36, 3. http://www.awf.org/documents/SPRING01.pdf (accessed 17 November 2005)

Dunn, A. (1995) *Summaries of Some Recent Project Approaches to Conservation and Development*. Rural Development Forestry Network, ODI. http://www.odifpeg.org.uk/publications/rdfn/18/d-i.html (accessed 17 November 2005)

EA-Ecoconsult (2002a) Ecolodges and travel sites in East Africa. http://www.ecotourism.8m.net/about.html (accessed 17 November 2005)

EA-Ecoconsult (2002b) Porini ecotourism camp-Amboseli, Sarara ecotourism lodge. http://www.ecotourism.8m.net/whats_new.html (accessed 17 November 2005)

EA-Ecoconsult (2002c) Busingiro ecotourism site. http://www.ecotourism.8m.net/catalong.html (accessed 17 November 2005)

Earthfoot (2003) The Tanzanian Cultural Tourism Coordination Office. http://www.earthfoot.org/guides/tcto.htm (accessed 17 November 2005)

East Africa Safari (nd) Boundary Hill Lodge. http://www.eastafricansafari.info/bound.htm (accessed 17 November 2005); East Africa Safari (nd) Tarangire Conservation Area. http://www.eastafricansafari.info/tarang.htm (accessed 17 November 2005)

Eastern Arc (2002) Eastern Arc Mountains Information Source. http://www.easternarc.org/ (accessed 17 November 2005)

Echtner, C.M. (1999) Tourism in sensitive environments: Three African success stories [Uganda]. In: Singh, T.V. and Singh, S. (eds) *Tourism Development in Critical Environments*. Cognizant Communication Corporation, New York, pp. 149–162.

Eco and Culture Tours (nd) Day tours on Zanzibar. Eco & Culture Tours Zanzibar. http://www.ecoculture-zanzibar.org/HTML/e_daytours.htm (accessed 17 November 2005)

EcoCurrents (2005) The Maasai: More resources, more responsible ecotourism. *EcoCurrents* (TIES) 1st quarter 2005, 9.

Eco-Resorts (2002) About eco-resorts. http://www.eco-resorts.com/AboutUs.php (accessed 17 November 2005)

Eliah, E. (2000) Pleasing the tourists and saving the fish. June 2000. WWF International Newsroom. http://www.panda.org/news/features/story.cfm?id=1975 (accessed 17 November 2005)

Enchanted Landscapes (2004) Kaya Kinondo. http://www.enchanted-landscpes.com/ecotourism/kaya.htm (accessed 17 November 2005)

Environmental Business Finance Program (2004) Campi Ya Kanzi, Kenya. In: *Ecolodges: Exploring Opportunities for Sustainable Business*. EBFP Ecolodge publication. International Finance Corporation. http://ifcln1.ifc.org/ifcext/enviro.nsf/Content/EBFP_Ecolodge (accessed 17 November 2005)

ESOK (Ecotourism Society of Kenya) (2004a) Welcome to ESOK. http://www.esok.org/ (accessed 17 November 2005)

ESOK (Ecotourism Society of Kenya) (2004b) Communities and ecotourism. http://www.esok.org/ (accessed 17 November 2005)

ESOK (Ecotourism Society of Kenya) (2004c) Visitors can now choose. http://www.esok.org/ (accessed 17 November 2005)

FAO (2004) Alternative livelihoods developed to protect World Heritage Site in Uganda. 3 December 2004. FAO Newsroom. http://www.fao.org/newsroom/en/field/2004/51674/index.html (accessed 17 November 2005)

Fennell, D.A. (2003) Gorilla tourism in Africa. In: *Ecotourism: An Introduction*. 2nd edn. Routledge, London, pp. 161–163.

Forest Peoples Project (2003) Indigenous peoples and protected areas in Africa: From principles to practice. Conference held in Kigali, Rwanda, 4–7 September 2001. http://www.forestpeoples.gn.apc.org/ (accessed 17 November 2005)

Francis, J. (2002) Walking with the Maasai. http://www.responsibletravel.com/Copy/Copy100782.htm (accessed 17 November 2005)

Fratkin, E. and Wu, T.S.M. (1997) Maasai and Barabaig herders struggle for land rights in Kenya and Tanzania. *Cultural Survival Quarterly* Fall, 55–61.

Friends of the Earth (nd) Where should the IFC money go – Ecotourism example in Tanzania. Dubious development. http://www.foe.og/camps/intl/worldbank/ifcreport/section5.htm (accessed 17 November 2005)

Gaceru, G. (2003) A day at shrine of tranquility amid the murmuring trees. *Coast Express*, 4 July 2003. http://www.nationaudio.com/News/CoastExpress/04072003/Relax/Relax070720031.htm (accessed 17 November 2005)

Garcia, R. (2005) Pemba: Dual jewel of the Indian Ocean. *African Geographic* 13, 32–43.

Gastorn, K.G. (2003) *The Legal Environment for Tourist Investments on Village Land Outside Wildlife Management Areas*. Tanzania Wildlife Discussion Paper No. 36. GTZ. http://www.wildlife-programme.gtz.de/wildlife/publications.html (accessed 17 November 2005)

Gillingham, S. (1998) *Conservation Attitudes of Villagers Living Next to the Selous Game Reserve.* Tanzania Wildlife Discussion Paper No. 23. GTZ. http://www.wildlife-programme.gtz.de/wildlife/publications.html (accessed 17 November 2005)

Gillingham, S. and Lee, P.C. (1999) The impact of wildlife-related benefits on the conservation attitudes of local people around the Selous Game Reserve, Tanzania. *Environmental Conservation* 26, 218–228.

Githitho, A. (1998) Institutional challenges in conservation: The case of the sacred kaya forests of the Kenya coast. The World Bank/WBI's CBNRM Initiative. http://srdis.ciesin.org/cases/kenya-006.html (accessed 17 November 2005)

Githitho, A.N. (2002) The sacred Mijikenda kaya forests of coastal Kenya and biodiversity conservation. In: *The Importance of Sacred Natural Sites for Biodiversity Conservation.* UNESCO Man and Biosphere. http://www.sacredland.org/PDFs/Mijikenda_Kaya.pdf (accessed 17 November 2005)

Godde, P. (ed.) (1998) Budongo forest ecotourism project. In: *Community-based Mountain Tourism: Practices for Linking Conservation with Enterprise.* Synthesis of an Electronic Conference, 13 April–18 May 1998. Mountain Forum and The Mountain Institute. http://www.mountainforum.org/rs/pub/ec.cfm (accessed 17 November 2005)

Goldman, M. (2001) *Partitioned Nature, Privileged Knowledge: Community Based Conservation in the Maasai Ecosystem, Tanzania.* Environmental Governance in Africa Working Papers: WP No. 3. World Resources Institute, Washington DC. http://pdf.wri.org/eaa_wp3.pdf (accessed 17 November 2005)

Goodman, R. (2002) Pastoral livelihoods in Tanzania: Can the Maasai benefit from conservation? *Current Issues in Tourism* 5, 280–286.

Goodman, R. (2003) Pastoral livelihoods in Tanzania: Can the Maasai benefit from conservation? In: Luck, M. and Kirstges, T. (eds) *Global Ecotourism Policies and Case Studies.* Channel View Publications, London, pp. 108–114.

Goodwin, H. (2001) Contribution of ecotourism to sustainable development in Africa. Seminar on Planning, Development and Management of Ecotourism in Africa. Mozambique, 5–6 March 2001. http://www.world-tourism.org/sustainable/IYE/Regional_Activites/Mozambique/ (accessed 17 November 2005)

Grieves-Cook, J. (2002) Eselenkei Conservation Area. In: WTO (comp.) *Sustainable Development of Ecotourism: A Compilation of Good Practices.* WTO, Madrid, pp. 163–165.

GTZ (German Technical Assistance) (2004) Selous Conservation Programme. GTZ Wildlife Programme in Tanzania. http://www.wildlife-programme.gtz.de/wildlife/scp.html (accessed 17 November 2005)

Gutkin, S. (2004) Keeping it clear: Where the zebras and wildebeest roam. AP. Environmental News Network. http://www.enn.com/news/2004–03–23/s_14255.asp (accessed 17 November 2005)

Hackel, J.D. (1999) Community conservation and the future of Africa's wildlife. *Conservation Biology* 13, 726–734.

Ham, M. (1995) Cashing in on the silver-backed gorilla. In: *Features: Ecotourism Special.* Panos Institute, London.

Hamilton, A. (2000) The Rwenzori Mountains National Park, Uganda. *African Journal of Ecology* 38, 376–378.

Hamilton, A., Cunningham, A., Byarugaba, D. and Kayanja, F. (2000) Conservation in a region of political instability: Bwindi Impenetrable Forest, Uganda. *Conservation Biology* 14, 1722–1725.

Harman, D. (2001) Kenya's tourism industry grows 'greener'. *The Christian Science Monitor* 19 September. http://www.csmonitor.com/2001/0919/p7s2-woaf.html (accessed 17 November 2005)

Hatfield, R. (2003a) Ecotourism as a development tool [Il Ngwesi Group Ranch]. In: Watkin, J. (ed.) *The Evolution of Ecotourism in East Africa: From an Idea to an Industry.* IIED Series No. 15. IIED, London, p. 6.

Hatfield, R. (2003b) On Shompole. In: Watkin, J. (ed.) *The Evolution of Ecotourism in East Africa: From an Idea to an Industry.* IIED Series No. 15. IIED, London, p. 7.

Honey, M. (1998) Ecotourism in the shadow of Mt Kilimanjaro: Lessons from Kenya and Tanzania. *Contours* 9, 8–13.

Honey, M. (1999a) Kenya, The *mzee* of ecotourism in Africa: Early experiments, foreign aid, and private reserves. In: *Ecotourism and Sustainable Development: Who Owns Paradise?* Island Press, Washington DC, pp. 293–338.

Honey, M. (1999b) Tanzania: Whose Eden is it? In: *Ecotourism and Sustainable Development: Who Owns Paradise?* Island Press, Washington DC, pp. 220–262.

Houtzager, D. (2000) Shades of green: East Usambara Mountains. *The Swahili Coast.* http://www.swahilicoast.com/shades_of_green_east_usambara_mountain.htm (accessed 17 November 2005)

Igoe, J. (2002) The challenge to community conservation: A case study from Simanjiro, Tanzania. In: Chatty, D. and Colchester, M. (eds) *Conservation and Mobile Indigenous Peoples : Displacement, Forced Settlement and Sustainable Development.* Berghahn Books, Oxford.

Igoe, J.J. (2004) *Conservation and Globalization: A Study of National Parks and Indigenous Communities from East Africa to South Dakota.* Thomson/Wadsworth, Belmont, California.

Irandu, E.M. (2004) The role of tourism in the conservation of cultural heritage in Kenya. *Asia Pacific Journal of Tourism Research* 9, 133–150.

Johannesen, A.B. and Skonhoft, A. (2005) Tourism, poaching and wildlife conservation: What can integrated conservation and development projects accomplish? *Resource and Energy Economics* 27, 208–226.

Johansson, Y. and Diamantis, D. (2004) Ecotourism in Thailand and Kenya: A private sector perspective. In: Diamantis, D. (ed.) *Ecotourism: Management and Assessment.* Thomson Learning, London, pp. 298–312.

Johnson, I. (2004) Hand in hand [Il Ngwesi, Namunyak & Tassia, Kenya]. *Africa Geographic* 12, 69–73.

Johnstone, R. (2000) Talking ecotourism. *Swara* (East Africa Wildlife Society Journal) 22, 5–9.

Kabananukye, K. (1998) Community involvement in protecting forests in Uganda. The World Bank/WBI's CBNRM Initiative. http://srdis.ciesin.org/cases/uganda-008.html (accessed 17 November 2005)

Kaisoe, M. and Seki, W.O. (2001) The conflict between conventional conservation strategies and indigenous conservation strategies: The case study of Ngorongoro Conservation Area, Tanzania. Forest Peoples Project. http://www.forestpeoples.org/documents/africa/fpproj_tanzania_summ_eng.shtml (accessed 29 November 2005)

Kamuaro, O. (2002) Ecotourism: Suicide or Development? *Voices from Africa* 6, Sustainable Development Part 2. http://www.unsystem.org/ngls/documents/publications.en/voices.africa/index.htm (accessed 17 November 2005)

Kareithi, S. (2003) *Coping with Declining Tourism, Examples from Communities in Kenya.* PPT Working Paper No. 13. Pro Poor Tourism. http://www.propoortourism.org.uk/13_Kenya.pdf (accessed 17 November 2005)

Kasulwa, S. (2000) The long march to success in Udzungwa. Feature Story. December 2000. WWF Tanzania. http://www.panda.org/news/features/story.cfm?id=2160 (accessed 17 November 2005)

Khalid, F.M. (2003) The application of Islamic environmental ethics to promote marine conservation in Zanzibar: A case study. IFEES. http://www.ifees.org/jour_art_pract.htm (accessed 17 November 2005)

Khatib, A.H. (2000) Ecotourism in Zanzibar, Tanzania. In: Dieke, P.U.C. (ed.) *The Political Economy of Tourism Development in Africa.* Cognizant Communication Corporation, New York, pp. 167–180.

Kibo Safaris (nd) The foothills of Kilimanjaro (The Sinya experience). http://www.kibo-safaris.com/camping_foothills.htm (accessed 17 November 2005)

Kileo, C. (2004) Tanzania's ecotourism program. http://www.africa-ata.org/entan21.htm (accessed 17 November 2005)

Kipuri, N. (nd) Indigenous peoples in Kenya – an overview. http://www.whoseland.com/paper6.html (accessed 17 November 2005)

Knickerbrocker, T.J. and Waithaka, J. (2005) People and elephants in the Shimba Hills, Kenya. In: Woodroffe, R., Thirgood, S. and Rabinowitz, A. (eds) *People and Wildlife: Conflict or Coexistence?* Cambridge University Press, Cambridge, pp. 224–238.

Kobb, D. and Olomi, D. (2001) *Institutionalising Cultural Tourism Activities: A Second Try.* SNV Netherlands Development Organisation, Arusha.

Kuriyan, R. (2002) Linking local perceptions of elephants and conservation: Samburu pastoralists in northern Kenya. *Society and Natural Resources* 15, 949–957.

Kutay, K. (2003) Masai land cultural safari: Beyond the looking glass. Wildland Adventures. http://www.wildland.com/trips/africa/100001/ken_tripreviews.aspx (accessed 17 November 2005)

Lamprey, R.H. and Reid, R.S. (2004) Expansion of human settlement in Kenya's Maasai Mara: What future for pastoralism and wildlife? *Journal of Biogeography* 31, 997–1032.

Lane, C. (1996) The views of Indigenous inhabitants. In: *Ngorongoro Voices: Indigenous Residents of the Ngorongoro Conservation Area in Tanzania Give Their Views on the Proposed General Management Plan.* Working Paper 29. Forests, Trees and People Program FAO, Uppsala, Sweden.

Langoya, C.D. and Aulo, G.M. (2002) Busingiro ecotourism site. In: WTO (comp.) *Sustainable Development of Ecotourism: A Compilation of Good Practices.* WTO, Madrid, pp. 255–258.

Langoya, C.D. and Long, C. (1997) *Local Communities and Ecotourism Development in Budongo Forest Reserve, Uganda.* Rural Development Forestry Network, Overseas Development Institute, London. http://www.odifpeg.org.uk/publications/rdfn/22/e-i.html (accessed 17 November 2005)

Lepp, A. (2002) Uganda's Bwindi Impenetrable National Park: Meeting the challenges of conservation and community development through sustainable tourism. In: Harris, R., Griffin, T. and Williams, P. (eds) *Sustainable Tourism: A Global Perspective.* Butterworth Heinemann, London, pp. 211–220.

Let's Go Travel (2004) Olarro Lodge. Let's Go Travel. http://www.let's-go-travel.net/?q=node/view/1833 (accessed 17 November 2005)

Levine, A. (2004) Local responses to marine conservation in Zanzibar, Tanzania. *Journal of International Wildlife Law and Policy* 7, 183–202.

Lewis, D. and Jackson, J. (2005) Safari hunting and conservation on communal land in southern Africa. In: Woodroffe, R., Thirgood, S. and Rabinowitz, A. (eds) *People and Wildlife: Conflict or Coexistence?* Cambridge University Press, Cambridge, pp. 239–251.

Lindkvist, L. (2002a) Tourism and conservation in protected and/or fragile ecosystems – A sustainable business opportunity? World Ecotourism Summit, Ecotourism Policy & Planning. Quebec Canada 19–22 May 2002. http://www.world-tourism.org/sustainable/IYE/quebec/cd/statmnts/pdfs/likene.PDF (accessed 17 November 2005)

Lindkvist, L. (2002b) Conservation and community based ecotourism – Basecamp Masai Mara. http://biodiversityeconomics.org/pdf/020405–32.PDF (accessed 17 November 2005)

Litchfield, C. (2001) Responsible tourism with great apes in Uganda. In: McCool, S.F. and Moisey, R.N. (eds) *Tourism, Recreation and Sustainability: Linking Culture and the Environment.* CABI, Wallingford, UK, pp. 105–132.

Loisaba Wilderness (2004) Loisaba-Maasai community. http://www.loisaba.com/maasai-community.htm (accessed 17 November 2005)

Loita Maasai (2004) Ecotourism. http://www.loita-maasai.com/getitem.php?cat=program&subcat= Ecotourism (accessed 17 November 2005)

Luca Safari (2002) The destiny of the Maasai. Campi ya Kanzi. http://www.maasai.com/maasai.htm (accessed 17 November 2005)

LWC (Lewa Wildlife Conservancy) (2004) Il Ngwesi Group Ranch. http://www.lewa.org/ilngwesi.php (accessed 17 November 2005)

LWF (Laikipia Wildlife Forum Ltd) (2004a) Laikipia tourism – towards a sustainable future. http://www.laikipia.org/safari_laikipia.htm (accessed 17 November 2005)

LWF (Laikipia Wildlife Forum Ltd) (2004b) Tassia Lodge. http://www.laikipia.org/hotel_tassia.htm (accessed 17 November 2005)

LWF (Laikipia Wildlife Forum Ltd) (2004c) Koija Starbeds. http://www.laikipia.org/koija-starbeds.htm (accessed 17 November 2005)

Maasai Environmental Resource Coalition (MERC) (2003a) MERC. http://www.maasaierc.org/ (accessed 17 November 2005)

Maasai Environmental Resource Coalition (MERC) (2003b) Consumptive tourism: General impacts and experiences of Maasai and other local communities. http://www.maasaierc.org/loliondo/consumptive. html (accessed 17 November 2005)

Maasai Trails (2004) About us. http://www.maasaitrails.com/aboutus.htm (accessed 17 November 2005)

Madoweka, S.A. (2002) Implementation of ecotourism projects in Uluguru mountain, Tanzania. Mountain Conservation Society of Tanzania. Conserve Africa International Post to Greentour Mailing List.

MAO (Maasai American organization (nd) The Siana Group Ranch. Maasai American Organization. http://www.maasaiamerican.org/siana location.html (accessed 17 November 2005)

Martyn, R. (2004) Wildlife or our life? *Developments: The International Development Magazine* 27. http://www.developments.org.uk/data/issue27/masai.htm (accessed 17 November 2005)

Maundu, P., Berger, D.J., Ole Saitabau, C., Nasieku, J.M., Kipelian, M., Mathenge, S.G., Morimoto, Y. and Hoft, R. (2001) *Ethnobotany of the Loita Maasai: Towards Community Management of the Forest of the Lost Child – Experiences from the Loita Ethnobotany Project.* People and Plants Working Paper 8. UNESCO, Paris. http://peopleandplants.org/wp/wp8.html http://bibpurl.oclc.org/web/4940 (accessed 17 November 2005)

Mbaria, J. (2003) 'Respectful' tourists among the Maasai. *The East African,* 6 October 2003. http://www.nationaudio.com/News/EastAfrican/06102003/Features/PA2-1.html (accessed 17 November 2005)

Melamari, L. (2001) Experience of Tanzania national parks on planning, development and management of ecotourism. Seminar on Planning, Development and Management of Ecotourism in Africa. Mozambique, 5–6 March 2001. http://www.world-tourism.org/sustainable/IYE/Regional_Activites/Mozambique/ (accessed 17 November 2005)

Miaron, J. (2003) The future of Amboseli: Implications of group ranches sub-division on pastoralism and conservation. *CORE-net* 6, 4–5. http://www.eawildlife.org/swara/index.htm (accessed 17 November 2005)

Monbiot, G. (1994) *No Man's Land.* Macmillan, London.

Monbiot, G. (1995) 'No man's land ....' *In Focus* (Tourism Concern) 15, 10.

Mowforth, M. and Munt, I. (2003a) The Maasai in Kenya and Tanzania. In: *Tourism and Sustainability: Development and New Tourism in the Third World.* Routledge, London, pp. 237–240.

Mowforth, M. and Munt, I. (2003b) Mountain gorilla conservation in Uganda, Rwanda and Zaire. In: *Tourism and Sustainability: Development and New Tourism in the Third World.* Routledge, London, pp. 240–242.

Mwamfupe, D. (1998) Demographic impacts on protected areas in Tanzania and options for action. *Parks* 8, 3–14.

Mwangi, G. (2002) Island's preservation based on Islam. AP. Deseret News. http://www.deseretnews.com/dn/view/0,1249,400007254,00.html (accessed 17 November 2005)

Myers, G.A. (2002) Local communities and the new environmental planning: A case study from Zanzibar. *Area* 34, 149–159.

Namara, A. (2003) Buhoma Rest Camp, Bwindi Impenetrable Forest, Uganda. In: Watkin, J. (ed.) *The Evolution of Ecotourism in East Africa: From an Idea to an Industry.* IIED Series No. 15. IIED, London, p. 8.

Ndunguru, I.F. and Hahn, R. (1998) Reconciling human interests with conservation in the Selous Game Reserve (Tanzania). International Workshop on CBNRM, Washington DC, 10–14 May 1998. http://srdis.ciesin.org/cases/Tanzania-Paper.html (accessed 17 November 2005)

Nelson, F. (2000) Sustainable development and wildlife conservation in Tanzanian Maasailand. *Environment, Development and Sustainability* 2, 107–117.

Nelson, F. (2004) *The Evolution and Impacts of Community-based Ecotourism in Northern Tanzania.* Drylands Issues Paper (E131). IIED, London.

Nelson, F. (2005a) Opportunities and challenges to ecotourism in Tanzania. *EcoCurrents* (TIES) First quarter 2005, 3, 5, 8.

Nelson, F. (2005b) In the valley of the mountain of god. *Swara* January–March, 56–58.

Nelson, F. and Makko, S.O. (2005) Communities, conservation and conflicts in the Tanzanian Serengeti. In: Lyman, M.W. and Child, B. (eds) *Natural Resources as Community Assets: Lessons from Two Continents.* Sand County Foundation, 121–146. http://sandcounty.net/assets/ (accessed 17 November 2005)

Nelson, J. and Hossack, L. (eds) (2003) *Indigenous Peoples and Protected Areas in Africa: From Principles to Practice.* Forest Peoples Programme. http://www.forestpeoples.org/publications/p_to_pafrica_eng.shtml (accessed 29 November 2005)

Ngomongo Villages (nd) From wasteland to eco-cultural tourist paradise: Reclamation of Ngomongo Villages quarry site. http://www.ngomongo.com/lang/eng/learnmore.htm (accessed 17 November 2005)

Norton-Griffiths, M. (1995) Economic incentives to develop the rangelands of the Serengeti: Implications for wildlife conservation. In: Sinclair, A.R.E. and Arcese, P. (eds) *Serengeti II: Dynamics, Management and Conservation of an Ecosystem.* University of Chicago Press, Chicago, pp. 588–604.

Norton-Griffiths, M. (1998) The economics of wildlife conservation policy in Kenya. In: Milner-Gulland, E.J. and Mace, R. (eds) *Conservation of Biological Resources.* Blackwell Science, Oxford.

Nzinjah, J. (2005) Sh48m to promote Rwenzori tourism. *New Vision* (Kampala), 17 May 2005. All Africa. http://allafrica.com/stories/200505171550.html (accessed 17 November 2005)

Ochieng, Z. (2004) From a barren quarry to a flourishing ecosystem. *News from Africa.* January 2004. http://www.newsfromafrica.org/newsfromafrica/articles/art_282004 (accessed 17 November 2005)

Oddie, C. (1994) *Enkop Ai: My Life with the Maasai.* Simon & Schuster Australia, East Roseville, NSW.

Odhiambo, N. (2000) Tanzania: Insensitive tourism abuses ethnic groups. *Tourism Concern* 10, 45–46.

Ogutu, Z.A. (2002) The impact of ecotourism on livelihood and natural resource management in Eselenkei, Amboseli ecosystem, Kenya. *Land Degradation and Development* 13, 251–256.

Okech, R. (nd) Sustainable ecotourism and local communities: Cooperation, compromise or conflict? Ecotourism Society of Kenya. http://www.esok.org/ (accessed 17 November 2005)

Okello, M.M. (2005a) An assessment of the large mammal component of the proposed wildlife sanctuary site in Maasai Kuku group ranch near Amboseli, Kenya. *South African Journal of Wildlife Research* 35, 63–76.

Okello, M.M. (2005b) Land use changes and human-wildlife-conflicts in the Amboseli area, Kenya. *Human Dimensions of Wildlife* 10, 19–28.

Okello, M.M. (2005c) A survey of tourist expectations and economic potential for a proposed wildlife sanctuary in a Maasai group ranch near Amboseli, Kenya. *Journal of Sustainable Tourism* 13, 566–589.

Okello, M.M. and Kiringe, J.W. (2004) Threats to biodiversity and the implications in protected and adjacent dispersal areas of Kenya. *Journal of Sustainable Tourism* 12, 55–68.

Okello, M., Seno, S.O. and Wishitemi, B. (2003a) Maasai community wildlife sanctuaries in Tsavo-Amboseli ecosystem, Kenya. *Parks (IUCN Journal): Conservation Partnerships in Africa* 13, 62–75.

Okello, M., Seno, S.O. and Wishitemi, B. (2003b) Principles for the establishment of community wildlife sanctuaries for ecotourism: Lessons from Maasai group ranches, Kenya. In: *Community Tourism: Options for the Future.* ATLAS International Africa Conference, Arusha, Tanzania.

Okungu, S.C. (2001) Kenya's strategy/programmes for the development and management of ecotourism in national parks and protected areas. Seminar on Planning, Development and Management of Ecotourism in Africa, Mozambique. http://www.world-tourism/sustainable/IYE/Regional_Activities/Mozambique/ (accessed 17 November 2005)

Ole Ndaskoi, N. (2001) Maasai wildlife conservation and human need: The myth of 'community based wildlife Management'. http://www.ogiek.org/faq/article-ndasoki-mas.htm (accessed 17 November 2005)

Olerokonga, T. (1992) What about the Maasai? *In Focus (Tourism Concern)* 4, 6–7.

Ongaro, S. and Ritsma, N. (2002) The commodification and commercialization of the Maasai culture: Will cultural manyattas withstand the 21st century? In: Akama, J. and Sterry, P. (eds) *Cultural Tourism in Africa: Strategies for the New Millennium.* Proceedings of the ATLAS Africa International Conference, December 200, Mombassa. ATLAS, Arnhem, pp. 127–136.

Porini (nd) Mara Intrepids, Mara Explorer. http://www.porini.com/gamewatchers/mara-intrepids.html (accessed 17 November 2005)

Porini (2004) Siana Springs Intrepids. http://www.porini.com/gamewatchers/siana-intrepids.html (accessed 17 November 2005)

Rahman, S. (2002) Kenya explorer. http://www.responsibletravel.com/Copy/Copy100846.htm (accessed 17 November 2005)

Redford, K.H., Godshalk, R. and Asher, K. (1995) Wildlife management for ecotourism in Tanzania. In: *What about Wild Animals? Wild Animals Species in Community Forestry in the Tropics.* FAO, Rome.

Reid, D.G. (2003) Cast study: Kenya. In: *Tourism, Globlization and Development: Responsible Tourism Planning.* Pluto Press, London, pp. 196–209.

Reid, D.G. and Sindiga, I. (1999) Tourism and community development: An African example. *World Leisure and Recreation* 41, 18–21.

Reid, D.G., Sindiga, I., Evans, N. and Ongaro, S. (1999) Tourism, biodiversity and community development in Kenya. In: Reid, D.G. (ed.) *Ecotourism Development in Eastern and Southern Africa.* Weaver Press, Harare, pp. 59–82.

Responsible Travel (2004) Kenya's community based tourism. http://www.responsibletravel.com/Copy/Copy100849.htm (accessed 17 November 2005)

Ringer, G. (2002) Gorilla tourism. *Alternatives Journal* 28, 17–21.

Russell, A.R. (2002) Shompole. Art of Ventures. http://www.shompole.com/eco.htm (accessed 16 August 2004)

Rutten, M. (2002a) Linking western tour operators with community-based protected areas in Kenya: Globalising paradise for whom? Digital Library of the Commons. http://dlc.indiana.edu/documents/dir0/00/00/09/14/index.html (accessed 17 November 2005)

Rutten, M. (2002b) *Parks Beyond Parks: Genuine Community-based Wildlife Ecotourism or Just Another Loss of Land for Maasai.* Drylands Issues Paper (E11). IIED, London.

Sacred Land (2004) The Kaya forests. http://www.sacredland.org/world_sites_pages/Kaya_Forests.html (accessed 17 November 2005)

Salehe, J. (2004) Ecotourism boosts the Kaya livelihoods. *EARPO News* (WWF Eastern Africa) Oct–Dec, 5.

Sand County Foundation (2004a) CBCN Tanzania hosts Laikipia wildlife forum study tour of community tourism ventures. 14 December 2004. http://www.sandcounty.net/newsroom/ (accessed 17 November 2005)

Sand County Foundation (2004b) Community based conservation network. http://www.sandcounty.net/programs/cbcn/ (accessed 17 November 2005)

Saruni (2005) Saruni, The lodge, The Masai Mara, The Maasai. http://www.sarunicamp.com/ (accessed 17 November 2005)

Save the Elephants (nd) Grassroots conservation programmes. http://www.savetheelephants.org/grassroots_main.htm (accessed 17 November 2005)

Sawe, C.T. (2002) Amani Nature Reserve in Usumbara Mountains, Tanzania. In: WTO (comp.) *Sustainable Development of Ecotourism: A Compilation of Good Practices.* WTO, Madrid, pp. 239–241.

Scheyvens, R. (2003) Local involvement in managing tourism. In: Singh, S., Timothy, D.J. and Dowling, R.K. (eds) *Tourism in Destination Communities*. CABI, Wallingford, UK, pp. 229–252.

School for Field Studies (2005) Summer 2005 – Kilimanjaro Bush Camp. http://www.fieldstudies.org/download/261_kenya_summer_syllabus_2005.pdf (accessed 17 November 2005)

Sebunya, C. (2002) Uganda's troubled tourism find women saviours. http://www.peopleandplanet.net/doc.php?id=1629 (accessed 17 November 2005)

SECUCE (2004) Kamani Forestry Reserve. SECUCE. http://www.serengeti.8m.net/custom.html (accessed 17 November 2005)

Seno, S.K. and Shaw, W.W. (2002) Land tenure policies, Maasai traditions, and wildlife conservation in Kenya. *Society and Natural Resources* 15, 79–88.

Serengeti Park (2000) FZS projects in Serengeti. Serengeti Park. http://www.serengeti.org/fzs_pj.html (accessed 17 November 2005)

Shompole (2004) Shompole Mara camp. http://www.shomploe.com/detailsnewcamp.htm (accessed 17 November 2005)

Sikar, T.O. (1996) Conflicts over natural resources in Maasai District of Simanjiro, Tanzania. *FTP Newsletter* 30. http://www-trees.slu.se/newsl/30/30sikar.htm (accessed 17 November 2005)

Sikar, T.O. (2002) SNV – Netherlands Development Organization: Tanzania Cultural Tourism Programme. In: *Tourism: A Catalyst for Sustainable Development in Africa*. WTO, Madrid, pp. 102–110.

Sikoyo, G. and Ashley, C. (2000) *Economic and Livelihood Impacts of Il Ngwesi Lodge, Laikipia, Kenya*. African Wildlife Foundation, Nairobi.

Sindiga, I. (1995) Wildlife-based tourism in Kenya: Land use conflicts and government compensation policies over protected areas. *Journal of Tourism Studies* 6, 45–55.

Smith, D.L. (2001) Maasai hopes and fears. People and ecotourism. Posted 2 July 2001. http://www.peopleandplanet.net/doc.php?section=10&id=1106 (accessed 17 November 2005)

Stephenson, D.J. (1999) The importance of the Convention on Biological Diversity to the Loita Maasai of Kenya. In: Posey, D.A. (ed.) *Cultural and Spiritual Values of Biodiversity*. UNEP. Intermediate Technology Publications, London, pp. 531–533.

Stewart, S. (2003) Good news stories. *The Weekend Australian*, Review-Travel, 12–13 April, R22–23, R27.

Sukkar, Y.A. (2002) Tourism as a tool for poverty alleviation in Ethiopia. In: *Tourism: A Catalyst for Sustainable Development in Africa*. WTO, Madrid, pp. 77–81.

Survival International (2003) Maasai-about. Tribal World. Survival for Tribal Peoples. http://www.survival-international.org/tc%20maasai.htm (accessed 17 November 2005)

Tassia Lodge (2002) Tassia Lodge. http://www.tassia.kenya.com/ (accessed 17 November 2005)

Taylor, G. and Johannson, L. (1996) Our voices, our words and our pictures: Plans, truths and videotapes in Ngorongoro Conservation Area. *FTP Newsletter* 30. http://www-trees.slu.se/speccase2/Ourvoices.html (accessed 17 November 2005)

TCTCO (Tanzanian Cultural Tourism Coordination Office) (2003) http://www.earthfoot.org/guides/tctco.htm (accessed 17 November 2005)

TESFA (Tourism in Ethiopia for Sustainable Future Alternatives) (nd) About TESFA. http://www.community-tourism-ethiopia.com/index_files/Page350.htm (accessed 17 November 2005)

Thomas, N. and Brooks, S. (2003) Ecotourism for community development: Environmental partnerships and the Il Ngwesi ecotourism project, northern Kenya. *Africa Insight* [Tourism: Africa's Key to Prosperity] 33.

Thompson, M. and Homewood, K. (2002) Entrepreneurs, elites, and exclusion in Maasailand: Trends in wildlife conservation and pastoralist development. *Human Ecology* 30, 107–139.

Tourism in Focus (2002) The hunting ecotourism conflict in Tanzania. *Tourism in Focus* (Tourism Concern) 42, 12–13.

Trekking Warrior (2004) Who we are. http://www.trekkingwarrior.com/html/our_staff.html (accessed 17 November 2005)

UCOTA (2003) Uganda Community Tourism Association. http://www.ucota.org.ug/

Uncharted Outposts (2004a) Campi Ya Kanzi. Chyulu Hills, Kenya. Property Profile. http://www.uncharted outposts.com/africa/webpages/properties/campi_yakanzi.php (accessed 17 November 2005)

Uncharted Outposts (2004b) Community projects. http://www.unchartedoutposts.com/africa/webpages/main/uoi_community.php (accessed 17 November 2005)

Uncharted Outposts (2004c) Kalacha. Chalbi Desert, Kenya. Property Profile.

UNDP (United Nations Development Programme) (2002) Equator Prize 2002 Winners – Il Ngwesi Group Ranch – Kenya. http://www.undp.org/ equatorinitiative/secondary/awards_winners.htm (accessed 17 November 2005)

UNDP (United Nations Development Programme) (2004) Equator Prize 2004 Finalists Community Stories – Africa. UNDP. http://www.undp.org/equatorinitiative/secondary/2004-finalists.htm (accessed 17 November 2005)

UNPO (2005) Maasai: The government found solution to Maasai Mara dispute. 11 March 2005. Unrepresented Nations and Peoples Organization. http://www.unpo.org/news_detail.php?arg=64&par=2127 (accessed 17 November 2005)

USAID (2002a) Generating rural incomes: Switching from cattle raising to conservation and tourism; Il Ngwesi Lodge: Linking business and nature, Laikipia, Kenya. http://www.usaid.gov/regions/afr/success_stories/kenya.html (accessed 17 November 2005)

USAID (2002b) Koija group ranch 'star beds' enterprise – a wilderness transformation. USAID/Kenya-Success Stories. http://www.usaid.gov/regions/afr/sso2/kenya7.html (accessed 17 November 2005)

USAID (2002c) Kasiagu community banda enterprise. USAID/Kenya-Success Stories. http://www.usaid.gov/regions/afr/sso2/kenya6.html (accessed 17 November 2005)

USAID (2002d) Mwaluganje community elephant sanctuary: From corn to conservation. USAID/Kenya-Success Stories. http://www.usaid.gov/regions/afr/sso2/kenya5.html (accessed 17 November 2005)

USAID (2003) Empowering women from coral garden conservation. Success Stories Kenya. http://www.dec.org/partners/afr/ss/ (accessed 17 November 2005)

van der Cammen, S. (1997) Involving Maasai women. In: France, L. (ed.) The Earthscan Reader in Sustainable Tourism. Earthscan, London, pp. 162–163.

van der Duim, R., Peters, K. and Wearing, S. (2005) Planning host and guest interactions: Moving beyond the empty meeting ground in African encounters. Current Issues in Tourism 8, 286–305.

Varat, J. and Anand, J. (2003) Maasai: Culture, colonization and change. Cultural Survival Voices 2. http://209.200.101.189/publications/csv/csv-article.cfm?id=52 (accessed 17 November 2005)

Verburg, D. (2003) Cultural Tourism as an Arena: A Case Study from Tanzania. MSc thesis, Wageningen University, Wageningen.

Victurine, R. (2000) Building tourism excellence at the community-level: Capacity building for community-based entrepreneurs in Uganda. Journal of Travel Research 38, 221–229.

Vieta, F.E. (2002) Ecotourism propels development but social acceptance depends on economic opportunities for local communities. Africa Recovery 13. Africa Recovery Center, United Nations, New York. http://www.un.org/ecosocdev/geninfo/afrec/vol13no1/tourism.htm (accessed 17 November 2005)

Waithaka, J. (2002) The role of community wildlife-based enterprises in reducing human vulnerability and environmental degradation: The case of Il Ngwesi ecotourism project, Kenya. In: Africa Environment Outlook. Case Studies. UNEP. http://africa.unep.net/casestudies/ilngwesi.asp (accessed 17 November 2005)

Waithaka, J., Waruingi, L., Wanakuta, E. and Maina, S. (2003) An ecological evaluation of Il Ngwesi community conservation project. http://www.conservationafrica.org/ecotourism_biodiversity.htm (accessed 17 November 2005)

Walpole, M. (2004) Community scouts promote conservation and livelihood security in the Mara ecosystem. Sustainable Development International 10, 119–121.

Walpole, M.J. and Leader-Williams, N. (2001) Masai Mara tourism reveals partnership benefits. Nature 413, 771.

Walpole, M.J. and Thouless, C.R. (2005) Increasing the value of wildlife through non-consumptive use? Deconstructing the myths of ecotourism and community-based tourism in the tropics. In: Woodroffe, R., Thirgood, S. and Rabinowitz, A. (eds) People and Wildlife: Conflict or Coexistence? Cambridge University Press, Cambridge, pp. 122–139.

Walpole, M., Karanja, G., Sitati, N.W. and Leader-Willams, N. (2003) Wildlife and People: Conflict and Conservation in Masai Mara, Kenya. Wildlife and Development Series No. 14. IIED, London.

Warinda, E. (2001) A socioeconomic survey and economic analysis of land use options in Shompole and Olkiramantian group ranches, Magadi Division. African Conservation Centre. Ecology. http://www.conservationafrica.org/Reports.htm (accessed 17 November 2005)

Warinda, E. (nd) Socio-economic survey: Imbirikani group ranch in Amboseli. African Conservation Centre. http://www.conservationafrica.org/Imbirikani-socioeconomic.htm (accessed 17 November 2005)

Watkin, J. (1999) Workshop series on conservation by communities in East Africa. African Conservation Centre. http://www.conservationafrica.org/ (accessed 17 November 2005)

Watkin, J. (2003a) Community workshops: Workshop series on conservation by communities in East Africa. African Conservation Centre. http://www.conservationafrica.org/RWS-brochure.htm (accessed 17 November 2005)

Watkin, J. (2003b) *The Evolution of Ecotourism in East Africa: From an Idea to an Industry.* IIED Wildlife and Development Series No. 15. International Institute for Environment and Development, London.

Watkin, J., Macharia, W., Inamdar, N. and Loehr, A. (2002) *Ecotourism in East Africa: The Responsible Business Opportunity.* African Conservation Centre, Nairobi.

Weaver, D. (1998) Ecotourism in Kenya. In: *Ecotourism in the Less Developed World.* CABI, Wallingford, UK, pp. 109–134.

Weber, W. (1993) Primate conservation and ecotourism in Africa. In: Potter, C., Cohen, J. and Jankzewski, D. (eds) *Perspectives on Biodiversity: Case Studies of Genetic Resources.* American Association for the Advancement of Science, Washington DC, pp. 129–150.

Weinberg, P. (2000) *Once We Were Hunters: A Journey with Africa's Indigenous People.* Mets & Schilt Amsterdam and David Philip, Cape Town.

Western, D. (1992) Ecotourism: The Kenya challenge. In: Gakahu, G.G. and Goode, B.E. (eds) *Ecotourism and Sustainable Development in Kenya.* Wildlife Conservation International, Kenya, pp. 15–22.

Western, D. (1994) Ecosystem conservation and rural development: The case of Amboseli. In: Western, D. and Michael, W.R. (eds) *Natural Connections: Perspectives in Community-based Conservation.* Island Press, Washington DC, pp. 15–50.

Wild, R.G. and Mutebi, J. (1996) *Conservation Through Community Use of Plant Resources: Establishing Collaborative Management at Bwindi Impenetrable and Mgahinga National Parks, Uganda.* UNESCO, Paris.

Wildland Adventures (2005) Masai Land Safari. http://www.com/trips/details/74/kenya_itn.aspx Masai Beading Safari. http://www.com/trips/details/185/kenya_itn.aspx (accessed 17 November 2005)

Wildwatch (2003) MIMCA celebrates first year of success. African conservation initiatives. http://www.wildwatch.com/conservation/action.asp (accessed 17 November 2005)

Williams, E. (2001) Involvement of local communities in ecotourism activities using tourism as a tool in sustainable community development – Uganda. Seminar on Planning, Development and Management of Ecotourism in Africa, Mozambique, 5–6 March 2001. http://www.world-tourism.org/sustainable/IYE-Main-Menu.htm (accessed 17 November 2005)

Willams, E., White, A. and Spenceley, A. (2001) *UCOTA – the Uganda Community Tourism Association: A comparison with NACOTBA.* PPT Working Paper No. 5. Propoor tourism, UK.

Wishitemi, B.E.L. and Okello, M.M. (2003) Application of the protected area landscape model in Maasai communally-owned lands of southern Kenya. *IUCN Parks Magazine* 13, 21–29.

WTO (2001) Seminar on Planning, Development and Management of Ecotourism in Africa. Mozambique, 5–6 March 2001. http://www.world-tourism.org/sustainable/IYE-Main-Menu.htm (accessed 17 November 2005)

WTO (2002a) Cultural Tourism Programme (CTP). In: WTO (comp.) *Sustainable Development of Ecotourism: A Compilation of Good Practices.* WTO, Madrid, pp. 243–246.

WTO (2002b) Ecotourism development in the Bishangari Nature Reserve. In: WTO (comp.) *Sustainable Development of Ecotourism: A Compilation of Good Practices.* WTO, Madrid, pp. 119–122.

WTO (2003a) Kibale Association for Rural and Environmental Development (KAFRED): A community based ecotourism project. In: WTO (comp.) *Sustainable Development of Ecotourism: A Compilation of Good Practices in SMEs.* WTO, Madrid, pp. 279–282.

WTO (2003b) Rwenzori mountaineering ecotourism project. In: WTO (comp.) *Sustainable Development of Ecotourism: A Compilation of Good Practices in SMEs.* WTO, Madrid, pp. 283–285.

WTO (2003c) Mnemba Island Lodge, Conservation Corporation Africa. In: WTO (comp.) *Sustainable Development of Ecotourism: A Compilation of Good Practices in SMEs.* WTO, Madrid, pp. 273–277.

WWF (2005) East Usambara forest landscape restoration. People and the Environment. Projects. WWF. http://www.panda.org/about_wwf/where_we_work/africa/where/eastern_africa/tanzania/projects/index.cfm?uProjectID=TZ0056 (accessed 17 November 2005)

Yunis, E. (2001) Conditions for sustainable ecotourism development and management. Seminar on Planning, Development and Management of Ecotourism in Africa. Mozambique, 5–6 March 2001. http://www.world-tourism.org/sustainable/IYE-Main-Menu.htm (accessed 17 November 2005)

Zaninka, P. (2001) Impact of (forest) nature conservation on indigenous peoples: The Batwa of southwestern Uganda – Case study of Mgahinga Mbwindi Impenetrable Forest Conservation Trust. Forest Peoples Project. http://www.forestpeoples.org/documents/africa/fpproj_uganda_summ_eng.shtml (accessed 29 November 2005)

Ziegler, F. (1998) Small-scale tourism in eastern Africa: Helpful or harmful to local communities? *Intercoast Network: International Newsletter of Coastal Management* 31. http://www.seacam.mz/icoastarticle.htm (accessed 17 November 2005)

5

Southern Africa: Ecotourism on Wildlife Conservancies and Communal Lands

This chapter reviews Indigenous ecotourism ventures on communal lands in southern Africa. These include wildlife conservancies in Namibia, Botswana, Zimbabwe and South Africa. With legal land titles and restitution of traditional lands, Indigenous groups are negotiating tourism joint ventures with private operators such as safari camps and lodges. Private operators and Park Boards support these new Indigenous ecotourism ventures by revenue sharing and community outreach programmes with communities living around conservation areas. Some Indigenous groups in southern Africa have developed their own community ecotourism ventures such as campsites, trails and tours, supported by conservation NGOs and local development agencies. In southern Africa, Indigenous groups also benefit from controlled trophy hunting on communal lands with income used to support community social services and community-owned tourism facilities (Lewis and Jackson, 2005). The chapter begins with a review of key issues for promoting Indigenous involvement in ecotourism on communal lands and protected areas. It then reviews Indigenous ecotourism sites in Botswana, Zimbabwe, Namibia and South Africa. Key factors and government programmes that support Indigenous ecotourism in southern Africa are discussed in the conclusion.

Introduction: Ecotourism in Southern Africa

In March 2001, a seminar on the planning, development and management of ecotourism in Africa was held in Mozambique. Organized by the WTO, the seminar was one of several global forums discussing regional issues on ecotourism, prior to the International Year of Ecotourism in 2002. Key themes for the seminar on ecotourism in Africa were ecotourism in protected areas, the involvement of local communities and management of ecotourism facilities and services (Dunn, 1995; Brown, 1998; Vieta, 2002). The seminar involved 150 participants from 22 African countries. Papers were presented on ecotourism in national parks (South Africa, Namibia, Tanzania, Uganda), the involvement of local communities in ecotourism facilities at protected areas (Botswana, Mozambique, Uganda, Ghana), at private games reserves (South Africa) and ecotourism activities at villages (Senegal, Tanzania). A key focus of the Seminar was involving local communities in ecotourism development and management and sharing the revenue from ecotourism. This included communities living within or near protected areas, ecotourism on community nature reserves and conservancies, land tenure and control, employment opportunities and sharing of benefits, and the role of community associations and NGOs in education and capacity building for community ecotourism. Suggested mechanisms for community benefits of ecotourism were joint ventures with the private sector, leasehold arrangements, revenue sharing and levies, donations, land ownership, tourism access rights linked to concession leases and equity shares in ventures. Limiting factors were a lack of government policies on ecotourism, minimal funding and support for community tourism, varied community rights to land, resources and wildlife, local access to national parks, forming partnerships with the private sector and marketing. Communities with legal land rights could best enter business partnerships and develop joint ventures in ecotourism (WTO, 2005). Village ecotourism projects were also developed as part of community-based natural resource management programmes implemented in Botswana, Namibia and Zimbabwe in southern Africa (Jones and Murphree, 2004; Child, 2005). Controlled trophy hunting with limited quotas and fees paid to local communities is seen as a form of ecotourism in southern Africa (Baker, 1997; Resource Africa, nd). These issues are examined for diverse Indigenous ecotourism ventures in Botswana, Zimbabwe, Namibia and South Africa.

Botswana

In 2001, Botswana developed a national ecotourism strategy based on conservation and sustainable development of resources and increasing jobs and tourism income in rural areas (Bentinck, 2002). Key tourism attractions in Botswana are wildlife, the wilderness areas of the Okavango Delta, Chobe, the Kalahari Desert and Makgadikgadi Pans, and San Bushmen culture. Botswana has a Bushmen (or Basarwa) population of 47,675 people (Mbaiwa, 2005a) and strongly promotes traditional Bushmen culture for tourism. However, most Bushmen live in poverty with limited economic opportunities. Others were removed in 1994 from the Tsodilo Hills, a Bushman rock art site and more recently since 2002 from the Central Kalahari Game Reserve (Survival International, 2005). In addition,

17% of Botswana is set aside as protected areas. Tourism generates US$413 million in foreign exchange, second only to the export of diamonds, and employs 10,000 people. In the 2004–2009 national development plan for Botswana tourism is recognized as a major economic driver with a budget allocation of US$68 million (Survival International, 2005). The government of Botswana supports a policy of 'low volume-high value' wildlife tourism, with high entry fees to protected areas (BWP150 per person per day) and a maximum of 24 beds in any lodge in a National Park or Game Reserve. Tourism attractions in the northern area of Botswana, mainly around Chobe National Park and the Okavango Delta, were often booked out and commercial operators sought alternatives in community areas. During the 1990s Botswana developed rural tourism with registered community trusts, controlled hunting areas and a community natural resources management programme.

Community-based Tourism in Botswana

Community-based tourism in Botswana began in the early 1990s at Nata Sanctuary and grew as hunting concession areas became available for community management through registered trusts. Tourism and hunting enterprises on community lands were part of the Community Based Natural Resources Management (CBNRM) programme implemented in Botswana and funded by USAID (Samson and Maotonyane, 1998). CBNRM grew out of wildlife, conservation and tourism policies during the 1990s that allowed local communities to gain economic benefits from wildlife, natural resources and tourism enterprises. These community enterprises were based on the legal designation of Wildlife Management Areas (WMA), 20% of Botswana, on reserved tribal lands used for hunting and gathering by the Bushmen (also known as San or Basarwa). The whole land area of Botswana was also subdivided into 163 Controlled Hunting Areas (CHAs) zoned for hunting or photographic tourism, managed by communities or leased to commercial operators. Local communities applied for a wildlife quota and formed a registered community trust (CBO) able to sublease land, sell wildlife quotas or form tourism joint ventures with private operators. Fourteen registered community trusts in Botswana were involved in hunting and tourism ventures by 2000 (Rozemeijer, 2000). The enterprises included trophy hunting, photographic wildlife safaris, campsites, guided tours, hunting and gathering trips, handicrafts and cultural activities such as dancing and storytelling (see Table 5.1).

The 1999 Botswana Tourism Development Programme also supported rural diversification of tourism products and local business involvement in tourism, including a policy for developing community-based tourism (Rozemeijer, 2000). The CBNRM programme and registered trusts enabled local communities to develop a range of tourism enterprises. Community involvement in Botswana tourism grew through the 1990s. The CBNRM programme in Botswana and an American university student developed websites for nine of these community-based tourism ventures

Table 5.1. Registered community trusts and tourism ventures in Botswana.

Trust name (2000)	CHA (area in km^2)	No. of villages (population)	Tourism activities	Economic benefits
Nqwaa Khobee Xeya Trust	KD 1 (12,225)	3 (850)	Wildlife joint venture (hunting and photographic), campsites, crafts, cultural tourism	BWP286,000 and 75 jobs
Nata Sanctuary	Central district	4	Lodge and campsite, birdwatching	BWP100,000 and 5 jobs
Gaing-O Community Trust	Central district	3 (900)	Cultural tourism: Lekubu Island	BWP60,000 and 3 jobs
Kgetsie Ya Tsie	Central district	15 (420 members)	Pottery, crafts, thatching grass	BWP2,595 per member
Kalepa	CH8 (1,085)	3 (4,000)	Wildlife JV (hunting and photo)	BWP360,000
Chobe Enclave Conservation Trust	CH1/2 (2,984)	5 (4,400)	Wildlife JV (hunting and photo) campsite, store, brickmaking	BWP882,000
Okavango Polers Trust	NG12	75 members	Mokoro safaris, campsite	BWP697,000 in 1999
Okavango Conservation Trust	NG22/23 (1,220)	5 (2,200)	Wildlife JV (hunting and photo[a])	BWP1,500,000 (2001), and 145 jobs
Okavango Jakotsha Community Trust	NG24 (589)	4 (10,000)	Photographic tourism subleases, guiding, campsites, crafts	Initial stage, 140 jobs
Mababe Zukutsama Community Trust	NG41 (2,181)	1 (400)	Wildlife JV (hunting and photo), campsite	BWP675,000 and 49 jobs
Khwai Community Trust	NG18, NG19 (1,995)	1 (360)	Sale of hunting packages Photographic tourism	BWP550,000 (2001) and 78 jobs
Okavango Kopano Mokoro Trust	NG32 (1,223)	6 (2,400)	Wildlife JV (hunting and photo) campsites	BWP1,155,000 (2001) and 100 jobs
Cgaecgae Tlhabololo Trust (Xai-Xai village)	NG4 (2,640) NG5	1 (400)	Wildlife JV (hunting), crafts, cultural tourism, photo safaris	BWP342,262 and 37 jobs
Sankuyo Tshwaragano Management Trust	NG33 and NG34 (870)	1 (345)	Wildlife JV (hunting), campsite, crafts, cultural village	BWP526,075 and 49 jobs
Phuduhudu Trust	NG 49 (1,180)	1	Hunting and photographic tourism	

[a]Hunting suspended in 2003
Gudigwa, Xaxaba, Mababwe, Khwai and Phuduhudu villages were all 100% San Bushmen; other villages were 50% San. Other groups were the Bayei, Bambukushu and Herero peoples. There were few San Bushmen people in Sankuyo village. CHA, Controlled Hunting Area; KD, Kgalagadi; CH, Chobe; NG, Ngamiland; JV, Joint Venture.
Sources: Rozemeijer (2000); Mbaiwa (2005a).

(Shewmake, 2002; CBNRM, 2003; Earthfoot, nd). Botswana Tourism (2001) also promotes three Bushmen community-based tourism ventures on its website. Traditional village leaders dominated some CBNRM projects and registered community trusts (e.g. Okavango Community Trust and Okavango Kopane Mokoro Community Trust). Other community trusts had a management structure based on equitable participation of family groups (e.g. KD1 and Xai-Xai village). In north-eastern Botswana, community tourism ventures included campsites, cultural villages, canoe tours, wildlife sanctuaries and hunting leases.

Trophy hunting joint venture agreements with private operators generated substantial community income during the 6 month hunting season. The community sold their wildlife quotas for valuable species such as lion, leopard, elephant, zebra, buffalo and large male ungulates to hunting operators. Safari hunting companies bid competitively for hunting rights to a concession area. Sport hunting quotas had to be paid in advance to community trusts with no refunds given if animals were not killed. The minimum safari hunting quota price was BWP40,000 for an elephant, BWP10,000 for a lion, BWP5000 for a leopard, BWP1500 for an eland and less than BWP1000 for other animal species (Gujadhur and Motshubi, 2000). Safari hunting joint ventures in community hunting areas provided money, meat from game animals and some local jobs mainly for men (tracking, skinning and tanning). Photographic wildlife safari tours were run in the non-hunting season (October–March). Community-owned campsites with guided tours, crafts and cultural activities catered to self-drive visitors and mobile safari companies. Bushmen handicrafts and culture was a key product in western Botswana.

In Botswana the tourism concessions paid lease fees ranging from BWP35,000 to BWP850,000 (average BWP230,045) and royalties ranging from 4 to 10% (av. 4.5%). Agreements were fixed at 5 years and renewable for two more 5-year cycles if operating conditions were met. Tourism concessionaires in Botswana also had responsibilities for conservation management (Humphrey and Boonzaaier, 2003). These community-based organizations promoted wildlife conservation but lacked marketing and entrepreneurial skills in managing

tourism, with poor distribution of benefits to trust members. Local people were not involved in tourism land use decisions or setting wildlife quotas (Mbaiwa, 2005b).

San Bushmen ecocultural tourism, western Botswana

From 1978 to 2003, the Netherlands Development Organization (SNV) played a key role in developing community-based tourism ventures in Botswana, particularly for San Bushmen in western Botswana. The Bushmen population of 47,675 San people (Mbaiwa, 2005a) lived in poverty with limited economic opportunities. They lived as squatters in town settlements and labourers on cattle ranches, supplemented with hunting and gathering activities. Some Bushmen communities also experienced the impacts of tourism on their communities with little or no economic benefits (Hitchcock, 1997; Thoma, 1998). SNV influenced land utilization and economic policies, organized and trained Bushmen in rural areas and supported local NGOs in forming partnerships with the government and private sector to develop tourism enterprises on hunting areas and farms managed with the Bushmen. Tourism aimed to use natural resources in a sustainable manner to generate rural income in this area. There was a steady demand for commercial hunting in Bushmen communal areas and a growing but smaller market for 'ecocultural' Bushmen tourism. SNV also regarded community-based tourism 'as a means towards empowering poor communities to take control over their land and resources, to tap their potential and acquire skills to design their own development' (Rozemeijer, 2000: 3). Four of these Bushmen tourism ventures in western Botswana were Xai-Xai village in hunting area NG4, the Dqae Qare Game Farm near Ghanzi, the joint venture Ghanzi Trail Blazers and three villages in controlled hunting area KD1 in the southern Kalahari.

Xai-Xai village

The village of Xai-Xai, located 10 km east of the Namibia border, managed controlled hunting areas NG4 and NG5 in north-western Botswana. The 400 people in Xai-Xai village were 80% Ju/'hoansi Bushmen ('the real people'), who were marginalized, and 20% Baherero people who were economically dominant. The village developed community-based tourism enterprises such as a wildlife hunting joint venture, crafts and cultural tourism activities, assisted by an SNV adviser from 1994 to mid-2001. Consultations were held at village forums and at household level, over a period of 4 years. Xai-Xai village established the Cgaecgae Tlhabololo Trust in 1997 to manage these tourism ventures. The first community tourism venture established in 1995 was Kokoro crafts. It had 80 members (75% women). A community land use plan zoned areas for hunting, photographic tourism, and a future lodge site. The Xai-Xai community provided horseback rides in the Aha hills, cultural tours staying overnight in grass huts and caving at Gchiwaba Caves. A safari hunting operator (Komtsa Safaris) also paid a land rental fee and trophy fee for each animal killed (mainly desert antelope), plus 22 seasonal jobs and game meat for the community. In 2000, Xai-Xai was awarded six elephants, two lions and four leopards on their wildlife quota, which increased their trophy hunting income to BWP380,000 per year. Hunting income was put into a Trust account and divided among 11 wards or family groups in Xai-Xai village.

In 1997, Xai-Xai also established their own cultural tourism business, with small groups of tourists taken on 2–3 day trips in the desert with 12–15 Ju/'hoansi Bushmen demonstrating hunting, gathering and cultural activities. This tourism income went to individual households. All the tourism activities generated income of BWP380,000 and 22 jobs at Xai-Xai village in 2000. Xai-Xai controlled cultural tourism for cultural preservation of Bushmen traditions, income and jobs for men and women, and to develop a niche in ecotourism. In 1999, Xai-Xai ran nine cultural tours earning BWP26,000 while more than 16 tours ran in 2000. Key issues were marketing partnerships with safari tour operators in Maun and managing tourism revenue. Tourism at Xai-Xai village provided jobs, income and a means of preserving unique Bushmen culture (Gujadhur and Motshubi, 2000; Rozemeijer, 2000).

Dqae Qare Game Farm, Ghanzi

The Dqae Qare Game Farm is located near Ghanzi, a large cattle ranching area in the Kalahari Desert. In 1993, the Kuru Development Trust (KDT) in D'kar asked the visiting Dutch Minister of Development Cooperation to buy a farm for local Bushmen. The 7500 ha Dqae Qare Game Farm was purchased in 1994 with funding of BWP1 million from the Netherlands and became a property of the KDT. It was developed as a Bushmen community tourism enterprise with funding from the Dutch government, European Community and Canada Fund used for a game fence, boreholes and BWP350,000 of game animals. A farm management committee was established in 1995 with 25 Bushmen residents from the nearby town of D'kar as members. KDT also employed a manager for the farm that combined commercial game animals with sport hunting and photographic tourism. SNV provided technical help to KDT in managing the farm and trained local Bushmen in skills to run the farm. Dqae Qare was the only game farm in Botswana owned by the Bushmen. Tourism operations on the farm began in 1998, with safari hunting, a guesthouse, and campsite, with cultural activities such as traditional dancing, storytelling and guided bush walks added in mid-1999. Other visitor activities were game drives, horse riding and donkey treks with overnight camping at beehive Bushmen huts and meetings hosted at the guesthouse (KFO, nd).

Capital investment in the farm and tourism assets from 1994 to 2000 was BWP3.1 million. Self-drive visitors, mobile tour operators and expatriates mainly visited the farm. In 2000, the farm had 1000 visitor nights generating income of BWP120,000. Thirteen local people were employed as guides, rangers, cleaners, caterers and receptionists. Funding from the Dutch government and technical help from SNV ended in 2000. The salaries and number of people working on the farm were reduced so that operational expenses could be met from tourism income (excluding the manager, insurance and depreciation of assets). Ownership of the Dqae Qare Game Farm was to be transferred from KDT to the D'kar Community Trust. However, the large scale of the Dqae

Qare farm project and its management complexity overwhelmed local Bushmen and KDT coordinators. Key issues were personnel management, role of the manager, lack of control by KDT, vehicles being misused by participants, alcoholism, and absenteeism and high salaries paid to project members. Large amounts of donor funding affected local ownership and commitment to the farm project while the goal of community management clashed with the idea of economic viability and business practices (Rozemeijer, 2000; van den Berg, 2000). Ecocultural Bushmen tourism, though, was a growing area of the farm.

Ghanzi Trail Blazers

Ghanzi Trail Blazers is a partnership between a private tour operator and the Xwiskurusa Trust Community that operate a 3500 ha farm in the Ghanzi district of Botswana. Tourists experience San/Bushmen culture on guided walks, through traditional dancing and accommodation. Permaculture Botswana helped develop this private agreement of the Xwiskurusa Trust with the tour operator, Ghanzi Trail Blazers, who employed 16 San/Bushmen. Training was provided for San youth and in handicrafts, while other San staff could obtain their guides licenses. In 2 years, the company had received 1000 tourists but, with start-up and marketing costs plus staff wages, was still to break even. The wages paid to local San staff was around US$9800 a year. The San/Bushmen also developed their own programme for the guided walks and dancing, but tired after 8 months or wanted to be at their traditional hunting areas in spring to gather natural resources. The San community, through the Xwiskurusa Trust, approved a tourist programme based on cultural activities with a head fee per tourist, employment of ten San people and a percentage of the profit (WTO, 2003d).

Southern Kalahari (KD1)

Three Bushmen settlements of Ukhwi, Ncaang and Ngwatle shared the management of controlled hunting area KD1 in the southern Kalahari, through the Nqwaa Khobee Xeya Trust. The Trust has a natural resources user lease for KD1 from the Kgalagadi Land Board. The 12,225-km^2 KDI hunting block also adjoined the Kgalagadi (Kalahari) Transfrontier Park. The two main ethnic groups in the area were the !Xoo Bushmen (70%) and the BaKgalagadi (25%) who farmed and raised livestock. SNV (from 1996 until 2002) and a Botswana national NGO, Thusano Lefatsheng, supported local Bushmen in developing tourism ventures in KD1. These included a wildlife joint venture for hunting and photographic safaris, campsites, crafts and cultural activities that generated BWP286,000 and 75 jobs in 2000 (Rozemeijer, 2000). During 1999, three safari companies placed bids for joint venture tourism rights at KD1. In 2000, the Trust had a 1-year lease with Safaris Botswana Bound for both hunting and photographic safaris with the company allowed to set up luxury tents in the community campsite. Additional community items were a radio and 100 blankets at each settlement along with sports equipment, stationery and T-shirts for local primary schools. Income from the hunting quota was distributed to the registered family groups in three communities. Hunting revenue was also to be re-invested in a local hardware store, petrol station, grinding mill and general dealer. The private sector operator employed local people as guides, cleaners and camp attendants while the Trust employed locals as bookkeepers, wildlife guides and administrators. Other local people sold crafts and baskets, demonstrated dancing or healing rituals, and led traditional hunting and gathering activities. Three community campsites and a cultural centre were constructed in 2000 along with a new entrance road and private lodge in Kgalagadi Transfrontier Park, both increasing tourism in KD1 (Flyman, 2001). However, other San Bushmen communities were removed from the 51,800 km^2 Central Kalahari Game Reserve to make way for diamond mining and tourism development (Weaver, 2000). Botswana promotes traditional Bushmen culture but the 2002 forced evictions of San Bushmen from this Reserve has led to court cases and one NGO boycotting tourism (Survival International, 2005).

Nata Sanctuary

Other community tourism ventures were located in the Makgadigadi Pans and the Okavango Delta in north-east Botswana. Nata Sanctuary preserved the Sowa pan, a breeding area for flamingos, pelicans and other birds and part of the Makgadigadi system. The sanctuary was established on a former cattle area and owned by four communities: Nata, Sepako, Maposa and Mmaxotae. After 3000 cattle were removed, the area was fenced and Nata Sanctuary opened to visitors in 1993. The community sanctuary preserved a sensitive natural area and won the 1993 Tourism for Tomorrow award. Income from entrance fees and camping fees at Nata Sanctuary went to village development councils for community projects and facilities. The Mmatshumo community also had a tourist campground and guided tours at Kubu Island, a San site at the edge of the Makgadikgadi Pans.

Community Tourism in Okavango Delta

The Okavango Delta in northern Botswana is a famous wilderness area with abundant wildlife. It covers 18,000 km^2 of wetlands, seasonal floodplains and woodland from the Namibia border to Maun. The Okavango area includes the Moremi Game Reserve, set aside by BaTawana chiefs, and numerous wildlife concessions used for exclusive tourist camps. About 122,000 people live in and around the Okavango Delta region, including 10,850 San people (Mbaiwa, 2005a). More than 40 tourist camps and lodges operate in the Okavango Delta, mainly owned by foreign tour operators and targeting up-market tourists from Europe, North America and South Africa. Most Okavango lodges are reached by charter flights from the gateway town of Maun, the office base for most safari tour companies. Tourism in the Okavango Delta generates annual income of US$350 million (NAD3.5 billion). Foreign domination of tourism in the Okavango has led to leakage of tourism revenue, expatriates in management positions, low salaries for local workers, weak linkages to local agriculture and the domestic economy, and a limited contribution to alleviating poverty in the region (Mbaiwa, 2003a, b, 2005a, b). Sandibe Lodge helped local women establish a vegetable and herb garden to sell produce while Nxabega Lodge employed over 200 rangers, guides, trackers and lodge staff (Buckley, 2003e). Lodge operators are constrained by short-term leases (increased to 5 years in 2003), high upkeep and operational costs, a new VAT tax, falling occupancy rates and erratic returns (Michler, 2004). In the 1990s though, the CBNRM project required safari operators to negotiate with local community trusts for hunting and tourism concessions in controlled hunting area. The trusts gained income from hunting and photographic joint ventures, community campsites and cultural villages. Local trust committees decided on income from leases, employment and other tourism benefits (Hoon, 2004).

Local communities are granted the right to use wildlife resources on communal lands or controlled hunting areas in the Okavango Delta. In 2001, there were 12 registered community trusts in the delta, with eight allocated controlled hunting areas (CHAs) for tourism. The Botswana government leased this land to community trusts for 15 years and allocated annual wildlife quotas. Most trusts sub-leased or rented land in their CHAs and sold wildlife quotas to safari operators, rather than directly running tourism businesses. In 2001, this generated total income of US$800,000 from tourism on trust lands. However, there was still little transfer of tourism management skills to local people who were now 'labourers and land lords' (Mbaiwa, 2005a: 103). The community trusts had a high reliance on funding from international conservation and development NGOs. The government of Botswana also recently created new policies to increase local participation and ownership of tourism in the Okavango Delta (AWF, 2004a, b). A few community-owned lodges now operate in the Okavango Delta, supported by Conservation International and the African Wildlife Foundation. However, these locally owned lodges have had limited government support for training staff and marketing community tourism ventures in the Okavango Delta (AWF, 2004a, b; Michler, 2004). Okavango lodge owners paid over BWP1 million annually in lease fees and wanted the government to use this income for training local communities about the tourism industry, and controlling illegal access in concession areas (Michler, 2004). River reeds, basket weaving resources and arable land were also becoming scarce resources for local people in the Delta (Mbaiwa, 2004; Kgathi *et al.*, 2005).

Sankuyo village, southern Okavango Delta

Sankuyo is a small village of Bayei, Bambukushu and a few San people at the southern edge of the Okavango Delta, 65 km from the regional town of Maun. The Bayei people introduced the *mokoro* (canoe) to the Okavango Delta. Supported by the African Wildlife Foundation, the Bayei people developed the Kaziikini community campsite and the Shandereka cultural village. The Sankuyo Tshwaragano Management Trust managed these community tourism facilities (Mearns, 2003; Mbaiwa, 2005b). The campsite included five private campsites, four *rondavels* (huts), a bar and restaurant. Guided game walks and self-drive game drives were provided. Tourist activities at the cultural village included dancing, basket weaving, setting animal traps, and a traditional healer throwing the bones to foretell the future. The campsite was a short walk from the cultural village while a free daily shuttle bus was provided from Maun. The People and Nature Trust handled bookings for the campsite and cultural village at Sankuyo. AWF worked with the Sankuyo community to improve their management of tourism, they helped develop the tourism product, obtained funding, organized benefits distribution and marketed the site (AWF, 2004a; STMT, nd). The Sankuyo community also had a hunting joint venture in controlled hunting area NG43. In 2000, hunting and tourism at Sankuyo generated BWP526,075 and provided 50 jobs (Rozemeijer, 2000).

Santawani Lodge, southern Okavango Delta

Santawani Lodge is located 80 km from Maun at the southern gate to Moremi Game Reserve.

The lodge has six private chalets with thatched roofs, a bar and reception area. The rebuilt lodge is community-owned and managed through the Sankuyo Tshwaragano Management Trust, representing 400 local households. The lodge employs 20 local residents who gained hospitality skills and experience by working in other private lodges and camps in the Okavango Delta. Santawani Lodge opened in June 2004. The lodge project was supported by AWF with funding from USAID to refurbish the lodge, and train local staff. A marketing strategy promoted this community venture to four-wheel-drive travellers from South Africa, the Regional Tourism Association of Southern Africa (RETOSA), at travel shows in the USA and at a booking office in Maun opposite the airport. AWF promoted wildlife conservation through sustainable community tourism enterprises. Santawani Lodge was located on a wildlife-rich conservation area of 8000 ha leased to the Sankuyo Trust. Revenue from the lodge supported a community social centre, orphanage, tourism courses and new toilets at each local household (AWF, 2004b).

Khwai, northern Okavango Delta

Khwai is a village of some 400 people from the Bukakhwae or 'river bushmen' located next to Moremi Game Reserve in northern Botswana. The Khwai Development Trust was formed in 1995 to promote ecotourism and a community safari business. The people of Khwai, through the Khwai Trust, had a traditional dance group for visitors, sold baskets, jewellery and other crafts at the Itekeng Craft Shop in Khwai and served traditional food such as water lily stew and guinea fowl. Game walks and night drives to see wildlife were allowed in the Khwai area but not in the Moremi Reserve. From 1995 to 1999 Khwai village insisted on running their own tourism operations. In 1999, Khwai auctioned off BWP1.2 million (US$240,000) of their hunting quota in controlled hunting area NG18, to different safari hunting companies. The community bought a four-wheel-drive to transport supplies and people and, in 2001, Khwai village built and operated two campsites, Xamotese and Zou, for hunters and other tourists (Khwai Development Trust, nd).

In 2000, the Khwai Trust sold hunting packages that generated income of BWP1.3 million. However, two senior members of the Khwai community defrauded the trust fund of BWP1.4 million (Michler, 2004). Community members and the board lacked financial management skills.

The Tsaro Game Lodge in the Khwai areas had been closed since 2001 as local people lacked the tourism marketing and management skills to run the lodge (Mbaiwa, 2005b,). The Moremi Game Reserve attracted 40,000 tourists annually, however, local people at Khwai were not involved in decision making and did not gain benefits from the Reserve (Mbaiwa, 2005c). Other issues in the Khwai tourism concession were uncontrolled vehicle access and off-road driving, groups camping outside designated areas and not paying camping or entrance fees (Michler, 2005). The Okavango Kopano Mokoro Trust, representing six villages and 600 people, also generated income of BWP1.1 million and 75 jobs from joint venture hunting and photographic safaris and a campsite in controlled hunting area NG32 (Rozemeijer, 2000). The high levels of income from hunting fees often supported community campsites and other cultural enterprises but further training was needed to run businesses.

Okavango Polers Trust, northern Okavango Delta

In the northern Okavango, the Okavango Polers Trust ran *mokoro* (canoe) safaris and a campsite in concession area NG12, generating income of BWP697,000 in 1999 for 75 members (Rozemeijer, 2000). The Polers Trust was formed in 1998 to provide ecotourism job opportunities for local people in the eastern part of the Okavango Delta. An expatriate was employed as the business manager. Tribal groups in this region were the BaYei, Bukakwe San (river Bushmen) and the Hambukushu. The Polers Trust employed 20 men as casual polers, who either owned their own *mokoro* (dug out canoe) or were using finance from the Trust to purchase their *mokoro*. Most *mokoro* were now fibreglass replicas, replacing wooden dug out canoes that leaked and only lasted 3

years. The polers all followed a code of conduct to use fibreglass canoes, dispose of rubbish, clean up campsites, conserve firewood, rotate islands used for camping, and to protect waterways and wildlife. Based at Seronga, the Trust organized *mokoro* trips in the Delta, managed the Mbiroba Camp, sold woven baskets at the booking office, and provided other services such as traditional meals and dancing. The Polers Trust ran for 2 years before receiving a grant of US$25,000 in 2000 to purchase a vehicle and subsidised wages over 5 years. The Okavango Polers Trust obtained a grant of US$233,200 from the African Development Fund in 2001 to build a restaurant, bar, ablution block, four chalets, a craft shop and library at the Mbiroba Camp. One hundred people were now employed by the Trust, who received total wages of US$133,320 in 2002. Fishermen and craftspeople also sold items to the camp. However, the government was slow to allocate land and issue a tourism licence to this independent Trust (WTO, 2003a; OPT, nd).

Gudigwa Camp, northern Okavango Delta

In 2003, Conservation International (CI) launched an ecotourism joint venture with Wilderness Safaris and the Bukakhwe San (Bushmen) at Gudigwa village on the northern edge of the Okavango Delta. Gudigwa village, with 800 residents, was the largest San Bushman village in Botswana. In 1998, CI held educational workshops in Gudigwa that prompted the local Bushmen to protect wildlife and develop a cultural village (Michler, 2004). A community organization, the Bukakhwe Cultural Conservation Trust, supported an ecotourism project with CI based on San Bushmen culture. The resulting Gudigwa Camp opened in 2003, located 5 km away from Gudigwa village and 65 km north-east of the town of Seronga. The camp is an 8-hour drive from Maun or reached by a charter flight. Funded with US$400,000 from Conservation International and the European Union, the camp includes eight grass huts modelled on Bushmen huts with solar-powered lighting and hot bucket showers. Visitor activities included guided bushman walks (Asato, 2003, 2005), traditional dance and songs, storytelling, traditional food tasting and sorghum beer, fire making, spear throwing and buying local crafts. The ecotourism camp is 100% owned by the Bukakhwe Trust with marketing and camp bookings handled by Wilderness Safaris. Gudigwa Camp provided alternative income for the village and rejuvenated traditional Bushmen culture, with tourism income funding community development projects. The camp manager and assistant manger were both local San Bushman and more than 20 staff worked at the camp on a rotational basis (Mbaiwa, 2005b). Young San people became proud of their culture and wearing traditional skins again. The camp received 50 international tourists in the first 6 months of operation (Michler, 2004). The camp also aimed to reduce hunting pressure on wildlife and influence the San to adopt sustainable land use practices. A fence dividing Bukakhwe San land and blocking wildlife movement was to be realigned (CI, 2003). Gudigwa Camp was also a CBNRM site for tourism ventures (Hoon, 2004).

Okavango Community Trust

The Okavango Community Trust represented five villages with 5000 people in the northern Okavango Delta. These five communities of Seronga, Gunitonga, Eretsha, Beetsha and Gudigwa were located by Chief's Island, an area in high demand for wildlife tourism and hunting (Hoon, 2004). Gudigwa Camp and the Gudigwa village of San people were also part of the Okavango Community Trust. During 2000/01 the five villages negotiated a contract and tourism concession terms with WP Safaris, with a 3–2 result leading to a renewal, though most individuals had voted for a re-tender (Hoon, 2004). The Trust also managed the 89,000 ha Duba and Vumbura concession areas, leased to Wilderness Safaris to operate four small camps (Duba Plains, Kaparota, Vumbura and Little Vumbura).

The partnership between the Trust and Wilderness Safaris involves annual lease fees, the purchase of annual hunting quotas (unused since WS has a no hunting policy), jobs for 120 local people, training and skills development. Motswana people were trained

locally to become lodge managers. The company also provided medical services and assisted in business planning for local enterprises. The high cost of lease fees, trophy hunting fees, salaries, investment in the camps and a short tenure meant the Okavango camps were a marginal business for Wilderness Safaris (WS, 2004).

Modumo Lodge, northern Okavango Delta

A local man, Modumo Sehitheng, and a non-citizen partner developed Modumo Lodge in the northern Okavango with a commercial loan from the Botswana National Development Bank. Born near Eretsha and Betsha villages, Modumo worked in private safari lodges where he learned about ecotourism and conservation. He noticed that wildlife numbers were decreasing around his local village due to local and safari hunting. In 1998, he formed a company with family members, lobbied authorities to stop hunting in the region, and applied to the Land Board for a concession to operate a safari lodge based on viewing wildlife. The annual lease fee was BWP60,000. Without financial or technical support from the government, a non-citizen helped design the lodge and provided collateral to finance the lodge. The 16-bed lodge was built with local labour and materials and employs 25 people from nearby villages. Wildlife numbers increased in the area with wild dogs, leopard and cheetah seen again. However, Modumo was disappointed with the lack of government support for training staff and marketing local community lodges in the Okavango Delta (Michler, 2004).

Zimbabwe

CAMPFIRE: Communal Areas Management Program for Indigenous Resources

Established in 1988, the CAMPFIRE project in Zimbabwe allowed local communities to manage natural resources such as wildlife on communal lands and to sell wildlife quotas to hunting operators. In the early 1980s, Rural District Councils were granted legal authority to manage wildlife resources. Fifty-three Rural District Councils were members of CAMPFIRE with authority to enter agreements with private wildlife operators and devolve wildlife revenue to wards and local villages (Jonga, 2003). Communities retained the income from wildlife ventures that was spent on village facilities such as schools, health clinics, roads and bridges, water bores, grinding mills, tractors and fences. In CAMPFIRE projects, wildlife conservation was linked to community benefits from safari hunting and wildlife tourism on communal lands that comprised 42% of Zimbabwe (Maveneke, 1998; Maveneke et al., 1998; Crawford, 2000; Heath, 2001; Murombedzi, 2001, 2003; ART, 2004; Parliament of Victoria, 2004; WWF, 2004a; Boniface and Cooper, 2005). The CAMPFIRE project operated in the mid-Zambezi River valley, south-east lowlands and Matabeleland, mainly in communal lands around protected areas that were wildlife-rich regions. The programme was managed by the CAMPFIRE Association with technical support from WWF and funded by USAID, the EU, and the Norwegian government development agency NORAD (WWF, 2004a). Local communities involved in CAMPFIRE leased safari hunting or photographic tourism concessions to private tour companies. By 1993, 23 CAMPFIRE districts earned revenue from wildlife tourism leases (Crawford, 2000). By generating local revenue from wildlife, CAMPFIRE reduced poaching of wildlife, improved attitudes to wildlife, reduced tree cutting and indiscriminate settlements, funded rural infrastructure, and increased household incomes by 15–25% in rural areas (Weaver, 1998; Scheyvens, 2002a).

Communal areas in 37 of Zimbabwe's 57 districts were involved in the CAMPFIRE scheme by 2002. In 1998, CAMPFIRE generated income of US$1.9 million for 3 million local people in 35 rural districts (WWF, 2004a). The 1999 CAMPFIRE income was US$2.75 million, with US$222 for 319,000 households (USAID, 2004). From 1989 to 2001, US$10 million was paid as dividends to local communities, representing 46% of total revenue earned (Jonga, 2003). Ninety-three per cent of this CAMPFIRE income was earned from sport hunting leases with just 2% of income (US$200,000) from tourism leases

(Maveneke et al., 1998). Hunting safaris were mobile, self-contained ventures that required few facilities and paid high trophy fees (e.g. US$8363 for an elephant in 2001). Ecotourism ventures required more visitor infrastructure and a higher level of services in land areas set aside for wildlife viewing rather than hunting. Most CAMPFIRE communities preferred the higher income from sport hunting rather than investment in ecotourism facilities (Baker, 1997; Buckley, 2003b; Murphree, 2003). The USAID funding from 1997 to 2000 focused on diversifying CAMPFIRE activities to include ecotourism ventures, crafts, fisheries and forestry products (USAID, 2004). CAMPFIRE initiated ecotourism ventures included the Sunungukai ecotourism camp and the Vhimba Wilderness Area. The Omay and Mukwichi communal lands in the Zambezi Valley of north-west Zimbabwe also had leases for game viewing ecotourism activities. In the Hurungwe District, a community entered a contract in 1993 with a private operator to run walking safaris from a tented camp. In 1994, the community built their own tourist camp of three rondavels (huts) and a campsite beside a river. Local people were more involved in these ventures than with hunting safaris negotiated by a council (Bird, 1995, 1997).

CAMPFIRE was consumptive ecotourism based on controlled sport hunting of wildlife (McIvor, 1994; Wilson, 1998; Sinclair and Pack, 2000; Scheyvens, 2002a). Conflicts within CAMPFIRE included the uneven distribution of benefits to areas with wildlife, access and infrastructure, disagreements between district councils and local villages, control of CAMPFIRE income by Rural District Councils and local elites, and land ownership disputes. Local households were not compensated for crop damage, livestock killed by wildlife, or resettlement to create community wildlife parks. Other factors affecting CAMPFIRE include the political turmoil and downturn in tourism since 2000, inflation, 70% unemployment, increased poaching, illegal hunting and the resettlement of people in wildlife and safari areas in Zimbabwe (Alexander and McGregor, 2000; Manwa, 2003; Virtanen, 2003). WWF and USAID support for CAMPFIRE ended in 2003. CAMPIRE mainly supported community-based tourism in eastern Zimbabwe (SAFIRE, nd).

Sunungukai ecotourism camp

The Sunungukai Ecotourism Camp was established in 1993 as part of the CAMPFIRE scheme in Zimbabwe. This camp was the first tourism venture run directly by local communities in CAMPFIRE (Crawford, 2000). Most other CAMPFIRE initiatives involved communities leasing their wildlife quotas to safari hunting operators or tourism leases for game walking and photographic safaris on communal lands in Zimbabwe. The Sunungukai camp was a non-consumptive ecotourism venture, adjacent to the Umfurudzi Safari Area, a protected area with scenic mountains. The Sunungukai camp with four chalets and a campsite was located on the Mazowe River 120 km north-east of Harare. The camp was built and managed by people from five rural villages with construction materials for the Sunungukai camp funded by the Zimbabwe Trust and New Zealand High Commission (Scheyvens, 1999). A Sunungukai management committee developed rules of natural resource use on fishing and forest use and also managed the ecotourism camp. Only single hook line fishing was allowed for local people and camp visitors while gold panning and crop cultivation was banned on the riverbanks (Odero and Huchu, 1998). Visitor activities at Sunungukai included viewing crocodiles and hippos, cultural tours of nearby villages, bird watching, fishing and guided walks to view cave paintings or wildlife. The Rural District Council organized bookings for the camp, oversaw financial records and provided transport for training and study tours (Scheyvens, 1999).

The camp was built on 1 ha of land at Kapandaro Village, with the land owner receiving 10% of camp proceeds and 5–10% paid in levies to the Rural District Council that provided technical support (Odero and Huchu, 1998). Local villagers became members of the project by paying ZW$10 and contributing free labour for camp construction and maintenance. Local people provided thatching grass and poles and made mud bricks to build the camp. In 1998, there were 65 community members of Sunungukai camp, mainly from the three closest villages. New members paid ZW$240 and provided 2000 bricks

(Scheyvens, 1999). The camp employed three local people and casual guides. With low occupancy rates (< 5%), the camp only paid its first dividend of ZW$120 to members in 1997 with 25% allocated for camp development, 15% to the district council and 5% to a primary school (Scheyvens, 1999, 2003). Tourism income was used for camp maintenance and to pay staff.

The camp was included in *Lonely Planet* and *Rough Guide* handbooks but the area lacked a two-way radio and telephones to book the campsite, while the Ministry of Transport removed road signs for the camp. The lack of tourism management experience and ad hoc support from local institutions, along with logistical difficulties and marketing issues limited community returns from this ecotourism venture (Scheyvens, 1999, 2003). The Sunungukai project promoted sustainable use of natural resources and the economic benefits of ecotourism for rural people. Crocodiles and baboons were no longer killed as they had been prior to the ecotourism venture. However, activities such as gold panning on riverbanks, fishing with nets and poaching from the adjacent safari area still took place due to limited income. Some members lost interest due to poor returns, with few people cutting grass around the camp. A canoeing venture with the nearby 'Hippo Pools' operator was suggested as a way to boost visitors at Sunungukai camp. The local African manager also did not support women working as tour guides at Sunungukai and preferred they do domestic camp tasks (Scheyvens, 1999, 2003).

Vhimba Wilderness Area

Vhimba is a remote rural area in south-east Zimbabwe near the border with Mozambique. This area has the last subtropical lowland forests in Zimbabwe with rich birdlife and other rare fauna. Vhimba is located to the south of Chimanimani Mountains National Park. Some 400–500 visitors a year visited the forests at Vhimba, with American and British bird-watchers brought on day trips. Some visitors paid ZW$10 to stay with local families. In 1974, local Ndau people were removed and not allowed to gather forest products when the forests were gazetted as reserves. The Ndau people had preserved the core area of each forest, with a ritual ceremony held to appease spirits. Local people derived income from selling bananas and citrus fruit (men) and wild forest fruit (women). In 1996, the Vhimba community was allowed to manage non-consumptive activities in the forest, charging visitor fees for entry, camping and bird watching tours. There was some poaching of butterflies, ferns and bird's eggs from the forest with local children trying to sell birds to visitors. The local community formed a committee to manage forest use and develop ecotourism; they visited the Sunungukai ecotourism camp and an up-market lodge joint venture at Mahenye. The community decided to build a chalet and campsites with an interpretive centre, forest trails and a crafts centre. Visitor activities included bird and butterfly watching, cultural tours and canoeing the Rusitu River. Local NGOs and government agencies developed a strategy for community-based ecotourism at Vhimba. Eighty per cent of ecotourism income was to be used for community development and 20% went to the Rural District Council. By 1998 the community had not yet obtained funding for the ecotourism venture, though a grinding mill and water supply projects were installed (Scheyvens, 1999). However, stone lodges and camping sites were developed at the Vhimba Wilderness Area and marketed by SAFIRE (Southern Alliance for Indigenous Resources), a Zimbabwe NGO supporting community tourism projects.

Hughes (2001) provides an alternative view of the Vhimba ecotourism project on Ngorima Communal Land. This fertile region supported banana plantations, fruit crops, tea and coffee. In Vhimba, fruit sales generated US$4851 in 1994 while the projected ecotourism venture would return US$1924. In 1996, a British expatriate received district council approval to develop backpacker lodges at Vhimba. A joint venture was proposed with the Vhimba community, still waiting on funding from CAMPFIRE to develop their ecotourism venture. However, the local Vhimba committee rejected this proposal. Local lodge owners and hotels proposed other tourism ventures on the Ngorima Reserve. The district council supported tourism training for locals and dis-

sauded the Vhimba from building their campsite. The conversion of farmland to tourism areas and the 2000 downturn in tourism reduced potential tourism income in the Vhimba area. A feasibility study of chalets at Vhimba projected start-up costs of US$290,754 (funded by international donors), for returns of US$1471 per hectare at full occupancy. Ecotourism investors in communal reserves received state and donor subsidies to protect natural areas while the CAMPFIRE programme encouraged local people to limit or sell their use of natural resources. Ecotourism projects such as Vhimba aided the commercial use of communal lands (Hughes, 2001).

Mahenye Safari Lodge

The Mahenye Safari Lodge is located next to the 5000 km^2 Gonarezhou National Park in south-east Zimbabwe. The lodge with eight thatched chalets is built among riverine forest of wild mango and sausage trees on Geyseni Island in the Save River. Mahenye Lodge is a joint venture with the local Shangaan community at Mahenye village. The lodge was developed as part of the CAMPFIRE programme with annual lease fees and a percentage of lodge revenue paid to Mahenye village (Murphree, 2000, 2001). Visitors at the lodge are shown a traditional Shangaan home, and told about the CAMPFIRE programme at Mahenye. Other attractions are a sacred forest near the village with numerous birds and plant species, canoeing on Save River, Chivirira Falls; game drives and walks in Gonarezhou, Tambahata pan for water birds, and sandstone cliffs of Chilojo. Chilo Gorge Safari Lodge, 5 km from Mahenye Lodge, was also developed with the Shangaan community (RLA, 2004).

In 1968, the Mahenye and other people were forcibly removed from Gonarezhou Park (Hove, 2000).

The Mahenye community owned 210 km^2 of land between the Save River and Rupembi River on the border with Mozambique. In 1987, the Mahenye community set aside 15,000 ha as a wildlife conservancy for hunting and ecotourism activities. International donors such as GTZ (Germany), USAID, the Netherlands, and WWF, and local NGOs such as the Zimbabwe Trust and

Africa Resources Trust supported the Mahenye CAMPFIRE project. Most of the funding went to local NGOs and the Rural District Council with little funding to Mahenye. In 2000, donor funding ended and a ward CAMPFIRE committee and local leaders now manage the Mahenye project. They set wildlife quotas with game guards monitoring wildlife and managing all village projects (ART, 2002). A tourist village was also constructed to present the traditional architecture and way of life.

The Mahenye community also sold hunting concessions for wildlife on their communal lands, as part of the CAMPFIRE programme. In 1991, Mahenye received US$19,111 as revenue from hunting safaris. With a limit on sustainable hunting of wildlife, the Chipinge Rural District Council and Mahenye community entered a commercial joint venture with the Zimbabwe Sun Group for a safari lodge based on game viewing (ART, 2002). In 1996, Mahenye community earned revenues of around US$6000 each from hunting safaris and the tourism lodge. In 1997, Mahenye Safari Lodge generated village revenue of US$15,516 and local wages of US$14,923 compared to hunting revenues of just US$6814 (Murphree, 2000, 2001; Hutton and Dickson, 2002). From 1997 to 1999, the tourism lodge generated more revenue than sport hunting leases for Mahenye. However, with the downturn in tourism, in 2000 revenue from Mahenye Lodge declined to ZW$396,980 while sport hunting revenues at Mahenye substantially increased to ZW$1,085,544. From 1990 to 2000, the total income generated at Mahenye from sport hunting was US$56,480 (58% of revenue) while the tourism lodge generated US$38,642 (40% of revenue). Revenue from hunting and tourism was allocated as household dividends, to pay a District Council levy, for wildlife management and for local community projects such as a school, clinic, borehole, grinding mill and a watering point for domestic livestock (Hove, 2000; ART, 2002).

Kairezi ecotourism project

The Kairezi ecotourism project started in 2000/01 with the construction of two campsites on the Kairezi River. The Nyanga Rural District Council initiated this CAMPFIRE project in 1998, with the campsites located in the Tangwena Resettlement Area. USAID funded the Kairezi ecotourism project on communal land next to the Kairezi River Protected Area. Protecting the trout fishing stocks and controlling the impacts of grazing, tree cutting, bushfires, and illegal settlements were key aims of the project. Local people were employed in fisheries management and as tour guides. The Nyanga Downs Flyfishing Club marketed the Kairezi ecotourism project and campsite, which mainly focused on maintaining and monitoring trout fishing stocks in the river. Tourism revenue at Kairezi was generated from sport fishing fees plus visitor accommodation in chalets or campsites. The Kairezi Development Trust managed this ecotourism project on behalf of the local community (WTO, 2003d).

Namibia

Namibia is a desert country between Angola, Botswana and South Africa that, in 1990, became an independent nation. From 1884, it was a German colony known as South-West Africa then ruled by South Africa from 1920. The spectacular desert scenery, wildlife, unique flora, vast wilderness areas and traditional cultures are key tourist features. The San people or Bushmen are one of the main Indigenous groups, with 38,275 San in Namibia and over 104,000 San in southern Africa (Mbaiwa, 2005a). The Herero, Himba (Jacobsohn, 1993; Bollig and Heinemann, 2004), Damara/Nama and Basubia are other tribal groups. Key tourist attractions include Etosha National Park, the Namib Desert dunes at Sossusvlei, and Fish River Canyon. Protected areas comprise about 15% of Namibia, mainly in the desert regions. Tourism is the fastest growing industry in Namibia, increasing at a rate of 8.5% per annum. Sixty per cent of tourists are from South Africa, 11% from Germany, and the rest from UK, Europe, North America and other African countries. The accommodation and transport infrastructure is well developed in Namibia (Echtner, 1999). However, citizens of European origin and expatriates dominate Namibia's private tourism industry. At the time of independence in 1990, 40.8% of land was allocated to Indigenous homelands, 43% to mainly white farmers, and 13.6% to conservation areas (Jones, 1998). Since independence, the Namibia Ministry of Environment and Tourism (MET, 2005a, b) implemented policies and legislation to develop communal area conservancies and community-based tourism enterprises. In June 1995, MET produced two key policies on Wildlife Management, Utilisation and Tourism in Communal Areas, and on Community-Based Tourism Development. These were supported in 1996 by amendments to the Nature Conservation Act and Regulations to allow conservancies to own, use and benefit from wildlife in communal land areas. A 1998 Tourism Act also gave communal conservancies the right to operate or lease tourism concessions on their lands. These policies and legislative change formed the basis for establishing communal area conservancies with community management of natural resources, local rights to earn income from wildlife, and the development of tourism ventures on communal lands. These wildlife conservation and tourism activities in registered communal land areas are supported by MET and the Namibia Community Based Tourism Association (NACOTBA) (Nicanor, 2001).

Communal Area Conservancies

Conservancies are unfenced communal land areas (45% of Namibia) registered as multiple use land areas and managed by an elected committee of community members. Community members have common property rights over wildlife and are legally entitled to generate income from wildlife resources in conservancies. Revenue goes directly to the conservancy rather than to district councils as in Zimbabwe's CAMPFIRE programme. The rationale for communal conservancies was community-based natural resource management and generating community income from wildlife resources in rural areas (Ashley, 1995, 2000; Ashley and Elliott, 2003; DeMotts, 2004; Vertefeuille and Benn, 2005). This matched the rights of commercial farmers that had

established 24 private wildlife conservancies (900 farms) in Namibia since 1968 (Jones, 1995, 1998; Jacobsohn, 2000; Barnes et al., 2002). Community members zoned land areas in conservancies for grazing, agriculture, exclusive wildlife use, and tourism, both safari hunting and wildlife viewing. Conservancies can recommend wildlife quotas, enter agreements with private tourism operators and establish their own tourism facilities on conservancy land. Members elect a committee that manages natural resources and distributes income from hunting and tourism activities (Jones, 1998). The first four communal area conservancies in Namibia, registered in 1998, were Nyae Nyae (northern Kalahari), Salambala (Caprivi), Torra and #Khoadi//Hoas (Kunene). All four conservancies manage tourism concessions including trophy hunting, wildlife lodges, and campsites (Miranda, 1999).

There were 31 communal conservancies covering over 78,000 km^2 or 22% of communal lands and representing some 100,000 members in these registered conservancies. Seventeen communal conservancies are adjacent to or located between state protected areas, providing an additional 47,515 km^2 of land for wildlife to roam (Bandyopadhyay et al., 2004). Twenty conservancies were located in the north-west region of Namibia, in desert and savanna areas inland from the Skeleton Coast, with seven conservancies in north-east Namibia mainly in the woodland region of the Caprivi Strip. Another 56 communities covering 5 million hectares and 50,000–60,000 people were also seeking registration as conservancies (Davis, 2003, 2004). By September 2005 there were 42 registered communal conservancies in Namibia (MET, 2005e). Conservancies employ community game guards for wildlife patrols and female resource monitors. Wildlife numbers have increased in communal area conservancies and ecotourism ventures or trophy hunting is a significant source of income for conservancies in the Kunene and Caprivi regions (WWF, 1999, 2001, 2004b; Barnes et al., 2001; Murphy and Halstead, 2003; DEA, 2004a, b; IRDNC, 2004; NACSO, 2004b). In 2002, 374 conservancy members had full-time tourism jobs, with another 3136 people involved in part-time work as trackers, craft makers and other services (Davis, 2003). A 2004 USAID study found that communal conservancies generated income from community-based tourism enterprises and campsites (35%), joint tourism ventures (27%) and trophy hunting (21%) (Novelli and Humavindu, 2005).

Since the early 1990s, WWF, USAID, UK, Canada, Sweden, Norway and other agencies provided donor funding for communal area conservancies and CBNRM in Namibia. WWF (2005a, b, c) has supported Project LIFE (Living in a Finite Environment) in Namibia to preserve wildlife and develop community conservancies in the Kunene desert region since 1993. Technical support and training for communal conservancies is provided by Namibian NGOs, such as Integrated Rural Development and Nature Conservation (IRDNC) in the Kunene (since 1982) and Caprivi regions, and the Namibia Association of CBNRM Support Organisations (NACSO) set up in 1999 with working groups on tourism and enterprise development (Baker, 2003). The Namibia Community Based Tourism Association (NACOTBA) supports conservancies in negotiating joint venture tourism leases or developing tourism facilities on their lands. Humphrey and Boonzaaier (2003) evaluated joint venture contracts for nine tourism concessions located on Torra, #Khoadi//Hoas and Omihana communal conservancies. Three had lease payments ranging from NAR3000 to NAR80, 454 while the annual return per tourist bed ranged from NAR914 to NAR3352 (average NAR1673). Six concessions paid royalties ranging from 0 to 12.5% (average 5.9%). For concessions with a fixed lease and royalty payment, the royalties were 5–6%. The private tourism agreements with conservancies ranged from 5 to 30 years (av. 18 years), plus concession income, employment, training, a camp and service contracts.

Community-based Tourism

Community-based tourism enterprises and joint ventures are a key land use on conservancies. Tourism on conservancies provides income, employment, involves community members in tourism decision-making and operations, develops skills and

provides an incentive for wildlife conservation. Community-based tourism ventures include cultural villages, craft outlets, campsites, rest camps, and tour guide associations. Ashley and Garland (1994) evaluated the financial viability and socio-economic impacts of four kinds of tourism ventures in communal areas: private up-market lodge (no community involvement), private up-market lodge (revenue sharing with community), joint venture up-market lodge, and community tourism enterprises such as campsites and crafts (see Table 5.2). The report emphasized communal areas attracting higher paying ecotourism markets. Other non-cash benefits were the extent of community control over tourism development and tourist interactions and donations of game animals to restock wildlife in communal conservancies. A 1994 Namibia Tourism Development Plan emphasized tourism opportunities on communal lands providing economic and conservation benefits, while growing ecotourism markets in rural areas (Ashley and Garland, 1994). In 2003, the MET supported the development of community lodges on conservancies (MET, 2005c).

In 2000, community-based tourism generated revenue of NAR1.5 million out of a total NAR3.5 million from CBNRM activities on conservancies. Joint venture lodges such as the Damaraland Camp in Torra Conservancy provided an additional NAR375,000 in revenue. Of this overall total, 46% was from community-owned tourism ventures, 23% from game donations (non-cash benefit), 12% from trophy hunting, 11% from joint ventures (Damaraland Camp), 3% from craft sales and 1% from cultural tourism. By 2005, income from CBNRM was expected to reach NAR10 million with joint venture tourism projected to be the largest source of income for conservancies. Joint ventures paid bed night levies, site rental fees, annual fees as a flat fee and a percentage of business income: with game for hunting, plus training and employment for locals. The market value of community resources in joint ventures was access to pristine land, utilization rights over wildlife in concession leases, and marketing ethical or cultural developments to ecotourists to offset costs of revenue sharing (Ashley and

Table 5.2. Community-based tourism development in Namibia.

Tourism approach	Possible enterprise	Examples
1. Investor-controlled venture with local employment	Hunting concession: professional hunters	Anova Safaris, Bushmanland
	Hunting concession: traditional trackers[a]	*Eastern Bushmanland*
	Luxury wildlife lodges in communal areas	Kunene and Caprivi
2. Private investor sharing revenue with the community	Luxury lodge with bed night levy paid to the local community	Lianshulu Lodge, East Caprivi
3. Outside investor in profit sharing joint venture with community	Luxury lodge with profit sharing between entrepreneur and the community	Damaraland Camp, Kunene
	Private and community enterprises[a]	*Lizauli Traditional Village set up with the help of Lianshulu Lodge*
4. Community-controlled enterprise	Up-market community campsite	Bagani campsite, West Caprivi
	Community campsite	Ongongo and Khowarib, Kunene Nganga and Ugab River, Kunene
	Community campsite	Salambala and Mayuni, Caprivi
	Basic campsite, cultural interaction[b] (*community dances, foraging walks, photos*)	*Makuri campsite, Bushmanland*
	Cultural village and craft sales	Lizauli Traditional Village, Caprivi Anmire Cultural Village, Kunene
	Tourist restcamp and cultural centre	Spitzkoppe, Usakos town, Erongo
	Bwabwata National Park campsites	Bumhill and Nambwa campsites

[a] 'Supply-driven' enterprises indicated in italics.
[b] Makuri campsite – revenue from cultural services paid to providers, campsite revenue goes in a community fund.
Bushmanland is now Otjozondjupa Region, Kunene Region was formerly Kaokoland and northern Damaraland.
Sources: Ashley and Garland (1994: 8); Rice and Gibson (2001); *NACOBTA Newsletter* (2003); IRDNC

Garland, 1994). Other tourism-related businesses included selling vegetables to lodges and firewood to campers; donkey-cart rides and *mokoro* (canoe) rides; guided walks; and a tyre repair centre and restaurant in the Kunene region. Tourism fostered local rural enterprises in communal lands (DEA, 2004a, b). The CBNRM programme also provides economic benefits for local people, with community game guards reinforcing the cultural connection to wildlife (Jones, 1999; Jones and Murphree, 2001).

The Namibia Tourism Development Programme, funded by NAR4 million from the European Union, supported CBNRM and community tourism projects from 1998 to 2005. From 2004, MET received a grant of US$7 million from the GEF for an integrated community-based ecosystem management project on registered conservancies. As part of

this, a community funding facility supported local income-generating projects such as the development or maintenance of tourism infrastructure, facilities and services, with conservancies contributing 10% in cash or kind to these projects (MET, 2005d, e). The Namibia Community Based Tourism Association (NACOTBA) also provides technical support, business training, legal advice and a booking system for conservancy tourism ventures.

Namibia Community Based Tourism Association (NACOBTA)

The Namibia Community Based Tourism Association (NACOBTA) was established in 1995. NACOBTA has a management committee of seven elected community members and a support staff of seven people that provides technical support and training to members. NACOBTA supports communal conservancies and other communities developing tourism ventures. The 54 members of NACOBTA include community campsites, rest camps, cultural villages, craft centres, museums, and community associations of tour guides. In February 2004, some 34 of these community tourism ventures were operating with others still in development. Most of the community tourism enterprises were located in the Kunene, Caprivi and Erongo regions of northern Namibia. In 2002, NACOBTA opened a booking office for these community-based tourism enterprises and established a Joint Venture Unit to facilitate the tendering and selection of private sector partners for rural communities developing tourism. In 2002, community tourism employed 160 full-time people and over 20 part-time staff, earned NAR3.2 million in gross income, NAR1.3 million in net income and paid NAR942,047 in salaries. The ventures attracted over 70,000 tourists in 2002 and over 90,000 tourists in 2004. Of total income earned in Namibia's CBNRM programme in 2002, 83% derived from tourism on communal areas. WWF, USAID, NACSO, the Green Development Fund, SIDA, Austria, Sweden and the EU all fund NACOBTA. The Association supports community tourism for rural development and building up local businesses aided by private investors (Wouter, 1999; Roe *et al.*, 2001; NACOBTA, 2003). NACOBTA was funded by USAID, mainly the joint venture unit, but needed to find other long-term funding. Service support to tourism enterprises on conservancies was being reduced, complying with standards set by the Namibian Tourist Board, but tourism marketing continued (NACOBTA, 2005). Support from the European Union for tourism development in Namibia also ended in June 2005.

Spitzkoppe community rest camp

In 1992, the Damara community constructed a tourist rest camp at Spitzkoppe, with funding and assistance from WWF, NACOTBA, Namibia Development Trust and other

agencies. Tourists had long visited the rock art at Spitzkoppe granite outcrops near the town of Usakos in the Erongo region of Namibia. The 1728 m Greater Spitzkoppe massif also attracted many climbers. This community project started with a few small campsites and donations from visitors then building materials, training, and loans were sought from NGOs to further develop the site. The rest camp around Spitzkoppe Mountain had two bungalows, 28 campsites, a restaurant and bar, and a crafts and cultural centre. Other tourist activities were donkey cart rides, hiking and climbing guides, cultural performances and a souvenir stall. The project aimed to create employment and income, sell gemstones and crafts to tourists and assist conservation of the area. Twenty community members were employed at the rest camp and trained in tourism and hospitality. A community development com-mittee was established to oversee all tourist activities and projects at Spitzkoppe rest camp. Entrance gates and a visitor reception area were added while signs advised visitors not to litter, drive off road or damage rock art at the site. Water conservation measures were put in place such as charging for water, water meters on taps and reusing shower water in toilets. Visitor numbers grew from 2300 in 1999 to about 5000 people in 2000 when the rest camp generated income of NAR220,000 (US$20,000). Revenue from Spitzkoppe went to a community trust and funded community development projects such as the primary school, support for the elderly and to help pay for funerals. A Damara community of 700 people lived at Spitzkoppe and ran the tourist rest camp. Day visitors paid entrance fees to the Spitzkoppe community, with income used to maintain paths and other facilities. An investment saving account was established with funds used to build the bar and restaurant and to upgrade visitor facilities. Spitzkoppe was also registered as a communal area conservancy and applied for an exclusive tourism concession. The community proposed a joint venture with a private investor to build a tourist lodge at the site (Gariseb *et al.*, 2002; Buckley, 2003a). In 2005, a new arts and crafts shop opened at Spitzkoppe (Kanzler, M., 2005). The new National Heritage Council managed other rock art sites in Namibia such as Brandberg and Twyfelfontein with 65% of visitor entrance fees used to pay for staff salaries, training of guides and other community projects. Local guides at these rock art sites now received only 35% of income (Kanzler, S.E., 2005).

Nyae Nyae Conservancy

The Nyae Nyae Conservancy was the first communal area conservancy in Namibia, registered in February 1998. The conservancy is located in the Okavango flooded savannahs of the northern Kalahari in north-east Namibia. It mainly includes Ju'/hoansi San Bushmen members, living around the village of Tsumkwe in the Otjozondjupa Region or East Bushmanland area. The Nyae Nyae conservancy has 2000 people spread over 30 villages. Herero herders also grazed their cattle in this area. South African and Namibian adventure travellers had long visited the area, camped freely, paid for dances and bought artefacts cheaply from Bushmen villages (Boynton, 1997; Wouter, 1999). In the mid-1990s, Nyae Nyae Bushmen approached local tour operators about visiting this area. The Bushmen sought a share of profits rather than just payment as guides and trackers. With the area declared a communal conservancy, the Bushmen were also restricted from hunting (Isaacson, 2001). To control access, off-road driving routes with signs were established, with campsites spread across the area. The Makuri campsite was built using local labour and materials (Ashley and Garland, 1994).

The Nyae Nyae Conservancy provides sport hunting of wildlife, guided cultural tours and a joint venture lodge. Income from Bushmen cultural activities such as tracking and food gathering trails exceeded income from bed night levies. With a local interpreter, visitors joined the Ju'/hoansi to track game, gather bush food and learn hunting techniques. The Bushmen wore their beaded traditional skins on tourist trips but hunters now used PVC pipes as a quiver to keep poisoned arrows dry (Weaver, 2000). A trophy hunting agreement worth NAR175,000 (US$30,000) over 2 years was negotiated soon after registration of the conservancy (Jones,

1998). The conservancy received over NAR3 million (US$280,000) in grants from WWF, the UK Department for International Development and the Nyae-Nyae Development Foundation of Namibia. NACOTBA and the Rossing Foundation also provided assistance in business training and craft development. The funding was used to build infrastructure including a wildlife-holding pen, purchase vehicles, to employ 20 local staff and train community members in tourism skills and wildlife conservation. The conservancy applied for tourism concession rights and negotiated with investors to build a tourist lodge. Income was derived from trophy hunting, donations and grants, and tourism. Community members participated in the translocation of hartebeest, oryx and other animals to replenish wildlife in the area. Illegal hunting of wildlife was also reduced in the conservancy area. Young Ju'/hoansi people joined in leading the guided tours, gaining cultural skills and knowledge (Gariseb, 2000; Buckley, 2003a). According to Epler Wood (2003), however, this 5-year aid project had limited success in funding a nature reserve on Ju'/hoansi Bushmen land, linked with ecotourism and hunting, with little support for Ju'/hoansi farmers and a lack of interest from some Ju'/hoansi in continuing a hunting and gathering way of life. For Wyckoff-Baird (2000) the conservancy allowed the Ju'/hoansi to manage wildlife and resources, although one local steward charged villagers fees to collect plant materials used for making craftwork.

#Khoadi//Hoas Conservancy

The #Khoadi//Hoas Conservancy covers an area of 3640 km^2 near Grootberg in the Kunene south or Damaraland region of northwest Namibia. The Damara/Nama name for the conservancy, with click sounds in the Khoi-Khoi language, means Elephant's Corner. Namibia government programmes to control desertification and range development and NACOSA funded the conservancy, along with technical support from WWF and the Namibia Nature Foundation. The Grootberg Farmers Association, a community-based group, also helped establish the conservancy in 1998. Tribal groups in the area included Damara/

Nama people with minority groups of Herero, Ovambo and San Bushmen. There were four main villages, eight farming districts and 10,000 people in the conservancy area. The conservancy area had up to 230 desert elephants and other wildlife with 80,000 ha set aside as an exclusive wildlife/tourism zone. Community tourism camping sites were located near wildlife watering points. The conservancy combined hunting, tourism campsites and livestock farming. Income was generated from trophy hunting and also from selling livestock. In 1999, hunting income provided NAR45,000 increasing to NAR144,504 in 2001 (NAR136,504 in cash and NAR8,000 in salaries). However, a private hunting operator in the area would not share revenue with conservancy members. After two years of negotiations about the new cooperative arrangements the Ministry of Environment and Tourism did not renew this hunting concession lease, forcing the operator to negotiate. There were also conflicts between traditional authorities and the inclusion of the Hobatere concession area as part of #Koahi//Hoas (Schiffer, 2004).

A funding gap also limited the development of tourism enterprises and wildlife management plans for sustainable wildlife utilization. The community employed ten wildlife shepherds to monitor wildlife and livestock, and wildlife poaching declined to almost zero. Tourism income was spent on local schools and to compensate local farmers for elephants damaging property (WWF, 2005a). In 2002, the conservancy covered 25% of its operating costs with a site negotiated for a new joint-venture lodge. The lodge would potentially generate over NAR200,000 a year in cash income. In 2004, #Khoadi//Hoas were still seeking a private investor for a tourist lodge at Klip River, a remote site with limited water (Goagoseb and Gariseb, 2000; Buckley, 2003a; NACSO, 2004c; Schiffer, 2004). However, the Grootberg Community Lodge with 12 luxury rooms opened on the #Khoadi//Hoas Conservancy in July 2005. The European Union (EU) provided funding of NAR4.5 million to develop the Grootberg Lodge, the first community-owned lodge, through the Namibia Tourism Development Programme (WWF, 2005b). A private business

partner, EcoLogistix, undertook staff training, maintenance and marketing for this community-owned lodge. A percentage of income and profits was paid to the conservancy, with the lodge expected to provide income of NAR300,000 in the first year of operation. The conservancy owned all fixed assets and 20 local people worked at the lodge. The conservancy also set aside 12,000 ha of land for tourism and conserved desert wildlife in this area (MET, 2005c).

Torra Conservancy

The Torra Conservancy covers 8000 km^2 of desert and semi-arid savannah in the Central Kunene Region, adjoining the Skeleton Coast Park. The Damara tribal group and Riemvasmakers, relocated from South Africa in the 1970s, manage the conservancy registered in 1998. About 1000 people live in the conservancy at Bergsig village and on remote farm posts spread around the arid area. IRDNC provided technical support and half the running costs for Torra in the beginning (Rice and Gibson, 2001). In mid-2001, Torra became the first financially self-sustaining conservancy, meeting management costs and making a profit. In the mid-1980s, IRDNC introduced community game guards at Torra to protect wildlife. Six game guards are employed at Torra, which is a key habitat for desert elephant and the endangered black rhinoceros. The Torra community was among the first to be granted wildlife harvest quotas and to sell sport hunting rights to selected wildlife in 1999. Torra also pioneered live game sales of 500 springbok. Another 847 springbok were captured for sale in 2003, with income of NAR211,750 going to Torra (45%) and shared with two neighbouring conservancies (WWF, 2003a). Commercial poaching has ceased in the Torra area with five cases of illegal hunting in 1998/99 and two small incidents in 2001. Once, meat from a trophy-hunted animal was stolen from the conservancy office (Jacobsohn, 2000; Long, 2002). Key issues for herders in the Torra Conservancy were stock losses due to predators, elephants raiding gardens, threats to human life and wildlife grazing pressure during times of drought (Long, 2002). With tourism increasing in the area, local residents opened a shop, a bar/restaurant and a tyre repair shop. A community campsite and third joint venture were also planned in the conservancy (NACSO, 2004c). In 2003, trophy hunting generated income of US$17,165 for Torra Conservancy. Torra also entered a new 3-year trophy hunting contract with Savannah Safaris for a minimum income of US$49,975 (WWF, 2003a). In 2004, Torra Conservancy won the UNEP Equator Initiative Award for managing sustainable hunting and ecotourism ventures. The US$30,000 award is for communities that conserve biodiversity and alleviate poverty in developing countries. The Conservancy started a breeding centre for sheep, goats and cows, to replace livestock killed by predators and thus stop farmers killing wildlife. The Torra Conservancy now covered its management costs and funded local community projects (WWF, 2005a).

Damaraland Camp

In 1996, Torra entered an agreement with Wilderness Safaris Namibia (WS) for an up-market tourist lodge, with 10% of profits paid to the conservancy (Jones, 1998). The Damaraland Camp was the first joint venture between a communal area conservancy and a private investor. The conservancy had a government lease for the land where the lodge was located (WTO, 2003c). The operator paid Torra an annual rent and a bed night levy. This generated income of NAR380,000 during 1997 to 1999. By 2002, the Camp was fully staffed and managed by local Torra residents. The current Damaraland Camp manager was a local woman who had started working as a waitress. During negotiations, members of Torra Conservancy pushed WS for more senior training and transferring ownership rather than a percentage increase in their share of revenue (Ashley and Jones, 2001). In 2007, the Torra Conservancy has the option to take over the camp as its own business, phased in over 5 years (Jacobsohn, 2000; Rice and Gibson, 2001). The Camp buildings, equipment and infrastructure were valued at US$458,000 in 2000 (WTO, 2003b).

The Camp staff received free housing, electricity and water. One staff member started pig farming using food waste from the Camp. Farmers living near the Camp gave up grazing areas and also supplied water in dry times, with a solar-powered pump at the lodge also serving the farm (Jacobsohn, 2000). At the start of 2004, total community income from the Damaraland Camp was NAR1.6 million. The nearby Etendeka Mountain Camp also voluntarily paid a bed night levy generating community income of NAR70,000 since 1995 (Rice and Gibson, 2001). By early 2002, the Torra conservancy had NAR1 million in its bank account, excluding salaries of eight conservancy workers and 12 staff at Damaraland Camp. Income from tourism was used at Torra for local job creation, training and education, an emergency fund, schools and community celebrations. In 2004, Damaraland Camp received the top Namibian eco-award for meeting 80% of criteria for sustainable tourism. The Camp employed one local person from each of 20 families living in the nearby village, to spread the economic benefits of tourism income among extended families. For 8 years, a local woman and former goat herder had managed this community-run Camp. She was the first black female manager of a tourism operation in Namibia. A female guide had also worked at the Camp for over 2 years, as the first female guide at Wilderness Safaris lodges in Namibia (WWF, 2005c).

Tsiseb Conservancy

The Tsiseb Conservancy is located south of Torra in the Namib Desert, near the Brandberg Mountains renowned for their Bushmen rock art, including the White Lady rock painting. The Brandberg Mountains Guide Service, a conservancy business, provided guided tours of the rock art sites. Local men started this guiding service in the 1990s concerned about graffiti and vandalism at the rock art sites and to gain employment. Tourists at the Brandberg Monument had to hire a local guide. In 2003, the White Lady Lodge was built in the Brandberg Mountains in partnership with a private business. The privately owned lodge, with stone chalets and tent sites, paid a monthly rental fee of US$3170 to the Tsiseb Conservancy. However, the remote desert lodge was not attracting enough guests to make these rent payments. In 2004, the Tsiseb Conservancy opened a new stone visitor centre with a craft shops, Internet café and booking office for tours of the Brandberg Mountains. The conservancy used its tourism income to purchase land in Uis and build the new visitor centre. The White Lady Lodge, Brandberg Mountain Guides and Tsiseb Tourism Information Centre, along with Damaraland Camp and the Grootberg Community Lodge, were promoted by WWF (2005a, b, c) for community conservancies involved in Project LIFE (Living in a Finite Environment) in Namibia.

Doro !Nawas Conservancy

In 2005, the Doro !Nawas Camp opened in the 407,300 ha Doro !Nawas Conservancy in northern Namibia. The camp was a joint venture between the conservancy, Wilderness Safaris and a Namibian company. The local community of 450 members in the Doro !Nawas Conservancy owned 40% of this new desert camp. The 16-room lodge, built near the edge of the usually dry Aba-Huab River, also employed 34 local people. The lodge was located near the San Bushmen rock engraving sites at Twyfelfontein (*Africa Geographic*, 2005; Namib Web, 2005). Wilderness Safaris also operated the successful Damaraland Camp in Torra Conservancy, used as a model for the Doro !Nawas Camp. The new camp was based on the values of community empowerment and conservation through tourism.

Puros Conservancy

In March 2000, Puros was the 10th communal area conservancy registered in Namibia. Managed by Herero and Himba people, the conservancy is located 55 km inland from the Skeleton Coast in the Kunene Region. The arid area of Puros includes the Hoarusib River where permanent springs provide water for desert elephants, other wildlife, local herding

people and their livestock. Poachers in the Hoarusib shot out elephants and black rhino by the early 1980s. However, with community game guards appointed at Puros, elephant returned after being absent for a decade and giraffe were reintroduced. The Puros area had 23 elephants along with ostrich, desert antelope and giraffe. Tourism operators using Puros paid a US$5 levy to the resident Himba community. By 1994, the community operated their own campsite (Jones, 1999). Women sold baskets woven from palm fronds to passing tourists, using the income to buy food, blankets, beads and utensils. The local community of less than 100 adults decided to form a conservancy to benefit from wildlife and tourism. Five months of negotiations were needed to agree on boundaries with adjacent communities. Conservancy members built a craft market and traditional Himba village for tourists. Other plans were for a community-managed campsite and a joint-venture tourist lodge. However, a wealthy Herero herder managed his own campsite at Puros that employed family members. He was prepared to contribute some income to a community development fund but refused to recognize the conservancy committee. This campsite was often full in the busy tourist season. The conservancy planned a second tourist campsite, linked with the cultural village and crafts, to provide more jobs and keep young people in the area. Tourism income was to be used for a drought relief fund. A VHF Radio at the conservancy office was used to contact a clinic or hospital and arrange transport (Jacobsohn, 2000). Other conservancies in the Kunene gained income from trophy hunting (US$37,200 at Ehirovipuka), a craft market built at Orupupa and contracts with three tourism operators at Marienfluss (WWF, 2003a).

Caprivi Strip

The Caprivi Strip is a 450-km-long panhandle of land in north-east Namibia, surrounded by Angola, Zambia, Zimbabwe and Botswana. The 20,000 km^2 area of woodlands, rivers and floodplains has 78,000 people from six tribal groups. Wildlife in the Caprivi area had been decimated by the Angolan war, uncontrolled hunting and by habitat clearance for farming. The CBNRM programme started in the Caprivi Region in 1990, supported by IRDNC. Ecotourism, game viewing and controlled trophy hunting were promoted as community-based tourism ventures (Ashley and La Franchi, 1997). The Caprivi Region has six registered communal conservancies representing 35,000 people in East Caprivi and more than 4000 people in West Caprivi. In 2003, the five conservancies of Salambala, Kwandu, Wuparo, Mayuni and Mashi received NAR200,000 each from trophy hunting. Community campsites were established at Salambala, Mayuni (Kubunyana), Bwabwata (Bumhill and Nambwa) and Wuparo, a trophy hunting joint venture at Salambala and a joint venture tourism lodge on Susuwe Island between Mayuni Conservancy and a Namibian tourist operator (Davidson, 2003; IRDNC, 2004). One lodge paid US$8000 to nearby communities from a bed night levy (Jones, 1999). Craft markets were established at Mashi, Sheshe and Ngoma in three conservancies, with Mashi earning NAR80,266 in 2003. A new Caprivi Land Board planned to charge lodges and campsites a fee; this could affect joint venture negotiations between private tourism investors and communal area conservancies that held tourism rights (WWF, 2003b).

Salambala Conservancy

The 92,000 ha Salambala Conservancy is located in the East Caprivi Region of Namibia, directly across the river from Chobe National Park in northern Botswana. The Basubia tribal group, with 19 villages and 7135 people, manages the conservancy registered in 1998. In 1995, the Salambala Forest in the central area had just seven impala, 20 kudu and transient elephant and buffalo. Salambala's wildlife had been poached during warfare around the Caprivi Strip from 1968 to 1989. Seventeen families lived in the forest where they grazed over 2000 cattle. In 1995, a 14,000 ha Core Wildlife Area was established around the Salambala Forest and 16 Basubia families voluntarily moved out of the forest.

The area was zoned for wildlife and tourism and livestock grazing was banned. Impala were reintroduced in 1999 and 2001, sponsored by WWF and MET. Wildlife watering points were established in the forest area that was fenced on three sides to exclude cattle. Eight community guards and three resource monitors were hired to protect wildlife and forest resources. Wildlife from Chobe has moved into Salambala, with 600 elephants, 1500 plains zebra, three lions prides (19 lions) and impala increasing to 250 in 2002. With increasing wildlife, in 1999 Salambala received a hunting quota of two elephants and gamebirds. A community campsite was also constructed. Despite ongoing conflict in the Caprivi region from 1998 to 2002, Salambala generated cash income from the campsite and trophy hunting used to pay operational costs and staff salaries. The Salambala community campsite is subsidized by trophy hunting income. In 2001, with total revenue of NAR242,921 (NAR149,300 in cash, NAR93,621 in salaries), the Salambala Conservancy paid NAR40,000 to the 19 villages and Basubia Tribal Authority. The hunting quota increased in 2002 and the Salambala conservancy expected to become self-financing (NACSO, 2004d).

Lianshulu Lodge, Mudume National Park

The Lianshulu Lodge is in the Eastern Caprivi Region of Namibia inside the Mudume National Park. The privately owned lodge supported community game guards and raised money for conservation, with revenue used to train game guards from nearby villages that helped protect local wildlife in the area. The luxury lodge paid a bed night levy to the local community. In a private–community partnership part of the lodge profits were also used to build a cultural village. The Liazuli Traditional Village was located next to Mudume National Park and staffed by local villagers. The village included traditional buildings, crafts and demonstrations of indigenous skills. Lizauli village attracted visitors from Lianshulu Lodge and other park visitors. Income from the cultural village funded community projects (Ashley and Garland, 1994; Echtner, 1999).

Bwabwata and Bagani, West Caprivi

Two community-owned campsites were established inside Bwabwata National Park in West Caprivi, following an agreement between the Ministry of Environment and Tourism and local communities in the Mayuni and Kwando conservancies. It was the first time communities were allowed to operate tourist facilities inside Namibia's protected areas; these park facilities are otherwise owned and operated by the Namibia government. IRDNC and NACOBTA assisted the communities to develop the park campsites and establish conservancies to manage wildlife on communal areas outside the park. The Bumhill and Nambwa campsites were built on the Kwando River, in wildlife viewing areas. The Karamacan Trust represented the communities managing these park campsites with income going to local people (*NACOBTA Newsletter*, 2003). A key attraction at Bwabwata National Park is the Popa Falls, visited by thousands of tourists each year. There are several lodges around Popa Falls, including one run by the Indigenous Barakwena people.

In the mid-1990s, the Kxoe San Bushmen used donor funding from NGOs to build the Bagani tourist campsite below Popa Falls in the Western Caprivi. The Kxoe San were given rights to land on the Kavango River, just below the waterfall at Popa, a key visitor attraction in northern Namibia. This up-market camp had four wooden decks perched above the rapids and under a canopy of gallery forest. However, a 1998 secessionist rebellion in the region and army intervention saw half the Kxoe San, including the chief and his senior adviser, flee into Botswana. In June 1999 the campsite area was cordoned off with razor wire and only a few Kxoe people were present (Weaver, 2000). The Bagani campsite also competed with the government-subsidized Popa Falls rest camp (Ashley and Garland, 1994). Further conflicts with Angola from 2000 to 2002 also affected the northern border region. Tourism in the Caprivi region is growing again, with a 2002 tourism plan for the Chobe floodplains fostering sustainable development for local people through ecotourism and lodges (Davidson, 2003).

South Africa

In 1994, the apartheid system ended in South Africa and was replaced by a democratically elected government. Black homelands ('bantustans') were abolished, with the two separate conservation and community agencies amalgamated into one government department representing all peoples in a province. Local people living around protected areas or claiming back land in these reserves were now involved in community development projects, especially ecotourism, to provide economic benefits and conserve natural areas (Foggin, 1996; Munnik and Mhlope, 2000; Mahony and van Zyl, 2001, 2002; Macie, 2002; Matlou, 2002; DeMotts, 2004; Kepe *et al.*, 2005). A 1996 tourism white paper promoted responsible nature-based tourism planning and development that supported community-owned reserves and tourism joint ventures between communities, conservation agencies and private operators. A 1997 white paper on the conservation and sustainable use of South Africa's biological diversity also stated that disadvantaged local communities should actively participate and benefit from tourism in protected areas (Scheyvens, 2002b; Font *et al.*, 2004). SANParks implemented this policy in protected areas through a social ecology unit that worked with communities living adjacent to parks and identified commercial tourism opportunities. In 2000, tenders for 13 tourism concessions in national parks (nine in Kruger) also included business and employment opportunities for disadvantaged local communities (Spenceley, 2004; Wolmer, 2004). There are also some 9000 private nature reserves and game farms in South Africa that include more land than all the state-run national and provincial parks (Buttner, 2004). Tourism in South Africa generates ZAR25 billion per year, or 8.2% of GDP. In 2004, South Africa had 6.5 million international visitors (WTO, 2005). It is the third main source of foreign exchange and jobs and a key driver of economic development in regional and rural areas (Groenewald, 2004).

The SA Department of Environmental Affairs and Tourism (DEAT) funds a Poverty Relief Programme and Tourism Enterprise Programme to provide rural tourism infrastructure, develop community tourism products, support local enterprises and improve tourism services. Spatial Development Initiatives (SDIs) also promoted private investment and community-based tourism projects in scenic rural areas such as the St Lucia wetlands and coastal region (Koch et al., 2002; Spenceley, 2004, 2005). A Rural Development Framework within South Africa's Reconstruction and Development Programme focused on building rural enterprises and social sustainability, as 11 million people in rural areas lived below the poverty level (Burns and Barrie, 2005). South African government policy also supports black economic empowerment (BEE). However, the tourism industry and wildlife safari businesses in South Africa are dominated by white-controlled tourist enterprises. In 2003, only 6% of all tourism business listed on the stock exchange had some level of BEE ownership, with just 17% of these under black management and control (15% male, 2% female) (Groenewald, 2004; WTO, 2005). South Africa also supports a Fair Trade in Tourism programme for community business ventures (FTTSA, 2004) and has implemented pro-poor tourism approaches in the private sector and also developed responsible tourism guidelines (Koch, 1994; Ashley and Jones, 2001; Seif, 2001; DEAT, 2002b; Koch et al., 2002; Fennell, 2003; Spenceley and Seif, 2003; Spenceley et al., 2004). Tribal communities in South Africa are involved with some tourism joint ventures in public conservation lands (e.g. Kruger NP), and on some private game reserves with up-market tourism lodges.

Kruger National Park

Kruger National Park is the main wildlife tourism attraction in South Africa. The park extends 335 kilometres along the Mozambique border and includes many private game reserves on the western side. Together, these cover an area of 20,000 km^2 protected for wildlife viewing of the 'Big 5' (elephant, rhino, buffalo, lion and leopard) and other species. The park receives around 5000 visitors a day and employs some 4000 people. However, local people were evicted to create the 2-million-hectare park and excluded from using

game, firewood or water resources. During the apartheid era, black people were legally restricted from entering Kruger Park (Magome and Murombedzi, 2003). In the 1960s, local people selling crafts at Skukuza, the main tourist camp in Kruger, were beaten, chased away and had their crafts confiscated (Spenceley, 2004). Some 2 million impoverished people live around the boundaries of Kruger Park, with limited infrastructure and job opportunities. Other up-market lodges in Kruger and adjoining game reserves had programmes to provide benefits to local rural communities (Spenceley, 2005). At Kruger, local people supplied linen, brooms and staff uniforms, sold crafts, worked as tour guides, and worked at a meat plant processing culled game (Wheal, 2001). The new SANParks policy of working with neighbouring communities allows local people to participate in decision-making and to sell products or tourist services in the park. In 2000, tourism concessions for nine sites in Kruger Park included empowerment plans (weighted at 20%) to involve local communities in business opportunities (e.g. garden produce, crafts, maintenance, transport, laundry and recycling centre), local training and employment and shareholding by disadvantaged groups (Spenceley, 2004). Revenue from financial penalties imposed on concessionaires in Kruger was directed to neighbouring communities but park revenue sharing of concession fees (ZAR202 million over 20 years) with local communities was not mentioned. New tourism concessionaires in Kruger Park such as safari operators, shop managers and caterers had to recruit 79% of employees from disadvantaged communities living near the park (WTO, 2005). Tourism concessions with SANParks had a 20-year agreement, paid royalties of 4 to 22.3% (av. 10.8%) and a minimum lease payment of 65% of bid royalties (Humphrey and Boonzaaier, 2003).

Makulele community, Kruger National Park

In 1995, the Makulele lodged the first tribal claim over land in a South African national park. In 1998, the Makulele community won their claim over 29,000 ha of land at the far northern end of Kruger National Park, bounded by the Limpopo, Pafuri and Levuvhu Rivers. They agreed to maintain conservation values and work in partnership with the National Parks Board. Some 3000 Makulele people were forcibly removed from this area of Kruger Park bordering Zimbabwe in 1969. This was the first land claim recognized in a South African national park, granting the Makulele land title and rights to commercial development. The Makulele community now included 8160 people living in two villages with livelihoods based on livestock farming, some cash income and limited trophy hunting on their land. Unemployment in this remote area was around 80%. In 1999, the Makulele claim area was designated a contractual national park for 50 years jointly managed by SANParks with the Makulele who retained rights to limited harvesting of wildlife and commercial tourism development including lodges, tented camps and wilderness trails. The Makulele Community Property Association was formed to reclaim land, then to guide land use and tourism development. The Makulele had electricity installed in their villages in September 2004 and would also receive compensation of US$450,000 from the South African government by 2008 (Koro, 2005).

The Makulele community supported research on the ecotourism potential of the claim area, with six or seven game lodges, a campsite, cultural tourism, and village homestays expected to generate revenue, alleviate poverty and provide jobs. Tenders were invited for tourism concessions at Makulele but only two bids were received (Koch *et al.*, 2002; PPT, 2004a). A feasibility study found the remote area was marginal for tourism receiving just 4% of visitors to Kruger Park. Matswani Safaris planned a 32-bed lodge in the Makulele area, providing 40 local jobs, paying annual rent of US$75,000. Wilderness Safaris planned to set up a tented-camp, paying a percentage of income. The lodges were expected to generate ZAR2 million in the first year (Skhalele, 2003; Turner, 2004). The Makulele further approved concessions for trophy hunting of elephant and buffalo, generating income of US$80,000 in 2000 and US$130,000 in 2001 for community projects. A community campsite and cultural

centre were also planned for self-drive visitors (Scheyvens, 1999; Mahony and van Zyl, 2001, 2002; Reid, 2001; Magome and Murombedzi, 2003; Spenceley, 2003).

The Makulele originally chose safari hunting over ecotourism, with SANParks reluctantly approving hunting in the Makulele portion of Kruger National Park. However, safari hunting reduced numbers of game, encouraged poaching of wildlife, and brought few job benefits for the Makulele people. The Makulele Community Property Association then developed ecotourism with private business partners.

Wilderness Safaris built The Outpost Lodge and Pafuri Camp in Makulele with jobs and training provided for local people. The Makulele also received a 25% equity stake in the lodge and camp from Wilderness Safari, receive some 40% of profits during the first 6 years, and obtain a percentage from every booking. Within 30 years, the Makulele have the option to take over full ownership of the lodge. The Mix hotel group now owned the lodge with the Makulele community receiving 10% of tourism revenue every 3 months. Tourism income from the lodge funded a visitor centre in the village with craft production and an amphitheatre along with bed and breakfast accommodation (Koro, 2005). To support ecotourism, other businesses were planned for local people in transport, clothing, fresh produce and a maintenance team for the lodge and camp (Groenewald, 2004).

Manyeleti Game Reserve

Other tribal groups also reclaimed their lands around Kruger National Park and manage tourism concession areas leased to private lodges. These claims included the Mnisi tribe in Manyeleti Game Reserve, a focus of commercialization for the Northern (now Limpopo) Province and supported by a SDI programme. Eight rural communities lived around the reserve and some had lodged land claims on the area. The Manyeleti reserve had three tourism concession areas with 74 beds, negotiated by the former Gazankulu homeland government with minimal income for the province and none to the reserve. In 2000, the 22,750 ha 'Big 5' reserve received nine tenders for four tourism concessions, that included local jobs and service provision, equity and profit sharing, and work for community businesses. Until land claims on Manyeleti were proven the government was not required to share concession fees (8–12%) or equity in tourism ventures with neighbouring communities (Mahony and van Zyl, 2001, 2002; PPT, 2004a). The Mdluli Tribal Authority faced similar issues in developing land inside and bordering Kruger as a contractual park and key asset for private sector investment in wildlife tourism (Spenceley, 2003).

Mthethomusha Game Reserve

The Mpakeni tribe owned the 8000 ha Mthethomusha Game Reserve with the CCA Bongani Mountain Lodge that opened in 1990 (Mahony and van Zyl, 2001). Guests at the lodge visited local communities, a *sangoma* or healer and San rock art sites. The tribal land in Mthethomusha bordering the eastern side of Kruger Park was used for grazing and farming up to 1985 but with poor grass and limited water the chief set aside the area for conservation. In 1986, fences were built and game reintroduced to the area. A local village that owned the Bongani reserve land had leased this area to the Mpumalanga Parks Board for 99 years. Money from the lease went into a community trust account. Operating rights for wildlife safaris and a game lodge in the Reserve were leased to BOE, a South African trust company, for 50 years. In turn, CCA subleased tourism operating rights from BOE for Bongani Mountain Lodge. The neighbouring villages of Luphisi had 6000 residents while Mpakeni had 4500 people. Sixty-eight per cent lived below the poverty line. The benefits of the reserve for the Mpakeni people are employment as lodge and maintenance staff at Bongani (57 out of 67), profit sharing, and a dance group (Burns and Barrie, 2005). They also sold vegetables to the lodge, had access to firewood, plants and thatching grass, received half of the meat from wildlife culling, and had a fruit and craft stall at the Kruger park entrance (Wheal, 2001). A local man who received a hospitality bursary at Bongani Lodge started a community project

producing arts and crafts, and a vegetable garden to provide more local benefits. He wanted more lodge guests to visit and sponsor community projects. The Parks Board also ran a buffalo breeding facility and allowed occasional buffalo hunting safaris in the reserve, in full view of guests at the Mountain Lodge (Buckley, 2003c). The community received income and meat, but hunting conflicts with the goals of ecotourism lodges.

Community Ecotourism in KwaZulu-Natal Province

Dukuduku forest, KwaZulu-Natal

The 5960-ha Dukuduku forest is the largest remaining coastal lowland forest in South Africa, located next to the Greater St Lucia Wetland Park (GSLWP) in Maputaland, the northern province of KawZulu-Natal. The Dukuduku forest was incorporated into GSLWP in 1994, when 6500 squatters and residents living in the forest agreed to move to a new village site north of the forest. At Dukuduku North (now Khula), resettled people were given half a hectare of land each with the Natal Parks Board (now KwaZulu-Natal Conservation Service) supporting forestry, gardening and health projects. With 90% unemployment, the community developed an ecotourism enterprise to benefit from the forest area. Local Zulu people formed the Dukuduku Development and Tourism Association (DDTA) and committee members visited tourism projects in other reserves managed by the Natal Parks Board (NTB). The NTB and DDTA jointly worked on a 'gateway project' for ecotourism development, linked with established tourism at the nearby Greater St Lucia Wetland Park, declared a World Heritage Area in 1999. Local people sold crafts and fruit to tourists along the road through the forest going to the town of St Lucia. Sales of baskets woven from *ncema* grass generated US$300,000 per year. The proposed ecotourism venture included accommodation in huts or tents (200 beds), a community campground, reception area, a cultural village and handicraft stalls. Local people were to be trained as guides, service staff and cultural centre staff.

Supported by NTB, the large ecotourism venture would provide employment, casual work for crafts people, and sustainable access to forest resources for crafts and construction. Outcomes of the Dukuduku ecotourism project were community organization and the infrastructure built. The Dukuduku North community would in future own the ecotourism project through a non-profit or private trust company (Honey, 1999; Scheyvens, 1999).

Other Zulu people remained in the Dukuduku forest with no services, under threat of forced removal. In 1996, some 20,000 people were estimated to be illegal occupants of the forest area. There were armed conflicts between local rebels in the forest and the conservation service over payments for harvesting *ncema* sedge used for making mats. An Mbuyazi Zulu chief also claimed forested land between Lake St Lucia and the sea, but received money as compensation. Local Zulu people sought to regain control of the forest and provide tourist services but only resettled people were involved in ecotourism projects by the KwaZulu-Natal Conservation Service. By 1999, just 270 families still living in the Dukuduku forest had registered to move to a resettlement area at the town of Monzi. A forest buffer zone at Monzi was made available for community ecotourism projects with a 200-bed camp proposed. Private investors were sought for these tourism ventures in the Dukuduku forest (Honey, 1999; Scheyvens, 1999).

Greater St Lucia Wetlands Park

The GSLWP and World Heritage Area included 220 km of forest, coastline and beaches, three major lakes (Lake St Lucia, Lake Sibaya and Kosi Bay), four Ramsar wetlands and eight game reserves. The park arose from a 1996 decision to ban sand mining and support conservation and nature tourism. Within 20 km of the park boundary were 500,000 impoverished local people. Some 4500 locals mainly work at removing introduced pines and gum trees. In 1998, there were just 350 tourism jobs (du Toit, 2005). There has been minimal progress with community ecotourism initiatives at GSLWP (Renard, 2001) while Zulu people valued

ongoing access to forest resources (Munnik and Mhlope, 2000; Brennan and Allen, 2001). However, 95% of local people supported GSLWP with Zulu residents positively linking nature conservation, tourism and better local economic welfare but hostile to the conservation agency on these aims (Picard, 2003). Land claims for 60% of GSLWP have been resolved, but others remain (du Toit, 2005). The GSL Wetlands Authority now has a policy of supporting private and community-based tourism development, and recognizing local access to key areas of the park. The community of Bhangazi, for example, was given financial compensation and access to 5 ha of land within GSLWP, formerly used for burials and ancestral ceremonies. They devised a business partnership to develop a 50-bed hotel on Bhangazi Lake, and another hotel at Cape Vidal Beach. Private business investors were sought for these ventures, co-owned by the community.

The Mabibi community has 68% shareholding ownership of the new Thonga Beach Lodge at Mabibi Beach. Operated by Isibindi Africa Lodges and opened in August 2004, the 22-bed six-star lodge cost ZAR8 million (US$1.2 million) to build (du Toit, 2005). Mabibi Beach has the southernmost coral reef in Africa with leatherback and loggerhead turtles nesting on the beach. Some 90% of jobs and training at the lodge went to 27 local Mabibi people, with a trust fund established to help pay for education, schools and clinics (Groenewald, 2004). Thonga Beach Lodge, located in the Maputaland Coastal Forest Reserve, was the first tourism concession in GSLWP (WWF-SA, 2005). Ten major tourism projects will see ZAR342 million (US$66.5 million) invested in GSLWP. Wildlife species worth ZAR25 million (US$3.8 million) were also reintroduced to the park. Other small business enterprises have been set up for local people, such as the Wetlands Craft Initiative, which supports 400 people, mainly women, in making crafts such as woven baskets to improve their livelihood (du Toit, 2005). The sustainable harvesting of fibrous plants from wetlands for tourism crafts is an issue, balancing local benefits with conservation and tourism (Dahlberg, 2005).

The Wildlands Conservation Trust (2005) supported other community ecotourism projects in GSLWP, such as the Mabibi Trust campsite and 2000-ha game reserve at Mabibi Beach, establishing the Muzi Pan Adventure Centre with the KwaJobe community for guided canoe trips and bird talks, and developing tourism at Khula village with local people starting a Zulu cultural village and restaurant. These ecotourism projects were part of the Green Futures approach to conserve biodiversity with sustainable local development. In Maputaland, tourism concessions paid for a lease at 10% of property value, and 4% of gross revenue as royalties. The leases for lodges in Maputaland ranged from 15 (operator) or 20 years (developer), while the community benefited from employment, training, shareholding, and 25% of leases and royalties (Humphrey and Boonzaaier, 2003).

Dlinza forest aerial boardwalk, KwaZulu-Natal

The 260-ha Dlinza Forest is located near the town of Eshowe in Zululand, KwaZulu-Natal Province. The coastal forest has over 65 species of birds and 80 species of butterfly. The 125-metre-long aerial boardwalk in the canopy of Dlinza Forest opened in 2000. A 20-m observation tower provides a panoramic view of the coastal and forest area. It is the first and still the only aerial forest boardwalk in South Africa. The Dlinza aerial boardwalk along with a visitor centre and souvenir shop was the key project in the TreeRoutes partnership between WWF-SA (2005) and Sappi, involving rural people in ecotourism ventures. The Eshowe area is a poor rural region with high unemployment. Six local guides work at the Dlinza boardwalk, with five being local Zulu women. Most of the women were previously unemployed single parents. The guides attended a 4-week training course run by Birdlife South Africa, learning about tourism, forest birds and Zulu myths and legends about the Dlinza forest. One female guide is now the assistant to the boardwalk manager, and attended a tourism expo in the city of Durban. Educational workshops for local schools are also run at the Dlinza visitor centre (WWF-SA, 2004). Dlinza forest was part of the Zululand Birding Route that developed birding eco-

tourism around Richards Bay and trained 20 local people as bird guides. This avitourism project received funding of ZAR2 million from Rio Tinto and Birdlife International (ZBR, 2002a, b).

Kosi Bay, KwaZulu-Natal

Kosi Bay is in the far north of KwaZulu-Natal, near the border with Mozambique. In 1988, Kosi Bay was declared a nature reserve with plans for a private luxury resort. Local people from the Kwadapha, eMalangeni and Nkovukeni tribes living and fishing in the Kosi Bay area were harassed into leaving but 130 families stayed on and were fenced in. In 1995, a local Durban NGO helped the remaining families at Kosi Bay develop a community-based ecotourism project in the nature reserve. Fundraising by the NGO was used to purchase a four-wheel-drive vehicle and a dinghy to ferry staff and tourists across a lake to a tented camp. Local people were trained in business and hospitality skills, with the camp manager paid by the NGO. The Wildlife Society of South Africa supported this ecotourism project. Tourists, fishermen and other interest groups began arriving from December 1994. By 1996, the campsite had occupancies of 70% and was economically viable. Further funding and contracts with external investors were needed to develop the project. However, the lack of legal land ownership discouraged private investors and meant the community could not gain access to low-interest loans. Some tourists were dissatisfied with camp security and the level of hospitality services. Rivalry between community members and conflicts with conservation agencies also affected the project. More effective decision-making procedures were required in future ecotourism initiatives at Kosi Bay. A community-owned hiking trail and accommodation in Kosi Bay were planned in 2001. The 16-bed Kosi Forest Lodge is now the only wilderness lodge in the Kosi Bay Nature Reserve. The estaurine lakes and coastline at Kosi Bay also attract many fishermen to the coastal reserve. From 2002 to 2005, Ufudu Flyfishing Experience had an exclusive contract with the kwaMvutshane community to use the Utshwayelo community campsite at the mouth of Kosi Bay during February and March. This provided contract employment for a few local people during a quiet time of the year (Ufudu, 2004). Ufudu was a catch-and-release flyfishing ecotourism business based in Durban. Ufudu also used the Umdoni and Nhlange camps on lakes in the Kosi Bay coastal reserve.

UMhlatuze Estaurine Sanctuary, KwaZulu-Natal

The UMhlatuze Estaurine Sanctuary was the site of a conservation and ecotourism development project supported by Ezemvelo KZN Wildlife, Wildlands Conservation Trust, Zululand Science Centre and Simunye Tourism Association. The Richards Bay Coal Terminal provided funding of ZAR200,000 for infrastructure and an education officer to run science programmes on mangrove and estuary ecosystems and their management. The estuary was one of the main sites for rare birds in South Africa. The Dube community mainly helped to remove pest plants from the Dube Coastal Forest and the estuary. A community tourism working group, comprising Bird Life South Africa, the Dube community and Simunye Tourism Association, identified several tourism options including a community campsite, guided fishing safaris, canoe trips and bird watching trips. Some youths who were illegally gill netting in the estuary undertook 1 year of training through a Nature Guide programme. This Dube community conservation project aimed to create alternative income through ecotourism (Ezemvelo KwaZulu Natal Wildlife, 2005a).

Hluhluwe-Umfolozi Park, KwaZulu-Natal

The Hluhluwe-Umfolozi Park was originally the exclusive hunting area of Shaka, the Zulu king. Impoverished rural communities with a total population of 600,000 people surround this national park in KwaZulu-Natal Province. In 1992, the Natal Parks Board (NTB) adopted a neighbour relations policy to work with local communities in a conservation outreach pro-gramme. They established 86 neighbour forums and environmental education programmes to increase understanding of both conservation and community needs. The NTB oversees the controlled local harvesting of natural resources such as thatching grass, reeds and mussels. Trees were cut in areas that need thinning out with the timber transported free within 10 km of the park boundary. NTB established a medicinal plant nursery and trained traditional healers in plant propagation and harvesting. Adjacent local communities also sold crafts to tourists around the park entrances or obtained funding to build more permanent craft stalls assisted by NTB. Culled wildlife was shared with local communities. In 1998, a community levy of ZAR5 was added to the Hluhluwe-Umfolozi park entrance fee (and all KZN parks/reserves) to fund community development projects.

The community levy was taken from the park entrance fee and first night's accom-modation, with 90% allocated to communities living around the park and 10% to a central fund for other areas (Ezemvelo KwaZulu Natal Wildlife, 2005b). Tribal members on park management boards decided on use of these community funds, controlling problem animals and other community issues (Foggin and Munster, 2000; Scheyvens, 2002b). KZN started a revenue sharing scheme with communities in the early 1990s.

Ten tribal authorities are represented on the Local Conservation Board for Hluhluwe-Umfolozi Park. In 1999, the Mpembeni com-munities decided to reinvest money raised from the park levy in park visitor accommodation. With tourism growing and secure employment for local people at the park, these communities invested in conservation and park accommodation for extra jobs and income (Kibirigi, 2003; Buttner, 2004). On their own, small-scale ecotourism ventures had limited direct economic benefits for local people. In 1996, community tourism accounted for 1% of tourism beds in KwaZulu-Natal (Brennan and Allen, 2001). Nature-based tourism, however, generated 25% of Province income and 80,000 jobs in 2002. In 2003, protected areas in KwaZulu-Natal hosted 440,772 visitors, with a 29% occupancy rate and 5% net profit. While park revenue from ecotourism had increased, there was a decline in overall occupancy, a low net return, and growing competition for nature products in the Province. Better marketing and extra services such as guided walks, game drives and adventure sports were needed to maximize the use of park facilities and also ecotourism income for communities (Ezemvelo KwaZulu Natal Wildlife, 2004). A community game hunting ecotourism enterprise was also started on community land stocked with wildlife from the park. However, the sealed road ended at the park boundary with poor road access to adjacent community areas around the park (Hill, 2004).

Conservation Corporation Africa

Conservation Corporation Africa (CCA) is a private company operating four game reserves and 37 up-market game lodges or safari camps in six African nations, with ten luxury lodges in South Africa (CCA, 2002). CCA lodges and reserves are purchased outright, or operated through concession leases and co-management agreements. Established in 1990, CCA employs 2500 people, generating tourism revenue from wildlife conservation, supporting field research and funding community development projects through its Rural Investment Fund (RIF). Donor agencies and private clients provided project funding for RIF with operating costs for eight staff met by CCA. From 1991 to 1997, RIF provided US$1 million to fund projects in communities living next to CCA lodges, largely in South Africa. The RIF programme was reduced in 1997 and put under the direct leadership of lodge managers (Christ, 1998). The Africa Foundation replaced the RIF, and is used to support communities living near CCA lodges and conservation areas and other ecotourism operators. It became a sole entity and charitable NGO (US/South Africa) in July 2000, funded by CCA guest donations and corporate donors. A 2001 hospitality bursary programme provided tourism training for ten students chosen from communities near CCA lodges. While only a few people or villages benefited, the Foundation still helped with rural development in prime tourism areas where government funding was limited (Burns and Barrie, 2005).

With a mission of caring for land, wildlife and people, CCA supports ecotourism ventures that are endorsed by local communities, funds community facilities and supports sustainable tourism development in rural regions. These key points are outlined in the CCA strategy for environmental conservation and sustainable community development (Wildwatch, 2003). CCA managers involved local communities in the operation of its ecotourism lodges, mainly through employment and local business ventures. Education and medical facilities were also provided in communities neighbouring CCA lodges. Co-management agreements of CCA with local communities included jobs and revenue sharing schemes. Other tourism operators followed this CCA model of sustainable ecotourism, conservation and community development (Christ, 1998; Buckley, 2003a; Carlisle, 2003). Most CCA lodges were in the wildlife-rich savanna of southern Africa but there were plans to operate in forest areas of East Africa. In KwaZulu-Natal, CCA rehabilitated farmland and reintroduced wildlife to Phinda game reserve. Phinda is the 'flagship' CCA project in Africa, supporting community projects in the Masaka tribal area.

Phinda private game reserve, KwaZulu-Natal

Phinda is a private game reserve north of Lake St Lucia in KwaZulu-Natal, owned and operated by CCA. In the late 1980s, CCA purchased 7500 ha of degraded farmland with further acquisitions building Phinda to 17,500 ha. Starting in 1990, CCA restocked Phinda with large game animals and predators. In 1991, the 44-bed Mountain Lodge was built and the 32-bed Forest Lodge opened in 1993. In 1997, two exclusive 12-bed lodges were added, Rock Lodge and Vlei Lodge. A tented walking safari camp was built in the sand forest. The Zuka Lodge with four cottages was built in western Phinda after boundary fences were removed. Phinda was funded with venture capital, 60% derived offshore. US$600,000 was spent building the Phinda Mountain Lodge with US$270,000 paid as local wages. In 1993, community construction teams were used to build the Forest Lodge, with US$345,000 (out of US$750,000) spent on wages for 110 local people and building materials. A local poacher caught at Phinda completed a community-imposed penalty of 3 months making bricks at Phinda. With a company loan, he established a brick-making business that employed 5–10 other local people. A charcoal-making business was also established at Phinda with 40 local people, while the collection of wood, grass, reeds, fruits, buffalo manure, medicinal plants and palm-wine was allowed (Carlisle, 2003). Organic waste was given to pig farmers while a sewing group made staff uniforms and children made recycled paper into welcome notes used at the lodges (Spenceley and Seif, 2003).

Three impoverished communities of 30,000 people surrounded the Phinda private game reserve, with 22,500 living within a 15-km radius. In 1993, Phinda established community development committees at Nibela, Mduku and Mnqobokazi, to represent local needs, receive funds and oversee the provision of facilities. Phinda supported development projects in the Masaka tribal area such as health clinics, 50 classrooms in schools, education bursaries, and literacy or skills training programmes. The Africa Foundation and Independent Development Trust funded these facilities and services for neighbouring communities at Phinda. In 10 years, over US$1 million was provided in development assistance. CCA also employed 300 local people (80% permanent staff) at Phinda providing economic benefits to 10% of the neighbouring population (Carlisle, 2003). Phinda reserve was included in a study reviewing pro-poor tourism approaches by the private sector that benefit local communities and businesses (Spenceley and Seif, 2003). A new digital centre at Phinda provides computer training for four communities at Mduku. Since 2001, five high school students near Phinda have completed a hospitality internship with CCA. While local people benefit from jobs, income, training, and community facilities, they had no real input in managing conservation and tourism activities at Phinda game reserve. Plans were made to involve local people in ecotourism by building their own lodges in the reserve but this did not eventuate (Brennan and Allen, 2001; Buckley, 2003c; Carlisle, 2003).

Wilderness Safaris

Wilderness Safaris (WS) is a southern African company that leases concession areas and operates 45 luxury tourist lodges and camps in seven African countries and the Seychelles. They support a range of 20 conservation and community projects, such as providing environmental education for children in the Okavango Delta, black and white rhino projects in Namibia and Botswana and local schools in Malawi and Zimbabwe. The WS Wildlife Trust funds development activities in communities living around their lodges and camps. This has contributed to half a million acres of land becoming wildlife reserves or conservancies. WS has formed a partnership or revenue sharing agreement with local communities at several locations. WS has operated the Damaraland Camp in the Torra Conservancy in north-west Namibia since 1996, with 10% of bed night revenue paid to the community along with annual lease fees. In Botswana, four WS camps are located on two concession areas that belong to five villages represented by the Okavango Community Trust (OCT). One hundred and twenty local people work at the Okavango camps and WS assists communities with business planning and health services. WS has a no hunting policy and must buy the annual hunting quota from OCT each year. The lease fees and hunting quotas make the Okavango camps a marginal business venture for WS. In South Africa, local communities have shares in the Ndumo and Rocktail Bay Lodges in KwaZulu-Natal, through a community trust scheme (Buckley, 2003e; Wilderness Safaris, 2004). Wilderness Safaris also recently built The Outpost Lodge and Pafuri Camp in the Makulele area of Kruger National Park, with a 25% equity stake, plus jobs and training provided for local Makulele people (Groenewald, 2004). The WS community partnerships programme has won the Imvelo Award in South Africa, WTO endorsement for best practise in ecotourism and a World Legacy Award (PPT, 2004c).

Rocktail Bay and Ndumo Lodges, KwaZulu-Natal

Rocktail Bay and Ndumo are two lodges operated by Wilderness Safaris in Maputaland or the far northern region of KawZulu-Natal, South Africa. Rocktail Bay opened in 1992 and Ndumo in 1995. Rocktail Bay was a fishing camp in a coastal forest reserve, with Ndumo in Madikwe Game Reserve on the Mozambique border (Magome *et al.*, 2000). WS obtained a 20-year lease for both lodge sites, with Ndumo in the area of the Mathenjwa Tribal Authority (> 20,000 people) and Rocktail Bay in the area of the Mqobela Tribal Authority (1566 people). The lodges are a partnership between WS (50%), the local community or tribal authority (12.5%) and the state conservation agency (KZN, 37.5%), through a lodge-owning company with shares and a lodge-operating company with WS as the lead partner. WS paid a lease rental fee to the lodge-owning company. KZN received rent and management profits through Isivuno, a tourism trust. The local communities had equity shares (12.5–14.5%) in the two lodges, through a community trust scheme. At Rocktail Bay, the kwaMqobela community had shares in both companies with dividends of US$15,287 since 1996 used to improve schools, roads and education bursaries. Overall, by 2001, the communities had received minimal income from financial dividends since neither lodge was profitable. In fact, WS drew on bank loans to pay out dividends to retain community support for the lodges. Benefits for local people were employment of 50 staff at the two lodges, with training and skills development and a low turnover of staff. The lodges used community taxi services and also arranged cultural visits to a traditional healer or *sangoma*. The taxi service generated ZAR29,000 a year while money from *sangoma* performances funds students and materials at a Sangoma Training School (PPT, 2004c, d). Hippo tours at Rocktail Bay used local guides with a fixed monthly fee paid to the community and a per tourist fee when hippos were seen. At Ndumo, the local community opened a caravan park on the edge of the game reserve (Honey, 1999).

WS contacted donor agencies to purchase bank shares on behalf of the communities and assisted with buying local goods and services such as food supplies, crafts, wood, stone and sand materials. However, more local infrastructure and tourism product development in Maputaland was required from the state conservation agency to increase occupancy at the lodges (Poultney and Spenceley, 2001; PPT, 2004c, d). A diving site permit obtained since 2001 helped to improve occupancy at Rocktail Bay Lodge. WS also paid US$18,287 annually to finance sea turtle surveys and monitoring at Rocktail Bay. In addition, WS obtained a loan of US$47,000 to increase the Mqobela share in the lodge to 49% (WTO, 2003e). By 2005, Rocktail Bay had occupancy rates of 70%, and employed 32 local people out of 45 staff. Community tours and local fishing guides were introduced, along with a beach cleaning initiative. Issues with the use of trust funds earned from the lodge saw the Mqobela Trust restructured to deliver more community benefits. A new 20-bed diving lodge and business partnership was planned with the adjacent Mpukane community, who also wanted to benefit from tourism at Rocktail Bay (PPT, 2004e). While WS endorsed community partnerships, lodge managers were cautious about implementing linkages with community partners (PPT, 2004c, d).

Mkambati Nature Reserve, Eastern Cape

The latest WS joint venture is Mtentu Camp in the Mkambati Nature Reserve in the Eastern Cape Region of South Africa. The coastal reserve is a biodiversity hotspot of endemic plants, with 23 waterfalls (three over coastal cliffs) and a colony of Cape Vultures. Local Pondo people reclaimed the reserve under the Land Restitution Act. They were forcibly removed from the area in 1920, with the nature reserve declared in 1976 in the former Transkei homeland area. The Mkambati Land Trust, formed in 2002, represents 40,000 Pondo and Xhosa people that live in seven villages inland from the Mkambati Nature Reserve. The Land Trust will maintain the nature reserve for conservation and plan to double the size of the reserve. The formal singing ceremony to return the nature reserve to Pondo people took place in October 2004 (WS, 2005). WS entered a partnership with the Mkambati Land Trust, Eastern Cape Nature Conservation and the Mantis Collection to develop tourism in the reserve with Mtentu Camp (van Rensburg and van Rensburg, 2004). Hence, in March 2004, WS managers accompanied the chiefs and headmen from the Mkambati Trust on an educational visit to Rocktail Bay and Ndumo Lodges (WS, 2005). WS also opposed construction of a new toll road and bridges crossing coastal Pondoland, with the wilderness setting promoting the growth of nature-based tourism in this area (Rogers, 2004; Queiros and Wilson, 2005).

Community Ecotourism in Eastern Cape Province

Mehloding hiking trail, Drakensberg Mountains, Eastern Cape

The Ukhahlamba Drakensberg Mountains are on the western border of KwaZulu-Natal Province, Eastern Cape Province and Lesotho. These scenic Drakensberg Mountains are a World Heritage Area and a Ramsar wetlands site. The 250,000 ha mountainous region was set aside mainly as a water catchment area, by proclamation and by the expropriation of tribal lands. Fire management and pest plant removal provided some direct income and skills training to neighbouring communities. The Mehloding community, based around the town of Matatiele in Eastern Cape, operates the Masakala Guesthouse and guided ecotours in this mountain area. The Mehloding Hiking Trail traverses the rural mountain areas of the southern Drakensberg, with accommodation in four different rondavels or chalets at scenic or access points. The local hostesses, Sindi, Nomsa, Kolu and Thenbeka, provided the meals, accommodation and also local entertainment at each chalet. Interaction with rural people, crafts, medicinal plants, rock art and cave initiation sites were part of the cultural aspects of these ecotours. The 4-day mountain trail could be done with full board or as a self-catered hike, with accommodation at the rondavels, and transfers. The Masakala Guesthouse, 8 km from Matatiele, included a traditional dinner and accommodation (Accommodate, nd). This ecotourism business was owned and operated by the Mehloding

Community Trust that represents 25 villages located next to the Ukhahlamba Drakensberg Mountains (Groenewald, 2004).

Amadiba Adventures, Wild Coast, Eastern Cape

Amadiba Adventures is a community-owned horse and hiking trail along a rugged and scenic section of the Wild Coast in the Eastern Cape region. The Amadiba Tribal Authority owned a 20-km stretch of coastal land between the Mzamba and Mtentu rivers, south of Port Edward, part of the former Transkei homeland. Local AmaMpondo people, poor subsistence farmers, lived in 500 homesteads in this area with high levels of poverty, 80% illiteracy and unemployment and lacking services such as electricity and piped water. The Amadiba trail was part of a Wild Coast community tourism initiative funded by the EU from 2000–2004 with support from WWF-SA (2003) and PondoCROP, a local NGO (Palmer et al., 2002). Government officials had proposed game lodges and hotels for the area but the chiefs and people of Amadiba invited PondoCROP to help establish a hiking business. The Amadiba trail first received tourists in June 1998 and in 2000 won an award as the best community tourism project in South Africa. Amadiba Adventures was one of the first ecotourism initiatives in South Africa owned and operated by an Indigenous community, with 500 local people benefiting from the trails (Groenewald, 2004). Five per cent of profits are put in a community trust fund and used for schools and a cattle dip. From October 2001 to June 2002, the Trust fund received ZAR50,000, with ZAR9981 from the trail. In 2001, the trail was running at 20% occupancy. PondoCROP marketed the trail and handled tourist payments (Ashley and Ntshona, 2003). The trail attracted school groups and 60% foreign tourists.

The 4–6 day Amadiba Trail goes from the Mzamba craft centre at Port Edward, down to the Mtentu River estuary and back again. The 25-km trail combined hiking and horse riding with river canoeing and waterfalls. Tented camps were set up for hikers at Kwanyana and Mtentu with catering and camp services provided by local people. Hikers could also visit local *shebeens* (pubs), see *sangoma* dancing, observe traditional ceremonies or join soccer matches with Pondo people in villages along the way. PondoCROP and the Amadiba Coastal Community Development Association (ACCODA) managed the Abadiba trail tourism project. ACCODA owned the tents and canoes used on the Amadiba trail. This community ecotourism venture supports 60–65 families with 80 people working as tour guides, caterers, cleaners, ferrymen, boat or tent owners and horse owners with horses used from different villages. Women worked as cooks, camp cleaners and trail guides or hosted visitors in their home. Locals owned these small enterprises and income of ZAR15 was paid per tourist per day. Amadiba Adventures had ten full-time guides, and 40% of trail income went to the service providers. From 1997 to 2001 Amadiba Adventures ran at a loss but a profit of ZAR200,000 was made in 2002 (Ndovela, 2003). Some camp staff at Mtentu collected money from solo hikers and fishermen, and then also claimed fees from ACCODA. Trail organization was improved in 2001 with a cell phone, salary payments into bank accounts and extra horse keepers, a reserve ferryman and a security guard added to the trail staff. ACCODA won an ZAR500,000 prize as the best community forum in the region, with the money used to build a new campsite for hikers at Salmon Rock and upgrade the Kwanyana camp on the Amadiba trail (Ashley and Ntshona, 2003; Ntshona and Lahiff, 2003; Rossouw, 2003).

The Mtentu Camp at Amadiba was also leased for 3 months each year to Ufudu Flyfishing, a catch-and-release ecotourism business that first visited Mtentu estuary in 1999/2000. After long discussions with government environmental agencies the ACCODA Trust was granted a permit for non-consumptive flyfishing at Mtentu that was then awarded to Ufudu Flyfishing. From 2001 to 2004 Ufudu had an exclusive contract with ACCODA Trust to use the Mtentu community campsite. Local staff were employed and trained by Ufudu during the summer flyfishing season at Mtentu from October to February. Horse rides, bush hikes and canoe trips with local guides were included as extra activities. In

2000, Ufudu paid ZAR39,000 to ACCODA (based on 12.5% of the daily rack rate) and ZAR46,000 as staff wages and for crafts. ACCODA members were expected to greet Ufudu guests and be present on payday when staff received their wages. Hikers on the trail used another campsite at Mtentu during this time while local people could no longer bring individual fishermen down to the river for a tip. In 2004, Wilderness Safaris won a public tender to operate two camps at Mtentu with Ufudu Flyfishing included in the bid. This would generate additional income and employment for Pondo people in the Amadiba area (Ashley and Ntshona, 2003; Pretorius, 2003; Ufudu, 2004). A proposed new toll road and bridges through coastal Pondoland, bringing more settlers, mass tourism and development, threatened both ecotourism and conservation (Rogers, 2004). Having previously lost land to tourist hotels in Port Edward, the Pondo people at Amadiba wanted to continue managing their community eco-tourism venture and concessions for local economic benefits (Rossouw, 2003).

Mbotyi campsite, Wild Coast, Eastern Cape

Amadiba Adventures was part of the longer Wild Coast Trails, with the Pondoland horse and hiking trail extending 110 km south to Port St Johns. At the Pondoland village of Mbotyi, north of Port St Johns, local Pondo people built and operated a community campsite. The coastal campsite was a joint venture with the Mbotyi River Lodge, and developed in 2002 with funding from the DEAT poverty alleviation programme for the Wild Coast. Pondo people owned and managed the Mbotyi campsite with local employment generated during building and operation. Local people built the campsite facilities of tent platforms, rondavels (round huts), a kitchen area and bathrooms. Directors of the Mbotyi River Lodge acted as mentors, setting up a management system and providing training and development for community members to run the campsite and operate as a legal entity. Local people were trained as guides, leading hikes to seven waterfalls, along with bird watching, fishing and horse riding trips. All community members with a horse could participate, with part of the income from horse riding trips used to maintain equipment and provide supplementary feed for horses. Mbotyi had the largest forest area on the Wild Coast, Waterfall Bluff, rare birds and ocean views of the sardine migration run attracting gannets, dolphins, whales and sharks (DSA, 2002a, b).

Matyholweni rest camp, Addo Elephant National Park, Eastern Cape

The 148,000 ha Addo Elephant National Park (AENP) is a major tourist attraction in the Eastern Cape. The 'Greater Addo' area has a new southern section with plans for a 120,000 ha marine park. In October 2004, the Matyholweni rest camp was opened in the southern section of the expanded park. The 12 chalets in the camp, named after the Xhosa phrase for 'in the bush', aim to bring tourism benefits to the local community. The camp was funded with a poverty relief grant of ZAR6.5 million from DEAT. The Mayibuye Ndlovu Development Trust was set up to receive 6–12% of the revenue earned from the camp. This Trust was registered in March 2005 to receive funds from tourism at the camp and the entrance levy. The Trust grew out of a Mayibuye Ndlovu Development Programme, a forum set up in the 1990s to engage with eight local communities living around the park. 'Mayibuye Ndlovu' is Xhosa for 'let the elephant return'. An access road was constructed to the southern end of the park, and this campsite, to link with other tourist roads in the park. In 2000, the Eyethu Hop-on Guides were also established in AENP, with ten local people trained as wildlife guides in 2000/01. The hop-on guides join tourists in their own vehicles, with others employed by private lodges or the park (Addo Elephant Park, 2005). The guiding service and new campsite were both supported by AENP.

Conclusion

Indigenous ecotourism ventures are mainly located on communal lands in southern Africa. These include wildlife conservancies in Namibia, Botswana, Zimbabwe and South Africa. With legal land titles and restitution of traditional lands, Indigenous groups are negotiating concessions for tourism joint ventures with private operators such as safari camps, lodges, and controlled trophy hunting. Land ownership, and tourism access rights linked to concession leases allow Indigenous groups to benefit from wildlife and ecotourism. Key factors such as legislation for community land ownership and resource rights over wildlife, new government policies on wildlife and tourism promoting community benefits, and government funded programmes for poverty relief, rural development, and community enterprise support these Indigenous ecotourism ventures. Success factors for entrepreneurs developing Indigenous ecotourism enterprises in southern Africa include high environmental quality and clear site boundaries, community partnerships, negotiation and social inclusion, and economic security based on land tenure and government policy underlying joint venture agreements (Parker and Khare, 2005). Private tourism operators on game reserves or concession areas leased from Indigenous groups, and also Park Boards both support revenue sharing and social outreach programmes with communities living around conservation areas. However, there are very few Indigenous-owned ecotourism ventures within national parks in southern Africa. New partnerships between Indigenous groups and park agencies or private operators include community campsites in Bwabwata National Park (Namibia) and joint venture lodges in 'contractual parks' (e.g. Makulele in Kruger National Park, South Africa).

Some Indigenous groups have developed community ecotourism ventures such as campsites, trails and tours, supported by conservation NGOs and local development agencies. Income from controlled trophy hunting on communal lands in southern Africa is often used to support community services and community-owned tourism facilities. In Zimbabwe, hunting income in the CAMPFIRE programme goes to District Councils while in Namibia and South Africa, income from trophy hunting goes to communal conservancies or tribal authorities. In southern Africa, community benefits of ecotourism are derived from joint ventures with the private sector, leasehold arrangements, equity shares in ventures, revenue sharing and levies, and funding from NGOs and foreign donors. Key issues were integrating community tourism with the mainstream tourism industry (SAFIRE, 2004), local access to resources in conservation areas, impacts of wildlife on livestock and crops, training and capacity building for staff and marketing Indigenous ecotourism ventures. In the Okavango Delta of Botswana, community land trusts for San Bushmen subleased land and wildlife quotas to safari operators or ran their own community tourism ventures. This promoted wildlife conservation and local economic benefits but communities required further social and political empowerment through training in managerial skills and use of trust funds, direct resource ownership and more input in land use or wildlife quotas allocated to tourism (Mbaiwa, 2005a). In southern Africa, communities with legal land rights or resource rights to wildlife could best negotiate business partnerships and joint ventures or develop their own ecotourism businesses. Private capital and support was needed for most of these tourism ventures.

Park agencies and community organisations were also crucial in developing Indigenous ecotourism.

References

Accommodate (nd) Melohding Hiking Trail. http://www.accommodate.co.za/Profile.asp?proID=49 (accessed 17 November 2005)

Addo Elephant National Park (2005) Minister proclaims new marine area for Addo Park and opens new camp to benefit local communities. Latest News 3 April 2005. http://www.addoelephantpark.com/latest.php (accessed 17 November 2005)

Africa Geographic (2005) Into Africa: A win-win situation. Africa Geographic 13, 84.

Alexander, J. and McGregor, J. (2000) Wildlife and politics: CAMPFIRE in Zimbabwe. Development and Change 31, 605–627.

ART (Africa Resources Trust) (2002) The Mahenye community conservation initiatives: Best practice case study in community conservation. http://www.zero.org.zw/programs/ART.pdf (accessed 17 November 2005)

ART (Africa Resources Trust) (2004) Wildlife and development series: CAMPFIRE. International Institute for Environment and Development. http://www.iied.org/pubs/ (accessed 17 November 2005)

Asato, L. (2003) The Camp's Grand Opening. Gudigwa Day 2: Dispatch. Expeditions. Investigate Biodiversity. http://investigate.conservation.org/xp/IB/expeditions/gudigwa/ (accessed 17 November 2005)

Asato, L. (2005) Expedition to Botswana's Gudigwa Camp. Conservation Frontlines Online. http://www.conservation.org/xp/frontlines/people/fieldnotes24.xml (accessed 17 November 2005)

Ashley, C. (1995) Community based tourism as a strategy for CBNRM: Options and potentials for achieving conservation and development through non-consumptive tourism in Namibia. In: Rihoy, E. (ed.) The Commons Without Tragedy? Strategies for Community-based Natural Resources Management in Southern Africa. SADC Wildlife Technical Coordinating Unit, Kasane, Botswana, pp. 56–94.

Ashley, C. (2000) The Impacts of Tourism on Rural Livelihoods: Namibia's Experience. Working Paper 128. Propoor Tourism, Overseas Development Institute, London, UK.

Ashley, C. and Elliott, J. (2003) 'Just wildlife?' or a source of local development? Natural Resource Perspectives 85. http://www.odi.org.uk/nrp/85.pdf (accessed 17 November 2005)

Ashley, C. and Garland, E. (1994) Promoting Community-based Tourism Development: Why, What and How? Research Discussion Paper No. 4. Ministry of Environment and Tourism, Windhoek. http://www.met.gov.na/pub_all.htm (accessed 17 November 2005)

Ashley, C. and Jones, B. (2001) Joint ventures between communities and tourism investors: Experience in Southern Africa. International Journal of Tourism Research 3, 407–423.

Ashley, C. and La Franchi, C. (1997) Livelihood Strategies of Rural Households in Caprivi: Implications for Conservancies and Natural Resource Management. DEA Research Discussion Paper 20. Ministry of Environment and Tourism, Namibia.

Ashley, C. and Ntshona, Z. (2003) Transforming Roles but not Reality? Private Sector and Community Involvement in Tourism and Forestry Development on the Wild Coast, South Africa. Research Paper 6. Sustainable Livelihoods in Southern Africa. http://www.ids.ac.uk/ids/env/SLSA/slsapubs.html (accessed 17 November 2005)

AWF (African Wildlife Foundation) (2004a) Heartland community lodges. Kazungula Heartland [Okavango]. http://www.awf.org/safari/ecokazungula.php (accessed 17 November 2005)

AWF (African Wildlife Foundation) (2004b) Africa's heartlands: Preserving wildlife by supporting local communities. *Africa Geographic* 12, 22–23.

Baker, J. (1997) Trophy hunting as a sustainable use of wildlife resources in southern and eastern Africa. *Journal of Sustainable Tourism* 5, 306–321.

Baker, L. (2003) NASCO: Supporting CBNRM in Namibia. Travel News Namibia. http://www.travelnews. com.na/index.php?fArticleId=799 (accessed 17 November 2005)

Bandyopadhyay, S., Shyamsundar, P., Wang, L. and Humavindu, M.N. (2004) *Do Households Gain from Community-based Natural Resource Management? An Evaluation of Community Conservancies in Namibia.* DEA Research Discussion Paper No. 68. http://www.met.gov.na/pub_all.htm (accessed 17 November 2005)

Barnes, J.I., MacGregor, J. and Weaver, C.L. (2001) *Economic Analysis of Community Wildlife Use Initiatives in Namibia.* DEA Research Discussion Paper No. 42. http://www.met.gov.na/pub_all.htm (accessed 17 November 2005)

Barnes, J.I., MacGregor, J. and Weaver, C.L. (2002) Economic efficiency and incentives for change within Namibia's community wildlife use initiatives. *World Development* 30, 667–681.

Bentinck, K. (2002) Developing a national eco-tourism strategy for Botswana. In: *Tourism: A Catalyst for Sustainable Development in Africa.* WTO, Madrid, pp. 15–25.

Bird, C. (1995) Communal lands, communal problems. *In Focus* 16, 7–8, 15.

Bird, C. (1997) Communal lands, communal problems. In: France, L. (ed.) *The Earthscan Reader in Sustainable Tourism.* Earthscan, London, pp. 157–161.

Bollig, M. and Heinemann, H. (2004) Nomadic savages, ochre people and heroic herders: Visual presentations of the Himba of Namibia's Kaokoland. *Visual Anthropology* 15, 267–312.

Boniface, B. and Cooper, C. (2005) CAMPFIRE: Local community involvement in safari tourism. In: *Worldwide Destinations Casebook: The Geography of Travel and Tourism.* Elsevier, Oxford, pp. 171–174.

Botswana Tourism (2001) Community-based tourism. Department of Tourism of Botswana. http://www.botswana-tourism.gov.bw/community/community.html (accessed 17 November 2005)

Brennan, F. and Allen, G. (2001) Community-based ecotourism, social exclusion and the changing political economy of KwaZulu-Natal, South Africa. In: Harrison, D. (ed.) *Tourism and the Less Developed World: Issues and Case Studies.* CABI Publishing, Wallingford, UK, pp. 203–221.

Brown, D. (1998) Participatory biodiversity conservation – rethinking the strategy in the low tourist potential areas of Tropical Africa. *Natural Resources Perspectives* 33, July. ODI Website. http://www.odi.org. uk/nrp/33.html (accessed 17 November 2005)

Buckley, R. (2003a) Spitzkoppe, Namibia; Khoadi Hoas Conservancy, Namibia; Nyae-Nyae Conservancy, Namibia. In: *Case Studies in Ecotourism.* CABI Publishing, Wallingford UK, pp. 33–34.

Buckley, R. (2003b) CAMPFIRE, Zimbabwe. In: *Case Studies in Ecotourism.* CABI Publishing, Wallingford, UK, pp. 29–30.

Buckley, R. (2003c) Conservation Corporation Africa; Phinda Private Game Reserve, South Africa; Bogani Mountain Lodge, South Africa. In: *Case Studies in Ecotourism.* CABI Publishing, Wallingford, UK, pp. 9–13.

Buckley, R. (2003d) KwaZulu-Natal Conservation Service, South Africa. In: *Case Studies in Ecotourism.* CABI Publishing, Wallingford, UK, pp. 35–37.

Buckley, R. (2003e) Wilderness Safaris, Southern Africa. In: *Case Studies in Ecotourism.* CABI Publishing, Wallingford, UK, pp. 23–24.

Burns, M. and Barrie, S. (2005) Race, space and 'our own piece of Africa': Doing good in Luphisi village? *Journal of Sustainable Tourism* 13, 468–485.

Buttner, G. (2004) Crossing the Atlantic: Game parks, reserves and communities. Planeta.com. http://www.planeta.com/planeta/04/0411samex2.html (accessed 17 November 2005)

Carlisle, L. (2003) Private reserves; The Conservation Corporation Africa model. In: Buckley, R., Pickering, C. and Weaver, D.B. (eds) *Nature-based Tourism, Environment and Land Management.* CABI Publishing, Wallingford, UK, pp. 17–23.

CBNRM (2003) Community based tourism in Botswana. http://www.cbnrm.bw/pages_sub_dir/CBT.htm (accessed 17 November 2005)

CCA (Conservation Corporation Africa) (2002) African safari – CC Africa. http://www.ccafrica.com/

Child, B. (2005) Principles, practice, and results of CBNRM in southern Africa. In: Lyman, M.W. and Child, B. (eds) *Natural Resources as Community Assets: Lessons From two Continents.* Sand County Foundation, pp. 17–50. http://sandcounty.net/assets/ (accessed 17 November 2005)

Christ, C. (1998) Taking ecotourism to the next level: A look at private sector involvement with local communities. In: Lindberg, K., Epler Wood, M. and Engeldrum, D. (eds) *Ecotourism: A Guide for Planners and Managers,* Vol. 2. The Ecotourism Society, Vermont, pp. 183–195.

CI (Conservation International) (2003) Botswana San Bushmen launch ecotourism project: Gudigwa Camp to reduce pressure on endangered wildlife. Press Releases 2 April 2003. http://www.conservation.org/xp/news/press_releases/2003/040203.xml (accessed 17 November 2005)

Crawford, S. (2000) Communal Areas Management Program for Indigenous Resources (CAMPFIRE). In: *Designing Tourism Naturally: A Review of the World Best Practice in Wilderness Lodge and Tented Safari Camps.* WA Tourism Commission, Perth, pp. 54–56.

Dahlberg, A. (2005) Local resource use, nature conservation and tourism in Mkuze wetlands, South Africa: A complex weave of dependence and conflict. *Geografisk Tidsskrift* 105, 43–55.

Davidson, A. (2003) Setting the stage for tourism development in Caprivi. *Conservation and the Environment in Namibia 2003/04,* 28–29.

Davis, A. (2003) Community based natural resource management in Namibia – an undeniable success. *Conservation and the Environment in Namibia 2003/04,* 8–9.

Davis, A. (2004) *Namibia's Communal Conservancies: A Review of Progress and Prospects.* NASCO (Namibian Association of CBNRM Support Organisations), Windhoek.

DEA (Directorate of Environmental Affairs) (2004a) Community based natural resource management (CBNRM): Enhancing conservation, development and democracy in Namibia? http://www.met.gov.na/programmes/cbnrm/Enhancing%20conse,%20devand%20dem.htm (accessed 17 November 2005)

DEA (Directorate of Environmental Affairs) (2004b) Namibia's community-based tourism policy – a simple guide. http://www.met.gov.na/programmes/cbnrm/cbtourism_guide.htm

DEAT (Department of Environmental Affairs and Tourism) (2002a) *Poverty Relief Programme.* http://www.environment.gov.za/ProjProg/PovRelief/index_PovRelief.htm (accessed 17 November 2005)

DEAT (Department of Environmental Affairs and Tourism) (2002b) *National Responsible Tourism Development Guidelines for South Africa.* http://www.icrtourism.org/sa/index.html (accessed 17 November 2005)

DEAT (Department of Environmental Affairs and Tourism) (2004) *Poverty Relief Programme, Tourism Business Development Programme.* http://www.environment.gov.za/ (accessed 17 November 2005)

DeMotts, R.B. (2004) Placing the local in the transnational: Communities and conservation across borders in southern Africa. In: Moseley, W.G. and Logan, B.I. (eds) *African Environment and Development: Rhetoric, Programs, Realities.* Ashgate, Aldershot, UK, pp. 189–212.

DSA (Discovering South Africa) (2002a) Magical Mbotyi river development. *Discovering South Africa – Eastern Cape,* September. http://www.dsa.co.za/dsa/ecsep02/magical2.html (accessed 17 November 2005)

DSA (Discovering South Africa) (2002b) Mboyti camp site – a mighty success story. *Discovering South Africa – Eastern Cape,* September. http://www.discovering-sa.co.za/ (accessed 17 November 2005)

Dunn, A. (1995) *Summaries of Some Recent Project Approaches to Conservation and Development.* Rural Development Forestry Network, ODI. http://www.odifpeg.org.uk/publications/rdfn/18/d-i.html (accessed 17 November 2005)

du Toit, J. (2005). Building blocks: Constructing the Greater St Lucia Wetland Park. *Africa Geographic* 13, 36–45.

Earthfoot (nd) Several community tourism projects offered by tribal people. Botswana Destination Index. Earthfoot. http://www.earthfoot.org/places/bw001.htm (accessed 17 November 2005)

Echtner, C.M. (1999) Tourism in sensitive environments: Three African success stories [Namibia]. In: Singh, T.V. and Singh, S. (eds) *Tourism Development in Critical Environments.* Cognizant Communication Corporation, New York, pp. 149–162.

Epler Wood, M. (2003) Community conservation and commerce. EplerWood Reports, October 2003. EplerWood International. http://www.eplerwood.com/images/EplerWood_Report_Oct2003.pdf (accessed 17 November 2005)

Ezemvelo KwaZulu Natal Wildlife (2004) *Corporate Strategic Plan 2004 to 2009.* Our Organisation Ezemvelo KZN Wildlife. http://www.kznwildlife.com/our_org.htm (accessed 17 November 2005)

Ezemvelo KwaZulu Natal Wildlife (2005a) Dube Conservation Based Community Development Project. http://www.kznwildlife.com/coast_dube.htm (accessed 17 November 2005)

Ezemvelo KwaZulu Natal Wildlife (2005b) Our Organisation-Community. http://www.kznwildlife.com/community.htm (accessed 17 November 2005)

Fennell, D.A. (2003) Ecotourism in the South African context. *Africa Insight* 33 (1&2). Tourism: Africa's Key to Prosperity. http://www.ai.org.za/africa_insight.asp (accessed 17 November 2005)

Flyman, M.V. (2000) Living for tomorrow in the southern Kalahari. Community based tourism in Botswana. http://www.cbnrm.bw/pages_sub_dir/CBT.htm (accessed 17 November 2005)

Foggin, T. (1996) The role of community participation in National Parks in Southern Africa. MA thesis, Roehampton Institute, University of Surrey, UK.

Foggin, T. and Munster, D.O. (2000) Enhancing links between rural communities and protected areas in KwaZulu-Natal through tourism – Abantu Bayasizana (people helping people) [Hluhluwe-Umfolozi NP, South Africa]. *The Journal of Tourism Studies* 11, 2–10.

Font, X., Cochrane, J. and Tapper, R. (2004) *Pay Per Nature View: Understanding Tourism Revenues for Effective Management Plans.* Report for WWF. Leeds Metropolitan University, Leeds, UK. http://www.leedsmet.ac.uk/lsif/the/documents/PayPerNatureView02.pdf (accessed 17 November 2005)

FTTSA (Fair Trade in Tourism South Africa) (2004) About Us, Fair Trade. http://www.fairtourismsa.org.za/ (accessed 17 November 2005)

Gariseb, G.G. (2000) The Nyae-Nyae Conservancy: Wildlife management and tourism development. In: WTO (comp.) *Sustainable Development of Tourism: A Compilation of Good Practices.* WTO, Madrid, pp. 127–128.

Gariseb, R., Swiegers, S. and Louis, M. (2002) Spitzkoppe community tourism restcamp project. In: WTO (comp.) *Sustainable Development of Ecotourism: A Compilation of Good Practices.* WTO, Madrid, pp. 193–196.

Goagoseb, D. and Gariseb, G.C. (2000) The #Khoadi//Hoas Conservancy: Wildlife management and tourism development. In: *Sustainable Development of Tourism: A Compilation of Good Practices.* WTO, Madrid, pp. 125–126.

Groenewald, Y. (2004) Who owns tourism? *Mail & Guardian Online* 30 November 2004. http://www.mg.co.za/articledirect.aspx?area=mg_flat&articleid=142983 (accessed 17 November 2005)

Gujadhur, T. and Motshubi, C. (2000) Among the real people in Xai-Xai. Community based tourism in Botswana. http://www.cbnrm.bw/pages_sub_dir/CBT.htm (accessed 17 November 2005)

Heath, R. (2001) Wilderness tourism in Zimbabwe. In: Smith, V.L. and Brent, M. (eds) *Hosts and Guests Revisited: Tourism Issues of the 21st Century.* Cognizant Communication Corporation, New York, pp. 153–160.

Hill, R. (2004) *Global Trends in Protected Areas: A Report on the Fifth World Parks Congress.* Rainforest CRC, Cairns. http://www.acfonline.org.au/uploads/res_protected_areas.pdf (accessed 29 November 2005)

Hitchcock, R.K. (1997) Cultural, economic and environmental impacts of tourism among Kalahari bushmen. In: Chambers, E. (ed.) *Tourism and Culture: An Applied Perspective.* State University of New York Press, Albany.

Honey, M. (1999) South Africa: People and parks under majority rule. In: *Ecotourism and Sustainable Development: Who Owns Paradise?* Island Press, Washington DC, pp. 339–389.

Hoon, P.N. (2004) Impersonal markets and personal communities? Wildlife, conservation and development in Botswana. *Journal of International Wildlife Law and Policy* 7, 143–160.

Hove, C. (2000) Zimbabwe – People and animals, a tense harmony. In: Weinberg, P. (ed.) *Once We Were Hunters: A Journey with Africa's Indigenous People.* Mets & Schilt, Amsterdam, and David Philip, Cape Town, pp. 103–120.

Hughes, D.M. (2001) Rezoned for business: How ecotourism unlocked black farmland in eastern Zimbabwe. *Journal of Agrarian Change* 1, 575–599. http://www.ies.wisc.edu/ltc/zimbabwe/conference.html (accessed 17 November 2005)

Humphrey, E. and Boonzaaier, W. (2003) *Joint Venture Decision Making Framework for Community-Based Natural Resource Management Areas.* Paper Prepared for WWF LIFE Program Namibia. http://www.propoortourism.org.uk/ppt_pubs_others.html (accessed 17 November 2005)

Hutton, J.M. and Dickson, B. (2002) Conservation out of exploitation: a silk purse from a sow's ear? http://www.taa.org.uk/TAAScotland/JonHuttonMar2002.htm (accessed 17 November 2005)

IRDNC (2004) The Caprivi programme. Integrated Rural Development and Nature Conservation [Namibia]. http://www.irdnc.org.na/caprivi.htm (accessed 17 November 2005)

Isaacson, R. (2001) *The Healing Land: A Kalahari Journey.* Fourth Estate, London.

Jacobsohn, M. (1993) Conservation and a Himba community in western Kaokoland. In: Lewis, D. and Carter, N. (eds) *Voices from Africa: Local Perspectives on Conservation.* WWF-US.

Jacobsohn, M. (2000) Namibia's Kunene region: A new vision unfolds. In: Weinberg, P. (ed.) *Once We Were Hunters: A Journey with Africa's Indigenous People.* Mets & Schilt, Amsterdam, and David Philip, Cape Town, pp. 122–146.

Jones, B.T.B. (1995) *Wildlife Management, Utilization and Tourism in Communal Areas: Benefits to Communities and Improved Resource Management.* Research Discussion Paper No. 5. Ministry of Environment and Tourism, Windhoek, Namibia. http://www.met.gov.na/pub_all.htm (accessed 17 November 2005)

Jones, B.T.B. (1998) Namibia's approach to community-based natural resource management (CBNRM): Towards sustainable development in communal areas. Scandinavian Seminar College. African Perspectives of Policies and Practices Supporting Sustainable Development in Sub-Saharan Africa. http://www.cdr.dk/sscafrica/jones-na.htm (accessed 17 November 2005)

Jones, B.T.B. (1999) Policy lessons from the evolution of a community-based approach to wildlife management, Kunene region, Namibia. *Journal of International Development* 11, 295–304.

Jones, B. and Murphree, M. (2001) The evolution of policy on community conservation in Namibia and Zimbabwe. In: Hulme, D. and Murphree, M. (eds) *African Wildlife and Livelihoods The Promise and Performance of Community Conservation.* Heinemann, Portsmouth, pp. 38–58.

Jones, B. and Murphree, M. (2004) Community-based natural resource management as a conservation mechanism: Lessons and directions. In: Child, B. (ed.) *Parks in Transition: Biodiversity, Rural Development, and the Bottom Line.* Earthscan, London, pp. 63–103.

Jonga, C. (2003) CAMPFIRE experiences in Zimbabwe. Global Transboundary Protected Area Network. http://www.tbpa.net/workshops_01.htm (accessed 17 November 2005)

Kanzler, M. (2005) Attempting Namibia's Matterhorn. 20 September 2005. News & Events. http://www.nacobta.com.na/ (accessed 17 November 2005)

Kanzler, S.E. (2005) Protecting rock art as part of conservation. Travel News Namibia. http://www.travel news.com.na/index.php?ArticleId=779 (accessed 17 November 2005)

Kepe, T., Wynberg, R. and Ellis, W. (2005) Land reform and biodiversity conservation in South Africa: Complementary or in conflict? *International Journal of Biodiversity* 1, 3–16.

KFO (nd) Dqae Qare game farm. D'kar Trust. Kuru Family of Organisations. http://www.kuru.co.bw/Game%20Farm.htm (accessed 17 November 2005)

Kgathi, D.L., Mmopelwa, G. and Mosepele, K. (2005) Natural resources assessment in the Okavango Delta, Botswana: Case studies of some key resources. *Natural Resources Forum* 29, 70.

Khwai Development Trust (nd) Khwai, Botswana. http://www.khwai.org/ (accessed 17 November 2005)

Kibirigi, R. (2003) The socio-economic impacts of tourism on poor rural communities: The Mpembeni community, Hluhluwe-Umfolozi Park, KwaZulu-Natal, South Africa. *Africa Insight* 33 (1&2).

Koch, E. (1994) *Reality or Rhetoric: Ecotourism and Rural Reconstruction in South Africa.* United Nations Research Institute for Social Development, Geneva.

Koch, E., Massyn, P.J. and Spenceley, A. (2002) Getting started: The experiences of South Africa and Kenya. In: Honey, M. (ed.) *Ecotourism & Certification: Setting Standards in Practice.* Island Press, Washington DC, pp. 237–263.

Koro, E. (2005) Success story: Community action lights up South African villages. People and ecotourism. http://www.peopleandplanet.net/doc.php?id=2446 (accessed 17 November 2005)

KZNTA (KwaZulu-Natal Tourism Authority) (2004) Zulu Cultural Villages. http://www.kzn.org.za/kzn/ (accessed 17 November 2005)

Lewis, D. and Jackson, J. (2005) Safari hunting and conservation on communal land in southern Africa. In: Woodroffe, R., Thirgood, S. and Rabinowitz, A. (eds) *People and Wildlife: Conflict or Coexistence?* Cambridge University Press, Cambridge, pp. 239–251.

Long, A.A. (2002) *Disentangling Benefits – Livelihoods, Natural Resource Management and Managing Revenue from Tourism: The Case of the Torra Conservancy, Namibia.* DEA Research Discussion Paper No. 25. Directorate of Environmental Affairs, Windhoek. http://www.met.gov.na/pub_all.htm (accessed 17 November 2005)

Macie, I.M.E. (2002) Assessing the participation of poor communities in tourism: Comparative case studies in pro-poor and community-based tourism initiatives in southern Africa. Master of Ecotourism Project. James Cook University, Townsville.

Magome, H. and Murombedzi, J. (2003) Sharing South African National Parks: Community land and conservation in a democratic South Africa. In: Adams, W.M. and Mulligan, M. (eds) *Decolonizing Nature: Strategies for Conservation in a Post-colonial Era.* Earthscan, London, pp. 108–134.

Magome, H., Grossman, D., Fakir, S. and Stowell, Y. (2000) *Partnerships in Conservation: The State, Private Sector and the Community at Madikwe Game Reserve, North-West Province, South Africa.* IIED, London.

Mahony, K. and van Zyl, J. (2001) *Case Studies of Makulele and Manyeleti Tourism Initiatives.* Practical Strategies for Pro-poor Tourism. PPT Working Paper No. 2. Pro-poor Tourism, UK. http://www.propoor tourism.org.uk/ppt_pubs_workingpapers.html (accessed 17 November 2005)

Mahony, K. and van Zyl, J. (2002) Impacts of tourism investment on rural communities. *Development Southern Africa* 19, 83–103.

Manwa, H. (2003) Wildlife-based tourism, ecology and sustainability: A tug-of-war among competing interests in Zimbabwe. *Journal of Tourism Studies* 14, 45–54.

Matlou, P.M. (2002) Ecotourism in South Africa. In: *Tourism: A Catalyst for Sustainable Development in Africa.* WTO, Madrid, pp. 47–49.

Maveneke, T.N. (1998) Local participation as an instrument for natural resources management under the communal areas management programme for indigenous resources (CAMPFIRE), in Zimbabwe. International Workshop on CBNRM, Washington DC, 10–14 May 1998. http://srdis.ciesin.columbia.edu/cases/Zimbabwe-Paper.html (accessed 17 November 2005)

Maveneke, T., Dzingirai, V. and Bond, I. (1998) Local participation as an instrument of conservation and development: The case of Campfire in Zimbabwe. Scandinavian Seminar College: African Perspectives on Policies and Practices Supporting Sustainable Development. http://www.cdr.dk/sscafrica/m&d&b-zi.htm (accessed 17 November 2005)

Mbaiwa, J.E. (2003a) The socio-economic and environmental impacts of tourism in the Okavango Delta, northwestern Botswana. *Journal of Arid Environments* 54, 447–468.

Mbaiwa, J.E. (2003b) Community-based tourism in Ngamiland district, Botswana: Development, impacts and challenges. In: Darkoh, M.B.K. and Rwomire, A. (eds) *The Human Impact on the Environment and Sustainable Development in Africa.* Ashgate, Oxford, pp. 379–402.

Mbaiwa, J.E. (2004) Prospects of basket production in promoting sustainable rural livelihoods in the Okavango Delta, Botswana. *International Journal of Tourism Research* 6, 221–235.

Mbaiwa, J.E. (2005a) Community-based tourism and the marginalized communities in Botswana: The case of the Basarwa in the Okavango Delta. In: Ryan, C. and Aicken, M. (eds) *Indigenous Tourism: The Commodification and Management of Culture.* Elsevier, Oxford, pp. 87–109.

Mbaiwa, J.E. (2005b) Enclave tourism and its socio-economic impacts in the Okavango Delta, Botswana. *Tourism Management* 26, 157–172.

Mbaiwa, J.E. (2005c) Wildlife resource utilization at Moremi Game Reserve and Khwai community area in the Okavango Delta, Botswana. *Journal of Environmental Management* 77, 144–156.

McIvor, C. (1994) *Management of Wildlife, Tourism and Local Communities in Zimbabwe.* United Nations Research Institute for Social Development, Geneva.

Mearns, K. (2003) Community-based tourism: The key to empowering the Sankuyo community in Botswana. *Africa Insight* [Tourism: Africa's Key to Prosperity] 33 (1&2).

MET (Ministry of Environment and Tourism) (2005a) Namibia's community based tourism policy – a simple guide. MET. http://www.met.gov.na/programmes/cbnrm/cbtourism_guide.htm (accessed 17 November 2005)

MET (Ministry of Environment and Tourism) (2005b) Community based natural resource management (CBNRM). Programme details. MET http://www.met.gov.na/programmes/cbnrm/cbnrmHome.htm (accessed 17 November 2005)

MET (Ministry of Environment and Tourism) (2005c) Namibia's first community owned lodge inaugurated. News release July 2005. http://www.met.gov.na/latestnews/lodge.htm (accessed 17 November 2005)

MET (Ministry of Environment and Tourism) (2005d) Integrated community based ecosystem management (ICEMA). Programmes. MET. http://www.met.gov.na/programmes/icema/icema.htm (accessed 17 November 2005)

MET (Ministry of Environment and Tourism) (2005e) Community funding facility (CFF). Information kit. MET. http://www.met.gov.na/programmes/icema/icema.htm (accessed 17 November 2005)

Michler, I. (2004) Delta blues & A way forward? [Modumo Lodge, Gudikwa]. *Africa Geographic* 12, 44–45.

Michler, I. (2005) Chaos in Khwai. *Africa Geographic* 13, 24.

Miranda, J.A. (1999) How people-power helps wildlife [Namibia]. December 1999. WWF International. http://www.panda.org/news_facts/newsroom/index.cfm (accessed 17 November 2005)

Munnik, V. and Mhlope, G. (2000) Uneasy paradise: A journey through Maputaland. In: Weinberg, P. (ed.) *Once We Were Hunters: A Journey with Africa's Indigenous People.* Mets & Schilt, Amsterdam, and David Philip, Cape Town, pp. 32–52.

Murombedzi, J. (2001) Committees, rights, costs and benefits: Natural resource stewardship and community benefits in Zimbabwe's CAMPFIRE program. In: Hulme, D. and Murphree, M. (eds) *African Wildlife and Livelihoods: The Promise and Performance of Community Conservation*. Heinemann, London.

Murombedzi, J. (2003) Devolving the expropriation of nature: The 'devolution' of wildlife management in southern Africa. In: Adams, W.M. and Mulligan, M. (eds) *Decolonizing Nature: Strategies for Conservation in a Post-colonial Era*. Earthscan, London, pp. 135–151.

Murphree, M.W. (2000) The lesson from Mahenye. In: Hutton, J. and Dickson, B. (eds) *Endangered Species, Threatened Convention*. Earthscan, London, pp. 181–196.

Murphree, M. (2001) Community, council and client: A case study of ecotourism development from Mahenye, Zimbabwe. In: Hulme, D. and Murphree, M. (eds) *African Wildlife and Livelihoods: The Promise and Performance of Community Conservation*. Heinemann, London.

Murphree, M. (2003) Lessons from non-lease tourism projects in the communal lands of Zimbabwe. In: Sihlophe, N. (ed.) *Leadership Lessons for Best Practice in Estuary Based Enterprise Development*. Part II – Case Study Presentations. Beahrs Environmental Leadership Program. University of California Berkeley. http://nature.berkeley.edu/BeahrsELP/reports/03safinal.html (accessed 17 November 2005)

Murphy, C. and Halstead, L. (2003) *'The Person with the Idea for the Campsite is a Hero': Institutional Arrangements and Livelihood Change Regarding Community-owned Tourism Enterprises in Namibia (Case Studies from Caprivi and Kunene Regions)*. DEA Research Discussion Paper No. 61. Ministry of Environment and Tourism, Windhoek.

NACOBTA (2003) Namibia Community Based Tourism Association. http://www.nacobta.com.na/ (accessed 17 November 2005)

NACOBTA (2005) Community-based tourism – from donor support to free market. 2 August 2005. News. http://www.nacobta.com.na/ (accessed 17 November 2005)

NACOBTA Newsletter (2003) Two new 'design' camps in national Park, Caprivi. *NACOBTA Newsletter*. August/September 2003. http://www.nacotba.com.na/ (accessed 17 November 2005)

NACSO (2004a) Conservancies. http://www.nacso.org.na/conservancies.htm (accessed 17 November 2005)

NACSO (2004b) Profile of #Khoadi//Hoas Conservancy. http://www.nacso.org.na/cons_profile/kHOADI_HOAS.htm (accessed 17 November 2005)

NACSO (2004c) Profile of Torra Conservancy. http://www.nacso.org.na/cons_profile/TORRA.htm (accessed 17 November 2005)

NACSO (2004d) Profile of Salambala Conservancy. http://www.nacso.org.na/cons_profile/SALAMBALA.htm (accessed 17 November 2005)

Namib Web (2005) Doro !Nawas Wilderness Safaris. Namib Web. http://www.namibweb.com/doronawas.htm (accessed 17 November 2005)

Ndovela, P. (2003) The challenges facing community owned eco-tourism enterprises: Lessons from Amadiba Adventures. In: Sihlophe, N. (ed.) *Leadership Lessons for Best Practice in Estuary Based Enterprise Development*. Part II – Case Study Presentations. Beahrs Environmental Leadership Programme. University of California Berkeley. http://nature.berkeley.edu/BeahrsELP/reports/03safinal.html (accessed 17 November 2005)

Nicanor, N. (2001) *Practical Strategies for Pro-poor Tourism: NACOBTA the Namibian case study*. PPT Working Paper No. 4. Pro Poor tourism, UK.

Novelli, M. and Humavindu, M.N. (2005) Wildlife tourism – wildlife use vs local gain: Trophy hunting in Namibia. In: M. Novelli (ed.) *Niche Tourism: Contemporary Issues, Trends and Cases*. Elsevier, Oxford, pp. 171–182.

Ntshona, Z. and Lahiff, E. (2003) *Community-based Ecotourism on the Wild Coast, South Africa: The Case of the Amadiba Trail*. Research Paper 7. Sustainable Livelihoods in Southern Africa. http://www.ids.ac.uk/ids/env/SLSA/slsapubs.html (accessed 17 November 2005)

Odero, K.K. and Huchu, P. (1998) Community-based ecotourism venture: The case of Sunungukai Camp, Zimbabwe. World Bank/WBI's CBNRM Initiative. http://srdis.ciesin.org/cases/zimbabwe-004.html (accessed 17 November 2005)

OPT (Okavango Polers Trust) (nd) Introduction. Several community tourism projects offered by tribal people. http://www.earthfoot.org/places/bw001.htm (accessed 17 November 2005)

Palmer, R., Fay, D. and Timmermans, H. (eds) (2002) *From Conflict to Negotiation: Nature-based Development on South Africa's Wild Coast*. HSRC, Pretoria.

Parker, S. and Khare, A. (2005) Understanding success factors for ensuring sustainability in ecotourism development in southern Africa. *Journal of Ecotourism* 4, 32–46.

Parliament of Victoria (2004) Zimbabwean case studies. In: *Inquiry into the Utilisation of Victorian Native*

Flora and Fauna. http://www.parliament.vic.gov.au/enrc_old/unff/report/util10-04.htm (accessed 17 November 2005)

Picard, C.H. (2003) Post-apartheid perceptions of the Greater St Lucia Wetland Park, South Africa. *Environmental Conservation* 30, 182–191.

Poultney, C. and Spenceley, A. (2001) *Wilderness Safaris, South Africa: Rocktail Bay and Ndumu Lodge.* Practical Strategies for Pro Poor Tourism. Working Paper No. 1. Pro Poor Tourism, UK. http://www.propoortourism.org.uk/safrica_sum.html (accessed 17 November 2005)

Pretorius, B. (2003) Ufudu fly-fishing operation: Lessons from a community private partnership. In: Sihlophe, N. (ed.) *Leadership Lessons for Best Practice in Estuary Based Enterprise Development.* Part II – Case Study Presentations. Beahrs Environmental Leadership Program. University of California Berkeley. http://nature.berkeley.edu/BeahrsELP/reports/03safinal.html (accessed 17 November 2005)

Pro Poor Tourism (2004a) *Case Study 2: The South Africa SDI and Community-Public-Private Partnerships (CPPP) Programme at Makulele and Manyeleti (Northern Province, South Africa).* Pro Poor Tourism, UK. http://www.propoortourism.org.uk/safrica2_sum.html (accessed 17 November 2005)

Pro Poor Tourism (2004b) *Case Study 7: St Lucia Heritage Tourism Programme.* Pro Poor Tourism, UK.

Pro Poor Tourism (2004c) *Case Study 1: Wilderness Safaris, Maputaland, South Africa: Rocktail Bay and Ndumu Lodge.* Pro Poor Tourism, UK.

Pro Poor Tourism (2004d) *PPT Facilitation at Wilderness Safari's Rocktail Bay Site: Analysis and Progress in 2003.* Pro-Poor Tourism Pilots in Southern Africa. Pilots Projects Reports. Summary Partner Scoping Reports. http://www.pptpilot.org.za/research.html (accessed 17 November 2005)

Pro Poor Tourism (2004e) Wilderness Safaris, Rocktail Bay Lodge. Pro-Poor Tourism Pilots in Southern Africa. http://www.pptpilot.org.za/Wilderness.html (accessed 17 November 2005)

Queiros, D. and Wilson, G.H.D. (2005) Doing it right the first time? Ecotourism on the wild coast of South Africa. In: Hall, C.M. and Boyd, C.M. (eds) *Nature-Based Tourism in Peripheral Areas: Development or Disaster?* Channel View Publications, Clevedon, pp. 203–217.

Reid, H. (2001) Contractual national parks and the Makulele community. *Human Ecology* 29, 135–155.

Renard, Y. (2001) *Practical Strategies for Pro Poor Tourism: A Case Study of the St. Lucia Heritage Tourism Programme.* Practical Strategies for Pro Poor Tourism. Working Paper No. 7. Pro Poor Tourism, UK. http://www.propoortourism.org.uk/ppt_pubs_workingpapers.html (accessed 17 November 2005)

Resource Africa (nd) Ecotourism fuelling development in southern Africa. *Fact Sheet No. 9.* Resource Africa.

Rice, M. and Gibson, C. (2001) Eco-tourism: Fact or fallacy? In: *Heat, Dust and Dreams: An Exploration of People and Environment in Namibia's Kaokoland and Damaraland.* Struik Publishers, Cape Town, pp. 135–153.

RLA (River Lodges of Africa) (2004) Mahenye Safari Lodge. http://www.riverlodgesofafrica.co.zw/mahenye.htm (accessed 17 November 2005)

Roe, D., Grieg-Gran, M. and Schalken, W. (2001) *Getting the Lion's Share from Tourism: Private Sector-Community Partnerships in Namibia.* Poverty, Inequality and Environment Series No. 1 (Volume 1, 2 and 3). Pro Poor Tourism, UK.

Rogers, D. (2004) A road runs through it [Wild Coast, South Africa]. *Africa Geographic* 12, 40–51.

Rossouw, R. (2003) A ride through real Africa [Amadiba Adventures, South Africa]. *Mail & Guardian* Online 2 June 2003. http://www.mg.co.za/content/13.asp?cg=0&o=21387 (accessed 17 November 2005)

Rozemeijer, N. (ed.) (2000) Community based tourism in Botswana: The SNV experience in 3 community tourism projects. Community based tourism in Botswana. http://www.cbnrm.bw/pages_sub_dir/CBT.htm (accessed 17 November 2005)

SAFIRE (Southern Alliance for Indigenous Resources) (2004) Community tourism action for Southern Africa (COTASA): Putting poverty at the heart of the tourism agenda. http://www.safireweb.org/ (accessed 17 November 2005)

SAFIRE (nd) Community based tourism. http://www.safireweb.org/html/cbt.htm (accessed 17 November 2005)

Samson, M. and Maotonyane, L. (1998) Community-based natural resource conservation and development: The experience of Botswana. The World Bank/WBI's CBNRM Initiative. http://srdis.ciesin.org/cases/botswana-001.html (accessed 17 November 2005)

Scheyvens, R. (1999) Dukuduku North community (South Africa), Makulele community (South Africa). In: *The potential for ecotourism to facilitate the empowerment of local communities in southern Africa: A summary report using selected case studies.* Massey University, New Zealand, pp. 33–41. http://geography.massey.ac.nz/staff/Scheyvens/index.html (accessed 17 November 2005)

Scheyvens, R. (2002a) Ecotourism: The CAMPFIRE programme in Zimbabwe. In: *Tourism for Development: Empowering Communities.* Prentice Hall, Essex, pp. 73–80.

Scheyvens, R. (2002b) The Natal Parks Board (NTB) and community conservation initiatives. In: *Tourism for Development: Empowering Communities.* Prentice Hall, Essex, pp. 91–93.

Scheyvens, R. (2003) Local involvement in managing communities. In: Singh, S., Timothy, D.J. and Dowling, R.K. (eds) *Tourism in Destination Communities.* CABI Publishing, Wallingford, UK, pp. 229–252.

Schiffer, E. (2004) *How Does Community-based Natural Resource Management in Namibia Change the Distribution of Power and Influence? Preliminary Findings.* DEA Research Discussion Paper No. 67. http://www.met.gov.na/pub_all.htm (accessed 17 November 2005)

Seif, J.A. (2001) Facilitating market access for South Africa's disadvantaged communities and population groups through 'Fair Trade in Tourism'. Fair Trade in Tourism South Africa, Pretoria.

Shewmake, S. (2002) Community based tourism in Botswana. http://www.cbnrm.bw/pages_sub_dir/ CBT.htm (accessed 17 November 2005)

Sinclair, M.T. and Pack, A. (2000) Tourism and conservation: The application of economic policy instruments to wildlife tourism in Zimbabwe. In: Dieke, P.U.C. (ed.) *The Political Economy of Tourism Development in Africa.* Cognizant Communication Corporation, New York, pp. 181–192.

Skhalele, D. (2003) The Makulele community private partnership: Lessons from a South African case study. In: Sihlophe, N. (ed.) *Leadership Lessons for Best Practice in Estuary Based Enterprise Development.* Part II – Case Study Presentations. Beahrs Environmental Leadership Programme. University of California, Berkeley. http://nature.berkeley.edu/BeahrsELP/reports/03safinal.html (accessed 17 November 2005)

Spenceley, A. (2003) *Tourism, Local Livelihoods and the Private Sector in South Africa: Case Studies on the Growing Role of the Private Sector in Natural Resources Management.* Research Paper 8. Sustainable Livelihoods in Southern Africa Project. Institute of Development Studies, Brighton, UK. http://www.ids. ac.uk/ids/env/SLSA/slsapubs.html (accessed 17 November 2005)

Spenceley, A. (2004) Responsible nature-based tourism planning in South Africa and the commercialization of Kruger National Park. In: Diamantis, D. (ed.) *Ecotourism: Management and Assessment.* Thomson Learning, London, pp. 267–280.

Spenceley, A. (2005) Nature-based tourism and environmental sustainability in South Africa. *Journal of Sustainable Tourism* 13, 136–170.

Spenceley, A. and Seif, J. (2003) *Strategies, Impacts and Costs of Pro-Poor Tourism Approaches in South Africa.* Practical Strategies for Pro Poor Tourism. Working Paper No. 11. Pro Poor Tourism, UK. http://www.propoortourism.org.uk/Anna_SA_sum.html (accessed 17 November 2005)

Spenceley, A., Goodwin, H. and Maynard, B. (2004) Development of responsible tourism guidelines for South Africa. In: Diamantis, D. (ed.) *Ecotourism: Management and Assessment.* Thomson Learning, London, pp. 281–297.

STMT (nd) Sankuyo Tshwaragano Management Trust. http://www.cbnrm.bw/pages_sub_dir/CBT.htm (accessed 17 November 2005)

Survival International (2005) Tourism and the Gana and Gwi bushmen. 9 March 2005. Tourism Factsheet. http://www.survival-international.org/ (accessed 17 November 2005)

Thoma, A. (1998) Focus on the San in Southern Africa. *Contours* 8, 14–17.

Turner, R.L. (2004) Communities, wildlife conservation, and tourism-based development: Can community-based nature tourism live up to its promise? *Journal of International Wildlife Law and Policy* 7, 161–182.

Ufudu (2004) The Ufudu flyfishing experience. http://www.ufudu.co.za/ (accessed 17 November 2005)

USAID (2004) Activity data sheet: Zimbabwe. http://www.dec.org/country/reports.cfm?region=africa3 &country=Zimbabwe (accessed 17 November 2005)

van den Berg, E. (2000) At the Dqae Qare game farm in Ghanzi. Community based tourism in Botswana. http://www.cbnrm.bw/pages_sub_dir/CBT.htm (accessed 17 November 2005)

van Rensburg, C. and van Rensburg, L. (2004) Mkambati people finally own their land! 26 October 2004. Mtentu Camp. http://www.wilderness-safaris.com/news/detail.jsp?newsitem_id=7947 (accessed 17 November 2005)

http://www.wilderness-safaris.com/news/detail.jsp?newsitem_id=5284 (accessed 17 November 2005)

http://www.wilderness-safaris.com/camps/camps.jsp?map_id=2588&method=menu

Vertfeuille, J. and Benn, J. (2005) Conservancy movement takes off in Namibia. People and ecotourism. http://www.peopleandplanet.net/doc.php?id=2557 (accessed 17 November 2005)

Vieta, F.E. (2002) Ecotourism propels development: But social acceptance depends on economic opportunities for local communities. *Africa Recovery* 13. http://www.un.org/ecosocdev/geninfo/ afrec/vol13no1/tourism.htm (accessed 17 November 2005)

Virtanen, P. (2003) Local management of global values: Community-based wildlife management in Zimbabwe and Zambia. *Society & Natural Resources* 16, 179–190.

Weaver, D.B. (1998) *Ecotourism in the Less Developed World.* CABI, Wallingford, UK.

Weaver, T. (2000) Kalahari, Namibia and Botswana: No respite for the San. In: Weinberg, P. (ed.) *Once We Were Hunters: A Journey with Africa's Indigenous People.* Mets & Schilt, Amsterdam, and David Philip, Cape Town, pp. 12–30.

Wheal, C. (2001) South Africa's new goldmine. Country report 23: South Africa. People and ecotourism. http://www.peopleandplanet.net/doc.php?id=1133 (accessed 17 November 2005)

Wildlands Conservation Trust (2005). Green Futures.http://www.wildlands.co.za/futures.html (accessed 17 November 2005)

Wildwatch (2003) CC Africa's six-point conservation strategy. http://www.wildwatch.com/conservation/strategy.asp (accessed 17 November 2005)

Wilson, A. (1998) Making people count [CAMPFIRE, Zimbabwe]. September 1998. WWF International. http://www.panda.org/news_facts/newsroom/features/index.cfm (accessed 17 November 2005)

Wolmer, W. (2004) Private-community ecotourism partnerships in southern Africa. Corporate social responsibility. Origo Cross-Sector News. Origo News. http://www.origonews.com/filemgmt_data/files/Private-community%20ecotourism%20partnerships%20in%20southern%20Africa.pdf (accessed 17 November 2005)

Wouter, S. (1999) Where are the wild ones? The involvement of indigenous communities in tourism in Namibia. *Cultural Survival Quarterly* 23. http://www.culturalsurvival.org/publications/csq/ (accessed 17 November 2005)

WS (Wilderness Safaris) (2004) About Wilderness Safaris. http://www.wilderness-safaris.com/ (accessed 17 November 2005)

WS (Wilderness Safaris) (2005) Mtentu Camp. Mkambati Nature Reserve. Wilderness Safaris. http://www.wilderness-safaris.com/camps/ (accessed 17 November 2005)

WTO (2003a) Okavango Polers Trust. In: *Sustainable Development of Ecotourism: A Compilation of Good Practices in SMEs.* WTO, Madrid, pp. 43–46.

WTO (2003b) Ghanzi Trail Blazers – Ked Trading Ltd. In: *Sustainable Development of Ecotourism: A Compilation of Good Practices in SMEs.* WTO, Madrid, pp. 47–50.

WTO (2003c) The Damaraland Camp: A partnership between the Torra Conservancy and Wilderness Safaris Namibia. In: *Sustainable Development of Ecotourism: A Compilation of Good Practices in SMEs.* WTO, Madrid, pp. 193–196.

WTO (2003d) Kairezi ecotourism project. In: *Sustainable Development of Ecotourism: A Compilation of Good Practices in SMEs.* WTO, Madrid, pp. 303–305.

WTO (2003e) Rocktail Bay Lodge & Ndumo Wilderness Camp. In: *Sustainable Development of Ecotourism: A Compilation of Good Practices in SMEs.* WTO, Madrid, pp. 251–253.

WTO (2005) South Africa: Tourism white paper and subsequent initiatives. In: *Making Tourism More Sustainable: A Guide for Policy Makers.* UNEP & WTO, Madrid, pp. 162–166.

WWF (1999) Ecotourism and conservation go side by side in Kunene. 20 May 1999. WWF-UK. http://www.wwf-uk.org/News/n_0000000192.asp (accessed 17 November 2005)

WWF (2001) Community conservancies in Namibia. In: *Guidelines for Community-based Ecotourism Development.* WWF International, Switzerland, 7.

WWF (2003a) CBNRM in Kunene. Bi-annual Technical Report. July–December 2003. http://www.irdnc.org.na/reports.htm (accessed 17 November 2005)

WWF (2003b) Caprivi CBNRM Programme Bi-annual Technical Report. July–December 2003. http://www.irdnc.org.na/reports.htm (accessed 17 November 2005)

WWF (2004a) Communal areas management program for Indigenous resources (CAMPFIRE). Working with Indigenous people: Zimbabwe. WWF. http://www.panda.org/about_wwf/what_we_do/policy/people_environment/indigenous_people/index.cfm (accessed 17 November 2005)

WWF (2004b) Sustainable wildlife management. Working with indigenous people: Namibia. WWF. http://www.panda.org/about_wwf/what_we_do/policy/people_environment/indigenous_people/index.cfm (accessed 17 November 2005)

WWF (2005a) Project LIFE – value of wildlife. Turning wildlife into diamonds. Project LIFE, Namibia. WWF. http://www.panda.org/about_wwf/where_we_work/africa/where/southern_africa/namibia (accessed 17 November 2005)

WWF (2005b) Project LIFE – How you can help. Visit the conservancy hotels and lodges. Project LIFE, Namibia. WWF. http://www.panda.org/about_wwf/where_we_work/africa/where/southern_africa/namibia (accessed 17 November 2005)

WWF (2005c) Project LIFE – community tourism. The Dam Camp. Project LIFE, Namibia. WWF.

http://www.panda.org/about_wwf/where_we_work/africa/where/southern_africa/namibia (accessed 17 November 2005)

WWF-SA (2003) Project on Wild Coast presented as case study for the World Summit. Newsroom. WWF-SA. http://www.panda.org.za/article.php?id=97 (accessed 17 November 2005)

WWF-SA (2004) Our living world: Dlinza forest 'girl guides'. *Africa Geographic* 12, 72–73.

WWF-SA (2005) Forests for life! *Africa Geographic* 13, 56–57.

Wyckoff-Baird, B. (2000) Environmental governance: Lessons from the Ju/'hoan Bushmen in northeastern Namibia. In: Weber, R., Butler, J. and Larson, P. (eds) *Indigenous Peoples and Conservation Organizations: Experiences in Collaboration*. WWF, pp. 113–135. http://www.worldwildlife.org/bsp/publications/ (accessed 17 November 2005)

ZBR (Zululand Birding Route) (2002a) Dlinza aerial boardwalk. http://zbr.co.za//boardwalk/index.htm (accessed 17 November 2005)

ZBR (Zululand Birding Route) (2002b) Special projects – Richards Bay avitourism marketing group. http://www.zbr.co.za//special-projects/bay-avitourism.htm (accessed 17 November 2005)

6

West Africa: Community-based Ecotourism in Forest Areas

Introduction: Ecotourism in West Africa

Ecotourism in West Africa is focused on remaining tropical rainforest areas and wildlife species such as chimpanzee, monkey, hippopotamus and crocodile (Ghana), tropical birds and giraffe (Niger). Ecotourism is mainly based in remnant forest areas of West Africa due to widespread rainforest clearing and poaching of wild animals in other areas caused by growing human populations. Countries in the West African region are also affected by political instability and armed conflicts, poverty, disease and corruption (Brown, 1998; Weaver, 1998). Indigenous peoples in this area include mobile pastoralist groups, the forest Pygmies in rainforest areas and also farming villages. A few West African countries have developed Indigenous ecotourism ventures, supported by conservation NGOs, aid groups and local tourism or park agencies. In Ghana, Gambia and Senegal, community-based ecotourism projects in local villages are focused around forest, wildlife and cultural activities. Local people also provide guiding and tourism services in rainforest areas such as Kakum National Park in Ghana and Tai National Park in Ivory Coast. Western lowland gorillas are a key attraction in the western rainforest areas of countries in central Africa (Sournia, 1997). The following sections review Indigenous ecotourism ventures in Ghana, Gambia, Senegal, Niger and the Ivory Coast along with lowland gorilla ecotourism in Cameroon and the Republic of Congo.

Ghana

Since the mid-1990s, the Ghana Tourist Board has supported community-based ecotourism and conservation in community forests and wildlife reserves at rural villages, together with local NGOs, the Nature Conservation Research Centre (NCRC, 2004) and the Ghana Wildlife Society (2003a, b). Ghana has less than 25% of closed forest remaining, with forest areas in remnant patches of 20–524 km² threatened by logging, mining and farming (GWS, 2003b). These community ecotourism projects aimed to generate income and assist the conservation of local ecosystems. The Ghana Tourist Board assisted with training and marketing for these community ecotourism ventures at key environmental sites such as remnant forests, wetlands and rivers and their wildlife. These ecotourism sites included the Amansuri wetlands, Tafi Atome monkey sanctuary, Afadjato nature reserve, Weichau community hippo sanctuary and Paga crocodiles. The canopy walkway in Kakum National Park is also reviewed.

Community Based Ecotourism Project

The Ghana Community Based Ecotourism Project (CBEP) began in 1995 as a collaborative venture between the Nature Conservation Research Centre (NCRC), Ghana Tourist Board (GTB) and 14 local communities (see Table 6.1). The NCRC is a Ghanaian conservation NGO promoting ecotourism and community conservation areas. A national steering committee for the project and CBEP coordination unit is steered by the Ghana Tourist Board. The NCRC worked with regional offices of GTB to oversee the ecotourism ventures. Villages established a tourism management team with local stakeholders to coordinate CBEP activities at each site. A US Peace Corps volunteer supported the local tourism teams. NCRC coordinated and implemented the ecotourism projects while GTB marketed the ecotourism activities and both provided training. In 2001, USAID funded the CBEP for 2 years while the Netherlands Development Agency (SNV) provided an ecotourism adviser with NCRC and a marketing adviser with GTB. The aim was to develop community-owned and operated ecotourism activities at key environmental sites in rural areas of Ghana. These included five wildlife sites, four landscape features, and five cultural experience or village sites. Tourism income and jobs were linked with the conservation of local ecosystems. Tourism revenue was used to develop the ecotourism sites and fund community facilities such as water pumps and schools. From 2001 to 2003, the CBEP improved ecotourism facilities (e.g. trails, toilets, visitor centres) and provided training on ecotourism service and tour guiding. Brochures and a website for NCRC were developed to market ecotourism in Ghana (Sikar, 2002). The website listed CBEP sites and other key attractions developed by conservation groups in the forest, Volta region and northern savanna of Ghana (NCRC, 2004). The CBEP sites were located in the savanna (seven), coastal plains of the Volta Region (four) and forest area (three).

Visitor revenue at these 14 ecotourism sites doubled in 2003 with tour operators featuring the sites. The Ghana Ministry of Tourism has given priority to ecotourism as a key sector for assisting with poverty alleviation in rural areas. The ecotourism project sites were assessed against basic criteria such as accessibility, visitor appeal, links with other attractions, local benefits and land tenure. With community consensus and support, other key sustainability criteria were community ownership structures, distributing benefits, involving youth and women, carrying capacity, poverty alleviation and conservation. These criteria were underpinned by funding support through loans

Table 6.1. Community-based ecotourism projects in Ghana.

CBEP Site	Region	Ecotourism attractions
Boabeng-Fiema	Savanna	Forest, 700 sacred monkeys (mona monkey, pied colobus), village
Paga	Savanna	Crocodiles, Chief's palace, slave market relics, village life
Siragu	Savanna	Crafts (pottery, basket, wall decoration), Chief's palace, market
Tanoboase	Savanna	Forest, nature trails, baboon, antelope, historic Bono shrine
Tongo-Tenzug	Savanna	Rock formations, sacred shrines and caves, village architecture
Wechiau	Savanna	Hippos, Black Volta River, trekking, birds, Lobi cultural tour
Widnaba	Savanna	Rare birds, elephants, traditional shrines, slave trade relics
Amedzofe	Volta	Forest, Mount Gemi, waterfall, hiking
Liate Wote/Tagbo Falls	Volta	Mount Afadjato, waterfall, hiking
Tafi Atome	Volta	Tropical forest, sacred Mona monkeys, traditional weavers, drummers
Xavi	Volta	Lotor River, canoe ride, birds, wildlife, Baobab grove, animist shrines
Boribi	Forest	Tropical rainforest, butterfly garden, arboretum
Bunso	Forest	Forest reserve, birds, butterflies, arboretum
Domama	Forest	Forest, rock shrines, River Pra, canoe ride, village life

Source: NCRC (2004).

and grants, and official by-laws reinforcing tribal laws to control activities and damage by visitors and community members at these ecotourism sites. However, government tourism agencies also lacked resources, skills and clear policy guidelines while taxes imposed on community tourism projects by District Assemblies were not being used to improve infrastructure and local services (WTO, 2005). Five of these community ecotourism sites in Ghana are reviewed below: Amansuri wetlands, Tafi Atome monkey sanctuary, Afadjato nature reserve, the Wechiau hippo sanctuary and the Paga crocodiles. The Kakum canopy walkway is also reviewed as a key nature tourist attraction in Ghana.

The first CBEP ecotourism site was at the twin villages of Baobeng-Fiema where Pied Colobus and Mona monkeys are considered sacred. Their monkey sanctuary opened to travellers in 1997. Other popular CBEP sites include the Tafi Atome monkey sanctuary (WTO, 2003a) and village with Kente cloth weavers; and Siragu with its geometrically painted adobe houses and women's craft cooperative. A fee of less than US$2 was charged per activity at CBEP sites affiliated with the NCRC. Other new community ecotourism sites in Ghana include a monkey sanctuary at Kokrobite, 25 km west of the city of Accra, and the bird-rich Amansuri Wetlands around the stilted village of Nzulezu (WTO, 2003b; Briggs, 2004). Local and international conservation NGOs supported these ecotourism sites.

Amansuri wetlands

The Ghana Wildlife Society (GWS) helped establish a community nature reserve at Amansuri wetlands. This wetland and lagoon area around the stilted village of Nzulezu has the largest intact swamp forest in Ghana with monkeys, marine turtles, birds and crocodiles. The Dutch government provided US$1 million to GWS for conservation and ecotourism activities at Amansuri Wetlands (GWS, 2003a). The Ghana Wildlife Society with BirdLife International has played a key role in conserving forests and wetlands as important

bird areas (IBA) supported by community ecotourism projects (Owusu, nd: Dei, 2000). Eight local communities were involved in the Amansuri Conservation and Integrated Development Project, initiated by GWS in 1997 and funded by the Netherlands Development Agency. Local people comprised 80% of the Amansuri project staff, with GWS promoting the area as an ecotourism destination. Environmental education, clean-up campaigns, and tour guide training were also provided. By 2001, the Amansuri Wetlands had received over 6665 visitors generating US$14,000 in income for the eight local communities involved. Other initiatives were a new visitor centre, broader walkway in Nzulezu stilt village, clean up of a 60 km beach and turtle watching. Amansuri has won the best community ecotourism award in Ghana (WTO, 2003a).

Amansuri was the largest ecotourism site in Ghana, in terms of size, villages, funding and income.

Tafi Atome monkey sanctuary

The Tafi Atome monkey sanctuary (WTO, 2003b) and village with Kente cloth weavers is located in the Volta region of Ghana. This CBEP site was supported by NCRC, a local NGO, with volunteers from the US Peace Corps assisting since 1995. The Netherlands and Japan funded this ecotourism project. The traditionally protected monkey sanctuary around the village had around 200 Mona monkeys. Believed to be messengers of the gods, the Tafi people had protected the monkeys for 200 years. Threatened by logging, hunting, farming and invasive pest species, the Tafi people sought help to protect the forest area. Each clan in the village donated land in the forest that was then declared as a monkey sanctuary. A grant from the Japanese government was used for reforestation and to build a visitor centre. From 2002 to 2004, USAID provided funding for new facilities, marketing and training. Local Tafi people worked as tour guides, forest stewards, or in shops, and also sold souvenirs or food to visitors. A guesthouse was built at the village. The Tafi Atome Monkey Sanctuary received about 150 visitors a month, generating US$350 in income. In the first 6 months of 2002, the monkey sanctuary received 908 visitors, generating tourism revenue of US$2100. Drumming, dancing and storytelling were also performed for tourists. The monkey sanctuary was threatened in 1999 when electricity lines were to be connected on poles through the forest; however, village protests meant underground electricity cables were laid. Other spin-off benefits from ecotourism were renovation of a school, streetlights, a chicken farm, and scholarships for local school children (WTO, 2003b).

Afadjato nature reserve

The Dutch government provided US$2 million over 5 years (1998–2003) for the Mount Afadjato Community Forest and key bird area. This forest area in the Volta region of Ghana had the rare golden cat along with numerous bird and butterfly species. The Afadjato community nature reserve and community ecotourism activities were established as an economic alternative to farming and tree cutting in the forest (GWS, 2003b). The project worked with chiefs and people of the Gbledi Traditional Area, developing tourist infra-structure and facilities, training local people and marketing ecotourism at Afadjato forest area. The community forest nature reserve and ecotourism at Afadjato was important as remaining forest areas of Ghana were threatened by logging, mining and farming.

Wechiau community hippo sanctuary

The Wechiau Community Hippo Sanctuary is located along a 40-km section of the Black Volta River in north-west Ghana. The sanctuary, one of the first community wildlife reserves in Ghana, is managed and operated by the local Daga, Lobi and Wala people of the region. The hippo sanctuary was established in 1999 by local people and traditional chiefs of Wechiau and Tokali. It now involves 22 local villages. The Ghana Nature Conservation Research Centre supported this community-based ecotourism project at

Wechiau. In West Africa, farmers are in conflict with hippopotamus that eat 50 kg of agricultural crops or riverside vegetation a night. Hippos are found in two remnant river populations in Ghana. The Wechiau sanctuary has 24 hippopotamus. In 2000, local leaders involved in the Wechiau hippo sanctuary received the 'community initiative of the year' award from the Ghana Tourist Board. In 2002, the Wechiau community prepared a sanctuary management plan to conserve the river area and derive income from ecotourism. Since 2000, Earthwatch volunteers have surveyed wildlife resources in the sanctuary, measured bird diversity, located hippo foraging plants and feeding grounds, and interviewed local people about farming practices (Earthwatch Institute, 2003a, b). This research information was integrated into the community management plan for Wechiau hippo sanctuary. Two local men trained by Earthwatch now work as guides for tourists visiting the hippo sanctuary. Local members of the Sanctuary Management Board received reports and attended Earthwatch meetings.

Paga crocodiles

Crocodiles are the main attraction at Paga, a small town in the far north of Ghana on the main road and river border to Burkina Faso. The 200 resident crocodiles are keepers of ancestral spirits, with a 300-year taboo on killing crocodiles and two perennial pools considered sacred. In 1998, elders of Paga appointed a local committee to work with a US Peace Corps volunteer to establish a community-based ecotourism activity based on crocodiles. Prior to this, guides and caretakers hustled visitors to the waterpools, threw a chicken at a crocodile then simply demanded money from tourists. A new visitor centre was built at Paga in 2000. Set fees were charged for each aspect of the visit to eliminate overcharging, commissions or aggressiveness. Guides hand-feed individual crocodiles, with up to 500 chickens fed in a month. Visitors closely observe and even touch the crocodiles, which 'suffer the indignity of being leaped on, prodded about and shooed off with a familiarity' (Briggs, 2004: 59). This type of wildlife interaction detracts from the ecotourism values of the site. However, local beliefs had conserved the crocodiles and also generated community benefits from tourism. [Ecotourism attractions in Cairns, North Queensland, also hand-feed large captive crocodiles while tourists handle small crocodiles with their jaws taped shut.] Other attractions at Paga are adobe houses, the Chief's palace and a former slave camp in rocky outcrops at Pikworo.

Kakum Canopy Walkway

The 330-m-long Kakum Canopy Walkway has six wooden platforms built around trees up to 45 m high and suspended walkways, slung from tree trunks with steel cables, 27 m above the ground. The canopy walkway, which opened in 1995, has spectacular views of the Upper Guinean rainforest. The walkway is 3 hours from Accra on a sealed road. The Kakum Canopy Walkway was designed and built by Conservation International, to provide tourism income for forest conservation. The 357 km² Kakum National Park was created in 1989. Kakum preserves a small part of the Upper Guinean rainforest that has been 90% cleared for timber and agriculture. A visitor centre opened in 1997 with displays on rainforest biology and the Akan culture of southern Ghana. Visitor numbers at Kakum National Park increased from 2000 in 1992 to 27,000 in 1996 and over 70,000 tourists in 1999, with 70% Ghanaian visitors. Domestic and foreign visitors at Kakum reached 170,000 in 2000 (Font et al., 2004). Wildlife at the park includes seven primate species (e.g. Diana monkeys, Campbells monkeys), 500 butterfly species, 269 bird species, forest elephant, bongo, antelope and duiker (NCRC, 2004). The park has guided hiking trails, interpretive walks about medicinal and other plant uses, a small campsite and a rainforest café that purchases produce from local farmers. Ghanaian food dishes are served at the park café and gateway village of Mesomagor. The Mesomagor bamboo orchestra perform music and traditional dances on Saturday in the park (CI, 2004).

The park entry fee was US$4 and the walkway user fee was US$10 (CI, 2004). Kakum National Park provided local employment and generated revenue for forest conservation (Buckley, 2003a). In 1996, the Kakum Canopy Walkway earned US$43,000 with additional income from park entry fees, gift shop sales and other revenue from local hotels. Revenue from the canopy walkway goes to the Ghana Heritage Conservation Trust (GHCT), and is used for conservation, operational costs, and community development projects (Vieta, 2002). The Trust received a US$2 million endowment from USAID in 2002. Tourism assets in Kakum, such as the walkway and visitor centre and rights to manage these businesses, were transferred to GHCT over a 2-year period. Tribal chiefs are included on the board for GHCT along with park staff, scientists, NGOs, local authorities and businessmen. The Kakum Canopy Walkway and souvenir shop now generates annual income of US$250,000 (Font et al., 2004). Some 2000 local people have park-related income and employment. Increasing entry fees from US$10 to US$37 for foreign tourists and US$3 to US$9 for local visitors would further boost park income and offset the opportunity costs of conservation limiting use of resources (Navrud and Vondiola, 2005).

The Ghana Wildlife Department also helped villagers around Kakum establish projects such as beehives and snail production (Omlund, 2001). These small enterprises compensated local people for not taking materials from Kakum Park. The forest at Kakum is sacred to local people, with the park located on Fante and Assin lands. Dei (2000) interviewed local people at five nearby villages who resented the restrictions in Kakum Park. Prior to 1989, local people used the area for farming, hunting animals and gathering plant materials. Of those interviewed, 33% were involved in park activities; however the Fante and Assin people felt excluded from the running of Kakum National Park. Local people considered the national park was important to conserve the environment (30%), other reasons (20%), for tourism (18%), and infrastructure development (16%), for employment (8%) and to protect the environment (6%). Local people were financially compensated for releasing land to the park.

However, park restrictions on traditional activities such as hunting and collecting forest products, thatch, poles and medicinal plants, intensified forest use by local people around the Kakum park boundaries (Dei, 2000).

Gambia

The Gambia, a small country around the River Gambia surrounded by Senegal, is mainly a beach resort and 3S (sun, sand, sea) destination for British, Dutch, German and other European tourists. The Gambia receives 100,000 tourists annually, most arriving on direct charter flights during the northern winter. There are ten ethnic groups in the Gambia, where half the population of subsistence farmers lives on less than one dollar a day. The Gambia has a Responsible Tourism Policy and an Association of Small Scale Enterprises in Tourism (ASSET) supporting local people involved in tourism. Large operators are adding up-country trips and canoe tours to their products (Goodwin and Bah, 2004). Some inland villages in the Gambia are developing ecotourism activities. The Gambia Tourism Authority promote ecotourism at Tumani Tenda, Makasutu Culture Forest, and other river camps.

Tumani Tenda Ecocamp

The Tumani Tenda Ecocamp is based in a mainly Jola village of 300 people and located on a tributary of the Gambia River. There are five extended families in the village, with four being Jola and one being Manjako (Jones, 2005). The people of Tumani Tenda own 140 ha of land including a community forest and cultivated land. The camp comprises six round houses of 13 rooms built of local materials and with fresh water supplied from village wells. The Tumani Tenda camp opened in 1999 and is run by 15 volunteers from the village that work as cooks, waiters, other service staff, and bird guides. The camp was built collectively; villagers also worked together to prevent bush fires and to stop other people felling trees in the forest. Tourists at Tumani Tenda Ecocamp experience Jola culture and village life.

Activities include bird watching, fishing, collecting oysters from mangroves, community forest and gardens, ox cart safaris, beekeeping, workshops on making soap and salt and batik tie-dyeing (ASSET, 2003). The Tumani area has 75 ha of forest and 175 species of birds. In 2001, some 200 tourists visited the camp with lower numbers in 2002 due to renovations (Jones, 2005). The Tumani Tenda Ecocamp is a member of the Association of Small Scale Enterprises in Tourism (ASSET), formed in 2001, which promotes the local benefits of Gambian tourism. Gambia is mainly a mass tourism destination for European visitors that stay at beach resorts on package tours.

The Tumani Tenda Ecocamp grew out of village efforts to improve their local forest and garden areas. Villagers at Tumani Tenda joined a community forestry programme in 1996, caring for Kachocorr forest. They constructed firebreaks, planted 3000 trees and developed forest management plans. Since 1990, more than 300 villages actively managed 6000 ha of forest in the Gambia (Bojang and Reeb, 1998). In 2000, the village of Tumani Tenda received full legal title and ownership of Kachocorr forest. Prior to this, in 1997, the village won a US$7000 award as the best environmental initiative in Gambia for their forest and horticultural gardens. The community wanted to use the award money to build an ecotourism camp. However, to avoid this cash award being mismanaged by villagers, the Gambia National Environmental Agency provided agricultural and forestry tools and machines instead.

Tumani Tenda received a grant of US$1000 from the British Volunteer Services Overseas to buy additional materials for the camp. Timber for the ecocamp came from the community forest. The village established a tourism camp committee and also built a restaurant in the river (Sanyang, 2001). Local men worked together to build a poultry hut to supply chicken and eggs to the camp and sell any surplus produce. Their venture was selected from 39 village ventures for funding. However, no accounts were kept for the ecocamp and some villagers were unhappy with the camp management. Of 35 people interviewed, tourism income from the ecocamp was identified as being used to pay school fees (26%), the annual village tax (17%) and employment (12%). Other additional income came from dancing tips (34%), tourist donations (1%) and craft sales (6%) The main environmental benefit of ecotourism was the retention of mangroves and forests which attracted birds and other wildlife of interest to tourists. Fast-growing tree species were used for timber and fuel wood. However, a fridge was purchased and a generator, since there were insufficient funds to buy solar panels (Jones, 2005).

Makasutu Culture Forest

The Makasutu Culture Forest is a 1000 acre nature reserve along the Mandina River in Gambia. The Makasutu reserve includes five ecosystems with diverse bird life, baboons, mongoose and lizards. The site includes a five-star ecolodge, Mandina River Lodge, a Base Camp hosting day visitors, the Baobab Cultural Centre with restaurant facilities and a dancing area, and guided wildlife or cultural tours in the reserve. The Makasutu Culture Forest officially opened in July 1999. Local people still live in the reserve and continue their daily life of fishing, collecting oysters and tapping palm wine. Visitors observe these daily activities, visit a *marabou* (holy man) and learn about history and myths. The reserve began with two Englishmen buying 4 acres of land in 1992. After 200 palm trees were cut down in the surrounding area, they purchased 1000 acres as a cultural reserve. Over the next 7 years, 15,000 trees were planted and 70 wells installed on the reserve. No trees were cut down in tourism development and buildings were designed to fit existing spaces between trees. Local people in neighbouring Kembujeh village were included in the ecotourism project. They were employed during construction, provide all the staff and lead guided tours in the reserve. Some 80 local people work at the reserve, and actively protect the local woodlands (GBG, 2004a; Makasutu, 2004).

The entry fee at Makasutu, open from 8 am to 6 pm, was 600 dalasi for a bird walk and creek trip being paddled in a dugout canoe and 800 dalasi with lunch and a cultural performance (GBG, 2004b). The Gambia Tourism Authority promoted ecotourism at Makasutu, Tumani Tenda and other river camps.

Birdwatching ecotourism

The Gambia has 570 bird species and birdwatching generates nearly a third of tourism revenue (Stratton, 2004). Local communities are protecting habitats with key bird species, supported by the West African Bird Study Association (WABSA), the Gambia Birding Group UK and bird tourism companies in the UK and the Netherlands. The community of Brufut with help from WABSA is protecting a remnant coastal forest area. An area of Brufut forest was fenced off to protect it from clearing and grazing. Visitors are charged 25 dalasi to enter the reserve with the community retaining 12 dalasi. WABSA is helping to define the forest area owned by the local community and encouraging British tour companies to pay the entry fee. The Brufut youths and environmental group is cleaning up the local forest while volunteer wardens monitor the area. The Exmoor Falconry Centre has funded the Brufut project. WABSA is sinking a well to form a pool area and also plan a bird hide to view Verraux Eagle Owls (GBG, 2004b). A warden's hut and mountain bikes are also needed at Brufut.

At Bansang Quarry, the local community is protecting a red-throated bee-eater colony of 50–70 birds. Half of the quarry was fenced off to protect the nest holes of these birds with the other half still used for local building materials. WABSA signed a management agreement for the quarry site with the local community. Gambia Birding Group UK funded the fencing materials and a hut for wardens at Bansang Quarry. Birdfinders, a British bird watching tour company, funded signs at the site. The Bansang quarry site was managed by WABSA. Members of a local youth group collected entry fees of 25 dalasi with 60% of this income going to the community. UK and Dutch bird tour companies were funding other WABSA birdwatching projects at Marakissa forest and Kartong in the Gambia.

The Gambia Birding Group also featured birdwatching tours at Tumani Tenda Ecocamp, with a local guide, Sanna Manneh, trained by the Makasutu Wildlife Trust. Local communities were encouraged to protect bird habitats while bird watching tourists spread income to rural areas (GBG, 2004a, b, c).

Senegal

The Senegal Ministry of Tourism and the National Commission on Sustainable Development has promoted ecotourism and sustainable enterprise projects since 1997. These include ecovillage study programmes organized through the EcoYoff Centre in the city of Dakar, and village-based ecotourism in the Djoudj National Bird Sanctuary in the Senegal River Delta. A Senegalese Ecovillage Network was established in 2002, with various clean up or training projects held at local villages. The Casamance region of southern Senegal had also developed and operated village tourism programmes since the 1970s.

Casamance village tourism

Village tourism in the southern Casamance region of Senegal began in the early 1970s, with initial support from a French ethnologist working in the area. During 1974–1991, some 13 tourism accommodation facilities with a total of 500 beds were built near local Diola villages supported by US$170,000 in aid funding from France and Canada. Eleven tourist camps were built in the Casamance region, a very traditional area of Senegal separated from the capital of Dakar by the small country of Gambia. The first tourist complex of round huts, a dormitory and amenities block was built in 1974 at the coastal village of Elinkine. Tourist facilities were built near villages with a population over 1000 people and restricted to 50 tourist beds or less. The villagers provided their labour to build the tourist huts using local materials such as wood, mud brick walls and straw roofs. Each tourist camp was planned and managed by a local village council of elected members with a team of six people overseeing day-to-day running of the tourism operations (Diouf, 2002; WTO, 2002). Training was provided for local villagers in guiding, hospitality and tourism operations.

Tourists joined in with village tasks, went on fishing boats, visited local beaches and observed wildlife. Tourist fees for accommodation and meals in 1990 were US$17 per person per day. By 1990, these villages received 20,000 tourists, 70% being French, earning tourism revenue of US$253,000 (Knights, 1993). One-third of this revenue paid the monthly salaries of local staff working at the tourism camps.

The remaining tourism revenue was used for schools, medical clinics, motorized fishing boats, agricultural equipment, water and sewerage systems, local mosques, interest-free loans to needy villages and seed funding for new businesses such as crafts, furniture making and market gardens. One village committee built a training centre teaching local people about sustainable fishing practices.

As with many Indigenous ecotourism projects, village tourism in Casamance combined both cultural and environmental aspects of ecotourism. The Casamance village tourism project increased awareness of environmental issues and local participation in conservation. Younger people with tourism work also stayed in the Casamance area rather than migrating to cities. Some negative impacts of village tourism were begging, westernization and tourism competition within villages, replacing a cooperative social system. Entrepreneurial locals set up restaurants or craft shops in their homes and provided guiding services or tours. Mass tourism resorts along the Casamance coastline, including Club Med, also saw the villages become a day-trip destination. The attitudes and behaviour of day-trip tourists conflicted with local people and overnight visitors staying at the villages interested in community ecotourism. Village tourism sites in the Casamance region had occupancy rates of 20% (Echtner, 1999; Buckley, 2003b). Tourism has further declined in the Casamance region due to the activities of separatist rebel groups. New ecovillages near Dakar are being developed in Senegal.

Ecovillages and sustainable development

The US 'Living Routes: Study abroad in ecovillages' programme has projects in

Senegal that focus on ecotourism and sustainable development in rural villages around Lac de Guiers, a main water supply. Organized through the EcoYoff Centre in the city of Dakar, the students spend 4–6 weeks living with Senegalese village families. Yoff is a 600-year-old fishing village on the Atlantic coast that, in 1996, hosted the Third International Ecocities and Ecovillages Conference in Senegal. Student projects on sustainable development are completed in five Senegalese ecovillages of Wolof and Serer people. US students work with village ecotourism committees to develop integrated ecotourism projects and participate in other sustainable development projects such as revegetation, solar energy, rural education and protecting endangered species. Students also work with staff from the Senegal Ministry of Tourism and National Commission on Sustainable Development, along with the World Bank and the UNDP. The 14-week-long Senegal programme cost US$2335 (Living Routes, 2004).

Djoudj National Bird Sanctuary

The Djoudj National Bird Sanctuary covers an area of 16,000 ha in the Senegal River delta. It is a Ramsar Wetland of International Importance and a UNESCO world heritage site. Local people were removed from the area when the bird sanctuary was declared in 1971. There are eight villages around the sanctuary, comprising people from three main tribal groups: Wolof, Moors and Peuls. Some local people worked as guides for tourists who went sport hunting in an area leased and managed by the Senegal Hunting and Gun Club. Conflicts with local people using natural resources in the sanctuary continued up until 1993. This included hunting, illegal fishing, illegal stays and animal theft (Diouf, 1997). After 1993, local people were consulted and involved in a new 5-year joint-management plan for Djoudi Bird Sanctuary. Volunteer village eco-guards monitored the sanctuary and educated local villagers about conservation. The inter-village conservation committee coordinated local views and decisions about ecotourism, reforestation, water management,

and forest pastures. The ecotourism committee coordinated local artisans who sold their handicrafts at a new craft store and eco-museum established in the bird sanctuary. A Moorish tent 'Khaima' was used to serve refreshments to park visitors. Three thousand tourists a year visited the Djoudj Bird Sanctuary, with the craft store visited by 1257 visitors in 1996/97. This generated CFA2.65 million from the sale of crafts and tea served at the Khaima tent, supporting 135 households (Diouf, 1997). A community-based bank fund was also established to finance village crafts and small business enterprises. Ecotourism benefited some local people living around the Djoudj Sanctuary but impacts on use of natural resources were not described.

Niger

Koure giraffe tourism

The last giraffe population in West Africa is found in the Koure region of Niger, 40 km east of the capital of Niamey (Ciofolo, 1995). Local farmers from Koure guide tourists in four-wheel-drives to view the giraffes. The trained guides in Koure know the regular trails and movements of the giraffes and the local ecology. The giraffes at Koure live year-round with farming communities and domestic cattle. The Dzarma people cultivate millet and vegetable gardens while Peulh and Tuareg herders also use the area. The free-roaming giraffes damage crops angering local farmers who chase them away (IRIN News, 2001). A giraffe conservation project in the mid-1990s funded by the EU and Netherlands Development Agency (SNV) supported local farmers and herders in managing natural resources, including giraffes (Le Pendu et al., 2000). Giraffe numbers at Koure doubled to 100; however numbers have fallen again to around 70. The giraffes in Koure and the neighbouring region of Dallol Bosso are threatened by poaching for meat, road accidents and desertification caused by tree felling. As a result, the giraffe population in Niger declined from 3000 to some 1911 giraffes by 1996/97. An education programme in Koure villages convinced local people the giraffes would provide sustainable income as a tourist attraction instead of killing giraffes for food. Tourists paid a set fee for a local guide, contributed to local development projects and purchased locally-made crafts (DTC, nd). As a result, farmers and guides have positive attitudes towards keeping giraffes in the area.

Both farmers and giraffes were affected by the 2005 drought and famine in Niger, with few tourists visiting this region.

Ivory Coast

Tai National Park

The Tai National Park in the south-west region of Ivory Coast was established in 1972. The 5340 km^2 park protects the largest tropical rainforest area remaining in West Africa. Tai National Park became a UNESCO Biosphere Reserve in 1978 and a World Heritage Area in 1982. Key tourist attractions in the park include 235 bird species, 11 species of monkey, forest elephant, the pygmy hippopotamus and chimpanzees that use wooden tools and stones to break open nuts to eat. Tourists observe chimpanzees habituated to human visitors, canoe the Hana River and climb Mt Nienokoue. Farming, illegal logging, gold panning and poaching of wild animals (chimpanzees, monkeys, deer) for bushmeat all threatened the park. Sixty animal poachers a year are caught in the park by forest guards whose equipment and subsistence costs are met by WWF. In 1988, WWF supported conservation efforts in the park that led, in 1993, to an integrated conservation project for Tai. WWF, GTZ (a German NGO), Dutch and Swiss groups and Ivory Coast park and forest agencies funded this project. This project supported management of the park with local Krou people living in surrounding areas and an ecotourism development plan. Ivory Coast has just 7% of forest cover, most within Tai National Park and the adjacent N'Zo Reserve. Hence, 11 community forests and alternative agricultural and forestry activities were supported in nearby villages. However, the local population has increased 1000% over the past 30 years with farms against the boundary of the park (Anhuf, 2000).

Nine tourism activity activities were established around the park with local people trained in conservation and sustainable development activities. In 1999, the 'Ecotel Touraco', a visitor reception centre with a 20-bed lodge of ten cabins, a restaurant and bar was opened in the village of Guiroutou at the south-west edge of the park. The visitor centre used solar energy, recycled rubbish and wastewater, and bought food produce from local farms. 'Ecotel Touraco' was German-managed but was to be handed over to local managers. The Ecotel resort attracted western ecotourists, scientists and birdwatchers. Young people were trained as tourist guides, employees at 'Ecotel Touraco' or as ecological assistants for research teams. The resort hosted several hundred tourists a year, with the park plan targeting 1500 visitors annually. Tourism income funded park patrols and environmental education programmes in local schools and villages. A canopy walkway and second research station were planned for the eastern part of the park in a secondary forest area, 35 km from the Ecotel site (Anhuf, 2000). Other conservation and farming projects were supported by WWF and GTZ at Comoe National Park in 1998 and at Ehotiles Islands National Park in 2000 (Bako, 2002; Debere, 2004; WWF, 2004).

Cameroon

Mount Cameroon Ecotourism Organisation

Mount Cameroon (4100 m) and five surrounding villages near Buea in south-west Cameroon are the focus of the Mount Cameroon Ecotourism Organisation (MCEO), established in 1999. Mount Cameroon is the second tallest peak in Africa, and the highest in west or central Africa. The peak is 36 km from the sea and 1 hour from Douala International Airport in Cameroon. MCEO was funded by the German Development Service (DED), German Technical Cooperation Agency (GTZ), and supported by the Cameroon Ministry of Tourism, local councils and the five local communities. Forest elephants, gorillas and chimpanzees were found in the Mount Cameroon forest. Local hunters were trained as guides to work for MCEO, helping to reduce hunting pressure on large animals. In 1999/2000, training seminars were held for 25 local guides and mountain porters. Trails used by hunters and farmers around the peak were designated as mountain treks of 1–5 days. Local villagers built a hut from traditional materials at Mann's Springs located at 2400 m. Porters, guides and tourists used this hut during the tourist season, that ran from November to July. Other income-producing activities were also supported such as crafts, traditional clothing, snail farming, and bee keeping. MCEO worked with a travel agency based in the city of Douala to promote ecotourism. MCEO also paid guides and porters to clean-up paths, trails and the mountain area used by tourists. The MCEO also maintained mountain huts, walking trails and lookout areas on Mount Cameroon.

Between September 2001 and July 2002, MCEO received 322 tourists, and employed 249 porters and 112 guides with a total of 114 guided tours and 757 days spent trekking on the mountain. Tourists paid set rates per day for guides, porters and the MCEO service. The total tourism revenue during this period was €6000 for guides and porters, and €3000 from other activities, with 60% placed in a reserve fund. Tourism income was distributed to MCEO (60%), Village Development Fund (32%), local councils (5%) and the Cameroon government (3%). One village used its share of tourism revenue to build an access road and renovate a communal building. Other villages constructed huts for health clinics and put in fire hydrants. Ecotourism also reduced the poaching of wildlife (WTO, 2003c).

Ebodje ecotourism project

Ebodje is a fishing village on the Atlantic coast of southern Cameroon. The Ebodje ecotourism project started in 1999 as part of the WWF Campo Ma'an conservation project. The village of Ebodje established an ecotourism committee with five councillors responsible for accommodation, culture, guides, food services and the ecotourism museum. Local guides from Ebodje lead tourists on forest walks to see local birds and wildlife, game traps, caves and a

camp of pygmy people. Other sea excursions include fishing, canoe trips, marine wildlife, nesting turtles and a sea turtle museum. These ecotourism activities at Ebodje were supported by SNV, the Dutch Cooperation Agency. SNV provided US$3300 to renovate three local houses as eco-lodges, and to build latrines in the village. SNV also trained ten guides and porters, and restaurant workers that volunteered to cook for tourists.

A further amount of SNV funding was to purchase beds, mattresses and paint for the eco-lodges. Local youths are paid by the village chief to patrol and monitor beach and forest areas for illegal activities. Local eco-guards from the village also reduced poaching of sea turtles and their eggs. The Ebodje ecotourism project was linked with sea turtle conservation that was part of the Campo Ma'an conservation project. Four sea turtle species were protected at Ebodje (Hawksbill, Leatherback, Green and Olive Ridley). 'Ebodje Ecotourism Village' is painted on a large sign at the village entrance.

Tourists at Ebodje paid an environmental compensation tax of CFA1000 (US$1.60) and a 10% surcharge on all other activities. Tourism revenues were evenly divided among the village and the ecotourism project office. Tourism has generated income of US$3000 and tourist service jobs (guides, porters, food and lodging). With the ecotourism project, beaches and trails are clean and sea turtle protection reached 87%. This success depended on both voluntary and paid support from villagers for ecotourism (WTO, 2003d).

Other local ecotourism projects are being developed by WWF in the 264,064 ha Campo Ma'an National Park, located 140 km inland. These include plans to build riverside bungalows and wildlife viewing towers in the village of Ebianemeyong. A canopy walkway, dugout canoe trips, recreational fishing and gorilla watching were also proposed. The park had an estimated 500 to 1000 gorillas and chimpanzees. The buffer zone of Campo-Ma'an included Bulu, Mvae and Mtumu ethnic groups and also Bagyeli Pygmies. Since the park was created in 2000, local access to hunting was reduced (Owono, 2001). Gorillas and elephants also destroyed agricultural crops planted by villagers. The Campo-Ma'an region has poor road access and a lack of infrastructure.

However, the village chief in one inland section of Campo-Ma'an has developed walking trails to the spectacular 25 m Memve'ele waterfalls in the park (van Bogaert, 2005a, b).

Lowland Gorilla Ecotourism, Southern Cameroon

Gorilla-based ecotourism for western lowland gorillas is being developed in the forests of southern Cameroon. Gorilla tourism aims to provide an alternative to logging forests and hunting great apes or other primates for bushmeat. Across West Africa, chimpanzees have declined by 75% and western lowland gorillas by 50% (Furniss, 2005). In Cameroon, local people can apply to manage Community Forests and Hunting Zones. Two villages in the Lomie region of south-east Cameroon, near the 5260 km^2 Dja Wildlife Reserve and World Heritage Site, were developing community-based gorilla tourism and research (Djoh and van derWal, 2001). Bantu farmers and Baka hunter-gatherers (Badjoule, Bulu, Nzime, Djem and Fang) occupy the periphery and buffer zone of the reserve. The villages of Karagoua and Koungoulou have included gorilla-based tourism in their forest management plans. A trail project habituating gorillas to human contact was being conducted in village forest areas by a local NGO, CIAD, with funding from the Netherlands (IUCN, SNV) and the International Fund for Animal Welfare. Villagers would provide services to scientific researchers and tourists, to supplement income from other sources. However, the gorillas were disturbed by poaching, with hunters earning CFA35,000–45,000 from killing and selling a gorilla for meat. In contrast, potential tourists would pay CFA140,000 each for a gorilla-watching permit. Commencing in 2000, two gorilla groups were tracked in the village forest areas, with two teams of four people for each gorilla group. The trackers were village hunters with each team supervised by an ex-gorilla hunter. Each village received income of CFA500,000 each month from the tracker salaries but only three trackers could keep up with the gorillas on a day-to-day basis. All of the trackers lost their fear of gorillas and wildlife became more abundant in the village

forest area where hunting ended 18 months previously. The number of gorilla contacts and length of time spent observing gorillas increased over the trial period in 2000. Other key issues for developing gorilla tourism were the legal status of the forest area, training local villagers, and sharing tourism income. Wildlifeline, a UK NGO, supported the Cameroon gorilla habituation programme with a special campaign to raise £30,000 for 2 years funding. The project aimed to legally protect lowland gorillas, train wildlife guards and ecotourism guides, produce tourism leaflets and brochures, and establish a poultry business to provide an alternative to hunting wildlife for bushmeat (Wildlifeline, 2004). However, logging roads were increasing the rate of hunting for bushmeat.

Other Lowland Gorilla Ecotourism Projects

Other projects habituating western lowland gorillas for tourism and research were conducted by WWF in Dzangha-Sangha (Central African Republic) and by ECOFAC in Lope Wildlife Reserve (Gabon), Monte Alen National Park (Equatorial Guinea) and Lossi Gorilla Sanctuary (Republic of Congo). The EU established ECOFAC in 1992 for conservation and rational use of forests in Centra Africa. ECOFAC supported the development of ecotourism in protected areas to generate income for area management. Gorilla tourism was developed as a key visitor attraction at Lope, Monte Alen and Lossi/Odzala. The programme provided infrastructure, equipment, and training for staff in these areas, and established partnerships with commercial tour operators (ECOFAC, 2004a). In Equatorial Guinea, a guesthouse, hiking trails and campsites were developed in Monte Alen NP, with tourism revenue funding community projects such as schools (Aveling, 1999; ECOFAC, 2004a). Guides and porters from the Fang people provided tourism services while groups of gorillas were followed daily at Essamalan, with a maximum of four people in a group with a ranger and guide. At Lope Reserve in Gabon, two gorilla families were visited by two groups of three people, a tracker and guide (ECOFAC, 2004b). The Indigenous involvement in these other lowland gorilla tourism projects was not reviewed.

Republic of Congo

Lossi Gorilla Sanctuary

In the 1990s, gorilla tourism was established in the Lossi area of the Republic of Congo, 15 km south-west of Odzala National Park. The village of Lengui-Lengui designated their traditional hunting ground as a wildlife sanctuary while Spanish primatologists working in the area since 1994 habituated two family groups of lowland gorillas to human contact (Aveling, 1999). These were the first lowland gorillas in central Africa habituated for tourism. The 250 km^2 Lossi Gorilla Sanctuary contained about 1200 gorillas (*National Geographic News*, 2003; Tsoumou, 2003). A 40 km^2 area in Lossi, a focus for research and tourism, included eight gorilla family groups with 139 gorillas in total. The villagers received a share of income from gorilla-viewing permits and guiding or service jobs (Bermejo, 1997). Tourism at Lossi was interrupted by the Congo civil war. In late 2002, an outbreak of deadly Ebola virus in the northern Congo killed 600–800 gorillas in Lossi, including the two gorilla families habituated for tourist viewing. In the core area, the Ebola virus killed 136 out of 143 lowland gorillas (80%) with only one group of six gorillas still found in this area (*National Geographic News*, 2003). This affected the local villagers who had created the Lossi sanctuary to benefit from gorilla tourism.

The Congo has a large area of central African rainforest and many Indigenous groups. However, security issues, lack of investment in tourism, poaching of wildlife and a lack of funding for protected areas in the Congo limit the potential of ecotourism (Inogwabini *et al.*, 2005).

Conclusion

Indigenous ecotourism ventures in West Africa are focused on remnant tropical rainforest areas (Ghana, Gambia, Ivory Cost and Senegal), and wildlife species such as tropical birds (Gambia and Senegal), chimpanzees, monkeys, hippopotamus and crocodiles (Ghana), giraffe (Niger) and western lowland gorillas (Cameroon, Republic of Congo). Forest areas and wildlife are under pressure due to forest clearing and poaching of wild animals caused by growing human populations. International and local conservation NGOs, aid groups and local tourism or park agencies have supported Indigenous ecotourism ventures to conserve forest areas and provide alternative local income. Local villages in Ghana, Gambia and Senegal have community-based ecotourism ventures focused on forest, wildlife and cultural activities. Guiding and ecotourism services are provided by local people in rainforest areas such as Kakum National Park in Ghana and Tai National Park in Ivory Coast and on village land near protected areas (e.g. Lossi Gorilla Sanctuary, Republic of Congo). Western lowland gorillas and chimpanzees are a key attraction in west and central Africa but their populations are declining due to Ebola disease and poaching. Local conflicts also affect the viability of community ecotourism ventures (e.g. Ivory Coast and Senegal). Drought, forest clearing, hunting and heavy reliance on using natural resources further mitigate against the conservation and use of natural areas for ecotourism, even in community nature reserves. Lack of capital, poor road access or infrastructure, along with limited marketing or support from government agencies also minimizes the number of ecotourism initiatives run by Indigenous groups. There were no Indigenous ecotourism projects discovered in Nigeria, Benin, Togo, Gabon, Liberia, Sierra Leone, Guinea, Guinea Bissau, Mali or Burkina Faso. In West Africa, there were virtually no Indigenous ecotourism ventures linked with private operators, one exception being the British-owned Makasutu Culture Forest in The Gambia. Most Indigenous ecotourism projects focusing on rainforest or wildlife rely on donor funding from conservation NGOs. This limits the effectiveness of local NGOs in fostering village-based conservation and ecotourism. With the exception of Ghana, government agencies for tourism, parks and wildlife also lacked the skills, resources and funds to develop and market community ecotourism ventures in rural areas.

References

Anhuf, D. (2000) The canopy crane in the Tai National Park (Ivory Coast). *ICAN Newsletter* 6, 6–7. http://www.evergreen.edu/ican/main/whatup6.3.pdf (accessed 17 November 2005)

ASSET (2003) Tumani Tenda Ecotourism Camp. http://www.asset-gambia.com/members/eco/tumanitenda.htm (accessed 17 November 2005)

Aveling, C. (1999) Lowland gorilla tourism in Central Africa. *Gorilla Journal* 18. http://www.berggorilla. de/english/gjournal/yexte/18central.html (accessed 17 November 2005)

Bako, O.L. (2002) Community-based project in the Tai National Park, Cote D'Ivoire. In: *Enhancing the Economic Benefits of Tourism for Local Communities and Poverty Alleviation.* WTO, Madrid, pp. 46–48.

Bermejo, M. (1997) Study of western lowland gorillas in the Lossi forest of North Congo and a pilot gorilla tourism plan. *Gorilla Conservation News* 11, 6–7.

Bojang, F. and Reeb, D. (1998) Community forest ownership: Key to sustainable forest resource management. International workshop on CBNRM, Washington DC, 10–14 May 1998. http://srdis.ciesin.org/cases/Gambia-Paper.html (accessed 17 November 2005)

Briggs, P. (2004) The scaly saga of Paga [Ghana]. *Africa Geographic* 12, 56–62.

Brown, D. (1998) Participatory biodiversity conservation – rethinking the strategy in the low tourist potential areas of Tropical Africa. *Natural Resources Perspectives* 33, July. ODI Website. http://www.odi.org.uk/ nrp/33.html (accessed 17 November 2005)

Buckley, R. (2003a) Kakum Canopy Walkway, Ghana. In: *Case Studies in Ecotourism.* CABI, Wallingford, UK, p. 43.

Buckley, R. (2003b) Casamance village tourism, Senegal. In: *Case Studies in Ecotourism.* CABI, Wallingford, UK, pp. 31–32.

CI (Conservation International) (2004) Kakum Canopy Walkway. The Ecotravel Center. Ecotourism Destinations. http://www.ecotour.org/destinations/kakum.htm (accessed 17 November 2005)

Ciofolo, I. (1995) West Africa's last giraffes: The conflict between development and conservation. *Journal of Tropical Ecology* 11, 577–588.

Debere, S. (2004) Travelling in Cote d'Ivorie. Safari Lodges in Africa. Siyabona Africa Travel. http://lodges.safari.co.za/Africa_Travel_Guide-travel/safari-lodge-travelling-in-ivory-coast.html (accessed 17 November 2005)

Dei, L.A. (2000) Community participation in tourism in Africa [Ghana]. In: Dieke, P.U.C. (ed.) *The Political Economy of Tourism Development in Africa.* Cognizant Communication Corporation, New York, pp. 285–298.

Diouf, A.M. (1997) Wetlands co-management: The case of the joint management of the Djoudj National Bird Sanctuary and its outskirts. The World Bank/WBI's CBNRM Initiative. http://srdis.ciesin.org/cases/ senegal-003-en.html (accessed 17 November 2005)

Diouf, P. (2002) Presentation du tourisme rural integre – Senegal. In: *Tourism: A Catalyst for Sustainable Development in Africa.* WTO, Madrid, pp. 41–46.

Djoh, E. and van der Wal, M. (2001) *Gorilla-based Tourism: A Realistic Source of Community Income in Cameroon? Case Study of the Villages of Koungoulou and Karagoua.* RFDN Network Paper 25e. July 2001. http://www.odifpeg.org.uk/publications/rdfn/25/e-iii.html (accessed 17 November 2005)

DTC (Dreamweaver Travel Centre) (nd) Niger: Land of desert and dreams. http://www.dreamweavertravel. net/nigerarticle.htm (accessed 17 November 2005)

Earthwatch Institute (2003a) Wildlife conservation in West Africa [Wechiau Community Hippo Sanctuary, Ghana]. Biodiversity Program. http://www.earthwatch.org/expeditions/oteng.html (accessed 17 November 2005)

Earthwatch Institute (2003b) Wildlife conservation in West Africa: Expedition Briefing [Wechiau Community Hippo Sanctuary, Ghana]. http://www.earthwatch.org/expeditions/oteng/oteng_04.pdf (accessed 17 November 2005)

Echtner, C.M. (1999) Tourism in sensitive environments: Three African success stories. In: Singh, T.V. and Singh, S. (eds) *Tourism Development in Critical Environments.* Cognizant Communication Corporation, New York, pp. 149–162.

ECOFAC (2004a) Making better use of forest helps the national economy – Ecotourism. ECOFAC Regional Programme. http://www.ecofac.org/EN/T2-BetterUse.htm (accessed 17 November 2005)

ECOFAC (2004b) Ecotourism. http://www.ecofac.org/Ecotourisme/indexEN.htm (accessed 17 November 2005)

Font, X., Cochrane, J. and Tapper, R. (2004) *Pay Per Nature View: Understanding Tourism Revenues for*

Effective Management Plans. Report for WWF. Leeds Metropolitan University, Leeds, UK. http://www.leedsmet.ac.uk/lsif/the/documents/PayPerNatureView02.pdf (accessed 17 November 2005)

Furniss, C. (2005) Seizing the moment: The Great Apes Survival Project. *Africa Geographic* 13, 40–51.

GBG (Gambia Birding Group) (2004a) Conservation. http://www.gambiabirding.org/cons.html (accessed 17 November 2005)

GBG (Gambia Birding Group) (2004b) Birding sites. http://www.gambiabirding.org/Sites.html (accessed 17 November 2005)

GBG (Gambia Birding Group) (2004c) The Gambia: 28th November-12th December 2003. Julian Hughes. http://www.gambiabirding.org/jhughesdec03.html (accessed 17 November 2005)

GWS (Ghana Wildlife Society) (2003a) Amansuri conservation integrated development project. http://www.ghanawildlifesociety.org/projects/amansuri.html (accessed 17 November 2005)

GWS (Ghana Wildlife Society) (2003b) Afadjato community forest conservation project. http://www.ghana wildlifesociety.org/projects/afadjato.html (accessed 17 November 2005)

Goodwin, H. and Bah, A. (2004) The Gambia: Paradise or purgatory? *Developments: The International Development Magazine* 27. http://www.developments.org.uk/data/issue27/gambia-paradise.htm (accessed 17 November 2005)

Inogwabini, B.I., Ilambu, O. and Gbanzi, M.A. (2005) Protected areas of the Democratic Republic of Congo. *Conservation Biology* 19, 15–22.

IRIN News (2001) Niger: Remaining giraffes endangered. IRIN News 23 November 2001. http://www.irin news.org/report.asp?ReportID=16020 (accessed 17 November 2005)

Jones, S. (2005) Community-based ecotourism: The significance of social capital. *Annals of Tourism Research* 32, 303–324.

Knights, P. (1993) *Tourism for Discovery in Senegal.* Environmental Investigation Agency, Washington DC.

Le Pendu, Y., Ciofolo, I. and Grosser, A. (2000) The social organization of giraffes in Niger. *African Journal of Ecology* 38, 78–85.

Living Routes (2004) Senegal: Ecotourism and sustainable development. Academic Programs. Living Routes. http://www.livingroutes.org/programs/p_ecotourism.htm (accessed 17 November 2005)

Makasutu (2004) Makasutu Culture Forest. The Gambia. http://www.makasutu.com/en/start.html (accessed 17 November 2005)

National Geographic News (2003) Massive great ape die-off in Africa – Ebola suspected. 6 February 2003. http://www.mongabay.com/external/020603_gorilla_ebola.htm (accessed 17 November 2005)

Navrud, S. and Vondiola, G.K. (2005) Using contingent valuation to price ecotourism sites in developing countries. *Tourism* 53, 115–125.

NCRC (Nature Conservation Research Centre) (2004) Discover Ghana's Ecotourism Destinations. http://www.ncrc-ghana.org/home.html (accessed 17 November 2005)

Omlund, M. (2001) Forest tourism: Exploring Ghana's treetops. http://www.peopleandplanet.net/doc. php?id=1137 (accessed 17 November 2005)

Owono, J.C. (2001) The extent and involvement of Bagyeli Pygmies in the management and development plan of the UTO Campo Ma'an, Cameroon. Forest Peoples Project. http://www.forestpeoples.org/ documents/africa/fpproj_cameroon_campo_maan_summ_eng.shtml (accessed 29 November 2005)

Owusu, E.H. (nd) The Ghana Wildlife Society and biodiversity conservation in Ghana. http://www.earth watch.org/europe/limbe/unpublimbe3.html (accessed 17 November 2005)

Sanyang, K. (2001) Tumani Tenda village-more than an eco-tourist camp. *Forest, Trees and People Newsletter* 44. http://www.ecoforestry.info/community.html (accessed 17 November 2005)

Sikar, T.O. (2002) SNV – Netherlands Development Organization: Tanzania Cultural Tourism Programme [Ghana]. In: *Tourism: A Catalyst for Sustainable Development in Africa.* WTO, Madrid, pp. 102–110.

Sournia, G. (1997) Tourism, wildlife and national parks in West and Central Africa. *Wildlife and Nature* 13.

Stratton, M. (2004) Behind the smile [Gambia]. *The Guardian.* 30 October 2004.

Tsoumou, C. (2003) Ebola kills 100 in Congo, wipes out gorillas. Reuters. 12 March 2003. http://www.mongabay.com/external/020603_gorilla_ebola.htm (accessed 17 November 2005)

van Bogaert, O. (2005a) A walk in the forest: Ecotourism Cameroon style. Stories from the Africa region. 3 February 2005. WWF. http://www.panda.org/about_wwf/where_we_work/africa/where/central_africa/ cameroon/news/index.cfm?uNewsID=18010 (accessed 17 November 2005)

van Bogaert, O. (2005b) Ecotourism Cameroon style. People and ecotourism. http://wwwpeopleandplanet.net/doc.php?id=2435

Vieta, F.E. (2002) Ecotourism propels development: But social acceptance depends on economic opportunities for local communities. *Africa Recovery* 13. http://www.un.org/ecosocdev/geninfo/afrec/ vol13no1/tourism.htm (accessed 17 November 2005)

Weaver, D.B. (1998) *Ecotourism in the Less Developed World.* CAB International, Wallingford, UK.

Wildlifeline (2004) Special campaigns – Great Ape project in Africa. http://www.wildlifeline.org/campaigns.cfm (accessed 17 November 2005)

WTO (2002) Village tourism program in Senegal. In: *Enhancing the Economic Benefits of Tourism for Local Communities and Poverty Alleviation.* WTO, Madrid, pp. 40–41.

WTO (2003a) Amansuri Conservation and Integrated Development Project (ACID). In: *Sustainable Development of Ecotourism: A Compilation of Good Practices in SMEs.* WTO, Madrid, pp. 111–114.

WTO (2003b) Tafi Atome Monkey Sanctuary. In: *Sustainable Development of Ecotourism: A Compilation of Good Practices in SMEs.* WTO, Madrid, pp. 115–117.

WTO (2003c) Mount Cameroon Ecotourism Organization (MtCEO). In: *Sustainable Development of Ecotourism: A Compilation of Good Practices in SMEs.* WTO, Madrid, pp. 59–64.

WTO (2003d) Ecotourism Project in Ebodje, a small fishing village. In: *Sustainable Development of Ecotourism: A Compilation of Good Practices in SMEs.* WTO, Madrid, pp. 65–70.

WTO (2005) Ghana: Community based tourism initiative. In: *Making Tourism More Sustainable: A Guide for Policy Makers.* UNEP and WTO, Madrid, pp. 149–152.

WWF (2004) Conservation and development of Tai National Park, Ivory Coast. WWF working in West Africa. Africa/Madagascar Programme. http://www.panda.org/about_wwf/where_we_work/africa/where/western_africa/ivory_coast/index.cfm?uProjectID=CI0004 (accessed 17 November 2005)

7

South-east Asia: Forest and Mountain Ecotourism, Hilltribes and Island Nations

This chapter reviews Indigenous ecotourism ventures located on tribal lands and protected areas of South-east Asia. Indigenous groups are found throughout the northern highland areas of the mainland Asian countries in the Mekong region and also the mountain or rainforest areas of the island countries of South-east Asia. These tribal or ethnic minority groups form a majority in some regions (e.g. hilltribes in northern Thailand, Laos and Vietnam; Ratanakiri Province, Cambodia; Yunnan Province, China; and Borneo). The chapter begins with a review of ecotourism in South-east Asia. It then describes Indigenous ecotourism projects in the mainland Mekong countries of Thailand, Vietnam, Cambodia, Laos and south-west China (Yunnan and Sichuan Provinces). Other Indigenous ecotourism ventures in the island nations of Indonesia, the Philippines and Malaysia, including Sarawak and Sabah in north-west Borneo are also reviewed. Key factors affecting the development of Indigenous ecotourism ventures in South-east Asia are discussed in the conclusion.

Introduction: Ecotourism in South-east Asia

Key drawcards in South-east Asian ecotourism include the rainforest and reef regions of Thailand, Malaysia and Indonesia and trekking tourism to see the hilltribes of northern Thailand and other areas. Other regional ecotourism attractions are marine protected areas around Sulawesi (Indonesia) and tribal longhouses and wildlife in Borneo. Ecotourism targets international visitors, is linked with cultural and adventure tourism products, and concentrated around resort areas in coastal and mountain regions of South-east Asia (Dowling, 2000; Weaver, 2002; Kontogeorgopoulos, 2003). Emerging ecotourism destinations are hilltribe trekking areas in northern Vietnam and Laos (Weaver, 2001) along with protected areas and minority groups in Cambodia. The Mekong Region of mainland South-east Asia includes many ethnic groups: 135 in Myanmar (Burma), 68 in Laos, 54 in Vietnam, 26 in Yunnan (China), 20 in Thailand and 10 in Cambodia. Ecotourism projects have been developed in Thailand, Indonesia and Malaysia since 1993 and in Vietnam, Laos, Cambodia and Yunnan Province (China) since 1999. Community-based ecotourism in the Mekong Region is at an early stage of development in protected areas and at tribal villages (Leksakundilok, 2004). National ecotourism plans have been prepared for Thailand (2001), the Philippines (2003) and Laos (2004). The impacts of forest clearing in South-east Asia (Mackinnon, 2005), dynamite fishing, political instability, low funding for protected areas and basic visitor infrastructure limit ecotourism to a few developed park areas near major tourist centres (Weaver, 1998a, b, 2001). With growing domestic and international tourism in South-east Asia, Indigenous communities are increasingly affected by tourism development but gain few economic benefits (Doco, 2002; Lasimbang, 2002; MRG, nd). 'There are currently few successful models for ecotourism in South-east Asia where benefits are being returned to local communities to encourage biodiversity protection' (Dearden, 1997). However, some Indigenous groups living in and around protected areas are now involved in conservation and ecotourism projects run by NGOs.

A regional meeting on *Community-based Ecotourism in South-east Asia* was held in Chiang Mai, Thailand in 2002, as part of the UN International Year of Ecotourism. The conference was organized by three Thai NGOs working in community tourism, the Responsible Ecological Social Tour Project (REST), the Project for Recovery of Life and Culture (PRLC) and the Regional Community Forestry Training Centre (RECOFTC). The meeting addressed key issues for developing ecotourism in protected areas, planning community-based ecotourism ventures and the impacts of tourism on local communities in South-east Asia, China and Nepal (Cochrane, 1993, 1996; Kinnaird and O'Brien, 1996; Pitamahaket, 1997; Ross and Wall, 1999, 2001a, b). Papers on implementing Indigenous ecotourism projects included tourism skills training at Yeak Laom in Ratanakiri Province (Cambodia), Semelai ecotourism at Tasek Bera, Pahang (Malaysia) and the Nam Ha ecotourism project (Laos). Papers about the impacts of tourism on Indigenous groups in South-east Asia included the Ifugao people in the Cordillera region (Philippines), and hill tribe tourism in Thailand and Sapa, Vietnam (RECOFTC, 2002; REST, 2002). These Indigenous ecotourism projects and tourism development issues affecting Indigenous tribal groups are reviewed in this chapter. For NGOs, community-based ecotourism promotes sustainable development and environmental conservation in South-east Asia.

In 1997, the Regional Community Forestry Training Centre (RECOFTC), based in

Thailand, hosted an International Seminar on *Ecotourism for Forest Conservation and Community Development*. This Centre supports community-based forest management and development in the Asia Pacific region. The ecotourism seminar involved 125 people from 20 countries with case studies reviewing the potential for community-based ecotourism to generate income and to help conserve forest areas. Key themes were local control of ecotourism to generate benefits, managing tourism impacts and training (Fisher *et al.*, 1997). An *Asia Pacific Ecotourism Conference* has also been held in Malaysia since 1999. The 2002 conference in Sabah covered planning, operating and marketing ecotourism ventures along with conservation and carrying capacity in protected areas (MATTA, 2002; Ecotourism Network Malaysia, 2004). Papers on Indigenous ecotourism in Malaysia included the Model Ecologically Sustainable Community (MESCOT) project in Batu Puteh on the Kinabatangan River (Sabah), Indigenous involvement in the Sukau Rainforest Lodge (Sabah) and ecotourism at Iban longhouses (Sarawak). These Indigenous ecotourism ventures in Sabah and Sarawak on the island of Borneo are reviewed in this chapter. The 2004 conference focused on ecotourism business development. The American Museum of Natural History also hosted a symposium, *Tiger in the Forest: Sustainable Nature-based Tourism in South-east Asia*, in New York in March 2003. The seminar covered ecotourism and biodiversity conservation in mainland South-east Asia, mainly in protected areas, with visitor fee use such as trekking permits in Nam Ha (Laos), guidelines for tour operators and tourism providing alternative income for local communities. The symposium also heard how the Sukau Rainforest Lodge in Sabah, Malaysia benefited Indigenous communities living in or near protected areas (AMNH, 2003).

Thailand

Hilltribe Trekking in Northern Thailand

The hilltribe villages of northern Thailand have been the focus of trekking tours since the 1970s. Some 100,000 visitors now go on hilltribe trekking tours around northern Thailand, organized by Thai companies and foreign tour operators (Cohen, 1989, 1996; Dearden, 1989, 1991, 1993, 1996). Treks from Chiang Mai, Chiang Rai and Mae Hong Son include overnight stays or even day visits to hilltribe villages. Northern Thailand is home to some ten ethnic minority or hilltribe groups, each with their distinctive cultural customs, colourful traditional dress, jewellery, handicrafts, huts and agricultural practices. The hilltribes originated from Tibet, southern China and Burma and migrated into Thailand over the past 150–400 years. These hilltribes from the Sino-Tibetan group include the Karen, Meo or Hmong, Lahu, Yao, Akha and Lisu people. Hilltribes from the Austro-Asiatic group include the Lua, H'tin, Khamu and the Mlabri, a small group of hunter-gatherers (Cohen, 1996). The hilltribes comprise about 1% of the total population in Thailand, with the 322,000 Karen comprising half of the hilltribes people (Intrepid Travel, 2002b). Most hilltribe villages in northern Thailand do not own their land, while major land use problems include deforestation caused by slash-and-burn agriculture and opium cultivation at higher altitudes. The hilltribe areas were opened for tourism to secure the border region, deter communism, develop the northern Thai economy and provide alternative income (Weaver, 1998a). Hilltribe trekking started as jungle tours for young backpackers; now half of the hilltribe treks are taken by older people up to 50 and include other soft adventure activities such as elephant rides and river rafting (Cohen, 1989; Dearden and Harron, 1992, 1994).

These hilltribe treks have brought few economic benefits and caused a range of social and cultural impacts in Akha, Hmong, Karen and Paduang villages such as begging, smoking opium, jealousy, tourism dependence, western clothing and social behaviours (Toyota, 1996; Johnson, 1997; Michaud, 1997; Bartsch, 2000). Hilltribe villages competed to attract tourists with one community guesthouse replaced by five family guesthouses in one Paduang village (Johnson, 1997). Hilltribe villages relying on tourism also reduced their land cultivation and lost fields allocated to them for planting crops to eat and sell. Some guides bought pipe loads of opium from villagers, and resold these at a profit to trekking tourists (Michaud, 1993; Chambers, 2000). Most of the hilltribes have no legal rights to land or Thai nationality rights with poor health and education services. The environmental impacts of hilltribe trekking include litter, water pollution, and bamboo cut for rafts causing habitat destruction and the decline of rare bird species (Brockelman and Dearden, 1990). Elephant rides were included in most trekking tours but the elephants, owned by northern Thai farmers, polluted the water, left dung and tore up plant foliage (Johnson, 1997). Plastic packaging generated more waste in hilltribe villages, while roads, electricity and television created more local demand for consumer goods and changed hilltribe culture (Leeja, 2003).

Most tour operators moved on to other villages and areas of northern Thailand, once a hilltribe village was spoiled by the impacts of trekking (Binkhorst and van der Duim, 1995; Johnson, 1997). A few tour operators maintained a good working relationship with hilltribe villagers, buying books and supplies for village schools, providing blankets and clothing and paying for regular visits by a doctor. Tour fees and donations were used to protect and improve the environment, with hilltribe villagers paid for monitoring and reporting poachers in the forest. Eco-friendly tour operators also reused bamboo rafts, and rotated their village visits, visiting each village only once a week with no more than six people. Many trekking tours, though, involved vanloads of 10–15 tourists taken to popular hilltribe villages (*Welcome to Chiangmai & Chiangrai Magazine*, 2004). For providing accommodation and rice, the village was paid 30 baht (US$0.75) per tourist. There was no other income from an entry fee or donations from tour groups, while the average family made US$40 per year from handicraft sales (Natural Focus, 2003a). Hilltribe trekking tours are also now offered in northern Laos and north-west Vietnam. In Thailand, hilltribe villagers often stage their culture by wearing traditional costume to sell handicrafts, work in craft markets, or to pose for paid photographs. Hilltribe people also worked in theme parks and 'tribal villages' owned by Thai entrepreneurs in north and central Thailand. In the 1990s, Paduang 'giraffe' women with brass coils around their neck were heavily promoted as a tourist attraction. The Paduang are a sub-group of Karen people and refugees from Burma (Cohen, 2001).

Intrepid Travel, an Australian tour company, visited Akha and Karen villages during their adventure tours in northern Thailand (2002a, b). A 4-day trek visited the Akha village of Baka located in mountain ranges 2 hours north of Chiang Rai. There were nine households and 40 people in this village, which lacked Akha ceremonial entrance gates or the annual Swing Festival. The Akha people had moved to this site from Myanmar and had no legal rights to land, while only two members had Thai identification cards. The villagers were forbidden from farming in a watershed area and instead worked on tree planting projects for the Thai Forestry Department. Intrepid began their village stays at Baka in 2000, with tourists sleeping in a separate hut. This income from tourist accommodation was shared among the nine households but there were local disputes about this. Local women also sold Akha handicrafts or provided leg and shoulder massages for tourists. Other income came from one Akha household selling soft drinks, bottled water and food (eggs, tinned fish) to tourists. This income was used to buy food, clothing, medicines and other items or to restock supplies of drinks. There were no direct conservation benefits from tourism at Baka and most Akha income came from tree planting.

A few NGOs promote trekking tours that bring economic benefits to hilltribe villages in northern Thailand (Palata Holiday Camp, nd; TEC, nd). The group, *Natural Focus*, developed ecotours with five hilltribe villages (two Akha, Lahu, Lisu and Mien) in the Doi Mae Salong area, north-west of Chiang Rai. A northern Thai NGO, the Hill Area and Community Development Foundation, established Natural Focus in 2000. They provided mountain life ecotours, plus craft workshops, volunteer projects and study/work programmes with hilltribe villages. Tourists were accommodated with hilltribe families in village homestays or in the Mountaintop Home, a dormitory and learning centre for Indigenous people (Natural Focus, 2003a, b). In this community-based ecotourism, villagers participated in planning and managing trekking or study tours that brought greater financial benefits and increased local awareness of both cultural traditions and nature conservation. Villagers also controlled the level of tourism (Leeja and Buchan, 2002). The Mirror Art Group, an NGO based in Chiang Rai, developed a hilltribe museum in a Lahu village with computers and video recording details of changing cultural traditions, such as wedding ceremonies, significance of clothing, and hunting skills (Macan-Markar, 2003). Thai government policies and modernization were causing the loss of cultural knowledge among hilltribes youth (Leeja, 2003). Funded by the Rockefeller Foundation, the museum educated both visitors and hilltribes people.

The *Project for Recovery of Life and Culture* (PLRC) is a northern Thai NGO promoting forest conservation and rural development with hilltribes in the Pai watershed of Ma Hong Son province. PLRC supports community organizations of the Karen, Lahu, Lisu and Shan people in maintaining forest resources for environmental conservation. The PLRC community-based tourism programme supports sustainable development among the hilltribes of Mae Hong Son. This hilltribe community tourism supports forest conservation, builds skills in tourism management and guiding, provides alternative income and employment, assists cultural preservation and increases awareness of tourism (Earthfoot, 2004a). Local hilltribe guides lead seven PLRC community tours of ethnic villages around Mae Hong Son. The tours visit Karen, Lahu and Shan villages, with village activities (weaving group, blacksmith, rice fields, fishing), learning about hilltribe history and culture, and accommodation with homestay families in each village. The 2–5 day treks visit a community forest and the summit of Doi Pui, the highest mountain in Mae Hong Son, waterfalls, and a rainforest area with great hornbills. Earthfoot (2004b), a responsible tourism agency and travel website, promoted the PRLC hilltribe treks.

The *Responsible Ecological Social Tours* (REST) project is a Thai NGO based in

Bangkok. Formed in 1994, REST promotes community-based sustainable tourism, with training and study tours at villages in north and south Thailand. The REST approach to community-based tourism is based around sustainable resource use, community control of tourism and educating visitors (REST, 2004). In 2000–2003, REST trained Thai staff with the Departments of Hill Tribe Welfare and Environmental Quality Promotion in community-based ecotourism and tourism management (Suansri, 2003). REST mainly helped local people to manage tourism in their home villages. The income from community tours is shared between REST (20%), local villagers hosting tourists (60%), with 20% contributed to a community fund for village facilities (Suansri, 2002). A REST 3-day/2-night tour is provided of Ban Huai Mee, a Karen hilltribe village of 22 households in Mae Hong Son province. The Karen villagers wore their traditional costume and derived income from handicrafts, orchids and tourism (food, guides, homestay, cultural show and donations). REST trained local Karen villagers in managing the tourism programme and activities, supported by the Canada Fund. The village hosted two groups of visitors a month, with homestay provision rotated between families to avoid jealousy and share income. At Ban Huai Mee, 15% of tourism income went to the Ecotourism Club managing the project, 5% to a village community fund and 80% to families providing accommodation and meals for tourists (Kwantu, 2001). Rather than leaving the village for jobs, young people learnt about Karen history, architecture, agriculture, religion and herbal medicine from elders, to become tour guides (Sukrung, 1997). Since 2001, the Karen villagers were also involved in an annual international training course on community-based tourism run by RECOFTC and The Mountain Institute.

The *Hill Area Development Foundation* (HADF) hosted an ecotourism workshop in Chiang Rai in early 2000. REST focused on environmental and social development for hilltribe villages in the Chiang Rai area. The ecotourism workshop was organized by the Thai Director of REST and John Sinclair from Australia, both winners of the Goldman Environmental Prize. REST aimed to generate income from ecotourism and promote forest conservation among the hilltribes in the Chiang Rai area. These included Lisu, Lahu, Yao and Akha hilltribes. The two-day workshop discussed ecotourism development issues with hilltribe villagers and development workers (Sinclair, 2000). These included the social impacts of tourism, villages competing to attract tourists and tour operators, and only a few families benefiting from tourism. To develop ecotourism among the Chiang Rai hilltribes, HADF needed to take a lead role as a marketing and coordinating agency to set fair tour prices and monitor visitation.

In the Umphang District, Karen villagers benefited from tourism based around the forest, river and wildlife in the Umphang Wildlife Reserve. Karen farmers worked as guides, punters on bamboo rafts, elephant mahouts, bus drivers, cooks and housekeepers and also ran guesthouses, travel agencies and restaurants. This scenic area, with 18,000 tourists annually, had government support for community ecotourism with projects from 1995 to 1998, such as tree planting, hilltribes tourism training, crafts, local produce and preserving traditional houses for homestay programmes (Hatton, 2002a).

Hilltribes in northern Thai national parks

Most national parks in northern Thailand include hilltribe villages and crop farming areas. The parks feature forest, waterfalls, mountains, 150 mammal species and many unique bird species. In a few cases, at Khlong Lan and Mae Wong parks, hilltribe villages were forcibly relocated outside park boundaries to prevent deforestation caused by slash-and-burn agriculture to feed growing populations. The hilltribes also hunt wildlife in and around park areas. According to Pleumarom (2002), the policy of the Thai Forestry Department is to remove hilltribe villages from protected areas. Use of natural resources in parks led to conflicts with national park officials while some hilltribe villagers worked at government-run tourist facilities or participated in park ecotourism projects to avoid eviction. At Doi Suthep-Pui National Park, near Chiang Mai, Hmong hilltribe villages are involved in reforestation efforts, with a community tree nursery, tree-planting efforts and protecting trees from forest fires. Hilltribe villages welcome tourists at the northern parks of Nam Tok Mae Surin, Doi Suthep-Pui and at Doi Inthanon, the main bird watching site in Thailand with 386 bird species (Elliott, 2001).

Doi Inthanon National Park

Doi Inthanon National Park is 60 km from the northern city of Chiang Mai and receives 1 million visitors a year, mainly Thai nationals. Birdwatchers and foreign tourists on the last day of a 3–4 day hilltribe trekking tour also visited the park (Hvenegaard and Dearden, 1998). The park has the highest peak in Thailand, with a summit road, three visitor centres, restaurants, bungalows and a campground. Doi Inthanon also has Karen and Meo (Hmong) villages and their agricultural plots. About 4500 people lived inside Doi Inthanon and another 12,000 people lived within 5 km of the park boundary. Local households used the park resources for fuel wood (88%), gathering plants (77%), construction materials (66%) and hunting (47%), with 40% of the park and 34% of surrounding forest encroached upon. Ecotourism was seen as a way to reduce hilltribe impacts on natural resources in the park (Dearden, 1996; Dearden et al., 1996). A Canada Fund project in the early 1990s developed the Ang-Ka Nature Trail and ecotour trails through Karen and Hmong villages that sold their handicrafts to tourists; however, little money went to local people (Dowling and Hardman, 1996). Working with park officers, Karen people at the village of Ban Mae Klang Luang in Doi Inthanon also started an ecotourism service with guided treks to see birds in the park and provide overnight accommodation. This enterprise has encouraged Karen villagers to stop hunting, preserve bird habitat through better agricultural practices and reduce flower plantations with heavy use of chemicals (Dearden et al., 1996; Emphandu and Chettamart, 1998; Elliott, 2001). Another project involved tree planting and reintroducing gibbons previously hunted out (Nepal, 2002). A small ecolodge with guiding services was proposed for visitors at one hilltribe village on the mountain. Tourism profits would fund village welfare projects and conservation activities (Dearden, 1997). Apart from this initiative, there is little hilltribe ecotourism in Thailand's northern national parks (Dearden, 1995).

Intrepid Travel (2002b) visited Khun Puai, a large Karen hilltribe village of 62 households and 400 people located close to the border of Doi Inthanon National Park. Plans to expand this park would include this Karen village located in the foothills. Tour groups had visited this village since the 1980s. The Intrepid treks to this village started in 1997, with an overnight stay during a 3-day trek. The Karen villagers were subsistence rice farmers, with women still wearing traditional dress and ornaments. Eleven households still followed animist beliefs while 51 households were Christian. Some Karen men sold flowers or worked as farm labourers. The villagers of Khun Puai also provided homestay accommodation, two porters, and one man gave massages for tour groups. Karen women sold handicrafts and clothing to visitors, generating 50–70% of the total income from tourism. The households directly involved in hosting tour groups (e.g. porters, accommodation) received a weekly wage. Tourism income was spent on purchasing rice, other foods, cotton, soap and schooling. The tour company also donated school clothes, books and vegetable seeds, cleaned up rubbish in the village such as discarded plastic packaging, and provided excursions for young Karen people. Village walks guided by Karen through forest areas and rice fields were suggested as an extra visitor activity.

Lisu Lodge

Lisu Lodge in northern Thailand is an ecotourism partnership between the Lisu hilltribe village of Dton Loong and an international tour company, the Asian Oasis Collection. The village of 750 people also has 20 Akha families. Lisu village members built the ecolodge that aims to protect hilltribe culture and increase the local benefits of tourism. Located 50 km north of Chiang Mai, the lodge was built on land leased from the village, with six guest rooms in the style of a hilltribe home. Opened in 1992, Lisu Lodge provides exclusive accommodation and contact with hilltribe culture for adventurous tourists (Muqbil, 1994; Seltzer and Grant, 2003). The lodge employs seven Lisu staff members and guides, including the manager who collaborates with Lisu village elders on cultural matters. The Lisu operate many of the tourist activities at the lodge such as guided tours of the village, four-wheel-drive tours, ox cart rides, trekking, rafting, elephant safaris and mountain biking. Family visits and Lisu cultural traditions are shared with visitors. A handicraft centre and shop at the lodge displays Lisu crafts such as silverware, woodwork, jewellery, weaving and embroidery. Treks from 1 to 4 days visit other hilltribe villages. Fact sheets at the lodge describe the hilltribes, Lisu culture and surrounding environment of the area. All food for Lisu Lodge was bought locally with villagers encouraged to grow new crops for sale. Lisu Lodge aims to preserve cultural diversity, encourage respect for Lisu culture, provide tourism income for hilltribes and provide a sustainable and profitable model of hilltribe ecotourism (REST, 2004). In 2000 and 2001, Lisu Lodge won ecotourism awards from Conservation International and Conde Nast *Traveler* magazine for preserving Lisu culture (Johansson and Diamantis, 2004; Lisu Lodge, 2005).

Vietnam

Ba Be National Park

Ba Be National Park, 250 km north of Hanoi, is a 500 km^2 area with the largest natural lake in Vietnam. Key features of the park include boating trips on Ba Be Lake, limestone cliffs and caves, forest, waterfalls, monkeys and 111 bird species. In 2000, Ba Be National Park received 28,000 visitors, with 3000 international visitors. The park also has small communities of Hmong and Dai hilltribe people. Park visitors can spend a night at a Dai stilt house in the village of Pac Ngoi, reached on a 30-minute boat ride up Ba Be Lake (Dye, 2001). In total, Ba Be Park has five ethnic

groups living in nine villages, with some villages farming flat lands near the shore of the lake. A community conservation and ecotourism project for ethnic groups in the park was implemented in 1999. The 4-year project was funded by the UN Protected Areas for Resource Conservation (PARC) programme with planning support from the World Conservation Union (IUCN). Staff from Vietnam's National Park Administration and Forest Protection Department implemented this ecotourism project.

Some 5 million people live within protected areas and special-use forests in Vietnam, with land allocation, work contracts, ecotourism and involving local people central to conservation (Bao, 2001).

Wildlife was decreasing in Ba Be Park due to forest clearing, hunting, harvesting of forest resources, and fish bombing by ethnic villagers. In 2001, programmes began with environmental education of villagers and greater park control of resource activities. An ecotourism strategy was also developed in consultation with communities living in the park, with ecotourism facilities and services providing economic benefits for villagers. Local residents rented boats to visitors and guided tours to villages and natural features around the lake. Local people owned and operated a restaurant at the boat landing while a lakeshore village developed homestays for visitors. Three ecotourism trails were also developed along with a park interpretation centre. These ecotourism facilities provided income and new jobs for residents in tour guiding, boat operation, accommodation, restaurants, and as park staff. The project included training for villagers in tour guiding and hospitality. Tourism work provided an alternative to logging, hunting and harvesting activities. A rural credit scheme or 'village assistance fund' was set up to help local people establish small tourism enterprises. The ethnic villages were also encouraged to retain their traditional customs and architectural styles, as a visitor attraction. A District Tourism Management Board was established to plan and coordinate ecotourism development in the park, however policy and planning for ecotourism differed between the province, national park and project team (Rihawi, 2002). Ecotourism in

Vietnam also needed to feature the cultural knowledge of Indigenous ethnic groups living inside parks or in buffer zones around nature reseves (Chung, 1999).

Cuc Phuong National Park

Cuc Phuong National Park, declared in 1966, is located 120 km south-west of Hanoi. The 22,200 ha park features two parallel ranges of mountains, limestone caves and the last primary tropical forest in northern Vietnam. In 2003, the park had 4227 foreign tourists and 56,236 Vietnamese visitors. Local people living in and around the park were mainly Muong people, the third largest of Vietnam's 53 ethnic minority groups. Park visitors could stay overnight at the Muong village of Ban Kanh, 15 km in from the park entrance. Other Muong people were resettled in a buffer zone surrounding the park. There were 2500 Muong people still living in the park and 50,000 Muong settlers around the park. The resettled Muong villagers struggled with poor farming land and had few benefits from tourism. Forest products in the park were illegally collected and used by villagers and wildlife poaching and logging still occurred illegally. The village of Ban Kanh, inside the park, had 116 people in 20 stilt-houses. The village was located beside a river and was used for overnight stays by foreign tourists trekking through the park. A park guide led visitors on a package tour to the village and paid the group fee of US$2–3 per group per night directly to the villagers. All tourists stayed with the village headman's family. The other village people gained some income from selling crafts, weaving and honey to visitors. In 1995, the villagers in Ban Kanh also received government loans and UNDP funding to invest in community projects (weaving, bee keeping, deer and lychees) in return for reforesting land areas that were returned to the park. With these new industries, the villagers' dependence on forest products was reduced. Unlike other resettled villagers in the buffer zone around the park, the Muong people in Ban Kanh had better access to resources, and had diversified their income-generating activities into cottage industries and tourism. Foreign NGOs, however, funded environmental education rather than community development projects (Rugendyke and Son, 2005).

Hilltribe tourism in Sapa

Sapa is a town in the north-west highlands of Vietnam, near the border with China. Located at 1600 m, Sapa is a former French colonial town undergoing a tourism boom with over 86 hotels built since 1992. The region attracts foreign tourists interested in the hilltribes and also Vietnamese tourists from the city of Hanoi. In 2001, around 50,000 tourists visited Sapa with 40% foreign tourists (Lipscombe, 2005). The Sapa region is home to five minority hilltribes, mainly from the Black Hmong (53%) and Red Dzao (24%) groups. These tribal groups practice shifting agriculture, cultivate opium and sell handicrafts at markets in Sapa. Local hill tribes comprised 85% of the Sapa district population but received few economic benefits from tourism. Four hilltribe families around Sapa operated homestays for trekking tourists, while a few people from hilltribes worked as porters or guides. Some 38% of international tourists went on hilltribe treks, staying overnight at four key villages (Lipscombe, 2005). The entrance fee to hilltribe villages around Sapa was set at 5000 dong by local district authorities but some international tourists refused to pay the fee as it was unclear what the money was used for (Koeman and Lam, 1999). Vietnam has promoted ecotourism development and minority cultures in mountain areas that received 10% of all international visitors (Luong and Binh, 1996).

In 1997, IUCN Vietnam and the Institute for Tourism Development Research conducted a 2-year pilot project on community-based sustainable tourism in Sapa. In 1998, the Dutch NGO, SNV (Netherlands Development Organization), continued this project work in Sapa on developing sustainable community-based tourism among the hilltribes. The SNV–IUCN community-based tourism project in Sapa district aimed to increase local benefits and reduce negative impacts of tourism on hilltribe cultures and the environment. Funded from 2000 to 2003, the US$208,820 project provided an information centre for tourists in

Sapa with cultural and environmental guidelines for visiting the hilltribes. The project also developed a tourism fee system, trekking tours and homestays in hilltribe villages, and training local stakeholders (ethnic minorities) in tourism skills and knowledge (Lipscombe, 2005). SNV worked with the Vietnam National Administration for Tourism in developing ecotourism guidelines (Amman, 2004; SNV Vietnam, 2004). A UK-based NGO, Frontier, has also conducted environmental education programmes for hilltribes in the Sapa area since 2001, to improve village use of natural resources and reduce impacts in protected areas. Since 1993, Frontier had conducted research on 14 protected areas in northern Vietnam (Hieu, 2001). However, the hilltribes around Sapa had little involvement in managing the Hoang Lien Son National Park, declared in 2002.

Outcomes of the IUCN–SNV community-based tourism project for Sapa hilltribes included a tourist fee policy for trekking and homestays with entrance gates at three hilltribe villages; new codes of conduct for trail guides and trekking; and three hilltribe homestays with tourist amenities. A Sapa tourism information centre and a cultural centre selling hilltribes crafts were also opened. Training was provided for hilltribe people in speaking English, tour guiding, hospitality and business management. The hilltribe trekking programme was well established with a trail system and management board. However, tourism in Sapa was dominated by Vietnamese-owned businesses. Poor education, language and business skills, discrimination, inter-ethnic competition and government policy that banned the collection of firewood and opium cultivation by hilltribes limited the tourism involvement by minority hilltribes. While IUCN–SNV supported the community benefits of ecotourism around Sapa, this was not linked to nature conservation (Lipscombe, 2005).

Cambodia

Cambodia Community-based Ecotourism Network (CCBEN)

The Cambodia Community-based Ecotourism Network (CCBEN) supports ecotourism projects that promote community development, cultural and social resources and conservation of natural areas. These community-based initiatives support poverty reduction and empowerment through ecotourism. Community ecotourism sites in Cambodia include Chambok, Yeak Laom and Osmose on Tonle Sap Lake. Chambok ecotourism site is a community forest area 100 km from the capital of Phnom Penh. Visitors learn about the forest and local history on guided walks with community members. Other activities include ox-cart rides, picnics along a river and a waterfall in nearby Kirirom National Park. Chambok encourages conservation and sustainable use of forest resources by the local community.

The non-profit Osmose Association Ecotourism provides ecotours on Tonle Sap Lake with a 1-day boat tour to the floating village of Prek Toal guided by local people who also provide paddleboats, food and accommodation. The US$60 tour of Tonle Sap Lake includes flooded forest, waterbirds, human activities and a floating village. Tonle Sap Lake was declared a Biosphere Reserve in 1997 with the core area of Prek Toal the most important biodiversity hotspot of the lake (Bonheur and Lane, 2002). The Osmose project also provides environmental education classes for local school children, supports poor families and helps to preserve the natural habitat and lifestyle of communities on Tonle Sap Lake (CCBEN, nd). Tonle Sap is the largest freshwater floodplain lake in the world, ranging from 3000 to 12,000 km^2 in area. The lake has a large fishing industry with 170 floating villages and 3.5 million people living on the surrounding floodplain. The flooded forest south of Prek Toal on Tonle Sap Lake is a refuge for breeding colonies of storks, ibis and pelicans, threatened by egg and chick collection. Since 2000, the Wildlife Conservation Society has funded and trained 25 local rangers in the Prek Toal Core Area to protect nesting colonies of large water birds, monitor bird populations and to prevent poaching of crocodiles and turtles. Half of the local rangers were former bird collectors. The waterbird colonies at Prek Toal were close to the temples of Angkor Wat and were being visited by more tourists. WCS was developing ecotourism guidelines to conserve the bird colonies and improve local income from tourism in the Prek Toal Core Area of Tonle Sap Lake (WCS, 2004; WWF Cambodia, nd).

Yeak Laom ecotourism project

Yeak Laom in north-east Cambodia is a commune of five Tampuen villages with 1500 people in Ratanakiri Province. The Tampuen were one of eight hilltribe minority groups in the province that together comprise 76% of the Ratanakiri region population (Tourism Cambodia, 2004). The 400 ha Yeak Laom protected area, near the provincial town of Banlung, has dense forest, a volcanic crater-lake, waterfalls and the unique culture of the Tampuen Indigenous people. The lake and forest area have spiritual significance for the Tambuen people who perform ritual offerings during harvesting, planting or family sickness. There were growing environmental impacts on the lake area such as litter and clearing the forest for agriculture. In 1995, the provincial authority and the International Development Research Centre (UK) implemented environmental protection and education activities with the Tampuen community around Yeak Yaom Lake who took over the project in 1997. The provincial governor approved a 25-year agreement for the Tampuen to manage Yeak Laom Lake and the surrounding protected forest area. Indigenous land rights were also included in Cambodia's new land laws, passed after 2001. A Yeak Laom Community Based Tourism Committee of ten elders was formed with one man and one woman from each of the five Tampuen villages. A working group of five people, one from each village, acted as liaison workers for tourism activities.

Ecotourism was developed at Yeak Laom to provide a livelihood and income for the Tampuen community. Trained Indigenous guides provided nature tours around Yeak Laom Lake, and cultural tours of Tampuen villages in the area. Traditional Tampuen dance and music performances were also arranged, along with overnight stays at Tampuen villages and farms for small groups. Facilities at Yeak Laom Lake included a cultural centre, a handicraft store, two swimming platforms and a walking trail around the lake. Tampuen community members managed visitor services at Yeak Laom Lake, worked at the cultural centre, and as tour guides. Training in tourism skills and management and English language was provided through a DRIVE (Developing Remote Indigenous Village Education) education project supported by AusAID and taught by volunteers from Australia and the UK. Income at Yeak Laom was generated from entry (US$1) and parking fees, a snack bar, hire of inner tubes and swimming vests, guided tours and craft sales. This income covered staff salaries with additional funding needed to maintain and improve visitor facilities (Yeak Laom, nd). Community-based ecotourism at Yeak Laom supported nature conservation and Tampuen cultural practices. The Tampuen tours at Yeak Laom were promoted on a responsible tourism website, Earthfoot.

Laos

Nam Ha ecotourism project

The Nam Ha ecotourism project is based around trekking trails and tribal villages in the Nam Ha National Biodiversity Conservation Area (NBCA) of northern Laos, bordering China and Myanmar (Burma). This mountainous region is home to 36 ethnic groups, including the Akha, Hmong, Khamu and Lanten tribal groups. Established in 1993, the 222,400 ha Nam Ha NBCA includes 25 tribal villages. Over 100 ethnic minority villages also border the Nam Ha protected area and depend on the harvest of non-timber forest products. The 20 NBCAs cover 12.5% of Laos, include many ethnic minority groups and are a magnet for ecotourism. At Nam Ha, the Wildlife Conservation Society worked with the Laos government on protected area and wildlife management. Launched in 1999 by UNESCO and the Laos National Tourism Authority, the Nam Ha ecotourism project assists local communities to establish cultural and nature tourism activities and supports conservation. The UNESCO chief technical adviser for the project was a US Peace Corps volunteer from Thailand. Nam Ha was the first community-based ecotourism project implemented in Laos (Ecotourism Laos, 2005a). Tour guides and ethnic community members providing tourism facilities were trained in sustainable tourism and resource conservation. Regulations were developed for carrying capacity, guide certification, trekking permits, impact monitoring, finance and administration, along with environmental and cultural guidelines (Schipani and Sipaseuth, 2002). The US owner of a guesthouse in the Luang Namtha province of northern Laos, also strongly supported the Nam Ha ecotourism project. They booked guests on trekking tours and supported local community projects while their website featured the Nam Ha area, cultural guidelines for visiting ethnic groups, and other local lodges and village stays such as the Ban Piang Ngam community lodge (The Boat Landing, 2005).

Laos is promoting ecotourism in its official tourism strategy, since nature and cultural tourism provide half of the tourism revenue in Laos. In 2002, Laos received 735,000 international visitors generating US$113 million as the main source of foreign exchange. Forests still cover half of Laos, with 12% as National Protected Areas, while there are 47 ethnic groups in the country (UNESCO, 2004). A *National Ecotourism Strategy and Action Plan* for Laos was developed in 2004 (SNV Laos, 2004; Ecotourism Laos, 2005b). The Laos National Tourism Authority oversees the Nam Ha ecotourism project, with technical assistance from the UNESCO Regional Office for Culture in Asia and the Pacific, and funding from New Zealand, Japan and the International Finance Corporation (UNESCO, nd). The EU Integrated Rural Development Project also provided €4500 for community tourism awareness seminars, study tours and tourist information material. Major external support for this ecotourism project ran from 1999 to 2002. However, other project staff, funding, materials and technical support for the Nam Ha ecotourism project were provided by The Netherlands (SNV), Germany (GTZ), Canada, New Zealand, a US tour operator, UN Drug Control Program, the Wildlife Conservation Society (USA) and the Asian Development Bank. The ecotourism project included field trips, testing trekking routes, visitor surveys, brochures, a cultural guidelines

poster, visitor information boards and village outreach and training. Specific ecotourism development activities were training village guides to lead treks in Vieng Phouhka District to see black-cheeked crested gibbon and guar (EU), and an Akha community ecotourism programme in Muang Sing with lodges, homestays and trekking tours (GTZ) (Ecotourism Laos, 2005b). Trekking permit and management fees are used to support conservation activities, trail maintenance and to monitor operations in the Nam Ha NBCA. Monitoring by tour guides included community satisfaction and economic benefits, cultural impacts, trail conditions and wildlife in Nam Ha. Trekking activities in Nam Ha generated gross revenue over US$21,000 from October 2000 to November 2001. The Nam Ha ecotourism project team won the 2001 UN development award for contributing to poverty alleviation in Laos (Schipani, 2002; Schipani and Sipaseuth, 2002). Local people in Nam Ha used tourism income to buy basic goods such as medicine, small goods, clothes, blankets and other items, including opium at one village (Lyttleton and Allcock, 2002). Cultural change was also occurring in the Nam Ha area and few Akha people still wore their traditional costume in accessible areas (UNESCO, 2001a; Gray, 2004).

The Nam Ha protected area had treks of 2–3 days and day treks to nearby ethnic villages, mountain biking and motorized boat trips on the Namtha River. Two treks began in 2000 with a 3-day trek to two Akha villages and a boat trip to a Lanten village added in 2001. The two Akha villages derived trekking income from selling food (68–71%), cooking (8–11%), selling handicrafts (14%) and accommodation (20%). Other income was derived from cardamom, livestock, rattan and vegetables (Lyttleton and Allcock, 2002). Trekking tours in Nam Ha were managed by the non-profit Nam Ha Ecoguide Service, supervised by the provincial tourism office in Luang Namtha. Independent trekkers and tour companies must hire local guides to ensure environmental and cultural guidelines are met in Nam Ha protected area. Profits from trekking fees were used to expand community-based ecotourism facilities and to support other development activities. Participating hilltribe villages gained income from food and lodging services, guiding and sales of handicrafts (Schipani and Sipaseuth, 2002). Trekking groups in Nam Ha NBCA visit selected tribal villages, with local guides explaining cultural customs. The groups are limited to a maximum of eight people, purchase food from tribal villages and pay 10,000 kip (US$1.30) per tourist to the villages. Trekking fees at villages were used for community welfare projects, schooling and medicine. Tourism income has reduced illegal logging and wildlife hunting by poor tribal people in the area. Tour guides earned US$5 a day rather than killing a bird for US$1, while women earned more cooking for tourists than collecting bamboo shoots (Gray, 2004). Villagers in the Nam Ha area received training in tour guiding, hospitality, English language and nature conservation (Holliday, 2002). From 2004 to 2007, the Nam Ha project included more training and support for local villages and also private sector involvement in ecotourism (UNESCO, 2004).

China

The province of Yunnan is the main focus for Indigenous ecotourism in China based on ethnic minorities and hilltribes found in this mountainous region next to Myanmar (Burma) and Vietnam. There are 56 ethnic or minority groups recognized in China, with many in Yunnan (Hatton, 2002b). Three million people live in north-west Yunnan, including 14 ethnic minority groups such as the Naxi, Tibetan, Yi, Mosuo and Bai peoples. The Naxi people are found around Lijiang, the Yi people near the eastern border with Sichuan Province and the Tibetans further north. The 280,000 Naxi people around Lijiang are descended from Tibetan nomads (Hatton, 2002b). This culturally diverse area of Yunnan Province is a major trade route between Tibet, Yunnan and South-east Asia (NYEA, 2002). Indigenous ecotourism projects in Yunnan Province include the Northwest Yunnan Ecotourism Association, Naxi people at Wenhai ecolodge, and Tibetan villages in Zhongdian County or 'Shangri-La', Khampa Caravan, and Jisha village. Baima Tibetan village tourism is also

reviewed for the Wanglang Nature Reserve for giant pandas in northern Sichuan.

Ethnic Ecotourism in Yunnan Province

Northwest Yunnan Ecotourism Association

The Northwest Yunnan Ecotourism Association was formed to develop and market local ecotourism ventures in the scenic Lashihai and Wenhai regions, 30 minutes from Lijiang. The UNESCO-heritage listed town of Lijiang attracted 300,000 tourists in 2003 (Clifford, 2004). Local Naxi people operated ecolodges, homestays and trekking, walking or cycling tours in this mountain area. The Association supported environmental protection, preserving the cultural heritage of diverse ethnic groups and community development. In 1999, The Nature Conservancy established the Yunnan Great Rivers Project with Chinese government agencies and funded a US$500,000 scientific study and action plan to conserve biodiversity in Northwest Yunnan (Bullock, 2002). Outcomes of this study were the 440 km^2 Three Parallel Rivers World Heritage Site in upper Yunnan. The Conservancy also supported smaller projects on ecotourism, alternative energy systems and management of nature reserves in north-west Yunnan. The Lashihai Watershed Green Tourism Program for sustainable tourism, Yunnan Great Rivers Project, and The Nature Conservancy supported a website for the Northwest Yunnan Ecotourism Association (2002). The website and community ecotourism were also supported by key local tourism operators including the Lashihai Xintuo Ecotourism Company, Nguluko Guest House run by a Naxi family in Nguluko village and the Khampa Caravan adventure travel company run by Tibetans. These local companies followed codes of conduct for ecotourists and tour operators in north-west Yunnan, supporting community ecotourism enterprises, purchasing local supplies, funding community projects, managing exchanges, and monitoring visitor impacts (NYEA, 2002). The Nature Conservancy also helped local governments to develop a Northwest Yunnan Visitor Centre to promote local ecotourism services and conservation activities in the region.

The mountainous region included four major rivers, forests and highland lakes such as Lashi and Wenhai Lake that attracted 57 species of migrating birds, including the black-necked crane, black stork and whooper swan. A nature reserve between the lakes included forest with black bears and 15 rhododendron species. Some 20,000 rural Naxi and Yi people also lived in the Lashihai-Wenhai watershed. They used solar panels for hot water and biogas pits but mainly followed a rural lifestyle with women wearing traditional clothing. Ecotourism aimed to provide the ethnic minority groups with an alternative to hunting, illegal logging, charcoal-making and hunting (NYEA, 2002). However, Yi villagers used donkeys to drag out logs cut illegally, while charcoal making still went on in the hills behind Wenhai Lake, reached by a new road in 2004 (Clifford, 2004).

The *Lashihai Ecotourism Company* and Wenhai Cooperative promoted community-based ecotourism. Local Naxi and Yi guides led small groups of two to ten people on walking and trekking tours in the area. The Nature Conservancy, together with environmental and tourism-related NGOs in Lijiang, supported the creation of these community ecotourism ventures (Crevoshay, 2002). The Lashihai Xintuo Ecotourism Company was owned and operated by local guides and community members who contributed 40% and 60%, respectively, to fund the business. Shareholders received dividends based on annual financial returns. Ten per cent of tourism profits were contributed to a fund for conservation activities and community development projects. Day tours from Lijiang visited Naxi villages around Lashihai Lake, had a lunch of local food, and visited the Buddhist Zhiyun Temple. Canoeing and bike tours were also offered. The conservation benefits of this project were not described.

Wenhai ecolodge, Northwest Yunnan

The Wenhai Cooperative comprised 56 Naxi households from the Upper Wenhai Village who bought shares and provided a loan to develop the Wenhai ecolodge. The renovated lodge with 12 rooms was based on a converted Naxi courtyard house. It was managed and staffed by local Naxi members of the tourism cooperative. Ten per cent of tourism profits went to a fund for conservation and community projects around Wenhai Lake (NYEA, 2002). Villagers learnt from the alternative energy systems such as biogas for cooking and heating a greenhouse, solar panels and a hydropower unit used at the ecolodge. The lodge was located in a valley at 3000 m and could only be reached on foot or by horseback. At the lower Wenhai village, several Naxi families also operated tourist homestays. The ecolodge and Naxi homestays provided a base for mountain trekking tours of the Wenhai area. Several trekking routes went from Lijiang up the flanks of the 5596-m Jade Dragon Snow Mountain to Wenhai Lake and more remote Yi villages on the upper slopes. Hikers on foot or riding horses enjoyed the mountain scenery and traditional culture of Naxi and Yi villages on 2–3 day trekking tours. All fees for tourism services went to local people working at the ecolodge or homestays.

Simon Fraser University in Canada started the Wenhai ecolodge project in the early 1990s. In 1995, local villagers from 56 households contributed a minimum of 60 yuan to a lodge cooperative. An earthquake in 1996 damaged the area and the lodge scheme was dormant for a time. Japanese aid money (US$35,000) was later used to renovate the ecolodge. Volunteers from the Nature Conservancy installed the alternative energy systems at the lodge, and also produced information boards and a handbook on the Wenhai area. The ecolodge reopened in November 2002 but the SARS epidemic devastated Asian tourism a few months later. Only four of 28 local guides trained by The Nature Conservancy stayed in the area, with most leaving to work in Lijiang. The ecolodge had only paid a dividend to local members twice in seven years (Schwinn, 2002). In early 2004, a local Naxi man took over the lodge, paid an annual management fee to the cooperative, hired local staff and kept the proceeds. By October 2004, only 80 tourists had stayed at the lodge (Clifford, 2004). Furthermore, a chairlift and golf course were built on the eastern side of Jade Dragon Snow Mountain for domestic Chinese visitors. Instead of benefiting local community development and ethnic cultures, large tour companies and the chairlift operator now dominated tourism in the area (Hatton, 2002b). Naxi villagers dressed Chinese tourists in traditional clothes for a paid photo opportunity. Only a few Naxi horsemen still made a small living from tourism on the mountain (Schwinn, 2002).

Sustainable tourism in Shangri-La

Since 1996, WWF has supported community-based conservation and sustainable development in the Zhongdian or Shangri-La region of Northwest Yunnan, between the Yangtze (Jinsha), Salween and Mekong Rivers. The mountain region, at elevations of 1500–5400 m, was a hotspot for biodiversity with endangered species such as the snow leopard and Yunnan golden monkey. Tibetan people comprise 80% of the total population of 58,168 in the Deqin Tibetan Autonomous Prefecture that includes Zhongdian County. Tourism to Deqin has only been allowed since 1999 (Schwinn, 2002). In July 2003, UNESCO declared this area of Northwest Yunnan bordering Myanmar (Burma) and the Himalayas (Tibet) as the Three Parallel Rivers World Heritage Site. The impacts of economic growth, logging, wood collection, urbanization and mass tourism threatened both Tibetan cultural traditions and the environment (Tisdell, 1996; Lindberg et al., 1997). Zhongdian County was renamed Shangri-La by the Chinese government in 2002 to market minority cultures and tourism (Hillman, 2003; Kolas, 2004). In 2002, the area received 128,000 visitors, a 10% increase over the previous year. Tourism generated income of US$474,000 at Zhongdian town, a 37% increase on the previous year. Tourism investors built a cable car up a sacred mountain, and planted tulip fields for Chinese tourists while fake homestays imitated Tibetan costumes and dancing. Sixty-three per cent of Tibetans and other ethnic minorities lived below the poverty line of US$75 and gained few benefits from tourism in Shangri-La (Liou, 2003).

The WWF Shangri-La Sustainable Community Initiative involved environmental education projects with Tibetan communities, including tree planting, biogas and solar energy installations, courses on nature conservation and Buddhism taught by monks, Tibetan schools and community centres and ecotourism training. WWF supported community-based ecotourism in Shangri-la with a workshop on bird identification for 40 local people, to help protect the habitat of the black-necked crane. Other courses on guiding tours, handicrafts and catering at homestays were planned for Tibetan villagers participating in ecotourism (Marston, 2004). At Baimaxueshan (White Horse Snow Mountain) Nature Reserve WWF worked with Tibetan schools and monasteries on environmental education. After a ban on logging in 1998, 95% of villagers relied on collecting non-timber forest products like wild matsutake mushrooms for a cash income. Tibetan students also planted 2000 trees and local hunters were employed on anti-poaching patrols. Since 2000, no illegal hunting or woodcutting have occurred.

Khampa Caravan, Northwest Yunnan

Khampa Caravan, an adventure tour company based in Gyalthang, was established in 2003 by three Tibetans from the Kham or eastern region of Tibet, now part of Northwest Yunnan, China. The Tibetan guides included former nomads, farmers, thangka-artists, herbalists and ex-monks. Tours visited Tibetan communities, Buddhist monasteries and pilgrimage sites in the Kham and Amdo regions of the eastern Tibet Plateau. Mountain trekking, rivers, gorges, and bird watching at the Lake Napa Nature Reserve, including the black-necked crane, were also featured. Their small group tours allowed visitors to experience the Tibetan highlands 'through indigenous eyes'. The company supported sustainable environmental practices (e.g. biogas, solar energy) and responsible tourism at local Tibetan villages. Food supplies were purchased from Tibetan farmers and nomads or from local markets. Tour leaders supported local development projects such as Trinyi ecolodge in

Gyalthang, building maintenance and new facilities at Lekerdo primary school in Lithang, and the Tashi Chompelling Education Centre for novice monks at Nyithong. On World Environment Day (5 June 2003), staff from Khampa Caravan helped clean up litter around Gyalwa Ringa Temple, a sacred site in Gyalthang. Villagers, monks, forestry officials and NGO staff also helped clean up the forest area around the temple (*Khampa Caravan Newsletter*, 2004). Khampa Caravan (2003a) was a member of the Northwest Yunnan Ecotourism Association and The International Ecotourism Society (USA).

At the Tibetan village of Trinyi, near Gyalthang, WWF funded an ecolodge and a community learning centre, built with volunteer labour and skills by local residents, using timber from an old house and biogas for energy. The Trinyi project was established in October 2001 and facilitated by a local man from Trinyi, the co-founder of Khampa Caravan, based in Gyalthang. Trinyi village had 252 people. The lodge used traditional adobe-style architecture to build a Tibetan *chikhang* or common house with a Buddhist stupa at the front. The Trinyi ecolodge opened in July 2003. The first floor was a dining area and stage for cultural shows with three bedrooms (15 beds) on the second floor. A basketball court was included for local youths, as an alternative to the karaoke bars and mahjong parlours in the town of Gyalthang. The ecolodge aimed to help local people conserve the natural environment, maintain Tibetan cultural traditions and gain equitable income from tourism. Instructors taught traditional Tibetan dancing and carpet weaving. Khampa Caravan (2003b) included the Trinyi Ecolodge, with dinners and a Tibetan cultural performance, in package tours of Gyalthang. Tibetan horse racing festivals were also organized for visitors. The Trinyi community learning centre supported Tibetan language and culture while tourism income from the ecolodge funded the rebuilding of a village school. Only two of 30 local Tibetan children were able to attend high school in Zhongdian due to poverty. Other environmental initiatives included cleaning up garbage in a local stream beyond the ecolodge, planting trees and managing a forest as a community nature reserve (Liou, 2003).

Jisha village ecocultural tourism, Northwest Yunnan

Jisha village is located in the Qianhu Mountains of Shangri La County in Northwest Yunnan. The snow-capped mountains include over 100 alpine lakes and three peaks considered sacred by the local Tibetan people. Jisha was a Kham Tibetan village of 79 households with a total of 446 people (CBIK, 2002). The forests around Jisha were heavily logged up until 1998, when the government ban on logging saw 400 local people lose their jobs. In 1994/95, logging had provided 50–70% of Jisha's income. Other people derived income from yak herding, barley crops and collecting wild mushrooms for sale. In 1999, an outside company with a contract from the Xiaozhongdian township government also planned to develop mass tourism in Jisha and the Qianhu (Thousand Lakes) Mountains. A new road provided access to the Jisha region. Local people were concerned about mass tourism, mainly litter and visitors bathing in sacred lakes. In 2000, the villagers started a horse-trekking business for tourists. In this National Forest land area, rules for environmental protection written on wooden boards by local people were seen as ugly and illegal by the township government (Sun, 2003). In 2000, a community-based research project identified threats to biodiversity in Northwest Yunnan. Responding to local concerns, a Chinese botanist and a Chinese graduate student of natural resource management developed an ecocultural tourism project managed by Jisha villagers (Li and Xie, 2003). Key principles were community ownership of ecotourism, benefit-sharing, managing tourism impacts, local participation in tourism decision-making and resource use, and funding ecological restoration. A website for the Jisha ecotourism project (in English) was created at the end of 2002 (CBIK, 2002).

The Jisha project, part of the Community Livelihoods Program at the Centre for Biodiversity and Indigenous Knowledge in Kunming, Yunnan, received funding of US$30,488 from a Dutch agency. Jisha village was selected as the pilot project for ecotourism due to its conservation and tourism significance, impacts of the logging ban and mass tourism, request for support from village leaders and the unique Tibetan/Naxi ethnic culture of the area. A village resource management committee oversaw the ecotourism programme and a village protected area based on Jisha collective forests (CBIK, 2002). In 2001, the Jisha villagers revived a traditional Tibetan farming celebration, the Dala Festival. In 2002, an agreement was signed with all Jisha residents and work began on a traditional Tibetan guesthouse in Jisha village. However, the outside company persuaded some illiterate villagers to sell their rights to develop mass tourism in the Qianhu Mountains for 40 years at US$6045 per year for 3 years. Two village heads also supported the mass tourism proposal. Despite this community division, Jisha villagers started building the community guesthouse at the end of 2002 and were paid for their efforts. The energy-efficient guesthouse featured solar energy, wall insulation, slow-combustion wood stoves and double-pane glass windows. Villagers favoured the distribution of tourism profits to each family while project managers preferred a community fund to assist with education, medical treatment and land restoration (CBIK, 2002). Some Jisha villagers went on a study tour to observe ecotourism at Wanglang Reserve (Sichuan) and the nearby homestay programme at a Baima Tibetan village. Lacking tourism expertise, the Jisha villagers sought a responsible company to manage and operate ecotourism and the Tibetan-style guesthouse in Jisha (Chen, 2003). Training in tourism and conservation was provided for villagers to manage the protected area and guesthouse. The Jisha village ecotourism project expected to receive tourists by mid-2003. However, government institutions and policies still supported mass tourism rather than community ecotourism in Yunnan.

Wanglang Nature Reserve, Sichuan

The 320-km^2 Wanglang Nature Reserve in northern Sichuan is home to 32 giant pandas. The mountain area between 2300 and 4980 m is a transition zone between the Tibetan Plateau and the Sichuan basin. Rare wildlife in the reserve includes golden monkeys, musk deer, takin antelope, red pandas, black and brown bears. Wanglang is one of 13 nature reserves in

northern Sichuan, home to 80% of remaining giant wild pandas in China. Logging was banned in the Wanglang reserve in 1963. The Wanglang Nature Reserve is a 7-hour drive north of the city of Chengdu in Sichuan Province. In July 2002, Wanglang was upgraded from a provincial to national level nature reserve with more government funding from the State Forestry Administration for conservation and ecotourism. A nation-wide ban on logging in China in 1998 had reduced funds to local government for conservation. With the end of local income from logging, threats to the nature reserve included poaching, woodcutting and the collection of non-timber forest products. The reserve was part of the Pingwu County Integrated Conservation and Development Project managed by WWF in Sichuan from 1997 to 2002. This project supported sustainable development of the nature reserve through environmental education, land use planning, micro-credit or loans to nearby villagers and ecotourism. WWF also funded staff training, a visitor information centre and a 50-bed ecolodge in the reserve. Wanglang reserve was the first international-standard ecotourism destination recognized in China, for promoting responsible travel, environmental conservation and economic benefits for local people.

The nature reserve worked with local communities on conservation and ecotourism activities. Two-thirds of giant pandas lived on land outside the reserve. Local villagers and skilled hunters were employed to patrol areas outside the reserve to look for signs of giant pandas and deter poachers. A Baima man was the only person to have seen a giant panda in the past 3 years, outside the reserve.

The Tibetan Baima people, a tribal group with animist beliefs, lived in the valley below Wanglang reserve. The 1400 Baima people of 325 households lived in small hamlets near the reserve. They lived by farming and collecting forest products. Some Baima people had grown rich from logging work and truck enterprises. With the end to logging, Baima people were constructing homestays for tourists. WWF provided Baima people with training on ecotourism and loans of 8000 yuan (US$1000) to build tourist guesthouses and other projects such as bee keeping, handicrafts and vegetable gardens. Mainly Chinese tour groups stayed at the Baima guesthouses, based around the village of Xiang Shujia, entertained with Biama dancing and drinking honey wine. Other Baima sold handicrafts. Some 20,000 tourists a year visited the Wanglang Nature Reserve (Doole, 2005a, b).

There were 300 beds in the Baima valley with more guesthouses being built. Old Baima dances and songs were revived for tourism, although Baima women still wore traditional costume in the fields. Tourists bought local honey, woven costumes and wooden masks from Baima people, with 150 yuan equal to a week's wage in the reserve. Mainly Baima people with logging income built guesthouses, using timber from their own timber plots rather than illegally taken from state land. Local Baima people working in the logging industry were previously hostile to reserve staff. The manager of the Wanglang nature reserve supported Baima community involvement in ecotourism, employing local people as drivers, tour guides, as staff at the ecolodge and on anti-poaching patrols. Baima elders and medicine men worked as cultural guides explaining medicinal plants in the reserve. WWF also recruited two teachers for the reopened local school, and paid them as part-time social workers. A Pingwu Tourism Festival in September 2002 attracted 10,000 people and members of ten ethnic groups. WWF promoted community-based ecotourism to the Sichuan Tourism and Ethnic Minorities Management Bureaus. Tourism income at Wanglang Reserve increased from 250,000 yuan in 2001 to 460,000 yuan in 2002. Ecotourism and other projects aimed to provide alternative income for Baima people, to reduce poaching and protect giant panda habitat in the nature reserve and adjoining areas (Li, 2002; WWF, 2003; Pearce, 2004). Fifty coaches a day now visit the Wanglang Reserve with the Baima homestays at full capacity and other new guesthouses owned by people from Beijing.

Indonesia

Indonesian Ecotourism Centre (Indecon)

The Indonesian Ecotourism Centre (Indecon), formed in 1995, develops and promotes community-based ecotourism in Indonesia. The Institute for Indonesia Tourism Studies, Bina Swadaya Tours and Conservation International initiated this organization to conserve natural areas and deliver economic benefits for local communities in Indonesia. The key mission of the Indecon Foundation (2004, 2005) is 'Conservation and community empowerment through ecotourism'. Ecotourism planning and development activities conducted by Indecon with local communities include the Togean Islands, Central Sulawesi, Gunung Halimun National Park, West Java and other projects in North Sumatra.

To help achieve sustainable ecotourism management in local communities, Indecon provides training courses on ecotourism planning, ecotourism perspective, interpretation, tour guide and field practice. Japan, New Zealand, Conservation International and The MacArthur Foundation all funded Indecon. Indecon staff participated in meetings held during the International Year of Ecotourism 2002 and also hosted the first International Ecotourism Business Forum in Bogor, Indonesia, in 2005.

Mountain Ecotourism in Java and Lombok

Gunung Halimun National Park, Java

The Gunung Halimun (Misty Mountain) National Park, established in 1992, is one of the last areas of lowland and montane forest in western Java. The 40,000-ha park has 500 plant species, 23 mammal species, including the Javan gibbon and grizzled langur, 200 bird species (18 endemics) and a diverse array of butterflies. 160,000 people also live in 46 villages in and around the park area (Harada, 2003). These include Indigenous Kasepuhan and Sundanese communities who continue to utilize natural forest resources. The Kasepuhan people have lived in the area for over 600 years. The Badui tribe of 1000 people in 35 villages also live and hunt in the jungle area (Smith, 1997a). The main park visitors are Javanese and expatriates from the city of Jakarta. In 1993, a consortium for the Gunung Halimun Ecotourism Enterprise Development

Project received funding of US$448,430 from the Biodiversity Conservation Network to develop community ecotourism enterprises and promote conservation in the park. The lead organization was the Biological Sciences Club, which provided field managers and office staff for the project. Other partners were the Wildlife Preservation Trust International, Centre for Biodiversity Conservation (University of Indonesia) and McDonalds, which promoted ecotourism and endangered species in Gunung Halimun Park on posters in their Jakarta stores during 1997 (Joy, 1998; Sproule and Suhandi, 1998; Buckley, 2003a). US$58,000 was used to build three community-owned guesthouses of five rooms in the north, south and east sections of the Park. Community members built these bamboo guesthouses in or near local villages. Access to the southern site of Panggunyangan was by a 1-hour walk passing through traditional villages. Existing walking trails to waterfalls and mountain tops were upgraded for visitors. A field manager was appointed for each ecotourism site, to oversee guesthouse operations and work with local communities. US$26,980 was spent on tourism workshops and training for managers, guides, porters and guesthouse staff employed at each site. Ten residents in each village were trained as guides.

The project provided income for local people through the sale of fresh food and handicrafts, entertainment, local transport (motorbike taxi, mini bus, truck) and monitoring activities. The guesthouse enterprises, built in a traditional style using bamboo, were 100% owned by community members. Electricity came from small hydropower systems. The three village lodges hosted 845 tourists from March 1997 to February 1998, generating total income of US$15,000 with 75% spent on accommodation and food, 8% on handicrafts and 7% on guides and porters. Thirteen million rupiah was paid in cash to enterprise members, providing 11% of household income for participating villages (Sproule and Suhandi, 1998). A percentage of tourism profits went to maintain community facilities such as buildings and bridges. From 2000, 10% of income went to the park agency, for monitoring and management of adjacent

areas. Ten per cent of tourism profits from the guesthouses also went to Yayasan Ekowisata Halimun (YEH) set up in 1998 to promote ecotourism in the park. YEH received 49 million rupiah in 1998 for tourism promotion and organic farming in the three project villages. Guidebooks, interpretive signs, maps, posters and leaflets were produced on the natural and cultural features of the park. Problems with the project were the lack of an accounting system, no set visitor carrying capacity, not enough training or funding for monitoring activities and a lack of local awareness about ecotourism (WTO, 2002c, 2003a). Other issues were disagreements between the Kasepuhan and Sundanese communities in the southern site, and compensation for village land used to construct the guesthouses, with a football field used at one site. It was not clear whether tourism income reduced activities by local villagers in the park such as collecting forest plants (Buckley, 2003a). The environmental impacts of military activities, gold prospecting and land cleared for tea farms in the middle of the park also degraded the biological value of Gunung Halimun Park (BCN, 1997). Local villagers also continued to cultivate paddy fields, and gather timber or forest resources (Harada, 2003).

In 2003, the Gunung Halimun ecotourism project received a grant of AUS$143,000 from the Australian office of the Great Apes Survival Project (GRASP) funded by UNEP and UNESCO. The park has around 700 silvery (Javan) gibbons, one of the largest populations in Java. The GRASP grant supported community ecotourism by funding maintenance work at the three guesthouses, upgrading a micro-hydro electricity plant at one site, a radio communication system to improve bookings, improved park signage, binoculars and field books for local guides, and computer equipment for the YEH office in Bogor. The ecotourism project with limited marketing had low visitor numbers with no income to fund maintenance work. By improving tourist facilities and tourist income for local villagers, the project aimed to reduce forest harvesting and increase local awareness of the silvery gibbon and protection of the forest area (GRASP, 2004).

Mount Bromo, Java

Bromo Tengger Semeru National Park in east Java is a 500-km^2 volcanic highland area including Mount Bromo, Mount Semeru, at 3676 m the highest peak in Java, and the Tenngger caldera. It has the highest visitation of any national park in Indonesia attracting 100,000–150,000 visitors annually in the 1990s, with 25–30% being foreign tourists. In 1995/96, park visitors paid US$100,000 in entry fees. The Kasodo Festival, a cultural ceremony, is held every 9 months on Mount Bromo, attracting 22,000–25,000 visitors. There are 50 Tenggerese villages around the park, a Hindu group distinct from lowland Javanese. Tenggerese villages on the main tourist route, such as Ngadisari, control tourism in the park. Village laws prevent non-Tenggerese from buying land or renting land for more than a year. Only Tenggerese people are allowed to own horses and four-wheel-drive jeeps taking visitors to the crater at Mount Bromo. Most local people at the village of Ngadisari earned their livelihood from tourism, employing people from other villages to work their agricultural land or collect grass fodder for tourist horses. The Tenggerese owned four of the six hotels around Ngadisari where foreign tourists stayed. Environmental impacts included villagers cutting fuel wood or grass fodder in the park, and tourist litter thrown down the caldera wall of Mount Bromo. There was little linkage between conservation and tourism, with park staff making money from tourism rather than protecting the area. The Tenggerese benefited economically through control of tourism access and accommodation, but these benefits mainly went to people in the village of Ngadisari (Cochrane, 2000; Buckley, 2003b).

Rinjani Trek ecotourism programme, Lombok

The 3-day Rinjani trek operates in Gunung Rinjani National Park on the island of Lombok. The 41,330-ha park, established in 1997 includes the 3726-m Mt Rinjani, the second highest volcanic peak in Indonesia. The active volcano, Mt Baru (2363 m) within the crater lake of Segara Anak below Mt Rinjani, last erupted in 1994. A further 66,000 ha of Protection Forest surround the volcanic park area. The slopes of Mt Rinjani include primary rainforest, monsoon forest and also dry savannah. Wildlife includes the black or silvered leaf monkey (*lutung*), long tailed grey macaque (*kera*), rusa deer, barking deer (*kijang*), wild pig (*babi hutan*), leopard cat (*bodok alas*), palm civet (*ujat*), porcupine (*landak*) and the sulphur crested cockatoo, an Australasian bird species at the western extent of its range. As with Mount Bromo in Java, local people on Lombok revered Mt Rinjani as a sacred place. Balinese and Sasak pilgrims visited the crater lake of Segara Anak to place offerings in the water and bathe in nearby hot springs (LN, 2004; LSP, 2004a, b). Since 1999, funding from NZAID has supported the Rinjani Trek ecotourism programme, developed with national park staff, tour operators and community groups from local Sasak villages. Prior to this, an ecoguide training programme run for local men at Senaru ended when a foreign NGO left and funding ceased (Lash, 1998).

There are 20 Sasak villages around Mt Rinjani, with the main visitor access from the village of Senaru in the north and also the village of Sembalun Lawang in the east. The 3-day Rinjani trek between the two villages went to the crater rim and/or the summit of Mt Rinjani, a volcanic crater lake and to hot springs. Trekking campsites are located at freshwater springs around the summit of Mt Rinjani. The Rinjani Trek Centre is located in Senaru, where trekkers paid park fees and hired local guides or porters. The trek centre includes displays on Sasak culture, the National Park, cultural guidelines, trekking and visitor activities in Senaru. In 2004, the Rinjani Trek won the World Legacy Destination Stewardship Award for protecting the cultural and natural heritage of Lombok. Management of trekking ecotourism at Rinjani was part of a wider New Zealand aid programme for the poorer eastern islands of Indonesia. Some 7% of NZAID's $8.2 million budget for Indonesia was dedicated to ecotourism development and poverty alleviation, by supporting community-based ecotourism in new protected areas (NZAID, 2004a, b).

At Mt Rinjani, local Sasak people, including

women, were trained as trekking guides to protect the volcanic landscape, and also sold local crafts. Community-run cooperatives coordinated trekking and tourist activities at the Rinjani Information Centre in Sembalun Lawang and the Rinjani Trek Centre in Senaru. A roster system was used for local guides and porters, village tours and handicraft sales. Trekkers hired local Sasak porters from the Senaru Porters Group based at the Trek Centre. Both villages also offered homestay (*losmen*) accommodation, a traditional cultural village, hill walks, waterfalls, cultural perfumers and local weavers. Income from park fees, village entry fees and other visitor activities was used to fund maintenance of the trails, conservation work, and tourism training and management activities in the Mt Rinjani area. Local people from Sasak villages were also included on the Rinjani Trek Management Board, along with park staff, tourism associations and key personnel from central and local government bodies (LSP, 2004a, b). A first for Indonesia, this board provided a model for community ecotourism. The Rinjani Trek Ecotourism Programme linked conservation, community and ecotourism for sustainable local livelihoods in a protected area of northern Lombok. The specific conservation benefits of the Rinjani Trek were not elaborated.

Marine Ecotourism in Sulawesi

Togean Ecotourism Network, Togean Islands, Sulawesi

The Togean Islands in Tomini Bay, central Sulawesi, include seven main islands and many smaller coral islands spread over 750 km², with a population of some 30,000 people in 37 villages. Seven ethnic groups include the Bobongko, Togean, Tojo, Salua, Bajau (sea gypsies), Gorontola and other groups from the Sulawesi mainland. The local people are mainly copra farmers and fishermen. Promoted as an adventure tourism destination, the Togean Islands receive around 5000 visitors annually and mainly attract young western backpackers. Southern Sulawesi receives 200,000 visitors while northern

Sulawesi has 40,000 visitors and central Sulawesi attracts 15,000 tourists (Suhandi, 2001). Accommodation in hotels, cottages and *losmen* on seven islands had a total of 152 rooms in 1997, an increase from 62 rooms in 1995. The islands are a key destination for scuba diving on coral reefs, other water sports, and Bajau culture. Endangered species found in the Togean Islands include the pig-deer or *babirusa*, cus-cus, rusa deer, Sulawesi hornbill, sea eagle, and the endemic Togian macaque, Togian tarsier (a small primate), Togian lizard and giant coconut crab. In 1997, the Indonesian office of Conservation International (CI) and a local NGO, the Indonesian Foundation for the Advancement of Biological Sciences (YABSHI), established the Togean consortium to protect habitat, conserve biodiversity and generate local income from ecotourism. The consortium established three locally managed tourist attractions, including: a wooden walkway in a mangrove forest (Lembanato village), a forest trekking path (Malenge village), and island handicrafts. Entry fees to the forest walk and mangrove walkway provided income for local communities (WTO, 2002d).

The consortium also assisted a group of local guides from seven villages to establish the Togean Ecotourism Network (JET) in 1997. With help from CI, this network coordinated the management and marketing of local ecotourism products, accommodation and visitor services, and handicrafts. The Japan (Keidanren) Nature Conservation Fund, the Poso district tourism office, and the Healthy Community Initiative funded these projects. The success of this project saw the provincial government stop extensions to logging concessions. The Togean Islands were declared a provincial ecotourism destination in 1996. The people at Lembanato village enacted traditional laws to protect the mangrove habitat around their walkway. Some income from tourism was set aside to restore the environment (Suhandi, 2001, 2002). The Togean Ecotourism Network won the 'Tourism for Tomorrow' award in 1998 and 2001 (Buckley, 2003c; CI, 2004). Despite the high level of biodiversity and endemic species, the Togean Islands had no legal status as a conservation area or nature reserve. In

October 2004, 362,000 ha of the Togean Islands were declared as a National Park.

According to Napthali (1997), educated professionals, medical workers, and outside businessmen dominated the Togean tourism industry. This limited the economic benefits of ecotourism to local tour guides and handicraft sales. CI and Seacology supported local people managing their own natural resources in the Togean Islands. In 2003/04, Seacology funded a new speedboat, radio equipment, and a guardhouse to patrol the area along with a new well and repairs to the mosque and pier at Tomil village. In return, the villagers established a 3200 acre no-take fishing zone coordinated by a dive company. There was little local involvement in marine ecotourism other than work at dive resorts.

Operation Wallacea, south-east Sulawesi

Operation Wallacea (OW) is a UK-based research organization linking scientific expeditions with ecotourism principles in local communities in Honduras, Egypt and in Sulawesi. Self-funded university students completed research projects on ecological or socioeconomic topics related to conservation and community development. In Indonesia, Operation Wallacea conducts environmental and ecotourism research in the islands of south-east Sulawesi, mainly in the Wakatobi Marine National Park declared in 1996 (OW, 2005a). Some 80,000 people live within the marine park boundaries. Indigenous peoples on Hoga and Kaledupa Islands in the Wakatobi Marine Park include the Bajau or sea gypsies and Indonesians. The Bajau villages on stilts are built over water in the intertidal zone with boats plying the channels. Since 1995, research tourism at Operation Wallacea in Sulawesi has supported and worked with local communities. The project uses homestay accommodation built, owned and operated by local people, while food, water, fuel and transport services and staff are hired or purchased locally. The town of Labundo Bundo is the Buton Island base for OW, which hosted 125 volunteers in 2002. In the Wakatobi Marine National Park, research students and scientists with OW are based at

Hoga Island and at satellite centres in Sampela, Ambeua and Darawa on Kaledupa Island. Hoga Island and Tomia Island were zoned for ecotourism. The OW research centre on Hoga Island was based at Adat House, built with funding from the World Bank in the early 1990s. A Dutch organization has also built huts for backpackers on Hoga Island, operated by two local people.

The World Bank and GEF projects supported the OW conservation research and management programmes in Sulawesi. In Wakatobi, a no-take fishing zone was set up on Hoga reef in 2000 and a fish aggregation device or *rompong* was installed near the Bajau village of Sampela, funded by the PADI Aware Foundation. These reduced illegal dynamite and cyanide fishing on the reef and supported sustainable fishing and tourism in the marine park (Johnson, 2003; WWF, nd). Local Indigenous groups had different perceptions of environmental impacts and ecotourism than western researchers (Benson and Clifton, 2004). Sampela village hosts over 200 students and academics from OW each year, providing an income for 50 local people. OW had a maximum of 15 visitors, at one time, in Sampela village. Research tourism is the largest tourist sector in the Wakatobi Park with about 14,000 bed nights in the 2004 season spread between the Operation Wallacea centres on Hoga Island, and in Ambuea and Sampela. Approximately Rp1700 million is spent mostly in the local economy from this activity, providing income to over 400 local people. The student volunteers also spent additional money in local shops and on crafts (imported from Bali). Total income from international tourism in Wakatobi in 2004 was estimated to be US$300,000 (Coles, 2004). Since 2000, OW research about the sociocultural impacts of ecotourism on local villages was conducted on Kaledupa and Hoga Islands in Wakatobi Park. These indicate positive impacts from tourism income and some social impacts from western clothing and behaviours on the Muslim population. Local people wanted more community development projects and grants to start small businesses to provide supplies (OW, 2005b). In 2004, the Wakatobi Islands became self-governing and OW suggested growth in research and dive tourism, plus developing up-market ecotourism (Clifton, 2004). In 2005, OW aimed to train 30 local people as Wakatobi tour guides (Coles, 2004).

Kandora Mountain Lodge, Tana Toraja, central Sulawesi

The Kandora Mountain Lodge is located 6 km south of the town of Makale, in Tana Toraja, part of central Sulawesi. The ecolodge was built in 1998 by local people, funded with a donation from KAS in Germany. The lodge accommodates 15 guests and is managed by WALDA, an Indonesian NGO. Torajan people are employed at the lodge as hospitality staff, construction and maintenance workers, and as tour guides. Kandora Lodge offers 2–3 day package tours visiting rural communities. Guests at the lodge joined one- or two-night trekking tours visiting Torajan cultural sites such a royal cliff face burial site at Suaya, a cave burial site at Tampangallo and the town of Potok Tengan, which commemorates the legend of the first Torajans that arrived from heaven. On the 3-day tour, tourists stayed overnight at Sangalla village in a traditional Torajan *tongkonan* house, with meals provided by villagers. Torajan guides explained local legends, history and culture on these tours (Adams, 2003). The lodge website provided ecotourism tips for trekking and village homestays on tourist behaviour and also wearing black clothes and bringing donations to a Torajan funeral. Tourist income for accommodation at Kandora Lodge and at Sangalla village benefited the local Torajan community (Kandora Mountain Lodge, nd). Operated as a private business, shares in the lodge were sold to local people to fund maintenance work. Friends of the World Bank, Volunteer Service Overseas (VSO) from the UK and the Responsible Travel website promoted this lodge. This prototype lodge was the only community ecotourism facility in Toraja Land (Responsible Travel, 2001). The 3000-km^2 Toraja highland area was a popular mass tourist destination in Sulawesi. In 1986, Tana Toraja was designated the second most important tourist destination in Indonesia, after Bali. The unique Toraja culture with cliff burial

sites, traditional houses, and funeral ceremonies attracted both western and Indonesian tourists, with visitor facilities at Rantepao and Makale. Native Torajan entrepreneurs owned local hotels and a few restaurants, while other Torajans worked as tour guides, service staff at tourist facilities, or sold crafts. Impacts of tourism included theft of funerary statues (*tau tau*) from burial sites, the sale of old Toraja artefacts, and changes to ritual ceremonies. Mass tourism had no benefits for the 75% of Toraja who were farmers and the traditional leaders who maintained religious and ceremonial traditions of the *Aluk To Dolo* ancestral Toraja beliefs (Crystal, 1989).

Mentawai cultural ecotourism, Siberut

The four Mentawai Islands of Siberut, Sipora, north and south Pagai, are located 150 km off the western coast of Sumatra. Around 64,000 Mentawai people live on these islands. The main island of Siberut is 86 km long and home to the Sakkudai people, an animist tribe with a few thousand people. The island has an area of approximately 500,800 hectares with a population of around 22,500, 90% of whom are Indigenous Mentawaians (Bakker, 1999). The hunter-gatherer Mentawai traditionally lived in clan longhouses (*umas*) and wore bark-cloth clothing. The Mentawai Islands have dense rainforest and unique wildlife, including four endemic monkey species. Most Mentawai trekking tours that visit Mentawai villages depart from the port city of Padang and take place on Siberut Island. Some 2400 tourists visited Siberut in 1999 but local people gained few benefits from tourism (UNESCO, 2001b). Rainforest logging and the relocation of Mentawai people to government villages are the main impacts in the Mentawai Islands. Siberut Island has 60% rainforest cover with a biosphere reserve managed to conserve both nature and culture (Smith, 1997b). Some 29,500 people, including Indigenous Mentawai people, live in the 1905-km^2 Siberut Biosphere Reserve, designated in 1981. Studies of primate ecology, land tenure/Indigenous rights, natural resource usage, and ecotourism were conducted (Kramer *et al.*, 1997; Sills, 1998). In

1993, western Siberut was declared a National Park. Trekking tourism and surf tourism have both grown on the Mentawai Islands. With more local autonomy since 1999, the Mentawai oppose logging and seek to share in tourism benefits (Persoon, 2003). Provincial and local governments also support sustainable tourism in the Mentawai Islands.

In 2003, an American evaluated the problems and needs of Mentawai people, visiting three clans still following a traditional way of life in the jungle. He worked with Mentawai people, guides and the Mentawai NGO, Citra Mandiri, to develop a strategy to empower the Mentawai people and protect Siberut. Mentawai people who were relocated to single family houses in government villages suffered poor health, food deficiency and poverty. The NGO Native Planet was formed to support Mentawai people. Native Planet organized Mentawai expeditions of 10–12 days on Siberut Island. The US$615 adventure tour for a group of eight people included Mentawai guides, porters and cooks. The tour included food and lodging with traditional clans at Mentawai villages, with taxes paid to the host village and food donated to host families. Trekking tourists joined daily activities such as weaving a thatched roof, making clothing from tree bark and using a bow and poisoned arrow. They also observed cultural ceremonies, including shamanic dances of medicine men (*sikeireis*) accompanied by drumming and chanting. A tour donation was made to the Mentawai Cultural Ecotourism Association, a non-profit group that supported independent tours and local Mentawai guides. The Association followed ecotourism guidelines and standards set by the NGO sponsors, Native Planet and Citra Mandiri, which aimed to protect and benefit Mentawai people and culture. Their tours and cultural documentation helped Mentawai people to preserve their way of life and protect ancestral lands (Native Planet, 2004). A 1996 survey of 370 foreign tourists in Siberut and west Sumatra found they would pay a visitor fee of US$23 to support conservation and Mentawai culture (Kramer *et al.*, 1997).

Native Planet and Citra Mandiri, along with Mentawai guides, also developed a Mentawai cultural tourism strategy to help preserve Mentawai culture and deliver local economic benefits from tourism. The strategy advocated controlled cultural ecotourism (services and fees), equitable distribution of tourism income, creating new tourism jobs, training Mentawai guides, tourism awareness and a food distribution programme for Mentawai families hosting tourists. Fees were negotiated for Mentawai tourism services such as host families, cultural activities, lodging, food distribution and guides. The fee schedule was developed with three host families, shamans (*sikeireis*) and their wives and guides. A bonus was paid to shamans for preserving traditional culture, but only if they were tattooed and wore traditional bark clothing. Basic fees were charged for daily activities such as shaman rituals, preparing sago and durian tree climbers. Special fees were charged for the *turuk* ceremony and dances. The Mentawai Cultural Ecotourism Association was formed to promote Mentawai guides and the fee schedule for host families. The local guides also gained Indonesian national guide licenses (Siberut, nd). While these strategies promoted Mentawai cultural preservation and local economic benefits from tourism on Siberut Island, the conservation and environmental benefits were not stated.

Kayan Mentarang National Park, Kalimantan

Kayan Mentaring National Park covers 1.4 million ha of mountainous tropical forest in north-east Kalimantan, adjoining the border with Sabah and Sarawak in east Malaysia. The remote park can only be reached by plane and longboat trips, though a new access road was to be constructed into this area. Several Dayak villages bordered the southern part of the park, with around 450 people. This area had received only 25 tourists. In mid-2001, however, a community-based ecotourism project was initiated in Kayan Mentaring, funded by WWF Indonesia and a Danish development NGO, DANIDA.

The residents of three Dayak villages were involved in ecotourism planning, training and visits to other ecotourism areas. Village ecotourism committees were set up and bathrooms built with shared community labour. The two smallest villages only wished to receive one or four to ten tourists per month and sell handicrafts. The larger village of 330 people, Long Pujungan, already had a guesthouse for 20 people and thought a minimum of 100 visitors a month was acceptable. This village was at the end of the planned new road into the Kayan Mentaring area. Men identified more benefits from ecotourism while women were more aware of the extra work in hosting tourists. However, conserving the forests and land area was more important to the Dayak people than ecotourism (Iiyama and Susanti, 2004).

At Pampang village, 30 km from the provincial capital of Samarinda in East Kalimantan, the Kenyah Dayaks commenced regular dance and music performances for tourists in 1998, along with handicraft sales. This village of 700 people, mainly Kenyah Dayaks who had migrated down to the coast, was declared a culture village (*desa budaya*) in 1991. The village lacked a traditional longhouse (*lamin*) but a new meeting longhouse, decorated with Kenyah carvings in 1999, was added as a performance venue. After lobbying from the traditional law chief, some minor improvements were made to the road and longhouse. Tourists arrived from Samarinda in minivans, sedans and motorcycles for the dance performance. The village charged tourists US$1 for a photo with the dancers in traditional dress. This income from ticket sales and photos was divided among the performers on the day. By 2000, the road to Pampang was in a poor state and other Dayak communities planned to establish their own culture villages. Non-Dayak people had also set up carving shops along the road to Pampang village (Schiller, 2001).

Philippines

In 2000, the Philippines had 1.8 million tourists with tourism revenue of US$2.5 million. Local elites and foreign investors dominate tourism in key island resort areas such as Palawan and Boracay. Indigenous Batak, Tagbanua, Pala'wan and Tao't-bato peoples live on Palawan. Limited attempts were made by UNESCO and a local government to develop community-based

ecotourism and fish farming at Ulugan Bay in Palawan (Chen Ng, 2002). Other Indigenous ecotourism projects focus on the Cordillera region of Northern Luzon, with 1.4 million tribal people. Overall, seven million Indigenous people live in the upland or mountain regions of the Philippines (Dulnuan, 2003a). The Philippines *National Ecotourism Strategy* promoted ecotourism ventures that benefited local communities. Hence, the Philippines Department of Tourism supported four pilot ecotourism projects during 2001–2003, with one of these involving Indigenous people in the Mt Pinatubo trekking tour. Since 2001, NZ aid money has funded the development of Indigenous ecotourism in mountain areas of Luzon, by improving the quality of ecotourism activities in local communities, skills development and supporting the recognition of Indigenous land rights (NZAID, 2004c). Other Indigenous groups such as the Ifugao have had minimal benefits from tourism around Banaue in the Cordillera region.

Mountain Ecotourism in Luzon

Mt Pinatubo Trek, central Luzon

The Mt Pinatubo Trek started in October 1999, part of a community tourism programme (*Kabuhayan sa Turismo*) launched to create jobs and alternative income for Indigenous groups living in the nearby villages of Tarlac and Pampanga provinces. The Indigenous Aetas people from six major clan-groups comprised most of the resident population around Mt Pinatubo. The Aetas believe Mt Pinatubo is the abode of their spirit guardian. They lived in a traditional hunting and gathering economy, also selling fruit, vegetables, forest products and craft souvenirs. After the eruption of Mt Pinatubo in June 1991, all the Aetas were forced to evacuate and resettle in other areas. A 1996 tourism plan for Mt Pinatubo included a road to the crater along with hotels, resorts and cabins for tourists. In June 2001, some 500 Aetas people aimed to reclaim their ancestral lands along the Mt Pinatubo mountain range including the US Clark Air Base (closed in 1992) built on former Aetas hunting grounds. The Philippines Clark Development Corporation aimed to turn the Mt Pinatubo area into an international tourist destination (Minority Rights Group International, 2001). Meanwhile, a new access trail to the middle of the Mt Pinatubo volcano passed through the Aetas villages of Juliana and Capas in Tarlac province. Some 60 Aeta people now worked as guides and porters for tourists visiting Mt Pinatubo. Since 1999, the Philippines Department of Tourism has organized an annual Mt Pinatubo Trek, to promote the volcano as an ecotourism destination and generate tourism income for the Aetas people. The registration fee of P1000 helped to fund the Mt Pinatubo Conservation Plan and Ecotourism Development Program, with a portion of trek proceeds donated to the community of Juliana where 80% of the 3000 residents are Aetas people (EManila, 2004). In 2002, the Mt Pinatubo Trek received awards for community-based sustainable ecotourism from PATA, the ASEAN Tourism Association and the Philippines Kalakbay Award.

During 2001–2003, the Mt Pinatubo trekking tour was one of four pilot ecotourism projects supported by the Philippines Department of Tourism (2002). The Mt Pinatubo project in central Luzon was based on Israel's community tourism programmes, with Indigenous Aetas residents hired as tourist guides, or selling handicrafts, refreshments and food (Vanzi, 2004). Funding from NZAID helped develop the treks around Mt Pinatubo, with Indigenous Aetas people trained in skills such as tour guiding and trek management. However, the conservation benefits of ecotourism around Mt Pinatubo were not elaborated, and this area was not a National Park. Since 2001, New Zealand provided funding of NZ$300,000 a year to develop the Philippines *National Ecotourism Strategy* supporting ecotourism ventures that benefited local communities. In 2004, a new 5-year strategy for NZ aid in the Philippines focuses on improving the quality of ecotourism activities in local communities, skills development and supporting the recognition of Indigenous land rights (NZAID, 2004c). From mid-2004, NZAID will support sustainable ecotourism in protected areas, managed by Philippine government agencies, local NGOs and the UNDP. At Mt Pulag National Park in northern Luzon, hikers pay a park entry fee of US$15 and hire local guides (Balcita and Solatre, 2000). Mt Pulag is a sacred place for the Indigenous Ibaloi, Kalanguya, Kankana-eys and Karaos peoples. Ibaloi people in the village of Kabayan Poblacion rented rooms at P100/night through the Kabayan Multi-Purpose Cooperative. A local museum featured Ibaloi culture with 120 burial caves found in the area. Other Indigenous involvement in ecotourism or conservation was not elaborated for Mt Pulag National Park.

Ifugao rice terraces, Banaue, northern Luzon

The Banaue rice terraces were listed as a living cultural landscape and World Heritage site in 1995. Indigenous Ifugao people constructed the rice terraces over 2000 years ago and still reside in the area. Forests buffered these rice terraces on steep mountain slopes. The Ifugao are one of seven tribal groups that comprise the Igorot or mountain peoples of the Cordillera or central mountain ranges in northern Luzon. Half of the Cordillera families lived below the poverty threshold. The Ifugao rice terraces at Banaue (and three other sites in Ifugao province) are a key tourist attraction in the northern Philippines for both domestic and international tourists. A 15-year tourism master plan for the Cordillera adopted an ecotourism framework with a community- and culture-based approach. However, by 2001, UNESCO listed the rice terraces on its endangered list due to the lack of a management and monitoring plan to preserve the rice terraces. Tourism plans focused on roads, hotels and other infrastructure rather than sociocultural support for the Ifugao people. Hotels and houses were built on to the rice terraces, reducing the environmental and cultural values of the landscape. Ifugao people also left for towns and cultivated other cash crops rather than following traditional rice farming practices with a lack of maintenance for the rice terraces. A 1997 study found that tourism to the Banaue rice terraces did not benefit the majority of the Indigenous Ifugao people. Tourism caused water distribution and rubbish problems, and also offended cultural customs (Dulnuan, 2002). During 2001–2003, tour operators and guides in Bauaue were the focus of an ecotourism pilot project. Local benefits of ecotourism were limited at Banaue, as tourists were not charged to visit the rice terraces.

Government tourism and development plans for the Cordillera region promoted ecocultural tourism. According to the Cordillera Peoples Alliance such ecotourism projects limited Indigenous access to ancestral land and resources while further commercializing Indigenous cultures (Carling, 2001). At Baguio City in the Cordillera region, Ifuago knowledge of forest and watershed management was the basis for a 1992 'Eco-Walk' education project, where local school children reforested a water catchment. Local NGOs and watershed management courses visited this ecotourism project in Baguio (Dacawi and Pogeyed, 2001). Recently, two Ifugao villages revived a farming ritual (*patipat*) last celebrated in 1944, with dancers beating on wooden shields to drive away rats and evil spirits that caused damage to the rice terraces (Yuson, 2000). Overall, there was little government or tourism industry support for preserving the Ifugao culture that created the rice terraces. The ecological and cultural integrity of the Ifugao rice terraces were affected by neglect, erosion, not enough water for rice irrigation, owners abandoning fields and building development on the terraces. These factors limited any contribution by tourism operators in preserving this cultural landscape (Dulnuan, 2002).

Around Sagada, local Indigenous people operated tourism businesses such as lodging, restaurants, handicrafts, souvenirs and transport or guiding services. These were set up by people with capital, with tourism not benefiting the 70% of locals who were farmers or farm labourers. The Indigenous People's Rights Acts of 1997 changed land tenure with titling of land used as collateral to obtain loans from banks and small areas of inherited lands consolidated for tourism businesses (Dulnuan, 2003a, b).

Malaysia

Orang Asli Ecotourism in Peninsula Malaysia

Semelai community-based ecotourism, Pahang

In 2001, Wetlands International (WI) initiated a community-based ecotourism project with the Indigenous Semelai people at Tasek Bera in the state of Pahang on Peninsular Malaysia. The Semelai are one of 18 Orang Asli Indigenous groups living on the Malay Peninsula. The Semelai people at Tasek Bera comprised 266 families (1476 individuals) living in 20 small settlements. Tasek Bera, a lowland freshwater swamp system including 6150 ha of wetlands, was declared a Ramsar site in 1996.

The lake ecosystem at Tasek Bera supports 200 bird species and 95 species of fish. The Semelai people fished at Tasek Bera, cleared swamp forest and burnt Pandanus and sedge areas to hunt turtles and clear waterways. Forty-five per cent of the Semelai people worked in oil palm and rubber plantations surrounding the wetlands and forest of Tasek Bera (D'Cruz, 1996). To address environmental impacts on the lake area, Wetlands International prepared a management plan for Tasek Bera that included the Semelai people. In the mid-1990s, a Danish group, DANCED, completed a 3-year study of the area in conjunction with the Pahang State Government and Wetlands International – Asia. They prepared a master plan for nature tourism development at Tasek Bera including community-based ecotourism with the participation of local indigenous communities, along with a visitor centre, fact sheets and booklets (Tagi, 2002; Ecology Asia, 2005; SNS, nd).

With US$50,000 funding from the UN Global Environment Facility (GEF), WI implemented a community-based ecotourism project with the Semelai at Tasek Bera in 2001/02. Ecotourism activities such as guiding and boat driving aimed to offset restrictions in hunting and resource use in the Ramsar site. The Semelai were encouraged to participate in and manage their own ecotourism enterprises, supported by training in English, tour guiding and business operations. Ecotourism guidelines and a registered community ecotourism organization, the Semelai Association for Boats and Tourism (SABOT), were developed at Tasek Bera. The community ecotourism project was delayed by conflicts among different groups, expectation of payments for training, some of the groups not contributing payments to SABOT, and recording tourism income earned by individual members. However, SABOT members also promoted environmental awareness in the Semelai community at Tasek Bera (Christensen, 2002). In 2003/04 WI received an additional US$50,000 grant from GEF for the Tasek Bera project, to train Semelai people as ecoguides, use of computers and book keeping, and marketing handicrafts (UNDP, 2004a).

Semai ecotourism and Rafflesia flowers, Ulu Geroh, Perak

The Indigenous Semai people are an Orang Asli group living at Ulu Geroh in the state of Perak. In 2001, the Malaysian Nature Society received a grant of US$2000 from the UN Global Environmental Facility (GEF) to conduct conservation training and ecotourism with the Semai. The Semai people helped identify Rafflesia and Rajah Brooke Birdwing butterfly sites within the Bukit Kinta Forest Reserve, adjoining the Ulu Geroh settlement, to be jointly promoted for ecotourism. In 2002, training courses were conducted for the Semai as nature guides, tour operators and manufacturing handicrafts (UNDP, 2004b). With funding from the Netherlands IUCN in 2000, the Malaysian Nature Society conducted a biodiversity audit of Rafflesia sites, terrestrial plants, birds and butterflies in the forest reserve, along with a socioeconomic survey of the Semai people. Rafflesia is the largest flowering plant in the world, with the *Rafflesia cantleyi* species in Bukit Kinta endemic to Peninsular Malaysia (MNS, 2005). Malaysia has eight of the 20 Rafflesia species found only in South-east Asia. Unlike Sabah and Sarawak, the three Rafflesia species on Peninsular Malaysia were not a protected species. The Rafflesia flower buds take 10 months to develop and are only open for a few days. The Semai people used to collect and sell the Rafflesia flower buds for 30–50 cents, used in Malay folk medicine for recovery after childbirth.

The Semai are now developing an ecotourism venture for tourists to see the Rafflesia in Bukit Kinta, a 68,565-ha forest reserve. At Kampung Ulu Geroh, the Rafflesia sites are located a 30–90 minute walk away in the jungle. The Semai control visitor access to the forest, monitor visitors and receive payment as tourist guides. The Semai are seeking permission from the Forestry Department to build a visitor trail to the Rafflesia sites. A small group of Semai visited Tasek Bera to observe the ecotourism venture run by Indigenous Semelai people. The Malaysian Nature Society advised the Semai to form an ecotourism cooperative and to create tour packages including Semai lifestyle, handicrafts, waterfalls and nature to benefit the village. In Sabah, the Rafflesia Conservation Incentive Scheme initiated in 1994 has allowed Indigenous landowners at Poring and Ranau on the edge of Kinabalu Park to earn visitor fees of 200–8000 ringgit annually from taking visitors to see flowering Rafflesia plants. At a family homestead in Kampung Kokob near Ranau, over 500 local and foreign tourists visited the site of *Rafflesia keithii* between 1995 and 1999 (Wild Asia, 2003). A similar tourism scheme for viewing Rafflesia is being developed for the Semai at Ulu Geroh (Li, 2004).

Dayak Ecotourism in Sabah

Model Ecologically Sustainable Community Tourism Project, Sabah

The Batu Puteh community comprising five villages of Indigenous Orang Sungai people living on the lower Kinabatangan River in Sabah established the Model Ecologically Sustainable Community Tourism Project (MESCOT) in 1997. Batu Putih is located on the main road from Sandakan to Lahad Datu in eastern Sabah. This community ecotourism project was driven by the loss of forest habitat due to logging and oil palm plantations. The 45 km^2 Supu Forest Reserve and the Kinabatangan Wildlife Sanctuary were also established around the community of Batu Puteh. This region has six types of forest, 200 bird species including nine of 11 hornbill species, and ten species of primate such as orang-utan and the proboscis monkey. WWF Malaysia, WWF Norway, the Sabah Forestry Department and the Sabah Ministry of Tourism supported the MESCOT activities at Batu Puteh. In 1996, the villagers from Batu Puteh approached WWF Malaysia for assistance in developing ecotourism.

MESCOT developed a Miso Walai homestay programme, along with a village boat service for tourists, MESCOT guides, Tulun Tokou handicrafts, a cultural performance group and jungle treks. Separate associations managed the boat services, village handicrafts and homestays programme. WWF Norway funded MESCOT training and tourism development from 1997 to 2001. Since 1997, village youths were trained in tourism planning and business skills. The first 4 years of MESCOT were spent on training local people in business and tourism skills, researching natural and cultural resources and planning ecotourism products. Voluntary community participation was achieved through consultation and the work of a village planning group for ecotourism.

The MESCOT tourism operations began in 2000. During 2000–2002, the Miso Walai homestay achieved around 1000 bed nights, generating income from 70,000 to 104,000 ringgit. Tourists joined in with daily village activities such as planting rice or gathering edible forest plants, went on boat rides and jungle treks or helped in reforestation and community activities. Prompted by MESCOT, the Sabah Ministry of Tourism established a Homestay Development Unit to develop and promote village accommodation for tourists. This Sabah homestay programme included Indigenous groups such as the Rungus (Kudat), Bajau (Kota Belud), Lundayeh (Long Pasia), Kadazan/Dusun (Papar) and the Orang Sungai of Batu Puteh (Sabah Tourism, 2005). The Miso Walai Homestay programme won the 2003 Malaysian Community Initiative Award. MESCOT directly employed 10–30 local people with another 100 people working part-time on a rotational basis. Twenty families were supported in the homestay operations, 60 people in the boat services, ten nature guides, over 30 elders and youth in the culture group and four coordinators. A MESCOT community fund also earned 9000 ringgit a year from tourism income, with the money used as loans to help villagers improve their housing facilities. The loans were repaid with money earned from tourism with the loan fund reused twice. In 2002/03, MESCOT and the local tourism groups formed a community-tourism cooperative (MESCOT, 2004).

The Batu Puteh community protected the Supu forest area from illegal loggers, fought forest fires and developed interpretive forest trails. The Menggaris Trail was a 3-hour walk through forest between the villages of Batu Putih and Mengaris. This walk along the riverbank featured wildlife, edible plants and burial sites. The forest and river areas were also cleared of rubbish, the local landscape was improved and a forest rehabilitation programme was implemented. The Batu Puteh community had formerly relied on work and income in the timber industry. In 1999, members of MESCOT were threatened and physically beaten by illegal timber poachers, hostile to conservation activities. Most of these people now work with MESCOT and join in with community tourism activities. A key area of MESCOT is forest conservation and rehabilitation activities in the lower Kinabatangan area (Fletcher, 1998). MESCOT planted 30,000 trees and restored a 50-ha area of degraded swamp forest. The Ricoh Corporation (Japan), Discovery Channel Singapore, WWF Norway and Netherlands, and Shell Malaysia supported this reforestation work (WWF Malaysia, 2000; WWF, 2001; WWF Malaysia, 2004). In 2004, MESCOT was a global finalist and won a merit award for community conservation in the UNDP Equator Prize.

Sukau Rainforest Lodge, Sabah

The Sukau Rainforest Lodge is located on the lower Kinabatangan River in eastern Sabah, close to the Kinabatangan Wildlife Sanctuary and ten minutes upriver from the village of Sukau, a community of 1000 people from the Orang Sungai or river people. Opened in 1995, the 20-room Sukau ecolodge was built and operated by Borneo Eco Tours. This company bought the land for the lodge from an Orang Sungai landowner, with assured employment for family members and also in boat charters. A son-in-law of the landowner started a boat-building business selling wooden boats to the lodge built in the traditional Orang Sungai style that held eight people. Borneo Eco Tours took two years to build the lodge and develop community support for ecotourism.

Initial problems were logging on the building site, theft of supplies for the lodge and implementing cash payments for locals used to bartering for services (Patterson, 2003). Local people and craftsmen were hired to build the wooden lodge on stilts and some of the furniture. The code of practice for Sukau lodge gave priority to local people in contracts and employment. Locals from Sukau village employed at the lodge included 13 of 15 full-time staff and five part-time staff (Teo, 2003). Other Orang Sungai families were hired to operate boats, supply building materials, and construct new facilities such as a river jetty and wooden boardwalk. Additional local income came from guests visiting fishermen at their houses and the purchase of seedlings to replant river forest with a local person paid to maintain the seedlings.

From 1995 to 1999, the lodge generated 500,000 ringgit for the local area, with an annual income of 150,000 ringgit (US$39,473) for the local economy from salaries, boat charters, and the purchase of fish and prawns from fishermen (Teo and Patterson, 2004, 2005). Local people were trained in English, guiding skills, hospitality and lodge operations. Forty-nine local families in Sukau were provided with rainwater tanks, and medical treatment was provided for one poor family. The lodge has since stopped implementing projects that create dependency in the local community. The Sukau Ecotourism Research and Development Centre was set up in 2000, with US$1 per visitor at the lodge, guest donations and funding from charity groups. The Centre channels funds to community and environmental projects such as tree planting and water tanks (BET, 2003; Teo, 2003; WTO, 2003b). The Sukau Lodge also had high operating costs and competed with four other lodges in the area. With price competition and low average occupancy of 35%, the company had to inject more funds to repay a 5-year bank loan of 500,000 ringgit (US$131,500). The loan was offset by a 60% investment tax incentive given by the Malaysian Ministry of Culture, Arts and Tourism for a minimum 20-room lodge. However, there were high costs in building and establishing Sukau lodge in a remote area with no electricity or other services. Sukau Lodge also competed with five

other river lodges. In 2004, the Lodge won a UN-Habitat award for Environmental Best Practice such as electric motors on boats and reafforestation, along with income generation and job creation to reduce poverty in the local community. Borneo Eco Tours and Sukau Lodge also supported a WWF Malaysia 'Partners for Wetlands' programme to manage tree planting and ecotourism on the Kinabatangan River. Local people from the village of Sukau also provided homestay accommodation and guiding (Ledesma, 2005).

Sabah Homestay Programme

The Sabah Homestay Programme is a community-owned accommodation service that was established and coordinated by the Sabah Ministry of Tourism in 2002. The Sabah homestay scheme was an extension of the Malaysia homestay programme launched in 1995. Tourists stay with local host families trained in the homestay programme, to experience village culture, daily life and nearby natural attractions. The homestay concept involves the whole community, takes place at new or traditional villages, generates extra income in rural areas and is monitored and supervised by a coordinating group for training and certification of homestay members (Ibrahim, 2004). The homestay programme also supports a government policy on village tourism, and markets homestay accommodation packaged with ecotourism, adventure tourism or educational tourism. These homestay packages and village locations were marketed on the Sabah homestay website, the Sabah Tourism Board, and by Borneo Native Homestay, a local operator in Sabah. The online directory of Sabah homestay operators included 11 villages or kampungs participating in the programme (see Table 7.1). These homestays involved tourist encounters with Indigenous groups including the Orang Sungai, Kadazan, Dusun, Rungus and Lun Dayeh peoples of Sabah. Around the Kinabatangan River, in eastern Sabah, these were Misowalai homestay, operated by Batuh Puteh community as part of MESCOT, and Kampung Bilit homestay. North of the capital of Kota Kinabulu, the host villages were Kampung

Table 7.1. The Indigenous villages involved in Sabah's Homestay Programme.

Business	Village	Location	Tribal group	Natural attractions
Misowalai Homestay	Batu Puteh	Kinabatangan	Orang Sungai	Wildlife, river, Supu forest
Kg. Bilit Homestay	Kampung Bilit	Kinabatangan	Orang Sungai	Wildlife, river, Bilit Hill
Kg. Pukak Homestay	Kampung Pukak	Kiulu	Dusun	River, rafting, jungle trekking
Mitabang Homestay	Kg. Tulung Matob	Kiulu	Dusun	River, jungle trekking
Taginambur Homestay		Kota Belud	Dusun	Rural area
Misompuru Homestay	Kg. Minyak	Kudat	Rungus	Rainforest, beaches, trekking
Bavanggazo Longhouse[a]	Tinangol	Kudat	Rungus	Rural area, trekking, beaches
Koposizon Homestay	Kg. Gana/Kinuta Kg. Kopimpinan/Limbahu	Papar	Kadazan	Rural area
Long Pasia Homestay	Long Pasia	Long Pasia	Lun Dayeh	Mountains, rainforest, rivers
Kg. Sinisan Homestay	Kampung Sinisan	Kundasang	Dusun	Rural area, mountains
Slagon Homestay	Kg. Kituntul Baru	Ranau	Kadazan	Rural area, hot spring, trekking
Tambunan Village Homestay	Kg. Keranaan	Tambunan		Rainforest, trekking, mountains

[a] Homestay – Sabah Tourism (2005).
Kg. = Kampung or village.
Sources: Sabah Homestay (2005).

Pukak Homestay and Mitabang Homestay at Kiulu, Taginambur Homestay at Kota Belud and Misomporu Homestay at Kudat. South of Kota Kinabalu, the operators included Koposizon Homestay in Papar and Long Pasia Homestay on the south-west border with Kalimantan. In central Sabah, around the foothills of Mt Kinabalu, the operators included Kampung Sinisan Homestay at Kundasang, Slagon Homestay at Ranau and Tambunan Village Homestay with ten host families in Kampung Keranen.

The homestay packages included a range of cultural activities, agricultural crops, fishing, sports, local foods and rice wine, along with rafting, river cruises, jungle trekking, nature walks and tree planting at Mitabang Homestay. The homestay programme utilized village resources (accommodation, activities and people), helped to maintain unique cultural practices and developed village tourism through a stringent selection policy, training of hosts, and linking homestays with surrounding products or activities. The steering committee for the Sabah Homestay programme included members from the Sabah and Malaysia Ministry of Tourism, Tourism Boards and Tourist Associations, three members from WWF (MESCOT, Partners for Wetland, Community Program), the Sabah Ministry of Rural Development and other local agencies.

The catalyst body or coordinating group included members of the various homestay operators and WWF, representing four community groups in the Kinabatangan river region (Sabah Homestay, 2005). The distribution of local income from homestays, tourism support for community projects, and the conservation benefits of village tourism were not explained.

Kiau Nulu village, Renau, Sabah

Kiau Nulu is a Dusun village near Mt Kinabalu in Sabah. The village comprised 86 households and 815 residents, with the majority being Christians. Only 15 people still followed animist Dusun beliefs. The villagers depend on farming and work as teachers or mountain guides in Kinabalu Park. Intrepid Travel, an Australian tour company, has brought tourists to Kiau Nulu village since 1995. A local leader in the village organized these tourist visits through the village headman and a development committee. Tourists stayed overnight in an accommodation hut owned by the Catholic Church. They had a meal with a local household and heard stories about the special cultural ties with Mt Kinabalu. Other individual households provided food and rice wine, worked as cooks, cleaned the visitor accommodation, led village walks and accompanied groups to Kinabalu as mountain guides. These duties were rotated among 25 households to share tourism income. Four-wheel-drive transport to Kiau Nulu village and to Mt Kinabalu was provided by a village cooperative and by a privately-owned vehicle. The village leader, who was the main host and guide, derived 80% of his income from tourism. His family also obtained a loan from Intrepid to build a restaurant at Kinabalu Park. The villagers mainly provided ecotourism services to Mt Kinabalu Park, with those speaking English or owning vehicles at an advantage. Other Dusun households at Kiau Nulu obtained less than 10% of their annual income from tourism, that was spent on food items, schooling and electricity fees. There were no local conservation benefits though a WWF project aimed to revive Dusun cultural practices (Intrepid Travel, 2002c).

Bavanggazo Longhouse, Kudat, Sabah

The Bavanggazo Longhouse is a ten-room lodge built by a cooperative of 14 Rungus people in 1992 in Tinangol, Kudat. The longhouse lodge, with bamboo flooring and a thatched roof, was built with financial assistance from the Sabah Tourism Board, private tour operators, and the Sabah government. It formed part of the Bavanggazo Cultural Village that featured traditional culture of the Indigenous Rungus people, a sub-group of the Kadazan/Dusun ethnic group, found mainly in Kudat and the Bengkoka peninsula in northern Sabah. Dwelling in traditional longhouses, the Rungus are also known for their beadwork necklaces and woven cloth. Visitors stay overnight at the Bavanggazo Longhouse lodge, participating in Rungus activities such as fishing, farming, making handicrafts, and visiting nearby Rungus villages to learn about gong making and bee keeping. The Kudat region is a 3-hour drive north of the city of Kota Kinabalu (Sabah Tourism, 2005).

   With limited publicity or support, the Bavanggazo Longhouse was under-utilized by tourists. The Rungus cooperative that built the lodge lacked experience in hospitality and

tourist marketing. The Sabah Tourism Board provided financial help for the longhouse lodge from 1996/97. Borneo Eco Tours also provided advice and technical assistance for 2 years to support this community tourism venture. They promoted tours to Bavanggazo Cultural Village and sold postcards of the Rungus Bavanggazo Longhouse. This industry support allowed the longhouse lodge to increase visitor numbers and income for the Rungus community at Tinangol (Kerschner, 2004). In 2004, some 1675 tourists stayed overnight at longhouses in Sabah, doubling since 2002 (*Traveltrade*, 2005). The website for the Sabah Tourism Board promoted the Bavanggazo Cultural Village and longhouse accommodation in the homestay section, while Classic Lodges also promoted the longhouse. There was no information on the distribution of lodge income or the conservation benefits of ecotourism.

Iban Longhouse Tourism, Sarawak

Iban longhouses are a key tourist attraction in Sarawak, a Malaysian state on the island of Borneo. The longhouse building, unique to Borneo, is a village under one roof, with family apartments joined together and a long communal gallery. Longhouse dwelling is still prevalent in Sarawak, with over 4500 longhouses still in daily use, especially among rural Iban people (Reed, nd). The hospitable Iban, comprising the largest ethnic group in Sarawak, are famed as former headhunters and for their warp ikat *pua kumbu* textiles. Rural Iban people live in multi-family timber longhouses with a tin roof and live by farming hill rice, fishing, cash crops such as pepper, and the sale of rainforest products. In 1991, over 16,456 tourists went on package tours staying overnight at an Iban longhouse (Zeppel, 1997). By 2004, around 18,200 tourists visited longhouses in Sarawak (*Traveltrade*, 2005). In a fast-developing region, this type of Iban 'longhouse experience' is found only in Sarawak, Borneo. These adventure tours, marketed as a 'River Safari', mainly visit select Iban longhouses located along the lower reaches of the Skrang, Lemanak, Engkari and Ulu Ai Rivers, in the Sri

Aman Division of Sarawak. This region is the main focus for Sarawak's Iban longhouse tourism, with road access to the rivers and being within a day's journey from the capital of Kuching. Iban people living on these rivers still continue a longhouse-based way of life, follow their animistic religion and practise traditional customs including *gawai* harvest or ritual festivals. Tour groups have visited Iban longhouses on the Skrang River since the mid-1960s, while regular Iban longhouse tours began on the Lemanak, Engkari and Ulu Ai Rivers in the late 1980s and early 1990s (Kedit and Sabang, 1993; Zeppel, 1997). In hosting tourist groups, Iban longhouse residents provide longboat transport and work as dancers, jungle guides, cooks and cultural demonstrators. Tourists joining Iban longhouse tours come mainly from Europe and the UK, USA, Canada, Australia and small numbers from Singapore and Japan. Guided Iban longhouse tours mainly comprise small groups of travellers, with two to eight people; group series tours with up to 20 people; and occasional larger incentive travel groups, with 25 to 60 people. The majority of tourists stay for one or two nights, sleeping in a guesthouse or inside the Iban longhouse. Tour operators pay Iban residents for all tourist services provided, at negotiated rates. Most tourists, however, remain unaware of these cash payments made to their Iban hosts.

Organized Iban longhouse tours are the result of agreements between local travel operators, based in Kuching, and select Iban longhouse communities. Sarawak tour operators negotiate with the *Tuai Rumah* (headman) and other longhouse residents before commencing guided tours. Issues discussed include the general organization of tour operations, the details of tourist accommodation and entertainment, and the payments made to Iban people for providing various tourist services. A longhouse tourism committee is formed and rosters are drawn up designating Iban people to perform certain tourist tasks. This includes the provision of longboat transport, cooking assistants, dancers, musicians, jungle guides, men to demonstrate cockfighting and using a blowpipe and other cultural activities as requested by tour operators. Iban people generally receive individual payments for the service they provide, while a standard tourist 'head tax' (*cukai pala*) is used for maintenance of the longhouse. From the total longhouse package tour cost, the Iban hosts get 20–30%. To avoid conflict and share income, Iban longhouse residents take their turn at providing visitor services. Hosting tourists is a community enterprise at Iban longhouses in Sarawak (Zeppel, 1997, 1998).

Ulu Ai Longhouse, Batang Ai, Sarawak

The Ulu Ai Longhouse is a rustic tourist guesthouse on the upper Batang Ai River operated by a tour company, Borneo Adventure, together with the Iban community of Nanga Sumpa. This Ulu Ai area, near the Kalimantan border, is next to Batang Ai National Park and the Lanjak Entimau Wildlife Sanctuary, established to protect wild orang-utans. The longhouse is reached by a 4 hour drive from the city of Kuching and a 1–2 hour longboat trip across the Batang Ai dam and up the Ulu Ai River. This Batang Ai area with clear flowing tree-lined rivers and primary rainforest is unaffected by logging. Borneo Adventure started visiting the Ulu Ai Longhouse at Nanga Sumpa in 1986. They aimed to bring visitors to experience the Iban longhouse and up-river lifestyle and to provide an incentive for the community to conserve the local wildlife such as orang-utans. Iban income from fishing and selling rattan or sandalwood was also depleted and tourism provided an alternative means of cash income. To reduce tourism impacts at the longhouse community of Nanga Sumpa, a separate guesthouse for up to 30 people was built from local materials using Iban labour. Borneo Adventure paid guesthouse fees (per person per night) to the Nanga Sumpa community that retained title to their land. Local Iban villagers are employed as boatmen, jungle guides, cooks and other assistants for hosting tourists. A longhouse tourism committee rotated work and shared tourism income among all the Iban villagers. There were no staged dance performances or other shows put on for tourists at Nanga Sumpa (Tarman, 1998). The Ulu Ai Longhouse received about 1000 visitors a year. Local fruit and vegetables were purchased from the Iban village while non-biodegradable rubbish and packaging was taken back to Kuching. The 22-room longhouse had a satellite receiver, televisions in most family rooms and fluorescent lights powered by a diesel generator (Barrus, 2004).

Iban guides received a daily wage and were paid a bonus when tourists saw orang-utans in the forest around Nanga Sumpa. With this cash incentive, sightings of wild orang-utan increased as members of the longhouse community noted the daily movements of orang-utans and warned if poachers were in the area. Iban people at Nanga Sumpa also revived their traditional stories and cultural lore about the links between the Iban and the orang-utan, referred to as 'grandfathers'. Longer treks of 11 days to see wild orang-utans, developed with three Iban communities in the Batang Ai, commenced in 2002 (Borneo Adventure, 2003). Iban income from long-house tourism also saw fish stocks recover in local rivers, with less need for selling fish down-river to obtain cash income. The community of Nanga Sumpa also sought to establish a 1 km² reserve on the state land area beyond the longhouse land and before the existing Batang Ai National Park, to be officially designated as village conservation land and managed for tourism by the Iban villagers. Tourism income allowed the Iban to focus on growing cash crops on existing farmland. This reduced the need to cut down forest areas for new agricultural land and thus retained more forest habitats for wildlife. However, there were few birds around Nanga Sumpa with the Iban limited to five shotgun cartridges a month to reduce over-hunting (Barrus, 2004).

The Iban longhouse community at Nanga Sumpa received significant economic benefits from tourism.

In 1999, 26 Iban families shared over RM300,000 (US$82,000) in tourism wages earned as guides, boat drivers and cooks, rental fees for the tourist guesthouse, and the sale of traditional handicrafts such as woven ikat textiles (US$10,000 in 1999). The tourism wages for Iban residents of Nanga Sumpa were around RM70,000 (US$20,000) a year. The accommodation or tourist guesthouse fees were paid to a longhouse trust fund managed by the

headman and used for longhouse maintenance, community projects, medical expenses, and interest-free loans. Borneo Adventure purchased ten outboard motors for individual Iban families who repaid their interest-free loans from their tourist earnings as boatmen. Since 1997, Borneo Adventure also paid RM10 (US$2.70) per client into a scholarship fund named for the late headman to help fund education for students from the Nanga Sumpa community. Some Iban people working with the Ulu Ai Longhouse project gained work at the Hilton Batang Ai Longhouse Resort that opened in 1993. Borneo Adventure also funded new foundation poles for the longhouse at Nanga Sumpa. In 2001, funding from CIDA (Canadian International Development Agency) was used to provide better drainage and a new sewage treatment facility at the longhouse (Borneo Adventure, 2003). While benefiting Iban residents, this also improved amenities for visiting tourists. Iban villagers at Nanga Sumpa were said to be taking on more managerial roles in tourism while the longhouse increased in size from 24 to 28 rooms or family apartments (Tarman, 1998). With the high level of investment in Iban wages and tourist facilities, overnight tours to the Ulu Ai Longhouse only delivered a 15% return to Borneo Adventure. The Ulu Ai Longhouse project won several awards for responsible tourism in 1995–1997 but information was limited to reports from Borneo Adventure and travel magazine articles about Nanga Sumpa (Tarman, 1998; Barrus, 2004). In 1998, Borneo Adventure also built a second tourist lodge at nearby Tibu longhouse in the Ulu Ai River area (Tarman, 1998; Basiuk, 2000; Buckley, 2003d; Wild Asia, 2004).

Nanga Stamang Longhouse, Engkari River, Sarawak

Nanga Stamang is an Iban longhouse on the Engkari River, located a 3 hour boat ride up-river from the Batang Ai dam, which is a 5 hour drive from the city of Kuching. In April 1992, a Malaysian tour company, Asian Overland Services (AOS), began taking regular longhouse tours to Nanga Stamang (Caslake, 1993). This company moved away from

Nanga Kesit longhouse on the Lemanak River, visited by many other tour operators. As an ecotourism operator, this company and their Chinese manager in Sarawak 'adopted' Stamang longhouse and negotiated all aspects of tourism with the community. This 'adoption' involved a formal contract between AOS and the *tuai rumah* or headman that guaranteed AOS exclusive rights to longhouse tourism at Nanga Stamang. Set prices were negotiated for various tourist services such as boat transport, cooking and accommodation. The main host for each tourist group at Stamang was the tattooed headman and his younger brother, the Penghulu or district head of the Engkari River. Their wives helped the AOS guide to prepare meals for the tourists and made up the sleeping mattresses. These two Iban leaders had adjacent family rooms in the middle of the longhouse and this area was the central focus for tourism at Nanga Stamang. All tourist meals were eaten in the headman's family room, sitting on woven mats, while the Iban cultural show usually took place on the gallery area in front of the Penghulu's family room (Zeppel, 1997). Apart from longboat transport, all other income from hosting tourists went to the community of Nanga Stamang rather than to individuals. To accommodate tourists at Stamang, AOS also provided new waterpipes, extra toilets, rubbish bins, a fire extinguisher and a radiophone to arrange boat transport. AOS also provided tourism familiarization trips to Kuching for longhouse residents of Stamang. Longhouse residents were encouraged to wear traditional costume for welcoming visitors and during cultural activities. Through ecotourism, AOS improved the standard of living, distributed tourism income to the longhouse and fostered Iban cultural preservation. Information on the steps taken by AOS to implement responsible tourism at Nanga Stamang was included as a boxed insert titled 'Adoption of Iban longhouse' in the AOS 1994 Malaysia tour brochure (Zeppel, 1998). However, Yea (2002) regarded this as a marketing device by AOS to give the appearance of 'sustainable, responsible tourism' at a new longhouse destination.

In March 1998, AOS had not brought tourists to Stamang longhouse since September 1997. Using tourism proceeds earned since 1992, the residents at Stamang constructed a new longhouse made of concrete and bricks, replacing the old wooden longhouse on stilts. As a result, AOS stopped bringing tour groups to Stamang and instead visited another Iban longhouse, Nanga Menyang, on the Ulu Ai River. The new tour was still advertised as Stamang with pictures of the old wooden longhouse and residents still featured in the AOS brochure. Building the new longhouse to improve their quality of life saw the Iban residents of Stamang lose their income from tourism. Another Iban longhouse on the Engkari River, Nanga Spaya, also saw a decline in tourism after building a new longhouse of modern materials. While longhouse leaders at Stamang travelled to Kuching to find other companies to bring tourists, the residents felt bound by the exclusive agreement signed by the headman with AOS. The residents at Stamang returned to cash crops for a reduced income (Yea, 2002). These Iban longhouse communities relied on external tour operators who could substitute localities and alter the appearance of Iban longhouses and traditional activities sought by tourists. In 1997, Nanga Ukom longhouse on the Engkari River signed an exclusive agreement with Singgai tours from Kuching, conditional on the headman adding bark walls, human trophy skulls, and ikat textiles in the communal gallery area while residents dressed in traditional attire for a tourist visit. Some 70% of tourists at Ukom were day trip visitors from the Hilton Batang Ai Longhouse Resort or Kuching. Sustainable longhouse tourism and economic benefits thus depended on the staged authenticity of Iban culture (Sangin *et al.*, 2000).

Skandis Longhouse, Kesit River, Sarawak

Skandis is a small Iban longhouse of 14 families (70 people) on the Kesit River in Sarawak. Since 1992, Intrepid Travel has brought small groups of 7–11 people on monthly visits to Skandis longhouse. Intrepid Travel is an Australian company promoting responsible travel and small group adventure tours in Asia, taking over 20,000 travellers each year. The 3-day adventure trip to Skandis longhouse involved two nights of accommodation in the longhouse, Iban parties, jungle walks and farm visits. Two pit toilets were built for the tour groups, who stayed in the longhouse and bathed in the river. Skandis longhouse is a 5 hour bus trip from Kuching and a 1–3 hour boat trip up the Lemanak and Kesit Rivers. Iban people at Skandis longhouse relied on rice farming, pepper crops, fishing, hunting and collecting forest products. The longhouse gained electricity in 1994, using a government grant to buy a generator, while an all-weather road was built to the nearby longhouse of Nanga Kesit, down-river from Skandis longhouse. Intrepid was the only company that regularly visited Skandis with occasional extra groups brought up from Nanga Kesit when their guesthouse was full. Tourism work such as cooking, jungle walks and boat transport, was shared among Iban households at Skandis. The Intrepid trips to Skandis were first organized by a Chinese Malay tour operator in Kuching with payments for boat transport, cooking and food initially going to the tour operator or to Nanga Kesit.

After 1997, the trips by Intrepid were organized directly by the Skandis headman. On arrival, tourists participated in a gift-giving ceremony and a welcome party with rice wine, Iban music and dance. The gifts of food and household items were divided evenly among the 14 Iban families. Other activities were a morning jungle walk to waterfalls or pepper farms, followed by swimming in the Kesit River or learning to make Iban handicrafts. A craft market was held on the second night, which provided 40% of the income from each tourist group. Intrepid paid individual Iban households for boat transport, guided walks, cooking and the headman's salary, with community payments made for accommodation (RM10 per visitor), food, lighting, gas for cooking, rice wine and the hire of musical instruments. Boat transport provided most individual income with this tourist service, along with jungle walks, cooking, and rice wine production rotated among the 14 households. Tourism income in the communal fund paid for longhouse celebrations along with medical expenses or food purchases. Iban women mainly gained income from craft sales, cooking and jungle walks (Yea and Noweg, 2000).

Income from tourism supported older families and allowed younger male household heads to remain at Skandis longhouse rather than moving to Kuching, Singapore or Brunei to obtain cash income. Household tourism income was spent on school fees and boarding accommodation, food and clothing. Iban people also wanted to perform dances and songs, and demonstrate blowpipe and cock-fighting activities for tourists. The conservation benefits of tourism at Skandis longhouse were not elaborated (Intrepid Travel, 2002d).

Nanga Kesit Longhouse, Lemanak River, Sarawak

The Lemanak River was promoted as an alternative to the Skrang River, for organized Iban longhouse tours. Since 1987, there was a substantial increase in tourist visitation to the Lemanak River, with the advent of new tour operators and other agencies moving away from the popular and long-visited Iban longhouses on the Skrang River. Regular tourist visitation began at Nanga Kesit longhouse in 1990. Several different tour companies visited Nanga Kesit, where tourists stayed in a community-owned guesthouse. In 1992, Nanga Kesit Longhouse hosted around 2000 tourists. Iban people maintained the guesthouse facilities and cooperatively provided tourist services. In contrast to other sites, longhouse tourism at Kesit was managed and run directly by the Iban community. A resident Chinese/Iban entrepreneur married to a local Iban woman controlled tourism at Kesit. As head of the longhouse tourism committee, he organized the building of the community guesthouse for tourists at the end of 1990. Iban people at Nanga Kesit regularly went to this entrepreneur's house, a modern two-storey house a short distance from the main longhouse building, to receive their 'pay' for providing tourist services. The house included a radio telephone to arrange bookings with tour operators, including guesthouse accommodation, longboat transport and any extra Iban cultural activities such as a *miring* ceremony. This local Iban management of tourism and guesthouse accommodation at Nanga Kesit represented a new initiative in Sarawak's longhouse tourism.

The author made a tourist visit to Nanga Kesit in June 1991, in the company of two French couples and a fellow Australian traveller. The guide for this particular visit was a young Iban woman who often brought tourists to this longhouse. On this visit, our tour group was introduced to the-then headman of Nanga Kesit, an older tattooed Iban man, who resided in the middle of the longhouse. Sitting down inside the headman's family room, our group ate tea and biscuits served by the headman's wife. After a brief visit, our group returned to the nearby guesthouse, with dinner cooked by the guide using food brought from Kuching. Our tour group returned to Nanga Kesit longhouse, later in the evening, for an Iban cultural show with traditional dancing, followed by a small handicraft sale. A striking memory was seeing small candles and kerosene lanterns lighting up the gallery area. After this entertainment, our group left to sleep in the nearby guesthouse, owned and operated by a private tour company in Kuching. Back in the longhouse, on the following morning, the performance of a small *miring* blessing ceremony was interrupted by the arrival of other French tourists who had spent the night in the community-owned guesthouse. Their evening entertainment had been provided separately in this other guesthouse. Our group then departed for a short jungle walk, with our guide explaining Iban use of jungle plants, followed by a delightful jungle picnic on the Kesit River, sitting beside clear-flowing freshwater and surrounded by rainforest trees.

Returning to Nanga Kesit in May 1992, to conduct fieldwork, the situation concerning longhouse tourism at this site had dramatically changed. The privately-owned wooden guest-house, where our group had stayed in 1991, was no longer in use with the outdoor dining area falling into disrepair. All tourists now stayed in the community-owned guesthouse constructed from wood and split bamboo, with a thatched roof. As previously mentioned, the key tourism figure at Nanga Kesit longhouse was now a resident Chinese/Iban entrepreneur who organized all tour bookings and activities. The culmination of this tourism-led social change was the election of the entrepreneur's Iban father-in-law, who worked for a medical clinic, as the new headman of Nanga Kesit in

1992. All tour groups now visited this entrepreneur's house, located near the main longhouse building. Other tourism-induced changes at Kesit longhouse were the proliferation of Iban handicrafts made for sale during the evening entertainment put on for tourists. This handicraft sale now occupied half of the galley area, with more than 40 people sitting behind groups of artefacts on display for tourists to look at and purchase. The Iban family of the local tourism entrepreneur resold handicrafts bought from souvenir wholesalers in Kuching. Longhouse tourism at Nanga Kesit was clearly a thriving community business. At the end of 1992, the local entrepreneur was organizing the construction of another tourist guesthouse at Lubok Subong longhouse, located across the river from Nanga Kesit (Zeppel, 1997, 1998). In contrast to Stamang longhouse, the Iban people at Kesit maintained control of tourism and customary culture.

Conclusion

This chapter reviewed Indigenous ecotourism ventures on tribal lands and protected areas of South-east Asia. Indigenous groups are found throughout the northern highlands of the mainland countries in the Mekong region, and also other mountain and rainforest areas in the island countries of South-east Asia. These tribal or ethnic minority groups form a majority in peripheral parts of this region such as Borneo and northern parts of the Mekong. However, there is limited Indigenous involvement in ecotourism projects in South-east Asia. With varied legal title to land and resource rights, or even lacking citizenship rights (e.g. hilltribes of Thailand), Indigenous groups are limited in their ability to develop or negotiate ecotourism ventures with government agencies or industry. Unlike southern and East Africa, there are very few ecotourism partnerships between private operators and Indigenous groups in South-east Asia. Exceptions include the Lisu Lodge in northern Thailand, Sukau Rainforest Lodge in Sabah and Borneo Adventure with the Iban community of Nanga Sumpa in Sarawak.

In trekking areas of northern Thailand and Sabah, and at Iban longhouses in Borneo, local households derived tourism income from visitor accommodation and transport services, craft markets, traditional massages, cultural activities, porters and food and drink sales at villages hosting tour groups. This benefited village leaders, those who spoke English, and those who owned infrastructure or transport (Intrepid Travel, 2002e).

With the support of local NGOs, development agencies and environmental groups (e.g. WWF, The Nature Conservancy), some tribal groups in South-east Asia have developed community ecotourism ventures such as homestay accommodation, guest-houses, mountain trekking trails and guided tours. These ecotourism projects aim to provide an alternative to income from logging, clearing forest areas for agricultural lands, hunting, or mass tourism for Indigenous groups. Income from ecotourism mainly helped Indigenous groups to meet the costs of food, domestic goods, education, and medical expenses. Tribal people also lived in and around many protected areas of South-east Asia, but few communities benefited from ecotourism

projects. Most park authorities supported a removal policy for Indigenous peoples and controlled the park facilities and guiding services, but a few areas (e.g. Nam Ha, Laos) supported local Indigenous groups in new ecotourism services. Indigenous groups that had a strong cultural link with sacred peaks also controlled mountain trekking trails and guiding services on Mt Bromo (Java), Mt Rinjang (Lombok) and Mt Pinatubo (Philippines). The conservation benefits of Indigenous ecotourism projects were limited in South-east Asia, due to ongoing use of natural resources for subsistence needs or cash income. Exceptions were the Rafflesia flowers on Indigenous lands in Malaysia and wild orang-utans in rainforest areas of south-west Sarawak with Iban longhouse communities. In South-east Asia, community-based ecotourism with Indigenous groups was still in the early stages of development. Government policies in South-east Asian countries still mainly supported mass tourism and resource usage rather than Indigenous rights or ecotourism projects.

References

Adams, K.M. (2003) The politics of heritage in Tana, Toraja, Indonesia: Interplaying the local and the global. *Indonesia and the Malay World* 89, 91–107.

Amman, M. (2004) Development and economic freedom: What will tourism bring to Sapa, Vietnam? Global Envision. http://www.globalenvision.org/library/3/704/ (accessed 17 November 2005)

AMNH (2003) Tiger in the Forest: Sustainable Nature-based Tourism in Southeast Asia. 20–21 March 2003. American Museum of Natural History. http://research.amnh.org/biodiversity/symposia/archives/tigerinthe forest/ (accessed 17 November 2005)

Bakker, L. (1999) Tiele! Turis! The Social and Ethnic Impact of Tourism in Siberut (Mentawai). Unpublished MA thesis in Cultural Anthropology, Leiden University, The Netherlands.

Balcita, J. and Solatre, J. (2000) Mt Pulag National Park. *Suhay* July–September 2000, 21–22. http://www.iapad.org/publications/profiles/profile_mt_pulag.pdf (accessed 17 November 2005)

Bao, T.Q. (2001) Lessons learned on the establishment and development of special-use forests in Vietnam in relation to socio-economic development in the last 10 years. First National Round Table, 14 September 2001. Protected Areas Development – Vietnam. http://www.mekong-protected-areas.org/vietnam/bao. htm (accessed 17 November 2005)

Barrus, J. (2004) Sizing up Sarawak. *DestinAsian*, August/September, 56–63, 84–86.

Bartsch, H. (2000) The impact of trekking tourism in a changing society: A Karen village in Northern Thailand. In: Michaud, J. (ed.) *Turbulent Times and Enduring People: Mountain Minorities in the South-East Asian Massif.* Curzon Press, Surrey, UK.

Basiuk, R. (2000) Borneo: Reaping the fruits of ecotourism. *UNESCO Courier*, May 2000, 31–32. http://www.unesco.org/courier/2000_05/uk/doss25.htm (accessed 17 November 2005)

BCN (Biodiversity Conservation Network) (1997) Ecotourism in the rain forest of western Java. http://www.worldwildlife.org/bsp/bcn/learning/ar97/97_java6.htm (accessed 17 November 2005)

Benson, A. and Clifton, J. (2004) Assessing tourism's impacts using local communities' attitudes toward the environment. In: Brebbia, C.A. and Mugica, M. (eds) *Sustainable Tourism.* WIT Press, Essex, UK.

Binkhorst, E. and van der Duim, V. (1995) Lost in the 'jungle' of northern Thailand: The reproduction of hilltribe trekking. In: Ashworth, G. and Dietvorst, A. (eds) *Tourism and Spatial Transformations: Implications for Policy and Planning.* CABI, Wallingford, UK.

Bonheur, N. and Lane, B.D. (2002) Natural resources management for human security in Cambodia's Tonle Sap Biosphere Reserve. In: *Environmental Science and Policy.* Elsevier.

Borneo Adventure (2003) The Red Ape Trail, and Nanga Sumpa Longhouse Drainage Project. http://www.borneoadventure.com/public/red_ape/default.asp (accessed 17 November 2005)

Borneo Eco Tours (BET) (2003) WTO selects SRL as model ecolodge. News & Articles. 30 July 2003. http://www.borneoecotours.com/news/details.asp?newsid=47 (accessed 17 November 2005)

Brockelman, W.Y. and Dearden, P. (1990) The role of nature trekking in conservation: A case-study in Thailand. *Environmental Conservation* 17, 141–148.

Buckley, R. (2003a) Gunung Halimun, Indonesia. In: *Case Studies in Ecotourism.* CABI, Wallingford, UK, pp. 66–68.

Buckley, R. (2003b) Mount Bromo, Indonesia. In: *Case Studies in Ecotourism.* CABI, Wallingford, UK, pp. 65–66.

Buckley, R. (2003c) Togian Islands, Indonesia. In: *Case Studies in Ecotourism.* CABI, Wallingford, UK, pp. 63–65.

Buckley, R. (2003d) Ulu Ai Longhouse, Sarawak. In: *Case Studies in Ecotourism.* CABI, Wallingford, UK, pp. 51–52.

Bullock, G. (2002) The Yunnan Great Rivers Project: In search of true 'ecotourism'. Regional Conference on Community-based Ecotourism in South East Asia. Chiang Mai, Thailand, 27 February–8 March 2002. http://www.recoftc.org/site/index.php?id=236 (accessed 17 November 2005)

Carling, J. (2001) Indigenous peoples, the environment and human rights in the Philippines: The Cordillera experience. http://www.asiasource.org/asip/carling.cfm (accessed 17 November 2005)

Caslake, J. (1993) Tourism, culture and the Iban. In: King, V.T. (ed.) *Tourism in Borneo: Issues and Perspectives.* Proceedings No. 4. Borneo Research Council, Kota Kinabalu, Sabah, pp. 67–90.

CBIK (Centre for Biodiversity and Indigenous Knowledge) (2002) Jisha village eco-cultural tourism project. http://www.ecoyunnan.org/ (accessed 17 November 2005)

CCBEN (Cambodia Community-based Ecotourism Network) (nd) Ecotourism sites in Cambodia. http://www.geocities.com/cambodiacben/sites.htm (accessed 17 November 2005); CCBEN (Cambodia Community-based Ecotourism Network) (nd) About CCBEN. http://www.geocities.com/cambodiacben/ (accessed 17 November 2005)

Chambers, E. (2000) Tourism and culture-tourism and ethnicity. In: *Native Tours: The Anthropology of Travel and Tourism.* Waveland Press, pp. 100–104.

Chen, L. (2003) Ecotourism to save nature. *China Daily,* 14 November 2003. CBIK Community Livelihoods. http://www.ecoyunnan.org/Jishaweb/chinadaily.htm (accessed 17 November 2005)

Chen Ng, M.A. (2002) The ethics and attitudes towards ecotourism in the Philippines. Eubios Ethics Institute. http://www2.unescobkk.org/eubios/ABC4/abc4313.htm (accessed 17 November 2005)

Christensen, P.C. (2002) Developing community-based ecotourism for the indigenous Semelai community in Tasek Bera, Pahang. IYE Regional Conference on Community Based Ecotourism in South-east Asia. http://www.recoftc.org/site/index.php?id=236 (accessed 17 November 2005)

Chung, V.T. (1999) Indigenous knowledge to diversify ecotourism value in Vietnam. In: *Proceedings: Workshop on Development of a National Ecotourism Strategy for Vietnam,* Hanoi, 7–9 September 1999. IUCN, VNAT & ESCAP, Hanoi, pp. 121–125.

CI (Conservation International) (2004) Strengthening local institutional capacity in the Togeans. CI Indonesia. http://www.conservation.or.id/site/modules/detail.daily.php?textid=2198727556420921 (accessed 17 November 2005)

Clifford, M. (2004) Eek-o-tourists and sad truths. *Weekend Standard* 27–28 November 2004. http://www.thestandard.com.hk/stdn/std/Weekend/FK27Jp04.html (accessed 17 November 2005)

Clifton, J. (2004) Evaluating contrasting approaches to marine ecotourism: 'Dive tourism' and 'research tourism' in the Wakatobi Marine National Park, Indonesia. In: Boissevain, J. and Selwyn, T. (eds) *Contesting the Foreshore: Tourism, Society, and Politics on the Coast.* Amsterdam University Press, Amsterdam, pp. 151–168.

Cochrane, J. (1993) Tourism and conservation in Indonesia and Malaysia. In: Hitchcock, M., King, V. and Parnwell, G. (eds) *Tourism in South-East Asia.* Routledge, London, pp. 317–326.

Cochrane, J. (1996) The sustainability of ecotourism in Indonesia: Fact and fiction. In: *Environmental Change in South-East Asia: People, Politics and Sustainable Development.* Routledge, London.

Cochrane, J. (2000) The role of the community in relation to the tourism industry: A case study from Mount

Bromo, East Java, Indonesia. In: Godde, P.M., Price, M.F. and Zimmermann, F.M. (eds) *Tourism Development in Mountain Regions*. CAB International, Wallingford, pp. 199–220.

Cohen, E. (1989) 'Primitive and remote': Hill tribe trekking in Thailand. *Annals of Tourism Research* 16, 30–61.

Cohen, E. (1996) Hunter-gatherer tourism in Thailand. In: Butler, R. and Hinch, T. (eds) *Tourism and Indigenous Peoples*. International Thomson Business Press, London, pp. 227–254.

Cohen, E. (2001) Thailand in 'touristic transition.' In: Teo, P., Chang, T.C. and Ho, K.C. (eds) *Interconnected Worlds: Tourism in Southeast Asia*. Pergamon/Elsevier Science, Oxford, pp. 155–175.

Coles, T. (2004) Suggestions for developing tourism in the Wakatobi Islands. Operation Wallacea. http://www.opwall.com/2004%20Trust%20tourism%20opportunities.htm (accessed 17 November 2005)

Crevoshay, F. (2002) Ecotourism in Yunnan. *Earth Island Journal*, Autumn, 13–14.

CRMP (Coastal Resource Management Project) (2002) About CRMP. http://www.oneocean.org/about_crmp (accessed 17 November 2005)

Crystal, E. (1989) Tourism in Toraja (Sulawesi, Indonesia). In: Smith, V.L. (ed.) *Hosts and Guests: The Anthropology of Tourism*, 2nd edn. University of Pennsylvannia Press, Philadelphia, pp. 139–168.

Dacawi, R. and Pogeyed, M. (2001) Eco-cultural tourism issues in the Cordillera region, Philippines. http://www.recoftc.org/ (accessed 17 November 2005)

D'Cruz, R. (1996) Case Study 7: Tasek Bera, Malaysia. In: Hails, A.J. (ed.) *Wetlands, Biodiversity and the Ramsar Convention*. Ramsar Convention Bureau, Switzerland. http://www.ramsar.org/lib_bio_1.htm#c4cs7 (accessed 17 November 2005)

Dearden, P. (1989) Tourism in developing societies: Some observations on trekking in the highlands of northern Thailand. *World Leisure and Recreation* 31, 40–47.

Dearden, P. (1991) Tourism and sustainable development in northern Thailand. *Geographical Review* 81, 400–413.

Dearden, P. (1993) Cultural aspects of tourism and sustainable development: Tourism and the hilltribes of northern Thailand. In: Nelson, J., Butler, R. and Wall, G. (eds) *Tourism and Sustainable Development: Monitoring, Planning, Management*. University of Waterloo, Waterloo, Ontario, Canada, pp. 165–178.

Dearden, P. (1995) Ecotourism, parks and biocultural diversity: The context in northern Thailand. In: Hiranburana, S., Stithyudhakarn, V. and Dhamabutra, P. (eds) *Ecotourism: Concept, Design and Strategy*. Srinakharinwirot University, Bangkok, pp. 15–42.

Dearden, P. (1996) Trekking in northern Thailand: Impact distribution and evolution over time. In: Parnwell, M.J. (ed.) *Uneven Development in Thailand*. Avebury, Aldershot, UK.

Dearden, P. (1997) Ecotourism and biodiversity conservation in Vietnam. Workshop on development approaches in highland communes. http://www.undp.org.vn/projects/vie96010/cemma/ras93103/ (accessed 17 November 2005)

Dearden, P. and Harron, S. (1992) Tourism and the hilltribes of Thailand. In: Weiler, B. and Hall, C.M. (eds) *Special Interest Tourism*. Belhaven, London, pp. 95–104.

Dearden, P. and Harron, S. (1994) Alternative tourism and adaptive change. *Annals of Tourism Research* 21, 81–102.

Dearden, P., Chettamart, S., Emphandu, D. and Tanakanjana, N. (1996) National parks and hilltribes in northern Thailand: A case study of Doi Inthanon. *Society and Natural Resources* 9, 125–141.

Department of Tourism (2002) Economic impacts and ecotourism – Pinatubo trekking. In: *National Ecotourism Strategy*. DOT, DENR & NZAID, Manila, p. 46.

Doco, G.D. (2002) Ecotourism and its impact on the lives of the Ibalois in Happy Hollow, Baguio City, Philippines. *Contours* 11.

Doole, C. (2005a) Going beyond the Great Wall: Ecotourism in China. News Article 18 July 2005. WWF. http://www.panda.org/news/ (accessed 17 November 2005)

Doole, C. (2005b) Pandas spur ecotourism Chinese style. People and ecotourism. Peopleandplanet.net http://www.peopleandplanet.net/doc.php?id=2529 (accessed 17 November 2005)

Dowling, R. (2000) Ecotourism in Southeast Asia: A golden opportunity for local communities. In: Chon, K.S. (ed.) *Tourism in Southeast Asia: A New Direction*. Haworth Hospitality Press, New York, pp. 1–20.

Dowling, R. and Hardman, J. (1996) Ecotourism in Asia: The Thailand experience. In: Richins, H., Richardson, J. and Crabtree, A. (eds) *Ecotourism and Nature-based Tourism: Taking the Next Steps*. Ecotourism Association of Australia, Brisbane, pp. 73–78.

Dulnuan, J.R. (2002) The impacts of tourism on Indigenous communities: A case study of Banaue, Ifugao, Northern Philippines. Regional Conference on Community-based Ecotourism in South East Asia. Chiang Mai, Thailand, 27 February–8 March 2002. http://www.rest.or.th/training/ (accessed 17 November 2005)

Dulnuan, J.R. (2003a) The perceived impacts of tourism on Indigenous communities: A case study of Sagada, Mt Province. Third World Network. http://www.twnside.org.sg/title2/ttcd/SO-03.doc (accessed 17 November 2005)

Dulnuan, J.R. (2003b) *The Perceived Impacts of Tourism on Indigenous Communities: A Case Study of Sagada, Mt. Province.* PASCN Discussion Paper No. 2003-05. Philippine APEC Study Center Network. http://pascn.pids.gov.ph/pubdetails.phtml?pid=23 (accessed 17 November 2005)

Dye, M. (2001) Northern Vietnam. In: Holing, D. and Forbes, S. (eds) *Rainforests.* Discovery Travel Adventures. Insight Guides, Singapore, pp. 140–147.

Earthfoot (2004a) The Project for Recovery of Life and Culture (PLRC). http://www.earthfoot.org/guides/prlc.htm (accessed 17 November 2005)

Earthfoot (2004b) Seven community-based tours in ethnic minority villages. http://www.earthfoot.org/places/th005.htm (accessed 17 November 2005)

Ecology Asia (2005) Tasik Bera – Malaysia's first protected freshwater wetland. Eco-location. http://www.ecologyasia.com/html-loc/tasik-bera.htm (accessed 17 November 2005)

Ecotourism Laos (2005a) Ecotourism Laos. LNTA-ADB Mekong Tourism Development Project. http://www.ecotourismlaos.com/

Ecotourism Laos (2005b) Lao ecotourism projects. Ecotourism Laos. LNTA-ADB Mekong Tourism Development Project. http://www.ecotourismlaos.com/ecotourismprojects.htm (accessed 17 November 2005)

Ecotourism Network Malaysia (2004) Ecotourism Network Malaysia. http://www.ecotourism.com.my/ (accessed 17 November 2005)

Elliott, S. (2001) Northern Thailand. In: *The National Parks and Other Wild Places of Thailand.* New Holland, London, pp. 60–109.

EManila (2004) All set for the 6th Mt Pinatubo Trek. EManila Travel. 9 November 2004. http://emanila.com/travel/index.php?subaction=showfull&id=1099971134&archive=&cnshow=headlines&start_from=&ucat=16& (accessed 17 November 2005)

Emphandu, D. and Chettamart, S. (1998) What makes for a viable ecotourism site? In: Bornemeier, J., Victor, M. and Durst, P.B. (eds) *Ecotourism for Forest Conservation and Community Development. Proceedings of an International Seminar held in Chiang Mai, 28–31 January 1997.* RECOFTC Report No. 15. RECOFTC & FAO, Bangkok, pp. 61–70. http://www.recoftc.org/site/index.php?id=222 (accessed 17 November 2005)

Fisher, B., Durst, P. and Victor, M. (1997) Let's travel: Overview of the RECOFTC/FAO International Seminar on Ecotourism for Forest Conservation and Community Development. *Asia-Pacific Community Forestry Newsletter* 10, 1, 14, 18. http://www.recoftc.org/site/index.php?id=244 (accessed 17 November 2005)

Fletcher, P. (1998) The Lower Kinabatangan: The importance of community consultations in ecotourism development. In: Bornemeier, J., Victor, M. and Durst, P.B. (eds) *Ecotourism for Forest Conservation and Community Development. Proceedings of an International Seminar held in Chiang Mai, 28–31 January 1997.* RECOFTC Report No. 15. RECOFTC/FAO, Bangkok http://www.recoftc.org/site/index.php?id=222 (accessed 17 November 2005)

GRASP (2004) Silvery gibbon ecotourism proposal for Gunung Halimun National Park. Australian GRASP site. http://www.grasp.org.au/Projects/byapeprojectindex.htm (accessed 17 November 2005)

Gray, D. (2004) Laos discovers lucrative eco-tourism niche. 5 March 2004. Environmental News Network. http://www.enn.com/ (accessed 17 November 2005)

Harada, K. (2003) Attitudes of local people towards conservation and Gunung Halimun National Park in West Java, Indonesia. *Journal for Resources* 8, 271–282.

Hatton, M.J. (2002a) Umphang District: A community-based ecotourism project. In: *Community-based tourism in the Asia-Pacific.* CTC, APEC & CIDA. http://cullin.org/cbt/index.cfm?section=chapter&number=18 (accessed 17 November 2005)

Hatton, M.J. (2002b) Yulong Snow Mountain region. In: *Community-based tourism in the Asia-Pacific.* CTC, APEC & CIDA. http://cullin.org/cbt/index.cfm?section=chapter&number=6 (accessed 17 November 2005)

Hieu, L.X. (2001) Is environmental education a key management tool for protected areas of Vietnam? Australian Association for Environmental Education Conference, 15–19 January 2001, RMIT University Melbourne Australia. http://www.mesa.edu.au/aaee_conf/Le_Xuan-Hieu.PDF (accessed 17 November 2005)

Hillmann, B. (2003) Paradise under construction: Minorities, myths and modernity in northwest Yunnan. *Asian Ethnicity* 4, 175–188.

Holliday, G. (2002) ELT drives Laos ecotourism project. *The Guardian Weekly*, Education Guardian, 29 August 2002. http://education.guardian.co.uk/tefl/story/0,5500,782000,00.html (accessed 17 November 2005)

Hvenegaard, G.T. and Dearden, P. (1998) Ecotourism versus tourism in a Thai national park. *Annals of Tourism Research* 25, 700–720.

Ibrahim, Y. (2004) Homestay programme in Malaysia: Development and prospect. *ASEAN Journal on Hospitality & Tourism* 3.

Iiyama, Y. and Susanti, R. (2004) Community perspectives on ecotourism carrying capacity: Case studies from three bordering villages of Kayan Mentaring National Park, Indonesia. In: Pineda, F.D., Brebbia, C.A. and Mugica, M. (eds) *Sustainable Tourism*. WIT Press, Boston, pp. 37–46.

Indonesian Ecotourism Centre (2005) Indecon profile. http://www.indecon.or.id/about_us.html (accessed 17 November 2005)

Indecon Foundation (2004) Indonesian ecotourism network. http://www.indecon.or.id/ (accessed 17 November 2005)

Intrepid Travel (2002a) Chapter 7: Baka community and Intrepid Travel. Responsible Travel Research. http://www.intrepidtravel.com/rtresearch.php (accessed 17 November 2005)

Intrepid Travel (2002b) Chapter 8: Khun Puai community and Intrepid Travel. Responsible Travel Research. http://www.intrepidtravel.com/rtresearch.php (accessed 17 November 2005)

Intrepid Travel (2002c) Chapter 5: Kiau Nulu community and Intrepid Travel. Responsible Travel Research. http://www.intrepidtravel.com/rtresearch.php (accessed 17 November 2005)

Intrepid Travel (2002d) Chapter 4: Skandis community and Intrepid Travel. Responsible Travel Research. http://www.intrepidtravel.com/rtresearch.php (accessed 17 November 2005)

Intrepid Travel (2002e) Comparative review of case studies. Responsible Travel Research. Intrepid Travel. http://www.intrepidtravel.com/rtresearch.php (accessed 17 November 2005)

Johansson, Y. and Diamantis, D. (2004) Ecotourism in Thailand and Kenya: A private sector perspective. In: Diamantis, D. (ed.) *Ecotourism: Management and Assessment*. Thomson Learning, London, pp. 298–312.

Johnson, L.S. (1997) The role of the community in ecotourism – the impacts of tourism and possible alternatives from one community's perspective: Paeng Daeng Village, Chiang Dao. *Asia-Pacific Community Forestry Newsletter* 10, 15, 18, 24. http://www.recoftc.org/ (accessed 17 November 2005)

Johnson, M. (2003) Operation Wallacea – Wakatobi Marine Reserve. *Dive Log Australasia* 180 (July), 100.

Joy, R. (1998) Development of ecotourism enterprises in Gunung Halimun National Park, West Java. In: Bornemeier, J., Victor, M. and Durst, P.B. (eds) *Ecotourism for Forest Conservation and Community Development. Proceedings of an International Seminar held in Chiang Mai, 28–31 January 1997*. RECOFTC Report No. 15. RECOFTC/FAO, Bangkok. http://www.recoftc.org/site/index.php?id=222 (accessed 17 November 2005)

Kandora Mountain Lodge (nd) Welcome to Kandora Mountain Lodge. http://www.toraja.net/walda/index.html (accessed 17 November 2005)

Kedit, P.M. and Sabang, C.L. (1993) Tourism report: A study of Skrang longhouse tourism. In: King, V.T. (ed.) *Tourism in Borneo: Issues and Perspectives*. Borneo Research Council, Kota Kinabalu, Sabah, pp. 45–58.

Kerschner, J. (2004) Creating wealth for local communities through tourism. *Borneo Post* 23 May 2004. http://www.borneoecotours.com/news/details.asp?newsid=50 (accessed 17 November 2005)

Khampa Caravan (2003a) Khampa Caravan: The real guide to the Tibetan world. http://www.khampacaravan.com/ (accessed 17 November 2005)

Khampa Caravan (2003b) Caravan communities. http://www.khampacaravan.com/files/communities.asp (accessed 17 November 2005)

Khampa Caravan Newsletter (2004) World Environment Day in Gyalthang. *Khampa Caravan Newsletter* 2. http://www.khampacaravan.com/files/newsletter.asp?id=109 (accessed 17 November 2005)

Kinnaird, M.F. and O'Brien, T.G. (1996) Ecotourism in the Tangkoko DuaSudara Nature Reserve: Opening Pandora's box? *Oryx* 30, 65–73.

Koeman, A. and Lam, N.E. (1999) The economics of protected areas and the role of ecotourism in their management: The case of Vietnam. Presentation to the Second Regional Forum for Southeast Asia of the IUCN World Commission for Protected Areas. http://www.ecotourism.org/index2.php?onlineLib/ (accessed 17 November 2005)

Kolas, A. (2004) Tourism and the making of place in Shangri-La. *Tourism Geographies* 6, 262–278.

Kontogeorgopoulos, N. (2003) Towards a southeast Asian model of resort-based 'mass ecotourism': Evidence from Phuket, Thailand and Bali, Indonesia. *ASEAN Journal of Hospitality and Tourism* 2, 1–16.

Kramer, R., Pattanayak, S., Sills, E. and Simanjuntak, S. (1997) *The Economics of Siberut and Ruteng Protected Areas*. Nicholas School of the Environment, Duke University, North Carolina. http://www.duke.edu/~subrendu/abstract.htg/bvsrep.html (accessed 17 November 2005)

Kwantu, K.A. (2001) Voice from Ban Huai Mee, Ma Hong Son Province. Voices from Communities. REST. http://www.ecotour.in.th/english.files/ (accessed 17 November 2005)

Lash, G. (1998) What is community-based ecotourism? In: Bornemeier, J., Victor, M. and Durst, P.B. (eds) *Ecotourism for Forest Conservation and Community Development Seminar*. RECOFTC Report No. 15. RECOFTC, Bangkok, pp. 1–12. http://www.recoftc.org/site/index.php?id=22 (accessed 17 November 2005)

Lasimbang, J. (2002) Impact of globalization and tourism: The case of Indigenous communities in Sabah, Malaysia. *Contours* 11.

Ledesma, L.V. (2005) Crossroads at Sukau. *Asian Geographic* 32, 44–53.

Leeja, J. (2003) The effects of mass tourism and globalization. Natural Focus Ecotour. http://www.natural focusecotour.com/FrameGlobalization.htm (accessed 17 November 2005)

Leeja, J. and Buchan, A. (2002) The impact of tourism: A case study from hill tribe communities. Outcomes of Conference on Community Based Tourism in Southeast Asia. RECOFTC. http://www.recoftc.org/site/ (accessed 17 November 2005)

Leksakundilok, A. (2004) *Ecotourism and Community-based Ecotourism in the Mekong Region*. Working Paper No. 10. Australian Mekong Resource Centre, University of Sydney, Sydney, NSW. http://www.mekong. es.usyd.edu.au/publications/working_papers/wp10.pdf (accessed 17 November 2005)

Li, B. and Xie, H. (2003) We share a dream in Jisha village. *Cultural Geography* 13. February. CBIK Community Livelihoods. http://www.ecoyunnan.org/Jishaweb/dream.htm (accessed 17 November 2005)

Li, N. (2002) Where the wild things are. Press Releases. 14 November 2002. http://www.wwfchina.org/ english/ (accessed 17 November 2005)

Li, T.C. (2004) Rallying for the Rafflesia. The Star Online, 17 February 2004. http://thestar.com.my/lifestyle/ (accessed 17 November 2005)

Lindberg, K., Goulding, C., Huang, Z., Mo, J., Wei, P. and Kong, G. (1997) Ecotourism in China: Selected issues and challenges. In: Oppermann, M. (ed.) *Pacific Rim Tourism*. CAB International, Wallingford, UK, pp. 128–143.

Liou, C. (2003) A sustainable future for Shangri-la. WWF Press Release, 19 May 2003. http://www.wwfchina.org/english/ (accessed 17 November 2005)

Lipscombe, N. (2005) Maintenance of cultural integrity in the face of cultural change: Tourism as an agent of cultural change in SaPa, Vietnam. In: Boyle, A. and Tremblay, P. (eds) *Sharing Tourism Knowledge: CAUTHE 2005 Conference Proceedings*. 2–5 February. Alice Springs: Charles Darwin University.

Lisu Lodge (2005) Lisu Lodge. http://www.lisulodge.com/ (accessed 17 November 2005)

LN (Lombok Network) (2004) Gunung Rijani National Park. http://www.lombok-network.com/rinjani/ (accessed 17 November 2005)

LSP (Lombok Sumbawa Promo) (2004a) Gunung Rinjani National Park. http://www.lomboksumbawa. com/rinjani/nat_park.htm (accessed 17 November 2005)

LSP (Lombok Sumbawa Promo) (2004b) Lombok's Rinjani Trek named as one of the four best destinations worldwide. Press Room, 9 June 2004. http://www.lomboksumbawa.com/press_room.htm (accessed 17 November 2005)

Luong, P.T. and Binh, N.V. (1996) Tourism activities and ethnic minorities groups in mountainous areas in Vietnam. UNDP. http://www.undp.org.vn/projects/vie96010/cemma/RAS93103/019.htm (accessed 17 November 2005)

Lyttleton, C. and Allcock, A. (2002) *Tourism as a Tool for Development: UNESCO-Lao National Tourism Authority Nam Ha Ecotourism Project: External Review July 6–18, 2002*. UNESCO Bangkok. http://www.unescobkk.org/index.php?id=486 (accessed 17 November 2005)

Macan-Markar, M. (2003) Hill tribes go high-tech to preserve way of life. IPS News. http://www.ipsnews. net/interna.asp?idnews=19235 (accessed 17 November 2005)

Mackinnon, K. (2005) Parks, people, and policies: Conflicting agendas for forests in Southeast Asia. In: Birmingham, E., Dick, C.W. and Moritz, C. (eds) *Tropical Rainforests: Past, Present & Future*. The University of Chicago Press, Chicago, 558–582.

Marston, A. (2004) Shangri-la residents develop community-led ecotourism projects. http://www.wwfchina. org/english/ (accessed 17 November 2005)

MATTA (2002) Apeco 2002 Profile of Speakers. http://www.ecotourism.com.my/ (accessed 17 November 2005)

MESCOT (2004) MESCOT: Batu Puteh community of Lower Kinabatangan. Nomination Form. Equator Prize 2004. UNDP. http://www.undp.org/equatorinitiative/pdf/EKZ/2004%20Finalists%20and%20winners/ 2004-0197_Nom_MESCOT_Malaysia.pdf (accessed 17 November 2005)

Michaud, J. (1993) Tourism as catalyst of economic and political change: The case of the highland minorities in Ladakh (India) and northern Thailand. *Internationales Asienforum* 24, 21–43.

Michaud, M. (1997) A portrait of cultural resistance: The confinement of tourism in a Hmong village in Thailand. In: Picard, M. and Wood, R.E. (eds) *Tourism, Ethnicity and the State in Asian and Pacific Societies.* University of Hawaii Press, Honolulu.

Minority Rights Group International (2001) Case Study 2: The Aetas of Central Luzon. Development Conflict: The Philippine Experience. http://www.minorityrights.org/Dev/mrg_dev_title4_philippines/mrg_dev_title3_philippines_7.htm (accessed 17 November 2005)

MNS (Malaysian Nature Society) (2005) The Ulu Geroh biodiversity audit. Science and Conservation. http://www.mns.org.my/science.php?op=display&id=6 (accessed 17 November 2005)

MRG (Minority Rights Group) (nd) The forests and indigenous peoples of Asia: Threatened people, overexploited forests. Minority Rights Group. http://www.minorityrights.org/Profiles/profile.asp?ID=5 (accessed 17 November 2005)

Muqbil, I. (1994) Lessons from the Lisu. *PATA Travel News,* March, 12–15.

Napthali, K. (1997) Togians: Ecotourism is not the answer. *Inside Indonesia* 51 (July–September). http://www.insideindonesia.org/edit51/kate1.htm (accessed 17 November 2005)

Native Planet (2004) Travel & ecotourism. http://www.nativeplanet.org/travel/travel.shtml (accessed 17 November 2005)

Natural Focus (2003a) Typical 'hilltribe' tour. http://www.naturalfocusecotour.com/FWhatisNaturalFocus.htm (accessed 17 November 2005)

Natural Focus (2003b) What is Natural Focus? http://www.naturalfocusecotour.com/FWhatisNaturalFocus.htm (accessed 17 November 2005)

Nepal, S.K. (2002) Involving indigenous peoples in protected area management: Comparative perspectives from Nepal, Thailand and China. *Environmental Management* 30, 748–763.

NYEA (Northwest Yunnan Ecotourism Association) (2002) Ecotourism in Northwest Yunnan. http://www.northwestyunnan.com/index1.htm (accessed 17 November 2005)

NZAID (2004a) Environment. http://www.nzaid.govt.nz/about/environment.html (accessed 17 November 2005)

NZAID (2004b) Indonesia fact sheet. October 2004. http://www.nzaid.govt.nz/ (accessed 17 November 2005)

NZAID (2004c) Philippines. http://www.nzaid.govt.nz/programmes/c-philippines.html (accessed 17 November 2005)

OW (Operation Wallacea) (2005a) Sulawesi home page. http://www.opwall.com/2004%20Sulawesi%20home%20page.htm http://www.projectaware.org/ (accessed 17 November 2005)

OW (Operation Wallacea) (2005b) Ecotourism studies. http://www.opwall.com/Reports/Index%20of%20previous%20reports.htm (accessed 17 November 2005)

Palata Holiday Camp (nd) Community based tourism at Palata Holiday Camp, Umphang, Tak Province, Thailand. http://www.geocities.com/palata_holiday_camp//200630 (accessed 30 January 2006)

Patterson, C. (2003) Ecotourism spotlight on Sukau Rainforest Lodge. *EcoTourism Management* Winter 2003. http://www.kalahari-online.com/ (accessed 17 November 2005)

Pearce, F. (2004) Field report: Wanglang Panda Nature Reserve. Journey to the Heart of China's Forests. http://www.wwfchina.org/english/ (accessed 17 November 2005)

Persoon, G.A. (2003) Conflicts over trees and waves on Siberut Island. *Geografiska Annaler: Series B, Human Geography* 85, 253–264.

Pitamahaket, P. (1997) The development of Kanchanaburi ecotourism co-operative: The first ecotourism co-operative in Thailand. In: Bornemeier, J., Victor, M. and Durst, P. (eds) *Ecotourism for Forest Conservation and Community Development.* FAO/RAP Publication 97/26. Bangkok, pp. 195–203.

Pleumarom, A. (2002) Community-based ecotourism: Miracle or menace? IYE Regional Conference on Community-Based Tourism in Southeast Asia, Chiang Mai, 3–7 March 2002. http://www.recoftc.org/documents/Inter_Reps/CBT_discusssion/Anita_Thailand.doc (accessed 17 November 2005)

RECOFTC (2002) Outcomes of conference on community based tourism in Southeast Asia. Regional Services. http://www.recoftc.org/ (accessed 17 November 2005)

Reed, M. (nd) Visiting longhouses. Sarawak Tourism Board. http://www.sarawaktourism.com/longhouse.html http://www.sarawak.com.my/travel_features/ulu/longhouse.html (accessed 17 November 2005)

Responsible Travel (2001) South Sulawesi eco lodge in Indonesia. http://www.responsibletravel.com/Accommodation/Accommodation100024.htm (accessed 17 November 2005)

REST (2002) Community based ecotourism in Southeast Asia. Chiang Mai, Thailand, 27 February–8 March

2002. Responsible Ecologically Sustainable Tours. http://www.rest.or.th/training/ (accessed 17 November 2005)

REST (2004) What is REST? http://www.rest.or.th/training/ (accessed 17 November 2005)

Rihawi, L. (2002) Community-based conservation and ecotourism at Babe National Park, Vietnam. In: *Enhancing the Economic Benefits of Tourism for Local Communities and Poverty Alleviation*. WTO, Madrid, pp. 43–46.

Ross, S. and Wall, G. (1999) Evaluating ecotourism: The case of North Sulawesi, Indonesia. *Tourism Management* 20, 673–682.

Ross, S. and Wall, G. (2001a) Wallace's line: Implications for conservation and ecotourism in Indonesia. In: Harrison, D. (ed.) *Tourism and the Less Developed World: Issues and Case Studies*. CABI, Wallingford, UK, pp. 223–233.

Ross, S. and Wall, G. (2001b) Ecotourism: A theoretical framework and an Indonesian application. In: McCool, S.F. and Moisey, R.N. (eds) *Tourism, Recreation and Sustainability*. CABI, Wallingford, UK, pp. 271–288.

Rugendyke, B. and Son, N.T. (2005) Conservation costs: Nature-based tourism as development at Cuc Phuong National Park, Vietnam. *Asia Pacific Viewpoint* 46, 185–200.

Sabah Homestay (2005) Sabah – Malaysian Borneo Homestay Programme. Sabah Homestay.

Sabah Tourism (2005) Accommodation. Homestay. Sabah Tourism Board. http://www.sabahtourism.com/accommodation.php?locateID=&typeID=&rateID (accessed 17 November 2005)

Sangin, S.E. *et al.* (2000) *Impact of Tourism on Longhouse Communities in Sarawak*. Unpublished paper, Faculty of Social Sciences, Universiti Malaysia Sarawak, Sarawak.

Schiller, A. (2001) Pampang culture village and international tourism in East Kalimantan, Indonesia, Borneo. *Human Organization* 60, 414–422.

Schipani, S. (2002) UNESCO-National Tourism Authority of Lao PDR Nam Ha ecotourism project awarded the 2001 United Nations Development Award. http://www.theboatlanding.laopdr.com/unesco.html (accessed 17 November 2005)

Schipani, S. and Sipaseuth, K. (2002) Community-based ecotourism in the Lao PDR: strengthening local capacity to conserve and protect the natural and cultural heritage within an economically viable framework. Outcomes of Conference on Community Based Tourism in Southeast Asia. RECOFTC. http://www.recoftc.org/ (accessed 17 November 2005)

Schwinn, C. (2002) Studying ecotourism in Yunnan. Asia Pacific Postcard from the Field. 30 April 2002. http://nature.org/wherewework/asiapacific/china/features/art7465.html (accessed 17 November 2005)

Seltzer, M. and Grant, S. (2003) Community Tourism News – Everyone's a Winner [Lisu Lodge]. BEST (Business Enterprises for Sustainable Tourism). http://www.sustainabletravel.org/ (accessed 17 November 2005)

Siberut (nd) The 'Mentawai Cultural Tourism' Strategy: Using tourism to preserve the Mentawai culture. Native Planet. http://www.nativeplanet.org/mentawai/ (accessed 17 November 2005)

Sills, E. (1998) Ecotourism as an Integrated Conservation and Development Strategy: Econometric Estimation of Demand by International Tourists and Impacts on Indigenous Households on Siberut Island, Indonesia. Unpublished PhD dissertation. Duke University, Durham, North Carolina.

Sinclair, J. (2000) Thailand 2000. http://www.sinclair.org.au/thailand/ (accessed 17 November 2005)

Smith, H.S. (1997a) Gunung Halimun. In: *Adventuring in Indonesia*. Sierra Club Books, San Francisco, pp. 107–110.

Smith, H.S. (1997b) Mentawai Islands. In: *Adventuring in Indonesia*. Sierra Club Books, San Francisco, pp. 236–239.

SNS (nd) Integrated management of Tasek Bera, Malaysia – support for the implementation of obligations under the Ramsar Convention. http://www.sns.dk/snscen/kontorer/16kontor/assist16.htm (accessed 17 November 2005)

SNV Laos (2004) Documents and publications: Sustainable tourism. http://www.snv.org.la/docseco.htm (accessed 17 November 2005)

SNV Vietnam (2004) Sustainable pro-poor tourism. http://www.snv.org.vn/OurProgramsDetail.asp?ID=20&show=2&SubId=20 (accessed 17 November 2005)

Sproule, K.W. and Suhandi, A.S. (1998) Guidelines for community-based ecotourism programs. In: Lindberg, K., Wood, M.E. and Engeldrum, D. (eds) *Ecotourism A Guide for Planners and Managers*, Vol. 2. The Ecotourism Society, North Bennington, Vermont, pp. 215–236.

Suansri, P. (2002) How has the local community in Thailand benefited from tourism? Definition of CBT. REST, Bangkok. http://www.rest.or.th/training/ (accessed 17 November 2005)

Suansri, P. (2003) *Community Based Tourism Handbook*. REST, Bangkok. http://www.rest.or.th/training/handbook.asp (accessed 17 November 2005)

Suhandi, A.S. (2001) Community-based ecotourism development at Togean Islands, Central Sulawesi, Indonesia. In: Varma, H. (ed.) *Island Tourism in Asia and the Pacific*. WTO, Madrid, pp. 176–183.

Suhandi, A.S. (2002) Community based ecotourism development conservation in the Togean Islands. In: WTO (comp.) *Sustainable Development of Ecotourism: A Compilation of Good Practices*. WTO, Madrid, pp. 155–157.

Sukrung, K. (1997) REST: a new approach to ecotourism. Bangkok Post, 20 December 1997. Voices From Communities. http://www.rest.or.th/training/ (accessed 17 November 2005)

Sun, M. (2003) Who respects our oath. *Cultural Geography*, 13. CBIK Community Livelihoods. http://www.ecoyunnan.org/Jishaweb/respect.htm (accessed 17 November 2005)

Tagi, K. (2002) Ecotourism in Malaysia: Current status and the effectiveness. In: *Interim Report FY 2001*. Environmental Education Project, Institute for Global Environmental Strategies, Japan.

Tarman, W. (1998) Up the Ulu – Nanga Sumpa 10 years on. http://www.sarawak.com.my/travel_features/ulu/nanga_sumpa.html (accessed 17 November 2005)

TEC (nd) Tourism and the Environment Concern Group (TEC). http://www.geocities.com/tec_groups/?200630 (accessed 30 January 2006)

Teo, A. (2003) Sukau Rainforest Lodge. In: *Sustainable Development of Ecotourism: A Compilation of Good Practices in SMEs*. WTO, Madrid, pp. 175–179.

Teo, A. and Patterson, C. (2004) Ecotourism in practice at Sukau Rainforest Lodge. News & Articles. 4 July 2004. http://www.borneoecotours.com/news/details.asp?newsid=48 (accessed 17 November 2005)

Teo, A. and Patterson, C. (2005) *Saving Paradise: The Story of Sukau Rainforest Lodge*. Sabah Handicraft Centre, Sabah, Malaysia.

The Boat Landing (2005) The Boat Landing Guest House and Restaurant. http://www.theboatlanding.laopdr.com/ghres.html (accessed 17 November 2005)

Tisdell, C. (1996) Ecotourism, economics and the environment: Observations from China. *Journal of Travel Research* Spring, 1–19.

Tourism Cambodia (2004) Ratanakiri: Back to nature with Cambodia minority. Attractions. Cambodia. http://www.tourismcambodia.com/Attractions/Ratanakiri/ (accessed 17 November 2005)

Toyota, M. (1996) The effects of tourism development on an Akha community: A Chiang Rai village case study. In: Parnwell, M. (ed.) *Uneven Development in Thailand*. Avebury, Aldershot, UK.

Traveltrade (2005) Longhouse living. *Traveltrade*, 18 May 2005, 19.

UNDP (2004a) Community-based eco-tourism for the Indigenous Semelai community in a Ramsar Wetland of International Importance – Tasek Bera, Pahang Project Fact Sheet http://www.undp.org/sgp/cty/ASIA_PACIFIC/MALAYSIA/pfs4467.htm (accessed 17 November 2005)
http://www.undp.org/sgp/cty/ASIA_PACIFIC/MALAYSIA/pfs6205.htm (accessed 17 November 2005)

UNDP (2004b) Local community-based ecotourism and conservation training for the indigenous Semai of Ulu Geroh, Gopeng, Perak. Project Fact Sheet. http://www.undp.org/sgp/cty/ASIA_PACIFIC/MALAYSIA/pfs4492.htm (accessed 17 November 2005)

UNESCO (nd) UNESCO-TNTA Nam Ha Ecotourism Project. UNESCO Bangkok. http://www.unescobk.org/index.php?id=486 (accessed 17 November 2005)

UNESCO (2001a) Nam Ha Ecotourism Project. http://www.unescobk.org/culture/namha/index.html (accessed 17 November 2005)

UNESCO (2001b) Siberut. Biosphere Reserve Information Indonesia. MAB Program. http://www2.unesco.org/mab/br/brdir/directory/biores.asp?code=INS+06&mode=all (accessed 17 November 2005)

UNESCO (2004) *The National Tourism Authority of Lao PDR-UNESCO Nam Ha Ecotourism Project, Phase II*. UNESCO Bangkok. http://www.unescobk.org/index.php?id=486 (accessed 17 November 2005)

Vanzi, S.J. (2004) Community tourism introduced in Pampanga, Tarlac rural areas. Philippine Headline News Online. http://www.newsflash.org/2004/02/ht/ht004502.htm (accessed 17 November 2005)

WCS (Wildlife Conservation Society) (2004) Tonle Sap. Saving Wildlife. Cambodia. http://wcs.org/sw-around_the_globe/Asia/Cambodia/Tonle-Sap (accessed 17 November 2005)

Weaver, D.B. (1998a) Ecotourism in Thailand. In: *Ecotourism in the Less Developed World*. CABI, Wallingford, UK, pp. 167–174.

Weaver, D.B. (1998b) Ecotourism in other parts of South-east Asia. In: *Ecotourism in the Less Developed World*. CABI, Wallingford, UK, pp. 174–179.

Weaver, D. (2001) Asia. In: *Ecotourism*. John Wiley, Milton, pp. 275–281.

Weaver, D. (2002) Asian ecotourism: Patterns and themes. *Tourism Geographies* 4, 153–172.

Welcome to Chiangmai & Chiangrai Magazine (2004) 'Eco-tourism' not always eco-friendly. *Welcome to Chiangmai & Chiangrai Magazine.* http://welcome-to.chiangmai-chiangrai.com/ecotourism_friendly.html (accessed 17 November 2005)

Wild Asia (2003) Rafflesia of the rainforest, the world's largest flower: Conservation of Rafflesia (Rafflesiaceae) in Malaysia. WildBorneo.net. http://wildasia.net/main/article.cfm?articleID=3 (accessed 17 November 2005)

Wild Asia (2004) Social principle: Visiting a traditional Iban longhouse. Responsible Tourism. Wild Asia. http://wildasia.net/RT/RT_social_01.cfm (accessed 17 November 2005)

WTO (2002a) Cambuhat river and village tour. In: *Sustainable Development of Tourism: A Compilation of Good Practices in Ecotourism.* WTO, Madrid, pp. 205–209.

WTO (2002b) Dolphin-whale watching tour. In: *Sustainable Development of Tourism: A Compilation of Good Practices in Ecotourism.* WTO, Madrid, pp. 211–213.

WTO (2002c) Community-based ecotourism enterprises in the Gunung Halimun National Park. In: *Sustainable Development of Ecotourism: A Compilation of Good Practices.* WTO, Madrid, pp. 151–154.

WTO (2002d) Community-based ecotourism development and conservation in Togean Islands. In: *Sustainable Development of Tourism: A Compilation of Good Practices in Ecotourism.* WTO, Madrid, pp. 155–157.

WTO (2003a) Community based ecotourism in Gunung Halimun National Park (GHNP). In: *Sustainable Development of Ecotourism: A Compilation of Good Practices in SMEs.* Madrid, WTO, 127–130.

WTO (2003b) Sukau Rainforest Lodge. In: *Sustainable Development of Ecotourism: A Compilation of Good Practices in SMEs.* Madrid, WTO. http://www.borneoecotours.com/news/details.asp?newsid=47 (accessed 17 November 2005)

WWF (2001) Capacity building for ecotourism in Sabah, Malaysia. In: *Guidelines for Community-based Ecotourism Development.* July 2001. WWF International, 5. http://www.wwf.no/pdf/tourism_guidelines.pdf (accessed 17 November 2005)

WWF (2003) Panda conservation in the Minshan landscape (Minshan Project). Giant Panda Programme. http://www.wwfchina.org/english/sub_print.php?loca=26 (accessed 17 November 2005)

WWF (nd) Sulu Sulawesi marine ecoregion. WWF International Corals Initiative.

WWF Cambodia (nd) WWF Indochina Programme Office. http://www.wwfindochina.org/ (accessed 17 November 2005)

WWF Malaysia (2000) The Model Ecologically Sustainable Community Tourism Project (MESCOT). Special Feature. http://www.wwfmalaysia.org/features/special/Mescot.htm (accessed 17 November 2005)

WWF Malaysia (2004) MESCOT awarded merit award at UNDP's Equator Initiative Prize. Press Releases, 19 February 2004. http://www.wwfmalaysia.org/newsroom/ (accessed 17 November 2005)

Yea, S. (2002) On and off the ethnic tourist map in Southeast Asia: The case of Iban longhouse tourism, Sarawak, Malaysia. *Tourism Geographies* 4, 173–194.

Yea, S. and Noweg, G.T. (2000) The reality of community: Iban women's participation in longhouse tourism in Sarawak. *Borneo Review* 11.

Yeak Laom (nd) Yeak Laom community-based ecotourism project. http://www.geocities.com/yeak_laom/ (accessed 17 November 2005)

Yuson, A.A. (2000) Dancing anew on the stairways to heaven. *Unesco Courier* December 2000. http://www.unesco.org/courier/2000_12/uk/doss6.htm (accessed 17 November 2005)

Zeppel, H. (1997) Meeting 'Wild People': Iban culture and longhouse tourism in Sarawak. In: Yamashita, S., Din, K.H. and Eades, J.S. (eds) *Tourism and Cultural Development in Asia and Oceania.* Universiti Kebangsaan Malaysia, Bangsi, pp. 119–140.

Zeppel, H. (1998) Entertainers or entrepreneurs: Iban involvement in longhouse tourism (Sarawak, Borneo). *Tourism Recreation Research* 23, 39–45.

8

Sustainable Development and Management of Indigenous Ecotourism

The main aim of this book was to review Indigenous-owned and -operated ecotourism ventures that benefit Indigenous communities and conserve the natural and cultural environment. Indigenous ecotourism was defined as 'nature-based attractions or tours owned by Indigenous people, and also Indigenous interpretation of the natural and cultural environment including wildlife' (Zeppel, 2003: 56). Indigenous involvement in ecotourism was examined through global case studies of Indigenous operators and providers of ecotourism products in the Pacific Islands, Latin America, Africa and South East Asia. These case studies illustrate how Indigenous groups are conserving natural areas and educating visitors, while developing and controlling ecotourism on Indigenous lands and territories. The growth of Indigenous ecotourism since the 1990s reflects the spread of tourism into natural areas and biodiversity hotspots still inhabited by Indigenous groups and also the legal recognition of Indigenous land rights. For many Indigenous groups, ecotourism provides an alternative to other extractive land uses such as hunting, grazing or farming; and the threat of incursions by logging, oil drilling or mining. Hence, ecotourism helps to conserve natural areas, wildlife and resources on tribal lands. It further involves Indigenous

peoples in managing tourism, culture and their own environment. Ecotourism, then, supplements a subsistence lifestyle and aids the transition to a cash economy for many tribal groups. Hence, the case studies presented in this book have refuted the common perception that Indigenous peoples have little involvement in ecotourism (Page and Dowling, 2002).

How various Indigenous communities develop and operate tribal ecotourism ventures in their traditional lands was a key focus of this book. The case studies described and analysed the approaches adopted by different Indigenous groups and communities in developing and operating ecotourism ventures, mainly in remote natural areas valued for biodiversity conservation. These studies considered the environmental, cultural and economic impacts of Indigenous ecotourism ventures in tribal areas of developing countries in Oceania, Latin America, Africa and South East Asia, particularly in tropical rainforest areas. The savannah and desert regions of Africa, along with the Andes Mountains of South America, are another key focus. The Asia-Pacific region, Latin America and Africa are a main focus for these community-based Indigenous ecotourism projects (Wesche and Drumm, 1999; Mann, 2002; SPREP, 2002; *Tourism in Focus*, 2002). In these developing countries, Indigenous ecotourism ventures are mainly implemented with the help of non-government agencies (NGOs) involved in conservation or community development projects. For many Indigenous peoples, controlled ecotourism is seen as a way of achieving cultural, political, environmental and economic sustainability for the community (Sofield, 1993, 2003; Butler and Hinch, 1996; Zeppel, 1998; Epler Wood, 1999a; Mbaiwa, 2005; Notzke, 2006). Opening up Indigenous homelands or reserves to ecotourism, however, involves a balance between use of natural resources, meeting tourist needs and maintaining cultural integrity. The case studies presented in this book assessed these key issues for Indigenous ecotourism as well as the approaches adopted by NGOs and Indigenous groups in establishing and operating ecotourism enterprises on tribal territories.

Indigenous Ecotourism on Tribal Lands

The case studies of Indigenous ecotourism reviewed in this book support conservation on tribal lands, and involve Indigenous people in decision-making and management of tourism and resources. These ventures include nature-based tourism products or accommodation owned by Indigenous groups, and Indigenous cultural tours or attractions in a natural setting. Cultural aspects of Indigenous ecotourism include the close bonds between Indigenous peoples and the environment, based on subsistence activities and spiritual relationships with the land, plants and animals. Specific ecotourism enterprises controlled by Indigenous people include cultural ecotours, ecolodges, hunting and fishing tours, cultural villages, and other nature-oriented tourist facilities or services. These were either Indigenous community-owned ecotourism enterprises or tourism joint ventures with the private sector. In most cases, Indigenous ecotourism involves 'tourism that is *based on indigenous knowledge systems and values*, promoting customary practices and livelihoods' (Johnston, 2000: 91). The case studies in this book highlight the conservation and community benefits of these different Indigenous ecotourism projects on tribal lands.

This includes preservation of community forests and wildlife as well as tourism income funding the basic infrastructure, facilities and services required by Indigenous communities. The focus is on the natural environment with ecotourism providing benefits for local communities. This accords with the definition of ecotourism as: 'responsible travel to natural areas that conserves the environment and *improves the well-being of local people*' (TIES, 2004). However, Indigenous ecotourism also includes sustainable tribal use of natural resources, securing land tenure, negotiating tourism contracts, and park revenue sharing of tourism income with neighbouring communities (see Table 8.1). The case studies presented in this book found that negotiating acceptable levels and types of Indigenous resource use is a key feature of many ecotourism projects and joint ventures on tribal territories.

Most of the Indigenous ecotourism ventures reviewed in this book are relatively new enterprises established with funding support from conservation and development NGOs, aid agencies and other foreign donors (see Table 8.2). Hence, the commercial sustainability of many Indigenous ecotourism ventures may be in doubt after this aid funding ends (Honey, 2003; Epler Wood, 2004). Natural disasters, political conflicts and continued resource exploitation also threaten the viability of small-scale Indigenous ecotourism ventures in remote areas. However, there is some government intervention and support for Indigenous ecotourism, mainly for communities living in or around protected areas or nature reserves of high tourism value. This includes the Maasai people on group ranches in Kenya and Tanzania, some parks in southern Africa, tribal groups in South-east Asia and Indians living in national parks or biosphere reserves in Latin America. In the Pacific Islands and West Africa, especially Ghana, community-owned forests and reserves are the main focus for conservation- and community-based ecotourism ventures with Indigenous groups.

The case studies of Indigenous ecotourism ventures in developing countries highlight the key role of government policies on Indigenous lands and tourism, along with legal recognition

Table 8.1. Key features of Indigenous ecotourism on tribal lands.

1. *Involves travel to natural destinations*
   Remote homelands, communal reserves,
   inhabited protected areas and tribal territories

2. *Minimizes impact*
   Minimize environmental and cultural impacts
   Sustainable tribal use of natural resources

3. *Builds environmental and cultural awareness*
   Tribal guides share environmental knowledge
   Reinforces Indigenous cultural links with land

4. *Provides direct financial benefits for conservation*
   Tourism funds conservation and community needs
   Tourist fees and lease fees, wildlife revenue, NGO funding

5. *Provides financial benefits and empowerment for local people*
   Park revenue sharing with local communities
   Legal land title to negotiate tourism contracts
   Lease land on tribal reserves and sell wildlife quotas
   Tourism business owned/co-owned by tribal community

6. *Respects local culture and sensitive to host countries*
   Promotes ecocultural tourism and learning
   Tourism complements traditional lifestyle

7. *Supports human rights and democratic movements*
   Tribal land rights and human rights recognized
   Indigenous political history acknowledged

Sources: Based on Honey (1999); Scheyvens (2002); Blake (2003);
TIES (2004).

of Indigenous land tenure and resource use rights. These national policies are shaped by international conventions on biodiversity conservation, cultural heritage and Indigenous rights, and the policies of the World Bank and other donor agencies on Indigenous peoples. Globally, Indigenous peoples occupy 20% of land, in areas of high biodiversity, compared to 6% in protected areas (WWF, 2005a). Hence, the growth of Indigenous ecotourism since the 1980s reflects the strong links between global initiatives on biodiversity conservation, Indigenous rights and the development of ecotourism (Lash, 1998; Honey, 1999; Weber *et al.*, 2000; Alcorn, 2001; Johnston, 2006; Notzke, 2006) (see Table 8.3). Ulloa (2005) refers to the western ideal of 'ecological natives' living in harmony with nature driving funding for conservation and also new forms of governance devised by Indigenous groups to advance their rights. International funding for the conservation of biodiversity hotspots, such as rainforests, and the global spread of tourism into remote natural areas have thus involved more Indigenous peoples in ecotourism projects.

The stages of Indigenous ecotourism development are: (i) tourism exploration of Indigenous peoples on tribal lands; (ii) involvement of the local community in providing tourism facilities; and (iii) tribal tourism development based on secure land titles and partnerships with tour operators (see Table 8.4). Legal land tenure such as a Certificate of Ancestral Domain Title provides a secure basis for Indigenous groups to negotiate contracts and leases with private tourism operators. Small Indigenous ecotourism ventures in the Pacific Islands, South-east Asia and West Africa are mainly in the tourism exploration or early involvement stage, while Indigenous groups with legal land titles in eastern and southern Africa and Latin America are developing joint ventures and their own community tourism. This stage includes tourism training and support for enterprise development from conservation NGOs.

Table 8.2. International agencies funding Indigenous ecotourism on tribal lands.

Finance agencies
The World Bank – International Finance Corporation (IFC)[a]
Inter-American Development Bank (IDB)
Asian Development Bank
African Development Bank
German Bank for Reconstruction and Development
European Union (EU)

Environment agencies
United Nations Environment Programme (UNEP)
Global Environment Facility (GEF)[a] – UNEP/World Bank
World Conservation Union (IUCN)
Food and Agriculture Organisation (FAO) Forestry
United Nations Educational, Scientific and Cultural Organisation (UNESCO)
South Pacific Region Environment Program (SPREP)

Development agencies
United Nations Development Programme (UNDP)
International Labour Organisation (ILO)
Department for International Development (DFID) UK
Overseas Development Institute (ODI) UK
USAID (USA)
AusAID (Australia)
NZAID (New Zealand)
JICA (Japan)
Netherlands Development Agency (SNV) Netherlands
DANIDA (Denmark)
SIDA (Sweden)
Canadian International Development Agency (CIDA) Canada
German Technical Assistance (GTZ) (Germany)
DED (Germany)

Tourism agencies
World Tourism Organization (WTO)
Pacific Asia Travel Association (PATA)
South Pacific Tourism Organisation (SPTO)
Pro-poor Tourism (PPT) (UK, Africa)

[a] IFC through the GEF funded the Small and Medium Enterprise Program (SME) since 1995.
IFC/GEF has funded the Environmental Business Finance Program (EBFP) since 2004.

In a similar manner, Smith (1999) refers to the stages through which Indigenous communities are progressing in contemporary times as survival, recovery, development and self-determination. These stages include survival of Indigenous peoples, languages, cultural practices and arts; the recovery of Indigenous territories, human rights and histories; the development of Indigenous lands and peoples, often in response to external threats, and self-determination in decision-making as a political goal. These steps involve Indigenous peoples in political mobilization and the assertion of their land rights.

Conservation NGOs such as WWF, The International Ecotourism Society (TIES), The Nature Conservancy, and Conservation International now play a major role in supporting Indigenous resource management and ecotourism projects (Epler Wood, 1999b; Sweeting and McConnel, 1999; Alcorn, 2001; WWF, 2001; Nature Conservancy, 2005). In fact, WWF adopted a policy on Indigenous peoples and conservation in 1996 that recognized the rights of Indigenous peoples to their traditional lands, territories and resources (Weber *et al.*, 2000; WWF, 2005a). These major international conservation NGOs provide

Table 8.3. Biodiversity conservation, Indigenous rights and ecotourism on tribal lands.

Biodiversity conservation	Indigenous rights	Ecotourism
1980s		
Biosphere Reserves	UN Working Group on Indigenous Populations (1982)	Ecotourism defined
World Heritage Areas	ILO Convention No. 169 on IP (1989)	
	UN *Draft Declaration on the Rights of IP (1989/90)*	
1990s		
GEF established (1991)	World Bank Policy on IP (1991)	Ecotourism Associations
UN *Convention on*	UN *International Year for the World's IP* (1993)	(USA, Australia, Kenya)
Biological Diversity (1992)	UN *Decade of the World's IP* (1995–2004)	
UN Earth Summit Rio (1992)	Indigenous Tourism Rights International (1995)	*Ecotourism: A Guide for*
IP Biodiversity Network (1997)	WWF Policy on Rights of IP (1996)	*Planners and Managers* (TES,
Ramsar Wetlands and IP	IP of Africa Coordinating Committee (1998)	1993/1998)
(1999)	Minority Rights Group International (1999)	
2000s		
World Summit on SD (2002)	UN Permanent Forum on Indigenous Issues (2000)	WTO *SD of Ecotourism* (2001/03)
World Parks Congress (2003)	Dana Declaration on Mobile IP and Conservation (2002)	WWF *Guidelines for CBE*
World Conservation Congress	Business for Social Responsibility Rights of IP (2003)	(2001)
(2004)	International Forum on Indigenous Tourism (2002)	Indigenous Ecotourism Toolbox
Protected Areas and IP	World Social Forum includes IP (2005)	UN *Year of Ecotourism* (2002)
(IUCN) (2000 and 2004)	UN *2nd Decade of the World's IP* (2005–2014)	*CBE Pacific Islands* (SPREP,
		2002)
		Rights and Responsibilities[a]
		(2003)

IP, Indigenous peoples; SD, sustainable development; CBE, community-based ecotourism;
UN, United Nations; ILO, International Labor Organisation; GEF, Global Environment Facility; WTO, World Tourism
Organization; WWF, World Wide Fund for Nature; TES, The Ecotourism Society; SPREP, South Pacific Region
Environment Programme; IUCN, The World Conservation Union.
[a] *Rights and Responsibilities: A Compilation of Codes of Conduct for Tourism and Indigenous and Local Communities*
(Honey and Thullen, 2003).

funding, staff and technical support for Indigenous ecotourism ventures that are located in global biodiversity hotspots such as rainforests. Increasingly, this funding for biodiversity conservation also involves alternative community development projects (e.g. ecotourism, organic agriculture, crafts). Most of these conservation NGOs are US-based organizations, with others from the UK and Western Europe, New Zealand and Africa (see Table 8.5). The majority of these environmental NGOs aim to conserve key ecosystems and their wildlife, while working with Indigenous groups still living in remote natural regions and protected areas. Some NGOs focus mainly on saving wildlife or a rare species (e.g. parrots and macaws in South America) in their natural habitats, while others focus on conservation in one specific region (e.g. Kenya/East Africa; and Operation Wallacea in Sulawesi, Indonesia). Local conservation NGOs and wildlife societies within one country and Indigenous associations

(e.g. Maasai Environmental Resource Coalition) also support Indigenous ecotourism (see also Table 8.8).

In addition to generating employment and income, there are often political motivations for Indigenous ecotourism. The case studies in this book support the fact that, for many Indigenous groups, ecotourism is used to reinforce land claims, acknowledge cultural identity and land ownership and to regain rights to access or use tribal land and resources. Ecotourism ventures also demonstrate that tribal land is being used productively to generate income and the ability of Indigenous groups to govern their own affairs and to manage businesses (Hinch, 2001, 2004; Weaver, 2001, 2006). For Indigenous peoples, then, sustainable ecotourism development is based on '*conservation of resources and empowerment of local people through direct benefits and control over ecotourism activities*' (Scheyvens,

Table 8.4. Stages of Indigenous ecotourism development.

	Exploration	Involvement	Development
Land Tenure	Traditional lands	Community reserves	Legal land title
Local System	Families, villages	Community organizations	Development organizations
Resources	Subsistence only	Subsistence and for sale	Limits on subsistence use
			Regulated commercial use
Funding	Local funds	Indigenous agencies	External donor agencies
		Conservation NGOs	(finance, aid, conservation)
Tourism	Independent visitors	Irregular tour groups	Regular ongoing tour groups
		Informal partnerships	Formal joint ventures and contracts
Marketing	Word-of-mouth	Flyers, direct sales	Website – community/tourism group
		Ethnic brokers (volunteers)	Wholesaled by other tour operators

Source: Based on the first three stages of Butler's (1980, 2005) resort life cycle model.

Table 8.5. Conservation NGOs supporting Indigenous ecotourism on tribal lands.

Conservation NGO	Area of operation
World Wide Fund for Nature (WWF)	Global (Africa, Latin America, Asia-Pacific)
The Nature Conservancy (USA)	Latin America, Indonesia, PNG
Conservation International (USA)[a]	Latin America, Africa, Indonesia, PNG
The International Ecotourism Society (TIES) (USA)	Latin America, Africa, China
Rare Conservation (USA)[b]	Latin America, Indonesia, China (Yunnan)
Rainforest Alliance (USA)	Latin America, Asia-Pacific, Africa (Guinea only)
Wildlife Conservation Society (USA)	Latin America, Africa, Asia
Seacology (USA)	Asia-Pacific
Macaw Landing Foundation (USA)	Latin America
Foster Parrots (USA)	Latin America
Sand County Foundation (USA)	Tanzania (East Africa)
Earthwatch Institute (USA)	Global
Friends of Conservation (UK, USA, Kenya)	Masai Mara Reserve, Kenya (East Africa)
Fauna and Flora International (UK, USA)	East Africa
Operation Wallacea (UK)	South-east Sulawesi (Indonesia)
Maruia Society (New Zealand)	Solomon Islands
African Wildlife Foundation (Kenya, Tanzania, Zambia, South Africa, USA)	East Africa, southern Africa
African Conservation Centre (Kenya)	Kenya
Maasai Environmental Resource Coalition (Kenya, USA)	Kenya, Tanzania
Africa Foundation (South Africa)	Southern Africa
Wantok Environment Centre	Vanuatu

[a] Conservation International (CI) – Critical Ecosystem Partnership Fund, Verde Ventures, Ecotourism Program, Conservation Enterprise.
[b] Rare Conservation – Rare Enterprises, Nature Guide Training, Nature Trails, Ecotourism Promoter Training, Ecotourism Alliances, Enterprise Development.

2002: 80). The case studies in this book indicate that government policies on community-based tourism and resource use rights, together with support from environmental NGOs, are essential for most Indigenous ecotourism and conservation projects on tribal lands to be successful.

Empowerment and Community Development

According to Honey (1999: 25), ecotourism 'directly *benefits the economic development and political empowerment of local communities*; and fosters respect for different cultures and for human rights'. Key themes in the published research and case studies of Indigenous ecotourism reviewed in this book include community development (Ashley and Roe, 1998; Russell, 2000; Fennell, 2003; Suansri, 2003; Briedenham and Wickens, 2004); empowerment (Scheyvens, 1999, 2000, 2002; Sofield, 2003; Spenceley, 2004; WTO, 2005) or self-determination (Johnston, 2003, 2006; Hinch, 2004); and sustainable tourism/ecotourism (Robinson, 1999; Epler Wood, 1999a, b, 2002; WTO, 2003; Mat Som and Baum, 2004; Mbaiwa, 2005; Notzke, 2006). The case studies also reinforce the fact that marginalized Indigenous groups require support from NGOs, aid groups and government agencies to control and benefit from community ecotourism or joint ventures on their tribal lands (ANTA, 2001; Johnston, 2001; Smith, 2003). However, the primary focus of large environmental NGOs on biodiversity conservation and ecotourism often denotes that other Indigenous land uses may not be supported. For example, in Namibia a 5-year aid project funded a nature reserve on Ju/'hoansi Bushmen land, linked with ecotourism and hunting, with little support for Ju/'hoansi farmers (Epler Wood, 2003). The partial success of some ecotourism projects funded by NGOs and other aid donors indicates that remoteness, a lack of infrastructure and training limits the development of tourism in marginal areas.

Indigenous ecotourism and the conservation of natural areas depend on community development and local empowerment, through technical support, tourism training and new tribal tourism committees. Moreover, successful community-based ecotourism requires the empowerment of community members through local participation and control of tourism decision-making, employment and training opportunities, and increased entrepreneurial activities by local people. Empowerment also requires building local capacity to participate in tourism through basic tourism awareness courses along with training in languages, business and operational skills. This process of community empowerment through ecotourism needs to be supported by appropriate policies, education, training and partnerships (Lash, 1998; Masberg and Morales, 1999; Doan, 2000; Lash and Austin, 2003). Therefore, 'if ecotourism is to be viewed as a tool for rural development, it must also help to *shift economic and political control to the local community*, village, cooperative, or entrepreneur' (Honey, 2003: 23). However, this aspect of community control of ecotourism is often the most difficult aspect to achieve in practice. Some case studies in this book describe tourism conflicts between ethnic groups, villages and community sectors about ecotourism income and the dominance of local elites.

Scheyvens (1999, 2002) community framework included psychological, social, political and economic empowerment or disempowerment through tourism. Increased status and self-esteem, lasting economic benefits, community development and tourism decision-making are aspects of empowerment through tourism. This model accounts for local community involvement and control (or lack of control) over ecotourism or other ventures. The case studies in this book reinforce the importance of political, social and psychological empowerment based on Indigenous land rights. However, while Indigenous ecotourism provides economic benefits for individuals and for community development, most of these ventures rely on external funding support from NGOs. The additional factor of resource empowerment based on land rights and resource use underpin many successful Indigenous ecotourism ventures (see Table 8.2). Sofield (2003) also supports the view that tourism sustainability depends on empowering Indigenous communities, but that traditional community mechanisms had to be supported by legal empowerment. Environmental or institutional change to reallocate power and decision-making on resource use to local communities, supported and sanctioned by states, is also required. While the case studies presented in this book indicate there is progress in this area, the states still had final control of land use decisions.

Other issues arising from these case studies were the level of empowerment for women, young people and poor people in local communities (Scheyvens, 2002; Momsen, 2004). Gender issues were not addressed in the case studies of Indigenous ecotourism reviewed in this book. At the Sunungukai ecotourism camp in Zimbabwe, local women were restricted to cooking duties and discouraged from being tourist guides by local men (Scheyvens, 2002). In contrast, the Damaraland Camp in Namibia, operated by Wilderness Safaris, employs a local female manager, the first black woman to manage a tourism operation in Namibia; and also a local female guide (WWF, 2005b). Many case studies found ecotourism ventures favoured local elites with access to resources and those in positions of leadership who were mainly male. The guiding positions at community ecotourism enterprises or joint ventures were given to Indigenous people who could speak the dominant national language and/or a tourist language (e.g. English, French, German). There were few Indigenous people in management positions at these ventures, except for the Damaraland Camp (Namibia) and the Gudigwa Camp (Botswana).

Sustainable Indigenous Ecotourism

The sustainable development of ecotourism is based on the integrated elements of ecological, economic and sociocultural sustainability (WTO, 2001, 2003). Ecotourism is largely based on the conservation of biodiversity, mainly in protected areas, together with environmental education and minimizing the impacts of tourism in natural areas (Weaver, 2001; Page and Dowling, 2002; Buckley, 2003; Fennell, 2003; Diamantis, 2004). The economic benefits of ecotourism aim to assist nature conservation and provide returns to local communities, through employment, purchase of goods and services and fees. Community ecotourism and pro-poor tourism projects focus on poverty alleviation and conservation to provide alternatives to traditional subsistence economies and resource use in rural areas (Lash, 1998; Epler Wood, 1999a, b, 2004, 2005; Butcher, 2003; Honey and Thullen, 2003; IFAD, 2003; Roe et al., 2004). However, ongoing Indigenous use of wildlife and natural resources, particularly in protected areas, conflicts with the environmental standards and sustainability criteria of developed nations, western tourists, national

park agencies and conservation NGOs (Hinch, 1998; Robinson, 1999; Weaver, 2006). Hence, the case studies in this book found negotiating acceptable forms of local resource use is a key aspect or factor of many Indigenous ecotourism ventures. This includes private joint venture partners or national park agencies restricting Indigenous hunting, farming or grazing in key tourism areas as well as Indigenous groups declaring their own conservation zones or wildlife use provisions to benefit ecotourism.

A key premise in this book is: 'The nexus between land and culture defines sustainable tourism for Indigenous peoples' (Zeppel, 1998: 65). Hence, a framework for Indigenous ecotourism was developed which considered the environmental, cultural, economic and political factors that may limit or control tourism development on tribal lands (Zeppel, 1998, 2000; Dahles and Keune, 2002; Epler Wood, 2004) (refer to Table 1.5). Indigenous ecotourism takes place within a global tourism industry, which dominates marketing, transport, accommodation and visitor services (Butler and Hinch, 1996). Sociopolitical factors that affect Indigenous groups developing ecotourism include land and property rights. Guiding principles for ecotourism on Indigenous territories include community involvement and benefit, small-scale ventures, land ownership, empowerment and cultural sensitivity (Scheyvens, 1999; Hinch, 2001). 'Real' ecotourism, then, has to empower local people and provide financial benefits used for community development rather than individual economic enhancement by local elites (Honey, 2003). NGOs play a key role in channelling these broader benefits of tourism into conservation and community development (Barkin and Bouchez, 2002; Holden and Mason, 2005).

The 'successes' of Indigenous ecotourism ventures may also be measured in environmental, social or political outcomes (e.g. land rights) rather than in purely economic terms. In the framework for Indigenous ecotourism, the environmental and cultural impacts or benefits of ecotourism are treated equally with financial or territorial (i.e. political) outcomes for Indigenous groups. The case studies in this book found that economic and political criteria are often key motivators for Indigenous ecotourism, while environmental and cultural criteria are outcomes for Indigenous groups involved in ecotourism. For example, Gerberich (2005) applied cultural, environmental, socioeconomic and political factors to assess the sustainability of tourism on American Indian reservations. The political factors revolved around Indian sovereignty and tribal ownership of land and resources. Hence, tourism development on Indian reservations maintained tribal cultures and reinforced their autonomous powers. The case studies in this book also demonstrated that there are strong links between these four key criteria for sustainability and community empowerment (i.e. environmental, social, economic and political) through Indigenous ecotourism ventures on tribal lands (Table 8.6).

In summary, key factors for the sustainable development of Indigenous ecotourism ventures on tribal lands and protected areas are: (i) securing land tenure; (ii) funding or technical support from NGOs, foreign donors and/or government agencies for community-based ecotourism; and (iii) links with the private tourism industry. A recent forum reviewed priorities for funding and investment in small ecotourism enterprises, including

Indigenous projects, by development agencies, NGOs (Conservation International), and the private sector (Planeta, 2005). Another report reviewed the financial viability of ecolodges in developing countries, including joint ventures with Indigenous groups (IFC, 2005). According to Drumm (1998: 198), community-based ecotourism involves 'ecotourism programs which take place under the control and active participation of the local people who inhabit a natural attraction'. These ecotourism enterprises involve Indigenous communities using their natural resources and traditional lands to gain income from tourism. Furthermore, Indigenous ecotourism ventures involve nature conservation, business enterprise (or partnerships) and tourism income used for community development (Sproule, 1996, cited in Fennell, 2003).

Development and Management of Indigenous Ecotourism

Indigenous ecotourism occurs within a wider nature-based tourism industry dominated by non-Indigenous tour operators and travel agents. Ecotourism itself is part of a global

Table 8.6. Sustainability and empowerment within Indigenous ecotourism.

Environmental sustainability	*Resource empowerment*
Contribution to the conservation of natural areas	Tribal reserves and protected areas
Economic benefits for conservation	Maintain natural areas and wildlife
Educational and interpretation activities (host communities, tourists)	Environmental knowledge and training
Environmental practices (minimal impacts/sustainable resource use)	Manage resource use and land practices
Social and cultural sustainability	*Social empowerment*
Community involvement and benefits	Facilitates stakeholder interest and income
Community participation and decision-making	Communities seen as key stakeholders
Community ownership and joint ventures	Supports traditional or local authority
Cultural activities and presentations	Supports and reinforces cultural identity
Economic sustainability	*Economic 'empowerment'*
Finance and funding (private, donor agencies)	Reliance on NGOs and foreign donors
Marketing and promotion	Market – Internet, NGOs, rural tourism groups
Profitability (private operators, community facilities)	Limited income, develop local infrastructure
Business cooperation and regulation	Partner joint ventures, government agencies
Political sustainability	*Political empowerment*
Community organization and decision-making bodies	Tribal councils and tourism committees
Community knowledge of legal rights (land, resources)	Legal titles to land and resource user rights
Negotiate with government agencies	Revenue sharing and community projects
Strategic alliances and networks	Tribal associations, NGOs, industry partners

Sources: Scheyvens, 1999, 2002; WTO, 2001, 2003.

tourism industry. Developing countries attract 30% of all international tourists with a growth rate of 9.5% per annum since 1990. In addition, 19 out of 25 biodiversity hotspots favoured by ecotourism, most with Indigenous populations, are in the southern hemisphere (Christ *et al.*, 2003). As such, Indigenous ecotourism is part of a broader environment that is influenced by non-Indigenous tourism, conservation and development activities (Butcher, 2003; Mowforth and Munt, 2003; Ryan and Aicken, 2005; Johnston, 2006; Notzke, 2006). Hence, issues associated with Indigenous control of ecotourism and environmental, social or political factors that affect these enterprises need to be considered. Indigenous ecotourism ventures face the same issues of product development, marketing, competition, quality control, training and profitability faced by other small ecotourism businesses (Weaver, 2001). However, Indigenous ecotourism businesses also have other objectives, such as asserting territorial rights, maintaining cultural knowledge and practices, and providing local employment. Other intangible benefits of Indigenous ecotourism include empowerment, skill development, security, and community organization (Ashley and Jones, 2001; Scheyvens, 2002). Furthermore, the development of Indigenous ecotourism ventures is limited by poverty, land titles, lack of infrastructure on reserves, visitor access and remoteness, funding, resource use restrictions, internal community conflicts over tourism, lack of business knowledge, and forming commercial links with the tourism industry. Guaranteed tourism revenue from lease fees and bed night or tourist levies may provide more stable income and employment than community-owned ventures with greater local control over tourism (Walpole and Thouless, 2005). Small-scale Indigenous-owned ecotourism ventures, while conserving key natural areas, have local benefits but limited impacts or market linkages with mainstream tourism (Ashley and Mitchell, 2005). Hence, a variety of strategies, policies and practices are needed to support Indigenous ecotourism on tribal lands (see Table 8.7).

According to Epler Wood (2002: 45), Indigenous communities must have 'legal *control over land* and full legal rights to protect any businesses that they establish' for ecotourism to be used for sustainable development of tribal areas. The case studies in this book reinforce this key point, with most new Indigenous ecotourism ventures established on communal lands, Indigenous reserves and wildlife conservancies under the legal control of Indigenous groups. This includes both land rights and also some resource use rights for wildlife on tribal lands, mainly with wildlife hunting quotas in Africa. With this legal control, Indigenous groups can sub-lease land to other operators, negotiate contracts with joint venture partners as well as establish and run their own tourism ventures on tribal lands. Hence, Indigenous peoples with legal land titles are now landlords, partners or tourism service providers. However, there is limited development or transfer of business skills to Indigenous peoples and organizations involved in ecotourism. In many areas, more Indigenous input in land use, wildlife quotas and tourism decision-making is needed at both national and regional levels (Mbaiwa, 2005).

Marketing of these Indigenous ecotourism ventures and sites is mainly undertaken by NGOs promoting ecotourism, community tourism or rural tourism in developing countries (see Table 8.8). These include websites for the Ecotravel Centre of Conservation International, Redturs (Latin America), ACTUAR (Costa Rica), REST (Thailand) and Tourism Concern (UK, website and guidebooks). A few Indigenous tourism organizations market a number of ecotourism sites, such as RICANCIE (Ecuador) for Indian communities in the Cuyabeno Reserve, and the Toledo Ecotourism Association (Belize) for Mayan village guesthouses and homestays. Some well-established Indigenous ecotourism ventures, mainly ecolodges in South America (e.g. Mapajo, Chalalan and Kapawi) and Africa have their own websites. Community tourism ventures are promoted in Africa for Namibia, Uganda, Kenya, Tanzania, Botswana, Ghana and Gambia. However, apart from Ghana, Botswana and Sabah (Malaysia), there is little website promotion of these Indigenous ecotourism ventures by national tourism bodies. Southern Belize and Milne Bay (PNG)

Table 8.7. Strategies for sustainable development and management of Indigenous ecotourism.

Factors affecting community ecotourism	Tourism policies and practices
Land Tenure	Secure community tenure over land, wildlife and/or tourism rights Legal land titles or recognized communal titles; resource use rights
Tourism Policy	Government policies support community-based tourism ventures Community involvement and benefits a key criteria in formal sector
Land-use Planning	Land-use planning recognizes tourism and allows multiple land uses Government investment in infrastructure to develop regional areas
Tourism Marketing	National tourism bodies (or NGOs) marketing community tourism Linkages with private sector marketing of joint community tourism
Tourism Regulations/Standards	Regulations allow homestays; local benefits part of larger ventures
Tourism Training and Licensing	Tourism training for rural people supported by government or NGOs
Tourism Joint Ventures	Tenure and regulations allow communities to enter contracts or leases Incentives for private companies to negotiate with rural communities
Tourism Support Staff	Community support officers provide tourism information and advice Support and facilitate enterprise development with NGOs and government
Park Development	Park agencies support community tourism enterprises/concessions Park visitor levies used to fund community development projects
Business Credit/Incentives	Credit or loans for small community enterprises; industry linkages External donor/NGO funding of community tourism enterprises

Sources: Ashley and Roe, 1998; Scheyvens, 2002; Roe *et al.*, 2004.

are the only regional tourism associations promoting Indigenous ecotourism sites on their website. As a result, the growth of Indigenous ecotourism in tribal areas may not be matched by market demand for these products.

This book summarized information about Indigenous ecotourism ventures published in English in tourism books and journals, in reports and manuals from conservation NGOs, government organizations or ecotourism operators, and on websites for Indigenous communities or organizations. These selected case studies either described Indigenous ecotourism products and/or critically evaluated the operation of selected Indigenous ecotourism ventures in more detail. Limitations were the reliance on NGOs describing their involvement with Indigenous ecotourism projects. Only a few detailed studies have been published that critically review the involvement of NGOs, government agencies and the private sector in developing these Indigenous ecotourism ventures. Examples include Indigenous ecotourism on Maasai lands in East Africa,

conservation and community ecotourism in southern Africa, ecotourism in Fiji and some ecolodges or protected areas in Latin America.

Further research, therefore, is needed to critically evaluate Indigenous participation in ecotourism ventures on tribal lands. In particular, information is required on the business structure or tourism management model followed in these Indigenous enterprises, including the provisions in joint venture contracts for royalties, land rents and employment (Mbaiwa, 2005). The links between biodiversity conservation, Indigenous rights and ecotourism require more analysis. Visitor market demand for Indigenous tourism experiences on tribal lands also needs to be investigated (Ryan and Aicken, 2005).

Conclusion

This book has established a context for the study of Indigenous ecotourism as a global trend in new tourism. Tourists are increasingly

Table 8.8. Tourism and conservation organizations promoting Indigenous ecotourism on tribal lands.

The Nature Conservancy (USA) Ecotourism Destinations
Conservation International (USA) The Ecotravel Centre
Rare Conservation (USA)
The International Ecotourism Society (USA)
WWF International – Project LIFE (Namibia)
Tourism Concern (UK)
Eco-Resorts (East Africa)[a]
Namib Web[a] – Community based tourism (Namibia)
Earthfoot[a]
Responsible Travel[a]

Uganda Community Tourism Association (UCOTA) (Uganda)
African Pro-poor Tourism Development Centre (Kenya)
African Conservation Centre (Kenya)
Ecotourism Society of Kenya (ESOK) (Kenya)
African Wildlife Foundation (Kenya)
East African Wildlife Society (EAWLS) (Kenya)
Laikipia Wildlife Forum Ltd (Kenya)
Tanzanian Cultural Tourism Coordination Office (Tanzania)
Tourism in Ethiopia for Sustainable Future Alternatives (TESFA) (Ethiopia)
Namibia Community Based Tourism Association (NACOBTA) (Namibia)
Community Based Tourism in Botswana (CBNRM) (Botswana)
Southern Alliance for Indigenous Resources (SAFIRE) (South Africa)
Fair Trade in Tourism South Africa (FTTSA) (South Africa)
Association of Small Scale Enterprises in Tourism (ASSET) (Gambia)
Gambia Birding Group (Gambia)
Ghana Tourism Board (Ghana)
Nature Conservation Research Centre (Ghana)
Ghana Wildlife Society (Ghana)

Cambodia Community-based Ecotourism Network (CCBEN) (Cambodia)
Ecotourism Laos – Laos National Tourism Authority (Laos)
Indonesian Ecotourism Centre (Indecon) (Indonesia)
Togean Ecotourism Network (JET) (Sulawesi, Indonesia)
Responsible Ecological Social Tours (REST) (Thailand)
Sabah Homestay and Sabah Tourism (Sabah, Malaysia)
Northwest Yunnan Ecotourism Association (NYEA) (China)
Centre for Biodiversity and Indigenous Knowledge (CBIK) (China)

Network of Communitarian Tourism of Latin America (Redturs)
Community-based Rural Tourism in Costa Rica (ACTUAR) (Costa Rica)
Mexican Association of Adventure Tourism and Ecotourism (AMTAVE) (Mexico)
Ecomaya (Guatemala)
Toledo Ecotourism Association (Belize)
Network of Indigenous Communities of the Upper Napo for
Intercultural Exchange and Ecotourism (RICANCIE) (Ecuador)

Ecotourism Melanesia (PNG)[a]
Milne Bay Tourism Bureau (PNG)
Solomons Village Stay (Solomon Islands)[a]
Fiji Bure (Fiji)[a]
Wantok Environment Centre (Vanuatu)
Island Safaris of Vanuatu (Vanuatu)

[a] Privately owned tourism companies promoting Indigenous ecotourism ventures on their websites.

visiting Indigenous peoples and their tribal lands around the world. Areas of high biodiversity, such as tropical rainforest, are linked with surviving groups of Indigenous peoples. Indigenous ecotourism is defined as nature-based attractions or tours owned by tribal groups, which feature Indigenous cultural knowledge and practices linked to the land. Key factors driving Indigenous involvement in ecotourism include gaining legal rights to land, preventing other extractive land uses and cultural revival. Many Indigenous groups are now owners and operators or joint venture partners of ecotourism ventures located on traditional homelands and protected areas. The case studies of Indigenous ecotourism ventures reviewed in this book illustrate how and why different Indigenous groups are involved in ecotourism and conservation projects. There are common issues for Indigenous ecotourism ventures in Oceania, Latin America, Africa and South-east Asia. In particular, legal land titles promote Indigenous control over ecotourism on tribal lands and territories. These include Indigenous ownership of ecotourism ventures, leasing land, partnerships and joint ventures.

Ideally, Indigenous ecotourism will conserve natural areas, maintain Indigenous lifestyles and provide social and economic benefits for Indigenous communities. However, Indigenous ecotourism also operates within a broader framework of economic, political, cultural and environmental factors that affect sustainability and community empowerment. The challenge is for governments, NGOs and aid groups to support and provide legal and technical assistance for Indigenous groups developing ecotourism ventures. Further marketing support and effective linkages with the commercial tourism industry are also required to develop Indigenous ecotourism. The surviving bonds between Indigenous peoples and wild natural areas are important for ecotourism operators seeking new areas. The case studies in this book reviewed the expansion of ecotourism into remote wilderness areas that are Indigenous homelands, linked with the growing assertion of Indigenous land and resource rights. Hence, Indigenous lands, stewardship of natural resources and cultural identity are central to this trend of Indigenous ecotourism. The critical issue is whether governments, NGOs and the private sector can effectively develop ecotourism that benefits nature conservation and Indigenous groups.

References

Alcorn, J.B. (2001) *Good Governance, Indigenous Peoples and Biodiversity Conservation: Recommendations for Enhancing Results Across Sectors*. Biodiversity Support Program. WWF. http://www.worldwildlife. org/bsp/publications/ (accessed 17 November 2005)

ANTA (Australian National Training Authority) (2001) Indigenous Ecotourism Toolbox. ANTA Website. http://www.dlsweb.rmit.edu.au/toolbox/Indigenous/ecotourismtoolbox/ (accessed 17 November 2005)

Ashley, C. and Jones, B. (2001) Joint ventures between communities and tourism investors: Experience in Southern Africa. *International Journal of Tourism Research* 3, 407–423.

Ashley, C. and Mitchell, J. (2005) Can tourism accelerate pro-poor growth in Africa? Opinions. November 2005. Overseas Development Institute. http://www.odi.org.uk/publications/opinions/ (accessed 17 November 2005)

Ashley, C. and Roe, D. (1998) *Enhancing Community Involvement in Wildlife Tourism: Issues and Challenges*. IIED Wildlife and Development Series No. 11. International Institute for Environment and Development, London.

Barkin, D. and Bouchez, C.P. (2002) NGO-community collaboration for ecotourism: A strategy for sustainable regional development. *Current Issues in Tourism* 5, 245–253.

Blake, B. (2003) The tourism industry's codes for indigenous peoples. In: Honey, M. and Thullen, S. (eds) *Rights and Responsibilities: A Compilation of Codes of Conduct for Tourism and Indigenous and Local Communities*. Center on Ecotourism and Sustainable Development and The International Ecotourism Society. http://205.252.29.37/webarticles/anmviewer.asp?a=14 (accessed 17 November 2005)

Briedenham, J. and Wickens, E. (2004) Community involvement in tourism development: White elephant or empowerment? In: Weber, S. and Tomljenovic, R. (eds) *Reinventing a Tourism Destination: Facing the Challenge*. Institute for Tourism Zagreb, Zagreb, Croatia, pp. 167–177.

Buckley, R. (2003) *Case Studies in Ecotourism*. CABI, Wallingford, UK.

Butcher, J. (2003) New moral tourism, the third world and development. In: *The Moralisation of Tourism: Sun, Sand … and Saving the World?* Routledge, London, pp. 113–136.

Butler, R.W. (1980) The concept of a tourist area cycle of evolution: Implications for management of resources. *Canadian Geographer* 24, 5–12.

Butler, R. (ed.) (2005) *The Tourism Area Life Cycle: Theoretical and Conceptual Implications.* Channel View, Clevedon.

Butler, R. and Hinch, T. (eds) (1996) *Tourism and Indigenous Peoples.* International Thomson Business Press, London.

Christ, C., Hillel, O., Matus, S. and Sweeting, J. (2003) *Tourism and Biodiversity: Mapping Tourism's Global Footprint.* Conservation International and UNEP.

Dahles, H. and Keune, L. (eds) (2002) *Tourism Development and Local Participation in Latin America.* Cognizant Communication Corporation, New York.

Diamantis, D. (ed.) (2004) *Ecotourism: Management and Assessment.* Thomson, London.

Doan, T.M. (2000) The effects of ecotourism in developing countries: An analysis of case studies. *Journal of Sustainable Tourism* 8, 288–304.

Drumm, A. (1998) New approaches to community-based ecotourism management: Learning from Ecuador. In: Lindberg, K., Epler Wood, M. and Engeldrum, D. (eds) *Ecotourism: A Guide for Planners and Managers,* Vol. 2. The Ecotourism Society, Vermont, pp. 197–213.

Epler Wood, M. (1999a) Ecotourism, sustainable development, and cultural survival: Protecting Indigenous culture and land through ecotourism. *Cultural Survival Quarterly* 23.

Epler Wood, M. (1999b) The Ecotourism Society – an international NGO committed to sustainable development. *Tourism Recreation Research* 24, 199–123.

Epler Wood, M. (2002) Ecotourism and indigenous communities. In: *Ecotourism: Principles, Practices & Policies for Sustainability.* UNEP, Paris and The International Ecotourism Society, Vermont, pp. 44–45.

Epler Wood, M. (2003) Community conservation and commerce. EplerWood Reports, October 2003. EplerWood International. http://www.eplerwood.com/reports.php (accessed 17 November 2005)

Epler Wood, M. (2004) Evaluating ecotourism as a community and economic development strategy. EplerWood Reports, October 2004. EplerWood International. http://www.eplerwood.com/reports.php (accessed 17 November 2005)

Epler Wood, M. (2005) Stepping up: Creating a sustainable tourism enterprise strategy that delivers in the developing world. EplerWood Reports, October 2005. EplerWood International. http://www.eplerwood.com/reports.php (accessed 17 November 2005)

Fennell, D.A. (2003) Ecotourism development: International, community, and site perspectives. In: *Ecotourism: An Introduction,* 2nd edn. Routledge, London, pp. 150–170.

Gerberich, V.L. (2005) An evaluation of sustainable Indian tourism. In: Ryan, C. and Aicken, M. (eds) *Indigenous Tourism: The Commodification and Management of Culture.* Elsevier, Oxford, pp. 75–86.

Hinch, T. (1998) Ecotourists and indigenous hosts: Diverging views on their relationship with nature. Current *Issues in Tourism* 1, 120–124.

Hinch, T. (2001) Indigenous territories. In: Weaver, D.B. (ed.) *The Encyclopaedia of Ecotourism.* CABI Publishing, Wallingford, UK, pp. 345–357.

Hinch, T.D. (2004) Indigenous peoples and tourism. In: Lew, A.L., Hall, C.M. and Williams, A.M. (eds) *A Companion to Tourism.* Blackwell Publishing, Malden, MA, pp. 246–257.

Holden, A. and Mason, P. (2005) Editorial [NGOs and tourism]. *Journal of Sustainable Tourism* 13, 421–423.

Honey, M. (1999) *Ecotourism and Sustainable Development: Who Owns Paradise?* Island Press, Washington DC.

Honey, M. (2003) Summary of major principles regarding tourism and indigenous peoples and local communities. In: Honey, M. and Thullen, S. (eds) *Rights and Responsibilities: A Compilation of Codes of Conduct for Tourism and Indigenous and Local Communities.* Center on Ecotourism and Sustainable Development and The International Ecotourism Society. http://205.252.29.37/webarticles/articlefiles/rightsandresponsibilities.pdf (accessed 17 November 2005)

Honey, M. and Thullen, S. (eds) (2003) *Rights and Responsibilities: A Compilation of Codes of Conduct for Tourism and Indigenous and Local Communities.* Center on Ecotourism and Sustainable Development and The International Ecotourism Society. Reports. http://205.252.29.37/webarticles/anmviewer.asp?a=14 (accessed 17 November 2005)

International Fund for Agricultural Development (IFAD) (2003) *Indigenous Peoples and Sustainable Development: Discussion Paper.* Roundtable Discussion Paper for the 25th Anniversary Session of IFAD's Governing Council. IFAD, Rome. http://www.ifad.org/media/events/2005/ip.htm (accessed 18 May 2006)

IFC (International Finance Corporation) (2005) Ecolodge publication. Environmental Business Finance Program. http://www.ifc.org/ifcext/enviro.nsf/Content/EBFP_Ecolodge (accessed 17 November 2005)

Johnston, A. (2000) Indigenous peoples and ecotourism: Bringing indigenous knowledge and rights into the sustainability equation. *Tourism Recreation Research* 25, 89–96.

Johnston, A. (2001) Ecotourism and the challenges confronting indigenous peoples. *Native Americas* 18, 42–47.

Johnston, A. (2003) Self-determination: Exercising indigenous rights in tourism. In: Singh, S., Timothy, D.J. and Dowling, R.K. (eds) *Tourism in Destination Communities*. CABI, Wallingford, UK, pp. 115–134.

Johnston, A.M. (2006) *Is the Sacred for Sale? Tourism and Indigenous Peoples*. Earthscan, London.

Lash, G. (1998) What is community-based ecotourism? In: Bornemeier, J., Victor, M. and Durst, P.B. (eds) *Ecotourism for Forest Conservation and Community Development Seminar*. RECOFTC Report No. 15. RECOFTC, Bangkok, pp. 1–12. http://www.recoftc.org/site/index.php?id=22 (accessed 17 November 2005)

Lash, G.Y.B. and Austin, A. (2003) *The Rural Ecotourism Assessment Program (REAP): A Guide to Community Assessment of Ecotourism as a Tool for Sustainable Development*. The International Ecotourism Society.

Mann, M. (2002) *The Good Alternative Travel Guide*, 2nd edn. Earthscan and Tourism Concern, London.

Masberg, B.A. and Morales, N. (1999) A case analysis of strategies in ecotourism development. *Aquatic Ecosystem Health and Management* 2, 289–300.

Mat Som, A.P. and Baum, T. (2004) Community involvement in ecotourism. In: Weber, S. and Tomljenovic, R. (eds) *Reinventing a Tourism Destination: Facing the Challenge*. Institute for Tourism Zagreb, Zagreb, Croatia, pp. 251–260.

Mbaiwa, J.E. (2005) Community-based tourism and the marginalized communities in Botswana: The case of the Basarwa in the Okavango Delta. In: Ryan, C. and Aicken, M. (eds) *Indigenous Tourism: The Commodification and Management of Culture*. Elsevier, Oxford, pp. 87–109.

McLaren, D. (1998) *Rethinking Tourism and Ecotravel: The Paving of Paradise and How You Can Stop It*. Kumarian Press, West Hartford, CT.

Momsen, J.H. (2004) *Gender and Development*. Routledge, London.

Mowforth, M. and Munt, I. (2003) *Tourism and Sustainability: Development and New Tourism in the Third World*, 2nd edn. Routledge, London.

Nature Conservancy, The (2005) The Nature Conservancy and indigenous peoples. How we work-our partners. http://nature.org/partners/partnership/art14301.html (accessed 17 November 2005)

Notzke, C. (2006) *The Stranger, the Native and the Land: Perspectives on Indigenous Tourism*. Captus University Publications, North York, Ontario.

Page, S. and Dowling, R.K. (2002) Community-based ecotourism: Management and development issues. In: *Ecotourism*. Pearson Education, Harlow, UK, pp. 244–247.

Planeta (2005) Ecotourism emerging industry forum November 1–18, 2005. Planeta.com http://www.planeta.com/ecotravel/tour/emerging.html (accessed 17 November 2005)

Robinson, M. (1999) Collaboration and cultural consent: Refocusing sustainable tourism. *Journal of Sustainable Tourism* 7, 379–397.

Roe, D., Goodwin, H. and Ashley, C. (2004) Pro-poor tourism: Benefiting the poor. In: Singh, T.V. (ed.) *New Horizons in Tourism: Strange Experiences and Stranger Practices*. CABI, Wallingford, UK, pp. 147–161.

Russell, P. (2000) Community-based tourism. *Travel & Tourism Analyst* 5, 87–114.

Ryan, C. and Aicken, M. (eds) (2005) *Indigenous Tourism: The Commodification and Management of Culture*. Elsevier, Oxford.

Scheyvens, R. (1999) Ecotourism and the empowerment of local communities. *Tourism Management* 20, 245–249.

Scheyvens, R. (2000) Promoting women's empowerment through involvement in ecotourism: Experiences from the Third World. *Journal of Sustainable Tourism* 8, 232–249.

Scheyvens, R. (2002) *Tourism for Development: Empowering Communities*. Prentice Hall, Harlow, Essex, UK.

Smith, L.T. (1999) An agenda for indigenous research. In: *Decolonizing Methodologies: Research and Indigenous Peoples*. Zed Books, London, and University of Otago Press, Dunedin, NZ, 115–118.

Smith, M.K. (2003) Indigenous cultural tourism. In: *Issues in Cultural Tourism Studies*. Routledge, London, pp. 117–132.

Sofield, T.H.B. (1993) Indigenous tourism development. *Annals of Tourism Research* 20, 729–750.

Sofield, T.H.B. (2003) *Empowerment for Sustainable Tourism Development*. Pergamon, New York.

Spenceley, A. (2004) Responsible nature-based tourism planning in South Africa and the commercialisation of Kruger National Park. In: Diamantis, D. (ed.) *Ecotourism: Management and Assessment*. Thomson, London, pp. 267–280.

SPREP (South Pacific Regional Environment Programme) (2002) *Community-based Ecotourism and Conservation in the Pacific Islands: A Tool Kit for Communities*. SPREP, Apia, Samoa.

Suansri, P. (2003) *Community Based Tourism Handbook.* REST, Bangkok. http://www.ecotour.in.th/english. files/infocenter.htm (accessed 17 November 2005)

Sweeting, J. and McConnel, M.A. (1999) Tourism as a tool for biodiversity conservation. *Tourism Recreation Research* 24, 106–108.

The International Ecotourism Society (TIES) (2004) Definition and ecotourism principles. TIES. http://www.ecotourism.org/index2.php?what-is-ecotourism (accessed 17 November 2005)

Tourism in Focus (2002) Communities choosing ecotourism. *Tourism in Focus (Tourism Concern)* 42, 10–11.

Ulloa, A. (2005) *The Ecological Native: Indigenous Peoples' Movements and Eco-Governmentality in Colombia.* Routledge, London.

Walpole, M.J. and Thouless, C.R. (2005) Increasing the value of wildlife through non-consumptive use? Deconstructing the myths of ecotourism and community-based tourism in the tropics. In: Woodroofe, R., Thirgood, S. and Rabinowitz, A. (eds) *People and Wildlife: Conflict or Coexistence?* Cambridge University Press, Cambridge, 122–139.

Weaver, D.B. (2001) Indigenous territories. In: *Ecotourism.* John Wiley Australia, Milton, pp. 256–262.

Weaver, D.B. (2006) Indigenous territories. In: *Sustainable Tourism: Theory and Practice.* Oxford, Elsevier, pp. 143–146.

Weber, R., Butler, J. and Larson, P. (eds) (2000) *Indigenous Peoples and Conservation Organizations: Experiences in Collaboration.* WWF. http://www.worldwildlife.org/bsp/publications/ (accessed 17 November 2005)

Wesche, R. and Drumm, A. (1999) *Defending our Rainforest: A Guide to Community-based Ecotourism in the Ecuadorian Amazon.* Accion Amazonia, Quito.

WTO (World Tourism Organization) (2001) *Sustainable Development of Ecotourism: A Compilation of Good Practices.* WTO, Madrid.

WTO (World Tourism Organization) (2003) *Sustainable Development of Ecotourism: A Compilation of Good Practices in SMEs.* WTO, Madrid.

WTO (World Tourism Organization) (2005) Local control. In: *Making Tourism More Sustainable: A Guide for Policy Makers.* UNEP and WTO, Madrid, pp. 34–36.

WWF (2001) *Guidelines for Community-based Ecotourism Development.* July 2001. WWF International. http://www.wwf.no/pdf/tourism_guidelines.pdf (accessed 17 November 2005)

WWF (2005a) WWF statement of principles on indigenous peoples and conservation. WWF. Policy. http://www.panda.org/about_wwf/what_we_do/policy/indigenous_people/statement_principles.cfm (accessed 17 November 2005)

WWF (2005b) Project LIFE – community tourism. The Dam Camp. Project LIFE, Namibia. WWF. http://www.panda.org/about_wwf/where_we_work/africa/where/southern_africa/namibia/life/project/ (accessed 17 November 2005)

Zeppel, H. (1998) Land and culture: Sustainable tourism and indigenous peoples. In: Hall, C.M. and Lew, A. (eds) *Sustainable Tourism: A Geographical Perspective.* Addison Wesley Longman, London, pp. 60–74.

Zeppel, H. (2000) Ecotourism and indigenous peoples. *Issues: All Australian Educational Magazine*, 51, July.

Zeppel, H. (2003) Sharing the country: Ecotourism policy and indigenous peoples in Australia. In: Fennell, D.A. and Dowling, R.K. (eds) *Ecotourism Policy and Planning.* CABI, Wallingford, UK, pp. 55–76.

Index

Page numbers in *italics* refer to tables

—

Date Due